# FORENSIC TAPHONOMY

## The Postmortem Fate of Human Remains

*Edited by*

# William D. Haglund
# Marcella H. Sorg

**CRC Press**

**Boca Raton   New York   London   Tokyo**

| Publisher: | Robert B. Stern |
| Editorial Assistant: | Jean Jarboe |
| Project Editor: | Helen Linna |
| Marketing Manager: | Greg Daurelle |
| Direct Marketing Manager: | Bill Boone |
| Cover design: | Dawn Boyd |
| PrePress: | Kevin Luong |
| Manufacturing: | Sheri Schwartz |

**Library of Congress Cataloging-in-Publication Data**

Forensic taphonomy: the postmortem fate of human remains /William D. Haglund and Marcella H. Sorg
    p.  cm.
   Includes bibliographical references and index.
   ISBN 0-8493-9434-1
    1. Forensic taphonomy.    I. Haglund, William D.  II. Title.
QR749.H64G79 1996
616'.0149—dc20
for Library of Congress

96-81217
CIP

© 1997 by CRC Press, Inc.

No claim to original U.S. Government works
International Standard Book Number 0-8493-9434-1
Library of Congress Card Number 96-81217
Printed in the United States of America 1 2 3 4 5 6 7 8 9 0
Printed on acid-free paper

# Contents

## SECTION I
## Taphonomy in the Forensic Context

## SECTION II
## Modifications of Soft Tissue, Bone, and Associated Materials

*Chemical Underpinnings*

## 7 Preservation and Recovery of DNA in Postmortem Specimens and Trace Samples     109

Thomas J. Parsons and Victor Walter Weedn

## Soft Tissue

## 8 The Process of Decomposition: A Model from the Arizona-Sonoran Desert     139

Alison Galloway

## 9 Postmortem Changes in Soft Tissues     151

Michael A. Clark, Michael B. Worrell, and John E. Pless

## 10 Recognition of Cemetery Remains in the Forensic Setting     165

Hugh E. Berryman, William M. Bass, Steven A. Symes, and O'Brian C. Smith

# SECTION III
## Scavenged Remains

*Carnivore Scavenged Remains*

*Rodent Scavenged Remains*

## Scavenging by Insects

## Scavenging by Water Organisms

## SECTION IV
## Buried and Protected Remains

# SECTION V
# Remains in Water

# Preface

JOSEPH H. DAVIS

Taphonomy concerns the comprehension of multiple factors which play a role in the disintegration and scatter of a body and its accoutrements until they have been environmentally recycled and incorporated into the earth, its waters, its air, and its inhabitants. To this extent we may all claim immortality or reincarnation.

What happened concerns events remote from and close to the time of death, events that transpired at the time of death, and events in the immediate or long-term period after death. Study of contemporary case material has been useful in understanding of paleobiological fossil remains, a very long time indeed (Weigelt 1989).

The reader will find in this volume a range of facts and opinions dealing with fragmented evidence, for a dead body is evidence, evidence to be photographed, X-rayed, described, analyzed in depth, and correlated with circumstances. The objective is not to overlook crucial information that enables one to judge correctly what did happen and did not happen to the decedent.

In a narrower sense the chapters in this book deal with forensic matters — who was the person, what happened, and what evidence indicates presence or absence of culpability. In criminal law the body of the crime, corpus delicti, when homicide is suspected consists of three parts: the identity of the victim; determination that the death was not natural (or the presumption that the death is natural in the absence of evidence to the contrary); and that the death resulted from the criminal act of another.

When the body is intact and terminal events are well documented, the cause and manner (natural, accident, suicide, or homicide) of death and the corpus delicti — if a consideration — are relatively simple. Fortunately, most death investigations are simple and almost "self-solving." When evidence, the body is altered by nature, a calamity, or a criminal act, the investigative process becomes complicated. Attention to particular details is essential. At this point the reader is advised to pause, obtain, and retain for repetitive perusal, Alan Moritz's timeless article, "Classical Mistakes in Forensic Pathology," for it truly emphasizes much of the purpose of this book. The error of omission, failure to do what should be done, is as common today as it was a half century ago (Moritz 1956).

The determination of cause of death (that disease or injury which initiated the lethal chain of events, brief or prolonged) (Adelson 1974) and manner (natural, accident, suicide, homicide, NASH) is both circumstance and autopsy dependent. Some few autopsy interpretations are almost non-circumstance dependent as far as cause is concerned. A simple gunshot in the chest involving the heart is practically self-evident except for manner. A calvarium with a depressed fracture and a scattering of dog-chewed long bones is most certainly circumstance dependent. For decades a contract killer has been serving what we hope is a true life sentence in Florida. He abducted circuit court Judge Chillingsworth and his wife, took them on a boat into the Gulf Stream, threw them overboard, and made sure they drowned, never to be found. The corpus delicti was established purely by the circumstances absent any corporeal remains. In some cases noted in forthcoming chapters, a paucity of autopsy evidence, coupled with circumstance, sufficed to meet the legal requirements of conviction. Meticulous attention to detail and most careful correlation with all circumstances (ideally achieved by a close inter-action of police, crime scene technicians and consultive scientists at the scene and subse-quently) may readily lead to successful completion of an investigation.

Psychologists who have studied the phenomenon of proper medical diagnoses compared to less correct diagnosis have found what seems self-evident. Experience and adequate data are prerequisites for proper diagnoses. However, experience means diagnostic case solving — not just a technical bench level skill. Data means relevant data, for the most common error is overreliance upon noncontributory data (Jason 1978). For example, determination of postmortem interval of fauna evidence may not be relevant if one does not know when, in that specific location and time of year, the waves of flies and beetles began. Mere supposition based upon other geographic locations may or may not be correct.

This brings us to the consideration of the value of this book. Hopefully, it will stimulate the reader to appreciate the correlative study of decomposed and scattered remains and associated accoutrements and geological evidence. The reader should also develop a cautious attitude and test his or her conclusions about a body or its parts in the light of all other circumstances.

# References

Adelson, L.
    1974   *The Pathology of Homicide*. Charles C Thomas, Springfield, IL.

Jason, H.
    1978   Foreword. In *Medical Problem Solving. An Analysis of Clinical Reasoning*, edited by A.S. Elstein, L.S. Shulman, and S.A. Sprafka, pp vii–xi. Harvard University Press, Cambridge, MA.

Moritz, A.R.
    1956   Classical Mistakes in Forensic Pathology. *American Journal of Clinical Pathology* 26:1383–1397.

Weigelt, J.
    1989 [1989]*Recent Vertebrate Carcasses and their Paleobiological Implications*, translated by J. Schaefer. University of Chicago Press, Chicago, IL.

# Foreword

## GARY HAYNES

About 15 years ago, an old woman was badly savaged in a quiet Baltimore neighborhood. As an archaeologist who studies bone modification, I was asked by the police for my opinion about the perpetrator. I suggested a big dog had done it. When asked to finger a specific dog, I had to decline, because one big dog's bitemarks look much like another's. They wanted a careful presentation of the evidence from tooth puncture placement and depth, as well as solid arguments that clarified the meaning of that evidence. I could not do it, not with the information at hand. My caution was seen as indecision and I have never been called to assist in other maulings.

Archaeological indecision, unlike forensic indecision, does not send people to prison. But the pressure never lets up on archaeologists to offer opinions on fragmentary, indirect, or circumstantial evidence. To extract meaning from a confusing record, new ways must be created to analyze old data. One of the most significant new sets of methods is taphonomy, a word coined by the Russian fantasist and scientist Yefremov (1940) to mean the study of death assemblages in the fossil record. Taphonomy in the service of paleontology and archaeology has forced the textbooks to be rewritten several times over the last 20 years.

Perhaps the most visible example of this revolution is our interpretations about early hominid behavior. At first, paleoanthropologists were convinced that the close spatial association of animal bones, stone tools, and hominid remains in very early African sites indicated that Plio-Pleistocene hominids were hunter-gatherers who behaved much like ethnographically observed modern hunter-gatherers. But then scientists began noticing that certain bone assemblages bore signs of scavenging by carnivores, and an enthusiastic questioning using taphonomic methods soon swelled. Some investigators noticed cutmarks on bones, and argued that hominids were hunters who competed successfully with lions and hyenas for early access to animal carcasses; others noted the presence of carnivore toothmarks on the bones and argued that hominids merely scavenged from the chewed-up remains of lion kills.

Soon investigators were devising ways to go beyond merely noting the presence and absence of different kinds of marks. Some measured the marks carefully and calculated percentages of bone fragments showing different mark-shapes. Some experimentally produced marks with controlled processes such as hammerstone impact, measured the marks, and compared them to fossil marks. The arguments rage on, but I would say that most archaeologists and paleoanthropologists now believe the earliest stone tool-using hominids were scavengers who could gain only rather late access to carcasses of animals killed by savanna carnivores, such as lions, hyenas, or leopards.

The taphonomic reexaminations of Plio-Pleistocene bone assemblages have affected many other research agendas. Now we regularly expect archaeological interpretations of sites of any age to tell us about bone weathering stages, bone-to-tooth ratios, carnivore activity, and so forth. The way we understand hominid evolution and past human behavior has changed dramatically, thanks to taphonomy.

Perhaps the most eye-opening training for an archaeologist is to deal with explaining the present rather than the past. Few universities offer courses like this. The training would be called actualism, one of the forms that taphonomy takes. The great lesson of such study probably would be that we are still mastering the ability to explain quite simply (and to understand) the processes of the present — the bone-modifying, carcass-dispersing, site-creating processes that operate in the here and now. I have watched future sites in the making for 20 years, and every time I return to the field to observe animal bones leaving the biosphere and entering the lithosphere, I am astounded at the things that happen to them, things I have never seen before. Natural processes working on modern bone assemblages seem capable of making nearly anything happen. These complex, seemingly chaotic natural transformations do contain regularities and patterns, and are subject to many different laws of nature. But they continue to be poorly documented, and even more poorly explained.

This book's most enduring value may follow from its compilation of case studies and longitudinal follow-ups that reveal a wide range of taphonomic variability from similar bone-modifying processes. The contributions go far to show that, while there are actual patterns in nature, there are no trophic responses, i.e., no unvarying, automatic responses of bones and bodies to specified stimuli. Such variety should not dismay us, but it should make us much more cautious and critical in our taphonomic analyses.

An archaeologist's interest in the methods and perspectives of taphonomy is different from a forensic scientist's. Archaeologists commonly excavate bones of animals that prehistoric people killed, and the questions to be solved usually involve the degree of butchering and carcass-sectioning actually attributable to human behavior, as opposed to dog-scavenging, say, or some other nonhuman process. Forensic scientists need to determine whether foul play accounted for a death, and, if so, how that death occurred, and where and when it occurred. Archaeological uses of taphonomic analyses solve issues without life and death consequences. But that does not mean that taphonomic studies are irrelevant outside archaeology. It would be a shame if taphonomy were to continue being utilized mainly within the prehistoric sciences. There are many important clues about past events that analysts without a grasp of taphonomic studies will never see. Archaeologists have learned this lesson.

Recent publications by Haglund and others with an active interest in taphonomy demonstrate clearly that forensic sciences have an urgent need for taphonomic analyses, now more than ever. The ability of good taphonomic methods to indicate whether bodies were savaged by carnivorous scavengers, gnawing rodents, or a murderous human being, is especially needed in these days when criminals are unusually inventive in the ways they dispose of bodies and body parts. The great differences in weathering rates and dispersal patterns of corpses in deserts vs. those in forests, differences between underwater and terrestrial body dispersal, the different types of insect fauna attracted to bodies in different seasons and different locations, and so forth, are all part of the variability that in-depth actualistic and taphonomic studies can help describe and explain.

Many scientists like to believe that the weakest explanations have the shortest shelf-lives, but this simply is not true. All theories and hypotheses have potentially long lives, especially those difficult to test. It is through the testing and re-testing of propositions, hypotheses, and theories that newer, stronger explanations eventually emerge. Intuition and guesswork are the inspirations for theory, but without rigorous questioning the theories may never be truly validated. And because actualistic taphonomy can be a dirty, smelly, and very slow process, taking years to reach a state ready for conclusions, few people each year become involved in the research. It is an event worth celebrating when taphonomy and actualistic research are awarded another publication, especially one with an encyclopedic coverage like this volume, so that the old errors can be brought to light, and new information can be assimilated into the growing awareness that forensic scientists now have.

There are "cookbooks" and there are "bibles" in taphonomy, their billing depending on the editor's ambitions and the publisher's preferred idiom. I don't know whether the editors of this volume want to be one or the other, but I think it will outrank either category. It provides a wide range of case studies and a wide range of expert opinions about the meanings to be found in the different cases. Forensic scientists are discovering taphonomy, but in the same slow and hesitant way that archaeologists have done. Bill Haglund points out that the word "taphonomy" was not even considered worth a keyword listing in the main forensic journal not so long ago. And it is still hard to find it in the new crop of textbooks about archaeology or paleoanthropology, even though a growing proportion of researchers now take taphonomic analyses into consideration. Forensic scientists will find the word appearing more and more often in their own literature.

The intersection between one brand of taphonomy and another will continue to be oblique. Each kind of scientist must shape the actualistic studies that will reach special objectives. But both are learning to speak a common language, and each has something to offer the other. We are all trying to understand the processes of the present as a way of seeing the processes of the past in a new light.

My comments here have been intended first of all to rouse interest and concern for actualism and other brands of taphonomy among forensic specialists. As the editors point out, the taphonomic study of human remains is not going to become a flashy burgeoning subfield in medicolegal sciences, because opportunities to study how human beings leave the biosphere and enter the lithosphere are limited. Yet, there is already a respectable amount of literature about taphonomic processes affecting human remains, thanks to the kinds of research described in this volume.

One morning a long time ago I was walking alone in a prairie in search of wolf-killed bison carcasses. In the persistent rain my clothes became soaked, pages of my notebook fell apart under my pencil, and my fingertips puckered. Irritated, I wondered why I was doing this miserable stuff instead of traditional archaeology. Suddenly, about 200 yards away I saw four bison which had backed together rump to rump, and five wild wolves dashing at them and circling. I froze. The wolves kept it up only a minute or so, then trotted away. They were coming towards me. An old bison carcass had been scattered about the base of the willows where I crouched, and I realized they were returning to this killsite to finish it off.

About 30 feet from me the wolves fanned out around my willow bushes, and I knew they could see me. A gray male hunched tentatively in the grass to study me, the wet fur on his head furrowed from the rain. I knew he was going to leap on me and rip out my throat. I stood up and said hello, rather meekly. After looking at each other and at the other wolves who now were looking too, I started walking towards them. All but one noiselessly rushed away.

I walked into the open prairie where he and I faced each other at about 20 feet. The bison were still nearby, feeding with their heads bent down to the ground. No one would see me die or survive this. I think that wolf and I felt the same ferment of emotions, primarily trepidation, yet with an intuition that maybe both of us would live through this, both greatly curious, but with the troubling sense of not belonging together. Finally, I took its picture and then walked away, leaving it timidly pondering me from its place in the meadow.

What was I, an archaeologist, doing out there rooting around animal carcasses and irking the living animals? The brush with death left the connection with archaeology difficult to see for the moment. This question is not incidental or superficial, but must be faced by anyone who does the type of research described here and elsewhere in the mounting taphonomic literature. Not all taphonomists face scavenging by wild wolves. But we all encounter the present in a way that more traditional archaeologists and forensic scientists never will; we see patterns in the teeth marking the bones and in the skeletons losing elements to the scavengers. We are learning how nature moves those carcasses from biosphere to lithosphere, removing evidence about death (and life), but also about how nature sometimes leaves us just enough evidence to understand what happened when a life ended in the past.

# The Editors

**William D. Haglund, Ph.D.,** took the position as Senior Forensic Advisor for the International Criminal Tribunal for Rwanda in December 1995, a position from which he also serves as consultant for the International Criminal Tribunal for former Yugoslavia. For the previous 16 years Dr. Haglund was with the King County Medical Examiner's Office in Seattle Washington where he was Chief Medical Investigator. As well, he serves as an expert with the Physicians for Human Rights and in that capacity has been involved in missions in Central America, former Yugoslavia, and Rwanda.

Dr. Haglund received his B.A. degree in biology from the University of California at Irvine in 1969 and his Ph.D in physical anthropology from the University of Washington in 1991. Prior to this he graduated from the California College of Mortuary Science in 1964 and holds a State of California Embalmers license.

Dr. Haglund holds an Affiliate Assistant Professorship with the Department of Anthropology at the University of Washington and is involved in teaching law enforcement through the Washington State Criminal Justice Training Commission. He has served as an affiliate member of the Board of Directors of the National Association of Medical Examiners, is a past president of the Washington State Coroner's Association, and is a fellow of the American Academy of Forensic Sciences. He has also held committee memberships with the National Association of Counties (NATCO), the Washington State Crime Laboratory User Committee and, the United Nations Expert Group for Exhumation and Identification in former Yugoslavia.

Dr. Haglund has co-authored a training text for the professional death investigator, *Medicolegal Death Investigator.* He has authored chapters *Controversies in Maxillofacial Surgery,* the *CAP Handbook for Postmortem Examination of Unidentified Remains* and, the second volume of *Forensic Osteology.* Dr. Haglund's major interests and publications are in the areas of human rights, outdoor scene processing, forensic taphonomy, and human identification. He has served as a guest editor for the *Journal of Forensic Sciences* and *International Journal of Forensic Sciences.*

**Marcella Harnish Sorg, Ph.D., D.A.B.F.A.,** is a private consultant in forensic anthropology, and has been an associated faculty member of the Department of Anthropology, University of Maine, since 1977. She served at the University of Maine as Associate Director of the Center for the Study of the First Americans, Institute for Quaternary Studies, from 1983 to 1988, and in private business as Vice President of Sorg Associates from 1988 to 1996.

Dr. Sorg received her R.N. from Fairview Park General Hospital in 1969, her B.A. in psychology from Bowling Green State University in 1972, her Ph.D. in physical anthropology from The Ohio State University in 1979, and was certified by the American Board of Forensic Anthropology in 1984. She has served as Secretary and recently as President of the American Board of Forensic Anthropology. Dr. Sorg is a Fellow of the American Academy of Forensic Sciences, a Member of the American Association of Physical Anthropologists, and the Maine Medico-Legal Society, and co-founder of the Northeast Forensic Anthropology Association.

Dr. Sorg has authored over 20 publications in forensic anthropology, taphonomy, and genetic demography, and was co-editor of *Bone Modification.* She has served as consultant for over 275 forensic cases, and has analyzed skeletal remains from over 20 prehistoric sites in northern New England. She has done forensic research on scavenger modification of human remains as well as on the timing of epiphyseal union in the medial clavicle. Her current forensic research focuses on taphonomic approaches to remains exposed in both marine and terrestrial environments, particularly the estimation of postmortem interval.

# Contributors

**Thomas W. Adair, B.A.**
Crime Laboratory
Westminster Police Department
Westminster, Colorado

**J. M. Adovasio, Ph.D.**
MercyHurst College Archaeological Institute
Erie, Pennsylvania

**Bruce E. Anderson, M.D.**
U.S. Central ID Lab
Ft. Kamehameha, Hawaii

**William M. Bass, III, Ph.D.***
Anthropology Department
University of Tennessee
Knoxville, Tennessee

**Hugh E. Berryman, Ph.D.***
Regional Forensic Center
University of Tennessee
Memphis, Tennessee

**Shelley Boyle, B.A.***
Anthropology Board
University of California
Santa Cruz, California

**Richard H. Brooks, Ph.D.**
University of Nevada
Las Vegas, Nevada

**Sheilagh Brooks, Ph.D.***
University of Nevada
Las Vegas, Nevada

**Valerie J. Cervenka, M.D.**
University of Minnesota
St. Paul, Minnesota

**Michael A. Clark, Ph.D., M.D.***
Medical Science Building
Indianapolis, Indiana

**Bertita E. Compton, M.A.**
Department of Anthropology
Smithsonian Institution
Washington, D.C.

**Melissa Connor, M.A.**
Midwest Archaeological Center
National Park Service
Lincoln, Nebraska

**Pamela M. Mayne Correia, M.A.***
Department of Anthropology
University of Alberta
Edmonton, Alberta, Canada

**Kim Castellano, A.S., B.S.**
Douglas County Sheriff's Department
Castle Rock, Colorado

**Thomas A.J. Crist, M.A.***
John Milner Associates, Inc. and
  Temple University
Philadelphia, Pennsylvania

**Edward David, M.D., J.D.,**
Office of the Chief Medical Examiner
Augusta, Maine

**G. Clark Davenport, B.S.**
AGEISS Environmental Inc.
Denver, Colorado

**Joseph H. Davis, M.D. ***
Dade County Medical Examiner's Office
Miami, Florida

**John H. Dearborn, Ph.D.**
Department of Zoology
University of Maine
Orono, Maine

**Dennis C. Dirkmaat, Ph.D.***
Department of Anthropology
Mercyhurst College
Erie, Pennsylvania

**Gregory L. Fox, Ph.D.**
Western Archaeological and Conservation Center
Tucson, Arizona

**Diane L. France, Ph.D.***
Laboratory for Human Identification
Colorado State University
Fort Collins, Colorado

* Denotes first author

**Alison Galloway, Ph.D.***
Anthropology Board
University of California
Santa Cruz, California

**H. Gill-King, Ph.D.***
Department of Biological Sciences
University of North Texas
Denton, Texas

**Tom J. Griffin, B.A.**
Colorado Bureau of Investigation
Denver, Colorado

**William D. Haglund, Ph.D.***
Senior Forensic Consultant for the International
Criminal Tribunal of the United Nations

**David W. Hall, Ph.D. ***
KBN Engineering and Applied Sciences
Gainesville, Florida

**Robert D. Hall, Ph.D.**
University of Missouri
Columbia, Missouri

**Neal H. Haskell, Ph.D ***
Forensic Entomological Investigations
Rensselear, Indiana

**Dean A. Hawley, M.D.**
Indiana University Medical Center
Indianapolis, Indiana

**Gary Haynes, Ph.D.***
Department of Anthropology
University of Nevada
Reno, Nevada

**Molly A. Hickey, M.P.T.**
Thomas Jefferson Hospital
Philadelphia, Pennsylvania

**Thomas D. Holland, Ph.D.***
U.S. Army Central ID Lab
Hickam AFB, Hawaii

**Ian Hood, M.S., Ch.B.**
Medical Examiner's Office
Philadelphia, Pennsylvania

**Dick C. Hopkins**
Arapahoe County Sheriff's Office
Littleton, Colorado

**Susan B. Jimenez, B.Sc., M.S.**
Department of Anthropology
University of New Mexico
Albuquerque, New Mexico

**Boris Kondratieff, Ph.D.**
Department of Entomology
Colorado State University
Fort Collins, Colorado

**F. John Krolikowski, M.D.**
Professional Medical Consultants
Wellesley, Massachusetts

**John W. Lindemann, M.Sc.**
Broomfield, Colorado

**Marilyn R. London, M.A.***
Department of Anthropology
Smithsonian Institution
Washington, D.C.

**R. Lee Lyman, Ph.D.***
Department of Anthropology
University of Missouri
Columbia, Missouri

**Mary H. Manhein, M.A.***
Department of Geography and Anthropology
Louisiana State University
Baton Rouge, Louisiana

**Robert W. Mann, M.A.**
U.S. Army Central Identification Laboratory
Hickam AFB, Hawaii

**Richard T. Mason, M.D.**
Office of the Sheriff-Coroner
Santa Cruz County
Santa Cruz, California

**Jerry Melbye, Ph.D.***
Erindale College
University of Toronto
Mississauga, Ontario, Canada

**Charles F. Merbs, Ph.D.***
Department of Anthropology
Arizona State University
Tempe, Arizona

**Marc S. Micozzi, M.D.***
College of Physicians
Philadelphia, Pennsylvania

**Elizabeth I. Monahan, M.A.**
Department of Anthropology
University of North Carolina
Chapel Hill, North Carolina

**Turhon A. Murad, Ph.D.***
Department of Anthropology
University of California
Chico, California

**Stephen P. Nawrocki, Ph.D.***
Department of Biology
University of Indianapolis
Indianapolis, Indiana

**Al Nelson, A.S.**
Jefferson County Sheriff's Department
Golden, Colorado

**Tyler G. O'Brien, M.A.***
State University of New York
Binghamton, New York

**Douglas W. Owsley, Ph.D.***
Department of Anthropology
Smithsonian Institution
Washington, D.C.

**Hydrow Park, M.D.**
Medical Examiner's Office
Philadelphia, Pennsylvania

**Thomas J. Parsons, Ph.D.***
Armed Forces Institute of Pathology
Washington, D.C.

**John E. Pless, M.D.**
Indiana University Medical Center
Indianapolis, Indiana

**Babette C. Rathbun, M.L.S.**
Department of Anthropology
University of South Carolina
Columbia, South Carolina

**Ted A. Rathbun, Ph.D.***
Department of Anthropology
University of South Carolina
Columbia, South Carolina

**William C. Rodriguez, III, Ph.D.***
Office of the Armed Forces Medical Examiner
Washington, D.C.

**Walter F. Rowe, Ph.D.***
George Washington University
Washington, D.C.

**Henry F. Ryan, M.D.**
Office of the Chief Medical Examiner
Augusta, Maine

**Michael Schultz, M.D., Ph.D.***
Department of Anatomy
Georg-August-Universität
Göttingen, Germany

**Douglas D. Scott, Ph.D.***
Midwest Archaeological Center
Natl. Park Service
Lincoln, Nebraska

**Paul S. Sledzik, M.S.***
National Museum of Health and Medicine
Washington, D.C.

**O'Brian C. Smith, M.D.**
Regional Forensic Center
University of Tennessee
Memphis, Tennessee

**Lynn Snyder, Ph.D.**
Detartment of Anthropology
University of Tennessee
Knoxville, Tennessee

**Marcella H. Sorg, Ph.D.***
Department of Anthropology
University of Maine
Orono, Maine

**Jack Swanburg, A.S.**
Arapahoe County Sheriff's Office
Littleton, Colorado

**Kristin G. Sweeney, M.D.**
Office of the Chief Medical Examiner
Augusta, Maine

**Steven A. Symes, Ph.D.**
Regional Forensic Center
Memphis, Tennessee

**Vickey Trammell, M.A.**
Department of Biology
Arapahoe Community College
Littleton, Colorado

**Cecilia T. Travis, M.Sc.**
Colorado State Parks and Recreation
Littleton, Colorado

**Douglas H. Ubelaker, Ph.D.***
Department of Anthropology
Smithsonian Institution
Washington, D.C.

**Scott A. Wagner, M.D.**
St. Joseph Medical Center Laboratory
Fort Wayne, Indiana

**Arthur Washburn, Ph.D.**
Department of Anthropology
Temple University
Philadelphia, Pennsylvania

**Victor W. Weedn, M.D., J.D.**
Armed Forces Institute of Pathology
Washington, D.C.

**P. Willey, Ph.D.**
Department of Anthropology
California State University
Chico, California

**Michael B. Worrell, Ph.D.**
Indiana University School of Medicine
Indianapolis, Indiana

# Acknowledgments

We would like to acknowledge the goodwill and patience of our family members and friends, especially Claudia and Ed. We also thank Catherine Chmidling, Judith Cooper, Ralph Johnson, Laurie Labar-Kidd, Joy Sorg, Sharon Smith, and Karen Turnmire who assisted with the preparation.

We extend our gratitude to the American Academy of Forensic Sciences, which provided the forum for our initial symposium in 1993 and released those papers for inclusion in this volume. Finally, we acknowledge the support of the Office of the King County Medical Examiner, Sorg Associates, and the Department of Anthropology, University of Maine.

# Introduction to Forensic Taphonomy

WILLIAM D. HAGLUND
MARCELLA H. SORG

## Linking Taphonomy and Forensic Anthropology

The purpose of this volume is to explain and illustrate the link between taphonomy, i.e., the study of death assemblages, and forensic anthropology, the application of the methods and theories of physical anthropology and archaeology to the medicolegal investigation of deaths. Despite the seemingly obvious connection between the two fields, they have been poorly linked in practice.

In spite of long-standing forensic interest in taphonomy on the part of a few forensic anthropologists (Bass 1984; Brooks and Brooks 1984; Haglund 1991; Sorg 1986), there have been few references to "taphonomy" per se on the part of forensic authors. Taphonomy receives only three references in the second edition of the standard text by Krogman and Iscan, *The Human Skeleton in Forensic Medicine*, although this text does recommend "taphonomic analysis" of human remains (Krogman and Iscan 1986). In a 1987 manuscript, taphonomy was eliminated as a key word by an editor of the *Journal of Forensic Sciences* (Haglund et al. 1987). It was only after pleading for its inclusion by separate letter that "taphonomy" appeared as a key word in that journal in 1989. Since 1989, "taphonomy" as a key word appeared a second time in 1992, and four additional times by volume six of 1993.

It is odd, yet understandable, that relatively little research has been devoted to the taphonomy of contemporary human remains. This paucity stems from at least three sources: (1) the infrequency of opportunities for research due to the nature and treatment of human death in this society; (2) the continued limited involvement of archaeologists or physical anthropologists in forensic investigations, particularly scene investigations; and (3) the limited awareness of taphonomy on the part of mainstream forensic death investigators in medical examiner/coroner agencies (Haglund 1991).

Contemporary society's treatment of human death generally prohibits the use of modern remains for research for religious, ethical, and emotional reasons (Smith 1986). Such proscriptions often mean that research on recent deaths occurs only as a by-product of the medicolegal investigation. Similarly, there has been pressure by modern Native Americans to "repatriate" (i.e., rebury ancient human remains and to limit research studies upon them) (McGuire 1989; Ubelaker and Grant 1989; Webb 1987; Willey 1981; Zimmerman 1989).

Pragmatic forces drive forensic death investigations. Identification of the deceased and determination of the cause, manner, and time of death are primary concerns of the medical examiner/coroner. This is a medicolegal context and not conducive to research. Once the pivotal forensic questions are answered, there may be little perceived need, opportunity, or resources to pursue the investigations further, at least from the point of view of the death investigation bureaucracy.

The majority of death in the United States today occur in health-care facilities (70%) or in residences or other locations that ensure almost immediate discovery (Robinson 1981). Deaths of this nature are usually certified by individual physicians and are not subject to comprehensive review. This is in sharp contrast to deaths which occur from unnatural or suspicious causes, or deaths which occur without a medical attendant.

Sudden, unexpected deaths and natural deaths that occur in the absence of a physician usually receive some form of regional review by a coroner or medical examiner. But, even in the majority of these forensic cases, the immediacy of discovery combined with the (usually) indoor location of the remains eliminates circumstances conducive to conventional taphonomic processes. There are exceptional circumstances within particular forensic jurisdictions which can inflate the number of cases that provide taphonomic contexts, e.g., catastrophes, mass exhumations, and certain serial homicides.

The exceptional nature of the forensic cases which may come under the scrutiny of the anthropologist is not peculiar to contemporary populations. Indeed, for the last 100,000 years at least, human deaths have been handled in ritual fashion, frequently including burial. In paleoanthropology, as in forensic anthropology, it is the deaths which have not been attended and have not been ritually buried that have invoked the greatest need for taphonomic models. And the questions are the same: what is the cause and manner of death, what can we learn about the individual's biological and social identity, when did the death occur, how can we discriminate postmortem changes from perimortem trauma or antemortem characteristics.

In addition to the rarity of appropriate cases, a second impediment to the study of taphonomic processes in forensic cases is the limited involvement of archaeologists and physical anthropologists. The absence of a trained physical anthropologist or archaeologist at recovery sites has been decried by many (Howard et al. 1988; Rhine et al. 1988; Sigler-Eisenberg 1985; Warren 1984; Wolf 1986). Unfortunately, it continues to be the exception rather than the rule that anthropologists have routine access to forensic cases in which they could potentially offer information. This absence can result in limited information about the scene circumstances (Krogman and Iscan 1986). The anthropologist's involvement may be invited only when it becomes apparent that there are problems distinguishing animal from human bones, or when race, sex, stature, and age of human skeletal material is needed to aid establishing an identity — frequently too late to be involved in the scene investigation.

There has generally been a lack of awareness of the discipline of taphonomy on the part of forensic anthropologists and other forensic investigators. What has been proffered as taphonomic insight has usually been highly qualitative. For example, T.D. Stewart (1979), in his discussion of time since death, suggested that smell and color of bones, insects, amounts of adhering earth or amounts of associated flesh, weathering, and animal damage to bone could generate an "impression" of the postmortem interval. When one of us (WDH) participated in the Green River serial murder investigation, taphonomic questions became much more precise and salient regarding the effects of scavengers, characteristics that distinguish tooth marks from other marks on bone, expected disarticulation patterns, and scavenger modification of soft tissue. The forensic literature at that time (mid-1980s) offered little information about these phenomena.

There are some structural reasons for the lack of cross-fertilization between forensic anthropology and taphonomy. Most scientists who do taphonomic research tend to be investigating deaths which occurred in the prehistoric past; forensic anthropologists tend to investigate recent deaths. Second, the forensic literature is not marketed to the bioarchaeologists, archaeologists, and paleontologists who do taphonomic research. Third, the taphonomic literature is somewhat diffuse due to its multidisciplinary nature; and forensic anthropologists usually do not stay abreast of the large number of journals in which taphonomic research is published.

One goal of this volume is to bridge this gap and illustrate that taphonomic models and approaches can be of use in forensic contexts. But, the second and more ambitious goal is to showcase properly researched forensic cases and case series as a form of actualistic research of potential interest to taphonomists. We invite a richer interplay between these fields and between scientists.

## Definitions

Taphonomy was originally proposed as a term meaning the study of death assemblages, or the "laws of burial" (Efremov 1940). Bonnichsen (1989) extends the definition to encompass the study of "the accumulation and modification of osteological assemblages from a site formation perspective." Olsen (1980) takes a slightly different approach in his definition, focusing on reconstructing the life history of a fossil from the time of death to the time of recovery; for him, taphonomy includes all aspects of the passage of organisms from the biosphere to the lithosphere. Archaeologists are perhaps more likely to assume the unit of analysis is the site, whereas paleoanthropologists and paleontologists may be more likely to assume an individual (or group of) organism(s) to be the unit of analysis.

In theory, these broad definitions of taphonomy presume a multidisciplinary approach: biological, cultural, and geological. In practice, taphonomists have tended to come from the sister disciplines of paleontology and archaeology (Johnson 1985) as well as paleoanthropology. Primary goals emanating from these disciplines have included: (1) reconstructing paleo-environments; (2) determining which factors cause differential destruction or attrition of bone; (3) understanding selective transport of remains; and (4) discriminating human from nonhuman agents of bone modification.

Forensic anthropology shares at least the last three of these goals. However, due to the shorter postmortem interval, forensic anthropologists are also concerned with soft tissue changes, including decomposition rates and patterns, disarticulation, dispersion of body parts, and modification of both soft tissue and bone. In fact, traditional taphonomic studies can be said to suffer from, for want of a better phrase, the myth of flesh. This bias manifests itself in experimental research and analyses which treat skeletal elements as though they had always existed without the encumbrances of skin, muscle, ligament, and other soft tissue.

Key goals which underlie forensic investigations, overlap extensively those of taphonomy. These include: (1) estimating the time and circumstances since death; (2) distinguishing postmortem conditions which may serve to confound human identification and the determination of the cause and manner of death; and (3) identifying factors which relate to the survival of human remains and other evidence.

Forensic taphonomy, as we use the term in this volume, refers to the use of taphonomic models, approaches, and analyses in forensic contexts to estimate the time since death, reconstruct the circumstances before and after deposition, and discriminate the products of human behavior from those created by the earth's biological, physical, chemical, and geological subsystems. We argue here that the immediate postmortem interval which includes soft tissue decomposition should be a more explicit part of the taphonomic paradigm. And, to that end, forensic anthropology has an important role to play, both in testing traditional taphonomic hypotheses and approaches, and also in providing actualistic models from which to create new taphonomic approaches.

## Areas of Taphonomy Applicable to Forensic Anthropology

Research areas within taphonomy that have particular relevance to forensic anthropology include reconstructing the scene (referred to in taphonomic literature as site formation), and studies of transport and dispersal — including selective representation, bone modification due to perimortem trauma, scavenging, and diagenesis.

Forensic anthropologists who participate in scene investigations and recovery of human remains are faced with difficulties similar to those faced in archaeological excavations. First, the scene must be interpreted. From a taphonomic perspective, one important consideration is whether the site is a product of autochthonous (the same as where the death occurred) or allochthonous (different from where the death occurred) deposition.

Estimating the time since death is a difficult process in both forensic and taphonomic contexts, but one that needs to be done as part of the scene reconstruction. Obviously, the precision needed is much greater in forensic cases — frequently in terms of days, weeks, or months, whereas the margin of error in taphonomy may encompass hundreds of years. The forensic anthropologist must frequently use other organisms' biological patterns to construct timetable models. For example, knowledge of the life cycles of sarcosaprophagous insects helps determine time since death in the first two weeks, or seasonality thereafter. Understanding the growth patterns of plants can assist in both absolute and relative dating of features within the scene.

Studies of selective representation are of great interest in reconstructing pre- and post-deposition events. Incomplete remains may be the result of selective transport and dispersal by water, scavengers, or due to preservation effects. And these events may have occurred before or since deposition. Taphonomic models can assist with interpreting how a particular scene assemblage accumulated, how it came to have a given spatial patterning, and how different types of bone elements came to be associated.

Overlapping with research about selective representation is the rather voluminous taphonomic research about bone modification (see, for example, Bonnichsen and Sorg 1989). Included in that literature is research about the modification of external and internal bone structure, about fracture patterns and differentiation of human from nonhuman agents, and about the many other alterations of bone, such as cuts, scratches, polish, flakes, punctures, desiccation, and discoloration. The interpretative effort is complicated by the fact that different agents can produce the same alterations and, similarly, the same agent can produce many alterations.

The taphonomic research has produced many distinguished studies and a watershed of information potentially applicable in the forensic context. For example, models have been advanced for:

1. Disarticulation sequences of mammalian carcasses (Clark et al. 1967; Hill 1979; Toots 1965; Voorhies 1969; Weigelt 1989).
2. Scavenging of carcasses (Blumenschine 1986a, 1986b; Haglund 1991; Haglund et al. 1989).
3. Weathering of bones (Behrensmeyer 1978; Johnson 1985).
4. Fluvial transport of skeletal elements (Boaz and Behrensmeyer 1976; Behrensmeyer 1982). These research studies provide rich starting points from which to base forensic speculation.

This is not to say that traditional taphonomic information can be applied indiscriminately to the forensic context. Of necessity, much traditional taphonomic information suffers from biases innate to its origin in archaeology and paleontology. One obvious difference from the forensic context, already mentioned above, is the longer temporal interval encountered in archaeology and paleontology. This affects basic assumptions. For instance, bone density has been a major concern of traditional taphonomists to explain skeletal element survival frequencies. For the much shorter time spans of forensic settings, the relative anatomic position of a skeletal element may be more influential to its survival and recovery than its density. Density becomes more influential as time goes on.

Other themes of bias, specific to actual models, may confound application of taphonomic models to specific forensic contexts. Behrensmeyer's weathering model is biased toward the extremely arid conditions in which it was developed (Behrensmeyer 1978). More applicable are the shorter-term weathering characteristics specified in models of, for example, Johnson (1985). Scavenging and disarticulation have been examined by many investigators, but the focal questions are different, using varied carcass and scavenger models, and varied tissue type perspectives (Blumenschine 1986a; Haglund 1991; Haglund et al. 1989; Haynes 1980, 1982; Hill 1979; Toots 1965). Pervasive among these is a bias of portraying the bone already skeletalized, as explained earlier.

Despite these biases, it is clear that taphonomic models are not only applicable to forensic research, they can be extended and improved by forensic examples.

# Areas of Forensic Anthropology Applicable to Taphonomy

We hope to argue by illustration in this volume that forensic cases can function as modern analogs of uniformitarian processes which also occurred in the remote past. In particular, forensic cases are informative about the immediate postmortem interval, e.g., about the fate of soft tissue and about the modification of fleshed and skeletalized "green" bone.

Further, because it is frequently possible to discover many of the independent variables involved in the postmortem interval, a more thorough understanding of certain processes results. These include: (a) what happens to flesh and bone in different environmental contexts; (b) which modifications are the result of human vs. nonhuman agents or environmental factors; (c) patterns of modification of certain scavengers; (d) patterns of fluvial or other types of aqueous dispersion; (e) patterns resulting from natural disasters; and (f) patterns of immediate postmortem transport. Each of these topics is covered within these pages.

Less traditional contributions to taphonomic research are also represented in this volume. For example, studies of marine contexts (see Boyle et al.; London et al.; Rathbun and Rathbun; Sorg et al.) fill a vacant niche, in that virtually all of the traditional taphonomic studies have focused on terrestrial or fresh water contexts. Other relatively new areas illustrated here include the modification of remains by insects (Haskell et al.), interpreting plants and fibers (Rowe) and the degradation of DNA (Parsons and Weedn).

# Research Methods and Trends in Forensic Taphonomy

The majority of data of taphonomic relevance produced by anthropologists and other medicolegal death investigators are limited to cross-sectional case observations. As a consequence, articles and presentations relating to forensic taphonomy have been treated as anecdotal case reports, based on a limited number of examples (Bass 1984; Brooks and Brooks 1984; Sorg 1986). Such anecdotes, normal for developing fields, either appear as "case study" presentations at professional meetings or are incorporated into case reports that do not receive wide audience. Although noteworthy, such case studies are limited in their contributions to theory building.

Taphonomic studies involving surveys of large numbers of cases of human remains are in the minority (Galloway et al. 1989; Haglund et al. 1987; Morse 1983; Warren 1979). Most forensic anthropologists do not routinely see large numbers of cases. Prospective longitudinal observations in this area are the exception, including for example the decomposition studies at Knoxville (Rodriguez and Bass 1985) and Project PIG in Colorado (France et al. 1992). Experimental studies of fractures and saw marks are also excellent forensic contributions to knowledge about the modification of bone (Symes 1992).

## Suggestions for the Future of Forensic Taphonomy

Marshall (1989) itemized five hindrances to the future of research in his overview of bone modification and taphonomy. They include:

1. Lack of standard nomenclature
2. Dearth of comparative case studies
3. Unsynthesized and scattered data sets
4. Limited data sets
5. Researchers who lack a broad knowledge base appropriate for this multidisciplinary field

These problems are present in forensic taphonomy as well. However, forensic anthropologists can make a real contribution in offering well-documented comparative case studies, as well as by working to alleviate the other problems in their own research.

In particular, forensic taphonomists should be closely examining existing taphonomic models with an eye to refining them to our foreshortened temporal needs and to control for ideographic variation. We need to look more closely at our use of terminology, for example in descriptions of fractures, in what is meant by adipocere and saponification, and how we depict the condition of remains. We need to encourage the concept of collaborative case assemblages for research purposes. This might overcome some of the hobbling effects of low case volume and limited examples of particular types of cases in individual case loads.

The development of shared research paradigms is imperative. If the research plan is in place, data can be collected routinely in the normal course of the forensic investigation without interfering with the medicolegal process. And if data collection strategies are shared among practitioners, the data sets will be more comparable and broader-based.

An optimistic forecast for taphonomy was expressed by Clyde Snow in his discussion of decomposition and the dispersal of evidence in the Cattone and Standish *Outline of Forensic Dentistry* (1982): "Eventually, as data accumulates, it should be possible to devise more efficient search procedures for the recovery of evidence and also improve our estimates of the time of death by a fuller understanding of the taphonomic factors involved." We share his hope that these and other taphonomic research goals can be achieved through careful work and cooperation as this new field develops.

## References

Bass, W.M.
    1984  Will the Forensic Anthropologist Please Help? A Case of a Woman Eaten by Dogs. Paper presented at the 36th Meeting of the American Academy of Forensic Sciences, Anaheim, CA.

Behrensmeyer, A.K.
    1978  Taphonomic and Ecologic Information from Bone Weathering. *Paleobiology* 4(2):150–162.
    1982  Time Resolution in Fluvial Vertebrate Assemblages. *Paleobiology* 8:211–227.

Blumenschine, R.J.
    1986a *Early Hominid Scavenging Opportunities: Implications of Carcass Availability in the Serengeti and Ngorongoro Ecosystems.* British Archaeological Reports International Series 283, Oxford, U.K.
    1986b Carcass Consumption and the Archaeological Distinction of Scavenging and Hunting. *Journal of Human Evolution* 15:639–659.

Boaz, N.T., and A.K. Behrensmeyer
    1976   Hominid Taphonomy: Transport of Human Skeletal Parts in an Artificial Fluviate Environment. *American Journal of Physical Anthropology* 45(1):53–60.

Bonnichsen, R.
    1989   An Introduction to Taphonomy with an Archaeological Focus. In *Bone Modification*, edited by M.H. Sorg and R. Bonnichsen, pp. 1–6. Center for the Study of the First Americans, University of Maine, Orono.

Bonnichsen, R., and M.H. Sorg
    1989   *Bone Modification*. Center for the Study of the First Americans, University of Maine, Orono.

Brooks, S., and R.H. Brooks
    1984   Effects on Bone of Abrasive Contents in Moving Water. In *Abstracts of the First International Conference on Bone Modification*. Center for the Study of the First Americans, University of Maine, Orono.

Cattone, J.A., and S.M. Standish
    1982   *Outline of Forensic Dentistry*. Standish Year Book Medical Publishers, Chicago.

Clark, J., J.R. Beerbower, and K.K. Kietzke
    1967   Oligocene Sedimentation, Stratigraphy, Paleoecology, and Paleoclimatology in the Big Badlands of South Dakota. *Fieldiana: Geology Memoirs* 5:1–158.

Efremov, I.A.
    1940   Taphonomy, a New Branch of Paleontology. *Pan-American Geologist* 74:81–93.

France, D.L., T.J. Griffin, J.G. Swanburg, J.W. Lindemann, G.C. Davenport, V. Trammell, C.T. Travis, B. Kondratieff, A. Nelson, K. Castellano, and D. Hopkins
    1992   A Multidisciplinary Approach to the Detection of Clandestine Graves. *Journal of Forensic Sciences* 37:1445–1458.

Galloway, A., W.H. Birkby, A.M. Jones, T.E. Henry, and B.O. Parks
    1989   Decay Rates of Human Remains in an Arid Environment. *Journal of Forensic Sciences* 34:607–616.

Haglund, W.D.
    1991   *Applications of Taphonomic Models to Forensic Investigations*. Ph.D. dissertation, Department of Anthropology, University of Washington, Seattle. University Microfilms, Ann Arbor, MI.

Haglund, W.D., D.T. Reay, and C.C. Snow
    1987   Identification of Serial Homicide Victims in the "Green River Murder" Investigation. *Journal of Forensic Sciences* 32:1666–1675.

Haglund, W.D., D.T. Reay, and D.R. Swindler
    1989   Canid Scavenging/Disarticulation Sequence of Human Remains in the Pacific Northwest. *Journal of Forensic Sciences* 34:587–606.

Haynes, G.
    1980   Prey Bones and Predators: Potential Ecologic Information from Analysis of Bone Sites. *Ossa* 7:75–97.
    1982   Utilization and Skeletal Disturbances of North American Prey Carcasses. *Arctic* 35(2):226–281.

Hill, A.P.
    1979   Disarticulation and Scattering of Mammal Skeletons. *Paleobiology* 5(3):261–274.

Howard, J.D., D.T. Reay, W.D. Haglund, and C.L. Fligner
    1988   Processing of Skeletal Remains: A Medical Examiner's Perspective. *American Journal of Medicine and Pathology* 9(3):210–216.

Johnson, E.
    1985   Current Developments in Bone Technology. In *Advances in Archaeological Method and Theory*, Vol. 8, edited by M.B. Schiffer, pp. 157–235. Academic Press, New York.

Krogman, W.M., and M.Y. Iscan
    1986   *The Human Skeleton in Forensic Medicine.* Charles C Thomas, Springfield, IL.

Marshall, L.G.
    1989   Bone Modification and "The Laws of Burial." In *Bone Modification*, edited by R. Bonnichsen and M.H. Sorg, pp. 7–24. Center for the Study of the First Americans, University of Maine, Orono.

McGuire, R.
    1989   The Sanctity of the Grave: White Concepts and American Indian Burials. In *Conflicts in the Archaeology of Living Traditions*, edited by R. Layton, pp. 167–184. Unwin Hyman, London.

Morse, D.
    1983   Time of Death. In *Handbook of Forensic Archaeology*, edited by D. Morse, J. Duncan, and J.W. Stoutmire, pp. 124–127, 148–153. Rose Printing, Tallahassee.

Olsen, E.C.
    1980   Taphonomy: Its History and Role in Community Evolution. In *Fossils in the Making: Vertebrate Taphonomy and Paleoecology*, edited by A.K. Behrensmeyer and A.P. Hill, pp 5–19. University of Chicago Press, Chicago.

Rhine, S., B. Curran, S. Boydstun, S. Churchill, P. Ivey, and M. Ogilvie
    1988   Skeletonization Rates in the Desert. In *Abstracts of the 40th Annual Meeting of the American Academy of Forensic Sciences.* American Academy of Forensic Sciences, Colorado Springs, CO.

Robinson, M.A.
    1981   Informing the Family of a Sudden Death. *American Family Physician* 23(4):115–118.

Rodriguez, W.C., and W.M. Bass
    1985   Decomposition of Buried Bodies and Methods That May Aid in Their Location. *Journal of Forensic Sciences* 30:836–852.

Sigler-Eisenberg, B.
    1985   Forensic Research: Explaining the Concept of Applied Archaeology. *American Antiquity* 50:650–655.

Smith, K.G.V.
    1986   *A Manual of Forensic Entomology.* Comstock Publishing, New York.

Sorg, M.H.
    1986   Scavenger Modifications of Human Skeletal Remains in Forensic Anthropology. Paper presented at the 38th Annual Meeting of the American Academy of Forensic Sciences, New Orleans.

Stewart, T.D.
    1979   *Essentials of Forensic Anthropology.* Charles C Thomas, Springfield, IL.

Symes, S.A.
    1992   *Morphology of Saw Marks in Human Bone: Identification of Class Characteristics.* Ph.D. dissertation, Department of Anthropology, University of Tennessee, Knoxville.

Toots, H.
    1965   Sequence of Disarticulation in Mammalian Skeletons. *University of Wyoming Contributions in Geology* 4(1):37–39.

Ubelaker, D.H., and Grant, L.C.
  1989   Human Skeletal Remains: Preservation or Reburial? *Yearbook of Physical Anthropology*
  32:249–287.

Voorhies, M.
  1969   *Taphonomy and Population Dynamics of an Early Pliocene Vertebrate Fauna, Knox
  County, Nebraska.* Contributions in Geology, Special Paper, No. 1. University of Wyoming
  Press, Laramie.

Warren, C.P.
  1979   Verifying Identification of Military Remains: A Case Report. *Journal of Forensic
  Sciences* 24:182–188.
  1984   The Recovery of Human Remains: The Weakest Link in the Chain of Forensic
  Evidence. In *Abstracts of the 36th Meeting of the American Academy of Forensic Sciences,*
  Colorado Springs, CO.

Webb, S.
  1987   Reburying Australian skeletons. *Antiquity* 61:292–296.

Weigelt, J.
  1989   *Recent Vertebrate Carcasses and Their Paleobiological Implications.* Translated by J.
  Schafer. University of Chicago Press, Chicago.

Willey, P.
  1981   Another View by One of the Crow Creek Researchers. *Early Man* 3(3):26.

Wolf, D.J.
  1986   Forensic Anthropology Scene Investigations. In *Forensic Osteology: Advances in the
  Identification of Human Remains,* edited by K.J. Reichs, pp. 3–23. Charles C Thomas,
  Springfield, IL.

Zimmerman, L.J.
  1989   Made Radical by My Own: An Archaeologist Learns to Accept Reburial. In *Conflicts
  of Living Traditions,* edited by R. Layton, pp. 60–67. Unwin Hyman, London.

# SECTION I

*Taphonomy in the Forensic Context*

# Method and Theory of Forensic Taphonomy Research

1

WILLIAM D. HAGLUND
MARCELLA H. SORG

## Introduction

Taphonomy can be defined as the study of postmortem processes which affect (1) the preservation, observation, or recovery of dead organisms, (2) the reconstruction of their biology or ecology, or (3) the reconstruction of the circumstances of their death. As such, taphonomy can provide a bedrock for many types of forensic investigation. Developed within the disciplines of paleontology, archaeology, and paleoanthropology, taphonomy is increasingly acknowledged as part of the forensic anthropology toolkit (Micozzi 1991; Sorg 1986; Ubelaker 1991) Taphonomy's holistic purview of data collection and analysis in death investigation encompasses both the contexts of recovery and the subsequent laboratory examination and stretches the traditional boundaries of forensic anthropology.

The scope of forensic anthropology, historically focused on laboratory analysis of decomposed and skeletalized remains, is often extended to include recovery of remains, particularly in outdoor scenes. The outdoor recovery of remains is sometimes termed forensic archaeology. Proposed as early as 1976 (Morse et al. 1976), forensic archaeology has received increased acceptance as part of the role of the forensic anthropologist. As a result, methods of site investigation and processing, largely derived from archaeology, are frequently applied in forensic settings.

Forensic taphonomy is that part of forensic anthropology which focuses on reconstructing events during and following death by collecting and analyzing data about the depositional context, discriminating peri- and postmortem modification of the remains, and estimating the postmortem interval. It includes the application of archaeological search and recovery techniques, the laboratory analysis of the remains, and an understanding of unique and overlapping agencies of soft tissue and bone modification and distribution. Forensic taphonomy frequently includes applications from other disciplines of the natural and physical sciences. It differs from taphonomic studies in archaeology and paleontology in its focus on events in the recent past, the legal context, and the emphasis on chain of custody.

In paleoanthropology and bioarchaeology the physical anthropologist has been intimately involved in both the recovery and analysis of human remains in order to better frame and investigate disciplinary questions about biology and health. Similarly, in the forensic context, it is often appropriate for the anthropologist to coordinate taphonomic data collection and analyses among several disciplines concerning the outdoor death assemblage, specifically in posing and answering of forensic questions about the victim's biology, health, and circumstances of death.

Presence at the scene and expectations of taphonomic analysis engender a more ecological perspective. For example, questions regarding animal scavenging beg knowledge of topics such as animal behavior, diet, and territory size. Questions bearing on estimates of time since death beg awareness of rates of decomposition, weathering, and entomological issues. The mission of the taphonomically inclined anthropologist is to determine how the body has been influenced by and, in turn, how it has influenced its surroundings. In a sense, the remains are the centerpiece of an ecosystem within which chemical, physical, and biological influences have come into play.

## Taphonomy in the Forensic Context

Perspective shifts are common sequel when one field of study is applied in a different disciplinary context. Historically taphonomy has undergone paradigm shifts as it has been applied by various schools of taphonomists and successively to the disciplines of paleontology, paleoanthropology, and archaeology. For example, human cultural processes, of little concern to paleontologists, became a primary concern of paleontologists and archaeologists with respect to human subsistence patterns, scavenging vs. hunting, butchering, and transport of prey (Bonnichsen and Sorg 1989). This "refreshed" mission resulted in debate regarding the definition of taphonomy (Lyman 1994).

In forensic work the reach of taphonomy is extended in several ways. The forensic investigator, the archaeologist, and the paleontologist are concerned, in turn, with interpreting successively deeper levels of the past. Forensic investigation concentrates on the processes immediately surrounding death, the perimortem period, and spans a postmortem period of days, weeks, months and, less often, years. Central issues of time in medicolegal death investigation are concerned with estimation of the postmortem interval and on resolution of whether events occurred in the ante-, peri-, or postmortem interval. This is a qualitative difference from the concept of time as used by the paleontologist and archaeologist.

Second, as a consequence of the forensic focus on the most proximal period of carcass transformation, the usual emphasis in taphonomy on vertebrate skeletons and their postmortem changes has been broadened explicitly to include the soft tissue changes which are part of decomposition and differential preservation. Additionally, there are qualitative differences in the dynamics of cause and manner of death. These include high velocity gunshots and a host of trauma attendant to industrialized society. The behavior of human killers, for example, may introduce extreme variations of transport, dismemberment, or other disturbances of remains (Haglund and Reay 1993).

A third departure is the shift from concerns at the level of the population and taxon to the level of the individual. Rarely is specimen interdependence an issue. That is, taphonomists have focused on reconstructing the behavior and ecology of populations of organisms in the past, whereas the forensic investigator focuses on the biology of an individual as the unit of analysis. Characteristics unique to the individual found in the death assemblage contribute to discovering the identity as well as reconstructing the finer details of the cause and manner of death.

Finally, the forensic investigation is often burdened by multijurisdictional concerns and the ever-present spector of potential medicolegal consequences. Matters such as chain of custody, depositions, and court testimony come into play (Melbye and Jimenez, this volume).

## The Fidelity of Inference

Taphonomy has been portrayed as an historical science (Shipman 1981). Thus, taphonomists walk a thin line between the actions of reconstructing a unique event and understanding that event in the context of uniform processes. Lyman (1994:52–53) has reviewed the concept of actualism in taphonomy, noting that taphonomy includes both laws (immanent properties, or "immutable physical and chemical reactions that occur with predictable results regardless of spatio-temporal context") and context-specific aspects ("configurational properties…which are historical and mutable"). He asserts that "taphonomic research is founded in mythological uniformitarianism and immanent properties, or actualism." Such an actualistic approach disallows the possibility of agencies operating in the past which are different from those operating in the present, but does admit some variance in energy levels, sequences, or intensity.

General procedures for historical research include three phases: (1) obtain and order historical data; (2) determine present processes; and (3) confront the historical data with the present processes. The pursuit of answers to traditional taphonomic questions has satisfied this approach by analyzing prehistoric assemblages (Voorhies 1969) and conducting actualistic experiments using modern analogues (e.g., Brain 1967; Boaz and Behrensmeyer 1976; Voorhies 1969) or field studies (e.g., Behrensmeyer 1978; Blumenschine 1986a, 1986b; Coe 1978; Haynes 1981; Hill 1979). Such actualistic or neotaphonomic studies are used to make inferences about past phenomena that are assumed to be analogous. They allow observations in contemporary operating systems of both dynamic and static components (Binford 1981). These observations can be compared to the static evidence from the past. Past causation must then be inferred.

Haynes (1981) provides a useful illustration of actualistic methods in his investigations of bone modification by carnivores. Observations of the modifications produced by captive carnivores gnawing on bone were compared to those of wild carnivores preying on carcasses. These static results, including the pattern and character of tooth marks produced on the bone, were readily observed and, in turn, compared to similar patterns seen on fossil bones, allowing for the inference that they were produced by a similar agent or mechanism. Such analogies help re-visualize an unseen phenomenon from the past by asserting its similarity to a contemporary pattern whose production can be observed.

Critical to the application of actualistic models and the resulting inferences is the credibility of those models (Binford 1981; Gifford-Gonzales 1989). Elements influencing credibility include the investigator's rigor in exploring not only positive aspects of the analogy, but also neutral and negative aspects (Lyman 1994). Building up many series of potentially related analogies, a necessary step in the development of the field, presents then an enormous task in maintaining credibility. Gifford-Gonzalez (1981) suggests a nested set of analytical categories (see below) to aid in building these linkages. From this perspective, the certainty of the relation between, for example, the directly observable "traces" and their actualistically determined "causal agencies" is greater than that between the "trace," the inferred "actor," or the inferred "behavioral context:"

| | |
|---|---|
| Trace | Observed modification of the remains, e.g., a scratch on a bone, including formal attributes of size, shape, location, orientation, and frequency |
| Causal Agency | The immediate physical energy cause or process which produces the trace, e.g., the movement and abrasion of sand against a bone |
| Effector | The item or material which actually produces the trace, e.g., sand grains |
| Actor | The source of the energy force that creates traces, e.g., an ungulate with sand grains adhering to its hoof trampling a bone |
| Behavioral Context | The prehistoric systemic environment in which the taphonomic behavior took place, e.g., a herd of ungulates milling about a waterhole |
| Ecological Context | The type of ecosystem and environment in which the actors lived, e.g., African savanna |

As Lyman has pointed out (1994: 59), "…archaeological analogy often lacks the required causal relations between processes and effects…and also lacks the diagnostic criteria some believe are requisite to use of the actualistic method…. Without the establishment of causal relations between processes and effects (relevant linkages), attributes of phenomena used as signature criteria are inductively derived empirical generalizations." Because we cannot prove analogically based inferences, such conclusions are only probabalistic; if we can carefully demonstrate causal relations between processes and effects in the present, however, the inferences become highly probable. Lyman's critical stance points to the growth still required of taphonomists, and hence of forensic taphonomists. Although much forensic inference is based on case experience rather than experimental observation, experimentally derived conclusions from taphonomic studies may be utilized to strengthen such inferences if they are carefully evaluated for their appropriateness.

The discipline and care needed in applying analogies is great. It is similar to the discipline needed to apply a certain statistical test. Are the ecological contexts similar? What differences as well as what similarities between model and observation exist? Which aspects may be neutral? Could equifinality be a factor? Has the literature on this topic been sufficiently developed to deal with variations?

The shorter time frame in forensic cases makes it somewhat less problematic to apply neotaphonomic models. Nevertheless, problems raised by Binford (1981), Carlson and Steele (1992), and others about the inherent weakness of argument by analogy still apply. That is, even if the model appears plausible, other possible causes for the same taphonomic signature should be ruled out. And, despite the amount of useful information gained by juxtaposing systems of independent relational analogies concerning generic taphonomic themes such as carnivore activity or water transport, (Gifford-Gonzales 1989) cautions about the complexity and variability of ecological systems, as well as the variation in the simultaneous and/or sequential processes to which a skeletal element may be subjected, are still necessary (Lyman 1982). Working with such analyses in forensic contexts begins to generate a familiar ring. As forensic scientists, we are called upon to render judgment about certain bodies of evidence. We use several levels which fit comfortably with actualistic methods: not consistent, consistent, probable, highly probable, virtually certain.

Forensic observations may offer higher resolution to taphonomic questions. For a pragmatic example, Rodriguez (this volume), in examining postmortem photographs of a homicide victim, noted diptera larvae on the victims hands and fingers. These atypical loci of insect scavenging on a decomposing body suggested these locales might be defense-type wounds. Subsequent exhumation of the remains demonstrated cut marks on bones underlying the insect activity depicted in the photographs. The observations of the soft tissue in this case allowed for an inference of higher fidelity to be made than mere cut marks on bone would have allowed. Direct effects of cause of death and perimortem injury are often readily observable in soft tissue and may involve hitherto unrecognized agents not experienced with bare bone by traditional taphonomists.

## Comments About the History of Taphonomic Theory and Models

Five basic assemblage phases have been identified for the transition states from which living organisms pass from life to fossilhood (Clark and Kietzke 1967; Klein and Cruz-Uribe 1984). As summarized by Klein and Cruz-Uribe (1984:3) these include:

1. The *life assemblage* (the community of live animals in their "natural" proportions).
2. The *death assemblage* (the remains that are available for collection by people, carnivores, or any other agent of bone modification).
3. The *deposited assemblage* (the carcasses or proportions of carcasses that come to rest at a site).
4. The *fossil assemblage* (the animal parts that survive in a site until excavation or collection).
5. The *sampled assemblage* (that part of the fossil assemblage that is excavated or collected).

To these assemblages should be added the *analyzed assemblage*, that part of the sample assemblage identifiable or appropriate for analysis. Aside from a few points of departure, this scheme lends itself to transition states undergone by human remains in forensic contexts. As human remains pass from life to death, they are deposited or buried at one or more locations where they are modified. As remains pass through various assemblage stages they undergo transformations, and not all body parts have an equal chance of survival. Hence, the collected sample may represent a tiny and distorted reflection of the original organism in its original environment (Walker and Leakey 1978).

Survival of bones has been a traditional object of taphonomic interest (e.g., Behrensmeyer 1975; Binford and Bertram 1977; Brain 1967; Guthrie 1967; Lyman 1982, 1984, 1989). Walker and Leakey (1978) and White (1988) in discussing *Australopilthecus boisei* and *Homo* remains, viewed them as passing though successive taphonomic screens or filters, such as the actions of water or animals, each having the potential to bias the sample passing through and/or around it. The concept of taphonomic bias has been used by others (e.g., Behrensmeyer et al. 1979; Boucot 1953; Hill 1975; Western 1980).

What parts do survive depends upon the various taphonomic agents, modification themes, or "pathways" which act to destroy, import, or export them to or from a locale. Taphonomic pathways are defined as processes of dispersal, disarticulation, and modification, and include chronologies of taphonomic mechanisms, factors, agents, and processes affecting taphonomic histories and bone survival (Lyman 1982). Several major taphonomic pathways have been identified and much effort has been put into ascertaining their "signature biases," for example, human subsistence activities (Binford 1981, 1984; Blumenschine 1986a; White 1952), and the activities of scavengers (Dodson 1973; Haynes 1980).

Interestingly, the concept of the biasing effect of taphonomic pathways has not always been the dominant approach. Although the term taphonomy was coined by Efremov (1940), much earlier work had already been devoted to the topic under the overlapping terms of paleobiology (Abel 1912, 1935), biostratinomy (Wieglet 1989), and actuopaleontology (Richter 1928). Cadee (1991) traces this non-English development from the birth of paleontology with Cuvier and Lamarck in France to its translocation to the German-speaking part of Europe at the end of 19th century. A main thrust of German taphonomy was the reconstruction of the paleoenvironment. Unfortunately, the German attention to process, exemplified by Wieglet (1989), did not spread widely outside German-speaking countries. This has been attributed, in part, to language barriers, but also to anti-German sentiment with the rise of Hitler and national socialism.

It was the recognition of taphonomic agents' biases and the processes which cause them, which dominated taphonomic research up to the mid-1970s and was considered central to interpreting ancient environments (Western 1980). Gifford (1981) suggests that increasing the accurate resolution of prehistoric biocene is accomplished by determining the nature of the taphonomic overprint and "stripping it away." Accordingly, a major goal of traditional taphonomic studies has been to identify the specific agent or agents that cause specific modifications of bone, and to remove their "noise," in an effort to view the original organism.

Since the 1980s there has been a resurgence of a more integrated, process-oriented approach that echoes the German tradition of Weiglet, whose pioneering classic, *Recent Vertebrate Carcasses and Their Paleobiological Implications*, portraying the interaction of environmental factors with processes of death, disarticulation, transport, burial, and preservation, was translated in 1989. (For historical reviews of taphonomy, see also Cadee 1991; Gifford 1981; Johnson 1985; and Lyman 1994.)

Although much useful information has been gained by studies of bone modification pathways, analyses using this approach tend to be somewhat particularistic (Lyman 1982). Research concentrating on generic taphonomic themes such as carnivore activity or water transport clouds the reality that a body (or a skeletal element) may be subjected to a variety of simultaneous and/or sequential processes before its eventual collection and analysis. Forensic investigation suffers the additional burden of distinguishing typical taphonomic pathways from criminal or other human interference, analogous to that faced by paleoanthropologists who seek to discriminate the effects of human activity from nonhuman taphonomic agents. Thus, dropping a strict taphonomic pathway approach allows more attention to the importance of context, multivariate observations, and the accommodation of other disciplines in interpreting interplay between the remains and the agencies of their transformations.

## A Forensic Taphonomic Model

In building a taphonomic model it is necessary to incorporate the temporal and spatial needs crucial to forensic questions. On the most fundamental level, taphonomic processes can be portrayed as involving four dimensions: (1) objects; (2) space; (3) modification of the object(s); and (4) the cultural dimension.

The "objects" of forensic taphonomy are human remains. They may exist as complete bodies with soft tissue, separate body units consisting of articulated bony elements (Hill 1979), isolated bones or teeth, or specimens (bone or tooth fragments, as defined by Grayson (1984). In spatial terms, remains can be deposited on the surface, within other environments such as water, or buried. Human remains may stay at the site of death or deposition, or may be moved and/or modified by physical or biological factors which may preserve or destroy them. More complex depositional environments may involve a combination or succession of these contexts. Cultural factors may affect the fate of human remains, including the cause of death or various types of transport, as well as investigator bias in collection, curation, and analysis.

The course of taphonomic processes and the displacement of remains takes place in a temporal context. Two major temporal components are of particular concern to forensic investigators: (1) the perimortem interval, including the timing of specific events such as trauma as they relate to the time of death, and (2) the postmortem interval, between death and recovery. The interpretation of temporal components may be ordinal (sequence of events), interval (absolute time units), or ratio (relative to some other temporal sequence or "clock").

The postmortem period may also be subdivided into early and extended intervals of time following death. Frequently these are used in an ordinal sense, as we do here, to denote the loss of soft tissue (early) and the exposure and modification of bone (extended). However, these subcategories are not well related to absolute time units, except in particular locations and contexts.

A model proposed by Carlson and Steele (1992) can be adapted to interpret forensic taphonomic history. Taphonomic history has traditionally been equated with the history of bone modification; in contrast, forensic taphonomic history also includes the event of death and the process of soft tissue modification. Carlson and Steele suggest that at least two contexts in the taphonomic history of bone may potentially be reconstructed: the primary context (PC) and the secondary context (SC). The PC is that in which the modification of bone began, and usually denotes the original depositional context; the SC is that which has qualitatively different modification agents usually due to qualitative or quantitative alterations in the context. For example, a context change occurs when a bone is transported following disarticulation. Context switches may also occur without physical movement of remains, such as with the introduction of a chemical or behavioral change *in situ;* thus, a change in the chemistry of the remains due to loss of organic matter may subject bone to different taphonomic influences; for example, it may fracture differently. Alternatively, there may be multiple displacements between death and recovery. Carlson and Steele point out that the taphonomic history of remains found in a secondary context is much more difficult to reconstruct than those found in a primary context. Thus, it is important to differentiate primary from secondary contexts in order to evaluate the reliability of the reconstruction.

Forensic time needs can be incorporated into Carlson and Steele's model by further partitioning the postmortem interval. It is not only the spatial/temporal context in which bone becomes modified that is of interest to the forensic taphonomist, but the time preceding bone exposure which must be considered. Forensic taphonomic history includes the actual death event, the interval of bone exposure through modification of soft tissue, the potential interval of bone modification, and the point of discovery and collection. Of particular interest in medicolegal death investigation is the perimortem interval, the boundary between soft tissue modification and bone exposure, and the interval in which bone is exposed to modifying agents. These intervals may potentially overlap and lack distinct interval boundaries. An overall interval crucial to forensic death investigation is the elapsed time between death and recovery.

## The Perimortem Interval

Estimating the timing of injury is a particularly pesky problem to the forensic anthropologist, specifically discriminating antemortem from postmortem injuries to bone. In order to distinguish these periods, we must be able to determine the conditions under which certain taphonomic processes come into play. Because these processes are not precise, the boundary between life and death becomes blurred when viewed retrospectively. The circum- or perimortem interval is an ambiguous interval into which are lumped our inabilities to distinguish antemortem from postmortem occurrences.

To illustrate, the reaction of a bone to stress is dependent upon its moisture and fat content. Fractures to bone that are considered definitely antemortem are characterized by evidence of this moisture/grease content, such as the presence of greenstick or spiral fractures. Those that are definitely postmortem are characterized by clean, brittle breaks, frequently parallel or at cross section to the long axis of the bone. But moisture loss occurs over time, and there is no distinct point in time after which it can be said to have occurred.

## Postmortem Interval

Estimating the postmortem interval can be similarly imprecise. In order to more accurately determine elapsed time since death, the observations (traces) used to mark the passage of time from death to recovery need to be specified. Certain processes lend themselves to partitioning as stages of postmortem change, including decomposition (Clark et al., this volume), carnivore assisted disarticulation (Haglund, this volume), and weathering (Lyman and Fox, this volume). Such stages are conventions that "freeze frame" a process by defining an array of observable attributes that mark its presence. It is ideal to know the triggering event for a particular process and the variables which regulate or influence the rate of movement through that process, as well as to be able to measure the rate of change.

Unfortunately, these processes are complex, potentially overlapping, and context-specific. Furthermore, they are not well related to absolute time intervals. Although one may be able to judge where a set of remains falls within a sequence of stages, it is almost never possible to assign a narrow time interval.

For example, in order to estimate postmortem interval for skeletal remains exposed outdoors, it is necessary to make judgments about the time needed for decomposition. Dependent upon the process chosen to measure time's passage e.g., temperature, it is ideal to know the triggering event(s) of that particular process, and also to be able to measure the rate and the variables which regulate the rate.

Converting "traditional taphonomic time" to "forensic taphonomic time" involves determining the triggering event for the taphonomic phenomena being observed, the time from death to reach that triggering event, and the time necessary to reach the observed stage of the taphonomic phenomena being observed at the time of the bone's recovery. To illustrate, consider bone weathering (Lyman, this volume). Exposure of bone to the atmosphere is the triggering event that initiates weathering of bone. In order to determine time since death, an estimation of the time it took the bone to be exposed must be added to the time it took for the bone to reach the weathering stage observed at the time of its recovery.

## Awareness of Investigator Bias

In any study it is necessary to keep aware of investigator-related biases. These include the investigator's recovery perception, collection methods, curation, and analysis. For example, the sample collected may not be the total sample that has survived. Brain (1981) suggests a strong artificial bias in early collection procedures at Sterkfontein. White (1988) echoes this theme in his discussion of collection bias in the context of early hominid remains, and his comments are germane to both collection of fossil as well as recent bones. White points out that at the site of recovery, depositional context, skill and methodology of the searcher, and "search image" (what the collector is expecting to find or looking for) potentially skew what is recognized and collected. For example, remains of South African hominid fossils, which are embedded in breccia, require different search methodology than those of eastern Africa, which are exposed from erosional outcrops. A further example from paleontology is that early collectors of hominid remains focused on an isolated tooth search image, while more recent search images encourage more complete fossil recovery.

Collection bias may be the most identifiable weakness in processing of human forensic skeletal scenes. This can be attributed to the relative complexity of the scenes and/or lack of qualified personnel to process them (Haglund et al. 1990; Howard 1988; Warren 1984; Wolf 1986). Familiarity with nonhuman vs. human bones, recognition of partially represented bones or those of immature individuals, and decisions about search area perimeters come into play as potentially biasing factors. Initial discovery of human skeletal remains is most frequently hostage to lay recognition of human skeletal material. For the majority of such discoveries, it is the human skull which triggers recognition.

Recovery perception goes beyond recognition of anatomical parts. It includes the collector's perception and recognition of the context of associations of elements, characteristics of individual elements, and, in fact, any observations which can significantly affect recovery and analysis.

Curation bias may result from loss, misplacement, or degradation of collected material. Historically the most notorious example is the disappearance of the Zhoukoudian hominid specimens (Binford and Ho 1985; Binford and Stone 1986). This can happen in the forensic context as well. Too vigorous cleaning of specimens can destroy evidence, for example. Or, as discussed in Melbye and Jimenez (this volume), samples may be incorrectly or inadequately labeled.

White (1992) has summarized factors critical to the "Identification level of analysis." Bias in identification is influenced by investigator competence, conditions under which the analysis takes place, and context from which the original sample was removed. Competence involves experience and what Cornwall (1956) termed "a feeling" or "intuitive perception," and innate aptitude for morphological identification. According to White, conditions of analysis are also influenced by the time allotted for analysis, bench space, and lighting. In reference to context, White provides the example of skeletal elements that are not particularly diagnostic of one particular species, but, when found in association with identifiable bones of a particular species, can be identified. Context and associations are a too often neglected aspect of forensic scenes (see Dirkmaat and Adavasio, this volume).

# The Present State of Taphonomic "Information" in Forensic Science

As noted in the introduction to this section, the majority of taphonomically relevant information is the heritage of the literature of paleontology/paleoanthropology and archaeology; the contribution of forensics to taphonomy has been slim. Certainly taphonomically relevant information resides in the experiences of individual medicolegal investigators, but it will unfortunately remain sequestered with those individuals for lack of being published. These experiences, when published, appear for the most part as anecdotal reports (e.g., Bass 1984; Brooks and Brooks 1984; Sorg 1985). Their anecdotal nature provides limited basis for theory building or for fully understood variation.

Published accounts representing large series of taphonomically relevant cases are in the minority, although there are some notable exceptions which take the form of retrospective or prospective approaches. Retrospective studies which collate the experiences of a particular forensic jurisdiction overcome limitations of the anecdote. Examples are the reports by Galloway et al., on decay and mummification of human remains in the Sonoran desert, Boyle and Galloway on the taphonomy of drowning victims in the Monterey Bay area, and the series of marine cases from the Gulf of Maine by Sorg et al. (all this volume).

One positive aspect of retrospective studies is their concentration on a specific geographic area. This allows general principles to be articulated and fuller explication of ideogeographic variation to be made. Another retrospective approach attempts to collate the information on a specific topic from investigators of various jurisdictions, as Manhein has done on buried remains (this volume). Both approaches are vulnerable to criticisms of having to "normalize" variables, in order to compensate for nonuniform data collection and documentation. Interobserver error is a potent source of variation. Even when a single individual has been involved in all cases in a series, data collection approaches and methods tend to have varied over time, and attention to calibration is rare.

Prospective and experimental studies theoretically overcome some of these difficulties, but are rare in forensic taphonomy. The decomposition and insect succession studies at Knoxville (Bass, this volume; Rodriguez and Bass 1985) and project PIG in Colorado (France et al. 1992, and this volume) are exceptional examples. Experimental studies of fractures and saw marks represent significant contributions to knowledge about modification of bone (Symes 1992). Micozzi (1986 and this volume) presents an attempt to study effects of freezing and decomposition. Ubelaker (this volume) reports his attempt to duplicate trauma to a human phalange using a nonhuman animal model. However, we are still left with surprisingly little reported research aimed at solving specific forensic taphonomic questions.

Both experimental situations and field studies have advantages and drawbacks. On one hand, experiments permit isolation and control of variables (Lyman 1982) and the potential for a clearer understanding, unimpeded by unwanted variables. On the other hand, experimental conditions may introduce artificiality which, at times, is simplistic and not reflective of "natural" processes (Hanson 1980). Field studies attempt to avoid these pitfalls of simplicity and artifact. They fall into two major categories, cross sectional and longitudinal studies. Longitudinal studies offer the advantage of monitoring a phenomenon throughout its history. These are the sorts of observations made at the decomposition center at the University of Knoxville, Tennessee. Cross-sectional studies capture time-continuum phenomena at one point of time in the continuum and study it broadly. Cases investigated by forensic investigators often fall into this category (Haglund et al. 1989). Cross-sectional studies can be enhanced by increasing sample size, but are more dependent upon inference to fill in for time periods which lack direct observation (see Sorg et al., this volume).

## Summary

Taphonomy offers a body of knowledge particularly applicable to forensic questions. In turn, forensic cases offer a human-specific model for which many variables affecting death assemblages may be assessed. Relative to archaeological and paleontological assemblages, forensic skeletal cases potentially provide refined resolutions of the variables immediately subsequent to death and allow actualistic settings for cross-sectional taphonomic observations. Such actualistic observations can provide needed understanding of the taphonomic pathways to which archaeological human remains have been subjected.

Both taphonomy and the forensic sciences are multidisciplinary. Because of this, there is no tidy way to limit and focus their union. Nevertheless, we think that forensic anthropologists, because of their links with both human biology and archaeology, are in the best position to lead the way. We advocate an expansion in the practice of both forensic anthropology and forensic pathology to include more involvement in outdoor scene processing. The idea that methods from archaeology are useful in forensic investigations is augmented to suggest the models and approaches from taphonomy be integrated as well. Archaeology has been a leader among the historical sciences in the development of methods of searching for and collecting data in outdoor settings, from both two- and three-dimensional contexts. And these highly systematic methods are indeed finding increased acceptance in forensic scene processing. When the forensic anthropologist receives skeletal remains in the laboratory, she or he must infer the context of recovery. This inference is one step removed from the original context, and information will be lost. Indeed, any recovery process will, itself, bias the data collected at the scene, data that may be critical to the interpretation of the postmortem interval or other issues. Thus participation in recovery is critical.

We also propose that the theoretical perspectives from taphonomy are necessary to improve the interpretation of individual biology and history within the context of depositional environment. But we must go further than that. In order to assure that such involvement will actually result in improved investigations, we must take steps to improve the rigor and reproducibility of our techniques. This involves increased focus on both diachronic and synchronic data collection within forensic casework, as well as attention to experimental research.

Finally, we welcome the correction and criticism of our efforts. This volume represents a tentative first step in exploring new directions, within both forensic sciences and archaeology. We hope vigorous debate and fertile interaction will ensue.

## References

Abel, O.
  1912 *Grundzuge der Palaobiologie der Wirbeltiere.* Sweitzerbart'sche Verlagsbuchhandlung, Stuttgart.
  1935 *Lebensbilder aus der Tierwelt der Vorzeit.* 2nd ed. G. Fischer, Jena.

Bass, W.M.
  1979 Development in the Indentification of Human Skeletal Material (1968–1978). *American Journal of Physical Anthropology.* 51:555–562.
  1984 Will the Forensic Anthropologist Please Help: A Case of a Woman Eaten by Dogs. Presented at the 36th Meeting of the American Academy of Forensic Sciences, Anaheim, CA, February.

Behrensmeyer, A.K.
  1978 Taphonomic and Ecologic Information from Bone Weathering. *Paleobiology.* 4:150–162.

1975 Taphonomy and Paleoecology of the Plio-Pleistocene Vertebrae Assemblages East of Lake Rudolf, Kenya. *Museum of Comparative Zoology Bulletin* 146:473–578.

Behrensmeyer, A.K., D. Western, and D. Dechant-Boaz
1979 New Perspectives in Vertebrae Paleoecology from a Recent Bone Assemblage. *Paleobiology* 5: 12–21.

Binford, L.R.
1981 *Bones: Ancient Men and Modern Myths*. Academic Press, New York.
1984 *Faunal Remains from Klasies River Mouth*, Academic Press, New York.

Binford, L.R., and J.B. Bertram
1977 Bone Frequencies and Attritional Processes. In *Theory Building in Archaeology*, edited by L.R. Binford, pp. 77–153. Academic Press, New York.

Binford L.R., and C.K. Ho
1985 Taphonomy at a Distance: Zhoukoudian, "The Cave Home of Beijing Man." *Current Anthropology* 26:413–442.

Binford, L.R., and N.M. Stone
1986 Zhoukoudian: A Closer Look. *Current Anthropology* 27:453–475.

Blumenschine, R.J.
1986a Early Hominid Scavenging Opportunities: Implications of Carcass Availability in the Serengeti and Ngorongoro Ecosystems. *British Archaelogical Reports International Series* 283, Oxford, U.K.
1986b Carcass Consumption and the Archaelogical Distinction of Scavenging and Hunting. *Journal of Human Evolution* 15:639–659.

Boaz, N.J., and A.K. Behrensmeyer
1976 Hominid Taphonomy: Transport of Human Skeletal Parts in an Artificial Fluvial Environment. *American Journal of Physical Anthropology* 45:53–60.

Bonnichsen, R., and M.H. Sorg (editors)
1989 *Bone Modification*. Center for the Study of the First Americans, University of Maine at Orono.

Boucot, A.J.
1953 Life and Death Assemblages Among Fossils. *American Journal of Science* 251:25–40.

Brain, C.K.
1967 Hottentot Food Remains and Their Bearing in the Interpretation of Fossil Bone Assemblages. *Scientific Papers of the Namib Desert Research Station* 32:1–11.

Brain, C.K.
1981 *The Hunters or the Hunted? An Introduction to African Cave Taphonomy*. University of Chicago Press, Chicago.

Brooks, S., and R.H. Brooks
1984 Effects on Bone of Abrasive Contents in Moving Water. In *Abstracts of the First International Conference on Bone Modification*. Center for the Study of the First Americans, University of Maine at Orono.

Cadee, G.C.
1991 The History of Taphonomy. In *The Processes of Fossilization*, edited by S.K. Donovan, pp. 2–21. Columbia University Press, New York.

Carlson, D.L., and D.G. Steele
1992 Human-Mammoth Sites: Problems and Prospects. In *Proboscidean and Paleoindian Interactions*, edited by J.W. Fox, C.B. Smith, and K.T. Wilkins, pp. 149–169. Baylor University, Waco, TX.

Clark, S., and K.K. Kietzke
    1967   Paleoecology of the Lower Nodular Zone, Brule Formation, In the Big Badlands of South Dakota. *Fieldiana: Geology Memoirs* 5:111–129.

Coe, M.
    1978   The Decomposition of Elephant Carcasses in the Tsavo (East) National Park, Kenya. *Journal of the Arid Environments* 1:71–86.

Cornwall, I.W.
    1956   *Bones for the Archaeologist.* Macmillan Company, New York.

Dodson, P.
    1973   The Significance of Small Bones in Paleoecological Interpretation. *Contributions to Geology* 12:15–19.

Efremov, J.A.
    1940   Taphonomy: New Branch of Paleontology. *Pan-American Geologist* 74(2):81–93.

France, D.L., T.J. Griffin, J.G. Swanburg, J.W. Lindemann, G.C. Davenport, V. Trammell, C.T. Travis, B. Kondratieff, A. Nelson, K. Castellano, and D. Hopkins
    1992   A Multidisciplinary Approach to the Detection of Clandestine Graves. *Journal of Forensic Sciences* 37:1445–1458.

Gifford-Gonzalez, D.P.
    1989   Modern Analogues: Developing an Interpretive Framework. In *Bone Modification,* edited by R. Bonnichsen and M. H. Sorg, pp. 43–52. Center for the Study of the First Americans, University of Maine at Orono, ME.
    1981   Taphonomy and Paleoecology: A Critical Review of Archaeology's Sister Disciplines. In *Advances in Archaeological Method and Theory,* edited by M.B. Schiffer, pp. 365–438. Academic Press, New York.

Grayson, D.K.
    1984   *Quantitative Zooarchaeology.* Academic Press, Orlando, FL.

Guthrie, R.D.
    1967   Differential Preservation and Recovery of Pleistocene Large Mammal Remains in Alaska. *Journal of Paleontology* 41:243–246.

Haglund, W.D., and D.T. Reay
    1993   Problems of Recovering Partial Human Remains at Different Times and Locations: Concerns for Death Investigators. *Journal of Forensic Sciences* 38:69–80.

Haglund, W.D., D.T. Reay, and D.R. Swindler
    1989   Canid Scavenging/Disarticulation Sequence of Human Remains in the Pacific Northwest. *Journal of Forensic Sciences* 34:587–606.

Haglund, W.D., D.G. Reichert, and D.T. Reay
    1990   Recovery of Decomposed and Skeletal Human Remains in the Green River Murder Investigation: Implications for Medical Examiner/Coroner and Police. *American Journal of Forensic Medicine and Pathology* 11(1):35–43.

Hanson, C.B.
    1980   Fluvial Taphonomic Processes: Models and Experiments. In *Fossils in the Making,* edited by A.K. Behrensmeyer and A. Hill, pp. 156–181. University of Chicago Press, Chicago.

Haynes, G.
    1980   Prey Bones and Predators: Potential Ecologic Information from Analysis of Bone Sites. *Ossa* 7:75–97.
    1981   *Bone Modifications and Skeletal Disturbances by Natural Agencies: Studies in North America.* Ph.D. dissertation, Catholic University Press, University Microfilms, Ann Arbor, MI.

Hill, A.
  1975  *Taphonomy of Contemporary and Late Cenozoic East African Vertebrates.* Unpublished Ph.D. Dissertation, University of London.
  1979  Disarticulation and Scattering of Mammal Skeletons. *Paleobiology* 5:261–274.

Howard, J.D., D.T. Reay, W.D. Haglund, and C.L. Fligner
  1988  Processing of Skeletal Remains: A Medical Examiner's Perspective. *American Journal of Medicine and Pathology* 9(3):210–216.

Johnson, E.
  1985  Current Developments in Bone Technology. In *Advances in Archaeological Method and Theory*, Vol. 8, edited by M.B. Schiffer, pp. 157–235. Academic Press, New York.

Klein, R.G., and K. Cruz-Uribe
  1984  *The Analysis of Animal Bones from Archaeological Sites.* University of Chicago Press, Chicago.

Lyman, R.L.
  1982  *The Taphonomy of Vertebrate Archeofaunas: Bone Density and Differential Survivorship of Fossil Classes.* Ph.D. Dissertation, Department of Anthropology, University of Washington. University Microfilms, Ann Arbor, MI.
  1989  Taphonomy of Cervids Killed in the May 18, 1980 Volcanic Eruption of Mount St. Helens, Washington, U.S.A. In *Bone Modification*, edited by R. Bonnichsen and M.H. Sorg, pp. 149–168. Center for the Study of the First Americans, University of Maine at Orono.
  1994  *Vertebrate Taphonomy.* Cambridge University Press, Cambridge, U.K.

Micozzi, M.S.
  1986  Experimental Study of Postmortem Change under Field Conditions: Effects of Freezing, Thawing and Mechanical Injury. *Journal of Forensic Sciences* 31:953–961.
  1991  *Postmortem Change in Human and Animal Remains.* Charles C Thomas, Springfield, IL.

Morse, D., J. Stoutamire, and J. Duncan
  1976  A Unique Course in Anthropology. *American Journal of Physical Anthropology* 45(3):743–747.

Morse, D., J. Duncan, and J. Stoutamire
  1983  *Handbook of Forensic Archaeology and Anthropology.* Rose Printing, Tallahassee, FL.

Richter, R.
  1928  Aktuopalaontologie und Palaobiologie: eine Abgrenzung. *Senckenbergianna* 10(6):285–92.

Rodriguez, W.C., and W.M. Bass
  1985  Decomposition of Buried Bodies and Methods That May Aid in Their Location. *Journal of Forensic Sciences* 30:836–852.

Shipman, P.
  1981  *The Life History of a Fossil: An Introduction to Taphonomy and Paleoecology.* Harvard University Press, Cambridge, MA.

Sorg, M.H.
  1985  Scavenger Modification of Human Remains. *Current Research in the Pleistocene* 2:37–38.
  1986  Scavenger Modifications of Human Skeletal Remains in Forensic Anthropology. Paper Presented at the 38th Annual Meeting of the American Academy of Forensic Sciences, New Orleans.

Symes, S.A.
  1992  Morphology of Saw Marks in Human Bone: Indentification of Class Characteristics. Ph.D. dissertation, University of Tennessee, Knoxville.

Ubelaker, D.H.

  1991  Perimortem and Postmortem Modification of Human Bone. Lessons in Forensic Anthropology. *Anthropologie* 29:171–174.

Voorhies, M.

  1969  *Taphonomy and Population Dynamics of an Early Pliocene Vertebrae Fauna, Knox Country, Nebraska.* Contributions in Geology, Special Paper, No. 1. University of Wyoming Press, Laramie.

Walker, A., and R.E.F. Leakey

  1978  The Hominids of East Turkana. *Scientific American* 239:54–66.

Warren, C.P.

  1984  The Recovery of Human Remains: The Weakest Link in the Chain of Forensic Evidence. In *Abstracts of the American Academy of Forensic Sciences 36th Annual Meeting,* Colorado Springs, CO.

Weiglet, J.

  1989  *Recent Vertebrate Carcasses and Their Paleobiological Implications.* Translated by J. Schafer, University of Chicago Press, Chicago.

Western, J.

  1980  Linking the Ecology of Past and Present Mammal Communities. In *Fossils in the Making,* edited by A.K. Behrensmeyer and A. Hill, pp. 41–54. University of Chicago, Chicago.

White, T.E.

  1952  Observations on the Butchering Technique of Some Aboriginal Peoples: No.1 *American Antiquity* 17:337–338.

  1992  *Prehistoric Cannibalism at Mancos 5MTUMR-2346.* Princeton University Press, Princeton, N.J.

White, T.D.

  1988  Comparative Biology of "Robust" Australopithecus: Clues from Context. In *Evolutionary History of the "Robust" Australopithicines,* edited by F.E. Grine, pp. 449–484. A. de Gruyter, New York.

Wolf, D.J.

  1986  Forensic Anthropology Scene Investigations. In *Forensic Osteology: Advances in the Indentification of Human Remains,* edited by K.J. Reichs, pp. 3–23. Charles C Thomas, Springfield, IL.

# Context Delicti: Archaeological Context in Forensic Work

## 2

DOUGLAS D. SCOTT
MELISSA CONNOR

## Anthropological Archaeology and the Forensic Sciences

Reconstructing human behavior from physical evidence is a multidimensional jigsaw puzzle. Pieces of the puzzle are missing, damaged, and some are even camouflaged. The puzzle pieces come in seemingly incompatible data types — some are visual, some are in such microscopic form that it takes days of specialized analysis to show their existence, and in some cases the evidence is intangible, such as oral testimony. But practitioners of these two disciplines, each for totally different reasons, sit at their desks and doggedly persist in completing these puzzles — archaeologists and forensic investigators.

An archaeological site is analogous to a forensic scene in that the archaeologist needs to reconstruct the activities at a site, the location of those activities, and their sequence. Because of this similarity in goals, archaeological techniques, especially excavation techniques, are applicable in forensic contexts (Morse et al. 1976; Sigler-Eisenberg 1985). In return, forensic methods, such as firearms identification analysis and blood residue analysis, are effective in archaeology (Loy 1983; Scott 1989).

An archaeologist works within the constructs of anthropological paradigms. The strongest of these paradigms is that human behavior is patterned, and therefore the artifacts remaining as a result of that behavior are also patterned:

> The spatial structure of an archaeological site is the result of the nonrandom output of human activities which allocate structures, activities, and artifacts to specific loci within a site (Clarke 1977:10).

The patterning of human behavior is key to the concept that the study of the spatial arrangement of artifacts can be used to infer the behavior from which they result. Because of this, the spatial context of artifacts, including their relationship with the natural environment, is more important than the artifact itself. Removing an artifact from its context destroys much of its potential to help reconstruct human behavior.

The patterning of artifacts reveals site formation processes which include both cultural and natural forces. Natural forces include wind or water erosion, sedimentation, or animal scavenging. Cultural processes include agricultural activities, construction, or even an overnight camp. The study of taphonomy can help reconstruct such processes as initial site formation and subsequent modifications to the site. These are important contextual elements in assessing behavioral patterns through time, as well as dating the initial site formation and subsequent modifications. Taphomony, in fact, extends beyond human behavior to link all biological, chemical, and geological sciences.

Archaeologists, particularly historical archaeologists, can bring a knowledge of material culture to scene investigations. All societies use artifacts in the course of their daily lives. Artifacts can be and are used in a multitude of ways. Many times evidence of those uses are left behind as wear patterns on the object. Wear pattern analysis, akin to tool-mark examination, can tell much about an artifact's life history.

Material culture also changes in style and design through time. Most students of material culture can date an artifact by its manufacture and design. For instance, drink can pull-tabs were introduced on the market in 1962 (Dolphin 1977:33), providing a "no earlier than" date for associated material. Most modern artifacts or pieces of evidence can provide "no earlier than" dates of use. Artifact inclusion in an excavation may be fortuitous, but these ancillary pieces of evidence provide clues to the date of associated material.

Unraveling the data contained in physical evidence often requires the knowledge of an artifact expert just as the study of blood residue or tool-marks requires specialists. The goal of this paper is to show how archaeological techniques and concepts such as patterning and context are integral to the reconstruction of human behavior and can aid forensic scene investigation. Two examples are presented, one archaeological and one forensic. In both, the reconstruction of the behavior at the site/scene rests on not just the artifacts/evidence, but also on the context of the material.

One of the drawbacks to the use of archaeological techniques in forensic contexts seems to be the amount of time that painstaking archaeological excavation can consume. In some cases, there is no other method that will recover the same data. However, in the archaeological example below, a nontraditional technique is used to speed data recovery over large areas. This is a combination of metal detectors and electronic, computerized mapping that allows detailed recording of the spatial patterning in less time than required for most traditional maps.

# The Battle of the Little Bighorn as an Archaeological Forensic Scene Investigation

## Introduction

On June 26, 1876, George Armstrong Custer led approximately 210 men into the Little Bighorn Valley and onto the pages of American history. By about 5 p.m. that day, the main body of the command was destroyed, with no survivors, and their bodies lay scattered over the mile-square area now designated a national monument. Another element of the Seventh Cavalry, under the command of Major Marcus Reno, were still fighting for their lives, entrenched on a hill about four miles to the south.

The initial burial of Custer's command was about two days later, when the Indians had withdrawn and Reno's men were joined by soldiers under the command of General Alfred Terry. The June weather was hot, the bodies were decomposing, and the command had few shovels. The soldiers were unsure of the position of the Indians, but they were very sure they wanted to leave the valley before the Indians returned. For those reasons, the initial burials were rather haphazard. Visitors to the battlefield during the next few years frequently described human bone protruding from the area (Gray 1976) and several Army burial parties were sent to rebury the remains. Finally, in 1881, a burial party removed the remains to a mass grave on the top of Last Stand Hill.

Over a century after the battle, in 1983, a careless smoker threw a cigarette out a car window and started a grass fire that burned the battlefield area. The fire cleared the vegetation and visitors to the National Monument were startled to find human bone, cartridges, and other battle paraphernalia protruding from the ground. The National Park Service's Midwest Archaeological Center organized an archaeological inventory of the battlefield.

## Metal Detection

At first, we were daunted by the need to record precise locational data on the artifacts over the mile-square Park Service property in a limited period of time. Responding to that challenge, a methodology was developed that relied on metal detectors, an electronic data collector, an electronic distance meter, and advanced computerized mapping. The inventory procedure consisted of three sequential operations: (1) metal detecting; (2) recovery; and (3) recording. During metal detecting, artifacts were located and marked. A recovery crew followed and carefully uncovered subsurface finds, leaving them in place. The recording team then plotted individual artifact locations, assigned field specimen numbers, and collected the specimens.

The metal-detecting operations located subsurface metallic items with the use of electronic metal detectors. Concurrently, the surface was visually inspected. A metal detector crew consisted of a crew chief, metal-detector operators, and visual inspectors who also flagged the targets found by the detectors.

Detector operators walked in a line, following transects across the area to be inspected (Figure 1). While walking, the operators used a sweeping motion to examine the ground. Coils, usually 8 in. to 10 in. diameters, were held as close to the ground as possible to provide maximum vertical and horizontal coverage. Each operator covered a sweep of roughly 1.5 to 2 m, depending on the individual's height and technique. Closer spacing would have gained more detailed coverage and more detail of information on the presence of metallic debris.

A crew of five to eight operators was optimal for rapid areal coverage and supervision purposes. When a target was located, it was marked with a surveyor's pin flag. When the location was marked, the operator continued along the transect. Leaving the target not dug was the hardest part of the operation for the detector operator. However, if each operator stopped to dig each target the transect lines lost any semblance of order. In dense concentrations of metallic debris, it was necessary to recover the targets located and then re-detect the area multiple times to recover all the artifacts. The signal from larger metal objects obscured the signal from other smaller or less dense targets unless the larger objects were removed from the detector field. Metal shafts of surveyor pin flags also obscured nearby buried targets, so that a dense field of pin flags affected the targets found.

Metal detector brands were intermixed on the line, to avoid overlapping signals. Machines of one brand often use the same frequency to transmit their electronic signal, and, if placed in proximity, begin to "talk to one another." Machines of all brands were used in the non-discriminate mode, so that we were assured of finding all metallic debris, regardless of type. Brands used on the line, and all were effective, included Garrett, Fisher, White's, and Tesoro. Inexpensive "turn on and go" models were nearly as effective as the more complex machines. The more complex and more expensive machines allow for a greater level of fine tuning and ground control. For the experienced operator with knowledge of the vagaries of local soil types, these complex machines are a good choice. However, for the average, or less-experienced, operator the "turn on and go" machine has several advantages. Most are self-tuning to ground conditions and they offer a dial type discriminate mode. They are easily maintained and will take rougher handling than the more complex machines.

Each type, of course, has its advantages and disadvantages. The coils or loops are actually an antenna. The standard size for a search is an 8 or 10 in. diameter. Larger coils can be used for deeper penetration, but they loose sensitivity to smaller objects. Small coils, 3½ to 5 in. in diameter, are very sensitive to small objects, but lack depth penetration. The 8- to 10-in. diameter coil is ideal for most search operations.

## Recovery

The recovery crew followed the metal detectors, excavated the artifact locations marked by the pin flags, and then left the artifacts in place for recording. Traditional hand tools were

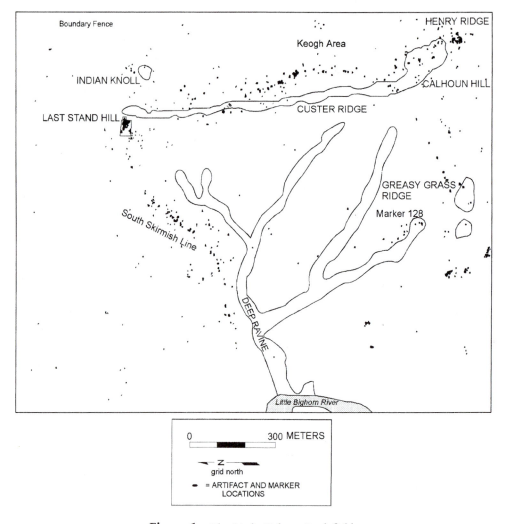

**Figure 1**    The Little Bighorn Battlefield.

used to dig, or scrape the earth away from, the artifact. No formal excavation unit was necessary, unless the goal of the recovery was to locate nonmetallic materials associated with the target. When other objects were found associated with the metal object, the crew chief decided whether to collect the object or mark it for later excavation. At the Little Bighorn Battlefield, nonmetallic objects included leather boots and animal and human bone.

The recovery team also used metal detectors to pinpoint the artifact. Excavation time was saved by using a small coil to pinpoint the artifact; otherwise time was wasted by digging a large area to recover a small object. Wire, nails, bolts, and other linear fasteners were notorious for giving ambiguous locational signals.

## Recording

As with any archaeological investigation the provenance data for interpreting artifact patterns was of paramount importance. Recording the data was crucial. The recording crew included the rod person and the transit operator, and people to assign field-specimen numbers and bag the specimens. Artifacts were assigned sequential field-specimen numbers beginning at some appropriate alpha or numeric field catalog designator. The recording crew also backfilled the artifact holes.

The project used a total station (combined transit and electronic distance meter) and an electronic data collector to record location and attribute data. Records were coded in the Sokkia SDR33 data collector, although a hand-written field-specimen catalog was also kept by a member of the recording crew as a backup. The electronic catalog was transferred from the SDR33 to a laptop computer on a daily basis. The Sokkia MAP program and Autodesk AutoCad programs were used for displaying the data.

Each artifact was piece-plotted as follows. The total station was set up at an established datum point. The rod person moved to the location of an artifact while another person filled out the bag for that artifact. The instrument operator read the distance and azimuth readings for each artifact location, and these were recorded electronically. The machine electronically converted the distance and azimuth to coordinate data, which were also recorded electronically. The instrument operator transmitted this information to the recorders at the artifact location either by a portable two-way radio or by voice. A radio is useful if the distance involved is much greater than several meters; otherwise the instrument operator will be very hoarse in several hours. The recorders at the artifact location entered the coordinate data into the hand-written field catalog that they kept, as well as a note on the type of artifact, and the field-specimen number. The rod person then radioed the artifact identification to the instrument operator who entered the appropriate artifact code in the electronic data collector from a designated set of codes. Meanwhile, the artifact was bagged and the rod person moved onto the next artifact. Using this technique, with the electronic data collector and a four-person recording crew, it was possible to piece-plot over 300 artifacts in an 8-h day.

Recent advances in the data collector capacity and reliability have nearly eliminated the need for hand-written back-up documents. However, written back-up documentation may be appropriate for some forensic scene investigations. Nevertheless, recording crew size can be reduced to two people if hand-written data are eliminated.

## Human Remains

The metal detectors frequently located metal objects that were associated with nonmetallic objects. Such was the case near Marker 128. Marble markers dot the field of the Little Bighorn, denoting where soldiers fell in battle. The markers were placed in 1890, although the bodies were supposedly exhumed and reburied in a mass grave in 1881. At Marker 128 (Figures 1, 2), the detector found boot nails, which were attached to a boot, which encased a skeletonized foot and a lower leg. A formal excavation unit was placed over the remains. About 20 cm north of the lower leg, a jumbled mass of bone was located. The jumbled bone extended 30 cm below the top of the mass. The outlines of a pit were not seen, but this was probably due to the homogeneity of the soil and the length of time since burial. The bones in the pit were jumbled and disarticulated, indicating reburial occurred after the flesh had completely decayed. When the marble marker was erected, the hole dug to set the marker intruded on the burial pit, scattering some of the bone. Rodents had also disturbed the burial, scattering small bones throughout the upper portions of the unit. Haglund (1992) noted a spectrum of possible rodent damage in addition to their being vectors of transport. In archaeological excavations it is common to see materials moved by rodents, by the motion of the soil caused by freezing and thawing, by insects, and by a number of other factors termed bioturbation.

The individual at Marker 128 was originally buried in his clothes, as buttons from his blouse and trousers were found, as were several fragments of army issue underwear cloth, and hooks and eyes, possibly from his campaign hat.

Examination by a forensic anthropologist (Snow and Fitzpatrick 1989) found the individual represented by the burial was male, about 22 years old and roughly 5 feet 6 inches tall. The soldier suffered from a congenital defect of the spine: the right lamina and inferior articular facet of the fifth lumbar is absent. While this had nothing to do with the battle, it

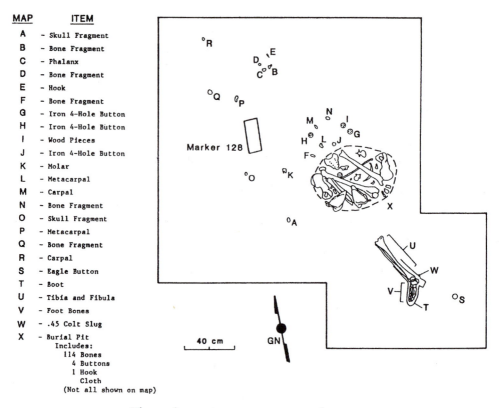

| MAP | ITEM |
|-----|------|
| A | – Skull Fragment |
| B | – Bone Fragment |
| C | – Phalanx |
| D | – Bone Fragment |
| E | – Hook |
| F | – Bone Fragment |
| G | – Iron 4-Hole Button |
| H | – Iron 4-Hole Button |
| I | – Wood Pieces |
| J | – Iron 4-Hole Button |
| K | – Molar |
| L | – Metacarpal |
| M | – Carpal |
| N | – Bone Fragment |
| O | – Skull Fragment |
| P | – Metacarpal |
| Q | – Bone Fragment |
| R | – Carpal |
| S | – Eagle Button |
| T | – Boot |
| U | – Tibia and Fibula |
| V | – Foot Bones |
| W | – .45 Colt Slug |
| X | – Burial Pit |

Includes:
114 Bones
4 Buttons
1 Hook
Cloth
(Not all shown on map)

**Figure 2**    Marker 128 excavations, plan view.

is probable that the trooper suffered pains in his lower back frequently, particularly when riding for long periods, as he would have been doing in the days before the battle.

Battle-related trauma was evident in the two gunshot wounds to the chest, the evidence for which was found on the ribs. One shot entered from the right and one from the left side. A fragment of a bullet was embedded in the left lower arm. This may be a third gunshot wound or a fragment of one of the other two bullets. In addition to the gunshots, both femurs showed three parallel cut marks near the proximal ends. Another cut mark was found on the collarbone.

The context of the skeletal material indicates a minimum of two burial episodes. As stated above, when excavated, one leg was in correct anatomical position, indicating it probably was not moved since the original burial when the body still included soft tissue. Differential weathering on the left side of many bones suggests that the left side of the skeleton was exposed after the soft tissue decayed and before the reburial. That most of the skeleton was jumbled indicates that it was reburied after the soft tissue had decayed, but probably before the 1881 construction of the mass grave. Thus, it is the context of the bones that allows the determination that there were two burials of this individual. In 1986, the soldier was buried for a third time, this time in the Custer National Cemetery. If the third time truly is charmed, he may now rest in peace.

## Firearms and Bullets

The battle of the Little Bighorn was fought primarily with firearms. The cartridge cases recovered from the battlefield were analyzed to determine how many weapons were represented within each caliber. Despite their corroded condition, about 90% of the cartridges could be analyzed. Detailed results of the firearms identification analysis are presented in Scott et al. (1989).

Firearms identification is the determination of types, calibers, and brands of firearms used. Class and individual characteristics are identified microscopically for each bullet or cartridge case. Microscopic comparisons are made between and among similar class characteristics to ascertain if there are matches at the individual characteristic level. If so, then the number of individual firearms represented can be reasonably determined.

The firearms identification analysis added to the history of the battle in a significant manner by using the piece-plotted locations of matched firing pin marks, and tracing the pathways of individual weapons. By combining the results of the firearms, identification analysis with the oral accounts of the witnesses present after the battle, in addition to the context of the cartridges recovered through the mapping procedure, the details of the battle came into focus. It became possible to reconstruct events and behavior at the Little Bighorn by combining physical evidence with historic documentation.

All the historic accounts agreed that Custer rode into the area from the southeast and deployed a group of men in a line facing a southerly direction (Figure 1). The quantity and types of cartridge cases and bullets, as well as their distribution, suggest that soldiers on this line faced intense fire from Indians south and east of that position. The Army-related materials consisted of cartridges in this position from a minimum of 15 Springfield carbines and two Colt pistols. Historical and artifactual evidence presented by Greene (1978) and artifacts recovered archaeologically suggest that the Sioux attacked from the south and southeast.

As C and L Companies deployed along the southern end of the ridge, the remaining three companies, E, F, and I moved along the ridge to the north. Captain Myles Keogh's Company I was left 300 yards in the rear of companies C and L, under the general command of Custer's brother-in-law, Lt. James Calhoun. Custer and the remaining two companies were apparently continuing their movement to the north in an attempt to enter the Sioux and Cheyenne village which lay just across the Little Bighorn River. While Calhoun was engaged on the southern end with Gall and many other Sioux warriors, Custer was forced back to the northern end of the ridge to the point now called Last Stand Hill.

Groups of Indians moved on the cavalry positions from the west, south, and north. As the various cavalry deployments took place to meet the Sioux and Cheyenne attacks, the soldiers were formed into a broad V-shaped pattern with Last Stand Hill at the apex to the north. Most of the cartridge cases associated with the soldiers were found in the area of the broad V-shaped deployment.

The firing must have been intense from both sides. The finds of spent cartridge cases and bullets certainly suggest this. Bullets fired from the soldiers' guns were found embedded in the ground, often within or at the front of the areas where quantities of Indian cartridge cases were found. Bullets in the calibers corresponding to the cartridge cases found at Indian positions were discovered embedded in the army positions. A few were even found in direct association with human remains.

From their positions under cover, and initially at a distance of up to 1200 yards from the soldiers, the Indians' fire began to take its toll. As the return fire from the soldiers began to slacken, the Indians moved in closer. From the south and east came Gall and the Sioux. They took positions close to Calhoun's line and poured intense fire into his men.

The heaviest fire came from the southeast from a ridge about 300 feet from Calhoun hill. The number of .44 caliber lever-action weapons in use here was substantial, with the cartridge cases indicating at least 23 Henry or Model 1866 rifles and at least six Model 1873 Winchester rifles. The cases also show that at least one Smith and Wesson revolver, two .44 caliber rimfire revolvers, and seven .50/70 caliber guns were also in use here. This area, referred to as Henryville or Henry Ridge, was perhaps also used to fire at the Keogh position.

More heavy Indian fire came from south and west of the Calhoun position on a lower portion of Greasy Grass Ridge. At least 22 .44 rimfire lever-action weapons, 13 .50/70 caliber guns, two Spencers, an unidentified .50 caliber rimfire, and one Model 1873 Winchester were in use in this area. The heavy fire from at least two areas with a combined firepower of at least 70 guns must have destroyed Calhoun's men. From the cartridge case distribution, it appears that Calhoun's position was overrun by the same Indians firing from Henryville and Greasy Grass Ridge. A few survivors from the Calhoun position may have attempted to join their comrades in Keogh's command. Cases from .45/55 cartridges with firing pin marks from two carbines were found in the Calhoun position; additional cases were scattered along a line toward the Keogh position, and finally intermixed with the Keogh group. It is also possible that these cases represent Springfield carbines recovered by the Indians and subsequently used against the soldiers. However, the casings were found in a coulee that could have provided some protection from the hostile fire from Henryville and Greasy Grass Ridge.

The cartridge case distribution suggests that as the Calhoun position fell, some Indians broke off and moved northwest toward Deep Ravine and the South Skirmish Line. These Indian groups were firing at ranges up to 500 yards into the soldiers on the South Skirmish Line. They brought to bear at least seven .44 caliber repeating guns, eight .50/70 guns, one Model 1873 Winchester, and several captured army Springfield carbines. As the Indians from the Calhoun fight moved toward Deep Ravine, they were joining an engagement already in progress.

The Indian attackers coming from the north and west met the men deployed from Last Stand Hill to the head of Deep Ravine. These soldiers fired at and into the Indians, perhaps halting their advance. The relatively small number of Indian cartridge cases found to the north and west of the South Skirmish Line suggests that the Indians attacking from this quarter were not as well armed as those attacking Calhoun.

Cartridge cases fired from some of the same Indian weapons used at Calhoun Hill and near Deep Ravine were also found near Last Stand Hill. These include at least three of the .44 caliber repeating guns. One .44 caliber gun was used at Henryville and Calhoun Hill in addition to coming into play at Last Stand Hill. Other repeating firearms were used against soldiers on the South Skirmish Line as well as Last Stand Hill. In addition, cartridge cases from other Indian weapons at Calhoun Hill and the Keogh position were found on and around a small hill northeast of Last Stand Hill. This Indian position provided some cover to the attackers as they fired into the knot of men on Last Stand Hill.

In summary, the cartridge case data suggest Indian movements along two broad lines. One was from south to north, from Calhoun Hill to Last Stand Hill through the Keogh position; the second was from Calhoun Hill and Greasy Grass Ridge to the South Skirmish Line, joining with the Indian group attacking from the north and west. These two broad movements converged at Last Stand Hill, suggesting that the hill was one of the last positions occupied by the Seventh Cavalry.

## The Koreme Execution Site: A Modern Crime Scene Investigation Using Archaeological Techniques

In 1988, the Iraqi government launched an offensive called the Anfel Campaign against the Iraqi Kurds. The results of this campaign on the village of Koreme were documented in detail by the Middle East Watch and Physicians for Human Rights (1993). This account is taken from that investigation. Witnesses in Koreme stated that the soldiers came into the village, and separated the villagers into three groups: women and children, old men, and young and adult men. A group of 33 young and adult men were separated from the last group. These men were made to form a line and asked to sit down. They did so, squatting on their heels, rather than sitting. The other villagers were led out of sight at this point.

Several young teenagers were pulled out of the line. After radioing to his superiors in a nearby community, the lieutenant ordered the remaining men shot. The soldiers opened fire at the squatting men. Some were killed immediately, others wounded, and six were missed altogether. There were 27 dead. The soldiers left the execution site without burying, or otherwise touching, the bodies. The remaining villagers were removed from the area that same day. Somewhere between a week and 3 weeks after the massacre, the Iraqi soldiers stationed nearby buried the bodies.

The investigation of the site and exhumation of the graves was carried out in 1992 by a team jointly fielded by Physicians for Human Rights and the Middle East Watch. The forensic team was headed by Dr. Clyde Snow, and James Briscoe acted as the Forensic Team Archaeologist. The team exhumed the graves and mapped the remaining village (all village structures had been destroyed through bulldozing and dynamiting). All cartridges and cartridge cases in the execution area were collected in a controlled manner.

## Method

The execution site was divided into two sections for controlled collection purposes. A metric grid was established along the firing line, and artifacts were collected in meter strips along the baseline. Each cartridge brass was plotted according to its position along the baseline and given a numerical designation before collecting. The numerical designation was plotted on graph paper and written on the artifact as each was located and collected. A second grid line, keyed to the firing line baseline, was set up along the victims line for collection of artifacts there. All materials located between the two lines and outside the grid were measured in relation to the grid baseline (Briscoe and Snow 1993:88).

This grid baseline allowed the detailed recording of the context of the material and the process used can be completed with equipment no more complicated than a 50-foot tape and some smaller tape measures.

The cartridges were sent to one of us (Scott) for analysis. There were a total of 124 cartridges cases collected. The locations of 63 cases were plotted using the method described above (Figure 3). Seventeen additional cartridges cases were recovered during the excavation of one of the graves (B-S). A final group of 44 cartridge cases was recovered in a pile near an olive tree about 20 m north of the piece-plotted cartridge cases.

The firing-pin analysis identified a minimum of seven individual weapons used in the execution. The weapons were all semi- or full-automatic 7.62 × 39 mm caliber firearms; AK-47 type firearms. Firing-pins from the 17 cases found in the grave and the 44 cases found under the tree matched with firing-pin marks from the piece-plotted cartridges. The matching groups were arbitrarily numbered 1 through 7, identified as separate weapons, and probably associated with individual persons. Among the cases are five unfired rounds found intermixed with the fired rounds. A single cartridge was a misfire. Weapon number 4 fired at least 15 rounds. Sometime during the shooting it had a round misfire that required it be cleared from the chamber by manually working the firing bolt. The condition of the gun's firing pin, as seen in the imprint on the primer, strongly suggests this gun was very dirty and possibly in poor condition.

The AK-47 and similar model firearms have a detachable magazine that usually contain 30 rounds. Assuming each weapon had a loaded 30-round magazine prior to the execution, it appears that weapons 1, 2, 3, 4, 5, and 7 fired at least one partial magazine each. Recovered cases indicate each minimally fired between 12 and 17 rounds, which is approximately one half of a full magazine. Weapon 6 fired at least 37 rounds, indicating it was reloaded at least once during the execution.

The distribution of the cases as piece-plotted shows two distinct clusters of cases (Figure 3). One group of six or seven cases lay in a western cluster. The second, and larger group, is 16 m to the east. A possible third cluster lay in a rough line to the north of the western group. There is a gap of about 16 m between the eastern and western clusters where only a single case was found. When the case matches are plotted, it becomes clear that the

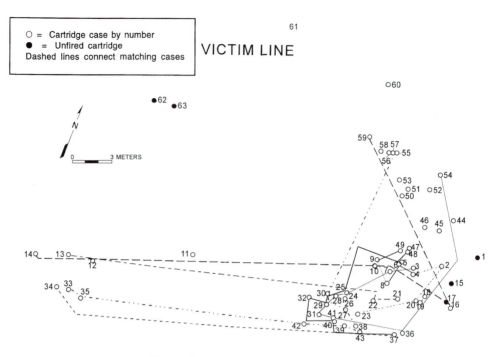

**Figure 3**   The Koreme execution site.

separation of cases is more apparent than real. Five weapons fired in the eastern and western clusters. The plotted matches in the western cluster suggest the individuals were aligned in a somewhat linear arrangement in this area. The eastern group demonstrates a much more bunched grouping.

The context of the cartridge cases suggests that the firing squad was linear and as the firing began, the men moved to the east in a random manner, clustering in an unorganized group. The absence of cases between the west and the east may be artificial in that the cases found in the grave and piled near the tree may imply someone collected the cartridge cases in the central area.

The case distribution show that weapons 2, 4, 6, and 7 moved to the north from the western cluster and fired one or more rounds each as they neared the line of victims. Weapon 6, which is the weapon that may have been reloaded with a new magazine during the execution, fired at least 12 rounds as it moved toward the victims. At least two rounds were fired within 10 m or less of the victims by weapon 6.

The ballistic evidence on the cartridge cases identified the minimum number of weapons and the minimum number of shots fired. Adding the context of the artifacts, however, the relationship of the cartridges to each other gave the interpretation a three dimensional quality. Using these relationships, Scott (1993) was able to interpret the movement of the shooters and their spatial relationship to the victims.

## Conclusions

The purpose of this volume is to demonstrate the link between the taphonomic study of death assemblages and forensic anthropology (Haglund and Sorg, Introduction, this volume). This paper focused on the archaeological concepts of context and spatial patterning to illustrate how anthropological method and theory is linked to the forensic sciences. That archaeologists can also learn from the forensic sciences is illustrated by the use of firearms identification analysis at the Little Bighorn battle site. The goal of archaeological methods and theory is to reconstruct human behavior. This is the same goal that governs forensic work, and many methods and theories are applicable to both contexts.

The methods and theories of anthropological archaeology were developed to recover and interpret the context of artifacts and relate them to the patterned behavior exhibited by those who left the artifacts behind. Analysis of these patterns relied on detailed recovery of the context of the artifacts. Documenting the context of the material is as important as the recovery of the material itself. In the past, the painstakingly detailed recovery techniques of archaeologists were frequently too slow to be of use in a forensic context. However, the new technologies of electronic, computerized mapping are making it possible to recover considerable detail in a short amount of time. The future possibilities of combining orthophotographic techniques with computerized mapping are exciting and make it unlikely that lack of time will be a recognized excuse for the lack of detailed data recovery in the future.

## Acknowledgments

The archaeological work at the Little Bighorn National Monument was funded by the Custer Battlefield Association. The work at Koreme was carried out under the auspices of the Physicians for Human Rights.

## References

Briscoe, J., and C.C. Snow
  1993 Archaeological Report on Koreme, Birjinni, and Jeznikam-Beharke Cemetery. In *The Anfal Campaign in Iraqi Kurdistan: The Destruction of Koreme*, pp. 85–96. Human Rights Watch, Washington, D.C.
  1977 *Spatial Archaeology*. Academic Press, London.

Dolphin, R.
  1977 *The International Book of Beer Can Collecting*. Castle Books, Secaucus, NJ.

Gray, J.S.
  1975 Nightmares into Dreams. *By Valor and Arms* 1:30–39.

Greene, J.A.
  1979 *Evidence and the Custer Enigma: A Reconstruction of Indian-Military History*. Putbooks, Reno.

Haglund, W.D.
  1991 *Applications of Taphonomic Models to Forensic Investigations*. Ph.D. dissertation, Department of Anthropology, University of Washington, Seattle. University Microfilms, Ann Arbor, MI.
  1992 Contribution of Rodents to Postmortem Artifacts of Bone and Soft Tissue. *Journal of Forensic Sciences* 37:1459–1465.

Loy, T.H.
  1983 Prehistoric Blood Residues: Detection on Tool Surfaces and Identification of Species of Origin. *Science* 220:1269–1270.

Middle East Watch, and Physicians for Human Rights
  1993 *The Anfal Campaign in Iraqi Kurdistan: The Destruction of Koreme*. Human Rights Watch, Washington, D.C.

Morse, D., D. Crusco, and H.A.G. Smith
  1976 Forensic Archaeology. *Journal of Forensic Sciences* 21:323–331.

Scott, D.D.
 1989   Firearms Identification for the Archaeologist. In *From Chaco to Chaco, Publication in Honor of Robert H. and Florence C. Lister,* edited by M.S. Duran and D.T. Kirkpatrick, pp. 141–151. Archaeological Society of New Mexico, No. 15, Albuquerque.
 1993   Firearms Identification of the Koreme Execution Site. In *The Anfal Campaign in Iraqi Kurdistan: The Destruction of Koreme,* pp. 103–107. Human Rights Watch, Washington, D.C.

Scott, D.D, R.A. Fox, Jr., M.A. Connor, and D. Harmon
 1989   *Archaeological Perspectives on the Battle of the Little Bighorn.* University of Oklahoma Press, Norman.

Sigler-Eisenberg, B.
 1985   Forensic Research: Expanding the Concept of Applied Archaeology. *American Antiquity* 50:650–655.

# The Role of Archaeology in the Recovery and Interpretation of Human Remains from an Outdoor Forensic Setting

# 3

DENNIS C. DIRKMAAT
J. M. ADOVASIO

## Introduction

In a forensic setting, much contextual information can only be acquired during the scene recovery phase of the investigation and is of most value when the information is gathered following standard archaeological methodological principles. This applies equally to urban or rural settings, fire scenes, and multiple fatality situations. Benefits are also realized by active participation in the autopsy and through postrecovery visits to the site for additional evidence. When included in the early stages, a forensic anthropologist who is trained in archaeological methodologies can make a significant impact on a forensic investigation in terms of: (1) locating and defining the scene; (2) ensuring maximal evidence recovery at the scene; and (3) more thoroughly addressing issues of personal identity and events surrounding and subsequent to the death, including postmortem interval or PMI (see also Killam 1990).

The use of archaeological methodologies during recovery has its greatest potential effects on the reconstruction of perimortem and postmortem events affecting the remains of the victim (more properly termed "taphonomy"). This chapter discusses basic archaeological protocols or "research paradigms" to be employed at forensic scenes and the benefits derived from their application to forensic investigation in general, and taphonomic reconstructions in particular. Discussions of case studies conducted by the authors illustrate concepts introduced in the text. The recovery methodologies discussed in this chapter have been very successful in producing rigorous data sets in strictly archaeological research contexts (e.g., Adovasio 1982; Adovasio et al. 1985, 1990; Carlisle and Adovasio 1982; East et al. 1989; Jorstad et al. 1986), and can be expected to do the same in the realm of forensic taphonomy.

It is hoped that what follows will demonstrate that:

1. Forensic archaeological techniques provide the most effective and efficient methods by which data are collected at an outdoor scene and as such have an important role to play in the forensic investigation involving decomposing human remains. Furthermore, that role is one that requires that the anthropologist become involved *prior* to the recovery phase of the investigation.
2. In order to actively and effectively participate in the multidisciplinary field of modern forensic investigation, forensic anthropology must encompass not only the laboratory analysis of wholly or partially skeletonized human remains, but also requires the collection and analysis of contextual information routinely obtained through standard archaeological techniques.

# Application of Archaeological Methods to Forensic Investigation

Archaeology and forensic investigation have much in common. Both are geared toward elucidating human behavior in a very precise way and both are based on exacting modes of data collection, data documentation, data processing, and data analysis. There is one critical difference — the factor of time, which has profound implications for both fields. Successful criminal or forensic investigations and successful archaeological studies are similarly oriented to reconstructing on the basis of physical evidence what happened at a "scene" in the past. For the archaeologist, however, the event to be reconstructed may be ten, twenty, or a hundred thousand plus years ago, evidence which contemporary jargon terms "very cold." Consequently, archaeologists have developed methodologies to locate, collect, analyze, and interpret what is often very ancient evidence. Most of these same techniques will work on what happened "yesterday" as least as well as they do on what transpired millennia ago.

David Hurst Thomas (1979) has observed that archaeology is primarily objects in their contexts, and all else is secondary. The same axiom applies to forensic investigations. Context is defined as "place in time and space," whether that space is a room an hour ago or a cave half a million years in the past. To understand the place of objects in their proper context is also to understand whether or not they are associated. Put most simply, all things found in the same place may not have "arrived" there at the same time, and even if they did they may not have come to their final destination as a result of the same set of activities or actions. If two or more objects do arrive in the same context as a result of the same depositional or emplacement process(es), they are in archaeological parlance "associated." If associated, these objects may be considered direct rather than circumstantial indications or reflections of a particular processual event in the past. Context and association are equally important in forensic investigation and, indeed, often have a legal gravity which only adds to their proper reconstruction.

Within contemporary North American archaeology, field research is normally a staged undertaking, composed of sequential episodes called phases. The perspective of phases is borrowed from cultural resource management (CRM) or "contract" archaeology. Phase I denotes a systematic archaeological reconnaissance of a previously unknown region or project area. Phase II designates the limited excavation of an identified but otherwise undefined site, the purpose of which is to characterize the site's stratigraphy, to determine the presence/absence of intact archaeological phenomena or features, and to assess its significance for future research. The term "Phase III" is usually applied to full-scale excavations or data recovery of a locality with demonstrated potential (as determined in phase II), while "Phase IV" refers to the analysis, interpretation, and presentation of recovered data in the form of a report. Very little modification is required to apply this staged approach and attendant procedures to forensic settings. More comprehensive descriptions of various aspects of these methodologies can be found in Dirkmaat (1996), Killam (1990), Morse et al. (1983), Skinner and Lazenby (1983), and Ubelaker (1989), among others.

A few cautionary remarks are in order regarding special concerns of the forensic anthropological investigation which distinguish it from a "standard" archaeological investigation. First of all, the chief concern of a forensic investigation is the legal acquisition of the evidence to be used in establishing links between suspect, victim, and crime, and potential legal testimony. A direct link must be established between the time of collection of evidence and the time that it is presented in court as admissible evidence. The person(s) recovering the material may be required to appear in court or respond to depositions to describe and defend any methods used, professional qualifications, and chain of custody concerns, as well as to answer a number of rigorous questioning sequences. Forensic investigations may involve multiple jurisdiction and multidisciplinary concerns that can include law enforcement personnel at the federal, state, and/or local level; the coroner/medical examiner's office; the forensic pathologist; and the district attorney's office. Careful pre-collection discussion with many or all of these participants is mandatory.

## Phase I: Systematic and Comprehensive Search Techniques

Searches for unlocated human remains are relatively rare and are most often conducted by law enforcement agencies on their own or with the solicited help of volunteer organizations. Most members of the law enforcement community are trained in search techniques, but their experience often does not extend to conducting searches for human remains — particularly remains that may have been deliberately buried (France et al., this volume; Morse et al. 1983). The forensic anthropologist, on the other hand, is trained to recognize subtle indications of a buried feature in the outdoor setting. These individuals can also provide rapid, on-site determinations as to whether bones are indeed human as opposed to animal, and differentiate forensically significant human remains from those derived from prehistoric or historic contexts. The efficacy of the search is greatly enhanced when a trained forensic anthropologist is an integral member of the search and recovery team. The forensic anthropologist may also evaluate the environmental, geologic, climatic, and biotic setting of the search area, critical in analyzing taphonomic factors affecting the cadaver.

### *The Successful Search Methodologies*

Extensive planning is required prior to entering the field. Factors to be considered in operationalizing the search include equipment, personnel needed and available, terrain (determined via aerial photographs and soil and topographic maps) and climatic/atmospheric conditions to be encountered, the time frame in which the search must be completed, jurisdictional matters (what Killam [1990] terms "political environment"), and general "plan of attack". All appropriate authorities such as land owners and law enforcement and medicolegal officials must be contacted, and permission or search warrants must be obtained.

Decisions regarding specific localities to be searched depend on suspect or informant (even victim) information and consideration of behavioral patterns of the suspect(s). Most graves involved in homicide cases are dug in a manner, time, and location that minimizes observation by other humans during the excavation process. This implies that the grave will be located in a relatively secluded spot, that it may not be deep, and that it was probably dug at night. These behavioral factors will aid in both the detection of the grave and in interpretations of events surrounding the initial excavation of the grave. These and other factors effecting the ultimate disposition of a body are discussed at length in Killam (1990) and follow what he terms a "principle of least effort."

Many of the searchers in a broad spectrum or "saturation" (Killam 1990) search covering a wide area will be relatively inexperienced volunteers. Prior to entering the field they should be thoroughly briefed regarding their role in locating the scene, the expected duration of search, distances to be covered, and importantly, what recognizable signs of a scene (natural and disturbed vegetation, soil features, and artifacts) are to be expected.

Search patterns are well established in both law enforcement and archaeology, and include strip or transect line search, grid search, and zone search (DeForest et al. 1983; Killam 1990; Morse et al. 1983; Saferstein 1990; Swanson et al. 1984). We have employed successfully a method whereby a first-wave of searchers walks in a straight, closely spaced line so that a 20 to 30% vision field of overlap is possible. The searchers mark the location, via a pin flag, of any and all potentially significant features or artifacts within their path. The forensic anthropologist and coroner/medical examiner or officer in charge follow the searchers and evaluate the flagged objects or features. If a significant feature or artifact is identified, the search process can move on to phase II — the more substantial evaluative process (see below). Cadaver dogs have been used successfully during this phase of the search to seek actively decomposing remains (Killam 1990).

If the surface reconnaissance is unsuccessful in locating the suspected grave, additional nonintrusive as well as intrusive methods can be employed depending on monetary resources, reliability of the information regarding location of the site, and time frame. Killam (1990), and Skinner and Lazenby (1984), among others, provide thorough descriptions of most of these techniques. In this regard, it is worth stressing that a wide array of highly sophisticated, high resolution, noninvasive search and detection techniques are now available to the archaeologist and have considerable potential for forensic investigation. These include the use of ground conductivity and soil resistivity meters, ground penetrating radar, and magnetometers, to name but a few (Weymouth 1986; Killam 1990).

## Phase II: Determination of Significance

Unlike conventional archaeological investigation, this phase of the forensic investigation is relatively short-lived. Surface finds are easily determined by the forensic anthropologist to be either human or nonhuman, and if human, whether they are forensically significant. If a buried feature is indicated, it may be evaluated via simple but thorough techniques, such as horizontal scraping with a trowel to identify differences in soil texture, coloration, compaction, and composition from surrounding undisturbed sediments, or even limited subsurface probing (Killam 1990; Owsley 1994). Such techniques provide determinations of whether a buried feature (grave) is present without actually encountering (and disturbing) the remains directly. If a significant feature is indicated, the project can quickly move into the recovery phase (Phase III). In summary, forensic anthropologist thus becomes an extremely valuable member of the search team in the following ways:

1. **Organization.**   Archaeologists are well trained and experienced in reading and interpreting aerial photographs and topographic and soil maps, anticipating and dealing with differing terrain and climatic/weather conditions, determining equipment needs, and directing and implementing successful search protocols. Additionally, most forensic anthropologists are employed in academic situations and are comfortable and effective at training volunteers and professionals in the concepts of patterned searches and preliminary identification of artifacts and features potentially related to the investigation.

2. **Differentiating human from nonhuman bone.**   An important consideration in searches conducted in rural areas is that very often complete and/or fragmentary animal bones will be encountered. The on-site presence of an anthropologist trained in the identification of both human and animal remains will considerably enhance the efficiency and effectiveness of the search through their ability to make rapid in-the-field evaluations of any potentially significant bone.

3. **Establishing forensic significance of human remains.**   The type and association of artifacts/physical evidence (including human bones) to depositional environment (i.e., context) will determine whether the remains are those of prehistoric Native Americans, Euro-American individuals disturbed from marked or unmarked cemeteries (Berryman et al. 1991; Huckaby et al. 1991; Rathbun 1990; Sledzik and Hunt 1995), or more recent and forensically significant individuals (generally <40 years since death). Archaeologists are trained and experienced in recognizing these types of associations and can provide rapid in-the-field preliminary determinations of age and significance of the remains.

4. **Identification of subsurface features indicative of a burial.**   Very subtle indications of a burial feature, including soil and disturbances and ruderal vegetation in a more recent burial as well as soil subsidence and enhanced vegetation in less recent burials (Morse et al. 1983; Skinner and Lazenby 1983), are best recognized by experienced forensic anthropologists during the initial surface reconnaissance. The detection of

obscured, poorly defined, or otherwise difficult to locate surface features via remote sensing is also most efficiently done by a trained archaeologist.

## Phase III: Context and the Recovery

It is likely that most human remains situated in outdoor settings will be disturbed in some way, either through curiosity or through ignorance; further disturbance must be prevented. In many cases the *modus operandi* has been the rapid removal of the remains accompanied by only cursory *in situ* documentation of the crime scene, resulting in the removal of the material from its primary depositional context with very little associated documentation which might facilitate its reconstruction. The unfortunate consequence is that the removal of remains — often crudely conducted using shovels and even heavy machinery — by its very nature results in destruction of the scene's context and hence, severely limits the resultant analysis and interpretation. The amount and caliber of information that is retrieved by trained forensic anthropologists as compared to law enforcement officials unfamiliar with archaeological methodology widens significantly when the remains have been purposefully buried (Killam 1990; Sigler-Eisenberg 1985).

## *Successful Recovery Methodologies: Surface Find*

Following the determination of the significance of the site, a perimeter is designated around the site (via police tape) within which access is strictly restricted to data collection personnel. Absolutely nothing within that scene is to be disturbed until the site is properly documented.

The first step entails comprehensive prerecovery documentation of the evidence by law enforcement personnel via written and oral notes, sketches, and extensive systematic photography with scales (DeForest et al. 1983; Saferstein 1990; Swanson et al. 1984). The forensic anthropologist should also thoroughly document the scene from the anthropological perspective and with the critical questions of taphonomy and circumstances surrounding the death event in mind. Standard forms can be developed which will aid documentation (e.g., Center for Social Development and Humanitarian Affairs [CSDHA] 1991). The following types of documentation are recommended:

1. Detailed written notes which describe the general setting (i.e., topography and vegetation), weather conditions, personnel involved, speculations, and any other general information that may be of value during interpretative phases of the investigation.
2. General sketches of the scene, preferably with scales, showing the relative position of the body and associated artifacts to major artificial and/or natural features.
3. Black-and-white and color 35 mm, medium-to-large format, and video photography of all aspects of the scene, progressing from general to specific views. Detailed photo notes must be taken of all still shots which include descriptions of camera settings and direction, orientation, and objective of the photograph. If a video camera is used, the shooting sequences must be steady (use a tripod if necessary), focused, and all panning shots unhurried. It is very important that the microphone on the camera be disengaged or muted, so that any and all inadvertent comments are not recorded and the evidence is allowed to speak for itself.

As with all of the documentation compiled throughout the course of the forensic investigation, all notes, photographs, and sketches made at the scene (and eventually in the laboratory) are potentially submissible in court; hence, they should be clear and legible, adequately labeled, and as precise as possible (see below).

Next, the area is carefully studied for additional physical evidence not identified during the preliminary evaluative phases of the project. This entails a more detailed search of the area, often with searchers on their hands and knees. Metal detectors are extremely useful for

**Figure 1** View of forensic scene following establishment of baseline and denuding of site (prior to removal of physical evidence).

finding metallic artifacts. Every effort should be made to find bullet slugs prior to their recovery on the sieving screens for important information relating the bullet to a particular gun may be retrieved from the striations on the slug. This evidence may be compromised if the slug is even lightly abraded against the wire mesh. If additional physical evidence is identified, it will be pin-flagged and documented as above.

The removal of all vegetation from the surface of the immediate vicinity of the site (Figure 1) will allow careful examination of surface topography as well as expose any additional physical evidence present on the surface (Adovasio 1982).

A permanent datum point must be carefully chosen in order that it can be easily relocated in the future. If possible, it should be located relative to a USGS benchmark or other permanent topographic feature. From this datum point, north-south and east-west baselines, the horizontal grid system employed in the investigation, and surface topography maps can be "shot-in" with conventional optional surveying equipment. The site or scene is now ready for final processing.

Prior to processing/recovery of the physical evidence, a second round of careful and comprehensive documentation is often required. In addition to the various classes of documentation described above, detailed plan view maps of the scene will be produced at this time. The location and orientation of all of the physical evidence visible on the surface relative to the physical setting can be mapped into the grid system established over the site. North–south and east–west dimensions can be taken relative to the datum point. Although, as indicated above, conventional instruments will suffice, more sophisticated mapping technology such as an infrared or laser theodolite can be used if available. The advantage of the more advanced equipment of this type is its capacity for rapid collection of spatial data and production of computer-generated site maps.

The physical evidence (including skeletal remains) visible on the surface may now be removed from its original position and carefully packed in order to prevent damage en route to the laboratory (see Berryman and Bass 1985; Howard et al. 1988). If the material is stratified, the removal proceeds layer by layer with careful documentation until all gross physical evidence has been collected. During this process, various samples should also be collected. Especially important are entomological specimens (see below), but it is also important to obtain flotation samples,* soil pH readings (Gordon and Buikstra 1981; White and Hannus 1983), palynological samples (used to reveal the geographic origin of an item and provide a link between an individual or item to the scene of the [Bryant et al. 1990]), and geochemical samples (Adovasio 1982) from the soil directly beneath the body. The remainder of this soil should be excavated to sterile either dry-screened or, preferably, water-screened through fine-mesh (⅛ in.) screens, with care taken not to damage bullet slug fragments.

One of the most important data sets to be collected during the recovery of human remains in a outdoor setting is insect fauna associated with the body, which are useful in establishing such issues as time since death, evidence of penetrating wounds, postmortem movement of the body, and even toxicological information (see Catts and Haskell 1990; Haskell et al. this volume, and Lord and Burger 1983; Rodriguez 1990).

## *Archeological Excavation Principles*

The discipline of archaeology has three primary and interdependent responsibilities: (1) the delineation of the site's stratigraphy from observed stratification; (2) the maintenance of context; and (3) the establishment of any associations between recovered materials. The terms "stratigraphy" and "stratification," which are *not* synonymous, are best viewed as being analogous to the pages of a book and the story which they tell. Stratification refers to the actual observed sequential layering of deposits (i.e., the pages in the book) while stratigraphy is the sum total of the processes whereby these layers accumulated (i.e., the story). The key to understanding stratigraphy is the successful identification of individual strata and their interfaces (i.e., contacts or boundaries differentiating one stratum from the other). All stratification adheres to certain basic "rules" or laws, often called Steno's principles, which include the laws of superimposition, original horizontality, lateral continuity, and intersecting relationship.

The law of horizontality dictates that the original declination of most individual strata is horizontal or flat, principally due to gravity. Superimposition asserts that for undisturbed depositional situations, the oldest strata are on the bottom or lower portion of a sequence, while overlying or higher depositional units are progressively younger.

The laws of lateral continuity and intersecting relationships are at once less self evident but also critical in the understanding of archaeological, geological, and forensic stratigraphy. Lateral continuity dictates that no matter how extensive the upper and lower boundaries or interfaces of a stratum may be, the material enclosed by these boundaries is broadly the same age. The key word here is *broadly*, because it is entirely possible that no two items found within a given stratum are *exactly* the same age or synchronous.

The law of intersecting relationships stipulates that the proper sequencing of stratigraphic phenomena is predicated on establishing where each anomaly — such as a burial pit — intersects a given surface in order to establish its age *relative* to other phenomena (Figure 2). If the stratification of a site can be correctly determined, then its stratigraphy can be delineated

---

* Flotation Samples: Feature fill samples of a standard size are routinely collected from the southwest corner of each excavation unit, from each natural stratum encountered (Skirbol 1982). These samples are then subjected to two types of flotation protocols in order to collect very small organic and artifactual remains. One involves the immersion of the fill sample in water, whereby one set of organics (usually floral remains) float on the surface and the other component remains on the bottom (bones and other compact organic materials and diminutive artifacts). The other flotation exercise involves immersion of sediment samples in a solution of hydrogen peroxide ($H_2O_2$) which maximizes the recovery of intact charred organics by minimizing the need for mechanical agitation. These methods ensure complete recovery and preservation of integrity of organic materials associated with the body. These organics may be used to resolve issues in a manner similar to that of palynological samples (see above).

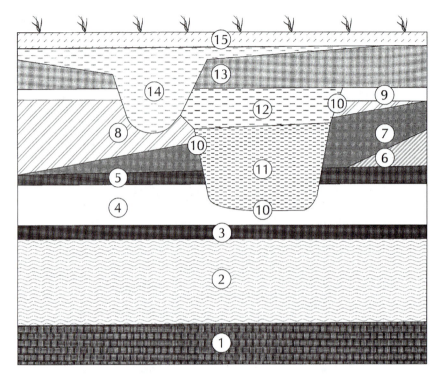

**Figure 2** Sequence of depositional events (a-g): (a) deposition of Strata 1–9; (b) excavation of Pit 10 into surface of Stratum 9; (c) initial infilling of Pit 10 by unit 11; (d) final infilling of Pit 10 by unit 12; (e) deposition of Stratum 13; (f) excavation and infilling of Pit 14 into surface of Stratum 13; (g) deposition of Stratum 15 and attendant plant growth.

and explained. Context, the position of any and all objects within a stratum relative to all other objects in all other strata, is critical. Once context has been established (via precise manual or computer-aided piece plotting), it may be possible to establish which items entered the depositional record as a result of the same process, and hence which items are associated.

## Successful Recovery Methodologies: Buried Human Remains

The preparation of the site for excavation follows the same guidelines established for recovery of the finds on the surface. As indicated above, site security must be established, comprehensive documentation of the site and all of its visible components must be made prior to excavation, the grid system must be emplaced, the site must be carefully denuded and searched for additional surface evidence, and a surface topography map must be produced.

The first step in the excavation of the burial feature is to delineate its plan view or horizontal outline, which can be accomplished via its horizontal exposure with a trowel. In many outdoor wooded settings, a very distinct demarcation between the darker, usually more compact humus layer and the often mottled, generally lighter and more friable grave fill will be evident and can require only a few centimeters of matrix removal. A plan view map and photo-documentation of the grave outline should be completed at this point.

Subsequent excavations should be restricted to the grave pit with the goal of determining: (1) the horizontal and vertical location in space of the body and all accompanying physical evidence, and (2) the original contour or profile of the grave pit. This is accomplished by carefully removing grave fill from the center to the margin of the feature, eventually exposing individual interred elements within the grave pit. It is strongly suggested that initially only half of the feature be excavated until bones or body portions are exposed (Figure 3). A profile map of the unexcavated portion of the grave which very clearly shows the position and

**Figure 3**    Example of proper excavation exposure and documentation of subsurface feature (feature 13, a prehistoric trash pit, 36ER243).

orientation of the body should then be produced and the profile photographed preferably in both black-and-white and color formats, with scales. Throughout the excavation, small tools such as trowels, dental picks, and hard- and soft-bristled brushes should be used. The use of wooden digging utensils will also prevent damage to bone.

Various samples may be taken from the grave fill, including soil and flotation samples (described in footnote). The remainder of the fill is either dry or water screened using fine-mesh hardware cloth or welded fabric($\leq$ ⅛ in.). Soil samples should also be taken from various regions of the body (thoracic, abdominal, pelvic regions). As with any of the archaeological methods previously described, complete and comprehensive documentation accompanies all stages of the excavation.

Partially decomposed remains are excavated in a manner similar to that employed for wholly skeletonized individuals — that is, complete horizontal exposure is first required. The process of removal of material from the burial pit may require minor modifications to the protocol, depen-dant on whether major portions of the body remain articulated due to soft tissue adherence.

Removal and packing of the remains follows the same routine as for surface remains (see above). Excavation continues until all of the grave fill has been removed. The use of metal detectors to locate slugs below the grave feature is suggested. Profile maps of the cross-section dimensions of the burial feature are then completed. These profiles are usually bidirectional and include north-south and east-west sections.

Employing the methodologies described above ensures that the positions of the body and associated physical evidence are thoroughly documented in three dimensions (see Sigler-Eisenberg 1985), that sequences of interment episodes in multiple occupancy burials can be recon-structed, and that any associated trace evidence such as footprints or tool marks can be recovered.

A recent phase III archaeological excavation of a partially destroyed prehistoric multiple interment ossuary feature required the development and implementation of revised recovery protocols (Dirkmaat et al. 1993). The dense concentration of friable and fragmentary commingled bones (Figure 4) rendered the data recovery process difficult. Rather than mapping each bone by hand, high-resolution photographs were taken with a large-format 6 × 7 cm camera and the resultant positives were enlarged to 12 in. by 18 in. Tracing paper was placed over the

**Figure 4**    Plan view of portion of prehistoric ossuary illustrates density of human remains.

positive and each bone was traced and labeled. The precise horizontal and vertical location of each fully exposed and entirely visible bone was noted and the bone then carefully removed. This process was conducted in multiple successive layers until the feature was completely excavated. All specimen provenience data were entered into Paradox, a computer database program, to aid in the production of computer-generated maps of the feature.

The cost in terms of time and money is minimal compared to the return of detailed contextual data available to help resolve even complicated cases. Most surface recoveries can be expected to last 4 to 10 hours, while excavations of buried remains may minimally take 1 to 3 days to complete.

In addition to documenting relationships of physical evidence at the scene, analyzing the relationship of the scene to its *environmental setting* is critical and often minimized or even overlooked. These data are especially relevant to taphonomic reconstructions. The role of geologic (e.g., soil composition and chemistry, site slope, surface and subsurface water movement), climatic (e.g., temperature gradients, amount of direct sunlight), elevational, and biotic (e.g., faunal scavengers, type and density of forest cover) factors in the ultimate disposition of the body following death must be carefully evaluated.

### Recovery of Remains from Fire Scenes

The anthropologist can make a significant contribution in the search for and recovery of cremated human remains in a fire situation (Bass and Berryman 1986; Bass and Marks 1990; Birkby 1991; Dirkmaat 1991; Heglar 1984; Maples and Mertz 1988). A common methodology utilized by fire investigators is to rake the coals and hope that an identifiable human bone or tooth turns up, thus disturbing the relationship between pieces. Much information can be garnered from the *in situ* identification of charred human remains, including: (1) location and orientation of body during the fire; (2) accurate and efficient identification and collection of fragmentary cremated human (and animal) skeletal elements; (3) field identification and documentation of obscured "precremation" trauma; and even (4) evidence of fire intensity or duration from effects on bones (Buikstra and Swegle 1989; McKinley 1989; Nelson 1992).

### Recovery of Human Remains at Multiple Fatality Incidents

Mass disaster scenes provide another arena of opportunity, little used until recently, for the unique skills of the forensic anthropologist in the recovery, documentation, and identification of multiple victims from a single cataclysm. As these types of situations increase in number (the result of terrorism, increase in number and size of planes and facilities, recent "ethnic cleansings," and "disappearings" staged by military governments, to name a few), the need for an anthropologist's active participation within a well-trained disaster response team is heightened.

Recently, due to efforts of such pioneers as Clyde Snow and others, the forensic anthropologist has been called upon to participate as a vital member of the disaster identification (Finnegan 1995) and even "human rights" teams (Burns 1995; Snow 1995) because of their experience dealing with fragmented, often heat-altered human skeletal remains. The recent efforts of a multidisciplinary team involved in the Mt. Carmel case is an excellent example (Warnick 1994). When the forensic pathologist, odontologist, and anthropologist are teamed, a very high percentage of the remains can be positively identified (Berryman et al. 1988; Sledzik and Hunt 1995).

One area of the multiple fatality incidents that may be minimized in importance is methodological approaches to the recovery of commingled and scattered remains. The anthropologist can provide valuable assistance — even guidance — during the recovery stage of the investigation, normally handled by a combination of law enforcement, fire, and/or armed service officials (Knight 1991; Randall 1991). As described above, systematic search techniques ensure maximal bone fragment and artifact recovery. The employment of comprehensive documentation and recovery methodologies also ensures collection of contextual information, which greatly benefits attempts to link disassociated remains, and ultimately, determine the identity of individual fragments.

## Site Visitation Following Removal of the Body

In situations in which the human skeletal remains arrive in the physical anthropologist's laboratory in a box, the person(s) analyzing the remains should, if at all possible, visit the scene to gather information which would compliment the analysis. The anthropologist, upon visiting the site following removal of the bones may:

1.  Recover more bones and/or teeth
2.  Determine whether remains are those from a prehistoric or cemetary burial (as discerned from the physical setting of the site, associated grave artifacts, configuration of the grave, and discoloration of the bones) or from a recent forensically significant feature
3.  Collect information on the extrinsic and intrinsic physical features of the site to resolve taphonomic issues relating to the spatial distributions and differential preservation of bone and tissue (e.g., site locational data relative to major geographic features, especially human activity centers [dwellings, roads]; soil samples at the body site for flotation, body fluid residue and pH levels [see above]; information regarding floral cover (e.g., the amount of sunlight available to "bleach" bone surfaces will play a crucial role in establishing time since death parameters); geologic/geographic features such as slope at the site and intermittent and permanent water course patterns; ambient temperature readings for the time period covered by the postulated postmortem interval [important for interpreting entomological data] and faunal communities in the area, especially predators and scavengers likely to modify bone)
4.  Collect evidence of insect fauna, relevant to establishing postmortem interval (see above), formerly associated with the body, which may have migrated away from the body in order to pupate (see Catts and Haskell 1990).

## Benefits of Forensic Anthropologist Involvement during the Recovery Phase

In summary, therefore, when human remains are carefully documented *in situ*, the following data sets can be collected:

1.  Detailed and comprehensive documentation of vertical and horizontal associations of human remains to potentially associated artifacts, and to their depositional environment
2.  Recovery of the maximum number of bones of the individual in surface scatter situations (Howard et al., 1988), and *all* bones in burial situations directly resultant from proper skeletal exposure techniques in conjunction with dry and wet sieving techniques
3.  Field identification and documentation of taphonomic processes affecting the distribution and preservation of skeletal and soft tissue elements (e.g., animal modification, physical features of the site, soil conditions, vegetation cover)
4.  Accurate reconstructions of the dimensions and excavation sequences of the burial pit and even the implements used to create the pit (e.g., flat-bladed vs. spade shovels)
5.  Expert witness testimony with respect to recovery methodologies and chain of evidence custody

## Phase IV: Laboratory Analysis and Report Preparation

The last phase of the forensic investigation and the point at which, historically, forensic anthropologists have most commonly entered the investigation is the analysis of human remains in the laboratory. The benefits of proper archaeological recovery to all of the major aspects of the comprehensive forensic anthropological analysis are outlined below.

### *Establishment of Identity*

Improvements in the recovery of physical evidence will benefit the identification process by maximizing the recovery of bone specimens of the individual. Often, small bones of the hands and feet, single-rooted teeth, and fragmentary bones are left behind in less rigorous recovery exercises that do not include dry and wet sieving.

### *Reconstruction of Perimortem Events*

Reconstructions of events and circumstances *at* death can be more accurately made through the implementation of rigorous archaeological recovery protocols.

From an osteological perspective, analysis of manner of death focuses almost exclusively on the presence/absence of skeletal trauma (Maples 1986; Morse 1983). Therefore, in cases of high velocity gunshot wounds, for example, which often result in extreme bone fragmentation, it is imperative that the maximum number of bone fragments be recovered (Figure 5) in order to accurately reconstruct wound defects (Berryman et al. 1994; Dixon 1984a, b; Huxley 1994; Peterson 1991; Smith et al. 1987). This information is used to determine origins, paths, sequences, proxomity and even the caliber of gunshot projectiles and ultimately, provide more corroborative evidence differentiating suicide from homicide.

The documentation of relative spatial relationships between the body, physical evidence, and the depositional environment will enhance the laboratory researcher's ability to identify factors contributing to the burial or surface emplacement episode, which may play a significant role in reconstructing manner of death. For example, the identification of patterns of skull damage consistent with blunt force trauma (possibly of a homicidal nature) may also indicate an accidental death, when associated with the body of a known rock climber found at the bottom of a cliff.

Finally, the employment of archaeological methodologies also ensures that no postmortem damage occurs to the skeletal material as a result of the recovery process itself. In many nonarchaeological recovery exercises, shovels, picks, and even heavy machinery cause damage to bone which may make complicate or confound the determination of peri- vs. postmortem damage.

### *Reconstructions of Postmortem Processes*

One of the primary goals of forensic investigation is reconstruction of the human role in events surrounding the death, especially the death event itself (e.g., original body location,

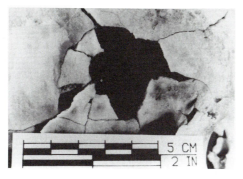

**Figure 5** Close up of perimortem damage and bone fragmentation patterns from a .38 caliber gunshot to the right side of a human cranium. The maximal recovery of very small bone fragments allowed for accurate determination of location and type (entrance vs. exit) of defect and identification of gunpowder residue on the edge of the defect indicative of a close range shot.

timing and sequence of events, number of people involved). Postmortem processes affecting the cadaver are studied in detail in order to filter out environmental (i.e., geologic, atmospheric, etc.) and biotic (i.e., plant and animal) factors. What is left, it is hoped, reflects human behavioral factors that account for the original location and disposition of the victim at death. Taphonomy, which has been defined in general terms as the study of "the fate of the organism after death" (Haglund 1991), therefore, plays a vital role in reconstruction of the death event by identifying and "weeding out" postmortem factors affecting the body.

In the forensic setting, taphonomic analyses provide information relevant to two important postmortem issues: what is the PMI, and how can we explain the differential representation of material and/or dispersal patterns of skeletal elements from their original anatomical position?

The reconstruction of PMI is especially difficult in extensively decomposed cadavers (Bass 1984). To some (e.g., Stewart 1979), it is a task sufficiently fraught with difficulties to suggest that consistent and accurate estimates (within weeks or even months) are generally not attainable. However, through rigorous taphonomic research employing standardized data collection and presentation methodologies, at least general standards can be developed that have some utility to a diversity of forensic settings.

The estimation of PMI most often focuses on the establishment of the rate of reduction of the body to a skeletal state (i.e., rate of decomposition and removal of soft tissue). Insect colonization and predation, and to a lesser extent bacterial action, have the greatest impact in reduction of the body. Analyses of insect activities provide the most accurate estimates of rate of decomposition. The effects of insect predation are most often measured indirectly through reconstruction of daily temperature regimes. Additional factors affecting this rate include season of death; presence/absence of wounds; amount of cover, including clothing and vegetation; amount of direct sunlight; immersion in water; and many other local environmental conditions. Chemical–physical tests (Krogman and Iscan 1986), including body fluid residue, may provide reasonable estimates of PMI. Less accurate estimates are derived from destruction sequences of clothing and other associated physical evidence (Morse and Dailey 1985; Rowe, this volume); floral evidence (Willey and Heilman 1987); faunal evidence (Willey and Synder 1989); and bone surface weathering patterns (Hill 1976; Behrensmeyer 1978).

The differential representation of human skeletal elements and/or dispersal patterns (from original anatomical position) of this material are also carefully studied in taphonomic analyses. The primary agents responsible for removing and displacing remains are animals (Haglund et al. 1989; Murad and Bayham 1990). Animal impact on skeletal assemblages is primarily studied through analysis of residual effects of gnathic activity on bone surfaces (Milner and Smith 1989). Carnivore chewing evidence and gnawing marks by rodents, which are rather easily identified, when combined with the analysis of distributional data can frequently provide cogent explanations of the ultimate disposition of remains from death to discovery.

Humans may also disturb remains by removing and/or scattering elements through dismemberment in fresh specimens or through disarticulation at natural joints in more extensively decomposed remains. Cut marks from sharp implements and/or striations produced by saw cuts provide highly informative clues that indicate human intervention.

Geological forces are also responsible for movement and even removal of remains from a scene. Gravitational forces involved in downslope movement and water transport (see Nawrocki and Pless, this volume) are two of the more important geological factors to be considered.

As described throughout this contribution, the best way to collect taphonomic data is through the use of archaeological recovery techniques that maximize the collection of contextual information. The inconsistent application of archaeological techniques, however, will generally not produce viable or usable taphonomic models. To date, with notable exceptions (e.g., Haglund 1991), taphonomic data derived from actual forensic cases (even when archaeological methods are used) are not generally useful for broad interpretations of postmortem factors, even in relatively restricted geographic regions, for these data are predominantly collected and presented in an anecdotal manner (Haglund and Sorg, this volume). Therefore, the standardization of data collection protocols in the field — like that fostered by contemporary archaeology, with its focus on comprehensive documentation of spatial relationships between all physical evidence and the physical, atmospheric, and depositional environments — is urgently required to allow for comparability of results. The role of burial depth, soil chemistry, exposure to moisture, temperature, sunlight, floral and faunal activity, exposure prior to burial, and many others factors can only be assessed following compilation of comparable data from a diversity of well-documented case studies and comparison with experimental and actualistic research (Binford 1981; Galloway et al. 1991; Hill 1976; Mann et al. 1990; Micozzi 1986, 1991; Rodriguez and Bass 1985). The forensic anthropologist plays an important role in the collection of all of this information in the field, preferably *in situ,* but also at autopsy (Tate 1990) and even on return visits following removal of the remains.

## *Report Preparation*

In order to achieve comparability of results that allow for production of syntheses and eventually "theory-building," a report (if not the final case report presented to law enforcement/medicolegal authorities) or data sheet must be prepared that provides at least an organized synopsis of results. Included in that report should be descriptions or lists of preserved soft tissue locations along with state of preservation/decomposition (e.g., soft desiccated, leathery desiccated, adipocere-like, wet, undifferentiated mass, etc.); insect activity; skeletal material recovered; bone surface modification ranging from weathering to burning, to animal chewing/gnawing; skeletal trauma; bone chemistry changes; and documentation of spatial distributions (three-dimensionally, if buried) of all physical evidence via sketches, photographs, plan view maps, and/or computer-generated images. Documentation of the depositional environment is important and should include slope calculations, forest type and cover, soil types, amount of direct sunlight, and type and location of clothing. Perhaps a regional or national repository for these reports is required that would allow for researchers to readily access data and proceed with compilation of data.

As an example of the benefits of systematic collection of this data, the primary author recently completed a study of taphonomic factors on estimates of PMI in the woodlands of western Pennsylvania (Dirkmaat and Sienicki 1995). The effects of season and location of death on decomposition/reduction processes were studied in six cases involving open air

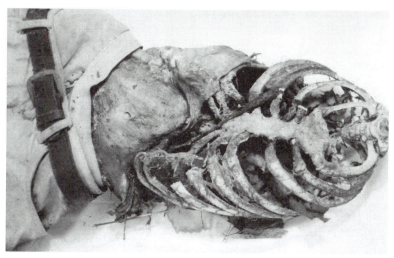

**Figure 6**   Example of partial decomposition of human remains in an outdoor setting. Note desiccated tissue over lower thoracic region and exposure of thoracic cage, although still articulated.

wooded sites located within an 80 mile radius of each other. The well-documented PMIs for
these cases included 2.5, 4.0, 6.5, 10, and 12 months. Most of the data noted above were
documented. Patterns regarding soft tissue destruction (see e.g., Figure 6) allowed prioritiza-
tion of factors such as temperature (indicating, primarily, insect activity), number of days
with temperatures above threshold levels, amount of direct sunlight, and clothing cover.
Though the sample size is small, a study of this sort provides a starting point by which a
regional sequence may be developed and estimates of PMI determined in unknown cases
more confidently and accurately.

## Case Studies in the Application and Benefits of Archaeological Recovery in Forensic Contexts

At the outset of this contribution, we expressed our hope that the pivotal role of forensic
archaeology in crime scene and forensic investigation could be demonstrated. Mindful that
a description of forensic archaeological methods and the specific benefits of those methods
is only a part of the equation, we now wish to present specific cases in which forensic
investigation has benefitted from the methodological protocols of forensic archaeology.

### Search and Evaluation

In a recent case in northwestern Pennsylvania, a dog recovered a human calotte which exhibited extensive damage from a gunshot wound. A 3-hour search covering a 2-mile diameter
area around the original find was conducted by approximately 100 volunteers following a
plan organized by a forensic anthropologist. The search identified over 20 sets of skeletal
remains, all of which, however, were determined to be nonhuman. The presence of the forensic
anthropologist during the search allowed for: (1) the organization of the search and briefing
of the volunteers, and (2) the on-site evaluation of all suspected burial features and physical
evidence, thus making for a very effective and efficient search. Although no additional human
remains were recovered, the search was successful because it then allowed for the investigation
to move to other arenas.

**Figure 7**   View of forensic scene involving three individuals prior to recovery.

## *In Situ* Recovery

Another recent case illustrates how the inclusion of the forensic anthropologist during recovery and at the autopsy allowed for well-established estimates of PMI and reconstructions of events surrounding the deaths of three associated individuals. The remains of these three individuals were discovered in deep woods by a hunter (Figure 7). The remains were not disturbed by law enforcement officials, and the coroner allowed the forensic anthropology team to recover the material. Following removal of leaf litter, the spatial distribution of the exposed remains (Figure 8) was carefully documented via infrared theodolite. Comprehensive written and photographic documentation of the material was accomplished, and finally, the bodies carefully removed. The autopsy of the remains, in this case conducted by the primary author, served to: (1) provide evidence of the identity of the victims through dental evidence, skeletal parameters, and associated clothing and other physical evidence; (2) (and in conjunction with field data) allow for the careful documentation of the state of decomposition of each victim (Figures 9, 10), which was then correlated with such variables as clothing, amount of direct sunlight, and orientation of the bodies; and (3) facilitate collection and documentation of entomological evidence. Information collected at autopsy allowed for a robust estimate of PMI which matched the time of disappearance. The laboratory analysis of the skeletal remains provided detailed analysis of trauma. Each individual had been shot in the head. By determining gunshot caliber, origin, and trajectory, and overlaying this information on the contextual data (Figure 11) collected at recovery (relative position and orientation of each of the victims) it was determined that a double murder and suicide best explained the deaths, and a triple murder could be ruled out.

## Site Investigation Following Removal of Remains

The skeleton of a 40-year-old male was found by hunters in a remote section of north-central Pennsylvania. Recovered with the remains was a wallet from which it was determined that a substantial sum of money was missing. The victim had suffered a gunshot to the head and a .44 magnum revolver was found associated with the body, but only three cranial fragments were recovered by law enforcement officers. The manner of death in the case at this point was unresolved. A search of the area by the primary author and two student assistants the following

**Figure 8**   View of forensic scene from Figure 7 following removal of leaf litter and vegetation in the immediate vicinity.

**Figure 9**   Close up view of partially decomposed human remains illustrating association of clothing, personal effects, and biological tissue, contextual information which was significant in reconstructing events surrounding death.

weekend revealed additional cranial and mandibular fragments which allowed for the reconstruction of the origin and trajectory of the gunshot. The death was ruled a suicide, as the gunshot originated from beneath the mandible and traversed the skull in a direction consistent with the victim holding the gun.

## Mass Fatality Incident

In early September 1994, a Boeing 737 (USAir Flight 427) crashed nose-first into a wooded, hilly section of Beaver County in western Pennsylvania on its approach to Pittsburgh International

**Figure 10**  Partial decomposition of human remains in an outdoor setting. Note desiccated tissue over bones of lower limbs resulting from exposure to direct sunlight.

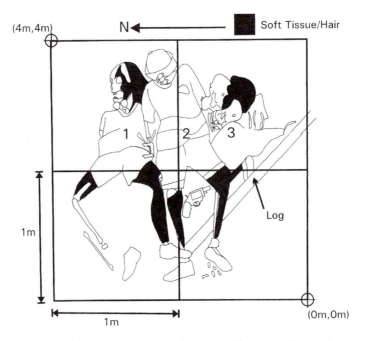

**Figure 11**  Plan view of forensic excavation showing grid system (1 m × 1 m units), spatial distribution of soft tissue, bone, clothing, and weapon. The collection of detailed contextual information at the crime scene prior to recovery allowed reconstruction of perimortem events, including the sequence of gunshots.

Airport. Following the determination that there were no survivors, the next step called for the efficient and expedient location and recovery of the human remains for final positive identification. A temporary grid system was walked off along the road leading to the crash site. However, due to the rough terrain and dense vegetation, the best the search teams could do was pin flag remains and roughly estimate their location relative to the grid. The forensic anthropological team arrived the next day and implemented a more exacting documentation methodology using an infrared theodolite which maps precise locations in three dimensions at an extremely high level of resolution. These data, collected via an electronic field notebook using software with an integrated database component, were processed in the laboratory to generate a very detailed, high-resolution map of the site showing the location of all identified human remains and aircraft parts, as well as the topography of the scene.

Forensic anthropology played a large role in the initial documentation of the human remains as they entered the temporary morgue, prior to final identification. Due to extreme fragmentation, the forensic anthropologist's unique knowledge of human osteology (especially when dealing with incomplete remains) allowed for the identification of remains that were little more than soft tissue with bone fragments. Furthermore, the forensic anthropologist's estimates of age and gender at the autopsy table helped to narrow the search for the victim's identity.

## Discussion

From effectively and efficiently locating the forensic site to the rigorous collection and documentation of all relevant evidence, standard archaeological methodologies enhance and maximize the amount and quality of data retrieved at the scene and thus aid the analyses conducted by both law enforcement officials and the forensic anthropologist in the laboratory.

The law enforcement and medicolegal communities have long recognized the value of physical anthropologists in the comprehensive analysis of human skeletal remains, especially for identification of unknown individuals. Forensic anthropologists have tended to enter forensic investigations following the removal of human remains from the scene, or have only rarely (usually in cases involving buried remains) visited the scene during recovery (Haglund 1991; Howard et al. 1988; Wolf 1986).

Today, however, more sophisticated questions regarding peri- and postmortem events are asked of anthropologists (Knight 1991), and these questions can only be addressed when well-documented contextual information is gathered along with the physical evidence during the recovery phase of the forensic investigation. The obvious solution is that when partially decomposed human remains are suspected, the full array of data recovery techniques should be brought into play in a highly integrated fashion during the investigation's incipient stages. The forensic anthropologist who is well trained in archaeological techniques is indispensable in integrating and fulfilling these objectives.

We suggest the role of the forensic anthropologist be revised in two ways. The forensic anthropologist should be a more active participant in the early stages of the field investigation, prior to recovery (Fulginiti et al. 1991). The data potentially obtained at this point (especially spatial distribution and orientation of physical evidence and biological remains to depositional environment) are most expeditiously collected via archaeological methodologies. Second, analytical protocols in the laboratory must be rearranged. Much of the evidence which may provide clues to events surrounding the death reside in the careful laboratory analysis of the entire skeletal, and importantly, soft tissue assemblage, which necessitates that the forensic anthropologist be one of the first individuals to examine the remains following removal from the scene (preferably alongside the pathologist at the autopsy). The skeletal elements present or absent; the condition of the remains (soft tissue as well as bone tissue); damage resulting from ante-, peri-, and postmortem modification; and other important information must be comprehensively documented at or prior to the autopsy. Only then should the remains be released to other experts (forensic odontologists, forensic artists, etc.) for specialized analyses.

The comprehensive gathering of contextual relationships of all physical evidence profoundly affects forensic investigation in two ways: (1) accurate reconstructions of certain types and sequences of events surrounding and subsequent to the death of the individual can be produced and used to corroborate or negate testimony; and (2) in instances in which background research data is weak or lacking (such as postmortem interval), data can be systematically collected and eventually compiled in order to produce more accurate taphonomic models or theories. Limited testing of these models can be accomplished through comparison with court testimony.

Here, we are proposing a redefinition of how forensic archaeology should fit within forensic anthropology and forensic studies generally. Forensic archaeology is defined by Morse and his colleagues as "the application of simple archaeological recovery techniques in death scene investigations involving a buried body or skeletal remains" (Morse et al. 1983: 1). This aspect of the forensic investigation is often considered distinct from forensic anthropology, which has been described as the "application of the science of physical anthropology to forensic problems" (Morse et al. 1983: 1) or as a "subfield of physical anthropology" (Bass 1987: 224). We believe it is now appropriate to reconsider this compartmentalization and include forensic archaeology as an integral component of the forensic anthropological repertoire, along with forensic physical anthropology.

At this point we would like to propose a revised definition of forensic anthropology, which incorporates a renewed emphasis on the field data recovery of contextual information which facilitates subsequent laboratory analysis. We suggest that the term "forensic archaeology" be used in reference to data collection activities carried out during the field recovery aspect of the entire discipline of forensic anthropology and not as a separate and distinct enterprise. Our proposed revision follows:

Forensic Anthropology involves the application of principles utilized in the anthropological subfields of archaeology and physical anthropology to forensic investigations. Archaeological principles are employed during the search for, recovery, and preservation of physical evidence at the outdoor scene, and emphasize documentation of contextual relationships of all evidence to its depositional environment. Physical anthropological principles are employed during the laboratory analysis of human remains and focus on reconstruction of identity and events surrounding and subsequent to death, often heavily reliant upon contextual data collected at the site.

We have specific recommendations for the role and practice of forensic anthropology and archaeology. First, practicing members of the professional forensic anthropological community must either be properly trained or experienced in applying archaeological principles to forensic situations (as well as the proper methodology for collection of entomological specimens as specified by professional forensic entomologists), or must associate themselves with professional archaeologists who are themselves trained in or have experience in excavations of forensic scenes. These archaeologists would work closely with the physical anthropologists and thus maximize the amount of information available to help identify the victim and reconstruct the circumstances surrounding the death of the individual. Second, information with respect to the benefits of employing proper archaeological techniques must be disseminated to all members of the medicolegal and law enforcement communities. This can take the form of presentations, special seminars, short courses, or workshops aimed primarily at these professionals (Berryman and Lahren 1984).

Stewart wrote in 1979 with reference to, among other educational efforts, a short course in forensic archaeology offered at Florida State University: "it remains to be seen how much more of the action forensic anthropologists will see as a result of these propagandizing and training activities" (pp. 30–31). We would propose that individuals specifically trained in the use of archaeological principles — either anthropologists or members of the law enforcement and medicolegal community — be routinely employed to recover human skeletal remains in outdoor settings; in this way, the taphonomic context, so important for answering basic forensic questions, will be properly documented and utilized in analysis.

# References

Adovasio, J.M. (compiler)
    1982  *The Prehistory of the Paintsville Reservoir, Johnson and Morgan Counties, Kentucky.* Ethnology Monographs 6. Department of Anthropology, University of Pittsburgh, Pittsburgh.

Adovasio, J.M., R.C. Carlisle, K.A. Cushman, J. Donahue, J.E. Guilday, W.C. Johnson, K. Lord, P.W. Parmalee, R. Stuckenrath, and P.W. Wiegman
    1985  Paleoenvironmental Reconstruction at Meadowcroft Rockshelter, Washington County, Pennsylvania. In *Environments and Extinctions: Man in Late Glacial North America*, edited by J.I. Mead and D.J. Meltzer, pp. 73–110. Center for the Study of Early Man, University of Maine, Orono.

Adovasio, J.M., K.J. Shaunessy, W.C. Johnson, W.P. Athens, A.T. Boldurian, R.C. Carlisle, D.C. Dirkmaat, J. Donahue, D.R. Pedler, and E.J. Sieman, III
    1990  Archaeology at the Howarth-Nelson Site (36FA40), Fayette County, Pennsylvania. *Pennsylvania Archaeologist* 60(1):32–68.

Bass, W.M.
    1984  Time Interval Since Death: A Difficult Decision. In *Human Identification: Case Studies in Forensic Anthropology,* edited by T.A. Rathbun and J.E. Buikstra, pp. 136–147. Charles C Thomas, Springfield, IL.
    1987  Forensic Anthropology: The American Experince. In *Death, Decay and Reconstruction: Approaches to Archaeology and Forensic Science*, edited by A. Boddington, A.N. Garland, and R.C. Janaway, pp. 224–239. Manchester University Press, Manchester, U.K.

Bass, W.M., and H.E. Berryman
    1986  Forensic Fire Scenes: Check Them Carefully. *Tennessee Forensic Headliner* 9(3).

Bass, W.M., and M.K. Marks
    1990  Fire Scene Investigation: The Role of the Forensic Anthropologist. Paper presented at the 42nd Annual Meeting of the American Academy of Forensic Sciences, Cincinnati.

Behrensmeyer, A.K.
    1978  Taphonomic and Ecological Information from Bone Weathering. *Paleobiology* 4:150–162.

Berryman, H.E., and W.M. Bass
    1985  Human Skeletal Remains: Recovery and Transportation. *Tennessee Forensic Headliner* 7(12).

Berryman, H.E., and C.H. Lahren
    1984  The Advantages of Simulated Crime Scenes in Teaching Forensic Anthropology. *Journal of Forensic Sciences* 20:699–700.

Berryman, H.E., J.O. Potter, and S. Oliver
    1988  The Ill-Fated Passenger Steamer "Sultana:" An Inland Maritime Mass Disaster of Unparalleled Magnitude. *Journal of Forensic Sciences* 33:842–850.

Berryman, H.E., O.C. Smith, and S.A. Symes
   1994   Cranial Gunshot Entrance Wound Diameter as a Function of Bullet Caliber. Paper presented at the 46th Annual Meeting of the American Academy of Forensic Sciences, San Antonio, TX.

Berryman, H.E., W.M. Bass, S.A. Symes, and O.C. Smith
   1991   Recognition of Cemetery Remains in the Forensic Setting. *Journal of Forensic Sciences* 36:230–237.

Binford, L.R.
   1981   *Bones: Ancient Men and Modern Myths*. Academic Press, New York.

Birkby, W.H.
   1991   The Analysis of Cremains. Paper presented at the 43rd Annual Meeting of the American Academy of Forensic Sciences, Anaheim, CA.

Bryant, V.M., Jr., J.G. Jones, and D.C. Mindenhall
   1990   Forensic Palynology in the United States of America. *Palynology* 14:193–208.

Buikstra, J.E., and M. Swegle
   1989   Bone Modification Due to Burning: Experimental Evidence. In *Bone Modification*, edited by R. Bonnichsen and M.H. Sorg, pp. 247–258. Center for the Study of the First Americans, University of Maine, Orono.

Burns, K.R.
   1995   Forensic Anthropology in Human Rights Missions. In *Proceedings of the American Academy of Forensic Sciences*, Vol. 1, p. 172. American Academy of Forensic Sciences, Colorado Springs, CO.

Carlisle, R.C., and J.M. Adovasio (editors)
   1982   Meadowcroft: Collected Papers on the Archaeology of Meadowcroft Rockshelter and the Cross Creek Drainage. Prepared for the Symposium "The Meadowcroft Rockshelter Rolling Thunder Review: Last Act," at the 47th Annual Meeting of the Society for American Archaeology, Minneapolis.

Catts, E.P., and N.H. Haskell (editors)
   1990   *Entomology and Death: A Procedural Guide*. Joyce's Print Shop, Clemson, SC.

Center for Social Development and Humanitarian Affairs
   1991   *Manual on the Effective Prevention and Investigation of Extra-Legal Arbitrary and Summary Executions*. United Nations Office at Vienna, Vienna, Austria.

DeForest, P.R., R.E. Gaensslen, and H.C. Lee
   1983   *Forensic Science: An Introduction to Criminalistics*. McGraw-Hill, New York.

Dirkmaat, D.C.
   1991   Applications of Forensic Anthropology: The Recovery and Analysis of Cremated Remains. Paper presented at the 43rd Annual Meeting of the American Academy of Forensic Sciences, Anaheim, CA.

Dirkmaat, D.C., and L.A. Sienicki
   1995   Taphonomy in the Northeast Woodlands: Four Cases from Western Pennsylvania. In *Proceedings of the American Academy of Forensic Sciences*, Vol. 1, pp. 158–159. American Academy of Forensic Sciences, Colorado Springs, CO.

Dirkmaat, D.C., C.A. Diefenbach, C. Burkett, C.A. Mertz, and L.A. Sienicki
   1994   Suicide or Homicide: A Multidisciplinary Approach to the Analysis of a "Mummified" Hanging Victim. Paper presented at the 46th Annual Meeting of the American Academy of Forensic Sciences, San Antonio, TX.

Dirkmaat, D.C., Compiler
   1996  *Field and Laboratory Methods in the Location, Recovery, and Analysis of Human Remains in a Rural Setting*. Manual prepared for Forensic Archaeology Short Course, Mercyhurst College, Erie, PA.

Dirkmaat, D.C., D.R. Pedler, J.M. Adovasio, C.L. Pedler, D.C. Hyland, J.T. Herbstritt, R. Buyce, and J. Thomas
   1993  Archaeological and Bioanthropological Investigation at the Orton Quarry Site (36ER243), North East Township, Pennsylvania. Paper presented at the 58th Annual Meeting of the Society for American Archaeology, St. Louis.

Dixon, D.S.
   1984a Pattern of Interesting Fractures and Direction of Fire. *Journal of Forensic Sciences* 29:651–654.
   1984b Exit Keyhole Lesion and Direction of Fire in a Gunshot Wound of the Skull. *Journal of Forensic Sciences* 29:336–339.

East, T.C., J.M. Adovasio, W.C. Johnson, J. Donahue, and T.F. Jorstad
   1989  *Archaeological Investigations at 36BK549, An Archaic and Woodland Lithic Workshop in Berks County, Pennsylvania*. University of Pittsburgh Anthropological Papers, No. 3, Department of Anthropology, University of Pittsburgh, Pittsburgh.

Finnegan, M.
   1995  Killed in Action — Body Not Recovered: Forensic Anthropology and Archaeology Applied to the Recovery of U.S. Military Remains in Vietnam. In *Proceedings of the American Academy of Forensic Sciences*, Vol. 1, p. 175. American Academy of Forensic Sciences, Colorado Springs, CO.

Fulginiti, L.C., T.L. Kahana, S. Fox, and A. Galloway
   1991  Crime Scene Involvement by the Forensic Anthropologist. Paper presented at the 43rd Annual Meeting of the American Academy of Forensic Sciences, Anaheim, CA.

Galloway, A., P. Willey, and L. Snyder
   1991  Bone Density Determinants of Carnivore Scavenging and Bone Survival. Paper presented at the 43rd Annual Meeting of the American Academy of Forensic Sciences, Anaheim, CA.

Gordon, C.C., and J.E. Buikstra
   1981  Soil pH, Bone Preservation, and Sampling Bias at Mortuary Sites. *American Antiquity* 46:566–571.

Haglund, W.D.
   1991  *Applications of Taphonomic Models to Forensic Investigations*. Ph.D. dissertation, Department of Anthropology, University of Washington, Seattle. University Microfilms, Ann Arbor, MI.

Haglund, W.D., D.T. Reay, and D.R. Swindler
   1989  Canid Scavenging/Disarticulation Sequence of Human Remains in the Pacific Northwest. *Journal of Forensic Sciences* 34:587–606.

Hegler, R.
   1984  Burned Remains. In *Human Identification: Case Studies In Forensic Anthropology*, edited by T.A. Rathbun and J.E. Buikstra, pp. 148–158. Charles C Thomas, Springfield, IL.

Hill, A.P.
   1976  On Carnivore and Weathering Damage to Bone. *Current Anthropology* 17:335–336.

Howard, J.D., D.T. Reay, W.D. Haglund, and C.L. Fligner
   1988  Processing of Skeletal Remains: A Medical Examiner's Perspective. *The American Journal of Forensic Medicine and Pathology* 9:258–264.

Huckaby, B.L., E. A. Murray, and A.J. Perzigian

    1991   Riverside Cemetery Remains: Reinterred or Discarded. Paper presented at the 43rd
    Annual Meeting of the American Academy of Forensic Sciences, Anaheim, CA.

Huxley, A.K.

    1994   The Dynamics of Gunshot Wounds on the Cranium: An Anthropological Analysis
    of Three Forensic Cases. Paper presented at the 46th Annual Meeting of the American
    Academy of Forensic Sciences, San Antonio, TX.

Jorstad, T., T. East, J.M. Adovasio, J. Donahue, and R. Stuckenrath

    1986   Paleosols and Prehistoric Populations in the High Plains. *Georchaeology* 1:163–181.

Killam, E.W.

    1990   *The Detection of Human Remains.* Charles C Thomas, Springfield, IL.

Knight, B.

    1991   *Forensic Pathology.* Oxford University Press, New York.

Krogman, W.M., and M.Y. Iscan

    1986   *The Human Skeleton in Forensic Medicine.* 2nd ed. Charles C Thomas, Springfield, IL.

Lord, W.D., and J.F. Burger

    1983   Collection and Preservation of Forensically Important Entomological Materials.
    *Journal of Forensic Sciences* 28:936–944.

Mann, R.W., W.M. Bass, and L. Meadows

    1990   Time Since Death and Decomposition of the Human Body: Variables and Obser-
    vations in Case and Experimental Field Studies. *Journal of Forensic Sciences* 35:203–211.

Maples, W.R.

    1986   Trauma Analysis by the Forensic Anthropologist. In *Forensic Osteology: Advances in
    the Identification of Human Remains*, edited by K.J. Reichs, pp. 218–228. Charles C
    Thomas, Springfield, IL.

Maples, W.R., and C.A. Mertz

    1988   Identification of the Cremated Remains in the Meek/Jennings Case. Paper presented
    at the 40th Annual Meeting of American Academy of Forensic Sciences, Philadelphia.

McKinley, J.I.

    1989   Cremations: Expectations, Methodologies and Reality. In *Burial Archaeology: Cur-
    rent Research, Methods and Developments*, edited by C.A. Roberts, F. Lee, and J. Bintliff,
    pp. 65–76. British Archaeological Series International Reports 211, Oxford, U.K.

Micozzi, M.S.

    1986   Experimental Study of Postmortem Change under Field Conditions: Effects of Freez-
    ing, Thawing and Mechanical Injury. *Journal of Forensic Sciences* 31:953–961.

    1991   *Postmortem Change in Human and Animal Remains: A Systematic Approach.* Charles
    C Thomas, Springfield, IL.

Milner, G.R., and V.G. Smith

    1989   Carnivore Alteration of Human Bone from a Late Prehistoric Site in Illinois. *Amer-
    ican Journal of Physical Anthropology* 79:43–49.

Morse, D.

    1983   The Skeletal Biology of Trauma. In *Handbook of Forensic Archaeology and Anthro-
    pology*, edited by D. Morse, J. Duncan, and J. Stoutamire, pp. 145–185. Rose Printing,
    Tallahassee.

Morse, D. and R.C. Dailey

    1985   The Degree of Deterioration of Associated Death Scene Material. *Journal of Forensic
    Sciences* 30:119–127.

Morse, D., J. Duncan, and J. Stoutamire (editors)
    1983   *Handbook of Forensic Archaeology and Anthropology*. Rose Printing, Tallahassee.

Murad, T.A., and F.E. Bayham
    1990   Northern California Examples of the Effect of Animal Scavenging on the Estimation of Postmortem Interval. Paper presented at the 42nd Annual Meeting of the American Academy of Forensic Sciences, Cincinnati.

Nelson, R.
    1992   Microscopic Comparison of Fresh and Burned Bone. *Journal of Forensic Sciences* 37:1055–1060.

Owsley, D.W.
    1994   The Use and Abuse of Probes in the Forensic Burial Search. Paper presented at the 46th Annual Meeting of the American Academy of Forensic Sciences, San Antonio, TX.

Peterson, B.L.
    1991   External Beveling of Cranial Gunshot Entrance Wounds. *Journal of Forensic Sciences* 36:1592–1595.

Randall, B.
    1991   Body Retrieval and Morgue Operation at the Crash of United 232. *Journal of Forensic Sciences* 36:403–406.

Rathbun, T.A.
    1990   Forensic Implications of Historical Cemeteries. Paper presented at the 42nd Annual Meeting of the American Academy of Forensic Sciences, Cincinnati.

Rodriguez, W.C. (compiler)
    1990   *Recovery, Examination and Evidence of Decomposed and Skeletonized Bodies*. Workshop Manual prepared for the 42nd Annual Meeting of the American Academy of Forensic Sciences Meeting, Cincinnati.

Rodriguez, W.C., and W.M. Bass
    1985   Decomposition of Buried Bodies and Methods That May Aid in Their Location. *Journal of Forensic Sciences* 30:836–852.

Saferstein, R.
    1990   *Criminalistics: An Introduction to Forensic Science*, 4th ed. Prentice-Hall, Englewood Cliffs, NJ.

Sigler-Eisenberg, B.
    1985   Forensic Research: Expanding the Concept of Applied Archaeology. *American Antiquity* 50:650–655.

Skinner, M., and R.A. Lazenby
    1983   *Found! Human Remains: A Field Manual for the Recovery of the Recent Human Skeleton*. Archaeology Press, Simon Fraser University, Burnaby, B.C.

Skirboll, E.
    1982   Analysis of Constant Volume Samples from Meadowcroft Rockshelter, Washington County, Southwestern Pennsylvania. In *Meadowcroft: Collected Papers on the Archaeology of Meadowcroft Rockshelter and the Cross Creek Drainage*, edited by R.C. Carlisle and J.M. Adovasio, pp. 221–240. Prepared for the Symposium "The Meadowcroft Rockshelter Rolling Thunder Review: Last Act," 47th Annual Meeting of the Society for American Archaeology, Minneapolis.

Sledzik, P., and D. Hunt
    1995   When the Dead Return, Part 1: The Hardin Cemetery Disaster. In *Proceedings of the American Academy of Forensic Sciences*, Vol. 1, pp. 154–155. American Academy of Forensic Sciences, Colorado Springs, CO.

Smith, O.C., H.E. Berryman, and C.H. Lahren
    1987   Cranial Fracture Patterns and Estimate of Direction from Low Velocity Gunshot Wounds. *Journal of Forensic Sciences* 32:1416–1421.

Snow, C.C.
    1995   A Decade of Work: Human Rights and Forensic Anthropology. In *Proceedings of the American Academy of Forensic Sciences*, Vol. 1, p. 172. American Academy of Forensic Sciences, Colorado Springs, CO.

Stewart, T.D.
    1979   *Essentials of Forensic Anthropology, Especially as Developed in the United States.* Charles C Thomas, Springfield, IL.

Swanson, C.R., N.C. Chamelin, and L. Territo
    1984   *Criminal Investigation.* 5th ed. McGraw Hill, New York.

Tate, L.R.
    1990   The Autopsy of the Decomposed Body. In *Recovery, Examination and Evidence of Decomposed and Skeletonized Bodies: An Anthropological and Entomological Approach,* compiled by W.C. Rodriguez, pp. 85–101. Workshop Manual prepared for the 42nd Annual Meeting of the American Academy of Forensic Sciences Meeting, Cincinnati.

Thomas, D.H.
    1979   *Archaeology.* Holt, Rinehart and Winston, New York.

Ubelaker, D.H.
    1989   *Human Skeletal Remains: Excavation, Analysis, Interpretation.* Taraxacum, Washington.

Ubelaker, D.H., and H. Scammell
    1992   *Bones: A Forensic Detectives Casebook.* HarperCollins, New York.

Warnick, A.J. (moderator)
    1994   In the Aftermath of the Branch Davidian Siege. Multidisciplinary session at the 46th Annual Meeting of the American Academy of Forensic Sciences, San Antonio, TX.

Weymouth, J.W.
    1986   Geophysical Methods of Archaeological Site Surveying. In *Advances in Archaeological Method and Theory*, Vol. 9, edited by M. B. Schiffer, pp. 311–395. Academic Press, New York.

White, E.M., and L.A. Hannus
    1983   Chemical Weathering of Bone in Archaeological Soils. *American Antiquity* 48:316–322.

White, T.D.
    1991   *Human Osteology.* Academic Press, San Diego.

Willey, P., and A. Heilman
    1987   Estimating Time Since Death Using Plant Roots and Stems. *Journal of Forensic Sciences* 32:1264–1270.

Willey, P., and L.M. Synder
    1989   Canid Modification of Human Remains: Implications for Time-Since-Death Estimates. *Journal of Forensic Sciences* 34:894–901.

Wolf, D.J.
    1986   Forensic Anthropology Scene Investigations. In *Forensic Osteology: Advances in the Identification of Human Remains*, edited by K.J. Reichs, pp. 3–23. Charles C Thomas, Springfield, IL.

# Chain of Custody from the Field to the Courtroom

4

JERRY MELBYE
SUSAN B. JIMENEZ

## Introduction

The primary role of the crime scene investigator is to attempt to collect all of the available evidence at the scene (Fisher et al. 1987). In cases where the death is recent, this is often less problematic. However, with the passage of time the evidence may be dispersed or altered by a variety of agents, natural and artificial. This is the essence of taphonomy (Efremov 1940). Although taphonomy usually focuses on changes to biological remains, nonbiological materials also undergo transportation, destruction, and modification. These materials frequently play an integral role in the reconstruction of the crime scene or, in taphonomic terms, the death assemblage.

Forensic anthropology has borrowed heavily from standard archaeological field methods (e.g., see Dirkmaat in this volume). There are, however, a number of unique adaptations (e.g., see Scott and Conner on the use of metal detectors in this volume). One important difference is the maintenance of a chain of custody. The principle of chain of custody is the establishment that evidence as found *in situ* is witnessed at time of discovery and that there is a continuous chain of custody up to presentation in a court of law. "Chain of custody" is used synonymously with "chain of security," "chain of evidence," and "continuity of evidence." Obviously, the defense can challenge any evidence if the chain of custody is broken at any point in time. Typically, in the standard excavation of prehistoric artifacts, soil samples, waste flakes, etc., the evidence is recorded, placed in labeled bags, and transported to a laboratory for analysis. The bags may sit in the laboratory for weeks with people walking in and out. The contents of the bags may be washed, catalogued, sorted, and stored by many different people at many points in time. No archaeologist considers the possibility that some person or persons might switch artifacts, falsify labels, or even steal waste flake. As archaeologists, we are a trusting lot — and probably rightly so. Rarely do we have to deal with dishonesty or theft, because our evidence has almost no monetary value. There are, of course, occasional examples of theft of archaeological specimens, and archaeologists have begun to tighten security. However, no archaeologist has to confirm his/her evidence in a court of law, and no person's freedom is dependent on the outcome of the analysis.

Forensic anthropologists must assume from the start that their evidence will end up in court. Evidence that is missing, mislabeled, mishandled, or degraded can be challenged. It is necessary to have a statement in the report outlining procedures taken for the maintenance of chain of custody. If evidence is challenged, it is necessaary to be absolutely candid regarding a possible, probable, or positive break in the chain of custody. We must be able to demonstrate that there has been no opportunity for the substitution of evidence (Galloway et al. 1990). The following are some basic guidelines for the maintenance of chain of custody.

0-8493-9434-1/97/$0.00+$.50
© 1997 by CRC Press, Inc.

1. **Field location, *in situ,* of all physical items.** This will include the usual log entry of the item, along with the horizontal and vertical location within the site.
2. **Identification marking of all physical items.** This will include appropriate containers with identifying labels or tags noting location and field number. Field numbers should never be changed.
3. **A separate log of all features.** These are features that cannot be preserved, such as a grave outline. Documentation should include scale drawings and location.
4. **A log of all photographs (including video tapes).** Photographs are critically important to document both physical items and features. It is recommended to keep three cameras on site: color, black and white, and Polaroid. Standard archaeological procedures of photographic documentation are appropriate.
5. **A chain of custody.** Every person who takes possession of any evidence must make a log entry of transfer. Further, while evidence is in each person's custody, a reasonable security must be maintained.
6. **Notebook.** Upon taking on a forensic case, one should begin a new notebook recording all events in chronological order beginning with the initial assignment. Who offered the job? Who was present? What is the nature of the assignment? What was the time of day? Note everything as it occurs. It is advisable to keep one bound notebook (not loose leaf) for each case. If this is done, there can be no question about the insertion or deletion of information that might compromise the chain of custody.

## Discovery of Evidence

Whether the discovery is on the surface or in the ground and whether the discovery is an artifact, human bone, animal bone, etc., the evidence should be witnessed. Most police agencies have a forensic evidence specialist who ideally should be assigned to the site. It is an important principle of forensic anthropology that we work as a team with investigating officers. The forensic identification specialists are a natural liaison between the investigation unit and the forensic anthropology unit. As evidence is recovered, the officer will act as witness. While it may not be critical that everything is witnessed, it is certainly advisable to reduce the possibility of a challenge in the courtroom. Following standard archaeological techniques, the evidence is noted for horizontal and vertical location, photographed, entered into a log book, and put in a marked bag. At the end of the day the evidence bags are "seized," e.g., they are taken into custody by the officer and locked in an evidence cabinet each night. The inventory of the evidence bags is entered into the forensic anthropologist's notes and signed by the officer. Also, the forensic anthropologist should sign the officer's notes to ensure correspondence. The officer should then place the bags in a box with a police seal, and enter the seal number into both notebooks. Typically, in the field it is impossible to predetermine everything that may constitute relevant evidence. The rule of inconclusiveness prevails. Swanson et al. (1988) state that, "... every available piece of evidence (should) be obtained and, where there is question as to whether a particular item constitutes evidence, to define it as such."

This process is repeated each day that the forensic anthropologist is in the field. This will ensure that there has been no contamination of the evidence. Additionally, before the forensic anthropologist leaves the site, she/he should make sure that a guard is posted to watch the site until she/he returns in the morning. This guard duty is undertaken by the police agency, and this should be arranged before excavation begins. It is now possible to testify unequivocally that there has been no contamination of either the site or the evidence extracted from the site.

## Analysis of Evidence

Under normal circumstances, at the end of an excavation the evidence will be locked up and sealed in a police station. Obviously, there may be evidence that is not within the expertise of the forensic anthropologists, e.g., bullets, clothing, insect casings, personal effects, etc. Evidence must be sorted to go to various experts in different laboratories. It follows that considerable time can be saved by bagging materials separately in the field in anticipation of transferring them to these various specialists. For example, one may excavate a pair of blue jeans with skeletonized contents and personal effects in the pockets. In this case, the bones, blue jeans, and personal effects are conveniently sealed in separate containers in the field. Subsequently, at the end of the excavation these sealed bags can be transferred with the seals unbroken.

Ideally, the dispersal of evidence is done by police officers in consultation with the forensic anthropologist and other interested parties such as the coroner/medical examiner. The inference of taphonomic dispersal is an important consideration at this point. Evidence is being dispersed (a new taphonomic problem?) and there must be feedback to the forensic anthropologist. Ultimately, one will need the reports of the various experts in order to interpret the field situation. If there is good rapport and teamwork the forensic anthropologist can ask for any expert reports and expect to be kept informed as data flows in. This is a two way street. Anthropological findings should be shared freely and quickly with these experts. This multidisciplinary approach maximizes the data that can be extracted from the crime scene.

At this time the forensic anthropologist formally takes possession of the bones (and occasionally the soft gooey bits that are attached). Depending on local coroner/medical examiner's policies, materials may be received at the morgue or directly from the police agency. He/she may be required to attend a formal autopsy by a forensic pathologist. Ultimately it is the responsibility of the forensic pathologist to identify and interpret pathology. A good working relationship with the forensic pathologist is essential. Regardless of local custom, the case notebook should be used to record the seal number, the date and time of the breaking of the seals, the persons present, and a confirmation of the contents.

In the event that the anthropologist is given possession of the bones to take back to his/her personal laboratory, this should similarly be documented in the case notebook. Once the bones are in the laboratory, it is advisable not to break the seals until one is ready to do the analysis. Further, the bones should be kept in a locked cabinet at all times when they are not being worked on. The anthropologist should keep the only key.

When the analysis begins, the seals are broken and documented in the notebook. The laboratory should be locked at all times — especially when one may be out for a few minutes. Traffic should be kept to a minimum. One may wish to consult with other experts or police officers; when this occurs, it should also be noted. In the event that someone else is doing photography, the anthropologist should be present.

Most forensic identification specialists have a large supply of police seals. They should be willing to provide a supply. At the end of the analysis, the bones should be boxed and sealed. The best place for them is the local coroner/medical examiner's office, but a personal locked cabinet in the laboratory is also possible.

This is considerably more of a bother than standard archaeological analysis of prehistoric specimens. But it is critical if the case goes to court. It is potentially a disaster, if the anthropologist performed a brilliant analysis, and then has the whole testimony dismissed because of lack of chain of custody.

## A Case Study

We have selected a recent case which will demonstrate some of the principles outlined so far. In fact, it is the reopening of an old case (1981) in which there had been no forensic anthropologist consulted, and this will demonstrate some of the problems when these guidelines have not been followed. The case is interesting because there are taphonomic implications which had not been considered earlier, and it also demonstrates that a forensic anthropology excavation can provide important evidence that standard police recovery cannot.

On September 19th, 1981, Ms. Smith (the name has been changed since the case is still pending) disappeared from her home in the east side of Toronto, Ontario. She was reported missing by family members. Shortly afterward, her car was found in a Toronto parking lot. Other than her unusual disappearance, the local investigating police found no evidence at the time to suggest foul play.

Almost exactly 5 years later (November, 1986), a human cranium was found in a mature maple forest at the bottom of a ravine about a 40-minute drive north of Toronto. A surface search by police recovered the fragmented human remains of about 15 infracranial bones in addition to the skull. Additionally, they recovered a number of nonhuman bones and assorted women's clothing. The cranium was inspected by a forensic odontologist, and Ms. Smith was positively identified as the victim. The 1986 investigation was entirely a standard police recovery (Table 1) including subsequent analysis by the forensic pathologist (Table 2). The only other comment on the bones in the forensic pathologist's report states: "I further examined these remains for evidence of antemortem injury. Although there had been postmortem deterioration of these bones, no evidence of before-death injury was found." No forensic anthropologist was contacted during either the recovery or analysis stage. Ms. Smith was presumed by the police to have been the victim of a homicide, but because of the lack of any clues there was little evidence to continue the investigation. The skeletal remains were returned to her family and cremated.

We were approached in October, 1991 by law enforcement officers from an Ontario regional police force and contracted to return to the site where the partial skeletal remains had been discovered in 1986. The case was being reopened on the basis of a possible link to a more recent homicide. During the investigation of this more recent homicide, the suspect was discovered to have known Ms. Smith. It was suggested to us that the focus of our excavation should be to recover any skeletal remains not recovered during the primary investigation of November 1986; and we were to examine these remains (if recovered) for any evidence that might suggest a link between the two homicides. Further, the body was missing in the second homicide. Anything that could be gleaned from the disposal of Ms. Smith was to be used in the search for the new victim.

The original police sketch map of the site where the remains were discovered was made available to us. Fortunately, the original datum point was still visible and the location was confirmed by police officers who had attended the scene in the 1986 investigation. Using this map we were able to determine the approximate area within which the skeletal remains and associated items of clothing, etc. had been located (see Figure 1). Unfortunately, other documents from the initial investigation were not so helpful. Upon examining the recovery list (Table 1) of field items by the police, we noticed something unusual about the forensic pathologist's report (Table 2). It was immediately obvious that the numbers did not correspond to the items on the list recovered from the field. Closer inspection of the forensic pathologist's report showed that the human bones had been renumbered beginning with the skull and ending with the toes. The bones were presented in anatomical order, much like the usual presentation in an anatomy text. There was no correspondence between the two lists, and no key for the renumbering process. The entire context of the position of the bones recovered in 1986 had been lost.

The police field recovery list (Table 1) was accompanied by a field map (Figure 1). It shows the location of items 1 to 18 and 21. Numbers 19, 20, and 22 to 30 are missing. A supplemental map (not shown here) shows three items located over 100 feet from this concentration. But their location does not correspond to that provided by a police officer who was on the scene back in 1986. The distance appears to be correct, but the direction is at least

**Table 1 Seized Exhibits from the Police Recovery**

| No. | Description |
| --- | --- |
| 1 | Two small pieces of blue cloth |
| 2 | Right shoe — ladies |
| 3 | Large piece of blue cloth with white cloth intertwined |
| 4 | Two pieces of blue cloth, one piece of white cloth |
| 5 | Small piece blue cloth, clothing tag |
| 6 | Three small pieces of blue cloth |
| 7 | Pieces of white bra strap, two clasps on strap |
| 8 | One large piece, blue cloth |
| 9 | Several pieces large and small blue cloth, small white cloth |
| 10 | One piece bone, approximately 5" |
| 11 | One gold ring |
| 12 | One pair, white womens panties, zipper intertwined with threads, tags |
| 13 | IUD birth control device |
| 14 | One large piece of white cloth |
| 15 | One small bone |
| 16 | Four pieces bone |
| 17 | Upper denture plate |
| 18 | Two bones |
| 19 | Small bone |
| 20 | Small piece, white cloth |
| 21 | Left shoe — ladies |
| 22 | Piece of white cloth, piece of brassier, piece of bone |
| 23 | Lower jaw bone, tooth, large piece of bone, small bone |
| 24 | Torn condom package |
| 25 | Three pieces of hard substance |
| 26 | Large bone, piece of blue cloth —ABRAHAM 12-11-86 |
| 27 | Pieces of blue and white cloth —POWELL 12-11-86 |
| 28 | Sixty-eight bags with small pieces of blue and white cloth found at excavation |
| 29 | Three bones, prop tags 65582, 65580 |
| 30 | Bone and material found 14+11–86 retained by ABRAHAM |

90° off. Further, that map lists the recovered items as #1, #2, and #3. This is impossible, because these numbers are also listed on Figure 1 in an entirely different location. What are these three items located over 100 feet away? The only item the officer remembers for sure is the cranium. This is probably true because the cranium is missing from the police list of items recovered (Table 1).

The 1986 recovery and analysis is a classic example of poor chain of custody. The forensic pathologists' report lists 16 human bones and 5 nonhuman bones. The police lists 18 bones recovered in the field. Adding the cranium brings the total to 19. If #2 and #3 on the supplemental field map are additional bony pieces, we have correspondence of 21 bones. What are the mysterious pieces #2 and #3 on the supplemental map? We have no way of knowing. Confusion resulted because the field numbers were ignored in the laboratory, and all the items were renumbered. Also, we are in serious trouble because the cranium from which positive identification was made is not on the list of items recovered, and is not noted on either field map. On the basis of hearsay we think the cranium is item #1 on the supplemental map, but the location is uncertain.

From Table 1, Figure 1, and the supplemental map (not shown), it is known that there are at least two clusters of skeletal material and associated artifacts: (1) the cranium plus two "mystery bones" and (2) the area of the infracranial bones, clothing, shoes, ring, and IUD, representing two dissimilar body regions. Assuming they had been reasonably articulated at time of death, it can be inferred that cluster (2) was the original location where the body

**Table 2  Forensic Pathology Report (November 30, 1986)**

| No. | Description |
|---|---|

### Human Bones

1. A skull devoid of teeth in the upper jaw
2. A lower jaw containing
   (a) Right and left incisor sockets
   (b) Right and left lateral incisors
   (c) Right and left canines
   (d) A left first premolar
   (e) A right first premolar socket; this tooth had fallen out postmortem
   (f) Right and left second molars
3. A complete upper denture which fitted the upper jaw
4. The right half of the first cervical vertebra
5. A left clavicle
6. The shaft of a left femur
7. The shaft of a left fibula
8. A right tibia
9. A right talus
10. A right medial cuneiform
11. The distal half of a left first metatarsal
12. A right second metatarsal
13. The distal two thirds of a left fifth metatarsal
14. The right proximal phalanx of the big toe
15. Two proximal phalanges of the toes
16. An intermediate phalanx

### Nonhuman Bones

1. A small animal vertebra, probably skunk
2. A part of a small animal jaw containing a major tooth
3. Two broken bird bones
4. Part of a wolf tibia

### Other Remains

1. An intrauterine contraceptive device

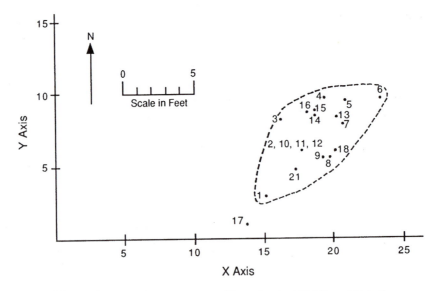

**Figure 1**   Map of items recovered by police in 1986 (from Table 1).

rested. It is more likely that it is from this area that the subsequent dispersal took place. This conclusion ultimately proved correct.

We used the 1986 datum plus the 1986 map to define an oval concentration area of about 5 feet by 8 feet. Over this general area we laid a larger gridded area of 19 one-meter squares. We did not orient the grid, however, to the traditional north-south axis. Instead, we laid out a base line along the edge of the intermittent stream (see Figure 2). This was our line-of-convenience. This ensured that none of our squares would be partially in the stream, and we could systematically excavate up the slope. The dashed line on Figure 1 (1986) is transferred to Figure 2 (1991). The 1986 recovery was a surface collection; we found some items below the surface in this area in 1991. In all, we recovered 51 items. We have omitted the animal bones from our map; these correspond to missing numbers on our 1991 map. However, we still have these items and their location documented in the entry log.

Topography has also been omitted for clarity on Figure 2; however, it is available. In general, there is a gradual rise from the stream to the N4 line. From the N4 line onward there is a very sharp incline, rising about 3 m for every 1 m of distance. The site is located in a ravine about 20 m deep, and has a flat bottom about 50 m across. The ravine is heavily wooded in mature maple trees with minimal amounts of undergrowth. Access to the site may have been from any one of three routes: along the stream bed about 50 m from the main road (gravel in 1981), an access lane immediately above the steep slope requiring coming down a rather precarious 30 m, and an access road on the other side of the ravine requiring at least 50 m from any parked car. Whatever the route, about 50 m or its equivalent appears to be the minimum distance from any parked car.

We noted a typical soil stratigraphy for the area. The first 20 to 30 centimeters (designated A-zone) is a rich organic layer developing from rotting leaves and twigs interspersed with occasional bones from small animals dying in the forest. Below this level is a distinctive yellow, mineral, sandy soil (designated B-zone) which continues beyond the interest of this excavation. There is gradual movement and mixing of materials in the A-zone in the area of interest because of the sloping downward to the stream.

We found numerous fragments of clothing consistent with the clothes discovered in 1986. While these fragments of cloth are more frequently near the surface, they were found throughout the A-zone. We suspect that some officers had shovels to randomly dig about here and there. Therefore, we cannot get too excited about location except in a very general sense.

Only three pieces of human bone were recovered during the course of the excavation (see Figure 2):

#20, A fragment of right scapula (44 × 46 mm) including a portion of the acromial spine (root) and the blade in the area of the supraspinous fossa. The spine is sheared or broken just medial to the root of the acromial process. At first we thought this to be a cut or slash. However, closer inspection under a stereo binocular microscope could not confirm this conclusion. It must remain simply as a possible cut.

#25, A distal phalanx from a hand — probably the third or fourth finger. Anatomical length and maximum length provide no new information. There is no evidence of pathological change.

#32, A fragment of a right clavicle includes part of the conoid tubercle. Both ends of the shaft are broken irregularly as if by crushing. These low energy crushing fractures are typical of carnivore trauma (Symes et al. 1994). Additionally, there are distinctive tooth marks on the surface which appear to be of canid origin.

During the course of trowelling at the bottom of the A-zone, we found the first evidence to suggest a probable manner of death: a bullet from a .45 caliber automatic weapon. Indeed, we found a total of five similar bullets near the bottom of the A-zone. Presumably, these had

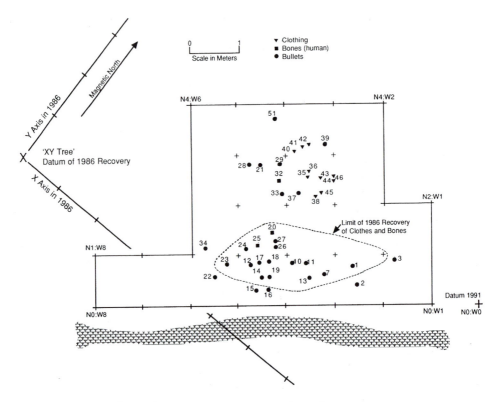

**Figure 2**   Map of items recovered by authors in 1991.

been missed in the 1986 police recovery because they were out of range of the metal detectors employed at the scene.

We had not excavated into the B-zone since the squares excavated at the outset had established that it was sterile. However, we reasoned that if five bullets had penetrated 25 to 30 cm through the A-zone, it was possible that additional bullets might have penetrated further into the supposedly sterile B-zone. The homicide detectives scanned our exposed B-zone with metal detector. Six additional bullets were located in the B-zone, bringing the total number of bullets to eleven. The bullets probably moved very little in the unstable A-zone because they were near the bottom. The ones in the B-zone, of course, were quite stable. Trajectory appears to be a different problem. The actual direction of the bullets appeared indeterminate. Some were pointing downward, while other were on their side. It is unknown whether there were several trajectories, slight movements in the soil, or that this is typical of the behavior of bullets fired into the soil. Further research is warranted on this problem. All these bullets are tightly grouped in an area of about 1 m × ½ m. It is interesting that the human torso is also roughly 1 m × ½ m. Apparently the bullets were all directed to the torso, since no bullet wounds were reported on the 1986 remains which included the skull, jaw, and legs. There is one enticing statement buried in the forensic odontologist's report from 1986. In his discussion of "radiolucent restorations" he mentions "A residual metallic fragment in the mandibular, left, first permanent molar area of the mandibular alveolus." No further comment is made. It may indeed be a fragment of a metallic restoration, but in the light of this new evidence, it also may be a bullet fragment.

Because we had noted and mapped the distribution of bits of bone, clothing, and bullets, we were able to reconstruct (infer) a scenario. The body probably lay on the ground as she was shot repeatedly with a .45 caliber pistol. Ballistic analysis indicates all the bullets were fired from the same weapon. Eleven bullets indicate that the gun was reloaded at least once with a new clip. The bullets probably all entered the torso because none of the extant bones bad any bullet wounds. The torso bones are mostly missing. She appears to have been left on the surface because in the 1986 recovery most of the bones and clothing were found on the surface. The bits of bones and clothing we recovered were found in the A-zone. Bones and clothing were found about 1 m down slope from the bullet cluster compatible with 10 years of A-zone formation and movement.

## Taphonomic Questions Addressed

**Are the bones human?**   Bones recovered in 1986 and 1991 include both human and non-human elements, all of which were identified. The animal bones appear to be random fauna from the forest and not related to the homicide occurrence.

**How many humans are present?**   There is no overlap among the 19 bones recovered in 1986 and 1991. While not conclusIve, the remains are probably from one individual.

**What is the time since death?**   There is no method that will provide a finer estimation than the circumstantial evidence discussed above. Additionally, no insect casings were recovered. An experimental biochemical analysis of bone tissue is currently part of a research project.

**What is the manner of death?**   No evidence was found in 1986. However, based on the 1991 evidence, there is a strong possibility that the victim was shot repeatedly with a .45 semi-automatic handgun. We cannot establish this inference conclusively because no bullet wounds have been noted on any of the bone elements. Nevertheless, the concordant distribution of the bones and clothing with the bullets cannot be ignored. It is possible that the bullets are from a different event, but this is far less likely than the possibility that the events are related.

**Why are the torso bones missing?**   Remembering that as many as eleven .45 caliber bullets had penetrated her body, there must have been considerable blood and exposed flesh. Extensive trauma to a body will tend to accelerate carnivore scavenging (Haglund et al. 1989; Haglund and Reay 1993). Remembering also that there is evidence of carnivore activity, the torso would have been of primary interest to predators.

**Why was the body not discovered for such a long period of time?**   The victim was noted as missing in late September, and she was left in a mature maple forest. Leaves would be falling, and they would continue to cover the remains until the winter snow. Even carnivore activity would be hidden in a matter of days.

**Why was the skull found so far from the body?**   Again, canids are the most likely perpetrators. Coyotes and wild dogs are common in the area. We have now noted three cases (including this one) in recent years with canid scavenging. Apparently, canids follow typical play behavior of domestic dogs (Rodriguez 1987). The human skull is not unlike a ball and it is probably played with by rolling it about. In none of the cases is there evidence of skull consumption. In all three cases, the skull was found some distance from the body. Unfortunately, the skull is no longer available for examination in this case. Signature canid puncture marks were not noted in the 1986 analysis. However, tooth puncture marks were not present on the skulls of the two cases noted above. While Rodriguez (1987) notes some cases of dog chewing, he has since observed that canid gnawing marks on the cranium are relatively rare.

# Conclusions

Taphonomic inferences obviously played an important part in determining the fate of Ms. Smith. Our interpretations are, unfortunately, not always based on hard evidence. If we had played a role in the 1986 recovery, there is no doubt we would be in a better position. The bones recovered in 1986 are not availible for re-analysis, and the context of the individual pieces recovered has been lost. As Haglund and Reay (1993) have noted, when the recovery of human remains is increasingly separated in time from the time of death, continuity suffers. No one in 1986 noted the presence or absence of trauma or canid scavenging. Considering these difficulties, the police investigators are very pleased that we were able to find as much as we did. They had been told by a pathologist at the outset that there would be no more evidence or bones after so many years.

The excavation covered 10 days in the field. During this period of time there seemed to be an endless number of curious police investigators visiting the site and each was duly noted. A forensic evidence specialist was assigned to the site. Though he was not present at all times, we were equipped with a cellular phone and he was called as we made important discoveries. He was always present at the end of the day to take custody of the evidence. We inventoried the bags for the day, noted them in our notebooks, and the evidence was locked up until the end of the excavation. Another police officer was assigned to protect the site until we returned the next morning. At the end of the excavation we received all the bony remains in a sealed carton, and analyzed the bones in our laboratory, maintaining chain of custody.

The suspected perpetrator in this case is under arrest for another more recent homicide. Should the police be able to connect the bullets with the suspect, we can expect to be testifying in court. There may be weaknesses in our inferences (which we recognize), but at least our evidence will be admissible because we followed basic rules of chain of custody.

# Acknowledgments

We wish to thank Detective Herb Curwain and Inspector Peter Holley, both of the Durham Regional Police, Oshawa, Ontario for their assistance and support. Further, we wish to recognize the cooperation of the Chief Coroner's Office of Ontario. There have been many changes instituted since the time of the 1986 investigation. The new Chief Coroner, Dr. James Young, has put together a new team that includes the routine use of forensic anthropologists. This team includes Dr. James Cairns, Deputy Chief Coroner, and Dr. David Chaisson, Chief Forensic Pathologist, who are strong advocates of forensic anthropology.

# References

Efremov, I.A.
 1940 Taphonomy: A New Branch of Paleontology. *Pan-American Geologists* 74:81–93.

Feder, H.A.
 1991 *Succeeding as an Expert Witness: Increasing Your Impact and Income.* Van Nostrand Reinhold, New York.

Fisher B.A, A. Svensson, and O. Wendel
 1987 *Techniques of Crime Scene Investigation.* Elsevier Science, New York.

Galloway A., W.H. Birkby, T. Kahana, and L. Fulginiti
 1990 Physical Anthropology and the Law: Legal Responsibilities of Forensic Anthropologists. *American Journal of Physical Anthropology Yearbook* 133:39–57.

Haglund, W.D., and D.T. Reay
    1993  Problems of Recovering Partial Human Remains at Different Times and Locations: Concerns for Death Investigators. *Journal of Forensic Sciences* 38:69–80.

Haglund, W.D., D.T. Reay, and D.R. Swindler
    1989  Canid Scavenging/Disarticulation Sequence of Human Remains in the Pacific Northwest. *Journal of Forensic Sciences* 34:587–606.

Rodriguez, W.C.
    1987  Postmortem Animal Activity; Recognition and Interpretation. Paper presented at the 39th Annual Meeting of the American Academy of Forensic Sciences, Anaheim, CA.

Swanson C.R., N.C. Chamelin, and L. Territo
    1988  *Criminal Investigation.* 4th ed. Random House, New York.

Symes S., H.E. Berryman, and O.C. Smith
    1994.  Large Carnivore Scavenging on Bone: Separating Taphonomic Features from Perimortem Fractures of Bone. Paper presented at the 46th Annual Meeting of the American Academy of Forensic Sciences, Boston.

# Taphonomic Applications in Forensic Anthropology

# 5

## DOUGLAS H. UBELAKER

## Introduction

The field of taphonomy was generally defined by Efremov in 1940 as the study of the processes by which organic remains pass from the biosphere into the lithosphere as the result of geological and biological processes. Interest in the field began within paleontology as the study of the fossilization process. Later, archaeologists recognized the importance of understanding taphonomic processes to properly interpret human modifications of organic materials.

Recently, taphonomic assessment has emerged as an important and vital component of forensic anthropological analysis. In particular, forensic contexts necessitate the reconstruction of perimortem and postmortem processes and the discrimination of natural from human-induced trauma. This paper reviews some of the taphonomic research which applies to such interpretations and presents case studies in which these approaches were used.

## Taphonomic Processes

Many processes can alter the appearance of bone and related organic materials after death (Morlan 1984; Shipman 1981). Factors in the transport and dispersal of skeletal elements include animals, gravity, or water and fluvial processes (Marshall 1989). The properties of the bones influence their reaction to these processes.

Animal-related processes include trampling, entrance fall, gnawing, and digestion. Physical factors include rockfall, water transport, sandblasting, weathering, burial, diagenic movement, volcanic shockwave, acid attack by roots, cryoturbation, release and breakup by bottom-fast ice, and mineralization by ground water (Marshall 1989). All of these can act independently or in unison to produce alteration of bones. Both animal and physical processes need to be understood in reconstructing the context of death and the sequences after death in forensic cases.

The usual sequence of disarticulation and scattering of mammal skeletons has been documented through studies by Hill (1979) in Lake Turkana, Kenya; Andrews and Cook (1985); and others. Hill and Behrensmeyer (1984) found the pattern of disarticulation to be very predictable. Human remains, exposed in outdoor scenes, can become disarticulated and scattered in a pattern similar to other large mammals. Knowledge about such patterns can be of use in scene recovery of remains and interpretation of missing elements.

Andrews and Cook (1985) documented the taphonomic processes operating on the carcass of a dead cow in Somerset, England during a 7.5 year period beginning in 1977. They found that trampling and movement by carnivores were the most significant factors leading to disarticulation and alteration of the remains. Eventually they found many fine striations, trough and V-shaped grooves, and depressions that were similar to those produced by human artifacts.

Miller found considerable variation in patterns of animal chewing. Miller (1969) adds that seasonal shifts involving freezing and thawing and/or wetting and drying can also alter bone.

Behrensmeyer et al. (1986) emphasize the important role of trampling in taphonomic bone change. Their experiments reveal that even at the microscopic level it is not always easy to distinguish alterations caused by tools from those produced by trampling and other taphonomic processes. Trampling marks in particular can mimic cut marks. They note "cutmark mimics can occur on bones subjected to trampling and original true cutmarks can be obscured by the same process" (Behrensmeyer et al. 1986:3). Discrimination of natural mimics from human-induced trauma can be critical in a forensic analysis. It is particularly important to be able to support a conclusion that natural processes cannot be ruled out.

Environmental assessment can play an important role in interpretation. The burial context, the presence of potentially abrading sand and gravel, and the pattern of the marks on the bones all provide clues (Behrensmeyer et al. 1986). The implication of this study for interpretation in archaeology and forensic anthropology is clear: taphonomic factors must be considered in judging possible tool marks on bone.

## Animal Chewing and Other Causes of Bone Breakage

Since animal chewing represents an obvious and well-known taphonomic factor, researchers have accumulated useful information on carnivore feeding patterns. In a study of 125 carcasses in the Arctic, Haynes (1982) documented considerable variation in the gnawing damage sustained by carcasses. Haynes (1983a) noted that different patterns of bone alteration resulted from canids, hyenas, bears, and felids.

Sutcliffe (1971) notes that bone-chewing animals are not confined to carnivores. The herbivores cattle, red deer, reindeer, muntjac deer, camels, giraffes, wildebeest, kudu, gemsbok, and sable antelopes also have been documented to produce chewing-type alterations on bones.

Research also has documented that the pattern of chewing varies for different bones, and that animal chewing can produce spiral fractures that frequently are interpreted as evidence of human activity in archaeology and potentially in forensic anthropology as well (Beebe 1983; Haynes 1980a,b; Morlan 1980).

In a study of bison and moose remains, Haynes (1983b) found that about 5% of the bones showed spiral fractures due to trampling and 8% due to carnivore activity. He suggested that up to 50% of the bones of smaller species may show such fractures. As noted by Hill (1976), the internal structure of bone strongly influences the nature of the fracture.

As a result of taphonomic research, archaeologists now routinely consider such factors in interpreting faunal remains to assess the number of individuals present (Aaris-Sorensen 1983), the possible products of the hunt (Binford and Ho 1985), and the possible use of tools.

Agenbroad (1989) reported the presence of spiral fractures that others might have interpreted as being of human origin on the bones of 34 mammoths excavated at a natural sinkhole trap in South Dakota. The remains date between 21,000 and 26,000 B.P., well before the presence of humans in the area. Agenbroad identified the following processes that modified the bones at the Hot Springs Mammoth Site: biological (trampling, torsion/falling, carnivores), hydrological (spring effluent, subaqueous down-slope movement), geological/structural (postdepositional movement), and mechanical (boulder fall, freezing, overbank fall).

Animal chewing, and other causes of bone breakage, can be confounding variables in forensic interpretations. On the one hand, such processes can obscure evidence of the cause and manner of death. On the other hand, some modifications such as spiral fractures with impact scars, can be difficult to interpret. It is necessary to examine the patterns using taphonomic models of animal modification and careful scene reconstruction.

## Weathering Patterns

In the taphonomic process, weathering represents the response of the bone to its immediate environment, e.g., soil, sun, etc. as opposed to carnivore modifications, trampling, fluvial transport, and geochemical changes (Behrensmeyer 1978; Miller 1975). From her research with bones of recent mammals in the Amboseli Basin in southern Kenya, Behrensmeyer (1978) recognized six progressive stages of bone weathering:

**Stage 0.** Bone surface shows no sign of cracking or flaking due to weathering. Usually bone is still greasy. Marrow cavities contain tissue; skin and muscle/ligament may cover part or all of the bone surface.

**Stage 1.** Bone shows cracking, normally parallel to the fiber structure (e.g., longitudinal in long bones). Articular surfaces may show mosaic cracking of covering tissue as well as in the bone itself. Fat, skin, and other tissue may or may not be present.

**Stage 2.** Outermost concentric thin layers of bone show flaking, usually associated with cracks, in that the bone edges along the cracks tend to separate and flake first. Long thin flakes, with one or more sides still attached to the bone, are common in the initial part of stage 2. Deeper and more extensive flaking follows, until most of the outermost bone is gone. Crack edges are usually angular in cross section. Remnants of ligaments, cartilage, and skin may be present.

**Stage 3.** Bone surface is characterized by patches of rough, homogeneously weathered compact bone, resulting in a fibrous texture. In these patches, all the external, concentrically layered bone has been removed. Gradually the patches extend to cover the entire bone surface. Weathering does not penetrate deeper than 1.0 to 1.5 mm at this stage, and bone fibers are still firmly attached to each other. Crack edges usually are rounded in cross section. Tissue rarely present at this stage.

**Stage 4.** The bone surface is coarsely fibrous and rough in texture; large and small splinters occur and may be loose enough to fall away from the bone when it is moved. Weathering penetrates into inner cavities. Cracks are open and have splintered or rounded edges.

**Stage 5.** Bone is falling apart *in situ,* with large splinters lying around what remains of the whole, which is fragile and easily broken by moving. Original bone shape may be difficult to determine. Cancellous bone usually exposed, when present, and may outlast all traces of the former more compact, outer parts of the bones. (Behrensmeyer 1978:151).

The Behrensmeyer weathering model can assist in understanding and reconstructing the postmortem interval (see Lyman and Fox this volume). Although in human forensic cases that interval is much shorter than in paleontological contexts, weathering changes can frequently be key to ruling out perimortem trauma.

## Forensic Anthropology Applications

Many of the paleontological and archaeological principles outlined above have direct utility in forensic anthropology (Micozzi 1991; Ubelaker 1989, 1991). Particular areas of application are: (1) estimation of postmortem interval (time since death); (2) environmental reconstruction or the detection of unknown postmortem scenarios; (3) reconstruction of postmortem events; and (4) distinguishing evidence of foul play from alterations caused by other taphonomic factors.

Taphonomic assessment of human remains differs from that of nonhuman animals not only in the structural differences between humans and nonhuman animals that may influence response to taphonomic forces, but especially in that human behavior frequently is involved normally in the postmortem treatment of the dead. Thus, with humans, postmortem interpretation includes not only the possible effects of weathering, trampling, etc., but also embalming, cremation, or other types of burning (Buikstra and Swegle 1989; Dawson and Santos 1990; Murray and Rose 1993; Nelson 1992), burial, coffin enclosure and many other cultural factors.

In the practice of forensic anthropology, taphonomic consideration has come to mean interpretation of all events affecting the remains between death and discovery. Since most forensic anthropologists also are experienced in aspects of archaeology and in the interpretation of archaeologically recovered human remains, they are most qualified to make such assessments. With many cases, taphonomic assessment represents the most important contributions made by anthropologists. This is especially true in the interpretation of skeletal evidence for foul play.

## Estimation of Postmortem Interval

Although the study of arthropods associated with remains and other factors can contribute to the estimation of the postmortem interval (Goff and Flynn 1991; Haglund and Reay 1993; Haglund et al. 1990; Schoenly et al. 1991, 1992; Skinner et al. 1988), usually such interpretations of largely skeletonized human remains involve assessment of their condition. Recent research and experience have documented how variable the rate of decomposition can be. Influencing factors can be the ambient temperature, amount of rainfall, clothing, burial type, burial depth, extent of animal chewing and disarticulation, extent of perimortem trauma, body weight, and general environmental conditions (Bass and Meadows 1990).

The pattern of postmortem change varies regionally and among microenvironments within each region. Galloway et al. (1989) document rapid bloating, but extensive mummification in the dry environment of southern Arizona. Tropical environments can involve skeletonization within 2 weeks (Ubelaker 1989). Freezing and thawing as well as mechanical injury can influence the process (Micozzi 1986). The formation of adipocere in wet environments can lead to exceptionally long-term preservation (Mellen et al. 1993).

The general pattern of disarticulation and bone weathering documented in experimental studies stemming from paleontological interests generally applies to humans as well. In fact, Bielenstein (1990) demonstrates that Behrensmeyer's (1978) stages of bone weathering match the sequence seen in modern forensic cases.

Much of the research on animal chewing of animal carcasses documented above also has been extended to humans. Different animals leave distinct patterns of tooth marks on human bone (Haglund et al. 1988; Haglund 1992; Miller and Smith 1989; Ubelaker 1989; Willey and Snyder 1989). The amount of carnivore activity varies considerably due to circumstances that shelter the remains from animal access and the human population density in the area (Haglund et al. 1988). With human remains, Haglund et al. (1989) document five stages of sequential alteration due to canid scavenging. These are (1) no bony involvement, (2) ventral thorax damage with one or both upper extremities removed, (3) lower extremity involvement, (4) only vertebral segments remaining articulated, and (5) total disarticulation. Obviously, previous trauma to the remains or other unusual factors may influence the sequence of change.

Research at the University of Tennessee in Knoxville also has shown that volatile fatty acids produced from soft tissue decomposition and anions and cations also from soft tissue may be detected within the soil beneath human remains. Measurement of these factors in controlled samples can allow accurate estimates of postmortem interval in some circumstances (Vass et al. 1992).

Experimentation and experience have revealed useful information on the decomposition process. Usually with surface burials, most odor and much of the soft tissue are gone within 6 months (depending upon the season). Sun bleaching, bone surface cracking, and the processes identified in Behrensmeyer's (1978) stages 2 through 5 usually indicate many months or even many years, depending upon the circumstances.

The variability in the rate of postmortem change can be impressive. Obviously, in arid environments such as coastal Peru or even the American southwest, mummification can occur naturally, leading to soft tissue preservation for hundreds or even thousands of years. In a tropical environment where remains are exposed to scavenging animals, a human body can be skeletonized within 14 days (Ubelaker 1989).

Such variability can occur even within a single site. At one South Dakota historic cemetery that had not been in use for several decades, a relocation project discovered some remains had been reduced to unrecognizable fragments while others were mummified and extremely well preserved.

Bass (1984) provides an excellent example of how difficult estimating time since death can be. His examination of the remains within the recently disturbed grave of a man who died 113 years previously revealed excellent soft tissue preservation, extensive odor and clothing as well. He initially suspected the remains were a recent deposit in the old grave. Later he learned that the remains actually were those of the man described on the tombstone. A cast iron coffin allowed the unusual preservation.

## Environmental Reconstruction

Although little has been written about the importance of environmental reconstruction from taphonomic indicators, in my experience, it can be of potential significance in forensic anthropology. Barnacles adhering to bones indicate exposure to salt water. Green algae stain frequently is present on remains from moist shaded areas. Soil embedded in orifices indicates previous burial. Bleaching of bone surfaces usually indicates prolonged sun exposure, although salt water can produce similar results. Adipocere usually indicates a wet environment.

Such observations usually reflect the known conditions surrounding the discovery site. Cobwebs are found within a skull recovered from a garage. Soil-filled bones with sun exposure are expected from remains found from a grave disturbed years ago in a sunny area.

Remains originating from previous burial in a cemetery also can be detected. Berryman et al. (1991) note that physical characteristics associated with the embalming process, artifacts associated with the coffin, devices used in embalming, and levels of chemicals in the soft tissue all provide clues to the remains' history.

## Sequence of Postmortem Events

Occasionally, taphonomic observations can be used not only to describe postmortem events, but also to determine their sequence. Mann and Owsley (1992) describe a case in which a skeleton was discovered in a farmer's field with a shotgun in association. A spent slug casing was present in the breech of the shotgun. Skeletal analysis revealed cranial fragmentation as well as numerous small round perforations in the pelvic area.

Although not all of the cranial fragments were present, those present were multicolored. Some fragments that articulated showed marked contrast in color, ranging from sun bleached white to a dark brown. Although no clear-cut exit or entry gunshot injury was found, the overall pattern of fracture was consistent with gunshot wound. The variability in coloration of anatomically adjacent fragments suggested that breakage occurred early in the postmortem interval. Microscopic examination coupled with infrared spectrometry of small particles imbedded within fractured cranial surfaces revealed them to be plastics containing cellulose nitrate, a known residue of gunpowder. All of these observations suggested "a perimortem close-range gunshot to the face or throat" (Mann and Owsley, 1992:1387).

In contrast, the alterations on the postcranial skeleton revealed a different pattern. Analysis revealed fractures of the right tibia, left scapula, and fifth lumbar vertebra, obvious plow cuts on other bones, alga stains on the mandible and the medullary cavity of the fractured right tibia, and 71 pellet-type perforations on the os coxae, right femoral head, proximal left femur, and the spinous process of the third lumbar vertebra.

Several taphonomic factors indicated that the pellet injury was sustained postmortem. Several of the perforations were located on the head of the femur with no injury to the corresponding area of the acetabulum area of the pelvis. This clearly indicated that the femur and pelvis were not articulated when the injury was sustained. Perforations also were present on the symphyseal surface of the left pubis with no damage to the corresponding area of the right symphyseal surface.

Small weathering cracks were present on the bones of the pelvis, indicating exposure of 2 to 3 years. Pellet perforations intersected several of the small cracks, indicating cracks had formed prior to the formation of the perforations. If the reverse had been true, the cracks would have terminated at the perforations and not have passed through them. Clearly the skeleton had been resting in the field long enough for the weathering cracks to form before the perforations were made. Taphonomic observations allowed the sequence of postmortem events to be established and the recognition that two events of gunshot trauma were present, one perimortem in the cranial area and another postmortem in the pelvic area.

## Pseudo-Trauma

Weathering cracks can resemble those produced by blunt force trauma. Trampling and carnivore chewing can cause spiral fractures similar to those caused by foul play-associated trauma. Fungus can cause a blackening of bones that simulates burning. Carnivore tooth marks can appear very similar to sharp force trauma. All of these factors call for detailed examination of such remains by an experienced forensic anthropologist (Ubelaker 1991).

## The Lady in the Cistern

At times evidence of foul play and taphonomic conditions that mimic foul play may appear on the same skeleton or even the same bone. In 1984 human remains were found within an unused cistern near a midwestern U.S. airport. The remains were identified by dental comparison as those of a young woman reported missing in 1975 (Ubelaker and Sperber 1988). Witnesses indicated she had attended a party hosted by a local Hell's Angels group on the night of her disappearance. Authorities found evidence of a fire in the basement of the house and noted that some wooden steps leading to the basement were missing. They suspected that after she had been killed, her attackers had attempted to burn the body before depositing it within the cistern. The theory was strengthened by the presence of a blackened distal femur. Analysis revealed, however, that the blackened area was produced by fungus growing within the damp dark cistern and was a postmortem phenomenon not related to foul play.

In contrast to this natural process, much of the outer structures of the face had been destroyed, apparently by an acid-like material (Figure 1). The destruction was too severe and too localized to represent a natural taphonomic process and thus had to represent foul play.

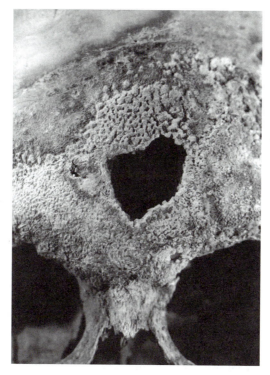

**Figure 1**    Localized destruction of skull due to acid-like substance.

Confronted with the evidence, the defense argued that perhaps the alterations had been produced within the cistern, with the skull in contact with caustic substances within the soil.

The soil had been tested and was found to be relatively neutral pH. The proof rested with the observation that the pattern of destruction extended across the occlusal plane from the maxilla to the mandible. The skull and mandible were not found in contact; the cranium had rolled off the skeleton and was resting on its side. The alterations on the bones had to have originated perimortem before decomposition when the bones were still articulated.

Additional alterations were observed on the top of the cranium. Roughly circular white circles were present. Initially it was thought they must be related to the destruction on the face, but the bone in the affected area was only whitened and showed none of the extensive bone loss seen on the bones of the face. Apparently the white dots were produced by sunlight beaming through perforations in the thick manhole cover above.

# Carl Weiss

In 1991, I was invited to participate in the exhumation and study of the remains of Dr. Carl Austin Weiss of Baton Rouge, LA. Dr. Weiss had been a 29-year-old ear, nose, and throat specialist in Baton Rouge when he was killed on September 8, 1935 (Ubelaker and Scammell 1992). He was accused of shooting former Governor and State Senator Huey P. Long and was in turn shot many times by Senator Long's bodyguards. Controversy followed the shooting, not only because, as a young physician with a family and house calls to make, Weiss was a very unlikely assassin, but also because a nurse who treated Long noticed he had a cut lip. When asked about the cut, Long replied: "That's where he hit me." Critics of the assassin theory argue that if Weiss hit Long with his fist, then he likely did not shoot him.

Careful reconstruction and study of the bone fragments included in Weiss' remains indicated that he had been shot at least 20 times, with about half of them coming from behind. Because of the historical controversy regarding the scenario that Weiss struck Long with his fist, I carefully examined the hand bones for evidence of trauma. Radiographs and visual examination revealed no apparent gross fractures. However, microscopic examination revealed a series of small fractures within the metacarpals of the right hand, raising the possibility that Weiss had sustained stress fractures of the metacarpal diaphyses but had not completely fractured the necks of the bones. However, additional analysis revealed similar small fractures on the diaphyses of the metacarpals of the left hand and on some of the metatarsals as well. Clearly the microfractures resulted from postmortem taphonomic factors and not from perimortem trauma.

Another unusual feature of the Weiss skeleton was a peculiar metallic blackening of the teeth. The black stain was located on the lingual aspects of most of the teeth but on the buccal surfaces of only the mandibular teeth. Analysis of the stain by electron-induced X-ray spectroscopy with a scanning electron microscope revealed a mercury composition. Had Dr. Carl Weiss consumed mercury turning him into a deranged killer? No. I reasoned that if such were the case, mercury would be dispersed throughout his system and would be detected within those structures growing at the time of death. Analysis of the basal extremes of body hair and toenails revealed no evidence of mercury.

The mercury on the teeth apparently originated from Weiss' amalgam fillings that were obviously deteriorating after 56 years in the ground. The released mercury concentrated on the lingual margins of the teeth in the immediate area. Weiss' marked dental overbite created the space through which some mercury managed to travel to eventually settle on the labial surfaces of the anterior teeth.

Coincidentally, a nonmetallic-looking black stain was present on many bones of the skeleton. Analysis revealed this stain to be primarily sulfuric in origin and likely originating from byproducts of soft tissue decomposition, held captive by the burial container.

Other interesting taphonomic features of the Weiss remains were small white crystalline deposits located throughout the postcranial skeleton. Analysis revealed these also were of sulfuric origin, likely originating from soft tissue decomposition. When the small deposits were removed, they left behind a small crater-like perforation in the bone cortex that perhaps to some would imitate a disease condition.

# Goochland, Virginia

In 1982, a skeleton was found by berry pickers in rural Goochland County, VA. A shoestring was present around the cervical vertebrae, indicating manual strangulation. The remains were brought to the National Museum of Natural History where forensic anthropologist J. Lawrence Angel observed an angular sheared planar surface on the distal end of a carpal phalanx. Angel's report noted, "A striking peculiarity is the diagonal cut amputating a 3 to 5 mm section of the distal joint of the basal phalanx of the left little finger (Figure 2). Does this come from the killer's removal of fingertips? from a defense slash (though there are no cuts on the facial bones)? from a postmortem cut? or, least likely, from accidental amputation by some kind of meat-packing machine shortly before death?"

The skeleton was later identified as being a young woman from Puerto Rico (Ubelaker and Scammell 1992). In 1991, a suspect was charged with the crime. The prosecutor in the case realized that cause of death was ligature strangulation but also focused on the possibility that in addition, her finger may have been amputated. The original examiner at the Smithsonian, Dr. Angel, had died in 1986 and the evidence of the altered phalanx apparently had been buried with the rest of the remains back in Puerto Rico.

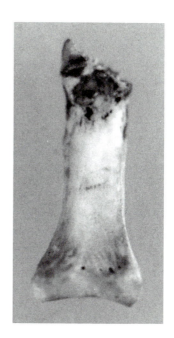

**Figure 2** Diagonal amputation of the left fifth proximal carpal phalanx.

Recognizing that I could not offer an opinion on evidence that I had not examined, I accepted the prosecutor's invitation to travel to Puerto Rico to supervise the exhumation of the remains and to try to locate the altered phalanx. In May, 1991, the remains were exhumed and examined in the nearby Medical Examiners Office.

Since Dr. Angel's examination, the remains had become stained dark gray, apparently by moisture and decomposing materials within the carton in which they were buried. The altered phalanx was found within a sealed plastic bag mixed in with the other remains and retained the original coloration. Some nonhuman animal bones were present, as well as evidence of extensive carnivore gnawing throughout the skeleton, including hand bones.

As noted by Angel, the left fifth proximal hand phalanx displayed loss of bone. A 3- to 7-mm section of this bone was missing from the lateral surface. The broken surface was roughly planar. Microscopic examination indicated irregular fracturing of the cancellous bone and slight irregularity in the axis of the cut or broken surface. Microscopic examination also revealed two alterations on the bone that were likely produced by carnivore chewing; one small indentation on the lateral surface immediately proximal to the cut or altered surface; and a small scratch on the superior surface near the midline. The cut or broken surface lacked the uniformly planar surface and pattern of evenly cut bone that would be expected if the bone had been cut with a sharp knife.

To reinforce my impression, I conducted a series of experiments. Chicken thighs and wings were purchased, recognizing that the cortical thickness and cancellous bones on the extreme ends were similar to those of the relevant aspect of human phalanges. The chicken parts were struck with a sharp knife, a dull knife, a digging tool and an axe. Parts were also tested by slamming them in the doors and hatchback of a 1974 Ford Pinto (the same model as that owned by the victim). One possible scenario suggested by the prosecutor was that the finger may have been damaged by the car door slamming on it during a struggle.

Following the testing, all of the chicken parts were defleshed, degreased, and examined grossly and microscopically. A planar pattern of fracture with irregular cancellous bone similar to that observed on the human phalanx was found on the chicken bones altered by a dull knife, axe, and the digging tool. Even one (the hatchback) of 16 tests of the Ford Pinto produced similar injury (Figure 3).

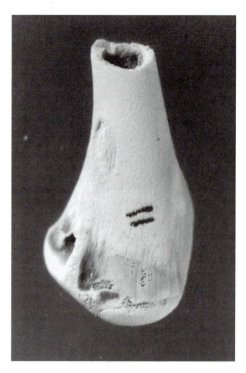

**Figure 3**  Typical pattern of amputation of chicken bone by a dull blade or straight edge.

I concluded that "the pattern of alteration is consistent with it being forcibly cut or broken with a dull (not sharp) blade or straight edge. In my opinion, this type of alteration could have been produced by the finger being struck with a dull knife, dull shovel, mattock, or similar instrument. Conceivably, this type of alteration also could have been produced if a car door was forcibly closed on the finger. It is also possible that a dog-size carnivore could have caused this damage with its posterior shearing teeth. Note that I have never before seen damage like this caused by carnivore chewing. Typically carnivore chewing will cause fractured and crushed bones with irregular jagged surfaces of the type seen with all other examples of alterations on this skeleton. The alteration on the left fifth phalanx is distinct from all of the other alterations in that it is relatively planar and evenly cut. Although such a cut by a carnivore would be very unusual, it is possible given the structure of the carnivore posterior teeth."

## Bones from the Cemetery: Recent or Old?

In July of 1991, a young woman was reported missing. Subsequent investigation revealed that she may have been abducted and killed, with the body buried in a local cemetery. In September, 1992, excavation of a likely unauthorized burial site within the cemetery recovered a number of bones thought to possibly represent those of the victim. The remains were submitted for analysis to the Department of Anthropology, National Museum of Natural History, Smithsonian Institution in Washington, D.C. through the FBI Laboratories.

Analysis revealed that the only bones present were a left scapula, one cervical vertebra, one left upper rib, one right foot navicular, one thoracic vertebra, one right metatarsal, and one cranial fragment. Neither soft tissue nor odor was present. All of the bones showed considerable surface cracking and exfoliation of the periosteal surfaces. Many areas of the bones were fragmented and/or eroded.

Analysis indicated that all bones likely originated from one individual, a young to middle-age adult female. Although this information was consistent with the age and sex of the missing person, the extent of weathering changes indicated the bones originated from an old grave in the cemetery and not the recent missing person.

In addition, the thoracic vertebra showed planar trauma on the proximal surface of the centrum. Sharp force trauma consisted of a wide, deep incision on the anterior surface of the centrum. The lack of soil adhesion, lack of erosion of the exposed trabeculae and a coloration pattern distinct from that seen on the other outer bone surfaces indicated the alterations had not been made perimortem but much more recently. They appeared to be typical of alterations made by a shovel.

Besides recovery damage, previous examiners of forensic remains may leave alterations on the bones that can be mistaken for perimortem trauma. With several cases, I have discovered definitive evidence of sharp force trauma only to realize that it was produced by a scalpel or striker saw during previous examination. White and Toth (1989) report that the measuring instruments of an anthropologist likely produced marks on a human fossil that others interpreted as being ancient cutmarks.

## Summary

Taphonomic interpretation has assumed a vital and unique place in the forensic anthropology tool kit. Consideration of taphonomic factors is essential in past environmental reconstruction, estimation of postmortem interval, reconstruction of the sequence of postmortem events, and the assessment of trauma and pseudotrauma.

## References

Aaris-Sorensen, K.
  1983   An Example of Taphonomic Loss in a Mesolithic Faunal Assemblage. In *Animals and Archaeology: Hunters and Their Prey*, edited by J. Clutton-Brock and C. Grigson, pp. 243–247. BAR International Series 163, British Archaeological Research, Oxford, U.K.

Agenbroad, L.
  1989   Spiral Fractured Mammoth Bone from Nonhuman Taphonomic Processes at Hot Springs Mammoth Site. In *Bone Modification*, edited by R. Bonnichsen and M.H. Sorg, pp. 139–147. Center for The Study of the First Americans, Orono, ME.

Andrews, P., and J. Cook
  1985   Natural Modifications to Bones in a Temperate Setting. *Man* 20:675–691.

Bass, W.M.
  1984   Time Interval since Death, a Difficult Decision. In *Human Identification, Case Studies in Forensic Anthropology*, edited by T.A. Rathbun and J.E. Buikstra, pp. 136–147. Charles C Thomas, Springfield, IL.

Bass, W.M., and L. Meadows
  1990   Time since Death and Decomposition of the Human Body: Variables and Observations in Case and Experimental Field Studies. *Journal of Forensic Sciences* 35:103–111.

Beebe, B.F.
  1983   Evidence of Carnivore Activity in a Late Pleistocene/Early Holocene Archaeological Site (Bluefish Cave 1), Yukon Territory. In *Carnivores, Human Scavengers and Predators: A Question of Bone Technology*, edited by G.M. LeMoine and A.S. Mac Eachern, pp. 1–14. Archaeological Association of the University of Calgary, Calgary.

Behrensmeyer, A.K.
1978 Taphonomic and Ecological Information from Bone Weathering. *Paleobiology* 4:150–162.

Behrensmeyer, A.K., K.D. Gordon, and G.T. Yanagi
1986 Trampling as a Cause of Bone Surface Damage and Pseudo-Cutmarks. *Nature* 319(6065):768–771.

Berryman, H.E., W.M. Bass, S.A. Symes, and O.C. Smith
1991 Recognition of Cemetery Remains in the Forensic Setting. *Journal of Forensic Sciences* 36:230–237.

Bielenstein, D.E.M.
1990 *Forensic Taphonomy: Definitions and Applications to Forensic Anthropology and Pale-oanthropology.* Unpublished master's thesis, George Washington University, Washington, D.C.

Binford, L.R., and C.K. Ho
1985 Taphonomy at a Distance: Zhoukoudian, "The Cave Home of Beijing Man." *Current Anthropology* 26:413–442.

Buikstra, J.E., and M. Swegle
1989 Bone Modification Due to Burning: Experimental Evidence. In *Bone Modification,* edited by R. Bonnichsen and M.H. Sorg, pp. 247–258. Center for The Study of the First Americans, Orono, ME.

Dawson, G.D., and J.F. Santos
1990 Differences in Final Arrangements between Burial and Cremation as the Method of Body Disposition. *Omega* 21:129–146.

Efremov, I.A.
1940 Taphonomy, a New Branch of Paleontology. *Izvestiya Akademii Nauk SSSR Lenin-grad, Biology Series,* 3, pp. 405–413.

Galloway, A., W.H. Birkby, A.M. Jones, T.H. Henry, and B.O. Parks
1989 Decay Rates of Human Remains in an Arid Environment. *Journal of Forensic Sciences* 34:607–616.

Goff, M.L., and M.M. Flynn
1991 Determination of Postmortem Interval by Arthropod Succession: A Case Study from the Hawaiian Islands. *Journal of Forensic Sciences* 36:607–614.

Haglund, W.D.
1992 Contribution of Rodents to Postmortem Artifacts of Bone and Soft Tissue. *Journal of Forensic Sciences* 37:1459–1465.

Haglund, W.D., and D.T. Reay
1993 Problems of Recovering Partial Human Remains at Different Times and Locations: Concerns for Death Investigators. *Journal of Forensic Sciences* 38: 69–80.

Haglund, W.D., D.T. Reay, and D.R. Swindler
1988 Tooth Mark Artifacts and Survival of Bones in Animal Scavenged Human Skeletons. *Journal of Forensic Sciences* 33:985–997.
1989 Canid Scavenging/Disarticulation Sequence of Human Remains in the Pacific Northwest. *Journal of Forensic Sciences* 34:587–606.

Haglund, W.D., D.G. Reichert, and D.T. Reay
1990 Recovery of Decomposed and Skeletal Human Remains in the Green River Murder Investigation: Implications for Medical Examiner/Coroner and Police. *American Journal of Forensic Medicine and Pathology* 11:35–43.

Haynes, G.

1980a Evidence of Carnivore Gnawing on Pleistocene and Recent Mammalian Bones. *Paleobiology* 6:341–351.

1980b Taphonomical Studies in North America: Analogues for Paleoecology. *American Quaternary Association, Abstracts of the Sixth Biennial Meeting,* p. 93. University of Maine, Orono.

1982 Utilization and Skeletal Differences of North American Prey Carcasses. *Arctic* 35:266–281.

1983a A Guide for Differentiating Mammalian Carnivore Taxa Responsible for Gnaw Damage to Herbivore Limb Bones. *Paleobiology* 9:164–172.

1983b Frequencies of Spiral and Green-Bone Fractures on Ungulate Limb Bones in Modern Surface Assemblages. *American Antiquity* 48:102–114.

Hill, A.

1976 On Carnivore and Weathering Damage to Bone. *Current Anthropology* 17:335–336.

1979 Disarticulation and Scattering of Mammal Skeletons. *Paleobiology* 5:261–274.

Hill, A.P., and A.K. Behrensmeyer

1984 Disarticulation Patterns of Some Modern East African Mammals. *Paleobiology* 10:366–376.

Mann, R.W., and D.W. Owsley

1992 Human Osteology: Key to the Sequence of Events in Postmortem Shooting. *Journal of Forensic Sciences* 37:1386–1392.

Marshall, L.G.

1989 Bone Modification and "The Laws of Burial." In *Bone Modification,* edited by R. Bonnichsen and M.H. Sorg, pp. 7–24. Center for the Study of the First Americans, Orono, ME.

Mellen, P.F.M., M.A. Lowry, and M.S. Micozzi

1993 Experimental Observations on Adipocere Formation. *Journal of Forensic Sciences* 38:91–93.

Micozzi, M.S.

1986 Experimental Study of Postmortem Change under Field Conditions: Effects of Freezing, Thawing, and Mechanical Injury. *Journal of Forensic Sciences* 32:953–961.

1991 *Postmortem Change in Human and Animal Remains: A Systematic Approach.* Charles C Thomas, Springfield, IL.

Miller, G.J.

1969 A Study of Cuts, Grooves, and Other Marks on Recent and Fossil Bone. I Animal Tooth Marks. *Tebiwa* 12:20–26.

1975 A Study of Cuts, Grooves, and Other Marks on Recent and Fossil Bone. II Weathering Cracks, Fractures, Splinters, and Other Similar Natural Phenomena. In *Lithic Technology,* edited by E. Swanson, pp. 211–226. Mouton Publishers, Paris.

Miller, G.J., and V.G. Smith

1989 Carnivore Alteration of Human Bone from a Late Prehistoric Site in Illinois. *American Journal of Physical Anthropology* 79:43–49.

Morlan, R.E.

1980 *Taphonomy and Archaeology in the Upper Pleistocene of the Northern Yukon Territory: A Glimpse of the Peopling of the New World.* Mercury Series Paper No. 94, National Museum of Man, Ottawa.

1984 Toward the Definition of Criteria for the Recognition of Artificial Bone Alterations. *Quaternary Research* 22:160–171.

Murray, K.A., and J.C. Rose
  1993  The Analysis of Cremains: a Case Study Involving the Inappropriate Disposal of Mortuary Remains. *Journal of Forensic Sciences* 38:98–103.

Nelson, R.
  1992  A Microscopic Comparison of Fresh and Burned Bone. *Journal of Forensic Sciences* 37:1055–1060.

Schoenly, K., M.L. Goff, and M. Early
  1992  A BASIC Algorithm for Calculating the Postmortem Interval from Arthropod Successional Data. *Journal of Forensic Sciences* 37:808–823.

Schoenly, K., K. Griest, and S. Rhine
  1991  An Experimental Field Protocol for Investigating the Postmortem Interval Using Multidisciplinary Indicators. *Journal of Forensic Sciences* 36:1395–1415.

Shipman, P.
  1981  *Life History of a Fossil: An Introduction to Taphonomy and Paleoecology.* Harvard University Press, Cambridge, MA.

Skinner, M.F., A. Syed, J. Farrell, and J.H. Borden
  1988  Case Report in Forensic Anthropology: Animal and Insect Factors in Decomposition of Homicide Victim. *Canadian Society Forensic Science Journal* 21:71–81.

Sutcliffe, A.J.
  1971  Similarity of Bones and Antlers Gnawed by Deer to Human Artifacts. *Nature* 246(5433):428–430.

Ubelaker, D.H.
  1989  *Human Skeletal Remains. Excavation, Analysis, Interpretation.* 2nd ed. Taraxacum, Washington, D.C.
  1991  Perimortem and Postmortem Modification of Human Bone. Lessons from Forensic Anthropology. *Anthropologie* 29:171–174.

Ubelaker, D.H., and H. Scammell
  1992  *Bones: A Forensic Detective's Casebook.* HarperCollins, New York.

Ubelaker, D.H., and N.D. Sperber
  1988  Alterations in Human Bones and Teeth as a Result of Restricted Sun Exposure and Contact with Corrosive Agents. *Journal of Forensic Sciences* 33:540–548.

Vass, A.A., W. Bass, J.D. Wolt, J.E. Foss, and J.T. Ammons
  1992  Time Since Death Determinations of Human Cadavers Using Soil Solution. *Journal of Forensic Sciences* 37:1236–1253.

White, T.D., and N. Toth
  1989  Engis: Preparation Damage, Not Ancient Cutmarks. *American Journal of Physical Anthropology* 78:361–368.

Willey, P., and L.M. Snyder
  1989  Canid Modifications of Human Remains: Implications for Time-Since-Death Estimations. *Journal of Forensic Sciences* 34:894–901.

# SECTION II

## Modifications of Soft Tissue, Bone, and Associated Materials

- *Chemical Underpinnings*
- *Soft Tissue*
- *Bone*
- *Associated Materials*

# Chemical and Ultrastructural Aspects of Decomposition

## H. GILL-KING

## Introduction

Living organisms are characterized by chemical processes which are highly organized. Superficial inspection of a recently deceased human reveals little change from the living state, yet the changes which will soon offend the senses and ultimately reduce the decedent to a collection of molecules have already begun. Western culture largely regards death as an event. In fact, it is a process. Not all cells die at once. The chemical activities which sustained cells and tissues only a short while earlier were orderly, well-catalyzed, and highly segregated within biological membranes inside the cytoplasm of cells. Failure of the heart pump and the ensuing deprivation of the tissues of oxygen sets in motion a series of events which leads to increasing chemical disorganization, failure of cellular metabolism and repair mechanisms, and, ultimately, the gross tissue effects commonly associated with the observable stages of decomposition.

The chemistry of living cells is characteristically (1) at low temperature, (37°C or thereabouts), (2) aqueous (for cells are mostly water), (3) highly catalyzed (by enzymes), and (4) well segregated into pathways which are associated with various lipid-bound membranes and organelles. In higher organisms the biosynthesis and restoration of these structures depends, in turn, upon a collection of chemical events referred to as central metabolism, a series of oxygen-requiring energy transformation reactions which drive biosynthesis. It is the increasingly anoxic environment following circulatory stasis which initiates the progressive disorganization of cellular chemistry and ultimately decomposition.

In death as in life the decomposing body remains for a time a dynamic system, both internally and in its interactions with the immediate environment. Following death, these interactions are profoundly influenced by the manner of disposition of the remains, i.e., buried, dumped, submerged, frozen, etc. A particular manner of disposal affords greater or lesser interaction with flora, fauna, and microbiota which, in turn, will influence the rate of decomposition. A particular mode of disposal will significantly affect ambient temperature, moisture, pH, partial pressure of $O_2$ and other gases, and the local chemical environment. These collectively act as the major constraints on the chemistry of decomposition.

## Physical and Chemical Constraints of Decomposition

### Temperature

The ambient temperature in which a decomposition proceeds may be related to altitude, latitude, burial depth, placement in water, air movement, or anthropogenic factors such as cold lockers, placement in wrappings, closed and or heated locations, or combinations of these.

The principle at work is Van't Hoff's rule, also known as the "rule of ten," or simply the temperature coefficient "$Q_{10}$". This physical principle states that the velocity of chemical reactions increases two or more times with each 10°C rise in temperature. All bodies move

0-8493-9434-1/97/$0.00+$.50
© 1997 by CRC Press, Inc.

through essentially the same stages of decomposition, but temperature is the most important variable influencing the "dwell-time" in a particular stage and the overall velocity of the process.

Living chemistry occurs near 37°C, and cooling or heating of the body to a different ambient temperature slows or speeds cell metabolism by affecting the cellular catalysts, enzyme systems that regulate most reactions. Enzymes as proteins are subject to denaturation, coagulation, and even crystallization at temperature extremes. As expected, mammalian enzymes are adapted to optimum activity near 37°C with a range of about 40 to 50°. A typical enzyme accelerates a cellular reaction $10^8$ to $10^{10}$ times (Freifelder 1983). The $Q_{10}$ coefficient for most intracellular enzymes is 1.1 to 3.0, meaning that each change of 10°C will speed or slow reactions from about one to three times, as long as the enzymes remain intact. Mammalian enzymes are usually completely denatured (broken into their constituent amino acid chains and fragments) at 60°, a temperature sustained by the enzyme systems of many plants and microorganisms which may interact with the decomposing body (Orten and Neuhaus 1977). Strictly speaking, statements about temperature effects on enzymes have meaning only if time is specified.

In addition to its implications for determination of postmortem interval, temperature may influence the likelihood of detection of remains by infrared instrumentation (Killam 1990) and by dogs or instruments sensitive to decomposition volatiles (McLaughlin 1974; Pella and Martinelli 1975). The effects of temperature on the onset and duration of rigor mortis are well known (Smith et al. 1978).

## Water

Water has several physical and chemical effects on the decomposing chemical system. Because of its high specific heat, water has a stabilizing effect on temperature. Chemically, water acts as a buffer moderating the effects of tissue and environmental acidity and alkalinity and ultimately serves as a source of hydrogen for biochemical reactions in all cells present, whether human, plant, or microbial. Water plays both a diluting role, affecting chemical concentration inside and outside of cells, and acts, in general, as a solvent for polar molecules of biological and nonbiological origin.

Water in which bodies are totally or partially submerged may accelerate or retard decomposition, depending upon whether it is salty or fresh, moving or still, or varying in either direction from normal pH. Water plays an important role in the osmotic environment of cells by virtue of the molecules and ionic species dissolved in it. The preservative effects of salty wet environments are summarized by Micozzi (1991). The presence of moisture in soil and air around the decompositus improves chances of detection by odor-sensitive means because decomposition gases are water soluble. Moisture in varying amounts encourages the growth of mycota, bacteria, and plants, and thus speeds the interaction of these with decomposing tissues. Indeed, from the point of view of these flora, the body is itself an important source of water.

Various hydrolase enzymes add available water to chemical bonds in order to break down large biological polymers which are important constituents of cells (e.g., carbohydrate, lipid, and protein hydrolysis). Yet, the activity of these enzymes is sensitive to concentration effects and pH, which are influenced by the amount of water present. Ambient atmospheric humidity assumes an important role when bodies are not immersed. High moisture content also theoretically promotes saponification in the presence of large amounts of lipid since water reduces the rate of oxidation of fatty acids, thus making them available for binding by salts at low pH (see "Adipocere Formation"); (Mant and Furbank 1957).

## Acidity and Alkalinity

Changes in intracellular, extracellular, and environmental pH are both cause and effect in the decomposition process. Initially, changing intracellular pH affects the progress of chemical reactions in cells by altering enzyme activity (Orten and Neuhaus 1977). As intracellular pH shifts, the activity of enzymes which catalyze central metabolic reactions slows, then ceases altogether as these proteins denature and/or coagulate. Initially, degradation of biomolecules lowers intracellular pH as free hydrogen and organic acids are liberated through denaturation of lipids and proteins and, as oxygen decreases further, through fermentation of carbohydrates to a variety of acids. The half-life of most intracellular enzymes is only a few hours, and, when these are depleted further, degradation may occur through nonenzymatic acid or alkaline hydrolysis.

Anaerobic and facultative bacteria in the soil (i.e., species of *Azotobacter*, *Rhizobium*, *Nitrosomonas*, and *Clostridium* spp. and in the large bowel (Enterobacteriaceae) also contribute to a decline in pH through fermentation. This increased acidity may be supplemented by humic acids in soils resulting from the decay of plant materials in well-vegetated areas. Lowered soil pH enhances the growth of ubiquitous fungi (Tortora et al. 1994) in the immediate decomposition environment which, in turn, act upon the remains. Lowered pH also enhances plant activity by increasing rates of nutrient uptake in rootlets; these as well as fungal hyphae may eventually invade tissues, accelerating physical reduction (Degaetano et al. 1992).

Thus, buried bodies create an acidic environment in surrounding soils early in the decomposition process and, after a considerable time, an alkaline one as proteolysis occurs. The latter might require weeks or months. These effects have occasionally had implications for the location of remains when marked variation from the characteristic pH of local soils could be detected, (Murray and Tedrow 1992).

## Partial Pressure of Oxygen

Bodies which are deeply buried, submerged, situated at high altitude (e.g., >3000 m), or left in man-made or naturally hermetic environments will decompose more slowly. Apart from the effects of lowered temperature usually afforded by these situations, there is retardation of oxidative processes. Water and waterlogged soils are oxygen deficient and therefore have a low redox potential. Conversely, soils and water which contain decaying organic materials become reducing environments, i.e., acidic. Dry soils, particularly if well aerated, have a high redox potential (Murray and Tedrow 1992). While mammalian cells are quickly affected by anoxia, the opposite is true for many soil bacteria which interact with bodies in graves (Tortora et al. 1994). Within cells, aerobic or anaerobic, the question of availability of oxygen is critical. Depletion of oxygen initiates the decomposition process, and the anaerobic conditions that follow stimulate the chemical activity of bacterial decomposers.

To say that various configurations of temperature, water, pH, and gases affect the viability of cells is ultimately to say that these variables are critical to enzymatic activity both in host cells and those of decomposers. The first few events in cell death, collectively known as autolysis, will result from enzyme failure due to lack of oxygen.

## Autolysis and Cell Death

A clear picture of acute, lethal cell injury requires some understanding of normal cellular biochemical activity, that is, of central metabolism. A living animal cell liberates potential energy locked in the covalent bonds of carbohydrates. This energy is used in a controlled way to drive biosynthesis (i.e., of lipids, carbohydrates, proteins, nucleic acids) for replacement and repair of organelles and membranes, cell products, and for cell division. This harnessing of bond energy is accomplished by enzyme-mediated reactions within fairly narrow limits of temperature, pH, and concentration of substrates, and it assumes the presence of oxygen as a final electron acceptor.

Along central metabolic pathways, energy is stored in the phosphate bonds of ATP (adenosine triphosphate) which can be moved about within the cell and coupled to various reactions. The most prominent source of ATP is the "electron transport chain" which occurs on the inner membrane of the mitochondrion. Here, ATP is created as a series of membrane proteins are successively reduced and oxidized by electrons removed from hydrogen. As these electrons move, the free energy liberated pumps the remaining hydrogen (as protons) to one side of the inner membrane, creating a gradient. Protons move down the gradient, crossing the membrane through special ports lined with the enzyme ATP synthase, which transfers the free energy of the moving proton to a phosphate bond, creating ATP, a process aptly called oxidative phosphorylation. The removal of oxygen as a final electron acceptor disrupts this production of ATP and, consequently, disrupts crucial biosynthesis. Oxidative phosphorylation may be interrupted by anoxia or by direct damage to the membrane itself or any part of the electron transport chain.

With circulatory stasis, the plasma and tissue (intercellular) pH decline quickly as the buffer systems fail. Within the cell there is a shift from the central metabolic pathway to a fermentative one in which pyruvic acid is anaerobically converted to lactic acid with an accompanying intracellular decline in pH. Although the fermentative pathway produces a small amount of ATP, it is unable to support normal levels of biosynthesis and repair.

Among the earliest effects of failing ATP production and biosynthesis is the loss of membrane structures. The unsaturated fatty acid tails of phospholipid molecules within cell membranes oxidize readily and are not replaced; nor are membrane transport proteins replaced (i.e., the electron transport chain fails). Without ATP for active membrane transport, the cell is unable to move essential molecules and ions against concentration gradients. Facilitated transport also fails as carrier proteins are lost through denaturation and nonreplacement. As a result, the cytoplasm and mitochondrial matrix are seen to swell as membrane selectivity is lost. Potentially destructive hydrolytic enzymes, previously compartmentalized within membrane-lined organelles, are disgorged into the cytoplasm where, activated by the decreasing pH, they begin to quickly denature molecules and remaining membrane (e.g., see Ito et al. 1991). Outer membranes supporting cell junctions finally disappear, causing cells to detach from each other, one of the events grossly observed in tissue necrosis. It should be noted that cells may be "dead" without tissue necrosis. For example, cell death is a normal event in tissues with high turnover (rapid mitosis) as in the gut lining and normal skin. The term necrobiosis is reserved for cell death in this instance.

The process of self-destruction of cells by enzymatic self-digestion, known as autolysis, occurs first in the most metabolically active cells, i.e., cells where characteristically high rates of ATP production are more sensitive to anoxia, and in secretory cells and macrophages which self-digest from their own stores of hydrolytic enzymes as these are decompartmentalized by membrane breakdown.

## Ultrastructural Correlates of Autolysis

Acute lethal cell injury is divided into two stages. These are "early reversible" (stage 1) and "late irreversible" (stage 2), and are described as follows:

### Stage 1

1. Anoxia or direct damage to mitochondrial membranes drastically reduces ATP production;
2. ATP-driven biosynthesis of important molecules fails;
3. Membrane-bound enzyme systems fail;
4. Failure of membrane pumps leads to osmotic imbalance, resulting in flooding of the cytocavitary network and swelling of the cell;

5. There is a shift to anaerobic fermentative pathways for ATP production to compensate for the loss of mitochondrial activity. Fermentation of lactic acid lowers cytoplasmic pH;

6. Increasing acidity causes nuclear chromatin to clump, thus suppressing RNA coding further reducing protein synthesis, including enzymes; and

7. Chromatin clumping leads to observable mitochondrial swelling.

## Stage 2

The irreversible phase is characterized by acceleration of the foregoing changes:

1. Denatured matrix proteins within the mitochondria appear as fluffy clumps ("matrical flocculent densities");

2. The protein portion of the cell cytoplasm is denatured also and appears as grainy densities or clumps;

3. Increased permeability of all membrane-bound organelles leads to leakage;

4. Powerful hydrolytic enzymes leak from damaged lysosomes and are activated at lowered pH. These leak into the nucleus irreversibly degrading chromatin ("karyolysis") and eventually all other structures within the cell.

5. As membranes are destroyed, the phospholipids released form visible concentric lamellar myelin bodies, a sign of end stage autolysis;

6. Leakage of hydrolytic enzymes into the intercellular spaces causes loss of cell-to-cell attachment. This effect is noted grossly as tissue necrosis. The most prominent microscopic feature of tissue necrosis is absence of cell nuclei. Macroscopically, necrotic tissue is usually paler and more friable.

These chemical and ultrastructural effects result in two distinct kinds of observable necrosis. In the brain complete enzymatic lysis results in liquefaction, hence liquefactive necrosis. This kind of necrosis usually produces a cavity. Coagulative necrosis is observed when there is significant denaturation of hydrolytic enzymes. In this type of necrosis there is preservation of the gross architecture of the tissues for some time, but with loss of cellular detail (e.g., skeletal muscle "paste"), (Ghadially 1975).

# The Order of Tissue Decomposition

The foregoing mechanisms of autolysis imply a general order in which the tissues of the body decompose. Tissues whose cells conduct the highest rates of ATP synthesis, biosynthesis, and membrane transport should fall apart first. The usual order is:

1. **Intestines, stomach, accessory organs of digestion, heart, blood and circulation, heart muscle.** Note that the large amount and variety of hydrolytic enzyme present in stomach, pancreas, and liver account for rapid deterioration of these and surrounding tissues. These include gastric and pancreatic lipases, numerous peptidases, carbohydrate-digesting amylase, and nucleotidases. Later on, the destruction of alimentary tissues is accelerated by the enteric bacterial flora through anaerobic fermentative pathways.

2. **Air passages and lungs.** These tissues contain large numbers of macrophages whose lysosomes release hydrolytic enzymes which are activated at lowered cytoplasmic pH. Contributing to the decomposition of the respiratory tree are bacteria which may invade these tissues in the absence of a functioning bronchociliary barrier or which may be present in aspirated materials.

3. **Kidneys and bladder.**
4. **Brain and nervous tissue.**  Neurons are among the most metabolically active, i.e., ATP-dependent, cells of the body and thus are often among the first to autolyze. Exceptions to this sometimes arise under wet conditions which promote saponification of the abundant lipid substance myelin (see "adipocere formation" below).
5. **Skeletal muscles.**
6. **Connective tissues and integument.**  Tissues whose ground substance contains the protein collagen are difficult to hydrolyze, and therefore among the last to decompose. Collagen, the most common protein in mammal tissues, has a unique triple-helical structure (Freifelder 1983; Orten and Neuhaus 1977) with strong inter- and intramolecular bonds. Collagen polypeptides exhibit "base-stacking" of the benzene rings of the amino acid phenylalanine. Additionally, hydrocarbon chains of several constituent amino acids (e.g., alanine, leucine, isoleucine, and valine) form tight hydrophobic clusters. The result is tissues which may last indefinitely, particularly in dry environments (Aufderheide 1981).

# Familiar Postmortem Phenomena

## Rigor Mortis

A concomitant of early autolysis is the characteristic stiffening of muscles known as rigor mortis. Rigor has its onset at about 2 to 6 hours postmortem. It begins with the muscles of the eyelids, neck, and, jaw, spreading over the next 4 to 6 hours, depending upon temperature, to all the muscles of the body including those associated with internal organs. Rigor persists for 24 to 84 hours, before the muscles again relax usually in roughly the same order in which they stiffened.

As the sarcoplasmic reticulum of muscle cells lose integrity, calcium ions flood into the contractile unit, or sarcomere, which consists of alternating parallel protein filaments of actin and myosin. Calcium unblocks binding sites on the actin, allowing the two molecules to bind via a cross-arm extending from the myosin. As the cross-arm retracts (i.e., uncocks) the actin is pulled along the thick myosin fiber. The sarcomeres are joined end-to-end so that when this action is summed over the length of the muscle it shortens and becomes rigid. Normally, ATP-driven active transport pumps the calcium back into the sarcoplasmic reticulum, thus allowing detachment of the actin–myosin complex and inducing relaxation. Since ATP is no longer available, the state of contraction persists as rigor (Marieb 1992).

Resolution of rigor involves structural changes in the myofibrils. Electron microscopic examination of the contractile unit reveals that the actin molecules become detached from the ends of the sarcomere, allowing the contractile unit to lengthen again. Muscle cells contain proteolytic enzymes called *cathepsins* which may promote this dissociation of actin from the ends of the sarcomeres, thus initiating the reversal of rigor (Mersmann 1991; Wheeler and Koohmaraie 1991; Whipple and Koohmaraie 1991).

The most important determinants of time of onset and duration of rigor are ambient temperature and the metabolic state at the time of death. Cold temperature accelerates and usually prolongs rigor, while warm or hot temperature delays it. In warm weather rigor may not develop fully. If the agonal state is characterized by high fever, or if there is vigorous activity and/or exertion, rigor may proceed more quickly. This is presumably due to the greater amounts of lactic acid present in recently active muscles. In any event, the degree of reduction in muscle pH will be determined by the size of glycogen stores available for anaerobic conversion to lactic acid within the muscle. Rapidly declining pH accelerates membrane dissolution, which promotes early release of calcium ions into the sarcoplasm (Marieb 1992; Mersmann 1991). As expected, body composition influences rigor through the surface area variable (i.e., cooling rates) and the lean body mass component (i.e., amount of skeletal muscle). For this reason rigor appears and resolves early in infants (Smith 1986).

## Putrefactive Effects

As the body's cells reach end-stage autolysis, an almost entirely anaerobic environment is created which favors the rapid growth of the bacterial inhabitants of the large bowel and, to a lesser extent, of soil bacteria. In the normal adult colon these endosymbionts consist of 96 to 99% anaerobes, (e.g., *Bacteroides* spp., anaerobic lactobacilli, clostridia, and anaerobic streptococci), and about 1 to 4% aerobes, (e.g., gram negative coliforms, enterococci, and small numbers of *Proteus* spp., *Pseudomonas* spp. and others) (Jawetz et al. 1982). Most of these organisms operate quickly upon host cells in their immediate environments, degrading carbohydrates, proteins, and lipids to various acids, gases, and other products which are the basis of color changes, odors, and bloating: the unpleasant sensory hallmarks of the anaerobic stage of decomposition aptly known as putrefaction.

Among the more prominent products of bacterial carbohydrate fermentation are the gasses methane, hydrogen, hydrogen sulfide, all detectable with several types of equipment (Morse et al. 1983), and carbon dioxide. Enteric flora produce a variety of organic acids as well: notably lactic, acetic, acetoacetic, and propionic acids. Collectively, these products are responsible for the early acidic environment created by the decomposing body. Other forensically important fermentation products are alcohols, (ethanol, butanol), and acetone (Davis et al. 1985). The difficulty of distinguishing bacterially fermented ethanol in putrefying tissues from that due to exogenous sources is a continuing challenge to forensic toxicologists (Helander et al. 1995).

Also prominent in decomposing bodies are some of the products of protein breakdown. Bacteria express exoenzymes which denature proteins to constituent amino acids. These are transported to the bacterial cytoplasm where endoenzymes remove either amine groups via deamination or carboxyl groups via decarboxylation (Figure 1). The sulfur-containing amino acids, i.e., cysteine, cystine, and methionine, are broken down by desulfhydralation to yield hydrogen sulfide gas (Figure 2) (Johnson and Case 1994).

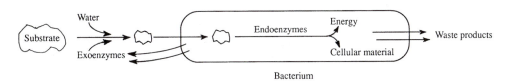

**Figure 1** Enteric and soil bacteria secrete exoenzymes which degrade molecules too large to be absorbed. Molecular fragments then pass into the bacterial cell where endoenzymes metabolize them for energy and synthesis. Some products of these reactions, including incidental cellular waste, are expressed as familiar decomposition volatiles or precipitates.

$$HSCH_2CH(NH_2)COOH \xrightarrow{\text{cysteine desulfhydrase}} H_2S + NH_3 + CH_3COCOOH$$

Cysteine                                   Pyruvic acid

$$H_2S \quad + \quad Fe \quad \longrightarrow \quad FeS \quad + \quad H_2$$

Hydrogen sulfide                      Ferrous sulfide
                                      (black precipitate)

**Figure 2** Amino acids containing sulfur atoms may be reduced by specific desulfhydrases to produce toxic hydrogen sulfide, ammonia, and pyruvic acid. Hydrogen sulfide will produce the familiar black precipitate, ferrous sulfide, in the presence of iron.

$$H_2N—\overset{\overset{\displaystyle H}{|}}{C}—\overset{\overset{\displaystyle H}{|}}{\underset{\underset{\displaystyle H}{|}}{C}}—\overset{\overset{\displaystyle H}{|}}{\underset{\underset{\displaystyle H}{|}}{C}}—\overset{\overset{\displaystyle H}{|}}{\underset{\underset{\displaystyle NH_3}{|}}{C}}—COOH \quad\xrightarrow{\text{ornithine decarboxylase}}\quad H_2N—CH_2CH_2CH_2CH_2—NH_2$$

putrescine
(1,4-butanediamine)

Ornithine                                                    Putrescine

**Figure 3**   A carboxyl group is removed from ornithine (decarboxylation), producing carbon dioxide and the foul-smelling toxic volatile putrescine.

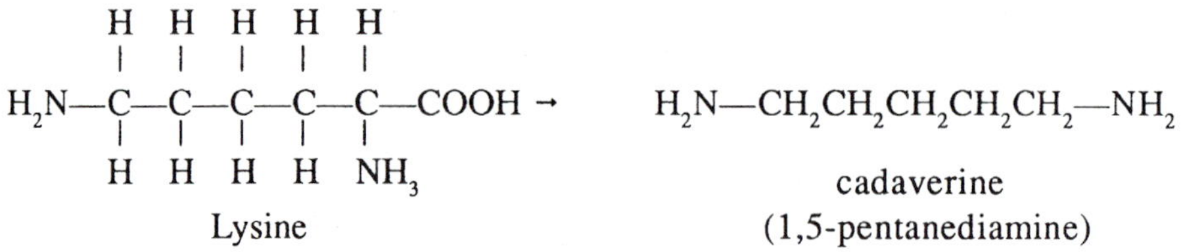

$$H_2N—\overset{\overset{\displaystyle H}{|}}{\underset{\underset{\displaystyle H}{|}}{C}}—\overset{\overset{\displaystyle H}{|}}{\underset{\underset{\displaystyle H}{|}}{C}}—\overset{\overset{\displaystyle H}{|}}{\underset{\underset{\displaystyle H}{|}}{C}}—\overset{\overset{\displaystyle H}{|}}{\underset{\underset{\displaystyle H}{|}}{C}}—\overset{\overset{\displaystyle H}{|}}{\underset{\underset{\displaystyle NH_3}{|}}{C}}—COOH \rightarrow \quad H_2N—CH_2CH_2CH_2CH_2CH_2—NH_2$$

Lysine                          cadaverine
(1,5-pentanediamine)

**Figure 4**   Lysine is decarboxylated (lysine decarboxylase), to form toxic cadaverine and carbon dioxide.

Two prominent decarboxylation products, putrescine and cadaverine, (Figures 3 and 4), are important for their characteristic foul decomposition odor. It is these two odoriferous signatures which are often detectable by cadaver dogs (Killam 1990). These two diamines are members of the family of highly toxic molecules known as ptomaines (Tiernay 1979). These, together with hydrogen sulfide and methane, are usually present in soils, well shafts, beneath houses, or in other closed environments where bodies may be decomposing. All are absorbable through unprotected skin and will displace or compete with oxygen as inspired gases posing considerable hazard for professionals involved in confined space recovery efforts. In the later stages of wet decomposition, the carbon dioxide liberated by decarboxylation reactions causes a slight upward shift in the pH of soils surrounding the decompositus.

Figure 5 illustrates the deamination of L-phenylalanine to phenylpyruvic acid and ammonia. In the presence of low soil pH, this ammonia, NH3, is converted to ammonium ($NH_3 + H^+ \rightarrow NH_4$) which is readily utilized by plants in the immediate environment in synthesizing a variety of organic compounds and generally enhancing growth. Acceleration of plant growth, particularly of forbes and some trees, by "nitrogen charging" from a nearby decompositus may result in a characteristic yellowing of otherwise healthy leaves, called chlorosis. The other deamination product, phenylpyruvic acid, combines with ferric iron ($Fe^{3+}$) in soil or circulatory tissues to form a greenish complex.

Temporary trapping of various volatile gases within the bowel creates bloating. Increasing pressure together with the action of bacterial exoenzymes allows gases to move through the circulatory system and to form "gas planes" by separating the necrotic tissue layers. The passive migration of enteric bacteria through circulation has been noted as well (Nehring et al. 1972). An interesting artifact of bloating occurs in shallow burials as earth is displaced by the expanding abdominopelvic cavity. As the gases escape, a depression is often left, which is accentuated later as the body wall caves in.

These gases are also the cause of flotation of submerged bodies. Water temperature is important in this connection, either speeding or slowing putrefaction, with the result that bodies submerged in very cold water may not achieve flotation until spring. Often the gas generated is sufficient to raise even substantially weighted or anchored bodies, or to pull them loose from their moorings, often at the expense of an extremity. Interestingly, bodies attaining

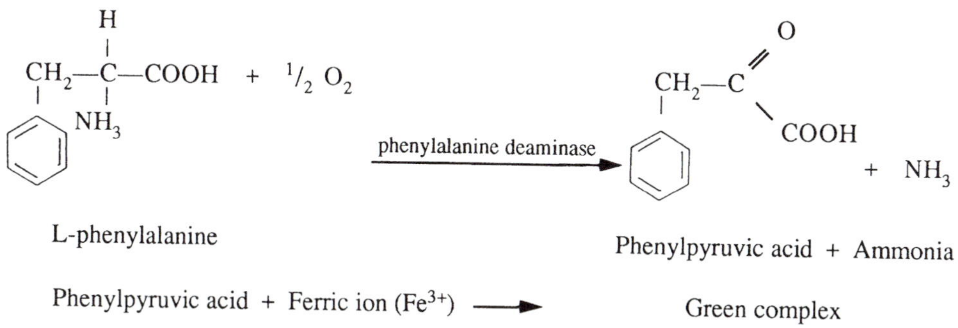

$$\underset{\text{L-phenylalanine}}{\underset{\overset{|}{NH_3}}{\overset{\overset{H}{|}}{CH_2-C-COOH}}} + \tfrac{1}{2} O_2 \xrightarrow{\text{phenylalanine deaminase}} \underset{\text{Phenylpyruvic acid + Ammonia}}{CH_2-C\overset{\overset{O}{\|}}{\diagdown} COOH} + NH_3$$

Phenylpyruvic acid + Ferric ion $(Fe^{3+})$ $\longrightarrow$ Green complex

**Figure 5**   Removal of the amine and a hydrogen atom from the amino acid phenylalanine produces phenylpyruvic acid and ammonia. The endoenzyme is phenylalanine deaminase. Note that if ferric iron is present, a green precipitate is formed. The ammonia generated may be added to hydrogen in the soil, forming ammonium which may accelerate plant growth in the immediate environment.

depths of about 180 feet may never achieve flotation because pressures at this depth (5.5 torr, or about 81 psi) keep the body from displacing a sufficient volume of water.

Color changes also accompany putrefaction. Aside from the purpling on dependent surfaces, livor mortis, there are color changes due to at least two decompositional phenomena. These are (1) degradation of hemoglobin and conversion of heme to a series of bile pigments, and (2) formation of precipitates of $H_2S$ within vessels and tissues.

Within a few hours after death, a greenish discoloration begins to spread over the anterior wall of the abdomen. Lysing pancreatic cells liberate a variety of hydrolases which attack biliary structures, releasing variously colored pigments into the circulation and tissues of the abdomen. These are eventually visible in the overlying skin. These colored pigments are produced principally within the liver as breakdown products of hemoglobin following digestion of worn out red blood cells, erythrocytes, by the spleen (Figure 6). The colors of the resulting bile pigments (Figure 7) depend upon their oxidation state. At death, this reservoir of pigment is responsible for the initial coloration observed as biliverdin moves through the tissues. Some of the biliverdin, which is green, may be reduced to bilirubin which is red. However, within the increasingly acidic tissue environment, bilirubin is quickly reduced to urobilin which is brown. In superficial tissues where oxygen may be more available, some biliverdin is converted to blue and yellow pigments. In death, hemoglobin and other hemoproteins, e.g., myoglobin, cytochrome, etc., may undergo degradation anywhere. Thus, heme breakdown eventually produces widespread pigment coloration effects in the body's tissues.

The cecum, located in the right lower abdominal quadrant, with its large population of enteric bacteria, ($10^8$ to $10^{10}$ organism per g-solid), produces a large quantity of $H_2S$, which combines with iron to produce the black precipitate ferrous sulfide. This reaction also occurs within the circulation as sulfur-containing amino acids (Figure 2) are broken down in the presence of lysing red cells by enteric bacteria within the circulation. The resulting sulfhemoglobin is a greenish-purple. As $H_2S$ accumulates within tissues and as oxidation of bile pigments continues within the circulation, there is a gradual change in coloration from green to purple to black. This effect is particularly noticeable in the superficial vessels which give the body a "marbled" appearance called suggillation. Color effects are variable in time of onset, depending primarily upon temperature and body composition, particularly the amount of subcutaneous fat present.

## Adipocere Formation

After fermentation has perfused the tissues with ethanol, the saponification ("making soap") of lipids produces adipocere. Also known as "grave wax," or "corpse wax," this grayish white caseous material often appears as early as a few days following death in warm moist conditions, or after much longer periods when a corpse with little fat is situated in an arid hot environment.

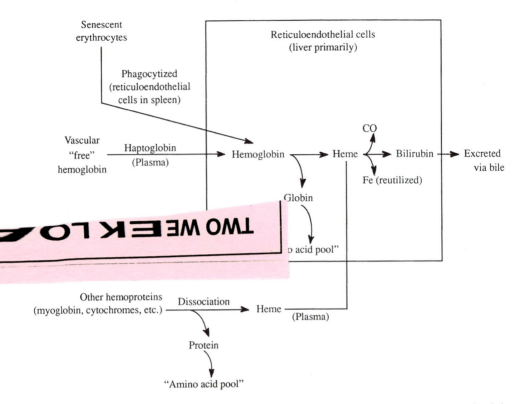

**Figure 6**   Heme from red cells, free hemoglobin, and other hemoproteins may be converted to bile pigments through several pathways during life as shown here. At death, pigments are released from the hepatic tissues into the abdomen and circulation. Further heme degradation may occur anywhere within the reticuloendothelial system.

$$\text{Urobilin} \xleftarrow{-H_2} \text{Urobilinogen} \xleftarrow{+4H_2} \text{Bilirubin} \xleftarrow{+H_2} \text{Biliverdin} \xrightarrow{-H_2} \text{(blue, yellow, etc.)}$$
$$\text{(brown)} \qquad\qquad \text{(colorless)} \qquad\qquad \text{(red)} \qquad\qquad \text{(green)}$$

**Figure 7**   Biliverdin, the predominant pigment, moves through a series of conversions by oxidation or reduction. Each intermediate has a characteristic color as shown.

Since its formation requires lipids, it is usually somewhat more evident in female and infant cadavera whose body composition has a higher fat component, and in obese individuals in general. The high water content of fat cells in the latter may offset the lack of moisture in a dry environment, for adipocere formation has been noted in shallow desert burials after only a few days (Mant and Furbank 1957).

    In the absence of enzymes, water and mild acidity are required for the hydrolytic cleavage of free fatty acids from glycerol (Figure 8). After a time, the carboxylic acids are attached to sodium or potassium ions present in tissue fluids of the decompositus at neutral or slightly alkaline intercellular pH (Figure 9). In some instances, modification of carboxylic acids by local bacteria may accelerate adipocerization (Gotouda et al. 1988). Initially, adipocere forms on the dependent parts of the body, utilizing sodium from the interstitial fluid, and later increasing amounts of potassium as cell membranes fail. Thus, the adipocere formed is a mixture of hard and soft varieties utilizing sodium or potassium, respectively, the former somewhat crumbly and the latter more paste-like. When bodies are deposited in water or soils with high mineral content, e.g., calcium which is water insoluble, sodium and potassium may be displaced, producing "hardening" (Figure 10).

$$\underset{\text{Neutral fat, or triglyceride}}{\begin{array}{l} \text{H} \quad \text{O} \\ | \quad \| \\ \text{H—C—O—C—CH}_2\text{—CH}_2 \cdots \text{CH}_2\text{—CH}_2\text{—CH}_3 \\ | \quad \text{O} \\ | \quad \| \\ \text{H—C—O—C—CH}_2\text{—CH}_2 \cdots \text{CH}_2\text{—CH}_2\text{—CH}_3 \\ | \quad \text{O} \\ | \quad \| \\ \text{H—C—O—C—CH}_2\text{—CH}_2 \cdots \text{CH}_2\text{—CH}_2\text{—CH}_3 \\ | \\ \text{H} \end{array}} \quad \underset{}{\overset{+3H_2O \atop +H}{\longrightarrow}} \quad \underset{\text{Glycerol}}{\begin{array}{l} \text{H} \\ | \\ \text{H—C—O H} \\ | \\ \text{H—C—O H} \\ | \\ \text{H—C—O H} \\ | \\ \text{H} \end{array}} \quad \underset{\text{3 fatty acid chains}}{\begin{array}{l} \text{O} \\ \| \\ \text{HO—C—CH}_2\text{—CH}_2 \cdots \text{CH}_2\text{—CH}_2\text{—CH}_3 \\ \text{O} \\ \| \\ \text{HO—C—CH}_2\text{—CH}_2 \cdots \text{CH}_2\text{—CH}_2\text{—CH}_3 \\ \text{O} \\ \| \\ \text{HO—C—CH}_2\text{—CH}_2 \cdots \text{CH}_2\text{—CH}_2\text{—CH}_3 \end{array}}$$

**Figure 8**   A neutral fat undergoes acid hydrolysis in aqueous solution with lowered pH. Fatty acid chains (carboxylic acids) are separated from glycerol as water is added to the ester bonds. Note that the number of carbons in the fatty acid chains is not specified, but will usually be an even number between 12 and 18. These chains will be saturated and unsaturated.

$$\underset{\text{3 fatty acid chains}}{\begin{array}{l} \text{O} \\ \| \\ \text{HO—C—CH}_2\text{—CH}_2 \cdots \text{CH}_2\text{—CH}_2\text{—CH}_3 \\ \text{O} \\ \| \\ \text{HO—C—CH}_2\text{—CH}_2 \cdots \text{CH}_2\text{—CH}_2\text{—CH}_3 \\ \text{O} \\ \| \\ \text{HO—C—CH}_2\text{—CH}_2 \cdots \text{CH}_2\text{—CH}_2\text{—CH}_3 \end{array}} \quad + Na^{+}Cl^{-} \longrightarrow \quad \begin{array}{l} \text{O} \\ \| \\ Na^{+}\text{—O—C—CH}_2\text{—CH}_2 \cdots \text{CH}_2\text{—CH}_2\text{—CH}_3 \\ \\ + H^{+}Cl^{-} \end{array}$$

**Figure 9**   Fatty acid chains take on sodium or potassium from the environment, i.e., from interstitial fluid, cell water, or ambient water, by removal of a proton from the carboxyl group, thus "saponifying," or becoming a soap. Addition of sodium produces "sapo durus" or hard soap, while the potassium addition results in "sapo domesticus" or soft soap. The reaction illustrated is not stoichiometrically balanced.

$$2C_{17}H_{35}C\overset{\displaystyle O}{\underset{\displaystyle O^{-}Na^{+}}{<}} \quad + Ca^{2+} \rightarrow (C_{17}H_{35}COO^{-})_2Ca^{2+} \downarrow \quad + 2Na^{+}$$

Sodium stearate
(soluble)

Calcium stearate
(insoluble)

**Figure 10**   Sodium stearate, a hard soap, loses its sodium ions in favor of calcium ions from the environment. The result is an insoluble product which contributes a more brittle quality to the adipocere if present in small proportions. This reaction is called "hardening."

Opinions concerning the relationship of adipocerization to postmortem interval (Bass 1984; Mellen, et al. 1993) should be weighed carefully against detailed information about soil chemistry, moisture, temperature, and available lipids. Saponification appears to depend upon a "sliding scale" involving relative amounts of fat and water. These compensate each other to such a degree that, over time, at least some adipocere will probably form. When both are abundant, its formation is imminent. Adipocere will be more lasting and more prominent in submerged bodies because of the insolubility of the nonpolar carboxylic acid tails. In soils with high redox potentials, there is some slowing of saponification as the availability of carboxylic acids, especially unsaturated ones, is reduced by autooxidation.

# Other Aspects of Postmortem Chemistry

In concluding this brief discussion of the chemical and structural features of autolytic and putrefactive phenomena, several other important aspects of postmortem chemistry should be noted.

## Sampling Issues

Questions concerning the best strategies for obtaining useable postmortem samples for bio-assay are complicated by redistribution phenomena. Concerns include interval, source, and selection of analytical methodology (Coe 1993). Attention has been focused on "chemical sanctuaries," or "pooling" phenomena for pharmaceuticals as well as biomolecules and their breakdown products (see Briglia et al. 1992; Hearn et al. 1991 ).

## Postmortem Interval

Chemical approaches to determination of time since death have focused on rates of breakdown or conversion of biomolecules and pharmaceuticals (Coe 1993) and on time required to establish new, temporary equilibria between materials where gradients were previously maintained. These approaches usually address short postmortem intervals (i.e., hours to a few days). Chemical techniques for determination of postmortem interval in more durable tissues, e.g., skin, bone, cartilage, etc., are less well developed. Recent approaches include UV-fluorescence (Yoshino and Kimijima 1991), degradation of lipids (Castellano et al.1984), immunohistochemical assays of connective tissue proteins (Betz et al. 1993), and attempts to examine rates of degradation of DNA and its components in hard tissue (Perry et al. 1988; Williams 1994; also see Parsons and Weedn in this volume).

## Extrapolation of Agonal State

Postmortem assays of a wide array of biomolecules provide clues to the agonal state. Aside from routine forensic toxicologic studies (Coe 1993; Saferstein 1990), experimental assays have shown promise in determination of conditions as various as metabolic diseases (Emery et al. 1988), rheumatoid arthritides (Gudbjornsson et al. 1991), and sudden infant death (Rognum and Sangstad 1991).

# Conclusion: Differential Decomposition of Hard Tissues

## Initial Factors

Once an organism dies, competition for the nutrients it represents intensifies to a greater or lesser degree, depending upon the context in which it is deposited. Initially, enteric and local soil bacteria, mycota, scavengers, plants, and insects quickly usher the remains through wet and dry stages of decomposition. The rate at which this occurs and the "dwell time" in a particular stage of decomposition is, as we have indicated, dependent upon physical factors of temperature, pH, concentration of reactants, availability of oxygen, and the presence of water.

As a body is reduced to hard tissues, decomposition begins to assume a different character. The pace of deterioration slows somewhat, and the size, shape, and hardness of bones become important in differential rates of decomposition. Skeletal components are affected differentially by scavenging. Small bones which may easily be removed tend to disappear first. Likewise, spongy, marrow-rich bones are often preferred by scavengers. Bones with thicker cortex are less susceptible to destruction than smaller ones and are less apt to be dispersed by wind and water. Flat bones are readily carried away by water currents and are also easily broken and scattered.

As remains decompose to predominantly hard tissue, their nutritive value and general vulnerability to animal forms large and small is proportionally reduced. In highly aerobic environments (e.g., surface depositions and shallow burials) decomposition is usually complete. It has been estimated that human remains without benefit of embalming or burial survive to fossilization on the order of thousandths of a percent of the population (Behrensmeyer 1984). In environments containing less available oxygen, little or no bioavailable water, or extremely low temperatures, the process takes longer and may even allow time for fossilization processes (Shipman 1981).

With passing time, the continued reduction of remains depends increasingly upon bacterial and plant activity. Eventually, as bacteria eliminate the collagen phase of hard tissues, there is a fundamental change in the chemical basis for decomposition. That is, the chemical breakdown of these tissues is no longer initiated by organisms, but is increasingly a matter of inorganic chemical equilibria between the soil or water medium and the hard tissues situated in it.

## Chemical Weathering and Diagenesis

An important factor in rates of bone destruction is surface area. Greater surface area means a higher degree of microrootlet invasion once the periosteal covering of bone is eliminated by bacterial action. Most importantly, the increased surface area of a bone also means a larger interface with ion solutions in soils. After the elimination of the organic collagen phase of bone, predominantly by the action of bacterial collagenase, the loss of mineral hydroxyapatite $[Ca_5(PO_4)_3 OH]$ proceeds by inorganic chemical weathering. Essentially, calcium ions in the apatite crystal move into the soil solution as they are replaced by protons at below normal pH. Phosphate may be removed by various metal ions (e.g., iron or aluminum) and precipitated as their salts (Lindsay 1979).

Accordingly, differential survival of hard tissues may be expected to follow regional variation in soil mineral and bacterial content. White and Hannus (1983) have predicted experimentally the expected rates of demineralization of bone for various components as a function of changing ratios of calcium and phosphate in a variety of soils.

Referred to as diagenesis, this exchange of ionic species between bones and their environments has implications for interpretation of antemortem disease states (Matthews et al. 1973), determination of the age of bone (Oakley 1971), and for the reconstruction of dietary patterns from the skeleton (Wing and Brown 1979).

Ultimately, accurate and meaningful interpretation of decomposing remains of the recently or long dead will depend on a clear understanding of the short- and longterm chemical aspects of taphonomy and the physical factors upon which they are based.

## References

Aufderheide, A.C.
    1981   Soft Tissue Paleopathology. *Human Pathology* 12:865–867.
Bass, W.M.
    1984   Time Interval Since Death, A Difficult Decision. In *Human Identification: Case Studies in Forensic Anthropology*, edited by T.A. Rathbun and J.E. Buikstra, pp. 136–147. Charles C Thomas, Springfield, IL.
Behrensmeyer, A.K.
    1984   Taphonomy and the Fossil Record. *American Scientist* 72:558–566.
Betz, P., A. Nerlich, J. Wilske, J. Tubel, R. Penning, and W. Eisenmenger
    1993   Immunohistochemical Analysis of Fibronectin, Collagen III, Laminin, and Cytokeratin in Putrefied Skin. *Forensic Science International* 61:35–42.

Briglia, E.J., J.H. Bidanset, and L.A. Dal Cortivo
    1992  Distribution of Ethanol in Postmortem Blood Specimens. *Journal of Forensic Sciences* 37:991–998.

Castellano, M.A., E.C. Villanueva, and R. VonFrenkel
    1984  Estimation of the Date of Bone Remains: A Multivariate Study. *Journal of Forensic Sciences* 29:527–534.

Coe, J.I.
    1993  Postmortem Chemistry Update: Emphasis on Forensic Application. *American Journal of Forensic Medicine and Pathology* 14(2) 92–93.

Davis, B.D., R. Dulbecco, H.N. Eisen, and H.S. Ginsberg
    1985  *Microbiology,* 3rd ed. Harper and Row, New York.

Degaetano, D.H., J.B. Kempton, and W.F. Rowe
    1992  Fungal Tunneling in Hair from a Buried Body. *Journal of Forensic Sciences* 37:1048–1054.

Emery, J.L., S. Variant, A.J. Howat, and G. Vawter
    1988  Investigation of Errors of Inborn Metabolism in Unexpected Infant Deaths. *Lancet* 2:29–31.

Freifelder, D.
    1983  *Molecular Biology,* 2nd ed. Jones and Bartlett, Chicago.

Ghadially, F.N.
    1975  *Ultrastructural Pathology of the Cell.* Butterworth, Woburn, MA.

Gotouda, A., T. Takatori, K. Terazawa, M. Nagao, and H. Tarao
    1988  Experimental Adipocere Formation: Hydration and Dehydrogenation in Microbial Synthesis of Hydroxy- and Oxo- Fatty Acids. *Forensic Science International* 37:249–255.

Gudbjornsson, B., A. Zak, F. Niklasson, and R. Hallgren
    1991  Hypoxanthine, Xanthine, and Urate in Synovial Fluid from Patients with Inflammatory Arthritides. *Annals of the Rheumatic Disease* 50:669–672.

Hearn, W.L., E.E. Keran, H. Wei, and G. Hime
    1991  Site Dependent Postmortem Change in Blood Cocaine Concentrations. *Journal of Forensic Sciences* 36:673–684.

Helander, A., O. Beck, and A.W. Jones
    1995  Distinguishing Ingested Ethanol from Microbial Formation by Analysis of 5-hydroxytryptophol and 5-hydroxyindolacetic Acid. *Journal of Forensic Sciences* 40:95–98.

Ito, T., T.R. Ando, H. Mayahara, H. Miyajima, and K. Ogawa
    1991  Postmortem Changes in the Rat Kidney: Histopathological, Electron Microscopic, and Enzyme Histochemical Studies of Postmortem Changes. *Acta Histologica, Chemica, et Cytochemica* 24:153–166.

Jawetz, E., J.L. Melnick, and E.A. Melnick
    1982  *Review of Medical Microbiology.* 15th ed. Lange Medical, Boston

Johnson, T.R., and C.L. Case
    1994  *Laboratory Experiments in Microbiology.* 4th ed. Benjamin Cummings, San Francisco.

Killam, E.W.
    1990  *The Detection of Human Remains.* Charles C Thomas, Springfield, IL.

Lindsay, W.L.
    1979  *Chemical Equilibria in Soils.* Wiley, New York.

Mant, A.K., and R. Furbank
    1957  Adipocere: A Review. *Journal of Forensic Medicine* 4:27–31.

Marieb, E.
  1992 *Human Anatomy and Physiology.* 2nd ed. Benjamin Cummings, San Francisco

Matthews, J.L., J.H. Martin, J.W. Kennedy, and E.J. Collins
  1973 An Ultrastructural Study of Calcium and Phosphate Deposition and Exchange in Tissues. In *Hard Tissues, Growth, Repair, and Remineralization,* pp. 187–211. Ciba Foundation Symposium 11 (n.s.). Elsevier Science, New York.

McLaughlin, J.E.
  1974 *The Detection of Human Bodies.* Andermac, Cincinnati.

Mellen, P.F., M.A. Lowry, and M.S. Micozzi
  1993 Experimental Observations on Adipocere Formation. *Journal of Forensic Science* 38:91–93.

Mersmann, H.J.
  1991 Postmortem Proteolysis in Longissimus Muscle from Beef, Lamb, and Pork Carcasses. *Journal of Animal Science* 69:617–624.

Micozzi, M.S.
  1991 *Postmortem Changes in Human and Animal Remains.* Charles C Thomas, Springfield, IL.

Morse, D., J. Ducan, and J. Stoutmire
  1983 *Handbook of Forensic Archeology and Anthropology.* Rose Printing, Tallahassee.

Murray, R.C., and J.C.F. Tedrow
  1992 *Forensic Geology.* Prentice–Hall, Englewood Cliffs.

Nehring, J.R., M.F. Sheridan, W.F. Funk, and G.L. Anderson
  1972 The Possibility of Postmortem Bacterial Transmigration. *Archives of Pathology* 93:266–270.

Oakley, K.V.
  1971 *Frameworks for Dating Fossil Man.* Aldine, Chicago.

Orten, J.M, and O.W. Neuhaus
  1977 *Human Biochemistry,* 9th ed. C.V. Mosby, St. Louis, MO.

Pella, R.I., and M. Martinelli
  1975 *Agriculture Handbook.* No. 489. USDA, U.S. Forest Service, Washington, D.C.

Perry, W.L., W.M. Bass, and W. Rigsby
  1988 Autodegradation of DNA in Human Rib Bone and Its Relation to Time since Death. *Journal of Forensic Science* 33:144–153.

Rognum, T.O., and O.D. Snagstad
  1991 Hypoxanthine Levels in Vitreous Humor: Evidence of Hypoxia in Most Infants Who Died of SIDS. *Pediatrics* 87:306–310.

Saferstein, R.
  1990 *Criminalistics: An Introduction to Forensic Science.* Prentice–Hall, Englewood Cliffs.

Shipman, P.
  1981 *The Life History of a Fossil: An Introduction to Taphonomy and Paleoecology.* Harvard University Press, Cambridge, MA.

Smith, G.C., G.R. Culp, and Z.L. Carpenter
  1978 Postmortem Ageing of Beef Carcasses. *Journal of Food Science* 43:823.

Smith, K.G.V.
  1986 *A Manual of Forensic Entomology.* British Museum of Natural History, London.

Tiernay, A.L.
  1979 *Contemporary Organic Chemistry.* W.B. Saunders, Philadelphia.

Tortora, G., C. Funke, and C. Case
  1994  *Microbiology: An Introduction,* 5th ed. Benjamin Cummings, San Francisco.

Wheeler, T.L., and M. Koohmaraie
  1991  A Modified Procedure for the Simultaneous Extraction and Subsequent Assay of Calcium-dependent Lysosomal Protease Systems from Skeletal Muscle Biopsy. *Journal of Animal Science* 69:1559–1565.

Whipple, G., and M. Koohmaraie
  1991  Degradation of Myofibrillar Proteins by Extractable Lysosomal Enzymes and M-calpain, and the Effects of Zinc Chloride. *Journal of Animal Science* 69:4449–4460.

White, E.M., and L.A. Hannus
  1983  Chemical Weathering of Bone in Archeological Soils. *American Antiquity* 48:316–322.

Williams, J.B.
  1994  Determination of Postmortem Interval by Changes in Nucleotide Pool Ratios Assayed by HPLC. Unpublished Ph.D. dissertation, Department of Biological Sciences, University of North Texas, Denton.

Wing, E.S., and A.B. Brown
  1979  *Paleonutrition: Method and Theory in Prehistoric Foodways.* Academic Press, New York.

Yoshino, M., and T. Kimijima
  1991  Microscopic Study on Estimation of Time since Death in Skeletal Remains. *Forensic Science International* 49: 143–158.

# Preservation and Recovery of DNA in Postmortem Specimens and Trace Samples

7

THOMAS J. PARSONS
VICTOR WALTER WEEDN*

## Introduction

Using DNA analysis, trace biological samples can now be used to determine individual identity, with a vanishingly small probability that the sample derived from any other individual. Further, we can now determine genetic sequences from organisms that died more than 100 million years ago. Such remarkable abilities are based on the preservation of DNA in nonliving samples, and we are only beginning to explore the extent to which genetic information can be retrieved after death. Advancements in this area have occurred rapidly in the last 5 to 10 years, and are based on recent developments in molecular biological technology, coupled with a greatly increased understanding of the genetic structure of individuals and populations — the fruit of basic research. Moreover, additional developments in both the power and ease of techniques to recover postmortem genetic information can be expected at an increasing pace for the foreseeable future. With the potential to provide exact information concerning species, sex, individual identity and familial kinship, such developments are having a revolutionary impact on forensic science. Other fields which will benefit greatly from access to genetic information from the past include archaeology, population genetics, evolutionary biology, taxonomy and epidemiology.

The aim of this chapter is to provide an overview of what is known about the preservation of DNA in postmortem samples, and how the genetic information can be recovered. Relevant characteristics of DNA and the genome will be reviewed, and substantial attention will be given to the methods that are employed in DNA analysis. Discussion of the preservation and recovery of DNA from various sources has been divided into two sections, one concerning a relatively short postmortem interval (up to, roughly, months or a few years), and the other focusing on what has been termed the field of "ancient DNA" analysis (from a few to millions of years). However, this distinction is somewhat arbitrary, as there is no precise division between what might be considered short-term and long-term preservation. In fact, it is the interaction between a sample and its environment that determines DNA preservation, and age *per se* is not an absolute indicator of DNA quantity or quality. Despite our consideration of techniques, this chapter is not intended as a laboratory guide. However, the attributes of various techniques must be kept in mind, as they dictate the amount and type of information that can be recovered and the ease and reliability of analysis. Importantly, particular samples may only be amenable to a subset of methodological approaches.

In general, the approach that is taken in a particular case is determined by the goal of the analysis, the type of sample available, and, necessarily, the technical resources available to

* The views expressed are those of the authors and do not necessarily reflect those of the U.S. Army or the Department of Defense.

the investigator. For example, distinguishing the remains of a small number of individuals from an accident site may only require quick tests based on an inexpensive, commercially available kit, while individualizing the source of a badly degraded, unassociated sample might require much effort and sophisticated laboratory equipment. We will discuss general trends relating to the preservation of DNA that may be observed from the existing body of information, but it should be emphasized that there are few absolutes concerning what sources may be amenable to genetic testing. Since each case is unique, no biological sample should be disregarded as a potential source for DNA recovery.

## DNA: Chemical Structure, Genomic Organization, and Variability

The genetic basis for heredity and the program for maintenance and development in all cellular organisms is encoded on strands of DNA (deoxyribonucleic acid). Unlike traditional serological markers, which represent expressed phenotypes, DNA defines the genotype of the individual. Hence, DNA sequence is the most detailed and variable source of genetic information available; in addition, it is present in all tissues. The size and structure of the DNA genome is such that all individuals, barring identical twins, can readily be shown to have a unique genetic profile. Biological evolution has produced DNA to function as a repository of information which molecular machinery must be able to access, interpret, and reproduce. Accordingly, an understanding of molecular biological processes permits easy access to the information in DNA. Furthermore, since the informational content of DNA is present in its primary chemical structure, this information is remarkably well preserved after death. In contrast, enzymatic markers must have intact secondary and tertiary structure to provide information.

### Biochemistry

DNA is a linear, double-stranded molecule, with the two strands hydrogen-bonded together and twisted to form a double helix. Each strand of DNA is a polymer of nucleotide subunits, consisting of a phosphate group, a deoxyribose sugar and a nitrogenous base, the latter being either a purine or pyrimidine ring structure. The nitrogenous bases are linked to the sugar by a glycosidic bond, and nucleotide monomers are linked in succession by phosphodiester bonds. The phosphodiester bonds occur between the 3′-carbon of one sugar residue and the 5′-carbon of the next, so that the linear chain of nucleotide subunits has a polarity, that is, a 5′ and a 3′ end. The two strands of the helix run with opposite polarity, and the planar nitrogenous bases from each strand point inward to form hydrogen-bonded pairs, like steps on a spiral staircase. The base pairing always involves one pyrimidine (C = cytosine or T = thymine) and one purine (A = adenine or G = guanine), adenine pairing with thymine and cytosine pairing with guanine. The linear sequence of bases in DNA constitutes its informational content. DNA determines the amino acid sequences of proteins using a triplet base code, and also codes for functional RNA molecules such as ribosomal and transfer RNA.

The two strands of the double helix can be separated in a process called denaturation. This is effected by any conditions that destabilize the hydrogen bonding between base pairs, such as increased temperature, low ionic strength, high pH, or the presence of chemical denaturants such as urea or formamide. Once denatured, the single strands of DNA will reanneal if conditions permitting hydrogen bonding are restored, and in solution, single stranded DNA will diffuse and hybridize to its complementary opposite strand. This sequence-specific reassociation is the basis for techniques that utilize hybridization probes which recognize specific genetic sequences. During probe hybridization, the degree of specificity required for annealing can be determined by adjusting temperature and ionic strength.

During DNA replication in the cell, the two strands of DNA are transiently separated, so that each may serve as a template for replication of a new opposite strand, complementary to the original. Replication of DNA in nature takes place by the linkage of the 5′ phosphate of an unincorporated nucleotide to the 3′ hydroxyl group on the elongating strand. *In vitro* enzymatic replication of DNA also occurs in this manner, and is the basis for the polymerase chain reaction (PCR, see below). Mutations are errors made in DNA replication, and these can be point mutations, where an incorrect nucleotide is incorporated, or insertions or deletions of one, several, or many bases. Mutations are rare events, and, if they occur in coding regions, are likely to be detrimental. However, mutations in noncoding DNA (see below) are less likely to be eliminated by natural selection. Additionally, because the genetic code is degenerate, point mutations in protein-coding genes do not always cause changes in amino acid sequence. These are silent or synonymous mutations, that are not immediately removed from the population by natural selection. Additionally, even changes in amino acid sequence can sometimes be tolerated. Over time, mutations give rise to various alleles at very many loci, which then spread in or are lost from the population according to genetic drift and/or selection, the latter being negligible for many apparently neutral changes (Kimura 1983).

## Genetic Variation and Repetitive DNA

The human genome is tremendously large and complex, exhibiting a high level of variation between individuals. There are roughly six billion base pairs per diploid human cell (~6 picograms), divided into 46 chromosomes in the nucleus. DNA in the nucleus is associated with histones and other structural proteins, and is coiled into a densely compact form. A separate, small genome exists in mitochondria in the cytoplasm, and this multicopy element accounts for roughly 0.1% of the total DNA. In addition to DNA that codes for protein or RNA, there is a large amount of DNA with no known function, much of which is repetitive (e.g., Cavalier-Smith 1985; John and Miklos 1988). 20 to 30% of the human genome consists of DNA that is moderately or highly repetitive (Singer 1982). "Satellite DNA" consists of tandemly repeated sequence elements that are found in very high copy number in chromosomal centromeres and telomeres. Other repeated elements are interspersed throughout the genome; these include LINE elements (long interspersed repeats) and SINE elements (short interspersed repeats). In primates, the most abundant SINE repeat is the Alu element, consisting of two head-to-tail repeats that are scattered throughout the genome, with a haploid copy number of nearly one million.

Other repeat elements are of great importance to forensic applications. Minisatellites are interspersed tandem repeats with a core repeat unit greater than ~7 base pairs (bp) in length. A typical repeat unit is ~15 bp in length and the size of the tandem array is normally from 0.5 to 30 kilobase pairs (kbp). In general, the fidelity of DNA replication during mitosis and meiosis is very high, but characteristics of tandem arrays cause them to experience mutation rates that are higher than normal. Point mutations, insertions, and deletions can occur within the array, but with higher frequency processes such as replication slippage and unequal crossing-over generate new copies that differ in the number of repeat elements (e.g., Jeffreys et al. 1988, and reviewed in Charlesworth et al. 1994). For this reason, minisatellites are also referred to as variable number of tandem repeat (VNTR) loci (Nakamura et al. 1987). Because these repeat elements are noncoding, mutational variants are tolerated by natural selection and many variants accumulate in populations over time. Minisatellite loci typically have many alleles, with the result that individuals are usually heterozygous. By typing individuals for their allelic patterns at multiple minisatellite loci, individual-specific profiles can be obtained. The first applications of DNA "fingerprinting" used probes that hybridize internally to minisatellite repeats (e.g., Jeffreys et al. 1985), resolving complex allelic patterns at many different minisatellite loci simultaneously. Subsequently, batteries of single-locus probes have been developed to permit identification based on discrete loci with well-defined population statistics (e.g., Jeffreys 1993).

Microsatellites, or STRs (short tandem repeats), are interspersed tandem repeats with a core repeat unit less than ~6 bp in length. Microsatellite tandem arrays are generally much smaller than minisatellites, with a mean length on the order of 100 bp. There are more than 30,000 separate microsatellite loci in the human genome (Weissenbach 1993). Microsatellites have many of the same properties as minisatellites, with loci showing high heterozygosity. However, because they are shorter they can be discretely typed on acrylamide gels to the resolution of a single repeat unit (see below). Further, their small size permits them to be reliably amplified using the polymerase chain reaction. This greatly enhances the utility of STR analysis for degraded samples. As diploid loci, both minisatellite and microsatellite VNTRs have great utility in parentage analysis, with offspring having one maternal and one paternal allele at each locus. However, the high mutation rate of these repetitive elements, up to a few percent per generation (Di Rienzo et al. 1994; Jeffreys et al. 1994), allows a small chance that a particular allele has mutated from one generation to the next. This potential cause of a false exclusion must be considered during analysis.

## Mitochondrial DNA

Mitochondrial DNA (mtDNA) has very different properties than nuclear DNA: it is present in high copy number, nonrecombinatorial, and maternally inherited (Brown 1985; Giles et al. 1980). Found in cytoplasmic mitochondrial organelles, mtDNA is a closed circular genome that codes for 13 proteins, 2 ribosomal RNAs, and 22 transfer RNAs. In humans, the mtDNA genome is 16,569 bp in length (Anderson et al. 1991), and somatic cells may have from 200 to 1700 mtDNA copies depending on the tissue type (Bogenhagen and Clayton 1980; Robin and Wong 1988). MtDNA is inherited solely from the mother, as virtually no mtDNA is transferred from sperm to the ovum. Animal mtDNA is extremely compact and conserved in its organization, with little or no noncoding DNA between genes. The only substantial section of noncoding DNA occurs in the displacement loop (D-loop), which contains the H-strand origin of replication. Mitochondrial DNA exhibits a roughly ten-fold faster rate of evolution (base substitution over time) than does nuclear DNA, possibly due to differences in DNA replication fidelity or repair efficiency (Brown et al. 1979). This high evolutionary rate has caused mtDNA to be an extremely important tool in population genetic and phylogenetic analysis within and between many species, including humans (e.g., Avise 1994; Cann et al. 1987).

Forensic identity testing has focused on the noncoding D-loop section of mtDNA. The D-loop has the highest frequency of nucleotide sites that are polymorphic, and, in humans, polymorphic sites are concentrated in two hypervariable regions, each roughly 300 bp in length. The average chance that unrelated individuals will have the same sequence over both hypervariable regions is less than 1% (Stoneking et al. 1991). As a rule, individuals have only a single type of mtDNA in all tissues, and, barring mutations between generations, this same type is shared by all maternal relatives. This important feature allows evidentiary samples to be compared to any maternal relative, with the expectation of an exact match. Of equal or greater significance is the high copy number of mtDNA, which permits its recovery under conditions where no intact nuclear DNA may persist. Accordingly, mtDNA plays a prominent role in "ancient DNA" analysis, and in other cases where only small amounts of degraded DNA are available. Generally it is thought that individuals are homoplasmic, having only a single mtDNA type for D-loop sequences. However, rare exceptions have been noted (Gill et al. 1994; Holland et al. 1994), and validation studies are ongoing at the Armed Forces DNA Identification Laboratory to determine the level of within and between generation heteroplasmy (the occurrence of multiple mtDNA types).

# Techniques for DNA Analysis

DNA can be isolated and tested from virtually any postmortem tissue, although after death it undergoes progressive fragmentation. Nevertheless, the sequence information remains in the DNA fragments so that the information is not completely lost despite even quite extensive fragmentation which occurs from decomposition. However, not all DNA testing is appropriate or possible when DNA is degraded. Traditional DNA fingerprinting using restriction fragment length polymorphisms (RFLPs) requires undegraded high molecular weight DNA, whereas analysis based on the polymerase chain reaction (PCR) can be performed on degraded and/or very minute samples. In cases of extreme degradation, mitochondrial DNA can often be obtained from skeletal or other remains when nuclear DNA cannot.

## DNA Extraction

DNA can be extracted from most tissue sources, including bone and biological fluid stains, using variations of standard organic DNA extraction protocols (e.g., Hochmeister et al. 1991a; Jackson et al. 1991; Kobilinsky 1992; Lee et al. 1991b; Sambrook et al. 1989). In general, fragmented tissue or ground bone is incubated in the presence of proteinase K and detergent to lyse cells and dissociate the DNA; then it is extracted with phenol/chloroform to remove other components such as proteins and lipids. After concentration, the DNA can then be quantitated by standard methods and analyzed for degradation on agarose gels. Inorganic extraction methods have also been developed, and the choice of extraction can be based on the type of analysis that will be performed. The rapid Chelex® method (Walsh et al. 1991) involves simply heating a small sample in the presence of a chelating resin that inactivates nucleases and dissociates DNA, but the resulting DNA is dilute and single-stranded and so can only be used for PCR. Chelex® and other commercially available DNA purification matrices have been compared for PCR applications (Akane et al. 1993; Comey et al. 1994). Recently, a simple silica-binding method has been successfully used for ancient DNA samples (Hoss and Paabo 1993); this, and more detailed consideration concerning DNA extraction from aged bone will be covered later in the section on ancient DNA.

## "Fingerprinting" by RFLP Analysis

Restriction fragment length polymorphism (RFLP) analysis of minisatellite VNTRs is the forensic DNA typing method that was first described and, initially, the DNA test most commonly employed by crime labs (reviewed in Kirby 1990). RFLP analysis is a method that directly assays the purified source DNA, distinguishing it from PCR-based methods which assay segments that have been artificially amplified. The first step in RFLP analysis is digesting the purified DNA with restriction enzymes that cleave the DNA at sequence-specific recognition sites (usually 6 bp in length) which occur randomly throughout the genome. Due to the large size of the genome, the resultant population of fragments has a virtually continuous size distribution. The DNA is then size-separated by electrophoresis on agarose gels, denatured into single strands, and, in a technique known as Southern blotting, transferred directly to an overlaid membrane where it becomes covalently immobilized. The membrane can then be immersed in solutions containing DNA probes which will hybridize to those immobilized DNA fragments that contain complementary sequences. These probes are labeled in such a way that their location, relative to size standards, can be determined on film through autoradiography or chemiluminescence. In this way, the restriction fragment size profile corresponding to particular genetic loci can be observed.

As mentioned earlier, classic fingerprinting probes bind to variable numbers of tandem repeat loci (VNTRs). The restriction enzymes employed are chosen to fall outside of the repeat array, so that allelic differences in array length are apparent. Multilocus probes (MLPs) recognize repeat sequences from a number of different VNTR loci, and produce complex patterns over a large range of sizes. A single multilocus probe can give a pattern that is highly specific for individualization. However, with MLPs it is not possible to determine which locus a particular band represents, so match probabilities cannot be accurately calculated, and mixed samples are not easily recognized. Therefore, most fingerprinting is currently performed with single-locus probes (SLPs), which have the additional advantage of increased sensitivity. SLPs are hybridized and washed under conditions that allow binding to only one specific locus and result in much simpler patterns, usually with one or two bands. The exclusion potential of just one SLP locus is not particularly large, but the Southern membranes can be stripped and reprobed with additional SLPs to result in combined random match probabilities of one in millions or even billions (e.g., Kirby 1990). Both MLPs and SLPs are highly informative in parentage analysis, as an offspring receives one allele from each parent for every locus.

RFLP typing, then, is a relatively low-technology means of obtaining very precise identity information. However, it has some serious drawbacks, especially for use with degraded remains. First, since the sample DNA is assayed directly, relatively high amounts of DNA are required. For single-locus probes, the minimum amount of DNA required is 10 to 50 nanograms, while for multilocus probes the amount is even higher. While this is a small fraction of the DNA that can be normally obtained from fresh sources (blood can yield 30 to 60 micrograms of DNA per milliliter, and fresh tissue can yield over a milligram per gram), amounts can be limiting for trace or low-yield samples. Of even greater detriment is the fact that substantially degraded DNA is not suitable for RFLP analysis. Target RFLP fragments may be many thousands of base pairs in length, and any DNA with an average length below this is generally unsuitable for RFLP analysis. Another disadvantage to RFLP testing is that it can take weeks to run a battery of SLPs on a particular sample. Further, the variation in allele size is essentially continuous, so determining a match requires operational criteria of "binning," where bands located within a specified narrow range are classed as one.

## Polymerase Chain Reaction

The ability to amplify DNA with the polymerase chain reaction is a primary tool in obtaining postmortem genetic information, and without it the field of ancient DNA analysis would likely not exist. The technique employs oppositely oriented specific primers that delineate a target locus. The sample DNA is heat denatured in the presence of nucleotides, primers, and a heat-stable DNA polymerase. After cooling, the primers anneal to their bindings sites and prime the replication of new copies of the target DNA. This process is then repeated, usually 20 to 40 cycles, resulting in the exponential amplification of a single DNA segment (e.g., Erlich 1989; McPherson et al. 1991; Saiki et al. 1988). Amplification can occur from a single molecule of starting DNA, and takes only a few hours. The resultant PCR "amplicon" can then be analyzed on agarose or acrylamide gels for length variation, cleaved with restriction enzymes for RFLP analysis (with direct visualization that does not require probe hybridization), assayed by "reverse dot blotting" with sequence-specific oligonucleotide probes, or sequenced (see below).

The sensitivity of PCR potentially enables results to be obtained from the minutest of biological samples, and from DNA that is badly degraded. Even if a majority of sample DNA is fragmented below the target size, a small percentage of intact copies will often persist and can be amplified. With degraded samples, however, efficiency of amplification drops off dramatically with increasing size of the target segment. This can cause negative results for larger allelic variants, and "allelic drop-out" can potentially confound analysis. Another disadvantage to PCR techniques is that impurities in DNA samples may inhibit the enzymatic reaction.

## PCR Contamination

The extreme sensitivity of PCR is also the cause of one of the greatest technical problems in its application: that of amplifying trace levels of contaminating DNA. This is particularly true with severely degraded or ancient samples, where template DNA can be present at extremely low levels or not at all, and is likely to be damaged to some extent. In such cases, even single copies of contaminating modern DNA can produce false positive results. Only DNA with sites matching the primers used for PCR is of concern, and contaminating DNA from bacteria or fungi will generally not cause problems. However, much forensic and ancient DNA work is performed on human specimens, and the potential for contamination by any person who has handled the sample or set up the amplification is quite strong. Samples that provide substantial quantities of template DNA are much less prone to be overwhelmed by trace contaminants, but caution must nevertheless be exercised. PCR products that have been previously amplified in the lab amplify very efficiently and are present in vast copy number (1/1000th of a microliter of a typical PCR product contains on the order of 10 million copies). Previously amplified fragments constitute a great contamination risk, and can out-compete even high quantities of authentic sample DNA during amplification.

Reviews of general practices and specific procedures to avoid the pitfalls of contamination may be found in Handt et al. (1994a), Hummel and Herrmann (1994), and Thomas and Paabo (1993). The following is a list of control experiments or criteria of authenticity that have been suggested for PCR investigations of ancient or highly degraded samples:

1. Laboratories where sample DNA is extracted and PCR is set up should be physically separated from laboratories where products of PCR amplification are handled; ideally, this would include separate ventilation systems.
2. Lab coats and laboratory equipment, etc…should be dedicated for use exclusively in the pre- and post-PCR laboratories.
3. Negative control experiments should be included at all phases. This must always include a mock extraction performed with no sample. Also required are control PCR amplifications with no template DNA added. All PCR controls should be made from the same PCR master mix as used for the sample of interest, differing only in the template DNA.
4. If possible, the same result should be obtained from at least two separate extractions of the same specimen, preferably from different parts of the specimen.
5. The DNA sequences or patterns obtained should make sense from a phylogenetic or population-genetic standpoint, when such criteria can be evaluated.
6. Due to fragmentation and damage of template DNA, authentic ancient DNA amplification should display an inverse relationship between amplification efficiency and the size of the amplified target.
7. In forensic applications where an evidentiary sample will be compared to a reference sample, it is desirable to analyze the evidentiary sample before the reference is analyzed. For extremely contamination-prone work such as mitochondrial DNA amplification, the reference sample should not even be brought to the laboratory until evidentiary analysis is complete. This precaution ensures that any contamination that occurs will falsely exclude, rather than falsely include, the evidentiary sample 1.

## Specific Techniques of PCR Analysis

Large bodies of knowledge concerning human polymorphisms have permitted the development of a number of simple and elegant PCR-based identity tests. Sequence-specific oligonucleotide

(SSO) probes have been devised to determine the allelic variants represented by PCR products for a number of loci. In "reverse dot blots," SSOs that exactly match the sequence of allelic variants at particular nucleotide positions are immobilized in spots on an assay strip. PCR products are hybridized to a series of SSOs (Saiki et al. 1989), and allele-specific hybridization is detected by a simple colorimetric assay — the spots turn blue. A commercial kit is available that types six alleles of the HLA DQA1 locus (Perkin Elmer AmpliType®), and another kit (Perkin Elmer AmpliType PM®) types alleles from five additional independent loci, amplified in a single multiplex PCR. The power of discrimination of SSO techniques is not as high as RFLP analysis of VNTRs, but produces random match probabilities on the order of one in 100 to one in thousands. The small size of the PCR targets, 138 to 242 bp, greatly enhances their utility for use with degraded DNA. An SSO kit is being developed to assay sequence variation in the human D-loop that could provide nearly as much potential for discrimination as complete sequence information (Stoneking et al. 1991).

PCR has also been very usefully applied to minisatellite VNTR loci, in what is known as "AmpFLP" (amplification fragment length polymorphism) analysis. The highly polymorphic D1S80 locus is the most widely used (e.g., Budowle et al. 1991), producing alleles that range in length from several hundred to over 700 bp. A commercially available kit (Perkin Elmer AmpliFLP D1S80®) designed for silver-stain detection in polyacrylamide gels, has an exclusion potential of roughly 95 to 98%. AmpFLPs are also used for other loci, such as S17S5 (Horn et al. 1989) and Apo B (Ludwig et al. 1989). A multiplex PCR system has been developed that uses automated fluorescent detection to assay a number of loci simultaneously, with much higher statistical power (Tully et al. 1993). For intact DNA, the sensitivity of PCR enables tests of smaller amounts of DNA than standard RFLP analysis, but the large size of minisatellite VNTR loci limits the application of this technique to DNA samples that are not extensively degraded.

An extremely promising PCR approach that has been developed recently is the analysis of STRs (Edwards et al. 1991; Hammond et al. 1994; Urquhart et al. 1994). STR arrays are much shorter than minisatellite VNTRs, and thus can be amplified from more extensively degraded DNA. Further, combined data from multiple STR loci have as much discriminatory power as does traditional RFLP analysis. A system to type four independent loci in a single quadruplex PCR has been developed (Kimpton et al. 1994). Dye-labeled PCR primers are used to enable automated fluorescent detection on denaturing polyacrylamide gels, so that a large number of samples can easily be typed in a day. Resolution down to single bases is possible, so alleles are typed in discrete rather than continuous classes. The system can be used with as little as 100 picograms of undegraded DNA, and has a random match probability on the order of 1 in ten thousand. The system has not been extensively characterized with degraded DNA, but preliminary results with even very small amounts of degraded DNA are promising (Armed Forces DNA Identification Laboratory unpublished results; Whitaker et al. 1995). Multiplex STR typing has now been employed in a seven-locus system (Urquhart et al. 1995), which includes sex-specific PCR targets from the amelogenin gene (Sullivan et al. 1993). Using this heptaplex system, random match probabilities are on the order of one in 10 million, and when combined with the quadruplex system become one in 5 billion, i.e., unique in the human gene pool.

The most detailed information available from amplified DNA is its complete nucleotide sequence. DNA sequencing continues to improve in ease and efficiency (e.g., Ellingboe and Gyllensten 1992), especially with the advent of automated techniques (Smith et al. 1986), but remains a labor-intensive and costly form of analysis. DNA sequencing is widely used in ancient DNA studies that focus on population genetics and evolutionary questions (see below), and is most frequently applied to mitochondrial DNA. In forensic applications, DNA sequencing is used for analyzing the mtDNA D-loop region (Wilson et al. 1993), but only a few laboratories are employing this approach. The powerful attraction of this method is that the mtDNA target is a high copy number element; samples that yield vanishingly small amounts of highly degraded DNA can often be typed even when other typing methods fail. MtDNA PCR primer sets standardly used at the Armed Forces DNA Identification Laboratory produce robust amplification from as little as 0.5 picograms of control DNA, 200-fold less than is required for STR analysis. However, the average random match probability for D-loop sequences is on the order of one in 100, so the statistical power of this approach is limited.

## "Short-Term" Postmortem Studies and Casework Examples

The stability of purified DNA is remarkably good, under a reasonably wide range of conditions. However, biological and environmental factors begin immediately after death to fragment and degrade DNA. The initial onslaught is to a great extent biological, stemming from endogenous biodegradative enzymes (autolysis) and exogenous microbial digestion (putrefaction). With the breakdown of cellular compartmentalization, DNA becomes exposed to cellular nucleases associated with DNA repair and metabolism. "DNases" include endonucleases that cut at internal sites within DNA strands and exonucleases that digest DNA from the ends. Tissues differ greatly in their concentrations of these enzymes; hence some are much better sources of DNA than others (additionally, some tissues are more densely cellular than others). Shortly after death, bacteria and other exogenous organisms proliferate and also digest DNA with nucleases.

Conditions that inhibit or retard nuclease activity and bacterial growth are those that favor the recovery of DNA. Cool or cold temperature and, especially, rapid dehydration are principal factors that inhibit these processes. If DNA avoids an initial aggressive course of biochemical attack, it may persist for very long periods of time. In this more extended phase, detrimental effects due directly to the physical and chemical characteristics of the environment become more important, although biological and environmental degradative factors are, of course, not wholly independent. One of the more important short-term environmental assaults is that of ultraviolet irradiation by sunlight. Longer-term environmental damage is discussed in the section on ancient DNA, below.

In the following sections, recovery of DNA from various sources in the relatively short postmortem period will be reviewed. A previous review is Kobilinsky (1992). A detailed review of sampling and storage procedures for samples to be used in forensic DNA analysis is Lee et al. (1991a).

### DNA Recovery from Cadaveric Tissues

A number of studies have compared DNA recovery from various postmortem tissues. Most of these are concerned with the recovery of high molecular weight (HMW) DNA that is suitable for RFLP analysis. The results of these studies are to some extent inconsistent and do not reveal definitive rules for predicting DNA recovery. However, some generalities may be observed. Bar et al. (1988) recovered HMW DNA from brain, lymph node, and skeletal muscle up to 3 weeks after death; kidney, spleen, and thyroid yielded HMW DNA up to 1 week, and liver lost all HMW DNA after 2 days. Within a tissue type there was an overall inverse relationship between DNA recovery and time since death, with degradation accelerated by increased temperature. The yield from blood in the body cavity was variable, and instances of good recovery were attributed to the presence of blood clots containing good quality DNA. Another study (Healy et al. 1990) found liver, spleen, cardiac muscle, and skeletal muscle to be poor sources of HMW DNA, diaphragm, lung and testes to be better, and skin, bone marrow, and bloodstains to be the best sources. Swarner et al. (1989) also concluded that DNA from liver degraded faster than that of heart muscle, spleen, and bone marrow. In a time-course study of 20 cadavers, brain tissue was the best source of HMW DNA, regardless of postmortem period from 1 to 30 days (Ludes et al. 1991). Kidney and heart samples often produced HMW DNA, while blood clots, liver, spleen, and lymph nodes more often yielded degraded DNA. Ogata et al. (1990) studied postmortem muscle samples and found that the degree of degradation increased from 21% at 1 day to 42% at 8 days. More than 90% of these samples were suitable for RFLP analysis after 3 days, but only 30% after 8 days. RFLP has also been used in the identification of a homicide victim found some days or weeks after death. Sufficient HMW DNA was obtained from peripheral blood sampled at the time of autopsy, as well as from muscle tissue sampled after the body had been stored at 3°C for 3 months (Haglund et al. 1990). Success with RFLP in this case may be related to the cool conditions in which the body had been found, 6°C. Overall, brain tissue seems to be one of the best sources of DNA, followed by muscle and blood, and then other internal organs. Liver is consistently a poor source of postmortem DNA.

The above studies indicate that in many instances DNA quickly becomes too degraded for use in RFLP analysis. In such cases, PCR approaches greatly extend the range of material that may be typed (Blake et al. 1992; Comey 1991; Erlich 1991). Gima et al. (1991) reported the PCR HLA DQA1 typing of partially cremated remains, and Sajantila et al. (1991) described DQA1 and D1S80 typing of charred human tissue of fire victims. Hochmeister et al. (1991b) reported successful PCR typing of samples buried for 3 months or immersed in water for 18 months; these samples failed for RFLP analysis. Similarly, highly degraded remains from casualties of the Persian Gulf war for which RFLP typing was not feasible were successfully typed by PCR of STR and HLA DQA1 loci (Wadhams et al. 1994). Amplification of D1S80, HLA DQA1, AmpliType PM®, and Quadruplex STR loci also provided extensive identity information on burned and highly degraded samples from the Waco, Texas mass disaster (Dizinno et al. 1995; Whitaker et al. 1995).

## Biological Fluid Stains

Dried body fluid stains are one of the most important sources of DNA for forensic applications. Because rapid dehydration inhibits enzymatic activity and microbial growth, DNA is often very well preserved in dried fluid stains. Extensive casework and validation studies have demonstrated that RFLP typing from dried blood and semen stains can be robust over periods of years, under many environmental conditions, on many substrates, and in the presence of many chemical and biological contaminants (e.g., Adams et al. 1991; Kanter et al. 1986; Laber et al. 1994; McNally et al. 1989a, 1989b; Yokoi and Sagisaka 1990). The types of insults that have been investigated include heat, humidity, ultraviolet and sunlight irradiation, dampness, and contamination with soil, acids, bases, gasoline, motor oil, bleach, detergent, lotion, and microorganisms. The most consistently detrimental insult appears to be contamination with soil, while sunlight, ultraviolet irradiation, increased temperature, dampness, and bleach also can promote degradation.

While no dried fluid stain should be disregarded as a source of HMW DNA, once again PCR techniques extend the range of samples which can be successfully typed. In one of many successful case applications, HLA-DQA1 typing was successful in typing an 11-year old semen stain (von Beroldingen et al. 1989a). Validation and casework studies have demonstrated the robust utility of HLA DQA1 typing (Blake et al. 1992; Comey 1991; Comey et al. 1993), and the polymarker AmpliType PM® system (Budowle et al. 1995; Herrin et al. 1994) in typing blood and semen stains. In a further demonstration of the high sensitivity of PCR methods, Hochmeister et al. (1991c) reported successful HLA DQA1 and D1S80 typing from dried saliva on cigarette butts.

## Miscellaneous Sources

Hair can yield sufficient DNA to be typed by various techniques. Hair roots, with associated cellular material, can be good sources of HMW DNA for RFLP analysis (Gill et al. 1987; Swarner et al. 1989). PCR techniques have been successful in typing single human hairs (Higuchi et al. 1988; Blake et al. 1992; von Beroldingen et al. 1989b). Likewise, amplification of DNA from hair of chimpanzees has permitted identification of subspecies using allele-specific probes (Morin et al. 1992). In another instance, mitochondrial DNA amplification of DNA from single hair roots has been used in human population genetic analysis (Vigilant et al. 1991). The high copy number of mitochondrial DNA even permits mtDNA amplification from hair shafts that have no associated cellular material. Because of this and the fact that individual hairs are commonly recovered from crime scenes, the FBI is developing a program for mtDNA testing of hair (Wilson et al. 1995).

DNA in urine has been successfully typed using the HLA DQA1 amplification system, enabling the identification of donors of urine samples for drug testing (Holland et al. 1993). Feces can also yield DNA for PCR applications, but can be technically difficult due to the presence of inhibitors of PCR. Mitochondrial DNA amplification from bear excrement yielded positive results, and identification of plant material in the bear diet was also possible, using primers for high copy number chloroplast genes (Hoss et al. 1992). The ability to type DNA from sources such as excrement and hair is of great benefit to studies of species that are rare or difficult to access, or when the subject animals would be unduly traumatized by direct sampling (Taberlet and Bouvet 1992). For example, amplification of microsatellite loci from baboon feces has advanced the prospects for determining paternity and relatedness in primate social groups (Constable 1995; Morell 1995).

## Bone and Teeth

Bone and teeth are extremely important sources of postmortem DNA, and are often the only samples available for analysis. Not only are bone samples more likely to persist due to their physical durability, but it appears that conditions within bone are relatively favorable for the preservation of DNA. This may be due to the comparatively low water and degradative enzyme content of bone, causing individual osteocytes or cementoblasts to undergo rapid mummification (Hummel and Herrmann 1994). Further, bone acts as a physical barrier to external factors such as ultraviolet light and microorganisms. There are roughly 20,000 osteocytes per cubic millimeter in compact bone (Martin and Burr 1989). Much of the bone matrix is composed of crystalline calcium phosphate (hydroxyapatite), which is known to bind to double-stranded DNA. Bone is by far the greatest repository of ancient DNA (Hauswirth 1994), and binding of DNA to the bone matrix may play a role in the long-term protection of DNA from chemical breakdown.

From relatively fresh compact bone, HMW DNA can be obtained at levels up to one microgram per gram starting material (Hochmeister et al. 1991a). Fresh, spongy bones, such as ribs, can yield 10- to 20-fold greater amounts of DNA (Lee et al. 1991b), but over the long term often does not yield DNA as reliably as compact bone (unpublished observations, Armed Forces DNA Identification Laboratory). In a controlled study where microbial activity was minimized, DNA from human rib bone was reduced to relatively low molecular weight within several weeks (Perry et al. 1988), but the comparatively high moisture content of spongy bone may cause more rapid degradation than in compact bone. RFLP analysis and PCR applications on relatively recent bone are discussed in Lee et al. (1991b). Hochmeister et al. (1991a) extracted DNA from bone of a number of decomposed bodies and found that while RFLP techniques gave results in some cases, more often the DNA was too degraded to produce RFLP patterns. However, PCR amplification of minisatellite and HLA-DQA1 loci was successful on samples up to 11 years old. These approaches were also successful on bone that had been buried for 3 months, or immersed in water for 18 months (Hochmeister et al. 1991c). Dental pulp appears to be a particularly good source of high molecular weight DNA, and in one case yielded sufficient DNA for RFLP analysis from severely incinerated remains (Sweet and Sweet 1995). Other studies have also obtained HMW DNA from dental pulp, but in some instances the DNA was degraded and useful only for PCR applications (Lawton et al. 1989; Schwartz et al. 1991; Smith et al. 1993; Yokoi et al. 1989).

The first use of bone in forensic identification involved an 8-year-old skeleton of a murder victim (Hagelberg et al. 1991b), using PCR amplification of microsatellite (STR) loci. Microsatellite loci were also amplified to identify the skeleton of Josef Mengele by comparison to the profiles of his wife and son (Jeffreys et al. 1992). STR and mtDNA analyses were also used in the identification of skeletal remains of members of the Romanov royal family, who were executed by the Bolsheviks in 1918 (Gill et al. 1994; Ivanov et al. 1996). MtDNA D-loop amplification and sequencing is the method of choice for highly degraded skeletal remains, and was also employed in the Romanov case, as well as in a case involving a 2-year-old skeletal fragment (Stoneking et al. 1991), and in the identification of individuals from teeth (Ginther et al. 1992). MtDNA amplification from bone exposed for decades to extremely harsh tropical environments often is successful in identifying the remains of American military personnel from the Vietnam conflict, when other PCR approaches are not successful (Holland et al. 1992). These cases, performed at the Armed Forces DNA Identification Laboratory, indicate very strongly the effect that environmental conditions have on DNA preservation. Bones recovered from tropical conditions of high heat, humidity, and microbial activity often present a greater technical challenge than bones that are many times their age, but recovered from less severe environments. In practical terms, forensic investigation of such "modern" cases overlaps with the field of "ancient" DNA analysis.

# Ancient DNA

The last decade has seen the emergence of what has been termed the "ancient DNA" field, and advances are continuing at an exciting rate (general reviews of the field at various stages are Cherfas 1991; Hagelberg 1994; Morell 1992; Paabo et al. 1989; Thomas and Paabo 1993). Among the more spectacular ancient DNA successes have been isolation of specific DNA sequences from insects trapped in amber up to ~120 million years ago (Cano et al. 1993), and from 17-million-year-old plant fossils (Golenberg et al. 1990). However, results from these exceptionally old samples have not yet won universal acceptance in the scientific community. Possibly of greater importance was the unequivocal demonstration that DNA can be amplified from aged bone (Hagelberg et al. 1989; Horai et al. 1989), and subsequent indications that authentic DNA can be obtained with fair regularity from even very ancient bone samples. This and other successes with a variety of ancient soft tissues have opened to scientific investigation tremendous resources of genetic information from the past.

## Successes and Applications of Ancient DNA Analysis

The first isolation of specific fragments of DNA from ancient sources came in 1984 when a group from Alan Wilson's laboratory at the University of California, Berkeley cloned sequences from an extinct equine, the quagga (Higuchi et al. 1984). This was followed by cloning of a segment of human DNA from an Egyptian mummy (Paabo 1985). However, the cloning efficiency of ancient DNA is so low that obtaining specific sequences is not generally feasible, and it was the successful application of PCR to ancient samples that truly gave life to the field of ancient DNA analysis (Higuchi et al. 1987; Paabo et al. 1988). Since then, DNA has successfully been amplified from many soft tissues, with a noncomprehensive list including such sources as an extinct marsupial wolf (Krajewski et al. 1992; Thomas et al. 1989), extinct flightless moa birds (Cooper et al. 1992), a 13,000-year-old extinct ground sloth (Paabo 1989), >50,000-year-old mammoth (Hoss et al. 1994), mummified humans (e.g., Haydon and Buikstra 1991; Nielsen et al. 1994; Salvo et al. 1989), human brain samples preserved in nonacidic peat bogs (e.g., Hauswirth et al. 1994a, 1994b; Lawlor et al. 1991), and archaeological samples of maize (Goloubinoff et al. 1993). Further, the great wealth of specimens housed in museums is now open to genetic analysis (e.g., Roy et al. 1994), which in one study allowed a direct comparison of ancestral and modern population structure in kangaroo rats (Thomas et al. 1990). In another notable case, representing the amplification length record for ancient DNA, a 1.7-kbp fragment of the opsin gene was amplified from the 150-year-old dried remains of John Dalton's eye, permitting a determination of the genetic basis of the famous scientist's color blindness (Hunt et al. 1995).

Ancient bone has proven to be an excellent source for recovery of DNA. Mitochondrial DNA has been amplified from many bone samples, with a success rate such that researchers can now undertake human population genetic analysis with meaningful sample sizes (Hagelberg and Clegg 1993; Horai et al. 1991; Kolman et al. 1994; Merriwether et al. 1994; Stone and Stoneking 1993; Turbon et al. 1994). In such studies, sequences from ancient bones can be compared to those from extant human populations to infer historical migration events; in this manner, the now extirpated prehistoric Easter Islanders were shown to be of Polynesian rather than South American origin (Hagelberg et al. 1994a). In nonhuman species as well, ancient bone DNA is being used to compare historical populations to modern populations (Hardy et al. 1994a, 1994b, 1995; Purdue and Patton 1992). In another case, ancient mtDNA sequences were used to determine the prehistorical range of the endangered Laysan duck (Cooper et al. 1996). MtDNA has been amplified from such ancient bone specimens as a 14,000-year-old sabre-toothed cat (Janczewski et al. 1992), a 25,000-year-old member of the horse family (Hoss and Paabo 1993), and ~150,000-year-old mammoths (Hagelberg et al. 1994b). In what appears to be the amplification length record from bone, a 900-bp mtDNA fragment was amplified from a 500-year-old human bone (Nielsen et al. 1994). DNA also appears to be well preserved in ancient teeth (Ginther et al. 1992; Hanni et al. 1990; Merriwether et al. 1994; Smith et al. 1993; Turbon et al. 1994; Woodward et al. 1994a). It may be that the exceptional hardness and high hydroxyapatite concentration of tooth dentin preserves DNA to an even greater extent than does bone. DeGusta et al. (1994) report amplification of mtDNA from various archaeological teeth, as old as 4700 years, from as little as 0.01 g of tooth material. Most work has been performed with mtDNA, but single-copy nuclear DNA has also been amplified from ancient bone (Corfield et al. 1992; Francalacci 1992; Hagelberg et al. 1991b; Hummel and Herrmann 1991; Jeffreys et al. 1992), as well as from ancient soft tissue (e.g., Hauswirth et al. 1994b; Lawlor et al. 1991).

There have been a number of cases where DNA has reportedly been amplified from samples that are millions of years old. The first such report was of high-copy-number chloroplast sequences amplified from 17-million-year-old plant compression shales (Golenberg et al. 1990), and a subsequent study also reported success from similar Miocene plant material (Soltis et al. 1992). The current record for ancient DNA, however, is from a 120- to 135-million-year-old weevil trapped in amber (Cano et al. 1993). Amplification and sequencing has been successful for other samples also trapped in amber, all of which are tens of millions of years old (Cano et al. 1992; DeSalle et al. 1992; Poinar et al. 1993). Given the extreme sensitivity of PCR to contamination with modern DNA, there is a high burden of proof concerning the authenticity of such profoundly old sequences, and doubt has been expressed regarding these results (see below). However, the fact that these sequences do not match those of modern taxa, but do group phylogenetically with sequences of expected evolutionary relatives remains difficult to explain by random contamination.

## Long-Term Degradation and Questioned Authenticity

Despite the many successes in ancient DNA, the recovery of specific DNA sequences from trace quantities of fragmented and damaged DNA is a remarkable feat, and the technical challenges should not be underestimated. Over time, DNA is susceptible to many forms of environmental damage and destruction (Imlay and Linn 1988; reviewed by Lindahl 1993a). These include hydrolytic cleavage of phosphodiester bonds and base linkages, oxidative damage to base and sugar moieties, and pyrimidine dimerization (greatly accelerated by ultraviolet irradiation). Spontaneous rates of many of these processes can be extremely slow in relation to biological lifetimes (e.g., Radzicka and Wolfenden 1995), but may be of great relevance to DNA recovery from very ancient samples.

Predictions have been made concerning the survivability of DNA based on its properties *in vitro*. Spontaneous depurination, which is accelerated by low pH and high temperature, is estimated to occur in neutral aqueous solution and moderate temperature at a rate of $\sim 3 \times 10^6$ sites per year per genome (Lindahl and Nyberg 1972), with strand breakage occurring soon thereafter (Lindahl and Andersson 1972). Extending figures such as these, there is an expectation that no DNA fragments greater than 800 bp will persist after 5000 years, fragments will be reduced to shorter than 150 bp by 27,000 years, and no purines at all will remain after 4 million years (Golenberg 1991). These considerations have, as a result, prompted Lindahl (1993a, 1993b) to sharply question the validity of results from million-year-old plus samples.

There is no definitive resolution to the contradiction between known properties of DNA *in vitro* and the spectacular ancient DNA reports. However, the ancient DNA researchers have done a good job of defending their techniques (Golenberg 1994a; Poinar 1993), and point to phylogenetic analyses that are consistent with authenticity. They suggest that empirical results should be given precedence over extrapolation of *in vitro* studies, and that specific environmental conditions, such as those in amber, may serve to protect DNA from degradation. For example, desiccation may limit hydrolytic damage (Golenberg 1991, 1994b; Paabo et al. 1989), but the strong affinity of DNA for water makes conditions for complete dehydration unusual (Lindahl 1993a). Anaerobic and reducing conditions may diminish oxidative damage, and the presence of environmental tannins or humic acids may retard the activity of degradative organisms, as well as chelate metal ions which catalyze oxidative DNA damage (Eglinton and Logan 1991; Golenberg 1994b). High ionic strength is known to diminish the rate of depurination (Lindahl and Nyberg 1972), and the association with chromosomal proteins or other biological molecules may favor preservation (De Leeuw et al. 1991). Additionally, as mentioned earlier, DNA might be preserved by binding to mineral surfaces (Romanowski et al. 1991), such as the hydroxyapatite matrix of bone.

Lindahl (1993b) included in his criticism a suggestion that further studies should concentrate on less spectacularly aged samples, on the order of 100,000 years, with authenticity demonstrated by identical results from multiple specimens and from multiple laboratories working on the same material. Two studies answered this challenge (Hagelberg et al. 1994b; Hoss et al. 1994) and produced sequences from six samples of mammoth tissue and bone, ranging in age from 10,000 to probably 150,000 years. The mammoth sequences clearly grouped together and were closely related to, but distinct from, elephant sequences. However, a report of sequence recovery from 80-million-year-old dinosaur bones apparently was not authentic (Woodward et al. 1994b). Subsequent analysis indicated that the supposed dinosaur sequences were actually from contaminated human DNA, in the form of nuclear pseudogenes that are homologous to mtDNA (Zischler et al. 1995).

## Characteristics of Ancient DNA

DNA recovered from ancient sources is invariably at least partially degraded and accessible to PCR in limited amounts. The single, relatively thorough characterization of ancient DNA (Paabo 1989) indicated that the DNA is, in fact, highly modified and damaged. Among 12 DNA samples extracted from dried soft tissue, with sources ranging from 4 years to 13,000 years, all but the 4-year-old sample had a high proportion of "AP sites" (sites where purine and pyrimidine bases have been lost), with greatly reduced levels of cytosine and thymine bases. AP sites permit DNA to form interstrand cross-links (Goffin et al. 1984), and electron microscopy indicated extensive strand cross-linking. Paabo (1989) noted that, beyond a short initial period, there was no correlation between the extent of DNA degradation and time since death. This has since been observed widely by other researchers, and indicates that specific environmental conditions play a more important role in determining DNA preservation than age *per se*. Paabo was unable to amplify sequences larger than 150 bp from the ancient sources, and concluded that this was the maximum length of functional templates. Other workers have subsequently succeeded in amplifying substantially longer fragments from ancient sources, and bone often yields longer amplification products than can normally be obtained from soft tissue (e.g., Cooper et al. 1992). In all cases, however, the maximum length is far below that obtainable from intact, modern DNA. This size limitation for amplified products is so universally observed that it has become a criterion for authenticity of a purported ancient sequence (Handt et al. 1994b; Paabo et al. 1988).

When analyzed on agarose gels, DNA extracted from aged or ancient bone typically appears to be partly or mostly of low molecular weight, but often with a certain high molecular weight component exceeding that normally obtained from ancient soft tissue (e.g., Tuross 1994). Many researchers consider that a majority of this DNA, especially the high molecular weight component, derives from invasive bacteria or fungi (e.g., Hagelberg 1994). Hagelberg et al. (1991a) reported that while similar quantities of total DNA were obtained from human bones of various ages and conditions, amplification success differed highly among the samples; the authors concluded that the DNA visible on gels was mostly of microbiological origin. Fisher et al. (1993) estimated by hybridization that ~1% of the DNA obtained from U.S. Civil War bones was of human origin. Nielsen et al. (1994) reported human-specific hybridization to only 0.001 to 0.002% of DNA recovered from ancient bone. However, this DNA also failed to hybridize to bacterial DNA, and hybridized only faintly to fungal DNA, and it may be that characteristics of ancient DNA cause it to be detected inefficiently in blotting/hybridization experiments. Nonetheless, Doran et al. (1986) obtained positive hybridization to apparently intact (16.5 kbp) mitochondrial DNA from 7000-year-old brain tissue. In another study, Brown and Brown (1992) performed size fractionation of DNA from human bones ranging up to 9000 years in age, and hybridized the two fractions (>500 bp, and 100 to 500 bp) to human-specific mtDNA and nuclear repeat probes. They reported no correlation between specimen age and the amount of hybridizing material, and saw positive hybridization to the high molecular weight fraction in most samples. A potential problem with this and other similar studies is that apparently high molecular weight DNA may actually be shorter chains that are cross-linked. Finally, one study (Tuross 1994) did observe a correlation between bone age and the amount of total DNA recovered: from a range of bone samples from 100 to 7000 years old there was on average a ten-fold difference in DNA yield between the oldest and the youngest. This study did not attempt to distinguish human from microbial DNA, but Tuross noted that the yield of DNA from buried bones never exceeded that from fresh bone, as might be expected if the DNA obtained were mostly bacterial or fungal in nature.

## Extraction of Ancient DNA

To a large extent, the nature of the total DNA extracted from ancient samples is not as important as whether authentic sequences can be amplified from the sample, and the size of the amplified fragments that can be obtained. While a variety of methods for extracting DNA from ancient bone and soft tissue have been reported, there have been surprisingly few studies that systematically compare the efficacy of various extraction methods relative to the ability to obtain authentic amplification products of various sizes (an exception is Fisher et al. 1993). Most bone extraction methods employ a standard organic extraction, with previous decalcification of the bone by incubation with EDTA (Corfield et al. 1992; Fisher et al. 1993; Francalacci et al. 1992; Ginther et al. 1992; Goodyear et al. 1994; Hagelberg 1994; Hagelberg et al. 1989 and 1991a; Hagelberg and Clegg 1991, 1993; Hardy et al. 1994a, 1994b; Hochmeister et al. 1991b; Hummel and Herrmann 1991; Turbon et al. 1994; Tuross 1994). However, it is clear that decalcification is not necessary for successful DNA extraction from bone (e.g., Fisher et al. 1993; Lee et al. 1991a; Nielsen et al. 1994; Merriwether et al. 1994; Smith et al. 1993), and the extent to which it is advantageous has not been documented. In the absence of decalcification, however, it is necessary that detergent be present in the extraction in order for DNA to be dissociated from the bone (unpublished results, Armed Forces DNA Identification Laboratory). Incubation with high concentrations of sodium phosphate has also been suggested as a means of dissociating DNA from the hydroxyapatite matrix of bone (Nielsen et al. 1994).

One of the biggest problems of extraction from ancient samples is the presence of inhibitors of PCR that frequently copurify with ancient DNA. The inhibitors seem to be environmental in origin (e.g., Cooper 1992), and may be mostly comprised of humic acids from the soil, and fulvic acid in particular (Tuross 1994). The commonest approaches to dealing with the inhibitor include diluting the DNA sample prior to amplification, increasing the amount of Taq polymerase used in amplification (Paabo et al. 1988), and adding bovine serum albumin to the amplification (e.g., Hoss et al. 1994). Other methods for removing the inhibitors involve additional steps at the end of standard extraction methods. These include gel excision (Janczewski et al. 1992), Centricon® filtration (Akane et al. 1993), precipitation with ethidium bromide and ammonium acetate (Dickel and Hauswirth 1992; Stemmer 1991), cesium chloride equilibrium density centrifugation (Bruce et al. 1992), ion exchange matrices (Akane et al. 1993; Goodyear et al. 1994), and spermidine precipitation (Persson 1992). An extraction method based on the binding of DNA to silica beads during incubation with guanidinium isothiocyanate (Boom et al. 1990) has recently been applied to ancient DNA (e.g., Cano and Poinar 1993; Hoss and Paabo 1993; Poinar 1994; van der Kuyl 1994), and apparently is highly effective at eliminating inhibitors of PCR. A systematic comparison of many of the most promising methods of DNA isolation from bone is currently being conducted at the Armed Forces DNA Identification Laboratory, to determine which produces the best template for amplification of authentic ancient DNA.

## Correlation with Bone Morphology

In bone as well as soft tissue, there is little correlation between successful amplification of DNA and the age of the specimen. However, there appears to be a correlation between DNA amplification success and the external gross morphological preservation of the bone, as well as the retention of microscopic matrix and cellular features (Hagelberg et al. 1991a, 1994; Hagelberg and Clegg 1993; Herrmann and Hummel 1994). An example of this correlation is seen in Hagelberg and Clegg (1993) where mtDNA amplification was obtained from 21 out of 38 attempted bones. Successful amplification was typically seen from dense bone with a characteristic yellow-waxy appearance, while brown, porous and fragile bones would more often fail to amplify. Similarly aged bones of these two types were sectioned, and microscopic analysis showed that the dense bone had almost perfect micromorphology, while the fragile bone which failed to amplify had no visible cellular organization. Microbial and fungal action are considered to account for a great deal of diagenetic degradation of bone (Bell 1990), and the type of damage seen in bones which frequently fail to amplify is similar to that incurred under microbial action (Hacket 1981; Hagelberg and Clegg 1993).

## "Jumping PCR"

Due to the damaged nature of ancient DNA, ancient DNA amplification is subject to a phenomenon known as "jumping PCR" (Paabo et al. 1989; Paabo et al. 1990), which may have both beneficial and detrimental effects. When template DNA has a strand break falling within the PCR target sequence, replication of this strand will not result in a full length copy of the target. However, in subsequent PCR cycles it is possible for replication products derived from the broken strand to bind to overlapping fragments from other templates, and thus to serve as primers for extension. In this way, recombinant PCR products can be formed. The benefit of this phenomenon is that it can allow amplification of lengths of DNA even when no unbroken template molecules of that length are present in original DNA sample (e.g., Golenberg 1991). In the case of a homogeneous target sequence, such as mitochondrial DNA, recombination between templates may cause no confounding effects. However, the tendency for the introduction of errors at jump sites can be a problem even for mitochondrial DNA if the original number of starting templates is very small, or if single cloned amplification products are analyzed. Further, products from ancient DNA can form recombinant chimeras with contaminating modern homologs. This was observed in the case of mtDNA amplified from the Tyrolean Ice Man (Handt et al. 1994b). When PCR is performed from diploid nuclear loci, jumping PCR can cause recombination between alleles. This has been seen in the case of HLA alleles from a 7500-year-old human soft tissue sample (Lawlor et al. 1991), and from HLA alleles from ~2000-year-old bone (Francalacci et al. 1992). Congruent results from multiple amplifications of the same sample seem to be the best concrete assurance that jumping PCR has not introduced errors into ancient DNA sequences.

## Conclusion

DNA often persists, to some degree, in a great variety of postmortem specimens, and in other trace biological samples. It is only in the last decade that the tools have been developed to permit access to this vast resource of genetic information, radically transforming forensic science and giving rise to the field of ancient DNA analysis. The extent of DNA preservation is very much dependent on many variables, both biological and physical, both short-term and long-term. As a result, there are no hard and fast rules to indicate whether a particular approach will be successful, and it is also unlikely that the quantity or quality of DNA can be used as a robust indicator of postmortem interval.

DNA fingerprinting by RFLP analysis was the first technique to permit sample individualization with high statistical surety, but the amount and quality of DNA required generally limits the applicability of this approach to a short postmortem interval, although in some cases (especially with dried fluid stains, or other well-preserved samples) typing can be accomplished even after months or years. However, the polymerase chain reaction permits DNA-typing from samples that harbor only tiny amounts of degraded DNA, greatly expanding the range of suitable specimens and acceptable postmortem intervals. Some robust and simple PCR-based typing methods lack the statistical power of traditional DNA fingerprinting, but amplification of STR loci combines great statistical power with the extreme sensitivity of PCR. Therefore, STR analysis is likely to develop as a dominant method in forensic science. Amplification of multicopy elements such as mitochondrial DNA further increases the range of samples that can be analyzed, permitting recovery from samples even millions of years old. However, when extremely sensitive PCR methods are used, contamination with modern DNA becomes a primary technical difficulty that must be addressed with great care.

The limits of DNA preservation and recovery from ancient or degraded samples have not yet been determined. As techniques have developed, the limits have been pushed back ever further. Future work on a greater range of samples will better define the extent of DNA preservation, and further technical developments will surely improve the ease, reliability, and power of testing. It is difficult to predict exactly what high technology developments, singly or together, will provide the next major advances, but there is no doubt that efforts in areas such as automation, miniaturization, and enhanced detection will bring DNA analysis even more to the forefront. Technical advances will also continue to be coupled with increased knowledge of genetic variation and the genetic determination of physical, developmental, and disease traits, further enhancing the power and range of application of DNA analysis.

## Acknowledgments

The authors wish to thank Diane McCauley and Marie Ricciardone for helpful comments on the manuscript.

## References

Adams, D.E., L. A. Presley, A.L. Baumstark, K.W. Hensley, A.L. Hill, S.A. Kim, P.A. Campbell, C.M. McLaughlin, B. Budowle, A.M. Giusti, J.B. Smerick, and F.S. Baechtel
     1991   Deoxyribonucleic Acid (DNA) Analysis by Restriction Fragment Length Polymorphisms of Blood and Other Body Fluid Stains Subjected to Contamination and Environmental Insults. *Journal of Forensic Sciences* 36:1284–1289.

Akane, A., H. Shiono, K. Matsubara, H. Nakamura, M. Hasegawa, and M. Kagawa
     1993   Purification of Forensic Specimens for the Polymerase Chain Reaction (PCR) Analysis. *Journal of Forensic Sciences* 38:691–701.

Anderson, S., A.T. Bankier, B.G. Barrell, M.H.L. de Brujin, A.R. Coulson, J. Drouin, I.C. Eperon, D.P. Nierlich, B.A. Roe, F. Sanger, P.H. Schreier, A.J.H. Smith, R. Staden, and I.G. Young
     1991   Sequence and Organization of the Human Mitochondrial Genome. *Nature* 290:457–465.

Avise, J.C.
     1994   *Molecular Markers, Natural History and Evolution.* Chapman and Hall, New York.

Bar, W., A. Kratzer, M. Machler, and W. Schmid
     1988   Postmortem Stability of DNA. *Forensic Science International* 39:59–70.

Bell, L.S.
     1990   Palaeopathology and Diagensis: An SEM Evaluation of Structural Changes Using Backscattered Electron Imaging. *Journal of Archaeological Science* 17:85–102.

Blake, E., J. Mihalovich, R. Higuchi, P.S. Walsh, and H. Erlich
     1992   Polymerase Chain Reaction (PCR) Amplification and Human Leukocyte Antigen (HLA)-DQalpha Oligonucleotide Typing on Biological Evidence Samples: Casework Experience. *Journal of Forensic Sciences* 37:700–726.

Bogenhagen, D., and D.A. Clayton
  1980  The Number of Mitochondrial Deoxyribonucleic Acid Genomes in Mouse L and HeLa Cells: Quantitative Isolation of Mitochondrial Deoxyribonucleic Acid. *Journal of Biological Chemistry* 249:7991–7995.

Boom, R., C.J.A. Sol, M.M.M. Salimans, C.L. Jansen, P.M.E. Wertheim-van Dillen, and J. van der Noordaa
  1990  Rapid and Simple Method for Purification for Nucleic Acids. *Journal of Clinical Microbiology* 28:495–503.

Brown, K., and T. Brown
  1992  Amount of Human DNA in Old Bones. *Ancient DNA Newsletter* 1:18–19.

Brown, W.M.
  1985  The Mitochondrial Genome of Animals. In *Molecular Evolutionary Genetics*, edited by R.J. MacIntyre, pp. 95–130. Plenum Press, New York.

Brown, W.M., M. George, and A.C. Wilson
  1979  Rapid Evolution of Animal Mitochondrial DNA. *Proceedings of the National Academy of Sciences U.S.A.* 76:1967–1971.

Bruce, K.D., A.M. Osborn, P. Strike, and D.A. Ritchie
  1992  Removal of PCR Inhibitory Substances from DNA. *Ancient DNA Newsletter* 1:12.

Budowle, B., R. Chakrahorty, A.M. Giusti, A.J. Eisenberg, and R.C. Allen
  1991  Analysis of the VNTR Locus D1S80 by the PCR Followed by High-Resolution PAGE. *American Journal of Human Genetics* 48:137–144.

Budowle, B., J.A. Lindsey, J.A. DeCou, B.W. Koons, A.M. Guisti, and C.T. Comey
  1995  Validation and Population Studies of the Loci LDLR, GYPA, HBGG, D7S8, and Gc (PM loci), and HLA-DQalpha Using a Multiplex Amplification and Typing Procedure. *Journal of Forensic Sciences* 40:45–54.

Cann, R.L., W.M. Brown, and A.C. Wilson
  1987  Mitochondrial DNA and Human Evolution. *Nature* 325:31–36.

Cano, R.J. and H.N. Poinar
  1993  Rapid Isolation of DNA from Fossil and Museum Specimens Suitable for PCR. *BioTechniques* 15:432–434.

Cano, R.J., H. Poinar, and G.O. Poinar
  1992  Isolation and Partial Characterization of DNA from the Bee *Proplebeia dominicana* (Apidae: Hymenoptera) in 25–40 Million Year Old Amber. *Medical Science Research* 20:619–623.

Cano, R., H. Poinar, N. Pieniazek, A. Acra, and G. Poinar
  1993  Amplification and Sequencing of DNA from a 120–135 Million Year Old Weevil. *Nature* 363:536–538.

Cavalier-Smith, T.
  1985  *The Evolution of Genome Size.* John Wiley, Chichester, U.K.

Charlesworth, B., P. Sniegowski, and W. Stephan
  1994  The Evolutionary Dynamics of Repetitive DNA in Eukaryotes. *Nature* 371:215–220.

Cherfas, J.
  1991  Ancient DNA: Still Busy after Death. *Science* 253:1354–1356.

Comey, C.T.
  1991  Validation of the HLA DQalpha Locus using the Polymerase Chain Reaction. *Crime Laboratory Digest* 18:129.

Comey, C.T., B. Budowle, D.E. Adams, A.L. Baumstark, J.A. Lindsey, and L.A. Presley
  1993  PCR Amplification and Typing of the HLA DQalpha Gene in Forensic Science. *Journal of Forensic Sciences* 38:239–249.

Comey, C.T., B.W. Koons, K.W. Presley, J.B. Smerick, C.A. Sobieralski, D.M. Stanley, and F.S. Baechtel
  1994  DNA Extraction Strategies for Amplified Length Polymorphism Analysis. *Journal of Forensic Sciences* 39:1254–1269.

Constable, J.J., C. Packer, D.A. Collins, and A.E. Pusey
  1995  Nuclear DNA from Primate Dung. *Nature* 373:393.

Cooper, A.
  1992  Removal of Colourings, Inhibitors of PCR, and the Carrier Effect of PCR Contamination from Ancient DNA Samples. *Ancient DNA Newsletter* 1:31–32.

Cooper, A., C. Mourer-Chauvire, G.K. Chambers, A. von Haeseler, A.C. Wilson, and S. Paabo
  1992  Independent Origins of New Zealand Moas and Kiwis. *Proceedings of the National Academy of Sciences U.S.A.* 89:8741–8744.

Cooper, A., J. Rhymer, H.F. James, S.L. Olson, C.E. McIntosh, M.D. Sorenson, and R.C. Fleischer.
  1996  Ancient DNA and Island Endemics. *Nature* 381: 484.

Corfield, V., S. Vandenplas, H.J. Deacon, and P. Van Helden
  1992  Ancient DNA Genotyping: HLA and CA Repeats by PCR. *Ancient DNA Newsletter* 1:31–34.

DeGusta, D., C. Cook, and G. Sensabaugh
  1994  Dentin as a Source of Ancient DNA. *Ancient DNA Newsletter* 2:13.

De Leeuw, J.W., P.F. Van Bergen, G.K. Van Aarssen, J.P.L.A. Gatellier, J.S. Sinninghe Damste, and M.E. Collinson
  1991  Resistant Biomacromolecules as Major Contributors to Kerogen. *Philosophical Transactions of the Royal Society of London Series B* 333:329–337.

DeSalle, R., J. Gatesy, W. Wheeler, and D. Grimaldi
  1992  DNA Sequences from a Fossil Termite in Oligo-Miocene Amber and their Phylogenetic Implications. *Science* 257:1933–1936.

Di Rienzo, A., A.C. Peterson, J.C. Garza, A.M. Valdes, M. Slatkin, and N.B. Freimer
  1994  Mutational Processes of Simple-Sequence Repeat Loci in Human Populations. *Proceedings of the National Academy of Sciences U.S.A.* 91:3166–3170.

Dickel, C., and W.W. Hauswirth
  1992  A Rapid Method for Clean-up of Ancient DNA. *Ancient DNA Newsletter* 1:9.

DiZinno, J., D. Fisher, S. Barritt, T. Clayton, P. Gill, M. Holland, D. Lee, C. McGuire, J. Raskin, R. Roby, J. Ruderman, and V. Weedn
  In press. The Waco, Texas Incident: The Use of DNA Analysis to Identify Human Remains. *Proceedings of the Fifth International Symposium on Human Identification*, pp. 129–131. Promega Corporation.

Doran, G.H., D.N. Dickel, W.E. Ballinger, O.F. Agee, P.J. Laipis, and W.W. Hauswirth
  1986  Anatomical, Cellular and Molecular Analysis of 8000 year old Human Brain Tissue from the Windover Archaeological Site. *Nature* 323:803–806.

Edwards, A., A. Civitello, H.A. Hammond, and C.T. Caskey
  1991  DNA Typing and Genetic Mapping with Trimeric and Tetrameric Tandem Repeats. *American Journal of Human Genetics* 49:746–756.

Eglington, G., and G.A. Logan
    1991  Molecular Preservation. *Philosophical Transactions of the Royal Society of London Series B* 333:315–328.

Ellingboe, J., and U.B. Gyllensten (editors)
    1992  *The PCR Technique: DNA Sequencing.* Eaton, Natick, MA.

Erlich, H.A. (editor)
    1989  *PCR Technology — Principles and Applications for DNA Amplification.* Stockton Press, New York.

Erlich, H.A.
    1991  The Application of PCR Amplification to Casework Analysis. *Crime Laboratory Digest* 18:127.

Fisher, D.L., M.M. Holland, L. Mitchell, P.S. Sledzik, A. Webb Wilcox, M. Wadhams, and V.W. Weedn
    1993  Extraction, Evaluation, and Amplification of DNA from Decalcified and Undecalcified United States Civil War Bone. *Journal of Forensic Sciences* 38:60–68.

Francalacci, P., M. Romani, S.M. Borgognini-Tarli, and L.L. Cavalli-Sforza
    1992  Chimeric HLA Alleles from Ancient Bones; Evidence of Museum Related Contamination? *Ancient DNA Newsletter* 1:16–17.

Giles, R.E., H. Blanc, H.M. Cann, and D.C. Wallace
    1980  Maternal Inheritance of Human Mitochondrial DNA. *Proceedings of the National Academy of Sciences U.S.A.* 77:6715–6719.

Gill, P., J.E. Lygo, S.J. Fowler, and D.J. Werrett
    1987  An evaluation of DNA Fingerprinting for Forensic Purposes. *Electrophoresis* 8:38–44.

Gill, P., P.L. Ivanov, C. Kimpton, R. Piercy, N. Benson, G. Tully, I. Evett, E. Hagelberg, and K. Sullivan
    1994  Identification of the Remains of the Romanov Family by DNA Analysis. *Nature Genetics* 6:130–135.

Gima, L., G.A. Sims, C. Konzak, J. Super-Mihalovich, and E. Blake
    1991  The Recovery, Amplification and DQ-Alpha Typing of DNA from Partially Cremated Human Remains. In *Abstracts of the 43rd Annual Meeting of the American Academy of Forensic Sciences,* p. 82. American Academy of Forensic Sciences, Colorado Springs, CO.

Ginther, C.L., L. Issel-Tarver, and M.C. King
    1992  Identifying Individuals by Sequencing Mitochondrial DNA from Teeth. *Nature Genetics* 2:135–138.

Goffin, C., S. Bricteux-Gregoire, and W.G. Verly
    1984  Some Properties of the Interstrand Crosslinks in Depurinated DNA. *Biochimica et Biophysica Acta* 783:1–5.

Golenberg, E.M.
    1991  Amplification and Analysis of Miocene Plant Fossil DNA. *Philosophical Transactions of the Royal Society of London Series B* 333:19–427.
    1994a Antediluvian DNA research. *Nature* 367:692.
    1994b DNA from Plant Compression Fossils. In *Ancient DNA,* edited by B. Herrmann and S. Hummel, pp. 237–256. Springer-Verlag, New York.

Golenberg, E., D. Giannasi, M. Clegg, C. Smiley, M. Durbin, D. Henderson, G. Zurawski
    1990  Chloroplast DNA Sequences from Miocene Magnolia Species. *Nature* 344:656–658.

Goloubinoff, P., S. Paabo, and A.C. Wilson
  1993 Evolution of Maize Inferred from Sequence Diversity of an Adh2 Gene Segment from Archaeological Remains. *Proceedings of the National Academy of Sciences U.S.A.* 90:1997–2001.

Goodyear, P.D., S. Maclaughlin-Black, and I.J. Mason
  1994 A Reliable Method for the Removal of Co-purifying PCR Inhibitors from Ancient DNA. *BioTechniques* 16:232–235.

Hackett, C.J.
  1981 Microscopical Focal Destruction (Tunnels) in Exhumed Human Bones. *Medicine, Science and the Law* 21:243–265.

Hagelberg, E.
  1994 Ancient DNA Studies. *Evolutionary Anthropology* 2:199–207.

Hagelberg, E., and J.B. Clegg
  1991 Isolation and Characterization of DNA from Archaelogical Bone. *Proceedings of the Royal Society of London Series B* 244:45–50.
  1993 Genetic Polymorphisms in Prehistoric Pacific Islanders Determined by Amplification of Ancient Bone DNA. *Proceedings of the Royal Society of London Series B* 252:163–170.

Hagelberg, E., B. Sykes, and R. Hedges
  1989 Ancient Bone DNA Amplified. *Nature* 342:485.

Hagelberg, E., L.S. Bell, T. Allen, A. Boyde, S. Jones, and J.B. Clegg
  1991a Analysis of Ancient Bone DNA: Techniques and Applications. *Philosophical Transactions of the Royal Society of London Series B* 333:399–407.

Hagelberg, E., I.C. Gray, and A.J. Jeffreys
  1991b Identification of the Skeletal Remains of a Murder Victim by DNA Analysis. *Nature* 352:427–429.

Hagelberg, E., S. Quevado, D. Turbon, and J.B. Clegg
  1994a DNA from Ancient Easter Islanders. *Nature* 369:25–26.

Hagelberg, E., M.G. Thomas, C.E. Cook, A.V. Sher, G.R. Baryshnikov, and A.M. Lister
  1994b DNA from Ancient Mammoth Bones. *Nature* 370:33–334.

Haglund, W.D., D.T. Reay, and S.L. Tepper
  1990 Identification of Decomposed Human Remains by Deoxyribonucleic Acid (DNA) Profiling. *Journal of Forensic Sciences* 35:724–729.

Hammond, H.A., L. Jin, Y. Zhong, T. Caskey, and R. Chakraborty
  1994 Evaluation of 13 Short Tandem Repeat Loci for Use in Personal Identification Applications. *American Journal of Human Genetics* 55:175–189.

Handt, O., M. Hoss, M. Krings, and S. Paabo
  1994a Ancient DNA: Methodological Challenges. *Experientia* 50:524–529.

Handt, O., M. Richards, M. Trommsdorff, C. Kilger, J. Simanainen, O. Georgiev, K. Bauer, A. Stone, R. Hedges, W. Schaffner, G. Utermann, B. Sykes, and S. Paabo
  1994b Molecular Genetic Analyses of the Tyrolean Ice Man. *Science* 264:1775–1778.

Hanni, C., V. Laudet, M. Sakka, A. Begue, and D. Stehelin
  1990 Amplification of Mitochondrial DNA Fragments from Ancient Human Teeth and Bones. *Comptes Rendus de l'Academie des Sciences Paris* 310:365–370.

Hardy, C., D. Casane, J.D. Vigne, C. Callou, N. Dennebouy, J.C. Mounolou, and M. Monnerot
  1994a Ancient DNA from Bronze Age Bones of European Rabbit (*Oryctolagus cuniculus*). *Experientia* 50:564–570.

Hardy, C., J.D. Vigne, D. Casane, N. Dennebouy, J.C. Mounolou, and M. Monnerot
1994b Origin of European Rabbit (*Oryctolagus cuniculus*) in a Mediterranean Island: Zooarchaeology and Ancient DNA Examination. *Journal of Evolutionary Biology* 7:217–226.

Hardy, C., C. Callou, J.D. Vigne, D. Casane, N. Dennebouy, J.C. Mounolou, and M. Monnerot
1995 Rabbit Mitochondrial DNA Diversity from Prehistoric to Modern Times. *Journal of Molecular Evolution* 40:227–237.

Hauswirth, W.W.
1994 Ancient DNA: An Introduction. *Experientia* 50:521–523.

Hauswirth, W.W., C.D. Dickel, and D.A. Lawlor
1994a DNA Analysis of the Windover Population. In *Ancient DNA*, edited by B. Herrmann and S. Hummel, pp. 104–121. Springer-Verlag, New York.

Hauswirth, W.W., C.D. Dickel, D.J. Rowold, and M.A. Hauswirth
1994b Inter- and Intrapopulation Studies of Ancient Humans. *Experientia* 50:585–591.

Haydon, R., and J. Buikstra
1991 Amplification and Analysis of HLA-DQA1 and D4S175 in Ancient Peruvian Mummies. *American Journal of Human Genetics* Supplement:460.

Healy, R.A., A.D. Colon, and L. Kobilinsky
1990 RFLP Analysis on DNA Isolated from Severely Compromised Postmortem Tissues: Comparison of Hae III and PST I Digests. Paper presented at the 1990 Meeting of the Northeastern Association of Forensic Scientists, Providence, RI.

Herrin, G., N. Fildes, and R. Reynolds
1994 Evaluation of the AmpliType® PM DNA Test System on Forensic Case Samples. *Journal of Forensic Sciences* 5:1247–1253.

Herrmann, B., and S. Hummel
1994 Introduction. In *Ancient DNA*, edited by B. Herrmann and S. Hummel, pp. 1–12. Springer-Verlag, New York.

Higuchi, R., B. Bowman, M. Freiberger, O.A. Ryder, and A.C. Wilson
1984 DNA Sequence from the Quagga, an Extinct Member of the Horse Family. *Nature* 312:282–284.

Higuchi, R., C.H. von Beroldingen, G.F. Sensabaugh, and H.A. Erlich
1988 DNA Typing from Single Hairs. *Nature* 332:543–546.

Higuchi, R.G., L.A. Wrischnik, E. Oakes, M. George, B. Tong, and A.C. Wilson
1987 Mitochondrial DNA of the Extinct Quagga: Relatedness and Extent of Postmortem Changes. *Journal of Molecular Evolution* 25:283–287.

Hochmeister, M.N., B. Budowle, U.V. Borer, U. Eggmann, C.T. Comey, and R. Dirnhofer
1991a Typing of Deoxyribonucleic Acid (DNA) Extracted from Compact Bone from Human Remains. *Journal of Forensic Sciences* 36:1649–1661.

Hochmeister, M.N., B. Budowle, J. Jung, U.V. Borer, C.T. Comey, and R. Dirnhofer
1991b PCR-based Typing of DNA Extracted from Cigarette Butts. *International Journal of Legal Medicine* 104:229–233.

Hochmeister, M., U. Eggmann, U. Borer, and B. Budowle
1991c Extraction and Typing of DNA from Compact Bone — A Tool for the Identification of Decomposed Bodies and Human Remains. In *Abstracts of the 43rd Annual Meeting of the American Academy of Forensic Sciences*, p. 82. American Academy of Forensic Sciences, Colorado Springs, CO.

Holland, M.M., D.L. Fisher, L.G. Mitchell, W.C. Rodriquez, J.J. Canik, C.R. Merril, and V.W. Weedn
    1992   Mitochondrial DNA Sequence Analysis of Human Skeletal Remains: Identification of Remains from the Vietnam War. *Journal of Forensic Sciences* 38:542–553.

Holland, M.M., R.K. Roby, D.L. Fisher, J. Ruderman, D.A. Lee, C.K. Bryson, T. Kuperschmid, R.S. Lofts, and A.J. Eisenberg
    1994   Identification of Human Remains Using Mitochondrial DNA Sequencing: Potential Mother-Child Mutational Events. In *Advances in Forensic Haemogenetics,* 5, edited by W. Bar and U. Rossi, pp. 399–406. Springer-Verlag, Berlin.

Holland, M.M., R. Roy, M.D. Fraser, and R.H. Liu
    1993   Application of Serological and DNA Methods for the Identification of Urine Specimen Donors. *Forensic Science Review* 5:1–14.

Horai, S., K. Hayasaka, K. Murayama, N. Wate, H. Koike, and N. Nakai
    1989   DNA Amplification from Ancient Human Skeletal Remains and their Sequence Analysis. *Proceedings of the Japan Academy Series B* 65:229–233.

Horai, S., R. Kondo, K. Murayama, S. Hayashi, H. Koike, and N. Nakaj
    1991   Phylogenetic Affiliation of Ancient and Contemporary Humans Inferred from Mitochondrial DNA. *Philosophical Transactions of the Royal Society of London Series B* 333:409–417.

Horn, G.T., B. Richards, and K.W. Klinger
    1989   Amplification of a Highly Polymorphic VNTR Segment by the Polymerase Chain Reaction. *Nucleic Acids Research* 17:2140.

Hoss, M., M. Kohn, S. Paabo, F. Knauer, and W. Schroder
    1992   Excrement Analysis by PCR. *Nature* 359:199.

Hoss, M., and S. Paabo
    1993   DNA Extraction from Pleistocene Bones by a Silica-Based Purification Method. *Nucleic Acids Research* 21:3913–3914.

Hoss, M., S., Paabo, and N.K. Vereshchagin
    1994   Mammoth DNA Sequences. *Nature* 370:333.

Hummel, S., and B. Herrmann
    1991   Y-Chromosome-Specific DNA Amplified in Ancient Human Bone. *Naturwissenschaften* 78:266–267.
    1994   General Aspects of Sample Preparation. In *Ancient DNA*, edited by B. Herrmann and S. Hummel, pp. 59–68. Springer-Verlag, New York.

Hunt, D.M., K.S. Dulai, J.K. Bowmaker, and J.D. Mollon
    1995   The Chemistry of John Dalton's Color Blindness. *Science* 267:984–988.

Imlay, J.A., and S. Linn
    1988   DNA Damage and Oxygen Radical Toxicity. *Science* 240:1302–1309.

Ivanov, P.L., M.J. Wadhams, R.K. Roby, M.M. Holland, V.W. Weedn, and T.J. Parsons.
    1996   Mitochondrial DNA Sequence Heteroplasma in the Grand Duke of Russia Georgij Romanov Establishes the Identity of the Remains of Tsar Nicholas II. *Nature Genetics.* 12: 417–420.

Jackson, D.P., J.D. Hayden, and P. Quirke
    1991   Extraction of Nucleic Acid from Fresh and Archival Material. In *PCR, A Practical Approach*, edited by M.J. McPherson, P. Quirke, and G. R. Taylor, pp. 29–49. Oxford University Press, New York.

Janczewski, D.N., N. Yuhki, D.A. Gilbert, G.T. Jefferson, and S.J. O'Brien
 1992 Molecular Phylogenetic Inference from Saber-Toothed Cat Fossils of Rancho La Brea. *Proceedings of the National Academy of Sciences U.S.A.* 89:9769–9773.

Jeffreys, A.J.
 1993 DNA Typing: Approaches and Applications. *Journal of the Forensic Science Society* 33:203–217.

Jeffreys, A.J., M. Allen, E. Hagelberg, and A. Sonnberg
 1992 Identification of the Skeletal Remains of Josef Mengele by DNA Analysis. *Forensic Science International* 56:65–76.

Jeffreys, A.J., N.J. Royle, V. Wilson, and Z. Wong
 1988 Spontaneous Mutation Rates to New Length Alleles at Tandem Repetitive Hypervariable Loci in Human DNA. *Nature* 332:278–281.

Jeffreys, A.J., K. Tamaki, A. MacLeod, D.G. Monckton, D.L. Neil, and J.A.L. Armour
 1994 Complex Gene Conversion Events in Germline Mutation at Human Minisatellites. *Nature Genetics* 6:136–145.

Jeffreys, A.J., V. Wilson, and S.L. Thein
 1985 Hypervariable "Minisatellite" Regions in Human DNA. *Nature* 314:67–73.

John, B., and G.L.G. Miklos
 1988 *The Eukaryote Genome in Development and Evolution.* Allen and Unwin, London.

Kanter, E., M. Baird, R. Shaler, and I. Balazs
 1986 Analysis of Restriction Fragment Length Polymorphisms in Deoxyribonucleic Acid (DNA) Recovered from Dried Bloodstains. *Journal of Forensic Sciences* 31:403–408.

Kimpton, C.P., D. Fisher, S. Watson, M. Adams, A. Urquhart, J. Lygo, and P. Gill
 1994 Evaluation of an Automated DNA Profiling System Employing Multiplex Amplification of Four Tetrameric STR Loci. *International Journal of Legal Medicine* 106:302–311.

Kimura, M.
 1983 *The Neutral Theory of Molecular Evolution.* Cambridge University Press, New York.

Kirby, L.T.
 1990 *DNA Fingerprinting.* Stockton Press, New York.

Koblinsky, L.
 1992 Recovery and Stability of DNA in Samples of Forensic Significance. *Forensic Science Review* 4:68–87.

Kolman, C., N. Tuross, R. Cooke, and E. Bermingham
 1994 Molecular Genetics of Contemporary and Ancient Amerind Populations in Panama. *Ancient DNA Newsletter* 2:17–18.

Krajewski, C., A.C. Driskell, P.R. Baverstock, and M.J. Braun
 1992 Phylogenetic Relationships of the Thylacine (Mammalia, Thylacinidae) among Dasyuroid Marsupials — Evidence from Cytochrome b DNA Sequences. *Proceedings of the Royal Society of London Series B* 250:19–27.

Laber, T.L., S.A. Giese, J.T. Iverson, and J.A. Liberty
 1994 Validation Studies on the Forensic Analysis of Restriction Fragment Length Polymorphism (RFLP) on LE Agarose Gels without Ethidium Bromide: Effects of Contaminants, Sunlight, and the Electrophoresis of Varying Quantities of Deoxyribonucleic Acid (DNA). *Journal of Forensic Sciences* 39:707–730.

Lawlor, D.A., C.D. Dickel, W.W. Hauswirth, and P. Parham
 1991 Ancient HLA Genes from 7,500 Year Old Archaeological Remains. *Nature* 349:785–788.

Lawton, M.E., P. Stringer, and M. Churton
  1989 DNA Profiles from Dental Pulp. *Proceedings of the International Symposium on the Forensic Aspects of DNA Analysis.* FBI Forensic Science Research and Training Center, Quantico, VA.

Lee, H.C., R.E. Gaensslen, P.D. Bigbee, and J.J. Kearney
  1991a Guidelines for the Collection and Preservation of DNA Evidence. *Journal of Forensic Identification* 41:344–356.

Lee, H.C., E.M. Pagliaro, K.M. Berka, N.L. Folk, D.T. Anderson, G. Ruano, T.P. Keith, P. Phipps, G.L. Herrin, D.D. Garner, and R.E. Gaensslen
  1991b Genetic Markers in Human Bone: I. Deoxyribonucleic Acid (DNA) Analysis. *Journal of Forensic Sciences* 36:320–330.

Lindahl, T., and A. Andersson
  1972 Rate of Chain Breakage at Apurinic Sites in Double-Stranded Deoxyribonucleic Acid. *Biochemistry* 11:3618–3622.

Lindahl, T., and B. Nyberg
  1972 Rate of Depurination of Native Deoxyribonucleic Acid. *Biochemistry* 11:3610–3618.

Lindahl, T.
  1993a Instability and Decay of the Primary Structure of DNA. *Nature* 362:709–715.
  1993b Recovery of Antediluvian DNA. *Nature* 365:700.

Ludes, B., P. Kintz, and P. Mangin
  1991 Evaluation of Postmortem DNA Stability by Single Locus Probes. In *Abstracts of the 43rd Annual Meeting of the American Academy of Forensics Sciences*, p. 70. American Academy of Forensic Sciences, Colorado Springs, CO.

Ludwig, E.H., W. Friedl, and B.J. McCarthy
  1989 High-resolution Analysis of a Hypervariable Region in the Human Apolipoprotein B Gene. *American Journal of Human Genetics* 45:458–464.

Martin, R.B., and D.B. Burr
  1989 *Structure, Function and Adaption of Compact Bone.* Raven Press, New York.

McNally, L., R.C. Shaler, M. Baird, I. Balazs, P. De Forest, D. Crim, and L. Kobilinsky
  1989a Evaluation of Deoxyribonucleic Acid (DNA) Isolated from Human Bloodstains Exposed to Ultraviolet Light, Heat, Humidity, and Soil Contamination. *Journal of Forensic Sciences* 34:1059–1069.

McNally, L., R.C. Shaler, M. Baird, I. Balaza, L. Kobilinsky, and P. De Forest
  1989b The Effects of Environment and Substrata on Deoxyribonucleic Acid (DNA): The Use of Casework Samples from New York City. *Journal of Forensic Sciences* 34:1070–1077.

McPherson, M.J., P. Quirke, and G.R. Taylor (editors)
  1991 *PCR, A Practical Approach.* Oxford University Press, New York.

Merriwether, D.A., F. Rothhammer, and R.E. Ferrell
  1994 Genetic Variation in the New World: Ancient Teeth, Bone, and Tissue as Sources of DNA. *Experientia* 50:592–601.

Morell, V.
  1992 30-Million Year Old DNA Boosts an Emerging Field. *Science* 257:1860–1862.
  1995 Getting the Poop on Baboon DNA. *Science* 267:615–616.

Morin, P.A., J.J. Moore, and D.S. Woodruff
  1992 Identification of Chimpanzee Subspecies with DNA from Hair and Allele Specific Probes. *Proceedings of the Royal Society of London Series B* 249:293–297.

Nakamura, Y., M. Leppert, P. O'Connell, R. Wolff, T. Holm, M. Culver, C. Martin, E. Fujimoto, M. Hoff, E. Kumlin, and R. White
1987  Variable Number of Tandem Repeat (VNTR) Markers for Human Gene Mapping. *Science* 235:1616–1622.

Nielsen, H., J. Engberg, and I. Thuesen
1994  DNA from Arctic Human Burials. In *Ancient DNA*, edited by B. Herrmann and S. Hummel, pp. 122–140. Springer-Verlag, New York.

Ogata, M., R. Mattern, P.M. Schneider, U. Schacker, T. Kaufmann, and C. Rittner
1990  Quantitative and Qualitative Analysis of DNA Extracted from Postmortem Muscle Tissues. *Zeitschrift für Rechtsmedizin* 103:397.

Paabo, S.
1985  Molecular Cloning of Ancient Egyptian Mummy DNA. *Nature* 314:644–645.
1989  Ancient DNA: Extraction, Characterization, Molecular Cloning, and Enzymatic Amplification. *Proceedings of the National Academy of Sciences U.S.A.* 86:1939–1943.

Paabo, S., J.A. Gifford, and A.C. Wilson
1988  Mitochondrial DNA Sequence from a 7000-Year Old Brain. *Nucleic Acids Research* 16:9775–9787.

Paabo, S., R.G. Higuchi, and A.C. Wilson
1989  Ancient DNA and the Polymerase Chain Reaction. *Journal of Biological Chemistry* 264:9709–9712.

Paabo, S., D.M. Irwin, and A.C. Wilson
1990  DNA Damage Promotes Jumping between Templates during Enzymatic Amplification. *Journal of Biological Chemistry* 265:4718–4721.

Perry, W.L., W.M. Bass, W.S. Riggsby, and K. Sirotkin
1988  The Autodegradation of Deoxyribonucleic Acid (DNA) in Human Rib Bone and Its Relationship to the Time Interval Since Death. *Journal of Forensic Sciences* 33:144–153.

Persson, P.
1992  A Method to Recover DNA from Ancient Bones. *Ancient DNA Newsletter* 1:25–27.

Poinar, G.O.
1993  Recovery of Antediluvian DNA: Reply to Lindahl. *Nature* 365:700.

Poinar, H.
1994  Glass Milk, a Method for Extracting DNA from Fossil Material. *Ancient DNA Newsletter* 2:12–13.

Poinar, H.N., R.J. Cano, and G.N. Poinar
1993  DNA from an Extinct Plant. *Nature* 363:677.

Purdue, J.R., and J.C. Patton
1992  Extraction and Analysis of DNA from White-tailed Deer Bones Recovered from Archaeological Sites in South Carolina, Illinois and Missouri. *Ancient DNA Newsletter* 1:28–30.

Radzicka, A., and R. Wolfenden
1995  A Proficient Enzyme. *Science* 267:90–93.

Robin, E.D., and R. Wong
1988  Mitochondrial DNA Molecules and Virtual Number of Mitochondria Per Cell in Mammalian Cells. *Journal of Cellular Physiology* 136:507–513.

Romanowski, G., M.G. Lorentz, and W. Wackernagel
1991  Adsorption of Plasmid DNA to Mineral Surfaces and Protection against DNase I. *Applied and Environmental Microbiology* 57:1057–1061.

Roy, M.S., D.J. Girman, A.C. Taylor, and R.K.Wayne
    1994  The Use of Museum Specimens to Reconstruct the Genetic Variability and Relation-
    ships of Extinct Populations. *Experientia* 50:551–557.

Saiki, R.K., D.H. Gelfand, S. Stoeffel, S.J. Scharf, R. Higuchi, G.T. Horn, K.B. Mullis, and H.A.
Erlich
    1988  Primer-Directed Enzymatic Amplification of DNA with a Thermostable DNA Poly-
    merase. *Science* 239:487–491.

Saiki, R.K., P.S. Walsh, C.H. Levensen, and H.A. Erlich
    1989  Genetic Analysis of Amplified DNA with Immobilized Sequence Specfic Oligonu-
    cleotide Probes. *Proceedings of the National Academy of Sciences U.S.A.* 86:6230–6234.

Sajantila, A., A. Stroem, B. Budowle, B. Karhunen, and L. Peltonen
    1991  The Polymerase Chain Reaction and Postmortem Forensic Identity Testing: Appli-
    cation of Amplified D1S80 and HLA-DQalpha Loci to the Identification of Fire Victims.
    *Forensic Sciences International* 51:23–24.

Salvo, J.J., M.J. Allison, and P.K. Rogan
    1989  Molecular Genetics of Pre-Columbian South American Mummies. *American Journal
    of Physical Anthropology* 78:295.

Sambrook, J., E.F. Fritsch, and T. Maniatis
    1989  *Molecular Cloning: A Laboratory Manual,* 2nd ed. Cold Spring Harbor Laboratory
    Press, New York.

Schwartz, T.R., E.A. Schwartz, L. Mieszerski, L. McNally, and L. Kobilinsky
    1991  Characterization of Deoxyribonucleic Acid (DNA) Obtained from Teeth Subjected
    to Various Environmental Conditions. *Journal of Forensic Sciences* 36:979–990.

Singer, M.F.
    1982  Highly Repeated Sequences in Mammalian Genomes. *International Review of Cytol-
    ogy* 76:67–112.

Smith, B.C., D.L. Fisher, V.W. Weedn, G.R. Warnock, and M.M. Holland
    1993  A Systematic Approach to the Sampling of Dental DNA. *Journal of Forensic Sciences*
    38:1194–1209.

Smith, L.M., J.Z. Sanders, R.J. Kaiser, P. Highes, C. Dodd, C.R. Connell, C. Heiner, S.B.H.
Kent, and L.E. Hood
    1986  Fluorescence Detection in Automated DNA Sequence Analysis. *Nature* 321:674–679.

Soltis, P.S., D.E. Soltis, and C.J. Smiley
    1992  An rbcL Sequence from a Miocene Taxodium (Bald Cypress). *Proceedings of the
    National Academy of Sciences U.S.A.* 89:449–451.

Stemmer, W.P.C.
    1991  A 20-Minute Ethidium Bromide/High-Salt Extraction Protocol for Plasmid DNA.
    *BioTechniques* 10:726.

Stone, A., and M. Stoneking
    1993  Ancient DNA from a Pre-Columbian Amerindian Population. *American Journal of
    Physical Anthropology* 92:463–471.

Stoneking, M., D. Hedgecock, R.G. Higuchi, L. Vigilant, and H.A. Erlich
    1991  Population Variation of Human MtDNA Control Region Sequences Detected by
    Enzymatic Amplification and Sequence-Specific Oligonucleotide Probes. *American Jour-
    nal of Human Genetics* 48:370–382.

Sullivan, K.M., A. Mannucci, C.P. Kimpton, and P. Gill
    1993  A Rapid and Quantitative DNA Sex Test: Flourescence-Based PCR Analysis of X-Y
    Homologous Gene Amelogenin. *BioTechniques* 15:636–641.

Swarner, S., R. Reynolds, and G.F. Sensabough
1989   A Comparative Study of DNA Extracted from Seven Postmortem Tissues. *Proceedings of the International Symposium on the Forensic Aspects of DNA Analysis*, p. 261. FBI Forensic Science Research and Training Center, Quantico, VA.

Sweet, D.J., and C.H. Sweet
1995   DNA Analysis of Dental Pulp to Link Incinerated Remains of Homicide Victim to Crime Scene. *Journal of Forensic Sciences* 40:310–314.

Taberlet, P., and J. Bouvet
1992   Bear Conservation Genetics. *Nature* 358:197.

Thomas, K., and S. Paabo
1993   DNA Sequences from Old Tissue Remains. *Methods in Enzymology* 224:406–419.

Thomas, R.H., W. Schaffner, A.C. Wilson, and S. Paabo
1989   DNA Phylogeny of the Extinct Marsupial Wolf. *Nature* 340:465–467.

Thomas, W.K., S. Paabo, F.X. Villablanca, and A.C. Wilson
1990   Spatial and Temporal Continuity of Kangaroo Rat Populations Shown by Sequencing Mitochondrial DNA from Museum Specimens. *Journal of Molecular Evolution* 31:101–112.

Tully, G., K.M. Sullivan, and P. Gill
1993   Analysis of 6 VNTR Loci by Multiplex PCR and Automated Fluorescent Detection. *Human Genetics* 92:554–562.

Turbon, D., A. Lalueza, A. Perez-Perez, E. Prats, P. Moreno, and P. Pons
1994   Absence of 9 bp MtDNA Region V Deletion in Ancient Remains of Aborigines from Tierra del Fuego. *Ancient DNA Newsletter* 2:24–26.

Tuross, N.
1994   The Biochemistry of Ancient DNA in Bone. *Experientia* 50:530–535.

Urqhhart, A., C.P. Kimpton, T.J. Downes, and P. Gill
1994   Variation in Short Tandem Repeat Sequences: A Survey of Twelve Microsatellite Loci for Use as Forensic Identification Markers. *International Journal of Legal Medicine* 107:14–20.

Urquhart, A., N.J. Oldroyd, C.P. Kimpton, and P. Gill
1995   Highly Discriminating Heptaplex Short Tandem Repeat PCR System for Forensic Identification. *BioTechniques* 18:116–121.

Van der Kuyl, A.C., J. Dekker, M.A.M. Attia, N. Iskander, W.R.K. Perizonius, and J. Goudsmit
1994   DNA from Ancient Egyptian Monkey Bones. *Ancient DNA Newsletter* 2:19–21.

Vigilant, L., M. Stoneking, H. Harpending, K. Hawkes, and A.C. Wilson
1991   African Populations and the Evolution of Human Mitochondrial DNA. *Science* 252:1503–1507.

von Beroldingen, C.H., E.T. Blake, R. Higuchi, G.F. Sensabaugh, and H.A. Erlich
1989a Applications of PCR to the Analysis of Biological Evidence. In *PCR Technology: Principles and Applications for DNA Amplification,* edited by H. Erlich. Stockton Press, New York.

von Beroldingen, C.H., R.K. Roby, G.F. Sensabaugh, and S.Walsh
1989b DNA in Hair. Proceedings of the International Symposium on the Forensic Aspects of DNA Analysis, p. 265. FBI Forensic Science and Training Center, Quantico, VA.

Wadhams, M.J., J. Kriss, and R.W. Cotton
1994   Success of RFLP and PCR Methods Using Samples from Military Casualties. In *Abstracts of the 46th Annual Meeting of the American Academy of Forensic Sciences.* American Academy of Forensic Sciences, Colorado Springs, CO.

Walsh, P.S., D.A. Metzger, and R. Higuchi
1991 Chelex 100 as a Medium for Simple Extraction of DNA for PCR-based Typing from Forensic Material. *BioTechniques* 10:506–513.

Weissenbach, J.
1993 Microsatellite Polymorphisms and the Genetic Linkage Map of the Human Genome. *Current Opinions in Genetics and Development* 3:414–417.

Whitaker, J.P., T.M. Clayton, A.J. Urqhart, E.S. Millican, T.J. Downes, C.P. Kimpton, and P. Gill
1995 Short Tandem Repeat Typing of Bodies from a Mass Disaster: High Success Rate and Characteristic Amplification Patterns in Highly Degraded Samples. *BioTechniques* 18:670–677.

Wilson, M.R., D. Polanskey, J. Butler, J.A. DiZinno, J. Replogle, and B. Budowle
1995 Extraction, PCR Amplification and Sequencing of Mitochondrial DNA from Human Hair Shafts. *BioTechniques* 18:662–669.

Wilson, M.R., M. Stoneking, M.M. Holland, J.A. DiZinno, and B. Budowle
1993 Guidelines for the Use of Mitochondrial DNA Sequencing in Forensic Science. *Crime Laboratory Digest* 29:68–77.

Woodward, S.R., M.J. King, N.M. Chiu, M.J. Kuchar, and C.W. Griggs
1994a Amplification of Ancient Nuclear DNA from Teeth and Soft Tissues. *PCR Methods and Applications* 3:244–247.

Woodward, S.R., N.J. Weyand, and M. Bunnell
1994b DNA Sequence from Cretaceous Period Bone Fragments. *Science* 266:1229–1232.

Yokoi, T., Y. Aoki, and K. Sagisaka
1989 Human Identification and Sex Determination of Dental Pulp, Bone Marrow and Blood Stains with a Recombinant DNA Probe. *Zeitschrift für Rechtsmedizin* 102:323–330.

Yokoi, T., and K. Sagisaka
1990 Haptoglobin Typing of Human Bloodstains Using a Specific DNA Probe. *Forensic Science International* 45:39–46.

Zischler, H., M. Höss, O. Handt, A. von Haeseler, A.C. van der Kuyl, J. Goudsmit, and S. Pääbo.
1995 Detecting Dinosaur DNA. *Science* 268: 1192–1193.

# The Process of Decomposition: A Model from the Arizona-Sonoran Desert

8

ALISON GALLOWAY

## Introduction

Each ecological area produces specific variations on the general or "typical" pattern of decomposition. Scientific analyses on the decay of human remains, therefore, must take into account local climatic conditions. Similarly, assessment of individual forensic cases must include weighting of the specific microenvironmental factors applicable to each particular case. Traditionally, investigators have relied upon their own experience in developing a method of translating the stage of decomposition into a rough estimate of interval since death. This ability requires exposure to a large number of cases before such a perspective is gained — an impractical and time-consuming process. Observers also bring with them biases in how they remember and perceive the importance of specific variables. An alternative is a retrospective study as explored in this paper.

The arid regions of the Arizona-Sonoran desert provide an example of how decomposition can vary with environmental factors. Here, large areas with low density habitation and a location along the international border and transcontinental highways result in bodies being deposited and remaining undiscovered for long periods of time. Rapid initial decay is induced by high temperatures but low humidity can produce indefinite preservation of some tissues.

In addition to the changes rendered by autolysis and bacterial activity, many studies have linked decay rates to insect activity and used the development of these organisms to assess both interval since death and seasonality in decomposition (Easton and Smith 1970; Motter 1898; Nuorteva 1977; Rodriguez and Bass 1983). The consumption patterns of nonhuman animals also have been observed to alter decay rates and the decomposition sequence (Bornemissza 1957; Burger 1965; Haglund 1991; Lane 1975; Payne 1965; Reed 1958; Shean et al. 1993). In the Southwest, both insects and vertebrate scavengers also affect the pattern of decomposition.

The influences of climatic patterns and other environmental factors were investigated in a retrospective study (Galloway et al. 1989). Autopsy and forensic anthropological reports from the southern portion of Arizona were reviewed to provide guidelines for estimating period since death, based on decay stages in closed structures, burials, and in the open. This study provides a model for producing a quantitative assessment of decay patterns on human remains which is tailored to the immediate environmental conditions.

## Materials and Methods

The Arizona-Sonoran desert is one of the four major North American deserts, an extensive area covering much of the northern Mexican state of Sonora as well as southern Arizona and portions of California. Although elevations range up to about 3000 feet on the more level areas, these are interspersed by rugged mountains. The vegetation is adapted to the arid conditions, predominated by cactus and creosote. Tall columnar cacti (saguaro, organpipe, etc.) are the most recognizable feature of this biosphere.

Southern Arizona enjoys hot, arid summers with mild winters (Sellers et al. 1985). Average high temperatures for the Tucson area regularly exceed 100°F during the months of June and July, while the winter highs, during December and January, are in the mid-60's. Low temperatures average about 30°F below the highs throughout the year. Summer nighttime temperatures remain high while, in the winter, night temperatures fall rapidly, often close to freezing. Humidity averages about 30%, but dips to 17 to 18% in the early summer. Precipitation is heaviest in the late summer "monsoon" season (July and August), when about 2 in. of rain falls per month. This rainfall is extremely heavy but of very limited duration. Flooding often occurs in the summer but, while the waters may rise very rapidly within the washes, they recede within 1 to 3 days. Winter rainfall is more gentle and peaks at under 1 in. per month. Total annual precipitation averages 9 to 11 inches. Consequently, large bodies of water are not plentiful except along the Colorado River.

The Human Identification Laboratory of the Arizona State Museum, University of Arizona, under the leadership of Dr. Walter Birkby, has acted as consultant for the Office of the Medical Examiner (OME), Pima County, Arizona for over 25 years. The OME serves many of the counties of southern Arizona. The anthropology laboratory has been responsible for forensic consultations and for a major training and research effort in forensic anthropology in this area. At the request of the OME, the anthropological team has examined many remains which have been recovered in various stages of decay. Their assistance has been requested for identification purposes, as well as assessment of trauma, pathology, and establishment of a biological profile.

In this study, 468 cases were selected from the Human Identification Laboratory records which potentially could yield information on the rate of decay. All these cases were under the jurisdiction of the Forensic Science Section, Arizona Health Sciences Center, University of Arizona which administered the Office of the Medical Examiner. Autopsies were performed by the OME in all cases.

## Photographic and Documentary References

Once selected, these cases were traced through OME and Human Identification Laboratory records for information on the duration of the postmortem interval, the circumstances of recovery, condition of the body, and the results of the investigation into the cause and manner of death. Photographic slides are taken of almost all cases at the time of examination by the anthropological team. These include basic identification views as well as documentation of lesions, clothing, trace evidence, and identifying marks. In some instances, these are supplemented by photographs made at the scene by law enforcement personnel. When more than one set of photographs is available, those taken closest to the time of discovery of the remains are used. Information on stage of decay could be assessed from photographs in only 245 cases. Photographs often do not provide information on the extent of internal maggot and other insect activity.

## Classification of Decay Stages

The remains are classified into five major categories: (1) fresh, (2) early decomposition, (3) advanced decomposition, (4) skeletonization, and (5) decomposition of skeletal material (see Table 1). The first four of these categories are roughly equivalent to those outlined by Rodriguez and Bass (1983). Within each of these classifications, secondary categories, which do not imply a sequence of events, are established, representing the overall condition of the remains. It is these latter categories which allow the more tailored assessments necessary to investigate local conditions.

**Table 1  Categories and Stages of Decomposition**

A. Fresh
   1. Fresh, no discoloration or insect activity
   2. Fresh burned
B. Early Decomposition
   1. Pink-white appearance with skin slippage and some hair loss
   2. Gray to green discoloration, some flesh relatively fresh
   3. Discoloration to brownish shades particularly at fingers, nose, and ears; some flesh still relatively fresh
   4. Bloating with green discoloration
   5. Post bloating following rupture of the abdominal gases with discoloration going from green to dark
   6. Brown to black discoloration of arms and legs, skin having leathery appearance
C. Advanced Decomposition
   1. Decomposition of tissues producing sagging of the flesh, caving in of the abdominal cavity, often accompanied by extensive maggot activity
   2. Moist decomposition in which there is bone exposure
   3. Mummification with some retention of internal structures
   4. Mummification of outer tissues only with internal organs lost through autolysis or insect activity
   5. Mummification with bone exposure of less than one half the skeleton
   6. Adipocere development
D. Skeletonization
   1. Bones with greasy substances and decomposed tissue, sometimes with body fluids still present
   2. Bones with desiccated tissue or mummified tissue covering less than one half the skeleton
   3. Bones largely dry but still retaining some grease
   4. Dry bone
E. Extreme Decomposition
   1. Skeletonization with bleaching
   2. Skeletonization with exfoliation
   3. Skeletonization with metaphyseal loss with long bones and cancellous exposure of the vertebrae

In addition to this decay classification, presence/absence data were collected, when possible, of (1) lividity (differential distribution of blood), (2) marbling, (3) skin slippage, (4) maggot activity, (5) dermestid and other beetle activity, (6) carnivore activity on flesh or bones, and (7) mold on remains or on clothing.

## Biological and Locational Information

Data on sex, age, and ancestral affinity of the individual were collected from police reports, autopsy assessment, or determination from the anthropological examination. Information on ancestry represents a mixture of sources and its relationship to the social classification of the individuals is unknown.

The latitude and longitude of the location of the remains are recorded to the nearest 15′ (U.S. Department of the Interior 1981). Elevation is taken to the nearest 500 feet. Whether the body was fully clothed or covered by other wrappings, partially clothed, or unclothed is also recorded. The location of the remains is classed as being (1) within a closed structure, (2) in water, (3) buried (including official cemetery burials with or without embalming), and (4) outside. The final category is subdivided, when possible, into whether the body was in the shade or in the sun.

## Interval Since Death

There were 189 cases in the final sample for which postmortem interval could be established. This set consisted of those cases for which documentation of dates that the person was "last seen alive" and the body was recovered were available, as well as the photographic records. For this study, the length of exposure was calculated as the difference between the date the individual was last seen alive and the date the remains were recovered. Overestimation of exposure was probable in many cases, as periods of time may have elapsed between the last known sighting of the person alive and the time of his or her death. In most, but not all cases, these dates were only determined through the establishment of positive or strong circumstantial identification of the remains. Since comparative records were less likely to be available as time since death increased and since other circumstantial evidence is often lost during this time, identification becomes more difficult and the number of useful cases in the upper ranges of decay is scarce.

Because of the retrospective nature of this study, certain errors and inaccuracies must be acknowledged. Since the initial autopsy and anthropological reports were not written with this study in mind, data are frequently missing.

## Results

Of the initial 468 cases selected for examination, 71% were of males, 28% of females, and 1% were unidentified as to sex. While the age range reached from infants to over 90 years old, mean ages were 33 years for women and 41 years for men. Most were of primarily European extraction (64%), while the remainder were mostly of Asian descent (18%), often Native American, or displayed a mixture of European and Asian traits (11%). Only 3% were of African ancestry.

Location for the discovery of the remains was outside in about 56% (N = 162) of the 292 cases for which it was recorded. 10% (N = 30) were buried and 27% (N = 79) were in closed structures. Approximately 7% (N = 21) were found in water. Clothing was noted in 266 cases of which 59% (N = 167) were found fully clothed, 19% (N = 53) partially clothed, and 16% (N = 46) unclothed.

The sex ratio of the 245 cases for which photographs were available significantly changes through the decomposition stages (Figure 1). Relatively fewer females (17%) are found during early decomposition, while a higher than expected number are recovered as skeletons (42%). While "racial" distributions fluctuate by stage of decay, no pronounced differences are visible.

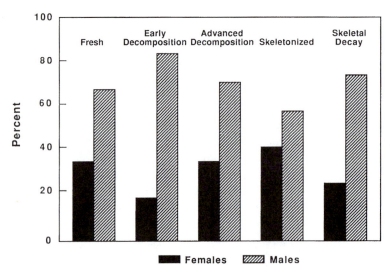

**Figure 1**   Distribution of the sex of individuals by decay stages (N = 245) (significant deviation at <0.005).

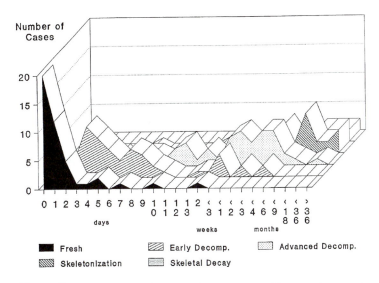

**Figure 2**   Distribution of remains by category and by time (N = 189).

Of the 189 cases for which the time between death and recovery could be reconstructed, 23% (N = 44) were classified as fresh, 28% (N = 52) in early decomposition, 28% (N = 53) in advanced decomposition, 15% (N = 29) skeletonized, and 6% (N = 11) in the final stages of decomposition (Figure 2). 31% of the remains (N = 58) were located within closed structures and 51% (N = 96) were found outdoors. In the latter category, 21 had been found in shaded areas such as in culverts, under wooded or bushy areas or under rock overhangs. Six cases were reportedly found in open sunny areas. This distinction could not be made in the majority of the open air cases. Of the remaining cases, 4% (N = 7) were found in water and 11% (N = 21) were buried. Of the latter group, three had been embalmed.

## Fresh Remains

Remains classified as fresh are usually found from the day of death through the seventh day following death. Remains retain a relatively fresh appearance beyond the day of death primarily during the cooler winter months (November to March). Lividity appears in about half of the cases autopsied on the day of death or the day immediately following. By the second day after death, lividity is found in all instances. No insect activity could be detected from the photographs, although deposits of eggs in the nose, eyes, mouth, and ears, and in the genital area, if exposed, have been seen during examination of bodies during this stage. None of these remains showed any carnivore activity.

## Early Decomposition

Reports of early decomposition range from the first day after death through as late as the fifth day after death. Maggots tend to appear with the onset of these changes and are noted by the second day. However, noticeable external maggot activity occurs in only 63% of the cases of early decomposition in which this factor can be assessed. Delay in this stage is again correlated with the time of year, with late fall and winter months producing slower rates of change. Bloating of the abdominal cavity is reported as early as the second day after death and accompanies moderate maggot activity and strong odor. Bloating is generally lost by the seventh day after death but is recorded as late as the thirteenth day. The termination of early decomposition is marked by the darkening of the skin and rupture of the abdominal gasses. This occurs as early as the third day but becomes more common after the eighth day following death. In some unusual instances it continues almost 2 months, but normally ends by 1 month after death. Delay in all these stages is slowed by burial or submersion in water. In this study, only a single case showed any carnivore activity on the bones or flesh.

## Advanced Decomposition

Advanced decomposition usually occurs at the fourth to tenth day following death but is sometimes delayed by cooler temperatures. In buried remains and those deposited in areas with high humidity, decomposition is rapid. These situations are conducive for maggot activity, which can reach extreme levels within short periods of time. Autolysis is usually accelerated and skeletonization or adipocere formation occurs rapidly. As seen in the previous stages, carnivore activity is very limited, affecting only two individuals at this stage.

## Mummification

In many cases in this arid region, the early decomposition is followed by dehydration of the outer surface of the remains. This marks a significant departure from the usual pattern of decomposition as outlined in more humid areas. The skin turns hard and leathery, forming a thick shell over the body. Despite this surface dehydration, the underlying tissues are frequently moist and continue to produce a strong odor. Initially these tissues are soft and pliable, but gradual dehydration turns them into a dark, viscous, adhesive paste. The surface shell of hard skin protects the internal portions of the body and slows the dehydration. Maggot activity continues unabated under this hardened material during the earlier portions of this process. Although the onset of this stage can occur as early as the third day, it is most frequent between the tenth day and one month. Gradually, the maggot activity wanes, and dermestid beetles take over much of the consumptive processes. Pupal cases from the migrating maggots are frequently found, primarily within the body cavities or in surrounding clothing. In some cases, molds appear along the underlying parts of the body or clothing.

This process results in a skeleton with bony exposure in less than half the body. Those regions of the body which are adjacent to the substrate are usually skeletonized while the uppermost regions, as well as the arms and legs, are covered with mummified skin. This situation first appears in the second month following death and may continue for as long as six to nine months following death.

Among the total remains of this study, 44 cases show some documentary or photographic evidence of mummification. These consist of 27% females (N = 12) and 73% males (N = 73). Of these cases, mummification is most often found in the scalp (78%) and face (69%). The chest and back are mummified in 59% and 57%, respectively, higher than the instances where there is abdominal mummification (49%). Interestingly the arms show a higher rate of mummification than the lower extremities: 60 to 62% in the upper limbs compared to only 53% in the legs.

Twenty-nine individuals, who show some mummification based on photographic evidence, can be matched to a general class of location. The majority of these (69%, N = 20) were found outside while seven (24%) were found within closed structures. One individual was found buried and one in water. Of the 28 individuals who can be classified by the type of clothing, 64% (N = 18) were found fully clothed or were believed to have been fully clothed at the time of death. Six (21%) were partially clothed and 4 unclothed (14%). This is close to the clothing distribution for the general sample.

## Skeletonization

The normal process of skeletonization in this area involves loss of mummified material, leaving remnants of desiccated material and the exposed skeletal elements. The retention of desiccated material is most common at the points of muscle and ligament attachment such as along the spine and at the articular ends of the long bones. This stage usually begins after two months of exposure although, in one instance, the skeletonized remains were recovered from an extremely warm house in late summer within 7 days following death. Desiccated tissue was not found in this sample after one year. The most common time period for this stage was two to nine months following death.

The termination of this stage was reduction to clean bone, with or without some greasy appearance. While this could appear as early as the third week, it normally required over six months exposure. Under protected conditions such as burial or dry shade, this stage could last for many years. Carnivore activity appeared to increase at this stage, as 25% of the individuals, in whom this could be determined, showed some indication of bone damage.

### Exfoliation and Decay of Skeletal Material

The last stage of decay was reported for remains found outside in unprotected environments. Bleaching first appeared in the second month, but became more common by the sixth month. Because remains may have been moved or uncovered during exposure the upper limit was not well documented. Exfoliation was reported as early as the fourth month but more likely at around one year to eighteen months. Carnivore activity was marked, being evident in two-thirds of the cases where it could be determined.

## Discussion

The results of this study show (1) the variety of cases which can be expected to be handled by forensic anthropologists in arid areas and (2) that a number of factors influence the decay process in this region. The detailed research of the University of Tennessee decay facility (Mann et al. 1990; Rodriguez and Bass 1983) has provided the medicolegal community with an excellent guideline of decay sequences. In comparison with the present study, remains exposed to insect activity but protected from rodents and carnivores remained fresh longer in the Tennessee experiment and had a longer period of bloating and greater seasonal variability in these earlier stages than seen in the Southwest. Inhibition of insect activity by dehydration in the arid areas lengthens the decay and dry stages. Decomposition changes were slowed during the winter months in Tennessee to a greater extent than in the present study.

Using the data generated in Tennessee, Mann and associates (1990) outlined the multiple factors which can alter the decay rate. The foremost of these was the ambient temperature which can hasten or impair the rate of insect infestation. The strength of this factor is exaggerated in the desert conditions where extremely high temperatures can result in rapid reduction of the body to a skeleton. Other factors mentioned by Mann include humidity, rainfall, soil pH, trauma to the body, access of insects to the body, depth of burial, carnivore or rodent activity, size and weight of body, surface, clothing, and embalming. In desert regions, humidity and temperature are inextricably linked and must be considered together. In the Southwest, rainfall is more of a factor in body transport than in alteration of the decay processes since the rains tend to be brief and heavy. Normal humidity is extremely low so that moisture is rapidly removed from the body to the surrounding atmosphere. Run-off of body fluids is often confined to the immediate substrate of the remains. In addition, the accelerated dehydration of the remains may also decrease the odor. This may lower the attraction of insects and carnivores to the body, as well as making the remains less olfactorily objectionable for people who may reside or pass near the site of deposition.

### Insect Activity

The primary insect types in southern Arizona are species of blow- and flesh flies. Less frequently, larvae of *Piophila casei*, commonly known as "cheeseskippers," are encountered. These usually are found on remains from cooler areas or higher elevations. Later decomposition is enhanced by the activities of the dermestid beetles, their larvae, and other beetle forms. These perforate the mummified skin and desiccated tissue. This allows easier separation of the remains by body segment.

Research on decay rates in dog and cat carcasses has been conducted within the Tucson area (Burger 1965). A seasonal rotation of blowfly species was noted. *Pharmia regina* was generally found during the winter months, while, in the summer, the most common blowfly was *Cochliomyia macellaria*. During the spring, the predominant form was *Phaenicia sericata*. Flesh flies *(Hystricocemina plinthopyga)*, *Calliphora* spp., and *Sarcophaga cessator* were also reported. A succession of flies was noted, beginning with *H. plinthopyga*, which was succeeded by *P. regina* and the other blowfly species.

The present study noted the difficulty with which the insects infest remains. In particular, the sarcophagids are dependent upon appropriate temperature and sunlight. A succession of cloudy days prevents egg-laying. If egg-laying does not occur within the first few days, the body is often too dried to be accessible. In extremely hot periods, the eggs must be laid in the shade to ensure viability of the young. However, in the cooler winter months, sunlight aided the development of the maggots. During the winter, larvae were only active during the day and skeletonization took five times longer than during the summer.

Insect activity is one of the numerous complicating factors which must be recognized in the present study. Unless the insects can lay eggs in the initial stages of decay, much of the surface will dry and become inhospitable to the larval stages which need both moisture and accessibility to air. This is the most probable reason for the high percentage of cases in early decomposition which do not exhibit external maggot activity. Maggot activity may begin later on the more internal tissues as these become accessible through autolysis.

## Carnivore and Scavenger Activity

Carnivores can also accelerate decomposition by disarticulating the remains, consuming soft tissue, and gnawing the skeletal material. Household pets are a contributing factor to the loss of flesh, especially in recently deceased remains found within closed structures. In the Southwest, carnivore activity, however, appears to occur during advanced decomposition, initial mummification, and skeletonization. Coyotes are the most abundant free-ranging scavengers in the Southwest, and both coyotes and dogs are known to transport desiccated body segments for consumption elsewhere. Bear and javelina also may be responsible for the consumption and transportation of bone. In two instances, bear was the suspected scavenger, and in both, the portions of the body consumed were already decomposed.

Haglund and colleagues (1989) reported on the carnivore activity on a series of human remains from the Pacific Northwest. There, scavenging appeared to begin quite early with entry into the flesh of the face and neck and into the abdominal regions resulting in complete evisceration. The majority of the cases reported in that study did show carnivore activity, in contrast to the much lower frequency reported in the Southwest where any carnivore activity is virtually absent until the skeletonization stage. Possible causes could be fewer numbers of feral dogs in the Southwest due to competition with coyotes, and avoidance of humans by coyotes until the odors of putrefaction are more advanced.

Rodents have been noted as being a major scavenger of human remains (Haglund 1992). Rodent damage can be recognized by the distinct parallel striae although these may not be seen on trabecular or smaller bones. This type of damage is also the case in the desert Southwest where packrats and other rodents frequently gnaw on skeletal material. In addition to accelerating the rate of bone decay after skeletonization, they are notorious for removal of smaller bones from the deposition site. Additional skeletal elements and other evidence are often found by dismantling nearby rat nests.

## Seasonal, Geographic, and Microenvironmental Differences

Seasonal differences are seen in the present data. When death is estimated to have occurred during the winter months, the remains retain a fresh appearance for up to a week, and bloating may not occur until about ten days following death unless the body is within a heated structure. Despite the differences in timing, the sequence of events is virtually identical.

At higher latitudes there also appears to be delayed decomposition. In the Southwest, the more northern areas are outside of the Arizona-Sonoran Desert, above the Mogollon Rim which forms the edge of the Colorado Plateau and are, therefore, also at higher elevations. These remains have been exposed to cooler temperatures, snowfall, and freezing weather during the winter months and more rain throughout the year. These conditions tend to inhibit dehydration of the soft tissues and decrease insect activity. Carnivore activity may be altered due to a shift in species frequencies at higher elevations and latitudes.

The major location types in this study were open air, closed structure, and burial. Exposure on the desert floor (150 to 1000 meters [500 to 3000 feet] elevation) in an unprotected area results in rapid bloating of the remains primarily between the second and fifth day after death (Figure 3A). There is then a transition toward dehydration of the upper surfaces, and mummification, noticeable in most cases by the eleventh day following death, may last until 1 month. Gradual loss of the mummified skin follows, taking about eight months and leaving only skeletal elements. Bleaching and exfoliation of the bones begins after this and continues until the skeletal elements are greatly reduced. These stages are not mutually exclusive, and there is usually retention of the articular cartilage and adherence of the intervertebral discs even as some bone surfaces are undergoing bleaching and cortical loss. Odor at this point is usually slight.

Confinement within a closed structure presents a different pattern of decay as these circumstances may prevent onset of mummification and accelerate decomposition (Figure 3B). Bodies found within houses, trailers, and other such buildings often show a slower onset of early decomposition. Bodies may retain a fresh appearance for three days following death. Bloating appears usually during the third day following death and is still frequently found at seven days. However, the retention of moisture most often quickly leads to exposure of the skeletal elements, usually found by the fourth month after death, but often much sooner. In some circumstances where drainage of body fluids or evaporation removes moisture, mummification may occur but may require about 2 weeks longer than if the body had been exposed outside.

Remains interred directly in the soil frequently show signs of very moist decomposition. Skin slippage and fungus development are common. Various stages of adipocere development have been observed even in shallow graves. These remains eventually show loss of all soft tissue, including those at the articular ends of long bones. Frequently there is also loss of much of the "greasy" appearance of the bone and loss of the brain tissues. At this time, decomposition odors are markedly absent. The bones do not show bleaching or exfoliation unless the body was protected from direct contact with the soil. Protected interments usually exhibit adhering pupae cases and may have dehydrated, flaking, dark tissue attached to the bones, not to be confused with the dehydrated, strongly adherent tissues found with surface exposure. Exposure of remains from shallow burials is common, producing differential decay.

Clothing, bedding, and other coverings also affect the rate of loss. Frequently clothing is displaced during the bloating stages, exposing the chest and abdomen. However, in those cases where clothing covered the body, decomposition appears to be retarded, particularly in the stage of advanced decomposition. Mummified remains often begin decomposition fully clothed.

The presence of major defects such as blunt force trauma and gunshot wounds also may contribute to the decomposition of the body. These provide access to the moist portions of the corpse for the insect forms while also maintaining air contact. However, Burger's study (1965) suggests that blowflies are less attracted to postmortem incisions than to the natural body openings. This is attributed to the competition for air which would occur under these

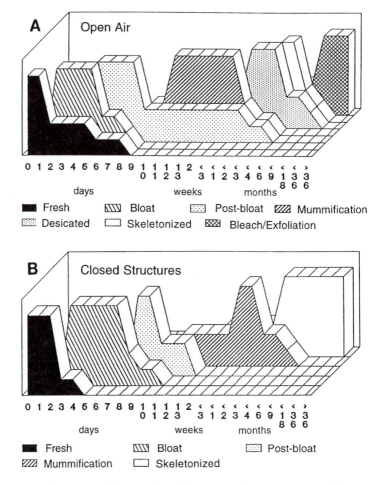

**Figure 3**    Stages of decomposition by time: (A) remains found in open air; (B) remains found in closed structure.

conditions. This may explain why, in some instances, indications of sharp force trauma are preserved in mummified skin and not lost to insect activity.

## Forensic Implications

The use of these guidelines should be viewed as a preliminary step in assessing interval since death. Gross decay rates cannot and should not replace more careful analysis of the remains for indicators of decay. Collection and analysis of entomological evidence (Catts and Haskell 1990) and analysis of soil solutions (Vass et al. 1992) should also be considered.

A rough preliminary assessment such as is provided by the retrospective study helps narrow the time range for initial searches for matching identifications. It will also highlight inconsistencies between the location and the stage or nature of the decay, suggesting that the remains have been moved or treated in ways which would alter the normal decay sequence, such as freezing, embalming, or wrapping in plastic. In lieu of gaining this perspective only through years of experience, the retrospective study permits rapid assessment of overall trends and important local factors.

For example, burial is of little concern in this area, occurring in only a few of the cases cited in the present study. In part, this may be due to the nature of the desert soils which are hard, thin, difficult to work, and almost impossible to replace without noticeable change to the surface of the ground. Dense caliche deposits often lie only a few inches below the surface making excavation of a sizable grave extremely labor intensive and time consuming. Concealment of the body often depends more on the isolation of the locality and minimal coverage of the remains with vegetation.

Expectations for particular types of cases are also revealed by this study. As with forensic cases at large, males greatly outnumber females. Interestingly though, the ratio differs by the stage of decomposition. It appears as if females are either likely to be found immediately postmortem or to be concealed in such a way that the body is skeletonized before discovery. Few cases of skeletonization are due to "in-ground" decomposition — burial of the remains is not a viable option for the perpetrator. Since many of the cases in this sample are deaths in suspicious circumstances, it is probable that we are seeing the results of deliberate placement of the body by the person or persons responsible or, in case of suicides, by the victim. These individuals are aware of land usage patterns, if not of the decay process, and act accordingly. In some cases, the body is deliberately left where discovery will be rapid, while in others, quick discovery is prevented by concealment of the body, usually in bushes or undergrowth.

## Summary

This study provides a model for producing an overview to local decay processes and establishing guidelines for estimation of the interval since death. In the arid Southwest, outside exposure with high temperatures and low humidity accelerates the early decomposition and results in surface dehydration/mummification of the soft tissues. The pattern, while generally following the more "typical" pattern, also varies due to reduction in the length of time available for insect infestation, the types of insects which can effectively utilize the remains, and the reluctance of carnivores to consume portions of the recently deceased body. Location of the body in terms of shelter and shade also appears to be important considerations.

## Acknowledgments

A version of this article appeared in the *Journal of Forensic Science* (1989, 34:607–616). The project was initiated by Dr. Walter H. Birkby and was completed with his guidance. I would also like to thank the Pima County medical examiners, Dr. Thomas Henry and Dr. Bruce Parks and the late Dr. Allen Jones, whose support for this project made it possible. The medical investigators, Mr. Morris Reyna, Mr. George Olson, and Mr. Ron Penning were responsible for compiling much of the data. The cooperation of the staff of the Forensic Sciences Section must also be acknowledged.

## References

Bornemissza, G.F.
    1957   An Analysis of Anthropod Succession in Carrion and the Effect of Its Decomposition on the Soil-fauna. *Australian Journal of Zoology* 5:1–12.
Burger, J.F.
    1965   Studies on the Succession of Saprophagous Diptera on Mammal Carcasses in Southern Arizona. Master's thesis, University of Arizona, Tucson.
Catts, E.P., and N. Haskell
    1990   *Entomology and Death: A Procedural Guide.* Joyce's Print Shop, Clemson, SC.

Easton, A.M., and K.G.V. Smith
    1970  The Entomology of the Cadaver. *Medicine, Science and the Law* 1:208–215.

Galloway, A., W.H. Birkby, A.M. Jones, T.E. Henry, and B.O. Parks
    1989  Decay Rates of Human Remains in an Arid Environment. *Journal of Forensic Sciences* 34:607–616.

Haglund, W.D., D.T. Reay, and D.R. Swindler
    1989  Canid Scavenging/Disarticulation Sequence of Human Remains in the Pacific Northwest. *Journal of Forensic Sciences* 34:587–606.

Haglund, W.D.
    1992  Contribution of Rodents to Postmortem Artifacts of Bone and Soft Tissue. *Journal of Forensic Sciences* 37:1459–1465.

Lane, R.P.
    1975  An Investigation into Blowfly Succession on Corpses. *Journal of Natural History* 9:581–588.

Lord, W.D., and J.F. Burger
    1983  Collection and Preservation of Forensically Important Entomological Materials. *Journal of Forensic Sciences* 28:936–944.

Mann, R.W., W.M. Bass, and L. Meadows
    1990  Time since Death and Decomposition of the Human Body: Variables and Observations in Case and Experimental Field Studies. *Journal of Forensic Sciences* 35:103–111.

Motter, M.G.
    1898  A Contribution to the Study of the Fauna of the Grave. A Study of One Hundred Fifty Disinterments, with Some Additional Experimental Observations. *Journal of the New York Entomological Society* 6:201–231.

Nuorteva, P.
    1977  Sarcophagous Insects as Forensic Indicators. In *Forensic Medicine: A Study in Trauma and Environmental Hazards*, edited by C.G. Tedeschi, W.G. Eckert, and L.G. Tedeschi, pp. 1072–1095. W.B. Saunders, Philadelphia.

Payne, J.A.
    1965  A Summer Carrion Study of the Baby Pig *Sus scrofa* Linnaeus. *Ecology* 46:592–602.

Reed, H.B.
    1958  A Study of Dog Carcass Communities in Tennessee, with Special Reference to the Insects. *American Midland Naturalist* 59:213–245.

Rodriguez, W.C., and W.M. Bass
    1983  Insect Activity and Its Relationship to Decay Rates of Human Cadavers in East Tennessee. *Journal of Forensic Sciences* 28:423–432.
    1985  Decomposition of Buried Bodies and Methods That May Aid in Their Location. *Journal of Forensic Sciences* 30:836–852.

Sellers, W.D., R.H. Hill, and M. Sanderson-Rae (editors)
    1985  *Arizona Climate: The First Hundred Years.* University of Arizona Press, Tucson.

Shean, B.S., L. Messinger, and M. Papworth
    1993  Observations of Differential Decomposition on Sun Exposed vs. Shaded Pig Carrion in Coastal Washington State. *Journal of Forensic Sciences* 38:938–949.

U.S. Department of the Interior
    1981  State of Arizona [map]. U.S. Geological Survey, Reston, VA.

Vass, A.A., W.M. Bass, J.D. Wolt, J.E. Foss, and J.T. Ammons
    1992  Time Since Death Determinations of Human Cadavers Using Soil Solution. *Journal of Forensic Sciences* 37:1236–1253.

# Postmortem Changes in Soft Tissues

# 9

MICHAEL A. CLARK
MICHAEL B. WORRELL
JOHN E. PLESS

## Introduction

The processes that reduce a human body to a skeleton through the postmortem destruction of soft tissues are complex. As with other biologic phenomena, there will be much variation from person to person and it is impossible to assign absolute times for any of the processes. The following discussion of decomposition is limited to bodies which have not been embalmed, since this process retards and, in some cases, completely prevents decomposition.

## Determination of Death and Early Postmortem Changes

In a hospital setting, determination of death usually involves the use of such instruments as the electrocardiograph and the electroencephalograph. The more traditional and time-honored methods of determination of cessation of vital function are simple and straightforward. The absence of a heartbeat over the left side of the chest or lack of an arterial pulse in the neck or the wrists means that the patient is dead. Listening for a heartbeat with an ear to the chest or with a stethoscope is the next level of sophistication. Cessation of breathing after death can be observed by noting the lack of chest movement as well as by listening to the airway with or without a stethoscope.

Changes which occur within the first 2 hours after death are referred to as early postmortem changes. These alterations are caused by lack of effective cardiac pumping of oxygenated blood resulting in a loss of the usual skin color. This "pallor" is first noticed in very light-skinned people as early as 15 to 30 minutes after death, but it may go unnoticed in dark-skinned persons. At the same time, the skeletal muscles of the body, including the sphincters, relax. It is during this period that fecal soiling may occur. In addition, if a body is moved during the period of muscular relaxation, regurgitation of gastric contents or "purging" may occur.

External and internal alterations of the eye occur during the early postmortem period. Externally, a dark band of dried corneal epithelium may be visualized across the front of the eyes since relaxation of the orbicularis oculi muscles of the eyelids exposes the corneas to air drying. This phenomenon is sometimes referred to as "tache noir sclerotique." By using an ophthalmoscope, sludging and intravascular coagulation of blood in the retinal vessels can be seen. This is sometimes called sausaging or boxcarring.

Following death, the blood gradually becomes acidic due to the accumulation of carbon dioxide and other chemicals released as the result of tissue breakdown (Cotran et al. 1994). This causes the activation of the intrinsic coagulation mechanism resulting in blood clots in both arteries and veins throughout the body. This generalized coagulation of the blood usually occurs at about the same time as the development of rigor mortis or stiffening of the muscles. As decomposition continues, the blood pH further decreases, and enzymes called intrinsic fibrinolysins are activated. These enzymes cause reliquification of the coagulated blood. This generally occurs at the same time as rigor mortis begins to dissipate.

## Late Postmortem Changes

Rigor mortis, algor mortis, and livor mortis are referred to as late postmortem changes because they are first observed beginning at 2 to 4 hours after death. These processes are independent of one another, but usually occur simultaneously.

Rigor mortis, or the postmortem stiffening of the muscles, is a reversible chemical change of the muscles. It begins in all skeletal muscles shortly after death, but is first noticeable in the facial muscles as tightening of the jaw at 2 to 3 hours postmortem. After 24 hours, the entire body will be rigid to the extent that it may be capable of supporting its own weight (Spitz 1993:27). As chemicals in the muscles are consumed, they relax by about 48 hours. Since rigor mortis is a chemical process, it is accelerated by heat. This means that if an individual dies following exertion or with a fever, rigidity will develop faster than in an individual whose body temperature is normal at the time of death. Rigor mortis does not cause muscular contraction and, Hollywood movies to the contrary, dead bodies do not sit up, grasp objects, or walk about due to rigor.

Algor mortis is the normal cooling of a body which takes place as the body equilibrates with the environment after death. The normal metabolic processes of the body which maintain a core temperature of 98.6°F during life cease at death and the body temperature will tend to approach the ambient temperature. In most circumstances this means that bodies cool after death at an approximate rate of 1.5°F per hour. If death occurs in a very warm environment, body temperature will rise after death. Elevated body temperature during life or hyperthermia will obviously modify postmortem changes in body temperature.

Livor mortis (also called livor or lividity) refers to the gravitational pooling of blood in dependent parts which occurs after death. In other words, the blood pools on the down side of the body because it is no longer being circulated by the heart. Livor can be first recognized as soon as 15 minutes after death by trained observers, but it is ordinarily first evident at about 2 hours postmortem. The normal color of livor mortis changes from red to purple as oxygen gradually dissociates from the hemoglobin of the red blood cells. This produces a pigment in the red cells called deoxyhemoglobin which is purple. When it is initially seen, Iivor mortis is nonfixed. This means that when a blunt object, such as the back of a finger, is drawn across an area of lividity, the pressure will force blood from the engorged capillaries resulting in an area of blanching which quickly refills. As the body cools (i.e., algor mortis), the fat in the dermis which surrounds the capillaries solidifies and pinches them such that pressure will no longer force blood away from the area of lividity. This phenomenon is called fixation of Iividity and it occurs at 4 to 6 hours after death or after rigor mortis is easily detected (Figure 1). It should be noted that in patients who are profoundly anemic or have lost large quantities of blood, lividity may not easily be seen.

Lividity typically varies from red to purple and becomes darker as the postmortem interval increases. Deviations from these normal colors can be of profound importance. Specifically, cherry red lividity is diagnostic of carbon monoxide poisoning until proven otherwise. Bodies that have been exposed to very cold temperatures soon after death will appear pink because the cold inhibits dissociation of oxygen from the hemoglobin. The least common cause of red lividity is cyanide poisoning, where the cyanide inhibits dissociation of oxygen by blocking the cytochrome oxidase enzymes. All of these changes look similar. To tell the difference, laboratory testing of the blood must be done and these results should be

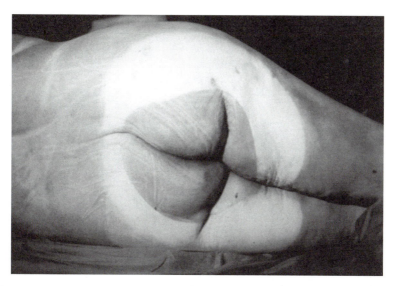

**Figure 1** This elderly lady with a history of heart disease, was last seen alive 24 hours prior to being found sitting upright in her bathroom on the toilet. Note fixed lividity with blanching in areas of pressure produced by the weight of the body.

compared with information from the scene of death. Finally, the death investigation and laboratory data must be the subject of interpretation by a forensic pathologist who then compares that information with the findings at autopsy.

## Tissue Changes

Now that early and late postmortem changes have been considered, we will begin a discussion of the changes which occur in the tissues eventually leading to skeletonization of the remains. The entire process is referred to as decomposition, and this process is further subdivided into autolysis and putrefaction.

Autolysis is a process whereby hydrolytic enzymes that are present in cytoplasmic granules in all cells, called lysosomes, are released into the cytoplasm. Autolysis is thought to be triggered by the decrease in intracellular pH which occurs as a result of decreased oxygen levels which occur after death (Cormack 1987). The hydrolytic enzymes in the lysosomes digest carbohydrates and proteins, while fats are affected to a lesser degree. Because the cell membranes are also disrupted during autolysis, these molecules are released and are utilized as nutrients by microorganisms (see below). Following death of the organism, homeostasis is no longer operative and all cells undergo autolysis beginning shortly after death. The time at which autolysis begins in different cell types and organs is quite variable. As a general rule, autolysis begins much sooner after death in those cell types which contain large numbers of lysosomes (e.g., pancreas) than in those which contain few hydrolytic enzymes (e.g., muscle). The process of autolysis is temperature dependent, and refrigeration of a body soon after death will retard the enzymatic self digestion of cells. Autolysis will be accelerated by ante-mortem fever, exertion, or a high ambient temperature.

The changes produced by autolysis initially can be seen only by use of a microscope, but as the process progresses the features can be seen with the naked eye. These changes will first be observed at about 48 hours after death. Externally, a phenomenon called skin slippage will be seen. In skin slippage, the postmortem release of hydrolytic enzymes by cells at the dermal–epidermal junction of the skin results in a loosening of the epidermis from the

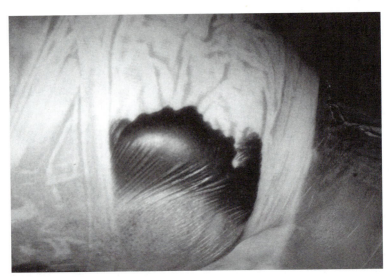

**Figure 2**   This individual died of a myocardial infarction but went undiscovered for some 72 hours. Note the large bulla at the dermal–epidermal junction

underlying dermis. As a result, the epidermis can be easily wiped off the dermis by the moving of a body. In addition, hair and nails become loose and, if not dislodged by moving the body, eventually fall off. It should be noted here that, horror fiction aside, hair and nails do not grow after death. If a body is found with head hair 3 feet in length and 3-in. long nails, these skin appendages were present at those measurements prior to death. Collections of fluid within the skin are called postmortem bullae (Figure 2). These accumulate at the dermal–epidermal junction in dependent portions of the body and are easily ruptured by moving the body.

Internally, autolysis will be noticed as a doughy consistency of the tissues as well as the staining of the intima of large blood vessels by postmortem hemolysis which is simply autolysis of the red blood cells. On the surface of the body, intravascular hemolysis will result in the outlining of superficial blood vessels by the blue color of deoxyhemoglobin, a process referred to as "marbling" (Figure 3).

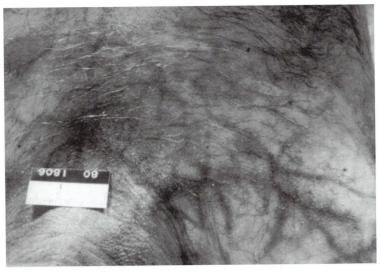

**Figure 3**   Note the prominent marbling caused by intravascular hemolysis in the skin of this man found approximately 48 hours after dying of natural causes.

During life, the normal homeostatic mechanisms of the body prevent bacterial over-growth, but, when homeostasis ceases with somatic death, the uncontrolled growth of endog-enous bacteria and fungi begins. This process is fueled by the copious quantities of carbohydrate, protein, and fat breakdown products which are released by autolysis. Many of the microorganisms produce large quantities of malodorous gases as well as pungent aromatic organic compounds. This is the stage at which decomposition is easily appreciated by the visual and olfactory senses. The rapid production and accumulation of gases causes both physical and chemical changes in the decomposing body which are superimposed on the autolytic processes described above. The physical changes of decomposition consist of alter-ations caused by accumulation of gases in the soft tissues as well as within the gastrointestinal and respiratory tracts. These changes are most prominent in the areas of the body which contain the most blood, since the red blood cells act as a food for the bacteria. Therefore, these putrefactive changes are more pronounced in areas of livor mortis. Ordinarily, the soft tissues of the face swell first and cause eversion of the lips (Figure 4). Then the abdomen becomes massively distended by gas and, in males, gas is forced from the peritoneal space down the inguinal canals and into the scrotum resulting in massive scrotal swelling. Extreme distortion of body contour occurs at this stage of decomposition which is commonly referred to as "bloating" (Figure 5).

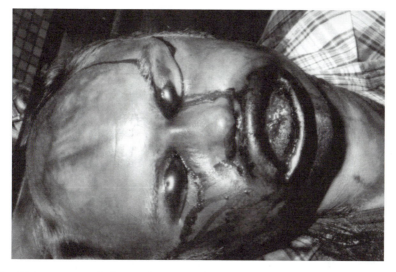

**Figure 4**    This picture is of a homicide victim who died of a gunshot wound of the chest. He was discovered approximately 96 hours after death. Note the eversion of the lips, face swollen by tissue gases, purge fluid from the nose and mouth, and bulla of the eyelids.

The chemical composition of the gas is complex and may not be uniform from body to body. A large component of the gas is hydrogen sulfide ($H_2S$), which is a small molecule that readily diffuses through the tissues. It also reacts with hemoglobin to form a green pigment, sulfhemoglobin. This pigment initially outlines superficial blood vessels and, as decomposi-tion proceeds, a generalized green hue may be seen in those portions of the body where livor mortis was most prominent.

The same processes which are visualized on the surface of the body also occur simulta-neously in the internal organs. Autolysis and putrefaction lead to destruction of the tissues and gas formation. As a result, large gas bubbles may be seen grossly in the liver and other solid organs. Decomposition of the contents and lining of the gastrointestinal tract form a dark, malodorous fluid called "purge fluid" (Figure 4) which flows freely from the nose and mouth due to gas pressure within the gastrointestinal tract. This phenomenon is frequently confused with either antemortem gastrointestinal hemorrhage or injuries.

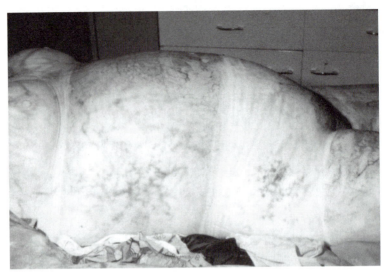

**Figure 5**   Extreme bloating of the abdomen accompanied by prominent marbling is demonstrated in this patient who died of heart disease.

## Modifications of the Decomposition Process

Postmortem modification of soft tissue, when unchecked by some means of preservation, leads to partial or complete skeletonization. This loss or removal of soft tissue from bone is quite dependent on environmental circumstances. The autolytic and putrefactive processes are entirely capable of completely skeletonizing a body. The soft tissue component is merely lost to the environment. The progression from fresh state to skeletonization is frequently modified by vertebrate and invertebrate animal activity and by factors in the environment.

Animal activity on postmortem remains may elicit the image of large carnivorous predators such as bears or lions feeding on the dead. That scenario, while fascinating, is, of course, rare. More frequently, vertebrate animals which modify soft tissue are of the domestic variety. Dogs and cats which are confined in a structure when an owner dies have been found to feed on the remains as a means of survival (Figure 6). When an individual dies in an exposed environment, those remains are subject to scavenging by carnivorous animals in that environment, be they domestic pets, livestock, or wild animals. Additional scavengers are encountered in aquatic environments (Haglund 1993). Fish and turtles are able to remove flesh from bone quite effectively (Figure 7).

While vertebrate animal activity does occur, it is the invertebrates, mainly insects, which are exquisitely capable of modifying soft tissue to the point of exposing the skeleton. Insect activity on postmortem remains is dependent on environmental conditions which determine the species of insects living in a particular areas at different times of the year (Schoenly 1992). In a tightly closed building, there may be little or no insect activity, especially during cold weather (Emson 1991). In warmer exposed environments, insects begin to work before or very soon after death (Catts 1990). Flies are most frequently associated with the death scene. Their larvae (maggots) dramatically alter soft tissue by their voracious feeding (Figure 8). Goff and Catts (1990) list a plethora of invertebrates which feed on animal flesh or body fluids and therefore alter the remains. Schoenly et al. (1992) describe recognizable and predictable patterns of successional activity among certain flies and beetles. In aquatic environments, other populations of invertebrates including crustaceans have the opportunity to feed on the flesh and fluids of the dead. Environmental exposures, in addition to animal activity,

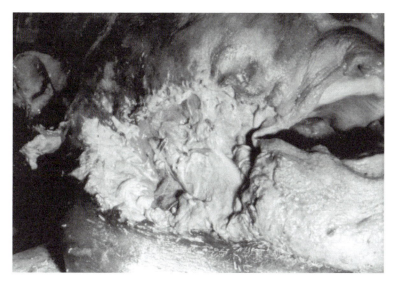

**Figure 6**   An elderly man died alone in his home of a massive heart attack. Note the area of missing tissue due to the activities of his dog which was trapped in the house with the victim for 3 days prior to discovery.

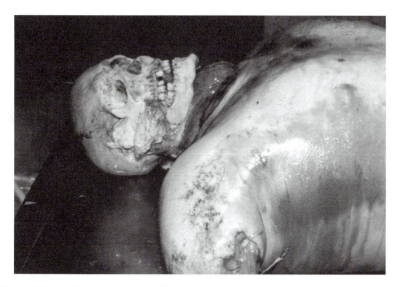

**Figure 7**   A 28-year-old male jumped off a ship at sea about 30 miles from shore, wearing heavy clothing covering everything except his head, hands, and legs. His body was recovered from salt water 3 weeks later. Partial skeletonization is due to marine animal activity.

are extremely important for determining the rate and degree of postmortem soft tissue modification.

Mummification of soft tissue occurs when the surrounding environment is very dry (Evans 1963). Mummies, such as have been encountered in Egypt, were prepared in ritualistic fashion using the hot, dry desert environment and often spices and herbs. Natural mummification takes place when death occurs and the body loses fluids to the environment via evaporation. Extremes of heat (Figure 9) or cold (Figure 10) can facilitate natural mummification.

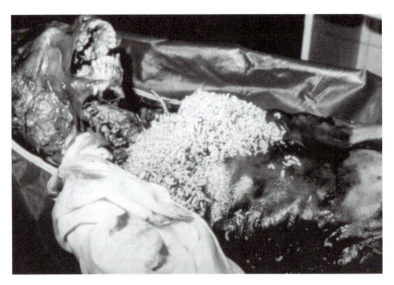

**Figure 8**    This homicide victim was stabbed to death and left in a cornfield during the summer. The body was discovered 2 weeks after being reported missing. Note the large mass of maggots and partial skeletonization.

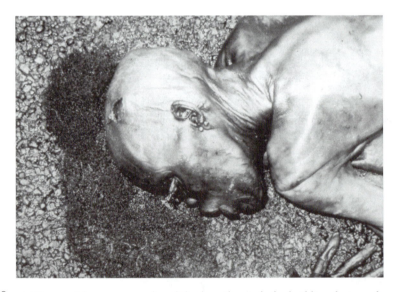

**Figure 9**    A 30-year-old woman was found dead on the roof of a building during a long summer drought. The woman had been dead for 3 to 4 weeks and exhibited total mummification with loss of hair, nails, and internal organs. Cause of death was undetermined.

Adipocere is a malodorous, cheesy, compound of fatty acids also referred to as grave wax (Evans). Adipocere formation occurs most commonly when tissues are submerged in cool water where the oxygen content is very low (Figure 11). Over time, adipocere has been seen to become hard and brittle even in aquatic environments (Haglund 1993). Adipocere forms in both embalmed and unembalmed bodies via the hydrolysis and hydrogenation of fats to fatty acids. This process requires the presence of water either from an exogenous source or from the body itself. Areas covered by clothing appear to produce conditions which favor adipocere formation (Mellen et al. 1993). Dehydration and mummification may accompany adipocere formation in bodies where little or no exogenous water is available. As fats are

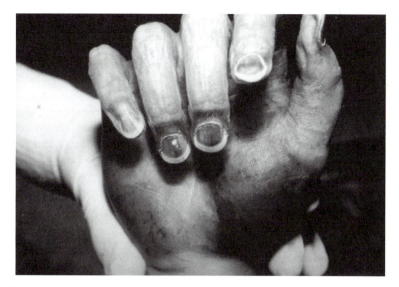

**Figure 10**   Mummification is apparent in the fingers of this 29 year old male who died in bed of a drug overdose. The conditions in the room included the air conditioning running at 60°F and an absence of insects.

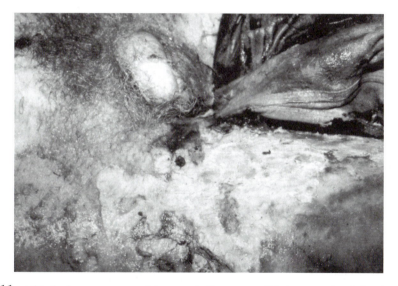

**Figure 11**   This body was recovered from a shallow water-filled grave after being buried for 3 weeks. Note the large area of white adipocere formation on the right upper thigh.

converted to fatty acid, the pH drops which inhibits bacterial growth and thereby promotes preservation of soft tissues (Mant and Furbank 1957). In an emaciated person, adipocere formation is limited at best, due to the lack of a suitable substrate, i.e., fat.

## Skeletonization

Skeletonization is the removal of soft tissue from bone. The process can be considered complete if all soft tissue is removed or partial if only portions of bone are exposed. A partially skeletonized body may proceed toward complete skeletonization with the appropriate circumstances. A buried body in a warm environment may skeletonize as rapidly as an exposed body in a mild environment. Depth of burial is also a factor, as is soil type, in determining the rate at which skeletonization proceeds.

Skin, muscle, and internal organs may be lost to the environment well before a skeleton becomes disarticulated. The ligaments, and to some extent tendons, which hold bones in place, will all be lost in time. According to Rodriguez and Bass (1985) disarticulation generally proceeds from the head downward (with the mandible separating from the skull and head from vertebral column) and from central to peripheral (from vertebral column to limbs).

Bone is broken down over time by physical breaking, decalcification, and dissolution due to acidic soil or water. Motter (1898) describes bones exhumed from a buried coffin, after 71 years, as having their general shape and form, but "easily crushed between thumb and finger." Bodies not in tombs or coffins therefore may in time disappear completely, or under appropriate conditions may become fossilized and preserved for millions of years.

## Decomposition Staging Scale

When information concerning postmortem changes and decomposition is arranged in a logical sequence, it is possible to construct a series of stages of decomposition. These stages are in a temporal sequence, but because of varying environmental conditions as well as variations in body habitus and causes of death, it is not possible to assign an absolute "time since death" to any of these stages (Micozzi 1991). This systematic approach to the degree of decomposition is useful for descriptive and comparative purposes. The final stage of decomposition, skeletonization, has been reported to happen as early as 3 days after death in very hot humid areas where fly larva and beetle activity is high, or in the case of frozen bodies, it may take millennia. At normal conditions of standard 30% humidity and temperature of 70°F the first seven stages of decomposition will appear roughly at 24-hour intervals postmortem (Table 1). Mummification is likely to occur in dry areas after the series of putrefactive processes have run their course. If the body is in an extremely hot environment (>100°F) the rapidity of dehydration may reduce the usual swelling of the body. Likewise, if the temperatures are below freezing, putrefaction may not occur as the bacteria are destroyed or rendered inactive. Postmortem changes are summarized and compared with the decomposition staging scale in Table 2.

## Autopsy of the Decomposed Body

An autopsy is an examination of a body performed after death: it includes both an external and an internal examination performed by a licensed physician specializing in pathology, or preferably, also certified in the subspeciality of forensic pathology. The objective of this medical procedure is to determine a cause of death and a manner of death as well as to collect any evidence which might be present either on or inside the body. An additional consideration in the case of decomposed bodies is that of identification. One of the classic mistakes in forensic pathology, as described in a definitive article by Alan Moritz (1956), is to regard the autopsy of a decomposed body as unrewarding. Although it may not be possible to determine a cause of death in some cases, many possible causes of death may be excluded by a careful autopsy performed on a badly decomposed body. As with any forensic autopsy, careful documentation in the form of photographs and written records is considered to be the standard of practice. In addition, a well-written report that can be easily understood by others is essential. In many cases, it is best to begin the autopsy by

**Table 1  Decomposition Staging Scale**

| Category | Stage | Changes |
|---|---|---|
| Putrid | I | Early putrid odor |
| | | Lividity fixed |
| | | Rigor waning |
| | | Tissues tacky |
| | II | Green discoloration of abdomen |
| | | Hemolysis |
| | | Intense livor |
| | | No rigor |
| | | Early skin slippage |
| | | Drying of nose, lips, and fingers |
| | III | Tissue gas on X-rays |
| | | Prominent hemolysis |
| | | Tissues soft and slick |
| | | Skin slips easily |
| Bloating | IV | Early body swelling |
| | | Discoloration of head |
| | | No discoloration of trunk |
| | | Gas in heart |
| | | Marbling |
| | | Bullae |
| | V | Moderate swelling |
| | | Discoloration of head and trunk |
| | VI | Maximal body swelling |
| Destruction | VII | Release of gases |
| | | Exhausted putrefied soft tissues |
| | | Total destruction of blood |
| | VIII | Partially skeletonized |
| | | Adipocere |
| | | Mummification |
| Skeleton | IX | Skeleton with ligaments |
| | X | Skeleton with no soft tissues |

taking a series of whole body X-rays with the clothing in place (Figures 12 and 13). This will help to locate objects such as keys which may play a pivotal role in the identification process. If dental fillings or appliances are in place, both an anteroposterior and lateral view of the skull should be taken to facilitate dental charting and identification. The frontal sinuses should also be included in the A/P view since frontal sinus X-ray patterns can be used for identification purposes (Marlin et al. 1991).

The collection of trace evidence is a critical part of the autopsy. The best rule of thumb to follow here is to think about what specimens may be needed at a future date, collect them, and preserve them in an appropriate fashion. In addition to saving body fluids (if available) for toxicology and serology studies, a sample of frozen skeletal muscle should also be saved for potential DNA analysis if appropriate. The temptation to wash off decomposed bodies with a fire-hose for 15 or 20 minutes before getting close enough to examine them should be avoided, since this procedure will result in the loss of valuable trace evidence.

**Table 2   Postmortem Changes**

| Time after Death | Postmortem Changes | Modifiers | Category | Stage |
|---|---|---|---|---|
| 0 minutes | Circulation and breathing stop | Temperature | See Table 1 | |
| | Pallor | Humidity | Early changes | |
| | Early lividity | Outdoor location | | |
| | Muscular relaxation | Indoor location | | |
| | Sphincters may relax | Submerged in water | | |
| 2 hours | Vascular changes in eye | | | |
| | Rigor mortis begins | | Late changes | |
| | Algor mortis begins | | | |
| | Lividity easily seen | | | |
| 4–5 hours | Coagulation of blood | | | |
| | Fixation of lividity | | | |
| 24 hours | Drying of cornea | | Putrid | I |
| | Re-liquefication of blood | | Tissue changes | II |
| 48 hours | Rigor dissappears | | | III |
| | Intravascular hemolysis | | | |
| 72 hours | Loss of hair and nails | | | |
| 96 hours | Skin slippage and bulla formation | Insect activity | Bloated | IV |
| | Bacterial overgrowth | Animal activity | | V |
| Days-months | Green discoloration | | | VI |
| | Bloating | | Destruction | VII |
| | Release of gasses | Mummification | | VIII |
| | Release of liquified internal organs | Adipocere formation | Skeleton | IX |
| | Gradual loss of soft tissues | | | X |
| | Partial skeletonization | | | |
| | Complete skeletonization | | | |

**Figure 12**   This body was recovered from a central Indiana cornfield in July. The victim had been dead for approximately 3 days. The clothing was in place prior to autopsy. Note the heavy maggot infestation.

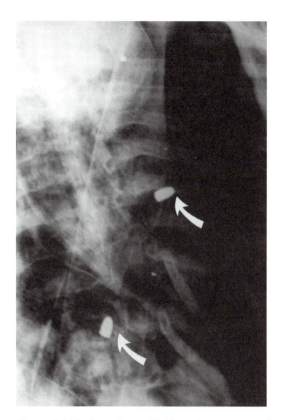

**Figure 13**   This is an X-ray of the body in Figure 12. Note the two projectiles present in the thorax and abdomen (arrows).

# References

Catts, E. P.
   1990   Analyzing Entomological Data. In *Entomology and Death — A Procedural Guide*, edited by E.P. Catts and N.H. Haskell, pp. 124–137. Joyce's Print Shop, Clemson, SC.

Cormack, D.H.
   1987   *Ham's Histology*. J.B. Lippincott, Philadelphia.

Cotran, R.S., V. Kumar, and S.L. Robbins
   1994   *Robbins Pathologic Basis of Disease*. W.B. Saunders, Philadelphia.

Emson, H.E.
   1991   The Case of the Empty Body. *American Journal of Forensic Medicine and Pathology* 12:332–333

Evans, W.E.D.
   1963   *The Chemistry of Death*. Charles C Thomas, Springfield, IL.

Goff, M.L., and E.P. Catts
   1990   Arthropod Basics — Structure and Biology. In *Entomology and Death — A Procedural Guide*, edited by E.P. Catts and M.H. Haskell, pp. 38–71. Joyce's Print Shop, Clemson, SC.

Haglund, W. D.
   1993   Disappearance of Soft Tissue and the Disarticulation of Human Remains from Aqueous Environments. *Journal of Forensic Sciences* 38:806–815.

Mant, A.K., and R. Furbank
  1957  Adipocere — A Review. *Journal of Forensic Medicine* 4:18–35.

Marlin, D.C., M.A. Clark, and S.M. Standish
  1991  Identification of Human Remains by Comparison of Frontal Sinus Radiographs: A Series of Four Cases. *Journal of Forensic Sciences* 36:1765–1772.

Mellen, P.F.M., M.A. Lowry, and M.S. Micozzi
  1993  Experimental Observations on Adipocere Formation. *Journal of Forensic Sciences* 38:91–93.

Micozzi, M.S.
  1991  *Postmortem Change in Human and Animal Remains.* Charles C Thomas, Springfield, IL.

Moritz, A.R.
  1956  Classical Mistakes in Forensic Pathology. *American Journal of Clinical Pathology* 26:1383–1397.

Motter, M.G.
  1898  A Contribution to the Study of the Fauna of the Grave. A Study of One Hundred and Fifty Disinterments, with Some Additional Experimental Observations. *Journal of the New York Entomological Society* 6:201–230.

Rodriguez, W.C., and W.M. Bass
  1985  Decomposition of Buried Bodies and Methods That May Aid in Their Location. *Journal of Forensic Sciences* 30:836–852.

Schoenly, K.
  1992  A Statistical Analysis of Successional Patterns in Carrion-Arthropod Assemblages: Implications for Forensic Entomology and Determination of the Postmortem Interval. *Journal of Forensic Sciences* 37:1489–1513.

Schoenly, K., M.L. Goff, and M. Early
  1992  A BASIC Algorithm for Calculating the Postmortem Interval from Arthropod Successional Data. *Journal of Forensic Sciences* 37:808–823.

Spitz, W.U.
  1993  *Spitz and Fisher's Medicolegal Investigation of Death.* 3rd ed. Charles C Thomas, Springfield, IL.

# Recognition of Cemetery Remains in the Forensic Setting* 10

HUGH E. BERRYMAN
WILLIAM M. BASS
STEVEN A. SYMES
O'BRIAN C. SMITH

## Introduction

From 1985 to 1989, 258 of the 3386 forensic science cases (7.62%) examined in the U.S. by anthropology diplomates were of historic origin (Rhine 1988). Increasingly, graves are exposed by construction, vandalism, and nature, despite state laws to protect them. As a result, bones or bodies from historic cemeteries find their way into the realm of forensic science investigation. Early recognition of characteristics associated with cemetery remains can reduce the time and effort spent on investigation. Recognition is enhanced by an understanding of the basic funerary customs of our culture, including preparation of the body for burial, artifacts accompanying the body, and accoutrements associated with the grave.

Embalming is perhaps the least understood of our funerary customs. According to the funeral industry, embalming, which involved the injection of chemicals into the vascular system and visceral cavity, is practiced for the disinfection and preservation of a body (Strub and Frederick 1967). The embalming fluid preserves the tissue by coagulating protein, which dehydrates and hardens the tissue, and thereby prevents bacterial growth. Although this tradition has existed for centuries, the practice has evolved considerably as a result of technical innovation and in answer to recognized needs.

Commonly used 19th century embalming chemicals included aluminum sulfate, potassium carbonate, copper sulfate, zinc chloride, arsenic, and bichloride of mercury (Strub and Frederick 1967; Oatfield 1956; Mendelson 1944). Early embalming was frequently performed in the home of the deceased, and usually involved the simple injection of the thoracic and abdominal cavities using a trocar and rubber bulb syringe. A cloth moistened with the preservative chemical was often placed over the face. In addition, the cranium was injected through the foramen magnum, the corner of the eye, or the nostril (Strub and Frederick 1967). Only the more sophisticated embalmers performed arterial injection, usually through the right brachial artery, using gravity flow or a bulb syringe and often requiring manual massage to disseminate the chemicals. Such early techniques were fraught with problems, as exemplified in the 1872 embalming of Cardinal Donnet:

> On his death, ... an outstanding surgeon was dispatched to Bordeaux to perform the embalming ... The fluid in this case was allowed to flow in by force of gravity, following drainage removal of the blood, and then it was further dispersed through

* Adapted for publication courtesy of *Journal of Forensic Sciences*, Vol. 36, 230–237, 1991.

the arterial tree and body by kneading and massage.... By the time this squeezing
… manipulative process had been applied from stem to stern, one intercrural stra-
tegic part had become quite turgid and assumed a grossly erectile character. The
organ proved so refractory on further manipulation that it had to be slit altitudinally
in order to release the pent-up fluid under pressure (Oatfield 1956).

Modern embalming using motorized injection has eliminated many of the earlier
mechanical problems involved with injection. The right carotid and femoral arteries are
common injection sites for arterial embalming, and the jugular or femoral veins the sites at
which blood is drained. The femoral arteries may be used to infuse the legs by directing the
fluid downward, or the fluid may be directed upward to inject the abdomen. If trauma or
disease obstructs the circulatory system, a combination of injection sites may be used (e.g.,
axillary, ulnar, radial, popliteal, or anterior tibial arteries). To embalm the body cavity, a trocar
18 in. (46 cm) long and 1/2 in. (12.7 mm) in diameter is inserted into the abdomen to aspirate
the upper chest and viscera, which are then injected with 16 to 32 oz. (0.47 to 0.95 liters) of
cavity fluid. The head is commonly embalmed through the carotid artery.

As a result of the embalming process and funerary rites, cemetery remains possess characteristics that can be used to identify their origin. The recognition of such predictors is
derived from the authors' experiences and observations with numerous forensic science cases
and in the excavation of cemeteries in various parts of the country (Bass and Bass 1975;
Garrow and Symes 1987; Garrow et aI. 1985; Owsley et al. 1987). Predictors of cemetery origin
include (1) the physical characteristics of the remains, (2) coffin/casket or embalming artifacts
recovered in association with the remains, and (3) the presence of embalmed tissue. Each of
these predictors may involve characteristics that are either consistent with or indicative of a
cemetery burial. The term "consistent" means that the trait cannot be used to exclude other
sources of origin for the remains, while the term "indicative" implies an exceedingly high
probability that the remains originated from a cemetery to the exclusion of other potential
sources.

## Physical Characteristics of the Remains

The differences in decomposition rates between embalmed and nonembalmed bodies have
been reported by Bass et al. (1988) and Meadows et al. (1988). According to their research,
embalming does not affect the sequence of events in the decomposition process, but it does
retard the rate and alter the areas of the body affected. Thus, the first evidence of cemetery
origin may be seen in an examination of the physical appearance of the remains. These physical
characteristics include fungal growth, the retention of head and facial hair, cracking and
flaking of the skin, fabric impressions in the skin, decomposition at pressure points, flaking
of cortical bone, differential decomposition, brain preservation, and cribriform plate fracture.

The dark, damp environment of the coffin/casket may stimulate a natural fungal growth
over the body. In addition, mold or other fungal spores may be present in the cosmetic makeup
often applied to the face and hands by the embalmer. The cosmetics may provide medium
conducive to fungal growth. The presence of mold on the skin, and particularly on the face
and hands, is consistent with cemetery remains.

Head and facial hair (such as eyebrows and eyelashes) may adhere to the skin of embalmed
cemetery remains whereas skin slippage may occur in nonembalmed, unprotected bodies
during the first 24 hours in a warm, moist environment. The presence of hair on forensic
remains is consistent with a cemetery burial or with a body that has been protected from the
elements to the extent that the skin can dehydrate.

In time, cracks will develop in the skin because of continual or extreme shrinkage, and
the skin takes on an appearance resembling old paint. Embalming fluid serves to preserve the

skin until it can dehydrate. The rate of skin shrinkage is affected by the extent to which the coffin/casket protects the body. The peeling characteristic of the skin, with its old paint appearance, results from the continued shrinkage of the skin, which decreases the surface area and elevates the margins. If the skin is still intact, the body was probably somewhat protected. Embalming fluid prevents the skin slippage that naturally occurs during decomposition. The presence of skin resembling old paint is consistent with cemetery remains.

Fabric impressions may occasionally be seen in the skin of the face. The pleated fabric in the lid of the coffin/casket may settle across the face. As a result, furrows may form in the skin, and occasionally the warp and woof impression of the weave may remain.

In coffin/casket remains, contact or pressure points of the body decompose first to expose the more superficial bony projections, such as the posterior aspect of the occipital bone, spinous processes of the vertebrae, and the spine of the scapula. Moisture or water may collect in the bottom of the coffin/casket and speed the decay of submerged portions of the body. In addition, these bony projections may exhibit excessive erosion relative to other parts of the skeleton. Differential erosion of bone in contact with the coffin/casket floor may result from the electrochemical action of the bone under local effects of temperature and moisture.

Cortical bone may flake and peel from the periodic wet and dry periods to which the bones are subjected. Superficial cortical bone becomes wet before deeper cortical bone and, during dry periods, the cortical surface dries first. This differential expansion and contraction produces flaking. Cortical flaking is prevalent in long bones, where the circumferential lamellar bone provides natural lines of cleavage. Also, mold on bone specimens is further suggestive of a dark, moist environment consistent with a coffin/casket.

The upper body or trunk may be more thoroughly embalmed and better preserved than the appendages, especially the legs. Collateral circulation near the site of injection acts as a shunt, to direct the embalming fluid along the path of least resistance and circumvent the more remote parts of the circulatory system. In natural decomposition, the upper body tends to decompose before the appendages. Bass et al. (1988) found that the legs and groin of an embalmed body demonstrated active decay relative to the trunk. The pattern of decomposition reflects the dispersal of the embalming chemicals through the body tissues. The gravity-flow method used for arterial embalming in earlier times was less effective in infusing the legs and removing gravitated blood than the mechanical pump commonly used today. However, it is still more difficult to embalm appendages than the head and thorax.

The brain may be preserved as a dry, hard mass in the cranial vault. Barring blockage, the brain is embalmed by infusion through the common carotid artery. The chemical preservation of the brain, in conjunction with the protection of the grave, provides the time and relatively dry environment necessary for it to dehydrate and form a solid, spheroid mass. If trauma or disease obstructs cranial circulation, fluid may be injected via the nostril into the cranial vault through the cribriform plate of the ethmoid bone. A trocar is used to aspirate the cranium and inject the fluid. Although injection through the nostril is not a common practice, the presence of a perforation in the cribriform plate is indicative of embalming. Care must be taken not to confuse gunshot or stab trauma to the cribriform plate with a trocar hole.

## Artifacts Associated with the Remains

With unmarked graves or cemeteries, artifacts associated with the coffin/casket or the actual embalming process provide some of the most reliable evidence of cemetery remains. Among the more recognizable of these artifacts are coffin handles, hinges, nails, and screws. Ornamental coffin trim may include cap lifters, cap plates, and decorative thumb screws.

Paraphernalia introduced into the body by the embalmer provide some of the most indicative evidence of cemetery remains. These artifacts (Figure 1) include eye caps, mouth formers, injector needles, trocar buttons, sutures, cotton packing, molding wax, and specific

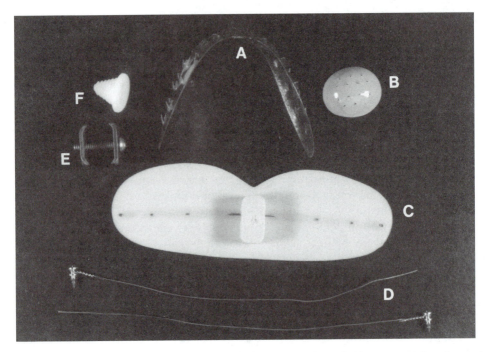

**Figure 1** Artifacts associated with the embalming process: (A and C) two examples of mouth formers; (B) eye cap; (D) injector needles; (E) mouth closure device; (F) trocar button, used to seal the opening from the trocar needle.

articles of clothing. Eye caps are thin, plastic disks use to keep the eyelid closed while preserving the contour of the globe. The disk is molded to produce a smooth, concave surface for direct placement over the globe of the eye. The convex surface is spiny to facilitate gripping of the inner surface of the eyelid. Not all embalmers use eye caps; some elect to use glue alone to seal the eyelids. The mouth former is similar in form and function to the eye cap. Made of perforated plastic, it is contoured to fit the teeth, with a smooth inner surface and a spiny outer surface. It facilitates the shaping of the lips and prevents them from opening. As with eye caps, use of the mouth former is not universal but is indicative of cemetery origin. Injector needles are stainless steel pins with attached wire. The pins are inserted into the mandibular and maxillary bone beneath the gum line and serve to anchor the wire which keeps the mouth closed. Small screws have also been used for this purpose. A plastic trocar button is used to seal the hole left by the trocar in the abdomen after aspiration and injection of the cavity. The button is threaded and is screwed into the trocar hole left in the skin. Trocar buttons may also be used to seal other defects such as gunshot or puncture wounds.

The presence and location of suture material, cotton packing, and wax can be indicative of cemetery remains. All injection sites are sutured, usually with waxed thread. Cotton packing can be used in all orifices of the body. Some embalmers use cotton to pack the nostrils, while others use it only when a trocar has been passed through the nostrils to inject the brain. Thus, cotton may be found in conjunction with a perforated cribriform plate. In cases of disfiguring trauma, wax is commonly used for cosmetic restoration of the face, and is resistant to decomposition.

The presence of specific articles used to clothe a body for burial is another source of evidence. Although practices may vary according to custom and region, men tend to be buried in suits, or at least a coat and tie. Women may be buried in a gown or in street clothes which may include gloves. Underclothes are commonly placed on the body, but shoes seldom are. Also, the clothes may be cut dorsally to facilitate dressing the embalmed body.

The presence of utilitarian associations may suggest that the remains are not from a cemetery. For example, money, keys, a lighter, and similar articles are associated with the living, not the dead. However, care must be exercised since the deceased may occasionally be supplied certain utilitarian items felt by the living to be important in the "second life."

Evidence of a previous autopsy may indicate that the death has been investigated. This evidence consists of a sutured Y-shaped incision used to close the chest and abdomen, and the sutured transverse incision of the scalp. The scalp incision is usually placed posterior to the ears and extends over the apex of the vault. The skull cap is sawn free from the cranium to allow removal of the brain.

## Presence of Embalmed Tissue

The identification of chemicals used in the early days of embalming (aluminum sulfate, zinc chloride, copper sulfate, arsenic, and bichloride of mercury) is less problematic than more recent alcohol- or aldehyde-based preservatives. Since alcohol is produced during decomposition, its presence alone is not evidence of embalming. An embalmed body will have alcohol concentrations exceeding those produced through normal fermentation; thus, the alcohol concentration and overall condition of the remains must be taken into consideration. Samples of muscle, organ, or bone tissue can be obtained for toxicological analysis. As much tissue as possible should be taken to ensure a sufficient amount for testing.

## Conclusions

Postmortem tissue changes provide subtle clues to the cemetery origins of remains, and when associated with more specific indicators, they can be used to corroborate such origins. However, it is the presence of artifacts specifically associated with a coffin/casket or with an embalmed body that provides the most conclusive evidence of cemetery origin.

## References

Bass, C.E., and W.M. Bass
   1975   *Removal of Graves from a 19th Century German Lutheran Cemetery in Wattburg, Morgan County, Tennessee.* Project No. RF-031-1 (18). Unpublished report prepared for the Tennessee Department of Transportation, Nashville.

Bass, W.M., R.W. Mann, and L. Meadows
   1988   Decay Rate of an Embalmed Body above Ground. Paper presented at the 40th Annual Meeting of the American Academy of Forensic Sciences, Philadelphia.

Garrow, P.H., and A. Symes
   1987   The Big Lazer Creek Unmarked Cemetery: A Multidisciplinary Investigation. Unpublished report submitted to the Fisheries Management Section of the Georgia Department of Natural Resources, Atlanta.

Garrow, P.H., S.A. Symes, and H.W. Case
   1985   Physical Anthropology and Archaeological Investigation of the Nancy Creek Primitive Baptist Church Cemetery, Chamblee, Georgia. Unpublished report submitted to Parsons, Brinckerhoff, Quade & Douglas, Inc./Tudor Engineering Co., Atlanta.

Meadows, L., R.W. Mann, and S.A. Symes
   1988   Embalmed Body Decomposition: Above Ground. Paper presented at the Spring Meeting of the Southern Association of Forensic Scientists, Memphis.

Mendelson, S.
  1944  Embalming from the Medieval Period to the Present Time. *Ciba Symposia* 6:1805–1812.

Oatfield, H.
  1956  *Literature of the Chemical Periphery — Embalming.* Advances in Chemistry Series, American Chemistry Society 16:112–142.

Owsley, D.W., M. Manhein, and M.K. Marks
  1987  Burial Archaeology and Osteology of Charity Hospital/Cypress Grove Il Cemetery, Near Orleans: Report of Investigation. Unpublished report submitted to the Louisiana Department of Transportation and Development, Baton Rouge.

Rhine, J.
  1988  *Dipomate Update Final Report.* American Academy of Forensic Sciences, Forensic Anthropology Section, Colorado Springs, CO.

Strub, C.G., and L.G. Frederick
  1967  *The Principles and Practice of Embalming.* 4th ed. L.G. Frederick, Dallas.

# Frozen Environments and Soft Tissue Preservation

# 11

MARC S. MICOZZI

## Introduction

The field of taphonomy has been actively considered in the forensic context for only about one decade. Many taphonomic studies have been carried out and observations made in an effort to further archaeologic interpretations of past human behavior and to make such interpretations more scientific. These observations and studies are now helping to make the estimation of postmortem interval in the forensic context more scientific (Micozzi 1991). When we first used the term "forensic taphonomy" in a window display at the National Museum of Health and Medicine, Armed Forces Institute of Pathology, during 1986–1987, the term was not familiar to many forensic scientists. This volume and others are serving to make the concepts and terminology of taphonomy more commonplace and useful in the forensic sciences.

The baseline temperature for most studies of taphonomic processes has been room temperature or within middle ranges. Changes in temperature tend to alter the rate but not the fundamental character of taphonomic change (Micozzi 1986, 1991). In frozen environments, however, the types of changes may be altered substantially, while the rates of change may slow to virtually zero. Freezing will, of course, preserve soft tissue while in the frozen state. After thawing, however, the effects of prior freezing may accelerate certain postthaw decompositional changes, while slowing others.

## Postmortem Preservation by Freezing

Immediate postmortem change is essentially a competition between decay and desiccation, and external factors such as temperature and humidity largely determine the outcome (Aufderheide 1981; Micozzi 1986). Natural preservation of soft tissues after death may occur through desiccation (drying), freezing and sublimation (freeze–drying) and fixation by mineral salts (niter, natron, salt peter), mineralized water, tannic acids, or other chemicals.

Preservation of soft tissue occurs with freezing through a process of sublimation, or freeze–drying, in regions within the Arctic and Antarctic circles, and at high altitude. Soft tissue preservation due to freezing over long periods of time has been observed in Scythian bodies from Middle East permafrost zones (Artamanov 1965). Scythian tombs in the Altai Mountains of Siberia were found to contain well preserved human remains (Rudenko 1970). Herodotus (IV:66–71) provides an early description of Scythian burial practices at the death of a king, who was eviscerated, mummified, entombed, and covered by stone cairns. Several frozen Siberian woolly mammoths (*Mammuthus primogenus*) have been well preserved, well studied, and are well known (e.g., Goodman et al. 1980).

Soft tissues have been preserved through freezing in circumpolar areas of North America and alpine areas during ancient and more recent times. A frozen, mummified body, complete with tattoos, was found on St. Lawrence Island, Alaska, dating from 400 B.C. (Smith and Zimmermann 1975). The body of a Neolithic voyager was found frozen in a glacier on the border between Austria and Italy with remarkable preservation of soft tissues, skin, and tattoos, dating from approximately 4000 to 6000 B.C. (Sjovold 1992). The body of arctic explorer Charles Francis Hall, who died of arsenic poisoning and was buried in 1871 at Thank-God-Harbour, Greenland, was exhumed and autopsied on site in 1968, with good preservation of soft tissue (Horne 1980). The preservative potential of arsenic itself is also noted, as in the case of Elmer McCurdy, a turn-of-the-century Western outlaw, embalmed with arsenic and preserved for a carnival show (Snow and Reyman 1984).

Soft tissue preservation under conditions of freezing is potentially ideal, but the practical limitations of discovery conditions often preclude examination prior to the onset of postrecovery deterioration (Aufderheide 1981). Further, exposure of soft tissues to alternating freeze–thaw cycles over time introduces confounding variables (Micozzi 1986). Depending upon latitude, season of death, and stratigraphy of placement in the ground, animal and human remains may be subjected to freezing with or without subsequent thaw. Wood and Johnson (1978) have illustrated zones of continuous and discontinuous permafrost world-wide, and maximum depths of frost penetration in seasonally frozen ground in the U.S. (Figures 1 and 2).

# Freezing and Postmortem Decomposition

Soft tissue which has not been naturally or artificially preserved is subject to the postmortem processes of putrefaction (anaerobic degradation) and decay (aerobic degradation). Whereas desiccation occurs under conditions of dryness, putrefaction takes place in the presence of moisture and moderate temperatures. No putrefaction occurs at temperature less than 4°C (the temperature of the average refrigerator). The inhibitory effect of refrigeration on bacterial growth is well known, and putrefaction does not occur in refrigerated mortuaries, as post-mortem bacteriological studies have often demonstrated (Decker 1978).

## Conditions of Bacterial Growth

Temperature has a direct effect on bacterial growth in both extremes of heat and cold, and in middle ranges. Freezing stops bacterial growth and preserves tissue by influencing cell division time, while boiling kills bacteria but destroys soft tissue. At temperatures below 55°F (12°C) bacterial reproduction is greatly retarded. At temperature between 32 to 41°F (0 to 5°C), bacterial multiplication stops entirely and the time required for a single bacterial cell division to occur approaches infinity (Binford 1978). Thus, 4°C provides an effective low temperature threshold below which bacterial growth is severely retarded.

At the other end of the scale is a high temperature threshold approaching the body temperature of most homeothermic animals. The susceptibility of bacteria to increased temperature, as well as decreased temperature, has been demonstrated under controlled conditions with respect to reduced decomposition rates of soft tissue (Aufderheide 1981). At high temperature, the time required for bacterial cell division approaches infinity. Thus it may be adaptive to develop a fever during infection in terms of retarding bacterial growth. However, in the temperature range immediately below this threshold, the highest rates of bacterial cell division occur. Therefore, decomposition due to bacterial action is rapid in environments characterized by temperatures between 60 and 95°F (15 and 37°C). At such temperatures, desiccation must be rapid and nearly complete in order to allow even limited preservation of soft tissue. With reduction in temperature to the 5 to 15°C range, the degree of desiccation required for preservation is reduced. Where temperatures are less than 5°C, the degree of

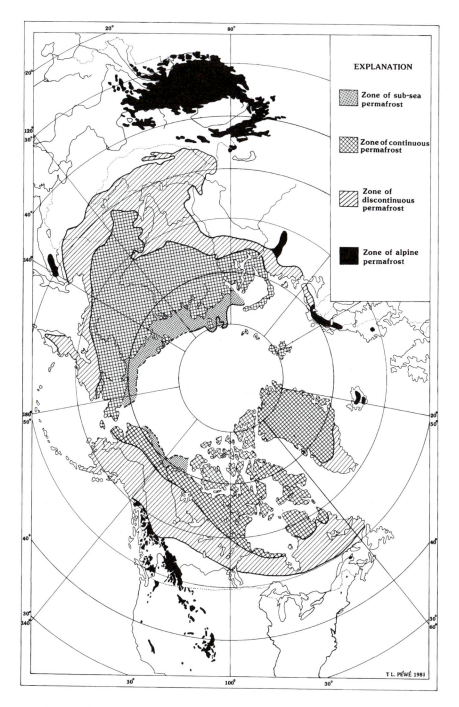

**Figure 1**  Zones of continuous and discontinuous permafrost worldwide.

desiccation required is minimal. Below 0°C, no desiccation is required (given sustained temperatures) since freezing is the most effective preservative technique. Prior freezing also retards bacterial growth after thawing at ambient temperature (Micozzi 1986).

It must be considered that the temperature of decomposing soft tissue may differ widely from the ambient air or soil temperature, due to the creation of an internal microenvironment by the action of bacteria (Payne 1965; Rodriguez and Bass 1983, 1985). At higher temperatures,

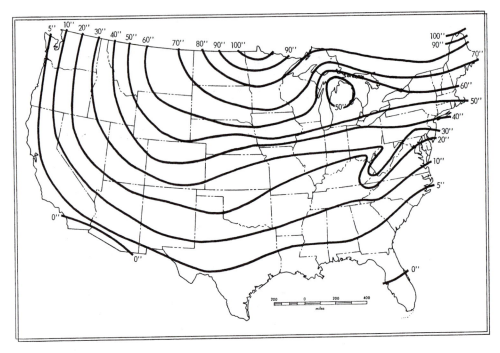

**Figure 2**   Maximum depths of frost penetration in seasonally frozen ground in the U.S.

desiccation occurs more rapidly but bacterial growth is also greater. Thus the outcome of this balance at a given temperature depends upon humidity.

## Freezing and Phases of Decay

Four phases of decay have been observed by both Reed (1958) and Johnson (1975). However, both studies used animals which had previously been frozen, and the extent to which decay processes in previously frozen tissue duplicates the behavior of fresh tissue is questionable (Micozzi 1986). Johnson (1975) described fresh, bloat, decay, and dry stages. The fresh stage persisted no longer than 2 days. The bloat stage was characterized by the build-up of gases due to predominance of anaerobic protein decomposition by bacteria (putrefaction), and persisted from 2 to 5 days under warm conditions. In a cold environment, or when the animal was exposed to alternating freeze–thaw cycles, this phase persisted for several weeks.

Variations in the duration of the various phases or stages of putrefaction and decay have been reported (Johnson 1975) by season of the year. Extensive freezing and lack of decay organism activity during winter preclude observation of definitive decay patterns during this season. Animals that have been subjected to freezing and subsequently thaw appear to decompose from the "outside in" with decay due predominantly to invasion by external soil organisms, while unfrozen animals decompose from the "inside out" with predominantly putrefaction due to enteric microorganism dissemination (Micozzi 1986).

## Effects of Freezing on Soil and Environmental Conditions

When human remains enter the soil matrix they are subject to a number of soil disturbance processes, or pedoturbation. Dynamic soil processes influence the deposition and placement of remains. These agents of attrition are quantitative vectors in that they have both magnitude and direction. The archaeologic matrix in which postmortem remains are embedded forms a system in which dynamics of soil formation and disturbance processes exercise a major influence.

Cryoturbation is soil disturbance by freeze–thaw action which also affects postmortem disposition of remains independently (Micozzi, 1986). This phenomenon is dependent upon the water content of soil and occurs in arctic, montane, and midlatitude regions where there is frozen ground. Continuous and discontinuous permafrost zones cover 25% of the surface of the earth, while seasonally frozen ground covers 50% (Figures 1 and 2).

Soil, like water, freezes from the surface downward. Freezing causes expansion of water, and hence soil, by conformational changes in crystalline water molecules at 4°C. Soil freezing has the same effect on capillarity as does surface evaporation of soil water, and the actual expansion of soil is even greater with freezing due to this effect. Ice heaving occurs due to frost pull or push depending upon the heat conductivity of bone in relation to soil. These freezing processes may result in several features: heaved soil and up-freezing of bone, mass displacement and involution, cracking and wedging, sorting and ground patterning into circles, polygons, nets, steps, and stripes.

Different geographic regions are subject to these processes to varying extents, and a site-specific index of pedoturbation may be developed with respect to climate, rainfall, seasonality, latitude, and other factors. The predominance of these processes may be estimated for a given site at a given time, but the temporal dimension must be added to determine changes in climate over time. Various combinations of processes may lead to specific feature formation in various regions. Gelifluction lobes occur at high latitudes and altitudes due to the action of graviturbation, cryoturbation, and secondary aquaturbation.

In addition to specific cryoturbative processes, whether or not a region is subject to frost quantitatively alters the character of many other pedoturbative processes. In frost zones, graviturbation will be manifest as gelifluction (rather than solifluction), as well as soil creep. Aquaturbation will be differentially manifest as cryostatic rather than artesian processes. The occurrence of these various specific topographic features at a given site may help identify the soil pedoturbative processes in operation over time.

There may also be subregional, site-specific variations in pedoturbative processes based upon topography and drainage. Cryoturbation causes resurfacing, while faunalturbation causes burial. In well-drained soil, faunal alterations predominate over cryoturbation, while in poorly drained soils, the opposite will pertain. As a result of all these processes, remains may alternatively sink into soil, concentrate into layers at various depths, become reoriented, thrust to the surface, or move horizontally on a plane or downslope, within soil. Processes occurring in short time-frame windows are superimposed upon the substrate of more gradual activities, and instantaneous events (seismiturbation or earthquakes) and rapid processes (graviturbation or landslides) are superimposed upon both.

## Experimental Study of Effects of Freezing and Thawing

A study was conducted in an experimental animal model under controlled field conditions to (1) observe the gross, histologic, and microbiological features associated with immediate postmortem change in soft tissue and skeletal remains; (2) determine the effects of freezing and thawing on patterns of postmortem change; (3) observe the effects of mechanical injury on postmortem change; and (4) compare the effects of freezing and thawing to those of mechanical injury (Micozzi 1986).

### Baseline

Baseline necropsies at 0 h revealed differences between the "fresh" and "frozen" animals. The freshly killed animals had normal gross and microscopic examinations, and the internal organs were distinct in color and consistency. The frozen–thawed animals had a normal external examination, but internal examination revealed gross loss of bloody fluid from oral and nasal apertures, indistinct internal organs and corticomedullary junctions of the kidneys, and hemolysis of blood. Microscopic examination revealed loss of nuclear detail in tissue cells.

## Day Two

Remaining pairs of animals were observed undisturbed in the field after 2 days (48 h). Insects (Hymenoptera, Coleoptera) and insect larvae were concentrated around carcasses and the surrounding areas. All frozen–thawed animals manifested greater external aerobic decomposition (decay) than the fresh-killed controls assessed by greater percent external hair loss, greater percent skin mummification, and greater percent loss of facial features. For the pair examined, the upper surface of the fresh-killed animal was intact (left eye present) and fully articulated. The undersurface (right) showed massive abdominal distention. The upper surface of the frozen–thawed animal showed focally denuded fur (left eye absent), partially mummified skin, and numerous ectoparasites. The undersurface was completely denuded, with skin focally decayed and flat abdominal wall. Internally, the freshly killed animal showed greater anaerobic decomposition (putrefaction) of abdominal fat and viscera, massive gastrointestinal distention, and "moth-eaten" lungs (right more than left). Insect larvae were present only in the anus and vagina. By contrast, in the frozen–thawed animal internally, the abdominal organs were preserved, lungs were intact, and gastrointestinal tract was not distended. However, there were insect larvae in the oral cavity, tracheobronchial tree, and abdominal wall, as well as anal and vaginal external orifices. Microscopically, the fresh animal showed histologic preservation of the skin, superficial insect larvae, marked autolysis of liver and other viscera, and bacterial overgrowth in the gastrointestinal tract.

The frozen animal showed decay of skin muscle, larvae in deep tissues, partial preservation of viscera, intact pulmonary and biliary trees, and bacterial overgrowth in the upper airway. Weight change in the fresh animal was 2% loss, and in the frozen 8% loss (including biomass).

## Day Four

After 4 days (96 h), both remaining pairs of animals displayed advanced decomposition with partial mummification and skeletonization, and insect larvae in abdominal cavities. Internally, abdominal and thoracic viscera were grossly absent in the fresh animal necropsied at this interval. The skeleton was fully articulated, except for the temporomandibular joint (TMJ). Insect larvae were present only in the right (ground contact) posterior thoracic region. In the frozen animal, internal organs were still partially preserved, but insect larvae were present throughout. The skeleton had undergone partial disarticulation (at TMJ, cervical vertebrae, symphysis pubis, and right knee), with forelimbs and thoracic cage completely articulated. Microscopic examination revealed extensive decay, large gram-positive bacterial rods, and multiple insect larvae. Weight loss was 83% of baseline in each animal at this stage.

## Day Six

After 6 days (144 hours), the remaining pair of animals showed no insects or insect larvae on the carcasses or in the surrounding areas. There was mummification and partial skeletonization. Partial disarticulation processes in the fresh animal (TMJ, atlantooccipital, cervical, and lumbar vertebrae, sternocostal junctions, symphysis pubis) continued to be less advanced than in the frozen animal (TMJ, cervical and lumbar vertebrae, costovertebral, sternocostal, lumbosacral, sacroiliac, pelvis-hip). The fresh animal had forelimbs fully articulated, but remnants of viscera were still present. Weight loss in the fresh animal was 72%, and in the frozen 87%.

A microbiologic succession sequence was observable from enteric to soil organisms over 6 days. The sequences in fresh and frozen organisms were similar in order, but it is evident from the gross, histologic, and microbiologic evidence that enteric microorganism growth proceeds more rapidly in the fresh animals, despite some initial contamination in the frozen animals.

## Decomposition and Disarticulation Patterns

In comparing the upper surfaces (exposed to air) to the lower surfaces (in ground contact), decomposition proceeded more rapidly on the side in contact with the ground in all animals, as compared to the other side in each. Animals that were killed by cervical dislocation at the start of the experiment showed rapid decay in the cervical tissue subjected to mechanical stress and injury.

A sequence of arthropod and microbiological succession, as well as patterns of decomposition and disarticulation, were discernable over the time interval. Using observations on all animals, a reproducible sequence of disarticulation can be reconstructed. Although the rates of disarticulation were slower in the fresh-killed animals than in frozen–thawed animals, the sequence in the two was the same, as determined by morphologic and biomechanical factors. The temporomandibular joint was the first to disarticulate in all animals. The atlantooccipital joint and cervical vertebrae followed in close succession. The cervical vertebrae disarticulated at this early interval, even in animals that had not been sacrificed by cervical dislocation.

Thus, the mandible and skull would have the first opportunity to become mechanically separated from the less-identifiable postcranial portions of the skeleton. The limbs have a tendency to remain intact during the immediate postmortem period. This pattern is consistent with the observed behavior of mammalian skeletal remains in archaeologic context (Hill 1977, 1979) Mammalian mandibles and skulls are often found in disassociation from postcranial skeletal remains. It has been suggested that some biologic agents and physical agents may accelerate the process of disarticulation, but do not alter its sequence (Gifford 1981). Freezing–thawing appears to be one such physical agent which accelerates rates of disarticulation, but does not alter the sequence, compared to fresh-killed animals.

In general, the frozen–thawed animals were more susceptible to invasion by insects and microorganisms from the outside, and aerobic decay of the skin and external surfaces. The fresh-killed animals were less susceptible to external decay, but putrefaction (anaerobic decomposition) proceeded more rapidly from within. It appears that the freeze–thaw cycle diminishes the capability of enteric organisms to grow and participate in postmortem putrefaction. The mechanical disruption of the tissues caused by freezing also weakens the skin, connective tissue, and joints, thus facilitating aerobic decay and skeletal disarticulation, and making internal organs more susceptible to invasion by foreign organisms and insects.

In summary, it appears that in frozen–thawed animals, postmortem decomposition proceeds from the "outside in" (predominantly decay); while in the fresh-killed animals, it proceeds from "inside out" (predominantly putrefaction). It is evident that studies of the various processes of postmortem change using frozen–thawed animals may not have given an accurate picture of the decomposition sequences and timing that would occur in fresh-killed animals for purposes of determining the interval since death. Such studies should be repeated using freshly killed animals. These findings have implications for the interpretation of human remains from individuals who die with, or without, injuries during the frost season in temperate climates. These remains may "winter over" and subsequently be discovered in the spring or summer, following one or more freeze–thaw cycles, and after the onset of postthaw decompositional changes.

## Effects of Freezing and Thawing on Soft Tissue: Case Illustration

A body with a gunshot wound to the head was discovered in a wooded area in mid-September 1983 wrapped with consecutive layers of plastic garbage bags and rope. Examination of the body revealed a bullet hole in the occipital–parietal region and a peculiar decomposition pattern of the body. Following a forensic reconstruction of autopsy findings, microscopic studies and other ancillary factors, it was concluded that the body had been frozen for over 2 years prior to its being dumped along a mountain road in Rockland County, N.Y. (Zugibe and Costello 1993).

The peculiar decomposition pattern (external aspects of the body markedly more decomposed than the visceral aspects and no intestinal or tissue distension) suggested that the victim may have been frozen for a period of time. Zugibe and Costello (1993) reasoned that freezing would either kill or alter the growth pattern of enteric flora. The external aspects of the body would be the first to thaw and, therefore, be directly exposed to microorganisms from outside the body. The head region showed more decomposition than the rest of the body because the perforation in the head would allow entrance of organisms from the outside. Moreover, if the body had indeed been frozen, the head may have decomposed more rapidly because of rapid thawing due to its small size. Tissue sections were evaluated for the presence of ice crystal artifacts in an attempt to confirm that the body may have been intentionally frozen prior to discarding it. Careful examination of heart muscle sections revealed features suggestive of ice crystal artifacts.

The body was subsequently identified as that of a man last seen alive about 2¼ years prior to the supposed time of death. This was fully corroborated almost 3 years later, when the New Jersey Attorney General's Office held a suspect named Richard Kuklinski in connection with a series of homicides, including this case. They indicated that the victim's body had been frozen, because one of their informants provided them with a sworn statement that he had observed a body hanging in a freezer compartment within Kuklinski's North Bergen, NJ, warehouse. This case was responsible for Kuklinski being dubbed the "Iceman," although this was purportedly the only victim that he froze.

The experimental study of laboratory animals frozen for a period of time after death, and then thawed, showed decomposition more marked externally than internally (Micozzi 1986). This study supported the preliminary observation and hypothesis proposed by Zugibe and Costello (1993) at the time of autopsy. The finding of ice crystal artifacts in the tissue provided them additional evidence that the body appeared to have been frozen prior to dumping it in Rockland County, NY.

The effects of freezing on tissue have been extensively investigated. Zugibe and Costello (1993) note the ice crystal artifacts are small disruptions of cellular structures within cells caused by ice crystal formation during freezing and thawing. During the freezing process, water is transformed into ice crystals with a rigid crystal lattice within the intracellular, extracellular, and intranuclear spaces, producing artifactual distortion of the tissue if the crystals are sufficiently large. The morphological features in the tissues can be recognized as empty spaces. Careful studies also reveal nuclear distortions due to the pressure exerted by the ice crystals (vacuolation around the nuclei). Repeated freezing and thawing disrupts cell organelles, releases enzymes, and produces diffusion of solubilizable constituents (Lillie 1965). The amount of distortion depends on the rate of freezing, the rate of thawing, the number of crystallation nuclei, the thermal conductivity properties of the tissue, and the tissue size and shape (Zugibe and Costello 1993).

The "Iceman" case provides a good example that caution must be exercised in interpreting the time of death in frozen environments. Although the perpetrator attempted to conceal the time of death in order to confuse the authorities, he was thwarted by careful observation and reconstruction of the autopsy findings and other ancillary studies (Zugibe and Costello 1993). In any case involving a decomposing body that has been dumped during the months of the year when the climate is cool or warm (not freezing), the medical examiner should consider the possibility of the body having been frozen prior to dumping. Zugibe and Costello (1993) proposed that the following observations be made: (1) whether decomposition is greater externally than internally; (2) whether there is significant intestinal distension or bloating; (3) whether the skin is pasty in consistency; and (4) whether tissue sections show evidence of ice crystal artifacts. The clothing of the victim may also be cleaned after checking for evidentiary material, and a list made of each item with a complete description. Following identification, one can then try to determine whether the victim was wearing the same clothing when last seen alive.

# References

Artamanov, M.L.
   1965   Frozen Tombs of the Scythians. *Scientific American* 212:101–109.

Aufderheide, A.C.
   1981   Soft Tissue Paleopathology — An Emerging Subspecialty. *Pathology* 12:865–867.

Decker, P.
   1978   Postmortem Bacteriology. *Bulletin of the Ayer Clinical Laboratory*, New Series 4(2):2–5.

Gifford, D.
   1981   Taphonomy and Paleoecology: A Critical Review of Archaeology's Sister Disciplines. *Advances in Archaeological Method and Theory*, Vol. 4, edited by M.B. Schiffer, pp. 365–438. Academic Press, New York.

Goodman, M., M.L. Barhhart, J. Shoshani, and A.E. Romero-Herrea
   1980   Molecular Studies on the Magadan Mammoth. In *Abstracts: Annual Meeting of the Paleopathology Association, p.* NF 4. Niagara Falls, NY.

Hill, A.P.
   1979   Butchering and Natural Disarticulation: An Investigatory Technique. *American Antiquity* 44:739–744.
   1977   Disarticulation and Scattering of Mammalian Skeletons. *Paleobiology* 5:261–274.

Horne, P.
   1980   The Death of Charles Frances Hall, Arctic Explorer. In *Abstracts: Annual Meeting of the Paleopathology Association, p.* NF 2. Niagara Falls, NY.

Johnson, M.D.
   1975   Seasonal and Microseral Variations in the Insect Populations on Carrion. *American Midland Naturalist* 93:79–90.

Lillie, R.D.
   1965   *Histopathologic Technique and Practical Histochemistry.* 3rd ed. McGraw Hill, New York.

Micozzi, M.S.
   1986   Experimental Study of Postmortem Change Under Field Conditions: Effects of Freezing, Thawing and Mechanical Injury. *Journal of Forensic Sciences* 31:953–961.
   1991   *Postmortem Changes in Human and Animal Remains: A Systematic Approach.* Charles C Thomas, Springfield, IL.

Payne, J.A.
   1965   A Summer Carrion Study of the Baby Pig *Sus scrofa* Linnaeus. *Ecology* 46:592–602.

Reed, H.B.
   1958   A Study of Pig Carcass Communities in Tennessee, with Special Reference to the Insects. *American Midland Naturalist* 59:213–245.

Rodriguez, W.C., and W.M. Bass
    1985  Decomposition of Buried Bodies and Methods That May Aid in Their Location. *Journal of Forensic Sciences* 30:836–852.
    1983  Insect Activity and Its Relationship to Decay Rates of Human Cadavers in East Tennessee. *Journal of Forensic Sciences* 28:423–432.

Rudenko, S.I.
    1970  *Frozen Tombs of Siberia,* edited and translated by M.W. Thompson. University of California Press, Berkeley, CA.

Sjovold, T.
    1992  The Stone Age Iceman from the Alps: The Final and the Current Status of Investigation. *Evolutionary Anthropology* 1:117–124.

Smith, G.S., and M.R. Zimmerman
    1975  Tattooing Found on 1600 Year Old Frozen Mummified Body from St. Lawrence Island, Alaska. *American Antiquity* 40:434–437.

Snow, C.C., and T.A. Reyman
    1984  The Life and Afterlife of Elmer J. McCurdy: A Melodrama in Two Acts. In *Human Identification: Case Studies in Forensic Anthropology,* edited by T. A. Rathbun and J. E. Buikstra, pp. 371–379. Charles C Thomas, Springfield, IL.

Wood, W.R., and D.L. Johnson
    1978  A Survey of Disturbance Processes in Archaeologic Site Formation. *Advances in Archaeological Method and Theory,* Vol. 1, edited by M.B. Schiffer, pp. 271–331. Academic Press, New York.

Zugibe, F.T., and J.F. Costello
    1993  "The Iceman Murder" — One of a Series of Contract Murders. *Journal of Forensic Sciences* 38:1404–1408.

# Outdoor Decomposition Rates in Tennessee

# 12

WILLIAM M. BASS, III

## Introduction

Shortly after arriving at the University of Tennessee, I became interested in the length of time since death, as I was receiving more partially decomposed bodies than I had while teaching at the University of Kansas from 1960 to 1971, where most of my cases were skeletal only. This chapter is a summary of some of the information that my graduate students and I have gained since 1972 when we began to conduct research on human decay rates. After 22 years there is still much to learn about this very complicated subject.

The forensic case that really initiated a concerned effort on research on length of time since death was the unauthorized excavation of a Civil War officer, Colonel William Shy. This case was the basis for a chapter in *Human Identification* by Rathbun and Buikstra (Bass 1984). In the Col. Shy case, I told the police we were looking for a 24- to 28-year-old white male who had been dead 1 year. Col. Shy, at the time of his death, was a 26-year-old white male. He had been buried 113 years before being unearthed by relic hunters.

There has been a tremendous amount of progress in forensic anthropology since then, but we still lag far behind in understanding human decay rates (Bass 1979). This realization was recently brought home in a case I had in December 1993. A fisherman launching his boat into the Tennessee River in Decatur County noticed a skull in about 2 feet of water (the water level was 8 feet below normal pool so the skeleton would normally have been under 10 feet of water). About 80% of the skeleton was recovered and sent to me for a forensic anthropology analysis. I reported to the law enforcement agencies that the skeleton was from a 24-year-old white female who was 5' 4" tall and had been dead at least 5 years. (She was reported missing from her home on 12-21-83 and was found 12-20-93). Although age, sex, race, and stature criteria are working, we still have a ways to go on length of time since death. However, while I missed the length of time Col. Shy was buried by 112 years, I underestimated the recent case by only 5 years.

We are learning something about decay rates, but most research has been on shorter lengths of time since death (Vass et al. 1992; Rodriguez and Bass 1983) than the skeleton from the Tennessee River. It is difficult for graduate students who wish to finish a master's thesis or a doctoral dissertation to undertake long research projects. There is still a substantial need for long-term research projects on many phases of human decomposition.

This article summarizes the results of the research at the University of Tennessee Anthropology Research Facility (ARF) as well as my 30 years of experience in the forensic field. In the case of the skeleton from the river, for example, although I felt the body might have been there longer, I chose the more recent end of the range. I tend to be cautious when giving law enforcement agencies dates, in order to avoid overestimating and having the investigator miss a possible suspect.

The major factor in decomposition is temperature; bodies decay much faster in summer than they do in winter. The primary process accelerating decomposition is insect activity, especially maggots. A body in Tennessee in July and August can go from what you and I know

0-8493-9434-1/97/$0.00+$.50

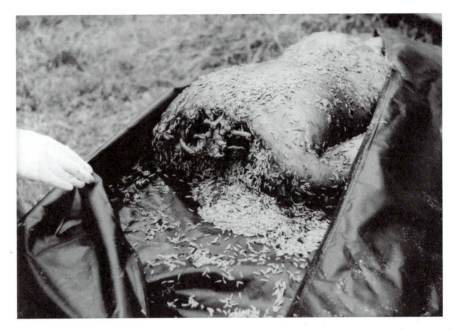

**Figure 1**　The remains of a 23-year-old black female whose body was in a semi-wooded area for 2 weeks before discovery. When the body was removed from the field a few hours before this photo was taken, very few maggots were visible. The body was placed in a black body bag; maggots emerged from the body cavity in the darkness.

to a complete skeleton in two weeks. Dale Stewart (1979: 71–72) reports an even faster time from Mississippi of a teen age girl who was almost a complete skeleton in 10 days.

To go from a flesh-covered body to a skeleton in such rapid time can only occur under the most favorable conditions of high temperatures and humidity, ample insect infestation, and the body shaded from direct sunlight. Maggots do not like sunlight, and if there is no overhead covering, they will leave the skin as an umbrella to protect them from the sunlight.

Figure 1 shows a body that had been in a semi-wooded area for 3 weeks before discovery. Before the body was placed in the black body bag only a few maggots were observed. This photograph was taken about one hour after the body had been placed in the bag. The maggots, sensing a dark environment, had left the body cavity to feed more actively on the skin.

I have often seen bodies in the field that look like they are in good shape only to find that no internal organs remain and only the skin above the ground has been left by the maggots to protect them from the sun. If you observe a body in the field, look at where the body and the ground meet, the ground/body interface, and you will notice that the skin has been eaten away about an inch or 2 above the ground surface. This allows air to circulate in the open space under the skin, and the skin will rapidly dry and turn to leather. What may at first appear to be a relatively intact body may under careful inspection be almost a complete skeleton held together by only the dry skin left by the maggots for protection from the sun.

Seldom do ideal conditions for a minimum time of skeletonization exist. We should be aware of how rapidly a human body will decay; but in our estimation of length of time since death, we must weigh the multitude of factors that affect decomposition.

The following information is based on the observation of literally hundreds of decaying bodies from both actual forensic cases and bodies under observation at the University of Tennessee Anthropology Research Facility (ARF). The times suggested for the appearance of various circumstances do not take into account the extensive destruction of soft tissue and bone that may be caused by most mammalian carnivores. ARF is surrounded by an outside chain link fence with a wooden privacy fence a few feet inside. This has effectively kept out the larger carnivores, although we do have problems with opossums. Opossums will eat flesh, as will most of the smaller mammals such as mice.

Small birds have been frequently observed on and around the decaying bodies, but they appear to be feeding on the insect larva rather than on the decaying soft tissue. Crows and even buzzards have occasionally been seen, but do not seem to be a major factor in human decay rates in Tennessee, with some exceptions. A few years ago one of my doctoral students, Emily Craig, was conducting hourly photograph and measurement projects on facial changes so that she could better understand facial reproductions. She observed a buzzard landing on the chest of the body during its first days of exposure. The buzzard walked down the body (we have photos of his footprints) and proceeded to peck a hole in the abdominal area and pull out the intestines. The buzzard fed on the intestines but did not bother the remaining parts of the body.

Many variables affect the decay rates of human cadavers. The presence of clothing or other material covering the body (furniture, old car seats, leaves, and brush) or whether the body is in open sun or shade are all important variables. Temperature and rainfall must be considered. We receive 50 to 60 in. of rain a year in Tennessee with most of the fain falling in spring and early summer. Falls are usually drier and we average 2 to 4 inches of snow during winter. The Anthropology Research Facility is in the Tennessee River Valley with typical daytime temperatures in the upper 80s to mid 90s during the summer. Temperatures for typical winter days range from the upper 20s to mid 40s. A summary article of this nature cannot cover all factors, but should be viewed as a baseline for your own interpretations.

## Summer Decay Rates (Bodies on Surface)

### First Day (Fresh)

Flies, most likely Calliphoridae or blowflies, will be attracted to the body within minutes of its deposit in a field. Flies are active when temperatures are above 5°F. Blowflies are most active from midmorning (9 to 10 a.m.) to early evening. Flies will lay their eggs in the body orifices (eyes, ears, nose, mouth, vagina, anus, and especially in any wound). The following characteristics may be present:

1. Egg masses will be white and may look like fine sawdust.
2. Veins under the skin may be turning blue or dark green.
3. Some body fluids may be seen around the nose and mouth.

### First Week (Fresh to Bloated)

During the first week the following observations may be made:

1. Maggots have hatched and are active in the face.
2. Lips may be distended because of the maggot mass under the skin.
3. Skin around the eyes and nose is eaten away exposing bone.
4. Beatles appear as a part of the sequence of carrion insect activity.
5. Skin slippage on the body is beginning.
6. Hair is beginning to slip from the scalp,.
7. Veins are prominent under the skin and are dark blue or dark green.
8. The odor of decay is present.
9. Body fluids may be flowing from the nose, mouth, and rectum.
10. Abdominal areas may be bloated.
11. Molds of various colors begin to appear on the body.

12. Mammalian carnivores may be active and will greatly speed up the decrease of soft tissue by eating the decaying tissue as well as bone.
13. Body fluids (volatile fatty acids) may have killed the vegetation immediately around the body.

## First Month (Bloated to Decay)

In the second through the fourth week, the following characteristics may be observed:

1. Maggot activity is much less and beetles are present on and around the decaying body.
2. Bloating is past and the body is in the decay phase.
3. If in the spring, birds may be using hair that has slipped from the scalp to build nests (Mann et al. 1990).
4. If the body has been covered most of the bones will be exposed where the soft tissue has decayed away.
5. If the body was not covered, the skin between the skeleton and the sunlight will be intact to protect the maggots from the sun. It will now be getting dry and leathery. If the body lies on its back the dry skin will be holding the ribs together.
6. Mammalian carnivores may be carrying off limbs and even the skull.
7. Molds (of various colors) have spread over the soft tissue and on the bones. The area around the body may be stained dark and the body may appear to have been burned. This is from the volatile fatty acids that have leached out of the body during the decay process.
8. If the body decayed on an incline, these volatile fatty acids will kill the vegetation as it flows from the body.
9. Adipocere may appear on a body decaying in a moist environment. If in the water, the adipocere will first be seen in the area from about 2 inches above to about 2 inches below the water line.

## The First Year (Dry)

After the first month and during the first year of exposure, the following may occur:

1. Bleaching of the skeleton has occurred from the sunlight.
2. The portions of the skeleton in the shade may have moss or green algae growing on them.
3. Rodent gnawing may be present along the crest or edges of bones (the eye orbits in the skull, the linea aspera of the femur, etc.).
4. Mice may be using the skull as a nest.
5. Wasps may build a nest in the skull if the skull was dry by late March or early April during the nest building period.

## First Decade (Bone Breakdown)

After the first year, changes in the remains tend to focus on deterioration of the bone tissue:

1. Surfaces of the bone are beginning to exfoliate or flake away. This is especially true in a moist environment. Moisture is the greatest factor in the deterioration of bone. If the body has decayed in direct sunlight, often longitudinal cracks will be seen on the long bones, especially the femur and tibia. This is because of rapid drying in a moist environment.

2. Roots of plants may be growing into or out of the bones. Nature has tended to cover the bones by annual leaf falls (mid-October in Tennessee). Large roots may have grown through the skull or sacrum.
3. Rodent gnawing can be extensive, with much of the bone having been eaten away.

## Winter Decay Rates (Bodies on Surface)

In general, all of the above processes slow down in cold weather. But the processes do continue; even on cold days, maggots will be active inside the body cavity. I have noticed numerous times during winter mornings, with the temperature in the upper 20s, that steam will be rising from the bodies because of the heat generated by the maggots. The whole decay process slows down, however, and the length of time for changes to occur will be greater.

1. Carnivores may be more aggressive during winter. I had a case a few years ago of a man who was missing only 2 days in a snow covered terrain. By the time he was found, dogs had eaten away the entire face, including the facial bones and the soft tissue of the neck down to the cervical vertebrae. The police had to fire their weapons to drive the dogs away from the body when discovered.
2. In cold weather the maggots will leave the skin as a protective layer from the elements (sun, wind, rain, and snow) and the skin will dry and turn to leather.
3. Factor in the change in climate when calculating length of time since death.

## Summary

Outdoor decomposition rates in Tennessee, as they do in all areas, depend on many factors, especially temperature and rainfall. Soft tissue decay can be complete in as short as 2 weeks in the summer and may be so slow in the winter that soft tissue above ground level may dehydrate and turn into leather.

I have not attempted in this review to cover decay rates in buried bodies (Rodriguez and Bass 1985) or in cemetery remains (Berryman 1991), both of which are included in this volume. Books of this nature are important because they aid the professional as well as the student in bringing together into a single volume literature scattered in many journals, theses, dissertations, and books. Let me apologize if I have not reported on an observation that you're particularly interested in. Look at some of the other chapters or set up and conduct your own experiment. If you do the latter, please publish your results, because it is by one research project or observation at a time that we have arrived with information to fill a volume this size.

## References

Bass, W.M.
  1979  Development in the Identification of Human Skeletal Material (1968–1978). *American Journal of Physical Anthropology* 51:555–562.
Bass, W.M.
  1984  Time Interval Since Death: A Difficult Decision. In *Human Identification: Case Studies in Forensic Anthropology,* edited by T.A. Rathbun and J.E. Buikstra, pp 136–147. Charles C Thomas, Springfield, IL.

Berryman, H.E., W.M. Bass, S.A. Symes, and O.C. Smith
  1991  Recognition of Cemetery Remains in the Forensic Setting. *Journal of Forensic Sciences* 36:230–237.

Mann, R.W., W.M. Bass, and L. Meadows
  1990  Time Since Death and Decomposition of the Human Body: Variables and Observation in Case and Experimental Field Studies. *Journal of Forensic Sciences* 35:103–111.

Rodriguez, W.C., and W.M. Bass
  1983  Insect Activity and Its Relationship to Decay Rates of Human Cadavers in East Tennessee. *Journal of Forensic Sciences* 28:423–432.

Rodriguez, W.C., and W.M. Bass
  1985  Decomposition of Buried Bodies and Methods That May Aid in Their Location. *Journal of Forensic Sciences* 30:836–852.

Vass, A.A., W.M. Bass, J.D. Wolt, J.E. Foss, J.T. Amnons
  1992  Time Since Death Determination of Human Cadaver Using Soil Solution. *Journal of Forensic Sciences* 37(5):1236–52.

# Microscopic Structure of Bone

# 13

## MICHAEL SCHULTZ

## Introduction

In physical anthropology and sometimes also in forensic medicine the microscopic structure of the skeleton is frequently neglected, although dry bones are primary sources of material for both scientific disciplines (cf. White 1991). Indeed, many macroscopically observable traits are only understandable on the basis of their microscopic structures. Therefore, microscopic investigations should be included in the routine examination of dry bones.

Particularly in paleopathology, a microscopic analysis should always be carried out when excavated human skeletal remains are examined for vestiges of diseases and cause of death. In the study of the etiology and epidemiology of diseases in prehistoric and historic populations, microscopic investigation is a necessity, especially for differential diagnosis (Schultz 1993).

As a rule, excavated skeletal remains are lacking in strength and elasticity. Frequently they are fragile and extremely brittle, because of the different processes of decomposition. Of course, the kind and the quality of the soil the dead person was buried in is the determining factor in the preservation of bone. Sometimes soil can even protect bone, e.g., if the earth contains manganese or copper (cf. Schultz 1986). Thus, a 4000-year-old skeleton can be much better preserved than the bones of a person interred 100 years ago.

Excavated dry bone no longer has the quality of fresh bone. As a result, archaeological bone should not be decalcified and cut with a microtome. These procedures can cause artifacts (e.g., microfractures, decay), and false diagnoses are almost unavoidable. Frequently, if the bone is very brittle, nothing will remain worth analyzing. Therefore, special techniques should be used to take samples and to produce histological specimens, e.g., epoxy resin-embedded ground sections (cf. Schultz 1988; Schultz and Drommer 1983). In forensic medicine, bone samples are frequently taken from fresh bone. In such cases, specimens can be made using well-known histological techniques following the decalcification process.

A detailed article (e.g., Hancox 1972; Schaffer 1930; Weidenreich 1930) would go beyond the limits of this contribution. Rather, the intent here is to provide a basis for understanding the microstructure of bone, using photomicrographs taken from ground sections made from archaeological bone.

## General Structures and Types of Bones

The external surfaces of bones have a hard and dense structure. If this structure is thin, it is called cortical bone (*corticalis*), if it is thick, it is called compact bone (*substantia compacta*). At joint surfaces, the bone is very smooth, showing no holes in the sense of blood vessel canals, and is called subchondral bone. The interior of bone consists of a spongy, porous substance called cancellous or trabecular bone (*substantia spongiosa*). This part of the bone represents the red bone marrow. In the bones of the skull vault, the spongy structure is the diploe (*diploë*); the cortical structures are the external (*lamina externa*) and the internal lamina (*lamina interna*). Long bones show a relatively large, tubular medullary cavity (*cavitas medullaris*) in their shafts, filled with the yellow bone marrow, which mainly consists of fat cells.

The human skeleton can be classified into three types of bones:

1. Short bones, which are blocky and irregular (e.g., vertebra). They are built up of cancellous bone which is covered by cortical bone.
2. Flat bones, which are flat and tabular (e.g., scapula, bones of skull vault). They are built up as described for short bones.
3. Long bones always have a tubular medullary cavity situated within the shaft and surrounded by compact bone, while the ends are made of cancellous bone which is covered by cortical bone (e.g., humerus, metacarpal). Due to bone growth, the shaft of a long bone is called the diaphysis, the expanded end of the shaft the metaphysis, and the ends of the bone with the articular surfaces the epiphyses.

Furthermore, it should be mentioned that some bones are partly filled with air (e.g., maxilla, frontal and temporal bone). The air-filled cavities are coated by mucous membranes and called paranasal sinuses and tympanum. These bones are termed pneumatic bones.

## General Histology of Bone

Bone, a relatively dense material in the sense of a matrix, represents the main calcified tissue of the skeleton of vertebrates. Other calcified tissues, including calcified cartilage, are the dental tissues enamel, dentine, and cementum. In pathological conditions, other tissues can also be calcified (e.g., ligaments, tendons, muscles). Characteristic cells are embedded in the matrix. In bone tissue, these cells are called osteocytes, which develop from osteoblasts which stem from connective tissue cells. Furthermore, the bone matrix is composed of collagen fibers, i.e., large protein molecules, crystals of a complex of calcium phosphate (hydroxyapatite) and a ground substance (glycosaminoglycans).

Osteoblasts secrete an, at first, amorphous substance called osteoid, a pre-bone tissue, which is calcified after a time by the deposition of calcium phosphate crystals. Bone tissue is resorbed by multinucleated giant cells called osteoclasts. The distribution and design of the collagen fibers characterize the different bone types: bundle bone, woven bone, and fine-fibered bone (Pritchard 1972). Important for growth and function of the bone tissue is a characteristic system of blood vessels and the hemopoietic tissue of bone marrow. Bony tissue is able to change its formation according to its function. For more detailed information, see Cormack 1987; Hancox 1972; Junqueira and Carneiro 1991a, 1991b; Pritchard 1972; Schaffer 1930; Weidenreich 1930.

## The Cells of Bone

### Osteoblasts

As noted above, osteoblasts stem from connective tissue cells, i.e., they are of mesenchymal origin. They are mainly concentrated beneath the periosteum and the surfaces of the bone trabeculae. Osteoblasts have very thin cytoplasmic extensions with which they communicate. They secrete an amorphous substance which is called osteoid and is rich in densely packed collagen fibers. Thus, osteoblasts are responsible for the synthesis of the organic substances of the bone (e.g., collagen, proteoglycans, and glycoprotein). After the deposition of calcium phosphate crystals, the osteoid becomes calcified, i.e., the osteoid is converted into bone.

## Osteocytes

In principle, an osteocyte is an osteoblast that has become embedded within the bone matrix. In their shape and form osteocytes resemble shrunken fibroblasts. The osteocytes lie in oval, flat holes called lacunae (Figure 1). Osteocytes also have very fine, filopodium-like cytoplasmic processes which are run through canaliculi. These canaliculi spread radially from the lacunae of the bone cells. The cytoplasmic processes of the osteocytes are directly connected so that the cells communicate by gap junctions. Developed osteocytes are situated in the calcified ground substance and arranged in rows. There are two different types of osteocytes: osteoblastic and osteolytic osteocytes. The first type is good for the conservation of bone tissue. If osteocytes of this type perish, the neighboring matrix is decomposed. The second is capable of disintegrating hard tissues (i.e., bone dissolution).

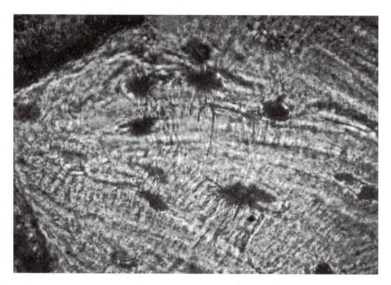

**Figure 1**   Lacunae of osteocytes with fine canaliculi. Femur. Early Middle Ages, Achsheim (Germany). Transverse thin ground section (50 μm). Microscopic view using normal light. Magnification approx. × 630.

## Osteoclasts

Osteoclasts are mobile, multinucleated giant cells which vary greatly in size and in the number of their nuclei; they carry out resorption of the ground substance. They stem from stromal cells of the bone marrow, probably mononucleate monocytes. Thus osteoclasts belong to a system of cells practicing phagocytosis. They probably do not originate by the fusion of several osteoblasts (Junqueira and Carneiro 1991a, 1991b). As a rule, they are found in sharply defined erosion bays, which are called Howship's lacunae. Microscopically, these lacunae look as though they were formed by something biting into external (e.g., surface of a bone trabecula, cf. Figure 2 and Plate 1) or internal surfaces (e.g., wall of blood vessel canal, cf. Figure 3 and Plate 2).

## Intercellular Bone Matrix

The intercellular substance is composed of organic (about 25%) and inorganic materials (about 50%) and of hydration water (about 25%). Because of the relatively high amount of inorganic material, bone is hard as stone. Pritchard (1972) notes that on average, collagen accounts for a third, and inorganic crystalline components for two-thirds of the dry weight of bone matrix.

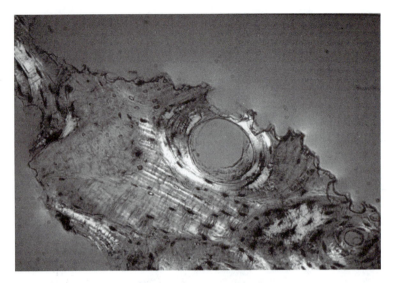

**Figure 2**   Howship's lacunae in surface of compact bone fragment. Frontal bone. Early Middle Ages, Sayala (Egyptian Nubia). Longitudinal thin ground section (50 μm). Microscopic view using polarized light and hilfsobject, red 1st. order (quartz). Magnification approx. × 100. (See color Plate 1 following page 212.)

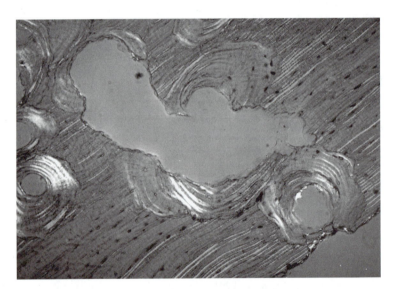

**Figure 3**   Osteoclasic resorption by Howship's lacunae spreading from a Haversian canal. Tibia. Late Classical Antiquity, Linz (Austria). Transverse thin ground section (50 μm). Microscopic view using polarized light and hilfsobject, red 1st. order (quartz). Magnification approx. × 100. (See color Plate 2 following page 212.)

## Inorganic Materials

The inorganic materials consist of bone minerals such as phosphate (about 50%), calcium (about 35%), carbonate (about 6 to 7%), as well as citrate, nitrate, sodium, magnesium, fluoride, and strontium (Junqueira and Carneiro 1991a, 1991b). These minerals build up the hydroxyapatite crystals. Their surfaces are coated by molecules of water.

## Organic Materials

About 90 to 95% of the organic bone tissue consists of masked fibers, called bone collagen. Furthermore, some proteins such as osteonectin, osteocalcin, and osteopontin, as well as proteoglycans and glycosaminoglycans are found in the intercellular matrix. The type of connection occurring between the hydroxyapatite crystals and the collagen fibers limits the hardness and the strength of the bone. While osteonectin is responsible for the connection between bone minerals and collagen, osteopontin determines the connection between bone minerals and cells (Junqueira and Carneiro 1991a, 1991b). The glycosaminoglycans of the ground substance essentially consist of chondroitin-sulfuric acids.

## The Micro-Architecture of Bone

As mentioned above, bone tissue can be classified according to the different structures of collagen fibers. Weidenreich (1930) described five basic types of bone tissue, of which three types are observable in human bone. Pritchard (1972) characterizes these three types as bundle bone, woven bone, and fine-fibered bone:

1. Bundle bone is characterized by its coarse parallel structure, and some of the coarse woven bone in the classification of Weidenreich.
2. Woven bone is a special type of the coarse woven bone described by Weidenreich.
3. Fine-fibered bone includes the parallel as well as the lamellated variety of bone in Weidenreich's classification.

Generally, bundle bone and woven bone are found in mammals only temporarily, because these tissues are, as a rule, associated with the growth and development of the skeleton. Both tissues are replaced by fine-fibered bone, with the exception of small areas (e.g., insertion of tendons and ligaments, margins of the sutures of the cranial vault, within the tooth sockets).

In the routine histological examination of human bone, only two types are strictly differentiated (cf. Hancox 1972; Junqueira and Carneiro 1991a, 1991b): woven bone and lamellar bone.

### Woven Bone

When bone is built up, it will, as a rule, develop primarily as woven bone. Thus, for instance, fetal bone, the cancellous bone found in repair tissue (*callus*), and the newly built bone structures observed in some tumors (e.g., osteosarcoma; cf. Figure 4 and Plate 3) represent typical woven bone tissue. It is characteristic for this type of bone that the collagen fibers in the ground substance, which form partly fine and partly coarse bundles, do not show typical orientation. This is the reason for the lack of lamellar structures. Within small bone trabeculae, however, the bundles of collagen fibers are relatively coarse. Microscopically, the osteocytes seem to be randomly scattered throughout the ground substance. Of course, there are also canals for blood vessels and nerves in woven bone tissue. In comparison to lamellar bone, in woven bone the stability due to minerals is reduced, but the number of osteocytes is increased. Therefore, woven bone is more resistant to traction and flexion.

### Lamellar Bone

Lamellar bone may be compact or cancellous. In the first instance, the vascular spaces are small, in the second, the vascular spaces are large and soft tissue cavities are also developed (Hancox 1972).

**Figure 4**    Primitive woven bone. Chondrosarcoma of distal femur. Middle Ages, Fritzlar (Germany). Transverse thin-ground section (50 μm). Microscopic view using polarized light and hilfsobject, red 1st order (quartz). Magnification approx. × 25. (For color see Plate 3 following page 212.)

Typical traits of lamellar bone tissue are lamellae and canaliculi. The lamellae are separated from each other very distinctly (Figure 5 and Plate 4). They are characterized by the presence of osteocytes and collagen fibers. Within each lamella, the collagen fibers have a typical orientation. The course and the angle of ascent of the collagen fibers alternate from lamella to lamella, i.e., the collagen fibers run contrary to each other. This orientation is of functional importance. Most of the fibers of two neighboring lamellae cross rectangularly. Within each lamella, some fibers show an acute angle in their course in comparison to the majority of fibers of the same lamella. Thus, a kind of fibrous lattice develops. Additionally a small number of fibers cross to the neighboring lamellae, resulting in a compound of fibers.

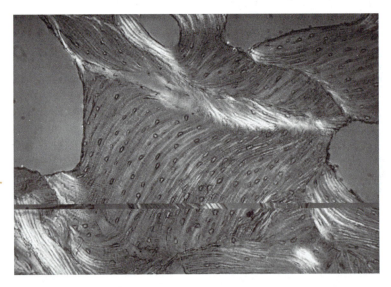

**Figure 5**    Lamellar bone, compact area. Tibia. Eneolithic (Late Neolithic) Age. Baštečki (Ukraine). Transverse thin ground section (50 μm). Microscopic view using polarized light. Magnification approx. × 100. (For color see Plate 4 following page 212.)

The microstructure of lamellar bone, particularly the course and the orientation of the collagen fibers which are birefringent, can be easily observed in polarized light (Figure 6). When collagen fibers look bright in polarized light, they are oriented transversely to the light beam, i.e., the light beam meets the fibers vertically (anisotropic). When the collagen fibers look dark, they are oriented approximately in the direction of the light beam, i.e., the light beam meets the fibers orthograde or obliquely (Figure 7 and Plate 5). Thus, the course of collagen fibers can be detected by polarized light. The orientations of the lamellae vary, but in the compact tissue of the diaphyses of the long tubular bones, the disposition of the lamellae is very regular.

**Figure 6**   Lamellar bone trabecula. Femur. Early Middle Ages, Achsheim (Germany). Transverse thin ground section (50 μm). Microscopic view using polarized light. Magnification approx. × 160.

**Figure 7**   Lamellar bone, Haversian system. Femur. Roman Age. Niğde-Hıdırlı (Turkey). Transverse thin ground section (50 μm). Microscopic view using polarized light and hilfsobject, red 1st. order (quartz). Magnification approx. × 160. (For color see Plate 5 following page 212.)

## *External and Internal Basic Lamellae*

The basic or circumferential lamellae cover a long tubular bone in the area of its shaft on the external (periosteal) and on the internal (endosteal) surfaces (Figure 8). The number of the external lamellae is greater than that of the internal lamellae. The internal basic lamellae do not represent a closed boundary, because small bone trabeculae of the cancellous bone of the metaphysis originate from these lamellae (Figure 9). All together, the number of external and internal basic lamellae decreases with age.

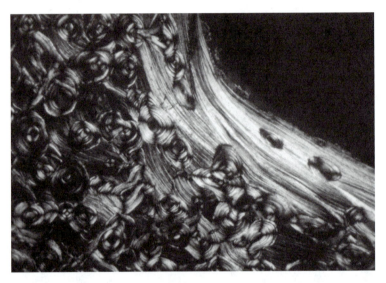

**Figure 8**   Lamellar bone, internal basic lamella. Roman Age, Niğde-Hıdırlı (Turkey). Transverse thin ground section (50 µm). Microscopic view using polarized light. Magnification approx. × 25.

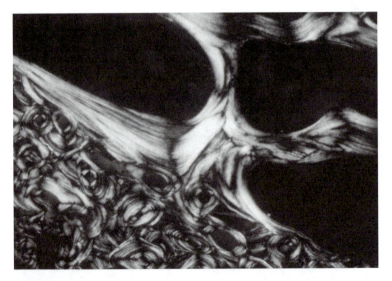

**Figure 9**   Lamellar bone, small bone trabeculae growing out from the remains of the internal basic lamella. Tibia. Roman Age, Niğde-Hıdırlı (Turkey). Transverse thin ground section (50 µm). Microscopic view using polarized light. Magnification approx. × 25.

**Figure 10**   Lamellar bone, compact bone substance with Haversian systems and interstitial lamellae. Femur. Roman Age, Niğde-Hıdırlı (Turkey). Transverse thin ground section (50 μm). Microscopic view using polarized light. Magnification approx. × 25. (For color see Plate 6 following page 212.)

## *Special Lamellae*

The most common type of special lamellae are those of the Haversian system, which are also called osteons. An osteon is a system of circular lamellae and is the unit of structure of compact bone tissue (Figure 10 and Plate 6). In the center of an osteon, the Haversian canal is situated containing blood vessels. The osteon includes a large number of lacunae, each containing an osteocyte. The canaliculi, which are associated with each bone cell lacuna, form a characteristic network. The lamellae and their osteocytes are oriented concentrically around this canal (see Figure 7). The alternation in the direction of the collagen fibers in the lamellae causes the optic phenomenon observed in transverse bone sections in polarized light (see Figure 7). The number of special lamellae per osteon varies between 3 and 20. This variation is caused by the growth process. When an osteon forms, the external lamella forms first and is then, of course, also the oldest lamella of the osteon (Junqueira and Carneiro 1991a, 1991b). The subsequent growth moves from the periphery to the Haversian canal. Thus, in old osteons, the lumen of the canal is restricted. Osteons are separated from each other and from other lamellae by a thin cement line which is built up of ground substance with a highly reduced collagen content.

The lamellae of the osteons are several centimeters in length. They branch frequently and can be connected to each other. As a rule, osteons mainly lie in the direction of the long axis of the bone. Thus, they run more or less parallel to the bone surface. Therefore, in cross section, the Haversian canal shows a round opening and the surrounded lamellae are ring shaped.

## *Interstitial Lamellae*

Especially in compact bone tissue, the irregular angular spaces between the osteons are filled with lamellae. These lamellae, usually called interstitial lamellae, are, as a rule, remains of osteons which have perished, or more likely, have been partly destroyed during the internal growth and reconstruction of the bone (Figure 10). The structure of interstitial lamellae and osteons gives the compact bone, in transverse section viewed by the microscope, the character of breccia.

### Blood Vessel Canals

In compact bone, two types of blood vessel canals can be observed: central or Haversian canals (*canales centrales*) and Volkmann's canals (*canales perforantes*).

The Haversian canals (see Figure 7) belong to a canal system which runs longitudinally through the compact substance of a long bone carrying blood vessels and nerves. They also contain connective tissue and special cells covering the bone surface. In individuals suffering from senile osteoporosis, fatty tissue is also found. The transverse diameter of such a central canal depends on the number of special lamellae, i.e., the larger the canal the more numerous the lamellae.

The Volkmann's canals run transversely through the compact bone, vertically entering the external or internal bone surface, crossing the external or internal basic lamellae and the special lamellae of osteons, and communicating with Haversian canals (Figure 11 and Plate 7) and also with the bone marrow cavity. Therefore, they do not have their own system of special lamellae. Their wall is, as a rule, only built up of one thin lamella. Blood vessels and nerves of the periosteum and the endosteum enter the Volkmann's canals.

**Figure 11**    Lamellar bone, Volkmann's canal. Femur. Roman Age, Niğde-Hıdırlı (Turkey). Transverse thin ground section (50 μm). Microscopic view using polarized light. Magnification approx. × 100. (For color see Plate 7 following page 212.)

The morphological situation described for compact bone tissue is also found in the trabeculae of the normal cancellous bone of adult individuals. Because of shapes and sizes of bone trabeculae in the different types of cancellous bone, its lamellation sometimes varies in structure, i.e., it is not as distinctly lamellated as the compact bone tissue.

## Periosteum, Endosteum, and Bone Marrow

The external and internal surfaces of bones are covered by connective tissue. The external structure is called periosteum, the internal structure endosteum. Surfaces of bone which are not covered by these structures are resorbed by osteoclasts.

### Periosteum

The periosteum consists of two levels of connective tissue:

1. *Stratum fibrosum* is the external layer of the periosteum, which is rich in collagen fibers forming a dense network and in fibroblasts. Bundles of collagen fibers entering the external bone matrix are called Sharpey's fibers. By means of these fibers, the periosteum is fixed to the bone surface.
2. *Stratum osteogenicum* is the internal layer of the periosteum representing the cambium layer, which contains many blood vessels, nerves, and cells, e.g., fibroblasts, (pre-)osteoblasts. This is the most important structure for bone regeneration (e.g., following fractures).

The blood vessels found in the periosteum branch out and enter the bone through the Volkmann's canals and a few larger canals whose openings are called nutrient foramina (*foramina nutricia*).

## Endosteum

As a rule, collagen fibers are seldom found in the endosteum, which represents only one layer of flattened cells of connective tissue. This thin structure covers the internal surface of bone, including the trabeculae of the cancellous bone and the walls of the blood vessel canals. The endosteum resembles the periosteum in some respects. It is also able to build up new bone.

## Bone Marrow

Areas of cancellous bone contain, especially in the skeleton of children and young adults, the red bone marrow which represents the blood-forming system. In young infants, red marrow is also partly found in the medullary cavities of the long tubular bones, in which, as a rule, the yellow bone marrow is situated. The yellow marrow contains mainly fat cells. As the red bone marrow belongs to the hemopoietic system, it will not be described further.

# Growth and Histogenesis of Bone

There are two different kinds of osteogenesis: intramembranous and chondral ossification.

1. During intramembranous ossification, bone originates directly in connective tissue (e.g., bones of skull vault, clavicle).
2. During chondral ossification, bone originates indirectly, i.e., primarily a cartilage model is formed which secondarily ossifies (most bones of skeleton, e.g., humerus). There are two kinds of chondral ossification: bone originates in the periphery of the cartilage model (e.g., diaphyses of long bones) and the process is then called perichondral ossification, or bone originates intracartilaginously (e.g., center of epiphyses) and the process is called endochondral ossification.

Chondrally ossified bones principally grow in their length in a growth or epiphyseal plate oriented roughly at a transverse level between the diaphysis and the epiphyses. The increase in diameter of bones is achieved by appositional growth. Bones, originating intramembranously, also grow by apposition. For more detailed information see Cormack 1987; Junqueira and Carneiro 1991a, 1991b; Schaffer 1930; and Weidenreich 1930.

In fetal and early infant life, the internal structure of bone is only dependent upon its origin. Later, the internal structure also depends on the functional stress experience during lifetime (cf. Currey 1984). Thus, especially in bones which originate by chondral ossification, the development of osteons can be easily studied. Sometimes, in some parts of the skeleton, cancellous bone is transformed into compact bone. In this case, the cavities of the cancellous bone which are usually filled with bone marrow become smaller and smaller, as osteoblasts, which cover the bone surface, put down layer after layer over the primary trabeculae. If this process continues, the primary marrow cavity containing the blood vessels of this area becomes very narrow. Then, thin bone lamellae are concentrically built up around the blood vessels and a primitive Haversian system (primary osteons) emerges.

In principle, the same procedure can be observed during very early infant life, when in the shaft of long bones the primary woven bone develops into primitive osteon bone. In some places which can be studied in the transverse section of a diaphysis of a long bone, the bone tissue begins to dissolve. This process, which is associated with the presence of osteoclasts, affects not only parts of the newly built primitive Haversian systems, but also the periosteal bone. In this way, small cavities (resorption holes) filled with blood vessels and embryonic bone marrow are formed. The destruction then stops, the activity of the osteoblasts starts, and a new generation of osteons (secondary osteons) originates by the concentric growth of lamellae around the blood vessels. In the same way, the third and the fourth generations of osteons grow. Remains of destroyed osteons survive as interstitial lamellae. The mechanism is the building up of osteons by bone apposition on the internal surfaces of lamellae of bone surrounding blood vessels. Thus, a progressive decrease in the size of the osteons and an increase of the compactness of bone can be observed.

## Acknowledgments

The author wishes to thank M. Brandt and Ingrid Hettwer-Steeger for preparing the ground sections and Cyrilla Maelicke for reading the English text.

## References

Cormack, D.H.
    1987  *Ham's Histology.* Lippincott, Philadelphia.

Currey, J.
    1984  *The Mechanical Adaptations of Bones.* Princeton University Press, Princeton, NJ.

Hancox, N.M.
    1972  *Biology of Bone.* Cambridge University Press, Cambridge, MA.

Junqueira, L.C., and J. Carneiro
    1991a  *Histologie. Zytologie, Histologie und Mikroskopische Anatomie des Menschen.* Springer, Berlin.
    1991b  *Basic Histology.* Lange Medical Publications, Los Altos, CA.

Pritchard, J.J.
    1972  General Histology of Bone. In *The Biochemistry and Physiology of Bone*, edited by G.H. Bourne. Academic Press, New York.

Schaffer, J.R.
    1930  Die Stützgewebe. In *Handbuch der Mikroskopischen Anatomie des Menschen, 2,* edited by F. v. Moellendorf, pp. 1–390. Berlin.

Schultz, M.
    1986  *Die mikroskopische Untersuchung Prähistorischer Skeletfunde: Anwendung und Aussagemöglichkeiten der Differentialdiagnostischen Untersuchung in der Paläopathologie,* pp. 140. Archäologie und Museum, Vol. 6. Amt für Museen und Archäologie Baselland, Liestal.

1988   Methoden der Licht- und Elektronenmikroskopie. In *Anthropologie. Handbuch der vergleichenden Biologie des Menschen, Vol. 1: Wesen und Methoden der Anthropologie* edited by R. Knussmann, pp. 698–730. Fischer Verlag, Stuttgart.

1993   Microscopic Investigation of Archaeological Skeletal Remains. A Convincing Necessity for Differential Diagnosis in Paleopathology. *American Journal of Physical Anthropology,* Suppl. 16: 175.

Schultz, M., and R. Drommer

1983   Möglichkeiten der Präparateherstellung aus dem Gesichtsschädelbereich für die makroskopische und mikroskopische Untersuchung unter Verwendung neuer Kunststofftechniken. In *Experimentelle Mund-Kiefer-Gesichtschirurgie: Mikrochirurgische Eingriffe,* edited by W. Hoppe, pp. 95–97. Stuttgart.

Weidenreich, F.

1930   Das Knochengewebe. In *Handbuch der mikroskopischen Anatomie des Menschen, 2,* edited by F. v. Moellendorf, pp. 391–520. Berlin.

White, T.D.

1991   *Human Osteology.* Academic Press, San Diego.

# Microscopic Investigation of Excavated Skeletal Remains: A Contribution to Paleopathology and Forensic Medicine

# 14

MICHAEL SCHULTZ

## Introduction

In paleopathology as well as in forensic medicine, not only dry bones, but also mummified tissues are examined by medical techniques such as radiology, endoscopy, and microscopy. During recent years it has been clearly demonstrated that microscopic investigation can add an abundance of data which can neither be seen macroscopically nor in radiographs (cf. Schultz 1986, 1988b, 1993a). Particularly, the examination of thin ground sections viewed in polarized light yields results which allow not only a diagnosis of diseases in macerated bone, but also gives important information about the state of preservation and the kind of post-mortem destruction. Thus, structures which cannot be detected in normal light can be observed and diagnosed in polarized light. Although Weber (1927) successfully used the microscopic examination in differential diagnosis of inflammatory bone diseases, little attention was paid to this relatively new technique in the following decades. Only when Hackett (1976) demonstrated the usefulness of microscopic analysis of thin ground sections was the technique revived, only to be neglected again after a short period of interest.

Kloiber (1957) was right when he described archaeological skeletons as "biohistorical documents." The term makes very clear the potential importance of the evidence gleaned from bones for archaeological and forensic science. It is basically of no consequence at all whether the findings are from animals or from human beings. Unfortunately, especially in Europe, the chances proffered by osteological examination are seldom utilized. The reason for this lies in the financial situation prevailing at present in most archaeological institutes and also in the lack of interest on the part of many archaeologists, who do not appreciate the wealth of information to be found in the results of osteological investigations. In the case of human skeletal remains, these are the primary source of information because they represent human individuals whose life and way of life are what archaeologists and historians are trying to explore (cf. Pfeiffer and Williamson 1991; Reeve and Adams 1993).

Paleopathology plays the dominant role in the investigation of living conditions and the ways of life of prehistoric and historic populations (cf. Schultz 1982). Paleopathology, an interdisciplinary field in which the fields of medicine, anthropology, and archaeology overlap, is concerned with examination of skeletons, human and nonhuman, recovered in archaeological excavations (cf. Moodie 1923; Tasnádi-Kubacska 1962). Hereby, individual cases (casuistics) and also causes (etiology) and the distribution and frequency of certain illnesses (epidemiology) are investigated. From a demographic point of view, causes and frequency of diseases in prehistoric and historic populations can be comparatively investigated diachronically for a limited habitat, or within the same time span or stage of civilization for different geographical regions (cf. Schultz 1987, 1993a). In many cases, the results of a paleopathological investigation can lead to the reconstruction of the living conditions of populations of days gone by or of the ecological conditions prevailing at those times (Schultz 1982). Thus, statements regarding availability of foodstuffs, living and working conditions, sanitary and hygienic conditions, and certain climatic and geographical influences can be made (cf. Schultz 1982).

Within the framework of interdisciplinary projects, paleopathology has, in recent years, been able to provide more and more information on living conditions of prehistoric and historic populations. The steadily increasing interest in the life of people in the past will, in the future, hopefully lead to increased use of the results from osteological research.

Not only can traces of illness be uncovered by microscopic analysis, but changes due to aging and function of parts of the skeleton can also be analyzed microscopically. This holds true even when the effects of heat and fire, occurring around the time point of death or after death, have led to typical changes in the bone tissue.

## Methods

In the course of a paleopathological investigation, archaeological skeletal remains are examined using macroscopic, endoscopic, radiological, light and scanning electron microscopic techniques. Of all these methods, microscopic investigation proves to be the most useful. A scanning electron microscope yields good diagnostic results, without any great technical difficulties. However, light microscopic investigations on thin ground sections or polished bone samples in normal or polarized light yield much more useful results (Schultz 1986, 1988b; Schultz and Drommer 1983). Microradiography also often yields useful supplementary information.

## Results

In this contribution, the most important applications of microscopic investigations of archaeological skeletal remains will be discussed with reference to only a few examples. The information is by no means meant to be exhaustive, since such a report would simply take up too much space. For the interested reader further information can be obtained from the literature (e.g., Schultz 1986, 1988b, 1993a,1993b; Grupe and Garland 1993).

### Determination of Alterations in the Compact Bone Tissue of the Long Tubular Bones due to Age

Since in the course of a lifetime the structure of bones, and therefore of the compact bone tissue, undergoes characteristic changes, various microscopic methods have been developed with the help of which a relatively dependable determination of the age of an individual can be made (e.g., Kerley 1965, 1969; Kerley and Ubelaker 1978; Ahlquist and Damsten 1969; Uytterschaut 1993). The histomorphological determination of age is particularly helpful, of course, when other methods prove to be unsuitable. Thus, it has become well established in many institutes of forensic medicine.

In principle, microscopic characteristics are dependent upon age. It is well known that the shafts of the long bones of children are not composed of osteon bones but rather of *schalenknochen*. Following the spreading of the blood vessels into the tissue, the first primary osteons slowly develop, under the steadily increasing physical strain, into the typical osteon bone. The number of osteons with relatively narrow lumina increases, i.e., the osteons move relatively closer together, and the ratio of external to internal basic lamellae in the overall cross section decreases with increasing age. In senile bones, the number of osteons usually

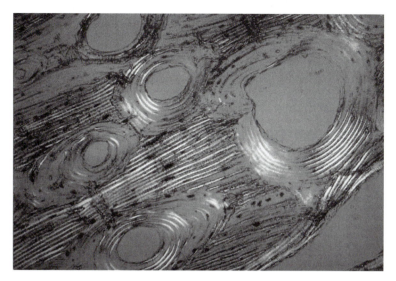

**Figure 1**  Old-age osteoporosis. Compact bone tissue of a femur of a senile male. Eneolithic Age, Baštečki (Ukraine). Magnification × 100. (For color see Plate 8 following page 212.)

decreases again. These are then characterized by a wide lumen (old age osteoporosis; Figure 1 and Plate 8).

## Determination of Alterations in the Compact Bone Tissue of the Long Tubular Bones due to Their Function

The skeleton adapts itself to the physical strain to which it is subjected with hypertrophy due to increased activity or atrophy due to inactivity. Although the skeleton is not as directly influenced by changes as are the muscles, distinct changes can be observed which allow conclusions to be drawn about the type and duration of physical strain. These changes affect not only the macroscopic appearance of the bone but also the microscopic structure. Therefore, microscopic investigation can sometimes throw light on antemortem restriction of function of the skeleton (e.g., paralysis following poliomyelitis; cf. Schultz 1982, 1986, 1988a).

As an example of an extreme case of atrophy due to inactivity combined with dystrophy, let us consider the skeleton of a 40- to 45-year-old man who lived in the Rocky Mountains between 1315 and 1680 A.D., in what is now the state of Arizona, in the Anasazi settlement Gran Quivira (Schultz 1982). The man suffered for several years from a serious case of rheumatic polyarthritis (probably the rhizomelic type of *morbus bechterew*). This disease led to an extensive ankylosis of the joints of the extremities in a bent position. Because this process continued for many years, probably decades, and movement in the ankylosed joints was no longer possible, the bone, as the results of the microscopic investigation showed, underwent fundamental changes in its compact structure in the sense of atrophy due to inactivity. The number of regular osteons was considerably reduced. A major portion of the osteons still present were degenerated. Most of the cross sections of the femur were full of tangential lamellae (Figure 2 and Plate 9).

## Problems Arising from the Time the Bones Lie in the Earth and Determination of Postmortem Damage due to Biogenic and Abiogenic Decomposition

The preservation of archaeological skeletal remains depends to a great extent on the surroundings. A bone which has spent a long time underground is usually different from one which, for example, was always kept in a sarcophagus in a vault. This means that the type and degree

**Figure 2**　Atrophy due to inactivity as a result of extensive ankylosis. Compact bone tissue of a femur of a mature male. Pre-Columbian age, Gran Quivira (Arizona, U.S.A.). Magnification × 25. (For color see Plate 9 following page 212.)

of microscopic damage of the bone usually gives insight into its surroundings. In damp surroundings, the bone shows different traces of damage (e.g., traces of algae growth, cf. Süßmann-Bertozzi 1984) from one from a dry environment. However, a bone stored in a dry environment can develop traces of algal or fungal growth due to improper storage after excavation. The skeletal remains from the charnel house of St. Martin's Church in Klosterneuburg (Lower Austria) provide us with an example of this problem (Figure 3 and Plate 10). A skeleton initially buried in sand or fine gravel will still also have typical grains of sand or crystals inside (e.g., sinuses, spongiosa spaces, marrow cavities). After a period of several decades or centuries, the remains were reburied in an area containing loess or humus earth. A microscopic examination can, in this case, reveal whether the skeleton found during the archaeological excavation was immediately buried where it was found or whether a secondary burial might have taken place. This question is often of importance in the case of poorly preserved or incomplete skeletons; it can, however, also be of interest in the search for the origins of certain relics.

　　Sometimes, the conditions prevailing underground in a grave can vary so much that a part of the skeleton can have completely disappeared in the course of decomposition. For example, perhaps the bones of the lower leg and its foot may be no longer detectable macroscopically (cf. Schultz 1978). The archaeologist will probably assume a case of amputation (Pauli 1978). A microscopic examination of a sample of earth from the region in which the bones can macroscopically no longer be seen can uncover the remains of human bone tissue, e.g., trabeculae of spongy bone (cf. Figure 4 and Plate 11) or compact bone islands. If the microscopic structures found correspond to the hard tissue of the macroscopically no longer visible bones, the loss of the limb antemortem can usually be excluded. Such investigations are also possible in the case of *leichenschatten* (corpse shadow, i.e., skeletons completely decomposed so that only a discoloration of the earth remains).

　　As described above, with enough experience, the age of an individual can be relatively reliably determined from cross sections of human long bones. Furthermore, these methods should be attempted in the examination of a *leichenschatten* (corpse shadow) or of a poorly preserved skeleton, since they yield relatively reliable results in the demographic analysis of a poorly preserved burial ground.

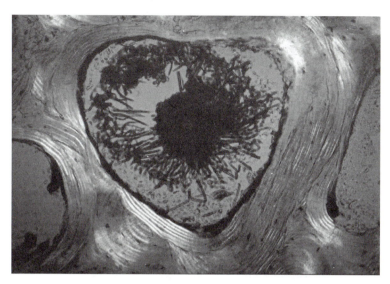

**Figure 3** Fungus (parts of "fruchtkörper," or fruiting bodies, "hüllhyphen," or hyphal sheath, and ascospores) in large blood vessel canal of compact bone tissue. Femur. Late Middle Ages, St. Martin's Church in Klosterneuburg (Austria). Magnification × 100. (For color see Plate 10 following page 212.)

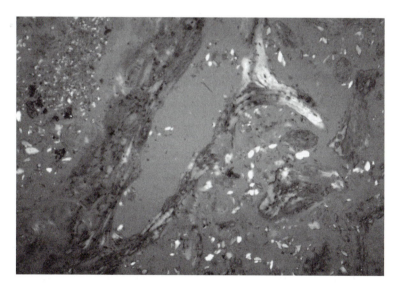

**Figure 4** Small fragments of bone in soil (*leichenschatten, or* corpse shadow). Eneolithic Age, Čertomlyk (Ukraine). Transverse thin ground section (50 μm). Microscopic view using polarized light and hilfsobject, red 1 st. order (quartz). Magnification approx. × 25. (For color see Plate 11 following page 212.)

Microscopic investigation usually allows complete segregation of human from animal bones (Harsányi 1978, 1993; Schultz 1986), even when only small bone fragments are available for study. This is of some interest differentiating between human and animal bones, when small fragments of long bones are found at an archaeological site in a pit showing evidence of cannibalism (e.g., fresh splintering of bone tissue, cut marks, discoloration due to fire).

Crystals developing during the time underground can sometimes bring about fossilization of a bone. This is, however, relatively seldom seen in prehistoric or historic skeletal remains. Newly crystallized structures can aggregate and almost completely break up inner structures of a bone (cf. Schultz 1986).

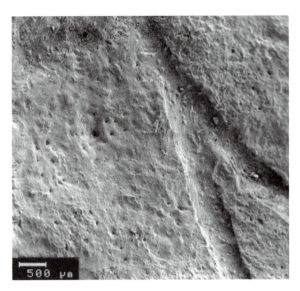

**Figure 5**    Vestiges of plant roots. External skull surface. Preclassic Age, Tehuacan (Mexico). Scanning electron microscope; bar = 500 μm.

Within the framework of a microscopic investigation of archaeological skeletal remains, traces of biogenic decomposition are of particular importance in the interpretation of results (Schultz 1986). Whether the bones are of human or animal origin is of no importance. The following types of damage which are often observed should be kept in mind.

## Damage Caused by Roots of Plants

Large roots leave distinctive traces on the surface of bones in the form of indentations (Figure 5). Often the roots grow through the bones leaving round holes which are sometimes misinterpreted as being vestiges of damage caused antemortem (e.g., tumor metastasis, pathway of growth of a fistula, trepanation, injuries caused by arrows). In long bones, large roots can grow for a considerable distance within the marrow cavities and then exit through a round hole.

Small and very small roots cause damage which to the inexperienced eye can only be distinguished from vestiges of antemortem disease with the aid of magnification. A reliable diagnosis can be achieved with a scanning electron microscope (Figure 6). Particularly in the internal lamina of the cranium, the traces of roots can be confused with antemortem alterations, because they resemble impressions of blood vessels as, e.g., can occur in the organization of an epidural hematoma (Figure 7) or in a hemorrhagic–inflammatory process of the meninges (Schultz 1987, 1990, 1993b). The development of fine root impressions can be explained as follows. Many plants need trace elements for their growth which are also present in bones (e.g., Ca). For the plants to be able to make use of these trace elements in the ground or in bones, they first have to be dissolved. The fine root hairs of some plants produce hydrogen ions. These react with the salts in the earth so that in the immediate environment of the root hairs a more acid milieu develops. This causes the bone to dissolve in the direction of growth of the fine roots. On the bone surface, root impressions develop. With the help of light or scanning electron microscopy, investigations of the impressions left by the plants can easily be distinguished from antemortem alterations (e.g., impressions of vessels).

Sometimes root impressions can, if they run straight, look like old traces of wounds, which apparently have left scars in the course of healing or have eroded in the earth. Microscopic examination of bone surfaces is eminently suitable for distinction between old and new traces of wounds. As an example, on the surface of a Bronze Age skull, the trace of a wound is visible from which, on the basis of the macroscopic examination, it cannot be said

**Figure 6**  Remains of roots, which, with the help of their fine root hairs, have dug their way into a human long bone. Tetelpan (Mexico). Scanning electron microscope; bar = 40 μm.

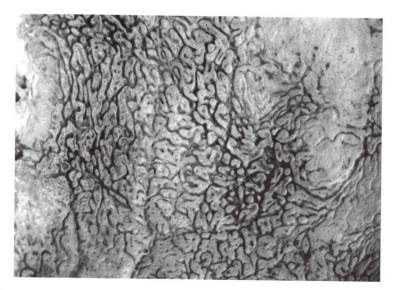

**Figure 7**  Organized epidural hematoma. Internal skull surface. Early Middle Ages, Schretzheim (Germany). Macrophotograph.

with certainty whether it occurred in the Bronze Age or was inflicted by the spade of the archaeologist. The surface of the wound shows signs of erosion. In the case of an "old" wound from the Bronze Age, usually, traces of erosion would be seen due to the length of time passed. The wound could, however, be an artifact. It is well known that bone lying in damp earth can often be cut with a spade like wet cardboard. Thus, a "new" gash can indeed occur. A "new" trace of a gash can look just as crumbly on the surface as an "old" one, if the bone substance is not completely brittle. These two kinds of traces can look so alike under magnification that they cannot be distinguished with certainty. The investigation of a thin ground section of a bone sample which is ground at right angles to the trace of the gash usually provides the answer. In the case of an "old" wound, the narrow erosion border which almost always develops would run not only along the original bone surface but would also follow

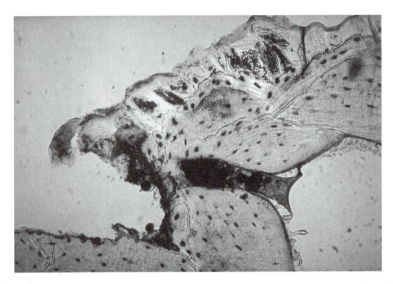

**Figure 8**  Growth vestiges of algae in compact human bone tissue. Radius. Early Middle Ages, Niens (Germany). Transverse thin ground section (50 μm). Microscopic view using normal light. Magnification approx. × 100.

the groove of the gash. In the case of a "new" trace, the narrow erosion border usually follows the entire original bone surface. It would not be found along the groove of the wound.

## Damage due to Fungi, Algae and Bacteria

Bones are also known to be affected under the earth by fungi, algae, and bacteria (Schultz 1986). The traces of damage due to fungi and algae appear in thin ground sections as horizontal or vertical channels which can sometimes converge to form large flat or tuft-shaped forms and even cause the entire bone tissue to disintegrate.

The channels with small lumina earlier seen by Wedl (1864) must be interpreted as pathways of growth of algae (Figure 8) (Schultz 1986; Süßmann-Bertozzi 1984), while the large, clearly tubular spaces (Figure 9) are the results of fungal growth postmortem (Schultz 1986; cf. Piepenbrink 1984). Because of their morphology and orientation, these "bohrkanäle," or bore channels, (Wedl 1864) were described by Hackett (1981) as "linear-longitudinal tunnels" or "budded tunnels" and represent, microscopically, typical patterns of damage.

Actinomycetes are bacteria which grow like mycelia. Streptomycetes belong to this group of microorganisms which are found in bones preserved in the earth and are immediately evident due to their typical growth traces (Figure 10) (Schultz 1986).

The hollow spaces arising from such damage are usually filled with the remains of fungi, algae and bacteria which secondarily colonize the buried bone. Tertiary colonization of other small organisms, such as mites and bacteria, may also move into the already affected structures (cf. Figure 11).

All these organisms in the disintegrating bone tissue live and die for many generations in buried bones. They reproduce and infiltrate the bone tissue over the course of centuries until it almost completely disappears. They are most easily identified by light microscopy with a phase contrast or a fluorescence microscope, but also with a scanning electron microscope (Schultz 1986, 1988b). It is interesting that different organisms do not infiltrate the same bone to the same extent throughout. In the course of a careful light and scanning electron microscopic investigation of specimens removed from archaeological skeletal remains, traces of fungi, algae, and bacteria are found in almost every bone. The extent of infiltration can vary enormously and depends on the milieu surrounding the bone. This knowledge is highly important for chemical and physical investigations with respect to possible sources of error. In this

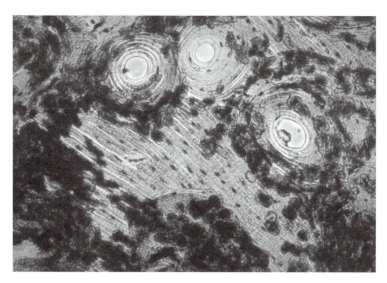

**Figure 9** Growth vestiges of fungi in compact human bone tissue. Femur fragment. Preclassic Age, Tetelpan (Mexico). Transverse thin ground section (50 μm). Microscopic view using normal light. Magnification approx. × 100.

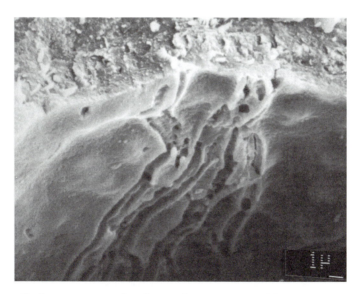

**Figure 10** Wall of Haversian canal with growth vestiges caused by streptomycetes. Long bone fragment. Preclassic Age, Tetelpan (Mexico). Scanning electron microscope, bar = 1 μm.

context, it should be remembered that certain minerals present in the earth (e.g., Cu, Mn) can have a strong preservative effect on bone tissue lying in the earth. In such cases, prehistoric bone tissue can show a morphology similar to fresh tissue. The most impressive example is copper impregnation of archaeological skeletal remains due to bronze jewelry lying directly on the bone surface (Schultz 1986).

## Damage Done by Insects and Their Larvae

Damage inflicted by insects and their larvae is relatively rare. This is probably due to the fact that insects living in bones in the ground are much more dependent on climate or certain geographical conditions than their phytogenic counterparts and, therefore, are seen less often.

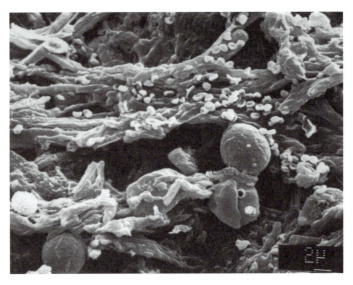

**Figure 11**   Filling of spongiosa spaces: fungal hyphae, fungal spores, and sporangia from actinomycetes. Spongy bone fragment. Relic, thought to be that of St. Martin, Middle Ages, Unterbillingshausen (Germany). Scanning electron microscope; bar = 2 μm.

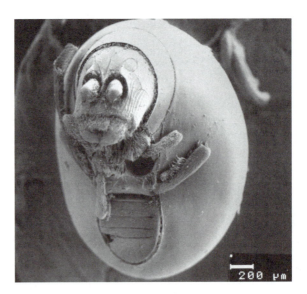

**Figure 12**   Hump spider beetle (*Gibbium psylloides*) found in old Egyptian mummy. Scanning electron microscope; bar = 200 μm.

On the other hand, traces of damage caused by small insects are only judged correctly in a few cases, since they are similar to traces of damage from roots and not easily recognized.

Mites or parts of mites (e.g., *exuvia*) are found relatively often in bones in the ground (Schultz 1986). Sometimes, tiny parts such as insect scales can be found, which, like pollen, probably enter the bones in a secondary manner (Schultz and Schwartz 1982; Schwartz and Schultz 1994). Now and again, pathways in the form of round channels are seen which are an indication of large insects or larvae (Schultz, in press). Bones found in dry and sandy regions apparently often show insect pathways and also parts of insect bodies which live in disintegrating bones (Figures 12 to 15). Similar situations have been reported for mummies (Curry 1979; Garner 1986).

**Figure 13**   Fragment of the extremity of an insect. Diploe of human skull. Early Middle Ages, Sayala, (Egyptian Nubia). Scanning electron microscope; bar = 40 μm.

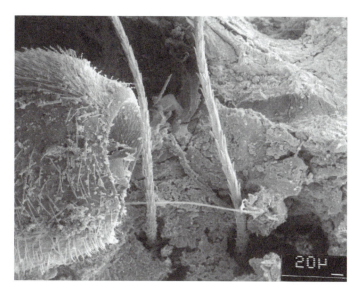

**Figure 14**   Fragment of the extremity of an insect (cf. Figure 13) and setae from at least two individuals. Diploe of a human skull. Sayala (Egyptian Nubia). Scanning electron microscope; bar = 20 μm.

It is striking that some insects can be observed quite frequently, especially in mummies stored in an exhibition room or in museum storage. The insect most frequently found seems to be the hump spider beetle (*Gibbium psylloides*) which lives not only in European museums (cf. Curry 1979; Schwartz and Schultz 1994), but is also closely associated with human habitats and is regarded as one of the most common storage species living in Europe and the Near and Middle East. Such specimens can be studied easily by scanning electron microscopy.

Sometimes in the skin of naturally mummified mummies small round holes are seen with a diameter of about 1 mm. These holes are produced by insects or their larvae (e.g., fly). Such holes are seldom observed in intentionally mummified corpses (Figure 16). The holes were made by the deathwatch beetle at a time when the mummy was housed in a museum

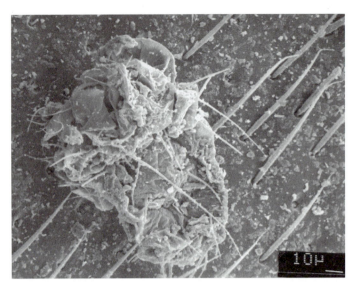

**Figure 15**   Remains of a mite on the wing cover of an insect found in the diploe of a human skull. Sayala (Egyptian Nubia). Scanning electron microscope; bar = 10 µm.

**Figure 16**   Holes made by deathwatch beetle. Mummified head of a Turk. Early Modern Age, Collection of Institute of Anthropology in Frankfurt-am-Main. Macrophotograph.

(cf. Schultz 1995). The result of the microscopic analysis of a mummified piece of skin with such a hole and the associated canal led to this diagnosis (Figure 17).

## Determination of Traces of Disease and How to Distinguish Them from Postmortem Alterations in the Sense of Pseudopathology

Determination of traces of disease is not always easy in archaeological skeletal remains, since factors influencing them during the time in the ground often cause morphological alterations which are similar to vestiges of antemortem processes (pseudopathology; cf. Wells 1967;

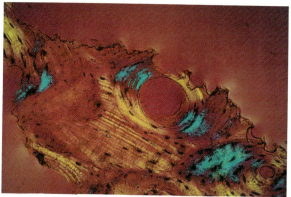

**Plate 1** Howship's lacunae in surface of compact bone fragment. Frontal bone. Early Middle Ages, Sayala (Egyptian Nubia). Longitudinal thin ground section (50 μm). Microscopic view using polarized light and hilfsobject, red 1st order (quartz). Magnification approx. × 100.

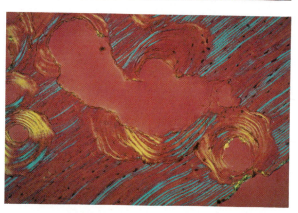

**Plate 2** Osteoclastic resorption by Howship's lacunae spreading from a Haversian canal. Tibia. Late Classical Antiquity, Linz (Austria). Transverse thin ground section (50 μm). Microscopic view using polarized light and hilfsobject, red 1st order (quartz). Magnification approx. × 100.

**Plate 3** Primitive woven bone. Chondrosarcoma of distal femur. Middle Ages, Fritzlar (Germany). Transverse thin ground section (50 μm). Microscopic view using polarized light and hilfsobject, red 1st order (quartz). Magnification approx. × 25.

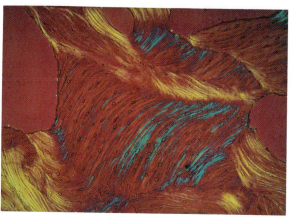

**Plate 4** Lamellar bone, compact area. Tibia. Eneolithic (Late Neolithic) Age. Baštečki (Ukraine). Transverse thin ground section (50 μm). Microscopic view using polarized light and hilfsobject, red 1st order (quartz). Magnification approx. × 100.

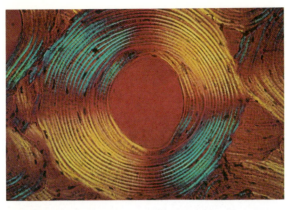

**Plate 5**  Lamellar bone, Haversian syste[m]
mur. Roman Age. Niğde-Hıdırlı (Turkey).
verse thin-ground section (50 μm). Micro[scopic]
view using polarized light and hilfsobject, [1st]
order (quartz). Magnification approx. × 160

**Plate 6**  Lamellar bone, compact bone sub[stance]
with Haversian systems and interstitial lar[nellae.]
Femur. Roman Age, Niğde-Hıdırlı (Turkey).
verse thin ground section (50 μm). Micro[scopic]
view using polarized light and hilfsobject, [1st]
order (quartz). Magnification approx. × 25.

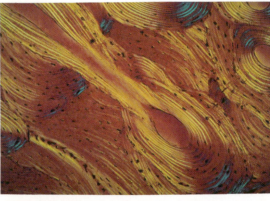

**Plate 7**  Lamellar bone, Volkmann's car[n]
mur. Roman Age, Niğde-Hıdırlı (Turkey).
verse thin ground section (50 μm). Micro[scopic]
view using polarized light and hilfsobject, [1st]
order (quartz). Magnification × 100.

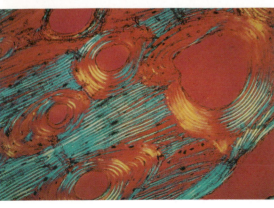

**Plate 8**  Old-age osteoporosis. Compact b[one tis]
sue of a femur of a senile male. Eneolith[ic]
Baštečki (Ukraine). Microscopic view using [polar]
ized light and hilfsobject, red 1st order (q[uartz).]
Magnification × 100.

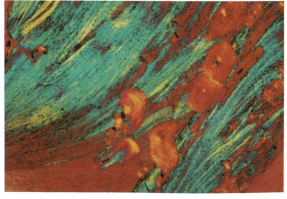

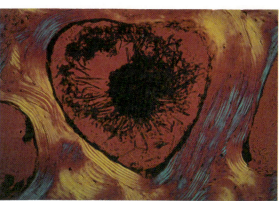

**Plate 9**  Atrophy due to inactivity as a result of extensive ankylosis. Compact bone tissue of a femur of a mature male. Pre-Columbian age, Gran Quivira (Arizona, U.S.A.). Microscopic view using polarized light and hilfsobject, red 1st order (quartz). Magnification × 25.

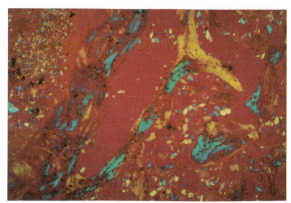

**Plate 10**  Fungus (parts of "fruchtkörper," or fruiting bodies, "hüllhyphen," or hyphal sheath, and ascospores) in large blood vessel canal of compact bone tissue. Femur. Late Middle Ages, St. Martin's church in Klosterneuburg (Austria). Microscopic view using polarized light and hilfsobject, red 1st order (quartz). Magnification × 100.

**Plate 11**  Small fragments of bone in soil ("leichenschatten," or corpse shadow). Eneolithic Age, Čertomlyk (Ukraine). Transverse thin ground section (50 μm). Microscopic view using polarized light and hilfsobject, red 1st order (quartz). Magnification approx. × 25.

**Plate 12**  Metastases of a malignant tumor (probably carcinoma of the breast). Howship's lacunae characteristic of a marked osteoclastic process. Clavicle of a mature female, Early Middle Ages, Sayala (Egyptian Nubia). Transverse thin ground section (50 μm). Microscopic view using polarized light and hilfsobject, red 1st order (quartz). Magnification approx. × 100.

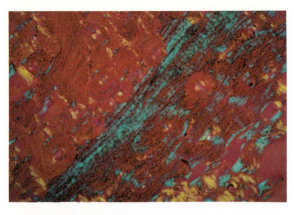

**Plate 13** Venereal syphilis in compact bone tissue with "grenzstreifen," or lineal border, in osteal area. Tibia. Early Modern Klosterneuburg (Austria). Transverse thin ground section (50 μm). Microscopic view using polarized light and hilfsobject, red 1st order (quartz). Magnification approx. × 25.

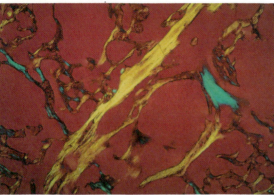

**Plate 14** Osteoplastic-osteoclastic metastatic carcinoma. Rib. Iron Age, Albersdorf (Germany). Transverse thin ground section (50 μm). Microscopic view using polarized light and hilfsobject, red 1st order (quartz). Magnification approx.

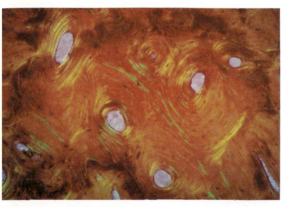

**Plate 15** Compact bone tissue of a femur of adult individual from the pre–Columbian San village in the Navaho Reservoir District, Mexico, USA). Characteristic alterations of bone collagen following a longer exposure to relatively low temperature (cf. bone collagen in Plates 1 and 2). Transverse thin ground section (40 μm). Microscopic view using polarized light and hilfsobject, red 1st order (quartz). Magnification approx. × 100.

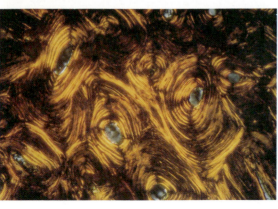

**Plate 16** Same as Plate 15 but using only polarized light without the use of quartz. Magnification approx. × 25.

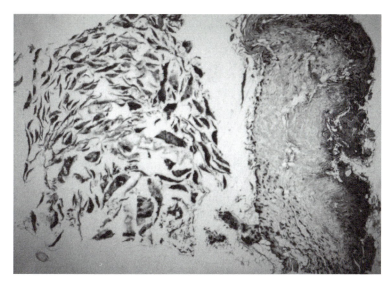

**Figure 17** Fill of canal made by deathwatch beetle. Same as Figure 16. Longitudinal thin ground section stained by fuchsin and methylene blue. Magnification × 25.

Schultz 1986). The results of microscopic investigations impressively show that alterations which were, macroscopically, seen as being due to disease prove to be postmortem when viewed microscopically (cf. Schultz 1986).

It also sometimes happens that, under the microscope, apparently postmortem traces of erosion are found to have occurred antemortem. For example, let us consider the case of a 35- to 45-year-old woman who lived in the early Middle Ages of Coptic Egypt in Sayala (Egyptian Nubia) (Schultz in press; Strouhal 1993). In her case, irregular holes in the vertebrae of the upper part of the skeleton and in the shaft of the left clavicle resembled, at first sight, traces of postmortem erosion processes. The microscopic investigation (Figure 18 and Plate 12) identified the alterations, beyond doubt, as vestiges of a metastasizing carcinoma (Schultz 1993a, and in press). This case is one of many examples demonstrating that microscopic examination is able to differentiate reliably between antemortem and postmortem alterations. Using microscopy, it can be demonstrated in many cases that apparently postmortem changes are caused by antemortem tumors and tumorous diseases, and that these diseases, sometimes called civilization diseases, were indeed more frequent (Schultz 1982, 1986, 1992) than can be supposed from the literature, which deals mainly with macroscopic and radiological investigations.

An important problem in diagnosing ancient diseases is the question of the probable presence of treponemal diseases in prehistoric and historic populations. This subject was intensively discussed at the congress "*L'Origine de la Syphilis en Europe avant ou après 1493*" which was held in Toulon (France) in November 1993 (Dutour et al. 1994). It is striking that with light microscopic techniques using polarized light, venereal syphilis (Figure 19 and Plate 13) can be reliably differentiated from hematogenous osteomyelitis (Schultz 1994a; Schultz and Teschler-Nicola 1987).

For paleopathological investigations on cremated bones, microscopic methods are also of high value. Even extremely slight traces of inflammatory processes of the meninges were identified in the cremated remains of a woman from the pre-Roman Iron Age in northern Germany (Schwissel, Schleswig-Holstein) (Kühl 1986; Schultz 1987). These changes due to disease were originally wrongly diagnosed in the macroscopic investigation as shrinkage fissures due to the heat (Figure 20).

**Figure 18**   Metastases of a malignant tumor (probably carcinoma of the breast). Howship's lacunae characteristic of a marked osteoclastic process. Clavicle of an adult-mature female, Early Middle Ages, Sayala (Egyptian Nubia). Transverse thin ground section (50 µm). Microscopic view using polarized light and hilfsobject, red 1st. order (quartz). Magnification × 100. (For color see Plate 12 following page 212.)

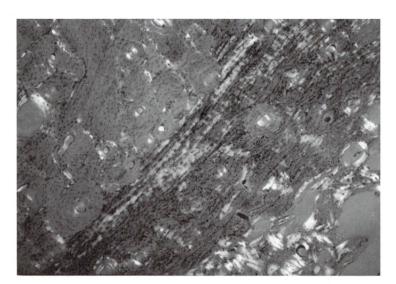

**Figure 19**   Venereal syphilis in compact bone tissue with "grenzstreifen," or lineal border, in periosteal area. Tibia. Early Modern Age, Klosterneuburg (Austria). Transverse thin ground section (50 µm). Microscopic view using polarized light and hilfsobject, red 1st. order (quartz). Magnification approx. × 25. (For color see Plate 13 following page 212.)

In another cremation from the pre-Roman Iron Age (cf. Kühl in press), also of a woman (Albersdorf, Schleswig-Holstein), traces of a carcinoma were diagnosed, the osteoplastic metastases of which had affected cranium, ribs, vertebrae, and also obviously metaphyseal parts of the long bones. During initial macroscopic investigation these osteoplastic metastases were incorrectly diagnosed as being spongiosa structures fused during the cremation process (Figure 21 and Plate 14).

**Figure 20**    Vestiges of epidural hematoma in cremated bones. Internal skull surface. Iron Age, Schwissel (Germany). Macrophotograph (cf. Figure 7).

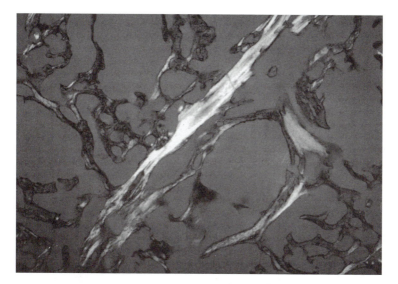

**Figure 21**    Osteoplastic-osteoclastic metastasis of carcinoma. Rib. Iron Age, Albersdorf (Germany). Transverse thin ground section (50 μm). Microscopic view using polarized light and hilfsobject, red 1st. order (quartz). Magnification approx. × 25. (For color see Plate 14 following page 212.)

## Determination of Effects of Heat and Fire on Bones

Discolorations can be observed in skeletal materials due to effects of heat or fire. Such observations are of particular importance in the further interpretation of results, since they are indications of burial practices, of cannibalism, of an accident, or an intentional incident (e.g., as in the case of battle).

It is not always possible to distinguish such vestiges macroscopically from postmortem influences. For example, a manganese impregnation of the bone can cause a discoloration surprisingly similar to discoloration due to fire. In this case, a microscopic investigation can

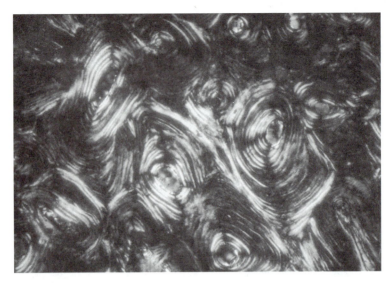

**Figure 22**    Compact bone tissue of a femur of an adult individual from the pre-Columbian Sambrito village in the Navaho Reservoir District (New Mexico). Characteristic alterations in the bone collagen following a longer exposure to relatively low temperature (cf. bone collagen in Figures 1 and 2 and Plates 6, 8 and 9.). Transverse thin ground section (40 μm). Microscopic view using polarized light. Magnification × 100. (For color see Plates 15 and 16 following page 212.)

rapidly expel all doubts (Grimm and Strauch 1957; Schultz 1986). Cremated remains, in contrast to unburned skeletal remains, are usually easy to judge even macroscopically (Teschler-Nicola and Schultz 1984). An important factor in heat-induced alterations in bone morphology is the temperature as well as the duration of exposure. Different temperatures lead to different morphological changes in the bone. Since the various degrees of heat-induced alterations in bone morphology as observed in archaeological skeletal remains have already been described elsewhere (Schultz 1986), we do not need to go into this problem here. Even relatively low temperatures (below 300°C) can apparently, when maintained over a longer time period, lead to characteristic changes which can usually be seen clearly in polarized light (Figure 22). The primary alteration is seen in the bone collagen. The shrinkage is often minimal and, as a rule, not measurable. Such changes can sometimes be linked to cannibalism (Schultz 1982, 1994b). For differential diagnosis, forms of preservation of the corpse for reasons of transport should be kept in mind (Schultz and Schmidt-Schultz 1991).

## Examination of Bone and Soil *in Situ*

One case should be mentioned to outline the importance of microscopic examination not only of isolated bone samples, but also of bones and bone fragments found in the ground *in situ* associated with earth or sand. In 1983, during an archaeological cooperation project between West Germany and the then Soviet Union, when a group of Eneolithic (Late Neolithic) to Early Bronze Age tumuli were excavated in the southern Ukraine, the author excavated a burial in which the skeleton was poorly preserved, and a difference in coloration of the surrounding soil drew his attention. Undestroyed bone tissue showing a reddish coloration on the surface of the bone, and successive layers of brownish and whitish soil under the bone, were sampled with a special tube. The content of this tube was carefully plugged and, when back in Göttingen (Germany), embedded in epoxy resin. Thin ground sections were then made from this sample (Schultz 1988b; Schultz and Drommer 1983). Microscopic analysis using normal and polarized light demonstrated the primary character of the differ-

**Figure 23**    Sample of soil containing layers of rotted reed and wood. Eneolithic (Late Neolithic) Age, Čertomlyk (Ukraine). Transverse thin ground section (50 μm). Microscopic view. Magnification approx. × 25.

ently colored structures: the reddish substance was identified as red ochre, the brownish substance probably represents a hide or a fur of an animal, and the whitish substance seems to be a layer of reed or a rotted mat made of reed (see Figure 23, which shows a similar specimen in which the rotted reed is layered with wood). Thus, about four or five thousand years ago, the corpse was placed on a hide or a fur which in turn was laid upon a reed mat put at the bottom of the grave, while the body was covered with red ochre (Figure 24). Similar microscopic investigations were carried out in several other burials with associated fragments of organic materials such as pieces of wood, with similar results. This example shows how the mode of interment can be reconstructed. Furthermore, the results demonstrate that skeletal remains and the associated soil can be examined *in situ* by special microscopic techniques. This could also be of major interest if archaeological bones are to be investigated by physical and chemical methods.

## Conclusions

Microscopic investigation of archaeological skeletal remains is carried out with very different aims in mind. It does not always yield a satisfactory result, due to technical difficulties that can arise in the embedding of specimens or preparation of ground sections. Sometimes, diagnostic problems arise when the structures observed in thin sections are open to more than one interpretation.

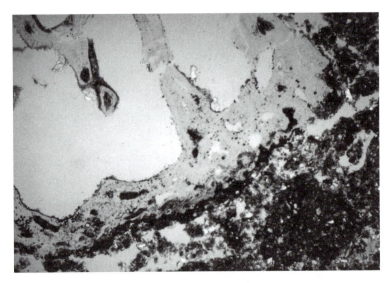

**Figure 24** Sample of soil containing fingerbone covered by red ochre. Eneolithic (Late Neolithic) Age, Čertomlyk (Ukraine). Transverse thin ground section (50 μm). Microscopic view. Magnification approx. × 25.

The least satisfactory results are achieved in histomorphological age determination. The methods recommended in the literature cannot always be compared with one another. Thus, a comparable collection of recent specimens of known age is always helpful, if prehistoric or historic samples are examined.

Changes in the shafts of long bones due to their function which are not always recognizable macroscopically are usually easy to diagnose microscopically. However, they are seen comparatively seldom.

Crematory remains are relatively reliably judged by microscopic techniques. This is particularly true of traces of effects of high temperatures. Determination of effects of lower temperatures is a little more difficult and is usually only possible if the bone is relatively well preserved, i.e., if it contains clearly more than about 75% of the original collagen content.

The difficulties in the diagnosis of vestiges of disease lie in the fact that for archaeological skeletal remains usually no soft tissue has been preserved. In recent pathology, the diagnosis is based on alterations within the cell due to disease or in pathological soft tissue structures. This is not possible in paleopathology. In the diagnosis of thin sections taken from archaeological skeletal remains, further criteria are, therefore, taken into account (cf. Schultz 1986, 1988a, 1988b). With the help of light microscopy using polarized light, the structure of the bone collagen can be determined and made use of for diagnosis, while microradiography can provide information on the degree of calcification at the particular level of cross section of the bone.

In the scientific investigation of archaeological skeletal remains, biogenic and abiogenic decomposition which affects the bones in the earth, and contamination occurring during archaeological excavations can cause great problems. These postmortem processes can falsify results of the scientific investigation by affecting determination of glycoproteins (blood group factors), of proteins and DNA, analysis of trace elements, and determination of stable isotopes, as well as various dating methods, such as amino acid racemization and the radiocarbon method ($^{14}$C) (cf. Schultz 1986) to a considerable extent.

These sources of error are, unfortunately, not considered carefully enough at the present time (cf. Price 1989) although attempts at a critical examination of such methods of investigation have been available for a relatively long time (Ambrose 1993; Berg et al. 1983; Pääbo et al. 1989; Richards et al. 1993; Sandford 1993). Undertaking a microscopic investigation before one of the chemical or physical methods can usually prevent the worst mistakes.

## Summary

The importance of microscopic investigations in the diagnosis of dry bones has been described. Alterations due to age and function, the problem of soil conditions and determination of postmortem damage (diagenesis, decomposition), diagnoses on the basis of vestiges of disease (including pseudopathology), and effects of heat and fire have been presented.

The results of the microscopic investigation show that the interpretation of results of a chemical or physical investigation should be treated with great care.

## Acknowledgments

The author wishes to thank M. Brandt and Ingrid Hettwer-Steeger for preparing the ground sections, Dr. P. Schwartz for scanning electron microscope pictures, Ingrid Hettwer-Steeger for preparing the slides for electron microscopy, Brigitta Smith and Anke Kreft for the microradiographs, Dr. Petra Carli-Thiele and Kerstin Kreutz for data technical help and last, but not least, Cyrilla Maelicke for reading the English text. Furthermore, the author thanks Mrs. Ingrid Kühl (Schleswig, Germany), Dr. C.F. Merbs (Tempe, AZ), Dr. Carmen M. Pijoan Aguade (Mexico City, Mexico), Dr. R. Protsch (Frankfurt am Main, Germany), Dr. E. Strouhal (Prague, Czech Republic), and Dr. C. Turner (Tempe, AZ) for bone samples.

## References

Ahlquist, J., and O. Damsten
  1969  A Modification of Kerley's Method for the Microscopic Determination of Age in Human Bone. *Journal of Forensic Sciences* 14:205–212.

Ambrose, S.H.
  1993  Isotopic Analysis of Paleodiets: Methodological and Interpretive Considerations. In *Investigations of Ancient Human Tissue: Chemical Analysis in Anthropology*, edited by M.K. Sandford, pp. 59–130. Gordon & Breach, Langhorne.

Berg, S., B. Bertozzi, R. Meier, and S. Mendritzki
  1983  Vergleichend-methodologischer Beitrag und kritische Bemerkungen zur Interpretation von Blutgruppenbestimmungen an Mumienrelikten und Skelettfunden. *Anthropologischer Anzeiger* 41:1–19.

Curry, A.
  1979  The Insects Associated with the Manchester Mummies. In *Manchester Museum Mummy Project. Multidisciplinary Research on Ancient Egyptian Mummified Remains*, edited by A.R. David, pp. 113–118. Manchester University Press, Manchester, U.K.

Dutour, O., et al.
  1994  *L'Origine de la Syphilis en Europe avant ou après 1493? [The Origin of Syphilis in Europe before or after 1493?]*, edited by O. Dutour, G. Pálfi, J. Bérato, and J.-P. Brun. Centre Archéologique du Var, Éditions France.

Garner, R.C.
  1986  Insects and Mummification. In *Science in Egyptology*, edited by A.R. David, pp. 97–100. Manchester University Press, Manchester, U.K.

Grimm, H., and R. Strauch
    1957  Schliffuntersuchungen am Knochen zum Nachweis einer Feuerbehandlung bei der Bestattung. *Ausgrabungen und Funde* 4: 262–264.

Grupe, G., and A.N. Garland
    1993  *Histology of Ancient Human Bone.* Springer-Verlag, Berlin/New York.

Hackett, C.
    1976  *Diagnostic Criteria of Syphilis, Yaws and Treponarid (Treponematoses) and Some Other Diseases in Dry Bones.* Sitzungsberichte der Heidelberger Akademie der Wissenschaften mathematisch naturwissenschaftliche, Klasse, 4, Springer-Verlag, Berlin, pp. 351–470.
    1981  Microscopical Focal Destruction (Tunnels) in Exhumed Human Bones. *Medicine, Science, and the Law* 21:243–265.

Harsányi, L.
    1978  Unterscheidung von Menschen- und Tierknochen. In *Identifikation*, edited by H. Hunger and D. Leopold, pp. 100–112. J.A. Barth, Leipzig.
    1993  Differential Diagnosis of Human and Animal Bone. In *Histology of Ancient Human Bone: Methods and Diagnosis*, edited by G. Grupe and A.N. Garland, pp. 79–94. Springer-Verlag, Berlin.

Kerley, E.R.
    1965  The Microscopic Determination of Age in Human Bone. *American Journal of Physical Anthropology* 23:149–164.
    1969  Age Determination of Bone Fragments. *Journal of Forensic Sciences* 14:59–67.

Kerley, E.R., and D.H. Ubelaker
    1978  Revisions in the Microscopic Method of Estimating Age at Death in Human Cortical Bone. *American Journal of Physical Anthropology* 49:545–546.

Kloiber, D.
    1957  *Die Gräberfelder von Lauriacum. Das Ziegelfeld.* Oberösterreichisches Landesmuseum, Linz.

Kühl, I.
    1986  Cremation of a Diseased Mature Female from Early Latène Period, North Germany. *Proceedings of the 6th European Meeting of the Paleopathology Association*, edited by F. G. Bellard and J. A. Sànchez, pp. 289–295. Madrid.
    In press  Leichenbrandanalysen zur Information auch für den Prähistoriker. Anthropologische Forschungen Wien. IV. Krebsmetastasen in einem Leichenbrand der vorrömischen Eisenzeit aus Schleswig-Holstein, Norddeutschland.

Moodie, R.L.
    1923  *Paleopathology. An Introduction to the Study of Ancient Evidences of Disease.* University of Illinois Press, Urbana.

Pääbo, S., R.G. Higuchi, and A.C. Wilson
    1989  Ancient DNA and the Polymerase Chain Reaction. The Emerging Field of Molecular Archaeology. *Journal of Biological Chemistry* 264:9709–9712.

Pauli, L.
    1978  *Der Dürrnberg bei Hallein III.* C.H. Beck, Munich.

Pfeiffer, S., and R.F. Williamson
    1991  *Snake Hill: An Investigation of a Military Cemetery from the War of 1812.* Dundurn Press, Toronto.

Piepenbrink, H.
    1984  Beispiele biogener Dekompositionserscheinungen an Knochen unter längerer Liegezeit. *Anthropologischer Anzeiger* 42:241–251.

Price, T.D.
 1989  *The Chemistry of Prehistoric Human Bone*. Cambridge University Press, Cambridge, MA.

Reeve and Adams
 1993  *The Spitalfield Project*. Vol. 1. *The Archaeology Across the Styx*. CBA Research Report 85, Council for British Archaeology, Walmgate, York.

Richards, M., K. Smalley, B. Sykes, and R. Hedges
 1993  Archaeology and Genetics: Analysing DNA from Skeletal Remains. *World Archaeology* 25:18–28.

Sandford, M.K. (editor)
 1993  *Investigations of Ancient Human Tissue. Chemical Analysis in Anthropology*. Gordon & Breach, Langhorne.

Schultz, M.
 1978  Pathologische Veränderungen an den Dürrnberger Skeletten. In *Der Dürrnberg bei Hallein III,* edited by L. Pauli, pp. 583–600. C. H. Beck, Munich.
 1982  Umwelt und Krankheit des vor- und frühgeschichtlichen Menschen. In *Kindlers Enzyklopädie: Der Mensch 2,* edited by H. Wednt and N. Loacker, pp. 259–312. Kindler-Verlag, Munich.
 1986  *Die mikroskopische Untersuchung prähistorischer Skeletfunde: Anwendung und Aussagemöglichkeiten der differentialdiagnostischen Untersuchung in der Paläopathologie,* pp. 140. Archaeologie und Museum, vol. 6, Amt für Museen und Archäologie Baselland, Liestal.
 1987  *Spuren unspezifischer Entzündungen an prähistorischen und historischen Schädeln: Ein Beitrag zur Paläopathologie*. Habilitationsschrift, Göttingen.
 1988a  Paläopathologische Diagnostik. In *Anthropologie: Handbuch der vergleichenden Biologie des Menschen,* Vol. 1: *Wesen und Methoden der Anthropologie,* edited by R. Knussmann, pp. 480–496. Fischer-Verlag, Stuttgart.
 1988b  Methoden der Licht- und Elektronenmikroskopie. In Anthropologie: *Handbuch der vergleichenden Biologie des Menschen,* Vol 1: *Wesen und Methoden der Anthropologie,* edited by R. Knussmann, pp. 698–730. Fischer-Verlag, Stuttgart.
 1990  Erkrankungen des Kindesalters bei der frühbronzezeitlichen Population vom Ikiztepe (Türkei). In *Gedenkschrift für Jürgen Driehaus,* edited by F.M. Andraschko and W.R. Teegen, pp. 83–90. Ph. v. Zabern, Mainz.
 1992  Nature and Frequency of Bony Tumors in Prehistoric and Historic Populations. *In Vivo* 6(4), pp. 439–441. Special Issue on Comparative Oncology, edited by H. E. Kaiser.
 1993a  Initial Stages of Systemic Bone Disease. In *Histology of Ancient Human Bone: Methods and Diagnosis,* edited by G. Grupe and A. N. Garland. Springer-Verlag, pp. 185–203, Berlin.
 1993b  *Spuren unspezifischer Entzündungen an prähistorischen und historischen Schädeln. Ein Beitrag zur Paläopathologie*. [*Vestiges of Non-Specific Inflammations in Prehistoric Skulls. A Contribution to Palaeopathology*.] Anthropologisches Forschungsinstitut Aesch (BL) and Anthropologische Gesellschaft, Basel.
 1994a  Comparative Histopathology of Syphilitic Lesions on Prehistoric and Historic Human Bones. In *L'Origine de la Syphilis en Europe avant ou après 1493?,* edited by O. Dutour, G. Pálfi, J. Bérato, and J.-P. Brun. Centre Archéologique du Var, Éditions Errance, pp. 63–67.
 1994b  Ergebnisse mikroskopischer Untersuchungen an archaeologischen Skeletfunden. Ein Beitrag zur Paläopathologie. *Beiträge zur Archäozoologie und prähistorischen Anthropologie,* Edited by M. Kokabi and J. Wahl. Forschungen und Berichte zur Vor- und Frühgeschichte in Baden-Württemberg 53:107–116.
 1995  A New Technique for Preparing Histological Specimens of Mummified Tissue. Una Neuva Técnica para Preparar Muestras Histològicas de Tejidos Momificados. II World Congress on Mummy Studies. Book of Abstracts 8.3.

In press    Ergebnisse mikroskopischer Untersuchungen an ausgewählten Skeletfunden. In *Die Anthropologische Untersuchung der Christlichen Skelete aus Sayala, Ägyptisch-Nubien,* edited by E. Strouhal. Denkschriften österreichischen Akademie Wissenschaften, philosophisch-historische. Klasse, Wien.

Schultz, M., and R. Drommer
1983    Möglichkeiten der Präparateherstellung aus dem Gesichtsschädelbereich für die makroskopische und mikroskopische Untersuchung unter Verwendung neuer Kunststofftechniken: Experimentelle Mund-Kiefer-Gesichtschirurgie. In *Mikrochirurgische Eingriffe,* edited by W. Hoppe, pp. 95–97. Thieme-Verlag, New York.

Schultz, M., and T.H. Schmidt-Schultz
1991    Ergebnisse osteologischer Untersuchungen an menschlichen Skeletfunden aus Milet. *Istanbuler Mitteilungen* 41:163–186.

Schultz, M., and P. Schwartz
1982    Ergebnisse der Untersuchung an den Knochenfragmenten aus dem Reliquiengefäss der Kirche St. Martin in Unterbillingshausen. *Plesse-Archiv* 18, pp. 71–76.

Schultz, M., and M. Teschler-Nicola
1987    Krankhafte Veränderungen an den Skeletten aus dem Karner der St. Martins-Kirche in Klosterneuburg, Niederösterreich. I–IV. *Annalen des Naturhistorischen Museums Wien* 89 A:225–311.

Strouhal, E.
1993    A Case of Metastatic Carcinoma from Christian Sayala (Egyptian Nubia). *Anthropologischer Anzeiger* 51:97–115.

Süßmann-Bertozzi, B.
1984    Einflüsse der Leichenfauna und mikrobiellen Saprophytie auf Blutgruppenbefunde an menschlichen Geweben. Medizinische Dissertation, Göttingen.

Tasnádi-Kubacska, A.
1962    *Paläopathologie: Pathologie der vorzeitlichen Tiere.* Gustav Fischer-Verlag, Jena.

Teschler-Nicola, M., and M. Schultz
1984    Jungneolithische Skelette der Badener Kultur aus Leobersdorf und Lichtenwörth, Niederösterreich. *Annalen des Naturhistorischen Museums Wien* 86 A:111–144.

Uytterschaut, H.
1993    Human Bone Remodeling and Aging. In *Histology of Ancient Human Bone: Methods and Diagnosis,* edited by G. Grupe and A.N. Garland, pp. 95–109. Springer-Verlag, Berlin.

Weber, M.
1927    Schliffe von mazerierten Röhrenknochen und ihre Bedeutung für die Unterscheidung der Syphilis und Osteomyelitis von der Osteodystrophia fibrosa sowie für die Untersuchung fraglich syphilitischer, prähistorischer Knochen. *Beiträge pathologische Anatomie, allgemeine Pathologie* 78:441–511

Wedl, C.
1864    *Über einen im Zahnbein und Knochen keimenden Pilz.* Sitzungsberichte der Kaiserlichen Akademie der Wissenschaften, mathematisch-naturwissenschaftliche Classe, 50:171–193. Vienna.

Wells, C.
1967    Pseudopathology. In *Diseases in Antiquity,* edited by D. R. Brothwell and A. T. Sandison. pp. 5–19, Charles C Thomas Publisher, Springfield, IL.

# A Critical Evaluation of Bone Weathering as an Indication of Bone Assemblage Formation *

# 15

R. LEE LYMAN
GREGORY L. FOX

## Introduction

A decade ago, Behrensmeyer (1978:161) defined six stages of bone weathering in subaerial/surface contexts, and suggested that once sufficient control studies were available, bone weathering features might "give specific information concerning surface exposure of bone prior to burial and the time periods over which bones accumulated." She conjectured how different taphonomic histories could produce different configurations of weathered bones, and emphasized those conjectures should be treated as "hypotheses which need testing through additional research on both recent and fossil bones" (Behrensmeyer 1978:162). In this paper, we offer detailed consideration of Behrensmeyer's (1978) seminal hypotheses and observations, referring to relevant actualistic and prehistoric data as necessary. We conclude that bone weathering data provide important taphonomic information, but those data do not necessarily reflect the duration of bone assemblage formation because (1) they are not structured to do so, and (2) many taphonomic factors are involved in the formation of an assemblage of weathered bone, some of which cannot be controlled in analyses of bone weathering data.

## Bone Weathering

Behrensmeyer (1978:150) characterizes bone weathering as the decomposition and destruction of bones "as part of the normal process of nutrient recycling in and on soils." She defines weathering "as the process by which the original microscopic organic and inorganic components of bone are separated from each other and destroyed by physical and chemical agents operating on the bone *in situ*, either on the surface or within the soil zone" (Behrensmeyer 1978:153). Thus, weathering is continuous through Time, involves mechanical and chemical changes to a bone's original integrity as a discrete object, and occurs in surface and subsurface contexts (see also Purdy and Clark 1987). In this paper we define "Time" as solar years because that "periodic system" (Kitts 1966) is the one to which Behrensmeyer (1978) relates the bone weathering process. We denote other periodic systems as "time" or "taphonomic time."

Behrensmeyer (1978:150) describes six weathering stages (Table 1) "to provide a basis for descriptive comparison with bones from other contexts, both fossil and recent." Descriptions are based on "easily observable criteria" (macroscopic and mechanical [e.g., fractures and flaking] rather than chemical) to insure the stages "can be readily learned and applied in the

* Adapted for publication, courtesy of *Journal of Archaeological Science*, Vol. 16, 293-317, 1989.

**Table 1   Definitions of Weathering Stages and Their Relationships to Years Since Death of Known-Age Carcasses**

| Stage | Range in Years Since Death | Definition of Weathering Stage |
|-------|----------------------------|--------------------------------|
| 0 | 0–1 | No cracking or flaking; greasy; soft tissue present |
| 1 | 0–3 or 4 | Cracking parallel to fiber structure (longitudinal) in long bones |
| 2 | 2–6 or 7 | Flaking of outer surface, usually associated with cracks; flakes are long and thin with one edge attached to bone; crack edge angular; exfoliation started |
| 3 | 4–15+ | Bone surface rough, fibrous texture; weathering only 1.0 to 1.5 mm deep; crack edges rounded |
| 4 | 6–15+ | Bone surface coarse, rough, and fibrous; large and small splinters loosely attached; weathering penetrates to inner cavities; cracks open |
| 5 | 6–15+ | Bone mechanically falling apart into pieces, very fragile |

From Behrensmeyer, A.K., *Paleobiology*, 4, 150–162, 1978. With permission.

field" (Behrensmeyer 1978:151). The analytic and interpretive purpose of the stages is denoted by (1) Behrensmeyer's (1978) use of the term "stage" which indicates the passage of Time; (2) her statement that types of bone weathering might be related "to specific processes acting over known periods of Time" (Behrensmeyer 1978:150); and (3) her discussion of weathering rates and exposure histories. Clearly Behrensmeyer perceives bone weathering to denote the passage of Time minimally measured at an ordinal scale, and the six weathering stages to measure that passage of Time.

Weathering is a function of Time, as it must be given Behrensmeyer's definition of weathering as a "process." What is not at all clear is the kind and scale (ordinal, interval, ratio) of time denoted by variously weathered bones. We must ascertain whether the periodic system of bone weathering stages unambiguously "permits consistent estimates of duration" measured by the period system of solar years (Kitts 1966:30).

By rate of weathering, we mean how quickly a bone passes through the weathering stages. Minimally, three factors control that rate. First, "small, compact bones such as patellas and phalanges weather more slowly than other elements of the same skeleton" (Behrensmeyer 1978:152). Second, bones of different taxa, especially those of different body size, weather at different rates (Behrensmeyer 1978, 1982; Gifford 1981). Third, "the less equable the immediate environment [in terms of temperature and moisture fluctuations] of the bone, the faster it should weather" (Behrensmeyer 1978:156). Many researchers note that burial markedly inhibits, but does not necessarily stop weathering (Behrensmeyer 1978; Boaz 1982; Potts 1986; Shipman 1981b; Todd and Frison 1986).

By duration of weathering, we mean the span of Time over which a bone is exposed to weathering agents. Exposure to those agents begins once soft tissues detach from the bones. Therefore, the manner in which hide, muscle masses, etc., are removed controls when exposure begins (Blumenschine 1986; Coe 1978; Hill 1979; Hill and Behrensmeyer 1984; Micozzi 1986; Todd 1983a,b). Frison (1974:25) notes that season of death may control how quickly after death a bone is exposed.

Because bones may, by definition, weather in subsurface contexts, identifying the temporal end of exposure is difficult. The literature indicates analysts tend to assume exposure ends once a bone is buried (Boaz 1982; Bunn 1982; Gifford 1980; Shipman 1981b). This may be because Behrensmeyer (1978:154) noted that buried bones of a carcass "frequently show no signs of weathering even when exposed parts are in stage 4 or 5." The definition of weathering, however, makes it clear that subsurface bones do weather, although perhaps at a slower rate than surface bones.

Miller (1975) described six bone weathering stages similar to Behrensmeyer's, based on observations of subaerial bones in a southern California desert. Miller (1975:217) defined weathering as referring to "the effects on bone of saturation, desiccation, and temperature changes," and, like Behrensmeyer, concluded that bones exposed to the atmosphere 20 to 30 years were so badly deteriorated that they had little chance of becoming fossilized. Miller's data corroborate Behrensmeyer's conclusions that subaerial bones become progressively more weathered through Time, tend to weather at different rates depending on microenvironmental context, and burial inhibits the rate of weathering.

The critical aspect of analyzing and interpreting bone weathering data involves converting that data into taphonomic time. Behrensmeyer (1978:157) readily accomplished that conversion because she had knowledge about one time scale in advance; her conversion amounted to arranging a weathered bone against a particular kind of taphonomic time: years since death of the animal contributing the bone. That conversion was successful: the weathering stage of a bone was closely correlated with years since animal death. Spearman's rho between each category of weathering stage and years since death represented in Behrensmeyer's (1978: Table 2-1) sample (N = 21) is 0.802 ($p < .002$) [we use ordinal scale statistics because there is no evidence to indicate Behrensmeyer's weathering stages reflect interval scale time (see below)]. That correlation no doubt prompted Behrensmeyer's suggestion that bone weathering data might reveal insights to the duration of prehistoric bone assemblage formation, but as will become clear, formation duration is a different kind of taphonomic time than years since death.

We suggest Behrensmeyer's weathering data were strongly correlated with Time measured as years since animal death because Time-related factors controlling weathering rates and durations were all controlled. Behrensmeyer recorded the single most advanced weathering stage apparent on the bones of each carcass she examined; thus all factors which might inhibit weathering rates or shorten exposure were effectively omitted for each carcass examined. Such omission enhances the correlation between the time since an animal's death and weathering stage. Spearman's rho improves from .802 when all represented categories of years since death (independent variable) and maximum weathering stage are considered (N = 21) to .914 ($p < .002$) when only the maximum weathering stage per years since death categories are considered (N = 11) (from Behrensmeyer 1978:Table 2-1). Behrensmeyer (1978:157) concludes "weathering stages appear to be predictably linked with Time since death." That is, the weathering stage displayed by a bone in her sample is a function of one kind of taphonomic time:

$$WS = f(YD) \tag{1}$$

where WS is weathering stage and YD is years since death. Prehistoric bone assemblages differ in important ways from Behrensmeyer's assemblage which produced the original correlation between (YD) and weathering. We now turn to a consideration of those differences.

## Characteristics of Prehistoric Bone Assemblages

Prehistoric bone assemblages typically contain various skeletal elements from multiple carcasses representing multiple taxa, often surficially deposited across different microenvironments at different times and having different exposure histories (Behrensmeyer 1984; Gifford 1981; Lyman 1987b. Thus, Equation (1) becomes complex:

$$WS = f(YD, SE, TX, ME, ED, AH) \tag{2}$$

where WS and YD are as above, SE is skeletal element, TX is taxon, ME is depositional microenvironment, ED is exposure duration, and AH is accumulation history. Inferring Time from weathered prehistoric bones requires conversion of Equation (2) to:

$$YD, ED, AH = f(WS, SE, TX, ME) \tag{3}$$

Recall that Behrensmeyer's sample involved correlating the greatest observed weathering stage per carcass with the years since death of the animal. Because her assemblage was a passive accumulation (see below), years since death and accumulation history were of equal duration. Because her assemblage was subaerial, the greatest observed weathering stage per carcass (what we later refer to as carcass stage) measured only surface exposure and not diagenetic effects. Recording only the maximum weathering stage per carcass on the ground surface resulted in exposure duration equaling years since death for each carcass. Equation (3) must be applied to prehistoric bone assemblages to ensure consideration of the three kinds of taphonomic time (years since death, exposure duration, accumulation history) and other relevant taphonomic variables. To clarify these aspects of Equation (3), we consider each variable in that equation.

## Weathering Stage

Behrensmeyer's weathering stages (1978: Table 2-1) each represent a discontinuous point in Time along the continuous process of bone deterioration: "the six weathering stages impose arbitrary divisions upon what was observed to be a continuous spectrum" (Behrensmeyer 1978:152–153) [Johnson (1985) defined six weathering "phases" spanning Behrensmeyer's first three stages]. Behrensmeyer (1978:153) indicates it is possible that "bones spend relatively longer periods within each stage than between them," but has little data to support that possibility, or to indicate the length of temporal gaps between stages. Gifford (1977:291) reported a sample of bones which progressed through stages 0 and 1 to stage 2 within 1 to 2 years, but which then remained in "stages 2 and 3 for several years," but later observed we may be unable to assign "absolute Time values to different stages" (Gifford 1981:418). That, plus Behrensmeyer's (1978:157) statement that "weathering stages are most useful in providing an estimate of minimum number of years since death [or exposure]" indicates the stages are at best an ordinal scale measurement of Time.

Identifying the weathering stage displayed by a prehistoric bone is relatively straightforward. The temporal significance of an observed stage is, however, obscure for a simple reason. Bones weather, by definition, in both surface and subsurface contexts (Behrensmeyer 1978; Todd and Frison 1986). Typically, however, analysts studying weathered bones are interested only in how long a bone was in surface context, and consequently the observation that surface bones of a carcass are typically more weathered than subsurface bones of that carcass is taken to mean weathering stops or slows to an imperceptible rate, even over $10^5$ or more years. While perhaps a reasonable assumption, we are unaware of any published empirical study establishing that assumption's validity. Explicit efforts to distinguish subaerial from subsurface weathering generally have been thwarted (Mehl 1966; Todd 1987; Todd and Frison 1986; Todd et al. 1987). Behrensmeyer's weathering stages simply characterize the physical and chemical breakdown of bone tissue over Time, regardless of subsurface or subaerial context. The relationship of that breakdown with the three kinds of taphonomic time is controlled by the weathering context and the values of the three other variables (skeletal element, taxon, depositional microenvironment) on the right side of Equation (3).

## Skeletal Element

Behrensmeyer (1978) suggested different bones from the same skeleton weather at different rates (see also Todd et al. 1987:68–70). Granting that many taphonomic processes are affected by the bulk density and/or porosity of the element undergoing alteration (Lyman 1984 and references therein), Behrensmeyer's suggestion seems reasonable. We simply do not yet know, however, which elements weather fastest, slowest, or at an average rate. Behrensmeyer (1978:152) suggested limb bone shafts might prove to be the "easiest to categorize." We wonder, however, if humeri might weather faster than radii and thus perhaps only one skeletal element should be studied. Even when this question can be answered, we must then consider whether the fastest weathering or the slowest weathering element should be chosen, or an element which weathers at an average or modal rate, and why that particular rate/element is chosen.

## Taxon

Behrensmeyer (1978:153) noted that her weathering stages were "only applicable to mammals larger than 5 kg body weight." Gifford (1981:417) later noted that "bones of roughly like-sized mammals of different taxa may weather at somewhat different rates due to constructional differences." In her control samples Gifford observed "more heavily constructed equid bones weathered at a somewhat slower rate than homologous bovid bones." Schafer (1972:24) reported "fences and tombstones in Holland made from bones of whale which have lasted for centuries," indicating these largest of all mammal bones are quite resistant to weathering. As with variation across different skeletal elements of one taxon, insofar as the bulk density and/or porosity of an element varies from taxon to taxon, Behrensmeyer's and Gifford's observations make sense. But, again a choice between the slowest, fastest, or a taxon known to weather at an average or modal rate may have to be made, and reasons for that choice offered.

## Microenvironment

By microenvironment we mean the environmental conditions of the place where a bone is deposited. That depositional "place" is discussed at two spatial scales by Behrensmeyer (1978): the general vegetational habitat of the depositional area, and the depositional locus specifics. She tends to discuss the former in regards to assemblages of bones and carcasses, and the latter in regards to individual bones. We consider each in detail.

Behrensmeyer (1978: Figure 10) presented data on 1534 carcasses distributed across six habitats. She recorded the most advanced WS per carcass, found all six weathering stages represented in all habitats, and suggested differences between the weathering data for each habitat could be accounted for by environmental differences affecting weathering rates and "changes in patterns of habitat utilization and/or mortality" (Behrensmeyer 1978:159). She concluded the latter explained some variation in weathering data, but not all variation could be so explained. We calculated Kolmogorov-Smirnov two-sample D statistics between all possible pairs of habitat weathering data (Table 2). Those statistics corroborate, in part, Behrensmeyer's conclusions. She suggests, for example, the open woodland and plains should be similar, and our D statistic indicates that is true. Behrensmeyer (1978:159) also suggests the swamp and dense woodlands are similar, having "modes in stage 1" rather than stage 2 because of "more equable environments with respect to weathering processes." Our D statistics indicate, however, the swamp and dense woodland data are different, and the dense woodland data are not significantly different from the open woodland and plains data. Behrensmeyer is thus appropriately cautious in noting that habitat effects on bone weathering have been obscured by changes over time in habitat utilization by the herbivores which contributed the bones. That latter factor falls under the rubric of what we label accumulation history, or one kind of taphonomic time.

Behrensmeyer (1978:158) suggested "localized conditions (e.g., vegetation, shade, moisture) are more important to bone weathering than overall characteristics of the [different] habitats." That is, the subaerial depositional microenvironment of a bone may inhibit or exacerbate the rate of weathering. Behrensmeyer's data indicate the size and internal density of vegetation patches in which bones are deposited are important parts of the depositional microenvironment. We suspect, based on data reported by Brain (1967), Cook (1986), and Miller (1975), the magnitude of seasonal changes in weather and durations of seasons are critical, and that the moisture content, temperature, and nature and texture of the sediment

**Table 2  Kolmogorov-Smirnov D Statistics between All Possible Pairs of Carcass Assemblages from Major Habitats**

| | Swamp (N = 322) | Dense wood (N = 312) | Open wood (N = 255) | Bush (N = 184) | Plains (N = 248) |
|---|---|---|---|---|---|
| Dense wood | D = .14 (1) $p <.01$ | | | | |
| Open wood | D = .16 (1) $p <.01$ | D = .04 (3) $p > .1$ | | | |
| Bush | D = .35 (1) $p < .01$ | D = .21 (1) $p < .01$ | D = .19 (1) $p < .01$ | | |
| Plains | D = .23 (1) $p < .01$ | D = .09 (1) $p > .1$ | D = .07 (2) $p > .1$ | D = .12 (1) $.1 > p > .05$ | |
| Lake bed (N = 213) | D = .26 (1) $p < .01$ | D = .12 (1) $p = .05$ | D = .10 (1) $p > .1$ | D = .09 (1) $p > .1$ | D = .06 (3) $p > .1$ |

*Note:* Number in parenthesis next to D statistic is weathering stage where D occurs.

Based on data in Behrensmeyer (1978).

on which a bone lies may also be important. Todd's (1983a, 1983b) data indicate that the presence of multiple, closely spaced carcasses tends to create a different microenvironment than when a carcass is isolated from other carcasses. Even if these localized, varying depositional microenvironmental conditions could be inferred from prehistoric evidence, we as yet do not know the magnitude of variation in them required to significantly alter weathering rates (Shipman 1981a:375). In other words, granting microscale variation in edaphic, climatic, and vegetational conditions across space, the spatial scale at which that microenvironmental variation will effect weathering rates is not at all clear. This problem seems to be analytically dealt with by implicitly assuming all bones within an archaeological or paleontological assemblage were deposited in the same depositional microenvironment (or at least one with variation insignificant to weathering rates). (Lithic analysts assume "lithic materials found in a single excavation unit at a site [were] exposed to the same environmental conditions if they were deposited at the same time" when dating lithics on the basis of weathering [Purdy and Clark 1987:235]). We suspect, however, that assumption becomes more tenuous as the total area sampled increases in size (see "Spatial Data" below).

## Years Since Death

A bone will not begin to weather until the animal contributing the bone dies, and soft tissue is removed from the bone (Behrensmeyer 1978; Miller 1975). Similarly, it seems logical to expect bone A will be more weathered than bone B, if Bone A "died" several years before bone B and all else is equal (every other variable in the equation has the same value for bone A and bone B). Given the strength of the correlation between years since animal death and carcass weathering stage in Behrensmeyer's sample (rho $\geq$ .8), if the analyst wishes to infer years since animal death from prehistorically weathered bones, the most advanced weathering stage for each carcass represented should be sought and recorded. All less weathered bones of a carcass reflect the influence of other variables in Equation (3).

Years since animal death can only vary between individual animals; it cannot vary within an animal. That renders years since animal death a significantly different kind of time than exposure duration or accumulation history. To infer years since animal death, the analyst must distinguish which bones make up a particular carcass; that is, the interdependence of bones must be determined and each set of bones from each carcass sorted from the complete collection. Controlling interdependence plagues efforts to calculate relative taxonomic abundances (Grayson 1979, 1984), but no good solution has been found in that analytic context. As Hesse and Wapnish (1985:88) note, "since different bones are likely to weather at different rates, weathering stage data cannot be used for grouping specimens of the same skeleton." We believe the only clear way to control interdependence and potentially detect variation in years since animal death between carcasses is by control of the skeletal elements examined. Specifically, recording the weathering stage as displayed by, for instance, only left femora will insure each observed stage derives from a different carcass. That interdependence of different weathering stage values recorded for one carcass must be controlled to allow inferences of years since animal death can be illustrated by example.

Assume, on one hand, we have a single left hindlimb of a bovid representing a single accumulation event: the bones are articulated. Assume also the bones of that hindlimb display stages 0, 1, and 2. Because we know the bones are interdependent and represent a single accumulation event, all weathering data can be interpreted as indicating variation in exposure duration per bone (variation in depositional microenvironment seems unlikely due to spatial contiguity), whereas the maximum weathering stage probably most accurately denotes years since death. On the other hand, assume we have a left tibia and a right femur that could, but may not be, from the same carcass. For one the weathering stage is 2, for the other the weathering stage is 3. Because interdependence is unknown, it is unclear whether the weathering stage displayed on the femur, or the tibia, or both should be recorded. If both are recorded and yet the bones are interdependent, variation in exposure duration, depositional microenvironment and/or skeletal element but not years since death, has been recorded if the accumulation histories of the two specimens are identical. Assuming only that both specimens were deposited in the same microenvironment and that skeletal element variation has not affected weathering rates, different accumulation histories and/or exposure durations must account for variation in the observed weathering stages. Ultimately, the most weathered specimen more accurately reflects the number of years since animal death than the less weathered specimen *if* the specimens derive from the same animal, but that is unknown.

## Exposure Duration

Given that exposure begins when insulating soft tissue is removed, two bones which died at the same time may or may not experience similar exposure durations, even if both are from the same carcass. Similarly, even if both are simultaneously exposed, the duration of their respective exposures may vary if the temporal end of exposure varies between the two. The magnitude of variation in weathering stage that can result from different exposure durations independent of other variables in Equation (3) is clearly indicated by Todd (1983b). In a sample of 20 paired left and right domestic cow femora from subaerial context, the members of only 8 pairs displayed the same weathering stage. Eight pairs differed by a weathering stage of one, three pairs differed by two stages, and one pair differed by three stages. From Todd's (1983b) description, it seems the only variable creating variation within pairs was exposure duration as the depositional microenvironment varied minimally between carcasses. Similarly, differences in when exposure started per specimen probably resulted in most variation between carcasses as all 20 cows died and were deposited at the same time (years since death was the same value for all carcasses), yet all six weathering stages were represented by the 40 femora. In another example, Todd (1983b:57, 70) reported bones in the "upper portion of the body" of a domestic cow were covered with hide and "still in an unweathered, fatty state" even though the animal had been dead approximately 22 months.

These observations indicate two important properties of exposure duration. First, exposure duration can vary within a carcass as well as between carcasses because it concerns individual bone specimens. Second, the exposure duration of a bone will always be less than or equal to the years since animal death. Thus exposure duration is a different kind of time than years since death because biostratinomic and burial factors control exposure duration, whereas thanatic factors control years since death, and the former factors may be independent of the latter. Given that, if the analyst wishes to infer years since death, it must be assumed

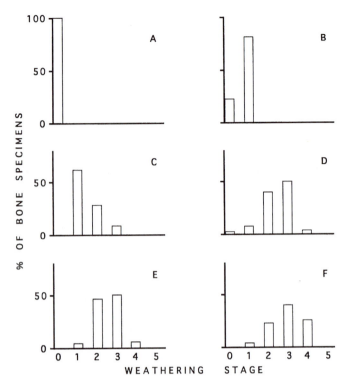

**Figure 1**   Changes in weathering profiles through time. (A) Theoretically all bones of a newly dead carcass will display weathering stage 0. (B) Surface bones of multiple carcasses dead <1 year. (C) Surface bones of multiple carcasses dead 2.5 to 3 years. (D) Surface bones of multiple carcasses dead 4 to 5 years. (E) Surface bones of multiple carcasses dead 6 to 10 years. (F) Surface bones of multiple carcasses dead 10 to 15 years. Data for B–F from Gifford (1977, 1982).

bones were exposed essentially immediately after animal death (YD = ED) for the maximally weathered bone of a carcass or carcass stage, which in turn presumes interdependence of bones making up a carcass can be ascertained.

Behrensmeyer (1978) presented her weathering data for surface carcasses in various forms. One of those forms is what we label a weathering profile: the percentage frequencies of bone specimens in an assemblage displaying each weathering stage. Behrensmeyer's (1978: Figure 9 and 10) profiles consisted of only the maximally weathered bone per carcass (or carcass stage), and thus each of her observations was clearly statistically independent of all other observations. Weathering profiles often serve as the focus of interpreting prehistoric weathered bones (e.g., Boaz 1982; Bower et al. 1985; Gifford 1984; Potts 1982,1984,1986; Shipman et al. 1981). Because such profiles probably consist of numerous interdependent elements (bones from the same carcass), they measure a different set of taphonomic variables (e.g., exposure duration and accumulation history) than Behrensmeyer's original profiles. The significance of that fact warrants detailed comment here.

We are aware of only one set of published data that sheds light on how the weathering profile of a carcass changes through time. Gifford (1977:290, 1984) provides weathering stage data for bones of multiple carcasses with known ages since death (Figure 1). All bones are from surface contexts, and if it is assumed that when an animal dies all of its bones begin at stage 0, then Figure 1 suggests a wave model for the weathering profile of a carcass through time. That model (Figure 2) assumes progressive weathering of all bones of a carcass from stage 0 through stage 5 through Time. Each bone weathers at a slightly different rate than every other bone, due to differences in bulk density of bone (Gifford 1981:417; Lyman 1984). The weathering profile of a carcass through Time thus takes the form of a unimodal wave

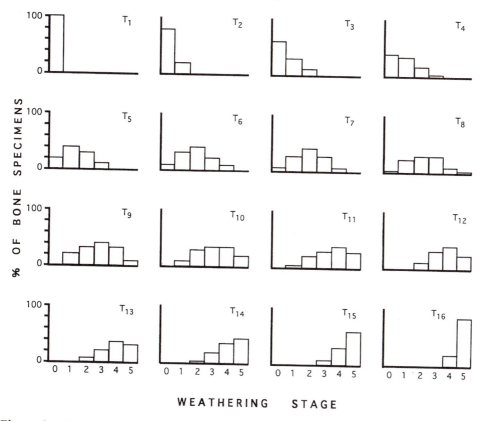

**Figure 2**    Wave model of weathering profiles through time for bones of a single carcass. The model is ordinal scale; i.e., no set temporal duration between profiles is implied. $T_{17}$ with 100% weathering stage 5, is not illustrated.

which moves across the series of weathering stages from left (stage 0) to right (stage 5). We note that because bones at stage 5 tend to deteriorate rapidly to dust, weathering profiles in which stage 5 is most abundant may be rare.

Deviations from the model (Figure 2) are expected, given variation in the exposure duration of bones of a carcass, depositional microenvironment for bones of a carcass, and other circumstances to which individual bones are subjected, but the model seems realistic *if* all bones from a single carcass remain exposed until stage 5. It illustrates that bones of a carcass collected and deposited at $T_1$ will have a different weathering profile than those collected and deposited at $T_2$, all else being equal, and they will both have a weathering profile different from those collected and deposited at $T_3$, all else being equal, etc. Because we cannot know when bones of a carcass, relative to $T_1$, were collected and deposited, especially for actively accumulated assemblages (see below), the analytic tendency seems to involve assuming all bones were collected and deposited when fresh or stage 0. (Lithic analysts assume "stone-workers will choose [unweathered] material for implement manufacture" when dating lithic tools on the basis of weathering [Purdy and Clark 1987:235]). While probably valid most of the time, we simply do not know how often the assumption is invalid. To explore that and related factors, we turn now to accumulation history.

## Accumulation History

By accumulation we mean to imply both active and passive (see below) addition of bone to the (future) fossil record, and both collecting/transporting of bones to their final depositional loci and their deposition on/in sediment. Behrensmeyer's sample of carcasses represents a passive accumulation [over a region] where predation [and death] occurs repeatedly" (Badgley 1986:336); all bones entered the subaerial 'fossil' record when at weathering stage 0. Accumulation is "active" when bones are collected and transported from, for instance, the location of the animals' death to another location where the bones were finally deposited. Under active accumulation, the transport monitoring perspective of a particular accumulation site — whether bones were only transported to the site, only away from the site, or both — ultimately seems critical to interpreting weathering data. Both active and passive accumulation of bones occurs over Time and can involve a single event (be of short temporal duration) or multiple events (be of long temporal duration). Active accumulation can be of a single element at a time or multiple bones of a partial or complete, single or multiple animals, whereas passive accumulation tends to involve a single animal at a time (Haynes 1988). In the following we first describe effects of collecting bones (implying active accumulation and thus transport), and then describe effects of depositing collected bones. Finally, we evaluate the cumulative effects of collection and deposition by describing some simulations using actualistic data.

A particular bone-collecting agent may gather bones on the basis of criteria that are independent of or interdependent with the weathering stage of a bone and/or the deterioration stages of the carcass being sampled. Gifford (1981:413), for example, hypothesizes that "the intensity with which carnivores accumulate bone as part of their denning or lairing behavior may be related to levels of interspecific competition in a given region." A carnivorous bone-collecting agent may select only those carcass portions that are least weathered (stage 0) and retain the most food value (Miller 1975; Richardson 1980) if prey carcasses are available in quantity. Dietary stress may alter that bone-collecting strategy to one focusing on bones at stage 0 or 1, perhaps with bones in stage 2 still articulated with less-weathered bones having food value. A geological process such as fluvial transport may select bones that have the least bulk density (Behrensmeyer 1975; Boaz 1982; Lyman 1984) rather than those that are least weathered. In fact, because it seems probable that weathered bones have lower bulk densities than unweathered specimens of the same element, weathered skeletal elements may be more readily transported by fluvial processes than specimens of those same elements that are not weathered.

It is well known that some birds and mammals prey upon live animals and/or scavenge relatively fresh carcasses in which bones would be stage 0 (e.g., Blumenschine 1986,1987; Brain 1981; Einarsen 1956; Haynes 1982). Richardson (1980:119) states that the bones of small prey are not disturbed by carnivores after about 6 months but that bones of large prey may be disturbed up to 12 months after death. Binford (1983:68–70) observed hyenas scavenging and collecting "relatively dry bones," some "from several different carcasses" near or as far as 100 m away from a water source. Haynes (1982:267) states "if wolves (*Canis lupus*) encounter remains of bison (*B. bison*) or moose (*Alces alces*) dead more than six months, efforts to gnaw bones generally are relatively slight. When food is scarce, the bones may be partly consumed. Isolated remains of prey animals smaller than caribou (*Ranaifer tarandus*) may suffer a great deal of dispersal and fragmentation by scavenging carnivores, even after months of aging." Behrensmeyer (1987:429) implies scavengers may exploit carcasses "over a period of several years after the kill." Mead and Sorg (1984:24) report wolves penned in a 10 acre enclosure gnawed bones "in a rather dry state." Porcupines (Brain 1980, 1981; Dixon 1984) and vultures (Mundy and Ledger 1976; Plug 1978) may collect bones displaying different weathering stages. Frison (1982:166) suggests long bones that have dried "for a few days, weeks, or even a year" would have made better expedient bone tools than fresh, greasy bone.

We are unaware of any study focusing on the weathering stages of collected bones; that is, we know of no weathering data derived from controlled contexts involving a single bone-collecting agent. What is known about the weathering stages of bones when collected by various taphonomic agents suggests that assuming bones were in stage 0 when collected may be invalid. We cannot ascertain, however, how often a scavenging carnivore may collect the

**Table 3  Taxon Collection Location and Microhabitat of Control Artiodactyl Carcasses**

| Carcass | Taxon | Collection Location | Collection Microhabitat |
|---|---|---|---|
| 10 | *Odocoileus hemionus* | Southwest Oregon | Grassland |
| 27 | | | Deciduous forest |
| 102 | | | Grassland |
| 104 | | | Deciduous forest |
| 107 | | | Deciduous forest |
| 108 | | | Grassland |
| 109 | | | Deciduous forest |
| 112 | *Cervus elaphus* | Southeast Washington | Coniferous forest |
| 119 | *Antilocapra americana* | Southeast Oregon | Sagebrush (*Artemesia*) grassland |
| 120 | *Bos taurus* | Southeast Washington | Grassland |

articulated hind limb of an animal dead for 8 to 10 months when the metapodial retains edible hide, tendon, and marrow while the femur has been defleshed and exposed since death (e.g., Haynes 1980).

Consideration of the deposition of bones reveals additional factors which obscure the temporal meaning of weathered bones. Because many archaeological collections of bones represent active collection of bones more or less continuously deposited over various Time spans, we believe inferring accumulation history (AH) from weathering data will often be impossible. Haynes (1988) reports bones in all weathering stages are found in both catastrophically and accretionally deposited assemblages (below, we consider recommended procedures for analytically solving this problem). Variation in the weathering stage displayed by bones in the former can be attributed to variation in exposure duration and/or depositional microenvironment (assuming skeletal element and taxon are controlled). In accretional or palimpsest assemblages, each time bones of fresh carcasses are added to a deposit already containing bones represents addition of bones with a weathering profile of $T_1$ to an assemblage with a profile of $T_{1+n}$, where n can be any value between 0 and 16, inclusively, according to the model in Figure 2. There are many ways for bones to accumulate in a locus and become spatially associated (Behrensmeyer 1987 and references therein). Those accumulation processes do nothing but obscure the relevance of weathering data for measuring an assesmblage's accumulation history.

To assess the interpretive consequences of not controlling when bones were accumulated (collected, and deposited or added together) relative to $T_1$ (Figure 2), weathering profiles were constructed for ten artiodactyl carcasses collected in the early 1980s (Table 3). All bones were collected from surface contexts, although some elements were partially covered with vegetation. All bone specimens, whether fragmented or complete, were assigned to a weathering stage on the basis of the most weathered portion of the specimen following Behrensmeyer (1978). While depositional environments and climates of the collection loci differ from those of East Africa where most previous bone weathering studies have been undertaken, the bones were easily assigned to Behrensmeyer's stages (Table 1). No data concerning the antiquity of death of the carcasses listed in Table 3 are available (i.e., YD is unknown), but such data are unknown and may be unknowable in prehsitoric contexts.

Four types of weathering profiles are represented by the carcasses (Table 4). Carcasses 27, 102, 107, 108, 119 display profiles similiar to $T_2$ in Figure 2. Carcasses 10, 104, and 109 have weathering profiles similar to $T_4$, and the weathering profile of Carcass 112 is similar to $T_5$. Finally, Carcass 120 exhibits a bimodal profile indicating the wave model (Figure 2), as noted earlier, is an inadequate characterization of variation in weathering profiles of single carcasses through time. The cause of this inadequacy is that the model does not account for different exposure durations and depositional microenvironments (see also Crader 1983:113).

**Table 4  Weathering Stage (WS) Profiles for Ten Control Artiodactyl Carcasses (see Table 3)**

| Carcass | WS 0 N | WS 0 % | WS 1 N | WS 1 % | WS 2 N | WS 2 % | WS 3 N | WS 3 % | WS 4 N | WS 4 % | WS 5 N | WS 5 % | Carcass Stage | Total NISP |
|---|---|---|---|---|---|---|---|---|---|---|---|---|---|---|
| 10 | 111 | 53.6 | 80 | 38.6 | 14 | 6.8 | 2 | 1.0 | | | | | 3 | 207 |
| 27 | 30 | 60.0 | 20 | 40.0 | | | | | | | | | 1 | 50 |
| 102 | 2 | 50.0 | 2 | 50.0 | | | | | | | | | 1 | 4 |
| 104 | 27 | 50.0 | 17 | 31.5 | 7 | 12.9 | 2 | 3.7 | 1 | 1.9 | | | 4 | 54 |
| 107 | 25 | 75.8 | 8 | 24.2 | | | | | | | | | 1 | 33 |
| 108 | 61 | 81.3 | 14 | 18.7 | | | | | | | | | 1 | 75 |
| 109 | 2 | 50.0 | 1 | 25.0 | | | 1 | 25.0 | | | | | 3 | 4 |
| 112 | 3 | 12.5 | 10 | 41.7 | 8 | 33.3 | 3 | 12.5 | | | | | 3 | 24 |
| 119 | 40 | 95.2 | 2 | 4.8 | | | | | | | | | 1 | 42 |
| 120 | 12 | 29.3 | 5 | 12.2 | 7 | 17.0 | 17 | 41.5 | | | | | 3 | 41 |

**Table 5  Weathering Stage (WS) Profiles for Ten Simulated Palimpsest Assemblages Derived from Table 4**

| Assemblage[a] | WS 0 N | WS 0 % | WS 1 N | WS 1 % | WS 2 N | WS 2 % | WS 3 N | WS 3 % | WS 4 N | WS 4 % | Carcass Stage | Total NISP |
|---|---|---|---|---|---|---|---|---|---|---|---|---|
| A | 15 | 23.1 | 15 | 23.1 | 15 | 23.1 | 20 | 30.7 | | | 3 | 65 |
| B | 29 | 50.0 | 18 | 31.0 | 7 | 12.0 | 3 | 5.0 | 1 | 1.8 | 4 | 58 |
| C | 29 | 50.0 | 19 | 32.8 | 7 | 12.0 | 2 | 3.4 | 1 | 1.8 | 4 | 58 |
| D | 73 | 63.0 | 19 | 16.3 | 7 | 6.0 | 17 | 14.7 | | | 3 | 116 |
| E | 7 | 21.9 | 13 | 40.6 | 8 | 25.0 | 4 | 12.5 | | | 3 | 32 |
| F | 172 | 60.9 | 94 | 33.3 | 14 | 4.9 | 2 | 0.7 | | | 3 | 282 |
| G | 126 | 46.3 | 95 | 34.9 | 29 | 10.7 | 22 | 8.1 | | | 3 | 272 |
| H | 54 | 62.1 | 9 | 10.3 | 7 | 8.0 | 17 | 19.6 | | | 3 | 87 |
| I | 138 | 52.8 | 97 | 37.2 | 21 | 8.0 | 4 | 1.5 | 1 | 0.4 | 4 | 261 |
| J | 141 | 49.5 | 107 | 37.5 | 29 | 10.2 | 7 | 2.3 | 1 | 0.4 | 4 | 285 |

[a]  Assemblage A, carcasses 112 and 120; B, 104 and 109; C, 102 and 104; D, 108 and 120; E, 102, 109, and 112; F, 10 and 108; G, 10, 112, and 120; H, 102, 119, and 120; I, 10 and 104; J, 10, 104, and 112.

The consequence of interpreting weathering profiles without controlling the weathering stage of the bones when they were accumulated is striking when selected profiles of individual carcasses are summed to simulate an active accumulation of carcasses. Table 5 illustrates the data for ten such simulations. Comparison of Tables 4 and 5 indicates the shape of the simulated profile is dependent on the carcass profiles from which it is constructed. As well, virtually all simulated weathering profiles suggest longer accumulation histories, and/or exposure durations and/or more years since death than single carcass profiles, often simply because of the addition of a few elements displaying weathering stages 3 or 4.

Additional weathering profiles were constructed under the assumption that bone-accumulating agents would collect one or both forelimbs or hindlimbs, of one or both sides of an animal. Only the weathering stages for long bones, metapodials, scapulae, and innominates were tallied, but all fragments of these elements were included (Table 6). Single accumulation events are potentially represented by single limbs, or any combination of limbs from a single carcass. Multiple accumulation events are potentially represented by any combination of limbs from multiple animals. These simulations indicate the weathering profile derived from a bone assemblage will depend on the profile of bones from particular carcasses, and how those carcasses are sampled. For example, the weathering profile for the right forelimb of carcass 10 is quite different than the profile for the left hindlimb of that carcass (Table 6). The forelimb

**Table 6  Simulated Weathering Profiles of Limb Bones Only Derived from Control Carcasses (Tables 3 and 4)**

| Carcass No. | Carcass Portion (Limb) | Weathering Stage 0 | 1 | 2 | 3 |
|---|---|---|---|---|---|
| 10 | L fore | 2 | 1 | 5 | |
| | L hind | 16 | 4 | | 1 |
| | R fore | 2 | 3 | 4 | |
| | R hind | | 11 | | |
| 107 | L fore | 4 | | | |
| | L hind | | | | |
| | R fore | 2 | | | |
| | R hind | 18 | 7 | | |
| 108 | L fore | 1 | 2 | | |
| | L hind | 3 | 4 | | |
| | R fore | 1 | 1 | | |
| | R hind | 4 | 1 | | |
| 112 | L fore | | 2 | 2 | 1 |
| | L hind | | 2 | 1 | |
| | R fore | | 3 | 2 | |
| | R hind | | 2 | 1 | 1 |
| 119 | L fore | 3 | 1 | | |
| | L hind | 3 | 1 | | |
| | R fore | 1 | | | |
| | R hind | 1 | | | |
| 120 | L fore | 1 | | 2 | 1 |
| | L hind | | 1 | | 3 |
| | R fore | | | 3 | 2 |
| | R hind | | | 1 | 3 |
| 107, 108, 119 | L fore | 8 | 3 | | |
| | L hind | 6 | 5 | | |
| | R fore | 4 | 1 | | |
| | R hind | 23 | 8 | | |
| | Fore (L and R) | 12 | 4 | | |
| | Hind (L and R) | 29 | 13 | | |
| | L (Fore and Hind) | 14 | 8 | | |
| | R (Fore and Hind) | 27 | 13 | | |
| 108, 119 | L fore | 4 | 3 | | |
| | L hind | 6 | 5 | | |
| | R fore | 2 | 1 | | |
| | R hind | 5 | 1 | | |
| | Fore | 6 | 4 | | |
| | Hind | 11 | 6 | | |
| | L | 10 | 8 | | |
| | R | 7 | 2 | | |
| 10, 112 | L fore | 2 | 3 | 7 | 1 |
| | L hind | 16 | 6 | 1 | 1 |
| | R fore | 2 | 6 | 6 | |
| | R hind | | 13 | 1 | 1 |
| | Fore | 4 | 9 | 13 | 1 |
| | Hind | 16 | 19 | 2 | 2 |
| | L | 18 | 8 | 8 | 2 |
| | R | 2 | 19 | 7 | 1 |
| 10, 112, 120 | L fore | 3 | 3 | 9 | 2 |
| | L hind | 16 | 7 | 1 | 4 |

**Table 6 (continued)   Simulated Weathering Profiles of Limb Bones Only Derived from Control Carcasses (Tables 3 and 4)**

| Carcass No. | Carcass Portion (Limb) | Weathering Stage | | | |
|---|---|---|---|---|---|
| | | 0 | 1 | 2 | 3 |
| | R fore | 2 | 6 | 9 | 2 |
| | R hind | | 13 | 1 | 4 |
| | Fore | 5 | 9 | 18 | 4 |
| | Hind | 16 | 20 | 2 | 8 |
| | L | 19 | 10 | 10 | 6 |
| | R | 2 | 19 | 10 | 6 |
| 10, 108, 112, 119 | L fore | 6 | 6 | 7 | 1 |
| | L hind | 22 | 11 | 1 | 1 |
| | R fore | 4 | 7 | 6 | |
| | R hind | 5 | 14 | 1 | 1 |
| | Fore | 10 | 13 | 13 | 1 |
| | Hind | 27 | 25 | 2 | 2 |
| | L | 28 | 17 | 8 | 2 |
| | R | 9 | 21 | 7 | 1 |

*Note:* Frequencies are absolute (NISP).

suggests an "age" of $T_6$ or $T_7$, whereas the hindlimb suggests an age of $T_3$ or $T_4$ (Figure 2). Similarly, the hindlimbs of carcasses 10, 112, and 120 produce a profile similar to $T_5$, while the forelimbs of those carcasses produce a profile similar to $T_6$ or $T_7$.

Because different bones of the same animal may display different weathering stages prior to burial due to variation in accumulation history, exposure duration, skeletal element, and/or depositional microenvironment, it seems we must find an analytic way to control interdependence. We have already suggested recording the weathering stage displayed by only one category of skeletal element per taxon (e.g., left femora) as one way to control for effects of interdependent bones displaying different weathering stages due to factors other than temporal ones. One could construct a weathering profile for each skeletal element category represented and compare the resulting profiles. Regardless, the analyst must realize that the greatest weathering stage represented in an assemblage from the right side or tail of a weathering profile indicates the maximum possible exposure duration for the assemblage (assuming taxon and skeletal element have been controlled). Whether it also represents the maximum years since animal death and/or aspects of accumulation history simply is unknown. To conclude it does requires assuming the maximally weathered bone(s) was accumulated when fresh (AH = ED), antiquity of death (YD) is directly correlated with accumulation history and exposure duration, and all bones entered the assemblage at the same time. To infer the entire weathering profile represents a particular accumulation history requires similar assumptions plus others noted earlier.

In sum, accumulation history can vary within as well as between carcasses, and the result is a bone's accumulation history will span the same or less time than years since death. Accumulation history thus represents a third kind of time, distinct from exposure duration and years since animal death. Because bones displaying weathering stages other than 0 may occasionally be collected as "riders" articulated with fresher bones (see above), a bone's accumulation history need not be the same duration as the bone's exposure duration. A bone's exposure history may begin before or after it is collected. As illustrated in the simulations, long-term deposition of bones in a locus can produce similarly skewed results. That problem is usually addressed by reference to spatial data.

## Spatial Data

Behrensmeyer (1978:161) suggested on one hand that a lack of variation in weathering of bones in prehistoric assemblages "may indicate catastrophic death, but could also mean that the local conditions (e.g., moisture, rapid burial) inhibited weathering of gradually accumulating skeletal remains." She suggested on the other hand that if most or all of the six weathering stages were represented in an assemblage, then attritional or long-term accumulation was indicated, but such variation "could also reflect highly variable microenvironmental conditions in which some bones of the same carcass could remain in stage 1 while others weathered more rapidly." In terms of Equation (3), a bone's accumulation history and its depositional microenvironment might have offsetting or conflating effects. She thus suggested the relative importance of accumulation history and depositional microenvironment could be ascertained by studying (1) spatial distribution and associations of variously weathered bones in the assemblage, (2) variation in the stages represented by bones from a single carcass (assuming interdependence can be controlled), and (3) relationships of various stages to their respective sedimentary environments. She further suggested that (1) if all stages were "homogeneously mixed in a single deposit," the assemblage was probably an attritional one, and (2) if only one stage was represented and the bones displaying that stage were spatially clustered, then the assemblage may or may not represent an attritional assemblage depending on "local variation in weathering conditions" (Behrensmeyer 1978:161). While clearly expressing due caution here, elsewhere in the same paper (1978:158) she states "it seems highly probable that [attritional surface assemblages] will all include some bones that are fresh, some that are slightly weathered, and some that are weathered." While perhaps true, the converse of this latter statement — the presence of all weathering stages denotes an attritional assemblage — is not necessarily true, because the presence of all weathering stages may reflect variation in depositional microenvironment, skeletal element, and/or exposure duration between specimens of a catastrophically generated assemblage. Behrensmeyer is obviously aware of that; hence her recommendation to study spatial and contextual data.

We constructed four spatial distributions of weathering stages. Three were generated with a random numbers table to approximate Behrensmeyer's "homogeneous mix," and one was subjectively built to simulate clustering (Figure 3). Viewing these assemblages from the perspective of Equation (3), several things not mentioned by Behrensmeyer in her discussion of interpreting spatial and contextual data become clear. First, Behrensmeyer's control sample was distributed across two-dimensional space: the ground surface. Interpretations of the spatial distribution of weathered bones must consider whether those bones under study were derived from three-dimensional space (e.g., a 3-D stratigraphic unit), or, a two-dimensional stratigraphically defined surface. This aspect is implied but glossed over by Behrensmeyer when she uses the term "deposit."

Stein (1987:340) notes geologists define a deposit as representing "one depositional event, during which time the sources, transport agents, and environment of deposition remained the same. The duration of such a depositional event is not often known. A single deposit may represent either continuous or abrupt deposition over either long or short periods of time." If bones are part of the constituent materials of a deposit, then by definition they may have been deposited rapidly or slowly over a long or short period of Time. Ignoring the important question of whether particular bones are intrusive to (and thus post-date formation of) the deposit (see Behrensmeyer 1987:433), the concern becomes one of deciding if we are to treat bones analytically as deposit constituents, or simply as inclusions in a deposit; that is, the analyst must decide if the bones represent a single depositional event as specified in the above definition of "deposit," or not. All bones in a deposit may or may not derive from the same source (e.g., taxon or habitat), and may or may not involve the same transport and depositional agent (e.g., fluvial action, hominids, carnivores). Those bones may have been deposited

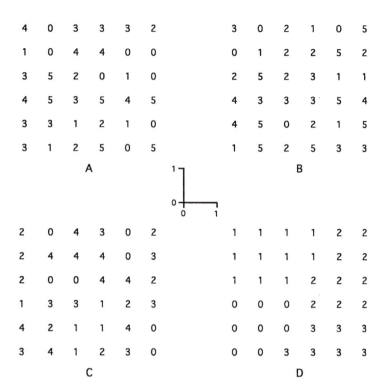

**Figure 3** Four simulations of spatial distributions of weathered bones. Each number signifies the weathering stage of a bone and the bone's location; NISP = 36 in all four simulations. Simulations A, B, and C are generated with a random numbers table; simulation D was subjectively constructed. Simulations A and B contain all weathering stages; simulation C contains only stages 0–4, simulation D contains only stages 0–3. See text for discussion of scale and orientation.

independent of the sediment-depositing agent. We believe most analysts have chosen to treat bones as inclusions in rather than constituents of a deposit. Evidence for that choice is twofold. First, consider the active bone-accumulating agents that are members of the Hominidae.

At one level, the simple act of accumulating a single ungulate hindlimb for consumption may involve a series of events including collection from the location of animal death, transport to the consumption locus, processing for consumption, consumption, and discard and burial of remaining parts. At a more general level, all acts of accumulating resources over a single day can be conceived as a palimpsest of resource accumulation events. At an even more general level, all acts of accumulating a particular resource during a single season can be conceived as a palimpsest of acts or events, or a set of related acts representing a specific kind of activity or seasonal event (Brooks 1982). Finally, all activities performed during a year (multiseason) can be considered a yearly activity or event. Because an event is a case of one, and a palimpsest is several events, analysts must be clear about the temporal scale at which an event, and thus a palimpsest, is defined. Because bone weathering stages differ along the temporal dimension in several-year increments, the finest level of resolution of bone accumulation events will involve sets of bones accumulated over one or more years, regardless of whether or not those sets actually represent one or more accumulation events as distinguished above. The second line of evidence for the analytic choice of treating bones as inclusions rather than constituents of a deposit concerns the fact that definition of a bone assemblage typically involves specifying spatial boundaries, the bones within the specified space making up the assemblage. Whether the horizontal and vertical boundaries of that spatially defined assemblage are isomorphic with, greater than, or less than the boundaries of a "deposit" is seldom clear in the analytic literature; hence we suspect bones are treated as inclusions within rather than constituent parts of a "deposit." This suspicion and its basis may be minor technicalities that pale in comparison to another aspect of "deposit" formation.

Spatial and contextual data may provide minimal insight to the formational history of an assemblage of weathered bones simply because while many techniques of spatial analysis are available, those techniques "do not [entail] assumptions that are logically consistent with the [potential] formation processes responsible for [the spatial arrangement of bones]" (Carr 1984:133). This aspect of the meaning of the spatial data in Figure 3 is emphasized by the fact we have not indicated on that figure whether those distributions are horizontal, vertical, or both.

The second aspect of spatial data not explicitly considered by Behrensmeyer is apparent in the fact that while we put a spatial scale in Figure 3, we did not indicate the size of the units on that scale. Are those units cm or km? Behrensmeyer's special units were km, whereas special units of many fossil collections are described in m and/or cm. This spatial difference may well relate to the fact that Behrensmeyer's sample of weathered bones was passively accumulated, whereas fossils collected by archaeologists and paleontologists often represent accumulations.

Third, even controlling spatial direction (horizontal, vertical) and scale (cm, mm, km), we would hesitate to interpret the spatial data in Figure 3. That is so because, even with taxon and skeletal element controlled, depositional microenvironment, years since animal death, and exposure duration are not (and cannot be) controlled if accumulation history is the variable of interest. Years since death and exposure duration are not necessarily equal for a bone, or between bones; nor is either necessarily equal to the duration of accumulation of a bone or equal between bones. Whether a bone's exposure duration is equivalent to its accumulation history or not is typically dealt with analytically by assuming a bone was collected and deposited (accumulated) when stage 0. Whether a bone's exposure duration is equivalent to the years since that bone died or not depends on how soon after death that bone was exposed. For one to conclude clusters of bones displaying the same weathering stage represent 4 accumulation events (in the case of Figure 3D) requires assuming all 36 bones were deposited in the same microenvironment, all 36 bones were exposed immediately after death (ED = YD), and members of each cluster experienced similar exposure durations and died at the same time; and inferring that only accumulation history varies between clusters. The analyst infers maximally weathered bones accumulated first and minimally weathered bones accumulated last. To conclude the clusters represent one instance of accumulation requires assuming each cluster was deposited in a different microenvironment or all members of each cluster died at the same time and experienced the same exposure durations, but that exposure durations and years since death varied from cluster to cluster, or both, such that accumulation histories do not vary from cluster to cluster. To conclude the "homogeneous" distributions represent attritional accumulations (Behrensmeyer 1978:161) requires assuming each specimen was exposed at death, depositional microenvironment did not vary significantly from specimen to specimen, and each specimen was accumulated when fresh (WS = 0) such that only accumulation history controls the variation from weathering stage to weathering stage. More simplistically, one assumes maximally weathered bones accumulated first and minimally weathered bones accumulated last (which in turn presumes interdependence has been controlled).

We thus believe spatial and contextual data will allow only minimal control of depositional microenvironment and accumulation history because the analyst must variously assume the values of these and the years since death and exposure duration variables as well. This is so because even with precise spatial data, we do not know the magnitude of microenvironmental variation (apparently assumed to be represented by spatial data and the distance and direction between specimens) that significantly controls weathering rates and exposure duration. That problem is well illustrated by Bunn and Kroll (1986:434) who maintain "bone weathering data do not effectively measure accumulation time [AH] at sites" but rather burial time [ED], because they have found "conjoining specimens of the same original bone that exhibit different weathering stages" in a prehistoric bone assemblage (Bunn and Kroll 1987:97). They acknowledge the requisite assumption here that "different bones of the same animal carcass necessarily accumulated at the same moment in time" (Bunn and Kroll 1987:97), but while mentioning the depositional microenvironment variable, they do not seem to realize their position also requires assuming depositional microenvironment did not vary between the conjoining pieces and thus only exposure duration could account for variation in weathering stage across those pieces. (Note: skeletal element and taxon are controlled because the pieces conjoin). Bunn and Kroll do not present spatial data for these conjoining pieces, but if they had, we doubt that data would have been illuminating for the reasons noted above.

Finally, we note that while Behrensmeyer's suggestions regarding the importance of spatial data superficially seem reasonable, we are unaware of any study of weathered prehistoric bones which reports such data. We find that perplexing, and wonder if that is the case for editorial reasons, or because, like us, other analysts are unsure that spatial data will provide the control Behrensmeyer originally proposed.

## Discussion

Behrensmeyer's (1978) observations indicated the potential that bone weathering data might reflect aspects of the temporal duration of bone assemblage formation as evidenced by the correlation of carcass weathering stage with years since the animal died. In the case of prehistoric bone assemblages, however, the simple Equation (1) takes on the complex form of Equation (3). Only two of the variables — skeletal element and taxon — can be readily controlled during analysis. Weathering can be controlled by presuming that Behrensmeyer's six stages characterize only subaerial weathering, and not subsurface deterioration. Behrensmeyer suggested spatial and contextual data would indicate how depositional microenvironment might be controlled, but we fail to see how that can be so because we do not know how much variation in depositional microenvironment is significant, and how much microenvironment varies across a given spatial unit. That lack of knowledge seems to be analytically "controlled" by assuming bones that are spatially close (from the same, spatially defined, assemblage) were deposited in similar microenvironments.

Behrensmeyer (1978:161) suggests exposure duration and accumulation history are the variables of interest when she states "weathering can give specific information concerning surface exposure of bone prior to burial and the time period over which bones are accumulated." Partial control of accumulation history is lent by assuming all bones were stage 0 when collected and all were simultaneously deposited (have the same accumulation history). In that case the weathering stage displayed by a bone is a function of its exposure duration. Because both exposure duration and accumulation history begin at or after animal death ($ED \leq YD$; and $AH \leq YD$), and because exposure begins at or after accumulation ($ED \leq AH$) in most archaeological cases, unravelling the temporal meaning of an assemblage of weathered bones is complex. Clearly, the most weathered bone in an assemblage has been exposed longest, insofar as skeletal element, taxon, and depositional microenvironment have not significantly affected weathering stage values. Even controlling skeletal element, taxon, depositional microenvironment, and weathering as noted above, we are not at all sure how the three kinds of taphonomic time — accumulation history, exposure duration, years since animal death — are to be analytically distinguished from weathering data, especially when those data are rendered as a weathering profile.

The kind of taphonomic time we have labeled years since animal death is ratio scale because the zero point is fixed at the date of an animal's death. Because exposure duration and accumulation history may be equal to or less than years since death (that is, start on the date of animal death or any time after animal death), they seem to be interval scale measures of Time; their zero points are free to vary. Weathering, as defined by Behrensmeyer (1978), could be construed as occurring over interval scale Time if uniform quantitative changes in bone deterioration (e.g., amino acid racemization) can be aligned with uniform Time intervals. The weathering stages presently used to characterize bone weathering seem at best to be ordinal scale measures of Time. Even if interval scale stages are eventually derived, it is clear such stages will only reflect exposure duration (assuming variation in skeletal element, taxon, and depositional microenvironment can be controlled, and assuming bones only weather in surface contexts), and may or may not reflect years since death or accumulation history.

Thus far we have attempted to keep the discussion simple. That the situation is, in fact, complex can be shown in three ways. First, Equation (3) includes only the major relevant variables. Other relevant variables that should perhaps be included on the right side of that equation include the mechanism or agent of animal death, the agent(s) by which bones are initially exposed from soft tissues, and the agent(s) of bone collection, transport, and deposition. For example, many late prehistoric hunters kill, butcher, and consume an animal within a very few days (Lyman 1987a and references therein), thereby effectively creating a situation where death, exposure, and accumulation all start at essentially the same time for the bones of a carcass. Limited actualistic data described earlier involving cases where the death agent differs from agents of accumulation and exposure indicate it is typical in those cases for (years since) death to start before exposure and before accumulation.

The second way to demonstrate the real world is more complex than Equation (3) involves realizing some bones will be variously buried, reexposed, and buried again, perhaps several times. Such processes serve to further the temporal disjunction between the end of exposure and (the beginning of years since) death. Bones are not necessarily buried upon deposition; taphonomic histories are much more complex than that (Lyman 1987b and references therein). Only detailed study of the sedimentological record may reveal the complexity of the exposure–burial history of the bones included in the deposit.

Third, the significance of Equation (3) for prehistoric bone assemblages can be made clearer if that equation is written as:

$$YD_i, ED_{ij}, AH_{ij} = f(WS_{ij}, SE_{ij}, TX_{ij}, ME_{ij}) \qquad (4)$$

where $i$ denotes the animal or carcass contributing the bone, and $j$ denotes the particular bone of carcass $i$ under scrutiny. Equation (4) underscores the importance of controlling specimen interdependence when interpreting weathering profiles. Each animal represented by a bone assemblage may have died at a different time, and each bone of each carcass may (1) have been exposed for a different duration; (2) have been accumulated at a different time; (3) have been deposited in a different microenvironment; (4) represent a different skeletal element, each with its own unique weathering rate; and (5) represent a different taxon, each with its own unique weathering rate.

Because her original correlation was between years since death and carcass weathering stage, with accumulation history and exposure duration known (bones accumulated at death, or $YD = AH$) or controlled (exposure duration controlled by recording the maximally weathered bone per carcass), Behrensmeyer (1978:162) correctly expressed concern, and emphasized her statements were "hypotheses which need testing." Our examination of the literature indicates virtually no testing has taken place. Instead, some analysts have taken Behrensmeyer's hypotheses as interpretive principles and applied them uncritically to bone assemblages (e.g., Boaz 1982; Bunn 1982; Gifford et al. 1980; Potts 1982; Shipman et al. 1981). Given our review, we are not at all surprised by disputes over the temporal meaning of bone weathering data (compare Potts 1984 and 1986 with Bunn and Kroll 1986 and 1987).

Behrensmeyer's actualistically based conclusions produce Equation (1). To apply those conclusions to assemblages of prehistorically weathered bone, however, requires use of Equation (3) [or more realistically, Equation (4)]. We believe only two of the variables in Equation (3) can analytically have rigorous values assigned to them: skeletal element and taxon. Few analysts actually control those variables; taxon is controlled in 7 of 14 case studies we have examined, and skeletal element is partially controlled in 4 of those studies (Boaz 1982; Bower et al. 1985; Bunn and Kroll 1986, 1987; Bunn et al. 1980; Gifford et al. 1980; Gifford-Gonzalez 1985; Lyman 1988; Potts 1982, 1984, 1986; Shipman et al. 1981; Todd 1987; Todd et al. 1987; Walker et al. 1988). Surprisingly, depositional microenvironment is controlled in only 4 of the 14 cases, despite its critical impact on weathering rates and thus inferred values of exposure duration and/or accumulation history.

It seems that analysts typically assume weathering stops once a bone is buried. Perhaps most surprising, despite the fact that Behrensmeyer's original correlation was between years since death and carcass weathering stage, the former variable is not even mentioned in any of the studies we reviewed. Instead, one of the other two kinds of taphonomic time — exposure duration and accumulation history — is inferred in those studies.

## Conclusions

Review of Behrensmeyer's (1978) seminal work on bone weathering reveals that weathering is a process, and thus reflects the passage of Time. Behrensmeyer's actualistic data indicate a strong correlation between the greatest weathering stage displayed by bones of a carcass and antiquity of death of that carcass. While Behrensmeyer phrased her observations carefully and emphasized the hypothetical nature of her conclusions, within a very few years those hypotheses were being used as principles to interpret assemblages of prehistoric weathered bones. Actualistic research aimed at gathering more data and testing the hypothetical conclusions has been much less frequently discussed in the literature.

We conclude that bone weathering data do not in any simple and direct fashion reflect Time, particularly the duration of bone assemblage formation. Bone weathering stages as a periodic clock can align themselves in various ways with the three kinds of taphonomic time, of which only years since death clearly and directly aligns itself with Time by definition. Exposure and accumulation independently begin any time simultaneous with or after death. Thus, weathering stages are not necessarily structured, insofar as they might somehow directly reflect exposure duration or accumulation history, to directly reflect years since death or Time. Taphonomic factors affecting weathering rates (depositional microenvironment, skeletal element, taxon) and durations (agents of exposure and burial) can only be analytically controlled in part and may further deflect weathering stage data from years since death and Time. We suspect that were we to significantly enlarge Behrensmeyer's (1978) original control sample of 52 carcass observations by study of all bones of, say, 200 carcasses of several taxa, the correlation of weathering stage with years since animal death would decrease remarkably due to within-and-between-carcass variation in accumulation history, exposure duration, skeletal element, taxon, and depositional microenvironment.

Researchers who have studied weathering of paleontological collections and inferred the duration of bone exposure have used that data in conjunction with data on the extent of (1) bone dispersal, (2) gnawing damage to bones, (3) disarticulation, (4) bone breakage, and (5) bone destruction (Badam et al. 1986:346; Barnosky 1985:340; Bown and Kraus 1981:46). That is, it appears paleontologists believe weathering data alone are inadequate to unambiguously indicate exposure and accumulation aspects of the taphonomic history of a bone assemblage.

Detailed data concerning weathering stages of bones when they are originally accumulated are needed. Additional data such as Gifford's (1977) on the weathering of individual bones in a carcass are needed as well. Conclusions based on interpretations of bone weathering patterns in archaeological assemblages, such as Potts' (1986:30) statement that "Olduvai hominids used their sites over a longer period than that practiced by recent hunter gatherers" require ethnoarchaeological data on bone weathering profiles at short term, long term, single and multiple occupation sites created by recent hunter-gatherers in order to build necessary analogs and bridging arguments. These and other necessary kinds of data are virtually non-existent at present.

Behrensmeyer (1978:152–153) suggested recording the "most advanced weathering stage covering more than 1 cm square" per bone specimen. Such a procedure may, however, mask precisely those data most relevant to assessing the duration of exposure. Behrensmeyer (1978:153) also noted that "bones are usually weathered more on the upper (exposed) than the lower (ground contact) surfaces," and Todd and Frison (1986:39) suggested bones subject to minimal post-burial movement might not be uniformly weathered on all surfaces. It can be conjectured, then, that a bone which displays a broad range of weathering stages may have undergone slow burial, or possibly, multiple burials and partial reexposure. This would seem particularly possible for a bone the long axis of which deviates from the horizontal.

There is much potential for bone weathering information that has not been intensively studied. Following Behrensmeyer (1978), readers are cautioned that much actualistic work remains to be done before any of the ideas expressed here become standard parts of taphonomic analysis. More importantly, it is our opinion that we are a long way from safely inferring Time of bone assemblage formation, let alone hominid behavior, on the basis of bone weathering data.

## Acknowledgments

We thank D. Gifford-Gonzalez, D. K. Grayson, L. C. Todd, and several anonymous reviewers who saw the value of this study but did not hesitate to point out weaknesses in its earlier versions. Thanks to W. R. Wood for lab space, and L. Stanley, W. Billick, D. Rogles, and M. B. Schiffer for encouragement and discussions.

## References

Badam, G.L., R.K Ganjoo, and Salahuddin
   1986   Preliminary Taphonomical Studies of Some Pleistocene Fauna from the Central Narmada Valley, Nadhya Pradesh, India. *Palaeogeography, Palaeoclimatology, Palaeoecology* 53:335-348.

Barnosky, A.D.
   1985   Taphonomy and Herd Structure of the Extinct Irish Elk, *Megaloceros giganteus*. *Science* 228:340–344.

Boaz, D.D.
   1982   *Modern Riverine Taphonomy: Its Relevance to the Interpretation of Plio-Pleistocene Hominid Paleoecology in the Omo Basin, Ethiopia*. Ph.D. dissertation. University Microfilms, Ann Arbor, MI.

Behrensmeyer, A.K.
   1978   Taphonomic and Ecologic Information from Bone Weathering. *Paleobiology* 4:150–162.
   1982   Time Resolution in Fluvial Vertebrate Assemblages. *Paleobiology* 8:211–227.
   1984   Taphonomy and the Fossil Record. *American Scientist* 72:558–566.
   1987   Taphonomy and Hunting. In *The Evolution of Human Hunting*, edited by M.H. Nitecki and D.V. Nitecki, pp. 423–450. Plenum Press, New York.

Binford, L.R.
   1983   *In Pursuit of the Past*. Thames and Hudson, New York.

Bladgley, C.
  1986   Counting Individuals in Mammalian Fossil Assemblages from Fluvial Environments. *Palaios* 1:328–338.

Blumenschine, R.J.
  1986   *Early Hominid Scavenging Opportunities: Implications of Carcass Availability in the Serengeti and Ngorongoro Ecosystems.* British Archaeological Reports International Series 283, Oxford, U.K.
  1987   Characteristics of an Early Hominid Scavenging Niche. *Current Anthropology* 28:83–407.

Bower, J.R.F., D.P. Gifford, and D. Livingston
  1985   Excavations at the Loiyangalani Site, Serengeti National Park, Tanzania. *National Geographic Society Research Reports* 20:41–56.

Bown, T. M., and M.J. Kraus
  1981   Vertebrate Fossil-Bearing Paleosol Units (Willwood Formation, Lower Eocene, Northwest Wyoming, U.S.A.): Implications for Taphonomy, Biostratigraphy, and Assemblage Analysis. *Palaeogeography, Palaeoclimatology, Palaeoecology* 53:335–348.

Brain, C.K.
  1967   Bone Weathering and the Problem of Bone Pseudo-tools. *South African Journal of Science* 63:97–99.
  1980   Some Criteria for the Recognition of Bone-Collecting Agencies in African Caves. In *Fossils in the Making,* edited by A.K. Behrensmeyer and A.P. Hill, pp 107–130. University of Chicago Press, Chicago.
  1981   *The Hunters or the Hunted? An Introduction to African Cave Taphonomy.* University of Chicago Press, Chicago.

Brooks, R.L.
  1982   Events in the Archaeological Context and Archaeological Explanation. *Current Anthropology* 23:67–75.

Bunn, H.T.
  1982   *Meat-Eating and Human Evolution: Studies on the Diet and Subsistence Patterns of Plio-Pleistocene Hominids in East Africa.* Ph.D. dissertation, Department of Anthropology, University of California, Berkeley, CA. University Microfilms, Ann Arbor, MI.

Bunn, H.T., J.W.K. Harris, G. Isaac, Z. Kaufulu, E. Kroll, K. Schick, N. Toth, and A.K. Behrensmeyer
  1980   FxJj50: An Early Pleistocene Site in Northern Kenya. *World Archaeology* 12:109–136.

Bunn, H.T., and E.M. Kroll
  1986   Systematic Butchery by Plio/Pleistocene Hominids at Olduvai Gorge, Tanzania. *Current Anthropology* 27:431–452.
  1987   Reply to Potts. *Current Anthropology* 28:96–98.

Carr, C.
  1984   The Nature of Organization of Intrasite Archaeological Records and Spatial Analytic Approaches to their Investigation. In *Advances in Archaeological Method and Theory,* Vol. 7, edited by M.B. Schiffer, pp. 103–222. Academic Press, Orlando.

Coe, M.
  1978   The Decomposition of Elephant Carcasses in the Tsavo (East) National Park, Kenya. *Journal of Arid Environments* 1:71–86.

Cook, J.
  1986   The Application of Scanning Electron Microscopy to Taphonomic and Archaeological Problems. In *Studies in the Upper Paleolithic of Britain and Northwest Europe,* edited by D.A. Roe, pp. 143–163. British Archaeological Reports International Series 296, Oxford, U.K.

Crader, D.C.
    1983  Recent Single-Carcass Bone Scatters and the Problem of "Butchery" Sites in the Archaeological Record. In *Animals in Archaeology, 1: Hunters and Their Prey*, edited by J. Clutton-Brock and C. Grigson, pp. 107–141. British Archaeological Reports International Series 163, Oxford, U.K.

Dixon, E.J.
    1984  Context and Environment in Taphonomic Analysis: Examples from Alaska's Porcupine River Caves. *Quaternary Research* 22:201–215.

Einarsen, A.S
    1956  *Determination of Some Predator Species by Field Signs*. Oregon State College Monographs Studies in Zoology No. 10, Corvallis.

Frison, G.C.
    1974  Archaeology of the Casper Site. In *The Casper Site: A Hell Gap Bison Kill on the High Plains*, edited by G.C. Frison, pp. 1–111. Academic Press, New York.
    1982  Bone Butchering Tools in Archaeological Sites. *Canadian Journal of Anthropology* 2:159–167.

Gifford, D.P.
    1977  *Observations of Modern Human Settlements as an Aid to Archaeological Interpretation*. Ph.D. dissertation, Department of Anthropology, University of California, Berkeley, CA. University Microfilms, Ann Arbor, MI.
    1980  Ethnoarchaeological Contributions to the Taphonomy of Human Sites. In *Fossils in the Making*, edited by A.K. Behrensmeyer and A.P. Hill, pp. 94–106. University of Chicago Press, Chicago.
    1981  Taphonomy and Paleoecology: A Critical Review of Archaeology's Sister Disciplines. In *Advances in Archaeological Method and Theory*, Vol. 4, edited by M.B. Schiffer, pp. 365–438. Academic Press, New York.
    1984  Taphonomic Specimens, Lake Turkana. *National Geographic Society Research Reports* 17:419–428.

Gifford, D.P., G.L. Isaac, and C.M. Nelson
    1980  Evidence for Predation and Pastoralism at Prolonged Drift: A Pastoral Neolithic Site in Kenya. *Azania* 15:57–108.

Gifford-Gonzalez, D.P.
    1985  Faunal Assemblages from Masai Gorge Rockshelter and Marula Rockshelter. *Azania* 20:69–88.

Grayson, D.K.
    1979  On the Quantification of Vertebrate Archaeofaunas. In *Advances in Archaeological Method and Theory*, Vol. 2, edited by M.B. Schiffer, pp. 199–237. Academic Press, New York.
    1984  *Quantitative Zooarchaeology*. Academic Press, Orlando.

Haynes, G.
    1980  Prey Bones and Predators: Potential Ecologic Information from Analysis of Bone Sites. *Ossa* 7:75–97.
    1982  Utilization and Skeletal Disturbances of North American Prey Carcasses. *Arctic* 35:266–281.
    1988  Mass Deaths and Serial Predation: Comparative Taphonomic Studies of Modern Large Mammal Death Sites. *Journal of Archaeological Science* 15:219–235.

Hesse, B., and P. Wapnish
    1985  *Animal Bone Archaeology*. Taraxacum, Washington, D.C.

Hill, A.P.
    1979  Disarticulation and Scattering of Mammal Skeletons. *Paleobiology* 5:261–274.

Hill, A.P., and Behrensmeyer, A.K.
  1984  Disarticulation Patterns of Some Modern East African Mammals. *Paleobiology* 10:366–376.

Johnson, E.
  1985  Current Developments in Bone Technology. In *Advances in Archaeological Method and Theory,* Vol. 8, edited by M.B. Schiffer, pp. 157–235. Academic Press, Orlando.

Kitts, D.B.
  1966  Geologic Time. *Journal of Geology* 74:127–146.

Lyman, R.L.
  1984  Bone Density and Differential Survivorship of Fossil Classes. *Journal of Anthropological Archaeology* 3:259–299.
  1987a Archaeofaunas and Butchery Studies: A Taphonomic Perspective. In *Advances in Archaeological Method and Theory,* Vol. 10, edited by M.B. Schiffer, pp. 249–337. Academic Press, San Diego.
  1987b Zooarchaeology and Taphonomy: A General Consideration. *Journal of Ethnobiology* 7:93–117.
  1988  Was There a Last Supper at Last Supper Cave? In *Danger Cave, Last Supper Cave, and Hanging Rock Shelter: The Faunas,* edited by D.K. Grayson, pp. 81–104. Anthropological Papers No. 66, American Museum of Natural History, New York.

Mead, J.I., and M. Sorg
  1984  Constructing Analogues of Bone Modifications Through the Study of Wolf Behavior. In *Abstracts of the First International Conference on Bone Modification,* pp. 23–25. Center for the Study of the First Americans, University of Maine, Orono, ME.

Mehl, M.G.
  1966  The Domebo Mammoth: Vertebrate Paleomortology. In *Domebo: A Paleo-Indian Mammoth Kill in the Prairie-Plains,* edited by F.C. Leonhardy, pp. 27–30. Contributions of the Museum of the Great Plains 1, Lawton, OK.

Micozzi, M.S.
  1986  Experimental Study of Postmortem Change under Field Conditions: Effects of Freezing, Thawing, and Mechanical Injury. *Journal of Forensic Sciences* 31:953–961.

Miller, G.J.
  1975  A Study of Cuts, Grooves, and Other Marks on Recent and Fossil Bones: II, Weathering Cracks, Fractures, Splinters, and Other Similar Natural Phenomena. In *Lithic Technology,* edited by E. Swanson, pp. 212–226. Mouton, The Hague.

Mundy, P.J., and J.A. Ledger
  1976  Griffon Vultures, Carnivores and Bones. *South African Journal of Science* 72:106–110.

Plug, I.
  1978  Collecting Patterns of Six Species of Vultures (Aves: Accipitridae). *Annals of the Transvaal Museum* 31:51–63.

Potts, R.
  1982  *Lower Pleistocene Site Formation and Hominid Activities at Olduvai Gorge, Tanzania.* Ph.D. dissertation, Department of Anthropology, Harvard University, Cambridge, MA. University Microfilms, Ann Arbor, MI.
  1984  Home Base and Early Hominids. *American Scientist* 72:338–347.
  1986  Temporal Span of Bone Accumulations at Olduvai Gorge and Implications for Early Hominid Foraging Behavior. *Paleobiology* 12:25–31.

Purdy, B.A., and Clark, D.E.
  1987  Weathering of Inorganic Materials: Dating. In *Advances in Archaeological Method and Theory,* Vol. 11, edited by M.B. Schiffer, pp. 211–253. Academic Press, San Diego.

Richardson, P.R.K.
   1980   Carnivore Damage to Antelope Bones and Its Archaeological Implications. *Palaeontologia Africana* 23:109–125.

Schafer, W.
   1972   *Ecology and Paleoecology of Marine Environments.* University of Chicago Press, Chicago.

Shipman, P.
   1981a Applications of Scanning Electron Microscopy to Taphonomic Problems. In *The Research Potential of Anthropological Museum Collections,* edited by A.M. Cantwell, J.B. Griffin, and N.A. Rothschild, pp. 357–385. *Annals of the New York Academy of Sciences* 376.
   1981b *Life History of a Fossil.* Harvard University Press, Cambridge, MA.

Shipman, P., A. Walker, J.A. Van Couvering, P.J. Hooker, and J.A. Miller
   1981   The Fort Ternan Hominoid Site, Kenya: Geology, Age, Taphonomy and Paleoecology. *Journal of Human Evolution* 10:49–72.

Stein, J.K.
   1987   Deposits for Archaeologists. In *Advances in Archaeological Method and Theory,* Vol. 11, edited by M.B. Schiffer, pp. 337–395. Academic Press, San Diego.

Todd, L.C.
   1983a Taphonomy: Fleshing Out the Dry Bones of Plains Prehistory. *Wyoming Archaeologist* 26:36–46.
   1983b *The Horner Site: Taphonomy of an Early Holocene Bison Bonebed.* Ph.D. dissertation, University of New Mexico, Albuquerque. University Microfilms, Ann Arbor, MI.
   1987   Taphonomy of the Horner II Bone Bed. In *The Horner Site,* edited by G.C. Frison and L.C. Todd, pp. 107–198. Academic Press, Orlando.

Todd, L.C., and Frison, G.C.
   1986   Taphonomic Study of the Colby Site Mammoth Bones. In *The Colby Mammoth Site,* edited by G.C. Frison and L.C. Todd, pp. 27–90. University of New Mexico Press, Albuquerque.

Todd, L.C., R.V. Witter, and G.C. Frison
   1987   Excavation and Documentation of the Princeton and Smithsonian Horner Site Assemblages. In *The Horner Site,* edited by G.C. Frison and L.C. Todd, pp. 39–91. Academic Press, Orlando.

Walker, D.N., G.C. Frison, D. Darlington, R. Reider, W.R. Latady, and M.E. Miller
   1988   The Hinrichs Mammoth Site, Converse County, Wyoming. *American Quaternary Association Program and Abstracts of the Tenth Biennial Meeting,* pp.159.

# Eskimo Skeleton Taphonomy with Identification of Possible Polar Bear Victims

# 16

## CHARLES F. MERBS

## Introduction

During the summers of 1967, 1968, and 1969, the author directed the recovery of Eskimo skeletons at a series of sites located northwest of Hudson Bay, along the western shore of Roes Welcome Sound, in the Northwest Territories of Canada (Merbs 1971, 1976). Two sites in particular produced large numbers of human skeletons: 127 from Kamarvik (LeHv-1), a coastal site south of Wager Bay (64°45′N, 87°10′W), and 190 from Silumiut (KkJg-1), a small island attached to the mainland at low tide north of Chesterfield Inlet (63°41′N, 90°05′W). The preservation of these skeletons varied greatly, with field-note comments ranging from good, including several examples of very good, to poor, very poor, and, in a few instances, fragments only. The mixed preservation limited the kinds of osteological analyses that could be carried out, but it also stimulated an interest in the pattern of preservation itself and the agents that produced it.

Silumiut and Kamarvik are similar in general appearance, with the most obvious archaeological features being the ruins of stone and sod winter houses and stone graves. Both sites have an initial radiocarbon age of circa A.D. 1200, a time when Eskimo occupation in the area is identified as Thule culture, and both show continued usage into historic (post-European contact) times. The people of the Thule culture appear to be the direct biological and cultural ancestors of the Inuit who reside in this region today.

Graves at both sites were constructed on the tundra surface, often directly on bedrock, and consisted of cairn-like rock tombs that enclosed human skeletons (Figure 1). Clad in animal skin clothing, or wrapped in a caribou skin shroud, the body was placed in a flexed position on the natural tundra surface, with the rock tomb then constructed around and over it. The inner chamber was approximately rectangular in shape, with dimensions that usually reflected the size of the body entombed, adult graves being larger than those of children, and those of adult males being even larger, at least on average, than those of adult females. Ethnographic reports indicate that it was very important that rocks forming the roof not rest directly on the body, lest the soul of the deceased become irritated by the weight or unable to breathe, and wooden crosspieces were sometimes used to support the roof. The presence of these wooden supports in a treeless land where even driftwood was scarce (McCartney 1977) proved too tempting for early explorers, particularly the Luke Foxe expedition that visited Silumiut in 1631, and many were removed and burned as firewood aboard ship (Miller 1894).

The pattern of bone preservation seen at the two sites may be attributed primarily to two factors: time since interment and local taphonomic conditions. The temporal factor covers a range of several hundred years, beginning around AD 1200 and terminating before 1631. One child burial at Silumiut was eliminated from the study because it was obviously very recent

**Figure 1**    Typical stone grave at Silumiut. (A) External; (B) internal.

and the excellent condition of these bones would bias the results. All but three graves contained a single individual, the exceptions being a child with an adolescent, an infant with an old adult female, and an infant with a middle adult female, all at Silumiut. One of the Kamarvik graves also contained the remains of two individuals, but this is interpreted as a special situation discussed later as a possible polar bear victim.

Individual burials are difficult to date, as most include few if any artifacts, and even when present, the artifacts may not accurately date the burial. Also, the bones are heavily encrusted, and to some extent even impregnated, with lichens and other organic materials that postdate the burial, thereby making $^{14}$C dating difficult and potentially unreliable. Only one burial, Sil-156, was actually dated by this method, producing a date of A.D. 1140 ± 70 (McCartney 1977), corrected to A.D. 1205 according to the correction curve of Stuiver and Suess (1966).

Local taphonomic conditions affecting preservation are numerous and varied, including a yearly freeze–thaw cycle, exposure to sunlight and drying, rock and soil acidity, weight of rocks resting directly on bones, growth of lichens and other vegetation on and even into bones, and gnawing of ground squirrels, foxes, wolves, and other animals. Although the results of distinct processes could often be identified on a bone, it was more often a combination of processes that was responsible for the bone's final appearance.

Presently, the average temperature in this area is very cold, but, as typical of the Arctic, it varies widely through the year. Recent temperatures recorded in nearby Chesterfield have ranged from –60°F in the winter to 86°F in the summer, with a mean January temperature of –24.8°F and a mean July temperature of 47.9°F (McCartney 1977). Various sources suggest that during Thule culture times, temperatures in the area may have been significantly colder during a time known as the Little Ice Age. Even during the warmest days of summer, the insulative and shading effect of a stone grave, plus the presence of permafrost near the surface, would keep the interior of a grave much cooler than the surrounding air. Nevertheless, the contents of the graves certainly experienced thawing during most if not all summers.

Microscopic plants found in damp, sealed graves appear to have done little more than give bones a greenish appearance, while disturbed graves were more likely to harbor lichens that grew on and into bones, giving them a pathological, neoplasia-like, appearance, and causing erosion of bone cortex. Severely disturbed graves that contained an accumulation of soil sometimes supported a wide variety of perennial plants whose roots penetrated bone to cause damage.

The Roes Welcome Lowland region of the Northwest Territories is characterized by flat expanses of exposed gneissic and impure granitic rocks, variously altered by glacial activity. Submersion following glacial retreat, and recent emergence due to isostatic adjustment, is still taking place (McCartney 1977). The graves were constructed of rocks broken free of bedrock, primarily by frost action, that ranged in size from too large to be moved by a single person, to small pieces the size of a person's fist, or smaller. The larger pieces were used to produce the primary grave structure — four walls and a roof (Figure 1A), and the angular, often straight-edged shape of these rocks allowed the construction of an inner chamber having approximately right angles. Progressively smaller stones were then added to the outside, essentially to seal the chamber. The smaller, outer rocks tended to camouflage the true structure of the graves, giving them the appearance of a simple stone pile.

Removal of the grave roof, if it had not already been removed prior to excavation, exposed the skeleton within. In some cases the bones appeared relatively undisturbed (Figure 1B), while in others they were in considerable disarray, with the cranium in particular likely to be separated from the remainder of the skeleton. Often the disturbance turned out to be superficial, however, with most of the bones closer to the floor retaining their anatomical relationships.

## Grave Environment and Skeletal Preservation

During the 1968 season, soil samples were obtained where possible from the floors of graves 105 through 186 at Silumiut and from all Kamarvik graves, and tested for acidity. In all cases the overall pH levels of floors tested were below 7.0 (acidic), ranging from 6.6 to 4.7 (Figure 2), with the floors at Kamarvik being slightly more acidic than those at Silumiut. Rare specific examples of pH levels above 7.0 (alkaline) were observed for soil in direct contact with limestone, an erratic in this part of the Arctic, that was sometimes used in a grave. Such usage was rare and does not appear to have affected overall skeletal preservation. The bones themselves produced pH readings in the 6.8 to 6.9 range.

The acidic environment of the grave floors was created primarily by the rock forming the grave structure, particularly the floor, with other contributors being decomposition of human organic material, material blown or washed into graves, and plants growing on grave floors. The effect of the acidity is seen most dramatically where rock was in direct contact with bone, as in the case of a mandible (Figure 3) found on the bedrock floor of a grave. Bone at the contact zone had simply disintegrated, giving the appearance of having dissolved. Pales et al. (1952) observed holes in Greenlandic Eskimo crania caused by this phenomenon and

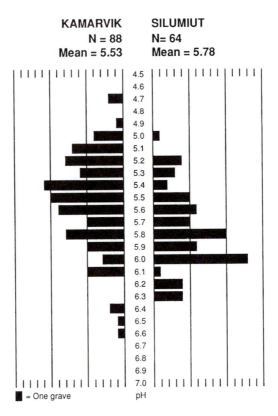

**Figure 2**   Acidity (pH) of soil on grave floors at Kamarvik and Silumiut.

**Figure 3**   Mandible showing destruction caused by contact with acid-producing bedrock grave floor.

cautioned against an interpretation of intentional trephination. Where rocks fell from the roof and rested on bones, the acid from the rock caused local destruction that could be confused with pathological lesions, such as those produced by carcinoma.

The acidic environment and dampness of the graves, occasionally in combination with pressure exerted by rocks that had fallen from the grave roof or walls, sometimes produced bone warpage having the superficial appearance of rickets, with long, thin bones being especially vulnerable. In one case a severely bowed fibula was exposed as a "pseudopathology" by its tibial mate, the latter being completely straight. In another case, a juvenile right tibia in contact with rock is bowed and considerably eroded, while the left tibia, lacking this contact, is straight and much better preserved (Figure 4).

**Figure 4**   Right tibia in contact with rock is bowed and considerably eroded, while the left tibia, lacking this contact, is straight and better preserved.

**Figure 5**   Right tibia with fractured midshaft; fibula intact.

Bones with unhealed fractures are rare, and those that do occur appear more likely due to falling rocks than perimortem trauma. A good example is a right tibia with a badly smashed midshaft, while the matching, much more delicate fibula is unaffected (Figure 5). The damage to the tibia obviously occurred well after death, after it and the fibula had become separated from each other in the grave.

Animal destruction of bone can be seen on many of the skeletons, particularly where the grave had been badly disturbed. The pattern of this destruction closely resembles that observed by Milner and Smith (1989) on bones having little overlying soft tissue and a thin cortex. The pattern of destruction on long bones is relatively uniform, usually beginning near the end where the cortex is thin. Common areas of bone destruction are the anterior surface of the proximal tibia, as observed by Haynes (1980) and Milner and Smith (1989), and the greater trochanter of the femur, as noted by Haynes (1980). The damage frequently had the effect of undermining the articular surface, often with little if any involvement of the articular surface itself (Figure 6A). Tooth marks are often evident, either as puncture marks through thin cortex roughly parallel grooving into the surface of the cancellous bone after removal of the cortex (Figure 6B), or as puncture marks through thin cortex into the underlying cancellous bone (Figure 6C) (see Milner and Smith 1989). Some of the puncture marks compare well in size with fox canines, while others appear too large for this animal and were more likely produced by wolves or dogs. Several bones found on the surface and not associated with specific graves, particularly femora, show more extensive gnawing, with the ends missing and only the shafts, with their thicker cortices, remaining. In some cases irregular shallow grooving of the cortical surface can be seen (see Haynes 1980). The margin of damage is irregular, similar to the situation noted by Haglund et al. (1988) and attributed to carnivore activity. These Eskimo bones had probably been chewed for a lengthy period by dogs or wolves, and specimens showing such extensive carnivore destruction were seldom encountered in graves.

A small amount of rodent activity, characterized by parallel grooving of the margin of damage (Haglund et al. 1988), was also noted. The chief culprits here were probably ground squirrels. One grave at Silumiut eluded discovery for 2 years because it was enveloped by the loose soil of a ground squirrel nest, and it was only through the squirrel's attempts to remove

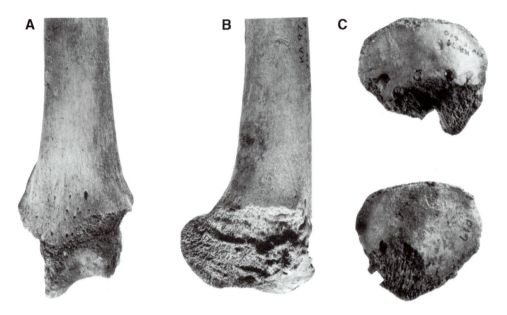

**Figure 6** Small carnivore activity: (A) destruction of femoral epicondyles and condyles. (B) femur with tooth grooving on epicondyle. (C) patellae showing destruction and tooth impressions.

bones from its lair that the burial was finally discovered. Some small bones, particularly those of the hands and feet, may have been removed from graves by lemmings, ground squirrels, or other rodents, and hidden away from the graves (Merbs 1962).

## Preservation by Bone and Age at Death

Skeletons from the two sites provided an opportunity to test some popular ideas about bone preservation and recovery, particularly whether certain parts of the skeleton are more likely to be recovered than others, and whether age at death can be a factor in bone recovery. Age at death was estimated using standard anthropological criteria, with individuals categorized as infant (0 to 3 years), child (3 to 12 years), adolescent (12 to 18 years), and adult (18+ years). The adult category was further subdivided into young (18 to 30 years), middle (30 to 45 years), and old (45+ years), along with a group of adults which could not reliably be placed in these subgroups. Sex in adults was determined according to standard anthropological criteria, but it did not turn out to be a significant determinant in skeletal preservation and is therefore not dealt with specifically in this report.

Skeletal inventory forms filled in by the author when the material was brought from the field were utilized to establish bone inventory scores. The forms provide information on the presence or absence of specific bones, with even a recognizable fragment considered as present. Qualitative information on preservation by skeletal region, and sometimes by specific bone, is also included. Scores were obtained for each individual using both the inventory data and the qualitative observations, with the results being quite similar. Inventory data were chosen for analysis in this study, however, because they deal with finer categories, were more complete, and were more objective than the estimated preservation scores.

Inventory data were divided into 14 categories with scores as follows: (1) cranial vault = 6 (frontal, 2 parietals, 2 temporals, occipital); (2) face = 6 (2 zygomatics, 2 maxillae, sphenoid, mandible); (3) scapula = 2; (4) clavicle = 2; (5) humerus = 2; (6) radius/ulna = 4 (2 radii, 2 ulnae); (7) carpals/metacarpals = 26 (16 carpals, 10 metacarpals); (8) sternum = 2 (manubrium, gladiolus); (9) vertebrae = 24 (7 cervical, 12 thoracic, 5 lumbar); (10) sacrum = 5; (11) pelvis = 2; (12) femur = 2; (13) tibia/fibula = 4 (2 tibiae, 2 fibulae); and (14) tarsals/metatarsals = 24 (14 tarsals, 10 metatarsals). Although the appropriateness of some of these categories is obvious, others are arbitrary and reflect little more than the preference of the author. The presence of ribs, phalanges, patellae, and other small bones was noted on the forms, but not included in the study. Scoring is based on presence or absence of a particular bone (or at least the ability to recognize it), with no attempt to estimate the proportion of bone still intact or the quality of preservation. Category scores range from 1.00 (all bones present) to .00 (no bones present), with incomplete inventories, such as 17 of 24 possible vertebrae, receiving intermediate scores (.71). Using these scores, it was possible to obtain mean scores for bone categories and for age groups. Because the two sites produced somewhat different scores, preservation at Silumiut being better on the whole than that at Kamarvik, the results are presented separately.

Very poor preservation of infant skeletons is seen in low inventory scores (Figure 7A). However, this group is underrepresented in general, either because the bodies had not been placed in tombs, or because the bones have since totally disintegrated. A number of small features that might have originally served as infant graves were found empty. However, even if all of these features did once contain skeletons, the number of infants would still appear to be too low, suggesting that simple exposure of infant bodies, leaving no trace today, had also been practiced. Cranial and leg bones are best represented among the infants that were recovered.

Skeletal recovery for the children is much higher, with scapulae, arm bones, and pelvises well represented (Figure 7B). The scores for adolescents are nearly twice those of the children, with reasonable numbers of clavicles and vertebrae now showing up in the inventories, but few hand and foot bones and sterna (Figure 7C). Although somewhat higher overall, particularly for arm bones, adult scores (Figure 7D) present an inventory pattern similar to that of adolescents. It is among the adults that the two sites show the greatest difference, with better representation at Silumiut than Kamarvik in nearly all bone groups and overall.

Bone representation closely follows age at death (Figure 8), with adults producing the highest scores (mean of 14 categories in Figure 7D), followed in order by adolescents (from Figure 7C), children (from Figure 7B), and infants (from Figure 7A).

Dividing the adult skeletons by age group, young adults show the best representation, followed in order by middle and old adults (Figure 8). However, the differences among the adult groups are small and the picture is obscured, especially at Kamarvik, by poorly preserved adult skeletons that could not reliably be assigned to age subgroups.

The range of individual scores varies little at the low end, with every age group having at least one individual with a score below .1, and often as low as .02 or .01, but it varies dramatically at the high end, with maximum scores of .24 for infants, .54 for children, .84 for adolescents, and .95 for adults.

## Grave Disturbance

At the time of excavation the graves showed various degrees of disturbance, with four categories established in the field: undisturbed (grave completely intact), slightly disturbed (some roof stones out of place), moderately disturbed (some roof stones removed), and heavily disturbed (most or all roof stones removed). Most roof stones removed prior to excavation ended up next to a grave, rather than in it, suggesting that much of the heavy disturbance was done to remove wooden roof supports, or simply to look into a grave, and did not result from natural collapse. To test the possible effect of grave disturbance on skeletal preservation, it was necessary to minimize the effect of age at death by limiting this part of the study to adults.

Grave disturbance does appear to have had an effect on skeletal preservation at both sites (Figure 9). Kamarvik shows a steady decline in inventory scores with greater disturbance, while at Silumiut the decline was abrupt and occurred between slightly disturbed and moderately disturbed graves.

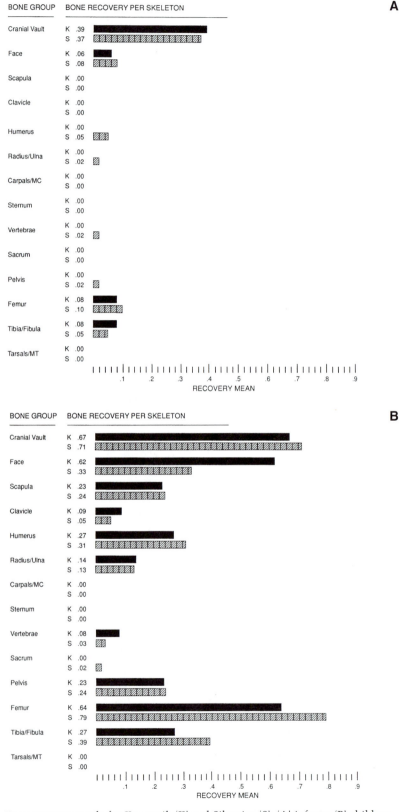

**Figure 7**   Bone recovery totals for Kamarvik (K) and Silumiut (S): (A) infants; (B) children.

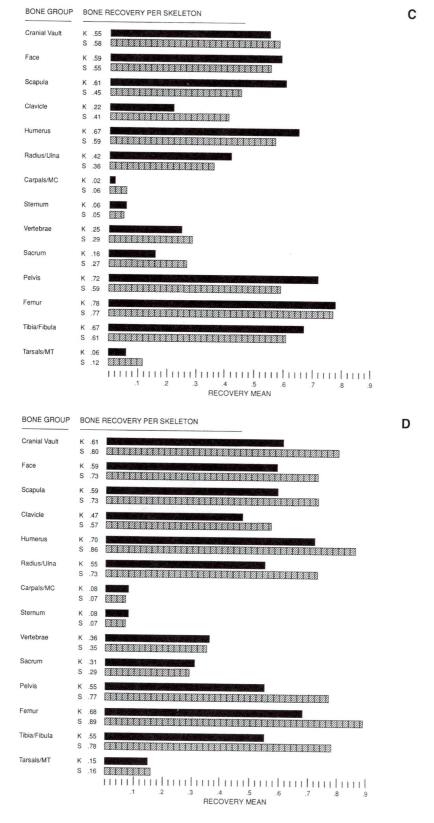

**Figure 7 (continued)** Bone recovery totals for Karmarvik (K) and Silumiut (S): (C) adolescents; (D) adults.

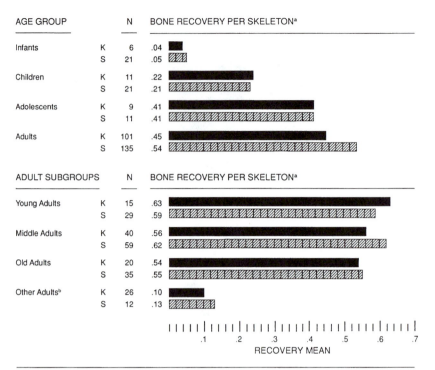

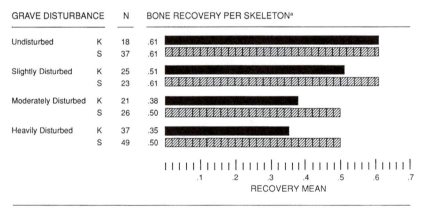

ᵃ mean of recovery in 14 bone groups

ᵇ adults that could not reliably be placed in any of the other three adult subgroups

**Figure 8**    Bone recovery totals for Kamarvik (K) and Silumiut (S) by age group.

ᵃ mean of recovery in 14 bone groups

**Figure 9**    Bone recovery totals for Kamarvik (K) and Silumiut (S) adults relative to grave disturbance.

## Grave Floor Composition and Acidity

Although the most common surface upon which the body was placed and the grave built was bare bedrock, other kinds of surfaces were noted. To test the possible effect of grave floor composition, graves were divided into two categories based on field notations: bedrock vs. other materials (nonbedrock). Analyzed separately were six graves built partly on bedrock and partly on some other surface. Again, to standardize this analysis only graves with adult skeletons were used.

**Table 1   Bone Recovery Totals for Kamarvik and Silumiut Adults Relative to Grave Floor Composition and Soil Acidity**

| Floor | Bone Recovery[a] | | Soil pH | |
|---|---|---|---|---|
| | N | Mean | N | Mean |
| **Kamarvik** | | | | |
| Bedrock | 50 | .32 | 29 | 5.4 |
| Part bedrock | 6 | .48 | 6 | 5.3 |
| Nonbedrock | 45 | .58 | 38 | 5.7 |
|   Rocks | 14 | .57 | 12 | 5.6 |
|   Pebbles | 5 | .48 | 4 | 5.6 |
|   Gravel | 7 | .59 | 7 | 5.6 |
|   Sand | 1 | .88 | 1 | 6.0 |
|   Clay | 1 | .37 | 1 | 6.1 |
|   Combination | 17 | .60 | 13 | 5.9 |
| **Silumiut** | | | | |
| Bedrock | 59 | .49 | 27 | 5.7 |
| Nonbedrock | 71 | .59 | 19 | 5.9 |
|   Rocks | 12 | .55 | 1 | 5.8 |
|   Pebbles | 17 | .59 | 4 | 5.8 |
|   Gravel | 16 | .62 | 8 | 6.0 |
|   Sand | 2 | .34 | — | — |
|   Combination | 24 | .61 | 6 | 5.8 |

[a]   Mean of recovery in 14 bone groups.

Skeletal inventory scores turned out to be lower for the bedrock graves at both sites, although the difference is much more dramatic at Kamarvik (Table 1). The six graves built partly on bedrock (listed as part bedrock), all at Kamarvik, produced an inventory score intermediate between those of the bedrock and nonbedrock graves, but closer to the latter.

The "soil" that had accumulated on the floors of graves was found to be slightly more acidic for the bedrock graves at both sites (Table 1). However, pH testing could not reliably be done for many of the bedrock graves, particularly those at Kamarvik (20 out of 49), because too little soil had accumulated on the floor. The slightly greater acidity recorded at Kamarvik might be due to a difference in bedrock composition at the two sites, something that was not tested. It must be noted that pH grave testing at Silumiut was done just in 1968, a year during which only graves at the eastern end of the site were being excavated; graves at the western end conceivably could have produced lower pH levels.

An important feature of bedrock floors is that often they did not drain as well as nonbedrock floors. This sometimes made excavation more difficult, particularly early in the summer, and the greater moisture content in these graves for a longer period during the summer may have allowed the acid to remain active longer, thus destroying more bone.

Nonbedrock grave floors were composed of rocks (including cobbles), pebbles, gravel, sand, clay, and a combination of these materials. The single clay floor was similar to bedrock floors in having poor drainage and poor bone preservation, but it recorded a higher pH. The three sand floors produced widely varying preservation results, ranging from .88 from a Kamarvik grave to .04 from a Silumiut grave. At both sites, gravel and combination floors produced slightly higher bone inventory scores than the nonbedrock averages.

## Polar Bear Scavenging and Predation

Three skeletons from Kamarvik show unusual patterns of destruction that suggest possible bear predation or scavenging. Polar bears occur in this region today, and undoubtedly did so

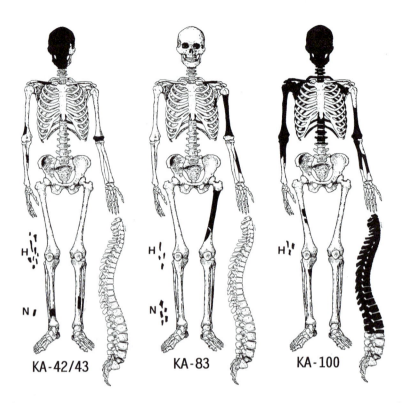

**Figure 10**   Bone parts recovered (darkened areas) from Kamarvik skeletons thought to reflect polar bear activity. H = human fragments; N = nonhuman fragments.

when the Thule people were living there. Merbs (1989) identified the skeleton of a probable polar bear victim from Kulaituijavik (64°34′N, 87°34′W), an early historic Eskimo site located south of Kamarvik.

Skeleton KA-83, an adult and thought to be male, based upon bone robusticity, consists of a clavicle, humerus, radius, rib, femur, and fibula, all from the left side and incomplete, a small fragment of posterior sacral wall, four unidentified fragments, and five nonhuman fragments (Figure 10). All bones show a pattern of sharp breakage with no gnaw marks. In addition, an 8-cm-long fragment has been separated from the distal end of the femoral shaft that was recovered at a point where the shaft consists of dense cortical bone measuring more than 6 mm in thickness. Considerable force was required to break this area of the shaft. All of the animal fragments are less than 6 cm in length, and the only one identified, a section of walrus rib, has sharply broken edges, along with a fracture line that bifurcates as it proceeds from the broken edge into the bone. Considerable force must have been exerted in the breaking of this rib, but no cutting or gnaw marks are present. The kind of damage observed on both the human and animal remains found in this grave are consistent with polar bear activity. However, the grave structure shows severe damage, suggesting that this may be an example of a bear scavenging a grave rather than predation. All of the animal bones plus the human fragments, which were found together on the grave floor, likely passed through the bear and were left behind by the animal in its feces. The situation here appears similar to that noted in a California forensic case involving a bear which is described by Murad and Boddy (1987), where a human finger was found in bear feces.

Skeleton KA-100 (Figure 10), robust, middle aged adult male, presents a very different picture. It lay in a large, well-constructed stone grave showing virtually no disturbance. Most of the upper skeleton was recovered, but missing were the left shoulder, both forearms and hands, and the ventral part of the thorax (sternum and all ventral rib ends). The vertebral column is complete through the third lumbar, with only the upper half of this vertebra present. Below the level of L5, the skeleton is represented only by several small fragments, two identified as femur, and one each as tibia and metatarsal. The picture presented is not one of persistent gnawing, but rather of parts of the body having been ripped away. It appears as though the victim's upper body, including the head, but missing the parts noted, was recovered and given a proper burial, along with fragments from the lower skeleton that were probably recovered from the bear's feces. This looks more like a case of bear predation than scavenging.

The skeleton from KA-42, another adult, consists only of fragments ranging from 3 cm to 8 cm in length, with scapula, clavicle, humerus, radius, and tibia, all from the right side, being recognizable (Figure 10). One of the fragments is clearly not human, and probably from a bird. Despite its meager contents, this grave showed no evidence of disturbance when first observed. The picture is consistent with these bone fragments having passed through the bear, collected in feces, and given proper burial in a full-size, well-constructed stone tomb. Nearby was another grave, KA-43, which seems to continue the story of KA-42. The KA-43 tomb (moderately disturbed) contained the skeleton of a middle-aged adult male with a high bone inventory score of .80. Along with this skeleton was a second skull, as well as three fragments representing left humerus (distal end), tibial shaft, and fibular shaft. The left side of the skull, which appears to be from an old adult female, is missing, including the lateral margin of the orbit, zygomatic arch, mastoid region, a portion of the tympanic plate and petrous portion of the temporal, and the ascending ramus and adjacent portion of the mandibular body. The bones are well-preserved and the edges are sharp, giving the appearance of having been broken with great force rather than gnawed or eroded away. The three postcranial fragments are very similar to those found in KA-42, and they too probably passed through the bear before being recovered for burial. The section of fibular shaft also shows the radiating fracture lines seen in the KA-83 walrus rib. It seems likely that the KA-42 and KA-43 fragments, along with the damaged skull in KA-43, represent the same individual, an elderly female who was killed and eaten by a bear. The fragments in KA-42 were probably found first and given a proper burial, while the skull and additional fragments were found later and were simply added to a later burial as it was taking place, or inserted into an existing grave.

## Conclusions

Preservation of ancient human skeletons at the Canadian Arctic sites of Kamarvik and Silumiut was determined by a number of factors, including the yearly freeze–thaw cycle, the general acidity of the environment, exposure to sunlight and drying, weight of rocks resting directly on bones, growth of lichens and other vegetation into bones, and mammal gnawing. Based upon inventory scores, age at death was an important factor in determining skeletal preservation, with adults showing the best preservation and infants the poorest. Young and middle adults show better preservation than old adults. Grave disturbance also played a general role in skeletal preservation, as adult skeletons from more heavily disturbed graves show poorer preservation than those from slightly disturbed or undisturbed graves. The composition of the grave floor was also a factor in determining bone preservation, with adult skeletons from graves with bedrock floors showing poorer preservation than those from nonbedrock floors composed of loose material such as pebbles, gravel, or sand. It was probably the poor drainage and wet environment created by the bedrock that was largely responsible for the poorer preservation in these graves, but bedrock floors also registered slightly lower pH readings than nonbedrock floors. Although the acid environment of graves certainly contributed to bone destruction generally, and sometimes in a very dramatic way, no significant correlation was found between skeletal inventory scores and specific pH readings.

Of particular interest are three graves showing unusual patterns of bone destruction. In one case a burial appears to have been scavenged by a polar bear, with fragments of animal bones left behind in the grave, probably in bear feces. In two other cases, the pattern is more that of predation, with the skeletons showing evidence of major trauma. In both cases the size and distribution of some of the human bone fragments suggest that they had passed through the bear and had been collected as feces by the Eskimos for burial.

# References

Haglund, W.D., D.T. Reay, and D.R. Swindler
    1988   Tooth Mark Artifacts and Survival of Bones in Animal Scavenged Human Skeletons. *Journal of Forensic Sciences* 33:985–997.

Haynes, G.
    1980   Evidence of Carnivore Gnawing on Pleistocene and Recent Mammalian Bones. *Paleobiology* 6:341–351.

McCartney, A.P.
    1977   *Thule Eskimo Prehistory along Northwest Hudson Bay.* Mercury Series, Archaeological Survey of Canada Paper No. 70. National Museum of Man, Ottawa.

Merbs, C.F.
    1962   A Case of Osteological Thievery. *Arctic Circular* 14:73–74.
    1971   Sir Thomas Rowe's Welcome. *The Beaver,* Outfit 301:16–24.
    1976   An Archaeological Study of the Eskimo Thule Culture in the Northwest Hudson Bay Area. *National Geographic Society Research Reports* 1968 Projects:247–254.
    1989   Trauma. In *Reconstruction of Life From the Skeleton,* edited by M.Y. İşcan and K.A.R. Kennedy, pp. 161–189. Alan R. Liss, New York.

Miller, C. (editor)
    1894   *The Voyages of Captain Luke Foxe of Hull, and Captain Thomas James of Bristol, in Search of a Northwest Passage in 1631–1632.* Hakluyt Society, Vol. 2. London.

Milner, G.R., and V.G. Smith
    1989   Carnivore Alteration of Human Bone from a Late Prehistoric Site in Illinois. *American Journal of Physical Anthropology* 79:43–49.

Murad, T.A., and M.A. Boddy
    1987   A Case with Bear Facts. *Journal of Forensic Sciences* 32:1819–1826.

Pales, L., E. Falck, and J. Lutrot
    1952   Les Perforations Posthumes Naturelles des Cranes Eskimo du Groenland. *Bulletins et Memoires de la Societe d'Anthropologie de Paris* 3(10):229–237.

Stuiver, M., and H.S. Suess
    1966   On the Relationship between Radiocarbon Dates and True Sample Ages. *Radiocarbon* 8:534–540.

# Human Variables in the Postmortem Alteration of Human Bone: Examples from U.S. War Casualties

# 17

THOMAS D. HOLLAND
BRUCE E. ANDERSON
ROBERT W. MANN

## Introduction

Taphonomy, in a traditional sense, has been the study of the transition of remains between death and fossilization, and thus has been the concern of archaeologists and paleontologists, but until relatively recently the study of taphonomic processes has not been routinely applied to human remains in contemporary forensic situations, such as homicides and aircraft crashes. Familiarity with the variables that contribute to the postmortem alteration of human remains allows researchers and investigators to more accurately interpret postmortem events and circumstances involving these remains.

The United States Army has had a long relationship with the anthropological community. The army first established Central Identification Laboratories (CILs) during World War II and continued the practice after the wars in Korea and Vietnam. Forensic and physical anthropologists associated with these efforts form an impressive list: Kerley, McKern, Snow, Stewart, Trotter, and others. In fact, few skeletal biologists or forensic anthropologists working in the United States today have not employed techniques first developed and pioneered for use on American war dead (e.g., McKern and Stewart 1957; Trotter 1970; and Trotter and Gleser 1952, 1958).

In its most recent incarnation, the U.S. Army Central Identification Laboratory, Hawaii (CILHI) serves as the executive agent for the United States government for the recovery and identification of U.S. personnel killed or listed as missing in action from past military conflicts. The number of missing or unaccounted for individuals includes over 2,000 individuals from the Vietnam war; 8,000 from Korea; 80,000 from various World War II theaters; as well as losses from a variety of Cold War incidents. While the mission is worldwide, the focus, certainly over the last several years, has been Indochina.

Because the goal of CILHI is the recovery and identification of human remains, it is no wonder that its scientists strive to better understand the taphonomic processes that alter the condition of the remains and impact on both their recovery and identification.

One aspect of taphonomy frequently dealt with at CILHI is postmortem alteration, willful or accidental, of human remains. It is important to know when, how and, possibly, by whom, human remains have been altered before reaching the laboratory. For instance, it may be vitally important to know whether bones unilaterally received (e.g., turned in by local villagers to Vietnamese officials who then turn them over to U.S. authorities) were burned as a result of slash-and-burn agriculture or from an aircraft crash. Knowing the circumstances of the alteration can provide evidence to support or refute witness information. If, for example,

0-8493-9434-1/97/$0.00+$.50
© 1997 by CRC Press, Inc.

information supplied by the local villager who initially handed in the remains is contradictory to the information contained in U.S. records for the incident, the scientists and field investigators must try to reconcile the differences. Contradictory evidence (including witness information) weakens a case because it imposes an element of doubt. If a villager turns in human skeletal remains that exhibit neither perimortem fracturing nor thermal alteration, yet states that he recovered the remains from the smoldering wreckage of a high-performance jet aircraft, one is justified in questioning the villager's credibility. In this case, the remains constitute the best evidence, and the witness testimony is severely undermined.

How important is witness testimony? In Vietnam era cases, the accounts of local villagers often are absolutely vital to the ultimate identification of an unaccounted for U.S. serviceman. If the Vietnam War was figuratively fought on the television sets of American homes, it quite literally was fought in the backyards of Vietnamese homes. The 1000 mph crash of a 26-ton F-105 Thunderchief in your manioc patch quite likely is one of the singular events in your life, and one that is difficult to ignore or forget. So are any human remains and mechanical wreckage that result. Often the sites visited by CILHI are in some of the most materially poor regions of the world, and at these locales there are few aircraft crash sites (these being the focus of the majority of CILHI's recoveries) that have gone untouched. Thus, unlike modern aircraft crash investigators, CILHI does not have the luxury of arriving on the scene while the patterns of wreckage and physical evidence are still fresh. Ours is an archaeological endeavor. By the time a CILHI Recovery Team is on site, 20, 30, even 50 years (in the case of WW II losses) after the incident, the trail may be unbelievably cold. Wreckage is gone, save for tiny bits of often unidentifiable melted metal and plastic; remains are scattered and deteriorated; the jungle has even reclaimed the pattern of scars left by impacting metal and flaming jet fuel. Very often it is the testimony of witnesses to the event that provides a crucial link on which the ultimate chain of identification is built. It is thus vital to be able to accurately evaluate the eyewitness accounts of not only the incident but of the subsequent events, processes, and conditions.

By understanding the taphonomic variables, CILHI scientists are better prepared to answer questions such as:

1. Why, in many cases, does an archaeological excavation team recover so few bones and teeth?
2. Where are the rest of the bones and teeth?
3. Why do excavation teams typically recover more remains of individuals who died as ground losses (e.g., infantryman shot) and were buried, than individuals involved in aircraft crashes?
4. Can a body ever be totally and completely consumed/destroyed by an explosion or fire?
5. What factors have resulted in the decay and, ultimately, destruction of human bones and teeth?
6. Which of the variables causes the most destruction of bones and teeth? Using examples, this paper will address some of the difficulties and questions arising through field and laboratory activities conducted by CILHI.

## Human Taphonomic Factors

Human remains suffer the same fate as anything else organic; the same taphonomic variables work their transformation on the remains of a U.S. serviceman lost in a war as they would on the remains of a musk deer or a water buffalo. Acidic jungle soils, monsoon rains, an undocumented variety of insect and bacteria, and year-round heat and high humidity without the benefit of a killing frost wreak their predictable havoc on the dead. And while the jungles of the Pacific rim are certainly some of the most inhospitable environments in the world for both the living and the dead, the remains of American war dead are exposed to an even greater range of disruptive forces, simply by virtue of their being American. This is particularly apparent with remains that have been unilaterally repatriated to the United States, that is, remains are turned over to U.S. officials rather than recovered at the incident location by a CILHI Recovery Team.

## Artifacts of Curation

We know that the skeletal remains of U.S. servicemen have been curated by foreign governments. For example, though this fact was for a long time adamantly denied by the Vietnamese government (this, understandably was and continues to be, a particularly sensitive political issue), details supplied by a Vietnamese "mortician" purportedly involved in the official "warehousing" of U.S. remains by his government, in fact illustrate how easily existing Vietnamese cultural practices were adapted to a political end. In Vietnam, especially in the northern provinces, bodies are placed in primary burials for a set period of time, generally around 36 months. At the end of this period, the (now skeletalized) remains are disinterred, cleaned, and reinterred at a different location in a small ceramic coffin approximately the size of a small footlocker. This custom seemingly was well preadapted to the need to dispose of deceased American servicemen, especially aircrews lost over the northern provinces of Vietnam. Having learned from their earlier experience during the French Indochina war that westerners will go to great lengths to get the remains of their dead back (the Vietnamese government in fact repatriated the skeletal remains of French soldiers in return for some economic considerations), the North Vietnamese Army established specific protocols for the retrieval and storage of remains of U.S. servicemen. These protocols built on the existing burial practices of the north and called for the initial interment of remains near the location of loss, disinterment of the bones some time after, cleaning and disinfecting the bones at a location in the north, and finally the placement of the bones in a small box. Instead of reburying this box as local custom prescribed, however, the remains were stored in a warehouse environment pending their return, for whatever leverage, to the United States.

In addition, these stored remains underwent periodic conservation. The "mortician" reported that an important part of his job included removing the bones from their boxes on a regular basis and drying them on a grate over a charcoal fire. This measure was taken to check mold growth on the bones (an important consideration given the high humidity of the region). After drying, the bones were then treated with an insect repellent solution of water and oil of citronella, and then were reboxed (without much apparent appreciation of the fact that reboxing bones damp with water and citronella may be the root of the mold problem).

Obviously, the more items are moved, the more deleterious are the things that can happen to them (perhaps not surprisingly our success at extracting and sequencing DNA from these warehoused remains has been mixed). The routine removal of skeletal remains from their box to a drying grate and back to their box creates the potential for commingling. This procedure introduces a novel form of bias into the taphonomic process in that it allows for the commingling of individuals who at one time may have been separated in both time and space (by distances of several hundred miles). Thus the detection of evidence of possible curation becomes essential in evaluating the circumstantial evidence surrounding a case.

## Vivianite Coloring

Over the years some remains recovered from Southeast Asia and brought to the CILHI for identification have been found to have what appears to be paint or some other surface application on many of the bones and some teeth. The substance typically appears in small clusters or patches, can easily be scraped off, and varies from gray to aqua to bright blue in coloration. Some members of the CILHI scientific staff initially interpreted the deposits as paint that had been applied to the outer surfaces of the remains, thus raising the question of why would anyone paint bones and teeth? Was it meant to somehow preserve the remains, was it done for some religious purpose, or was it an inventory means?

In 1992 the Vietnamese government unilaterally repatriated three sets of remains to the United States. The remains purportedly represented part of an American aircrew lost over North Vietnam in the early years of the war. Several of the skeletal elements were covered with large patches of this thick, bright-blue substance that resembled paint. Around most of the patches, the cortical surface of the bone seemingly had been abraded, in what some observers believed might have been an attempt to remove by sanding the suspicious substance. A sample scraping of the blue pigment-like substance from three of the bones was received and the sample sent to the Conservation Analytical Laboratory, Smithsonian Institution for compositional analysis. The analysis established that the bluish substance was not paint, but actually iron phosphate hydrate, a naturally occurring mineral known as vivianite that forms on some surfaces in contact with soils after a period of about 15 to 20 years (C. Timosa, personal communication).

This analysis thus established two significant facts: first, the bones and teeth were not painted (though they may still have been warehoused) and second, bones with vivianite have been in contact with soil for at least 15 to 20 years. Far from being the "smoking gun" that proved Vietnamese culpability on the warehousing issue, the vivianite deposits actually suggested that the remains were in contact with the ground for a rather lengthy period of time.

The presence of deposits of this type obviously allows the CILHI scientists to ascertain a minimal interrment interval. The laboratory can now provide a scientific explanation for the substance that in the past has been used to support the belief of purposeful alteration and "warehousing" of human remains by the Vietnamese. (Of additional note, vivianite, in a variety of hues, has now been detected on remains from Cambodia, Laos, Papua New Guinea, and the Philippines.)

## Bone Trading

As strange as any postmortem modification inflicted on bone by nature may be, nothing compares with that wrought by living humans. As the archaeological record will attest, the acquisition and alteration of human remains by other humans probably is as old as death itself. In modern-day Southeast Asia a veritable cottage industry exists for the sale and barter of U.S. remains, indeed, any skeletal element even suspected of being that of U.S. personnel; the result is that few Vietnam War era aircraft crash sites have gone undisturbed, regardless of how remote they may be.

During a Joint Field Activity (a U.S./Socialist Republic of Vietnam joint excavation in 1994) in Vietnam, one of the CILHI physical anthropologists was sent to Saigon to examine remains in the possession of a Vietnamese farmer who reportedly found them on his property. The remains were laid out and examined to determine whether they might be American. Racial affiliation can best be determined by a visual examination of the facial bones and teeth: Mongoloids generally have broad, flat faces, small nasal bones and shovel-shaped incisors; the shoveling refers to the raised lingual, i.e., tongue side, edges of the incisors. The teeth of indigenous Southeast Asian mongoloids also frequently have dark lingual staining (due to frequent tea drinking and their diet), and moderate to severe calculus and occlusal (i.e., biting surfaces) wear, widely believed to be a result of an abrasive diet. So, the combination of facial and dental features typically proves to be the most reliable indicator of race.

When this set of skeletal remains was examined, it was found that two nearly complete skeletons, including the small bones of the hands and feet, were present. The remains were in a good state of preservation and exhibited rootlet infiltration, some osseous destruction (commonly resulting from acidic soils), and were covered with reddish soil. All of the indicators were consistent with prolonged burial in the ground.

Examination of the cranium and mandible revealed that the remains were those of two young adult mongoloid males. What was unusual, however, was that the upper and lower central incisors were missing from both individuals. The bags containing the remains were examined, and ten loose teeth were found. This absence was brought to the attention of the attending Vietnamese officials who then stated that the farmer was actually a known bone dealer who tried to monetarily benefit by turning in remains believed to be those of missing American service members. Although he had frequently turned in human remains, he had yet to be reimbursed for his efforts because the policy of the United States and Vietnam is that remains will not be bought.

Using an interpreter, the anthropologist posed a series of questions to the "farmer" to ascertain what had happened to the missing teeth. The farmer first said that the teeth must have fallen out when the remains were gathered (exhumed) from the grave. Further questioning, however, revealed that the remains were taken from the ground and immediately placed in the bags — the bags were placed near the head, and the skulls and mandibles were placed in them — therefore it was unlikely that the teeth had simply fallen out and been lost.

What taphonomic process had been at work on the central incisors? From questioning, it became apparent that the bone dealer had learned, by watching previous examinations, that the central incisors provided significant racial information to anthropologists, so he simply had removed them. That he selectively removed the incisors is supported by the fact that ten single-rooted teeth (eight lateral incisors and two canines), also easily "lost," were nevertheless present in the bags. By removing the central incisors the trader hoped to pass the remains off as American.

The Vietnamese officials were subsequently notified that the remains represented two indigenous mongoloid males, and the dealer subsequently was arrested by Vietnamese police accompanying the U.S. investigation team. (It should be noted that the Vietnamese government appears to be cooperating fully with U.S. efforts, and the alteration of American remains described here seems to originate with private individuals.)

Perhaps an even better example of the extent to which the cash-for-bones mentality may go involves several sets of remains obtained by CILHI in 1990. The bones purportedly were those of U.S. servicemen lost during the Vietnam War. The remains supposedly were smuggled out of Vietnam by refugees who were, at that time, residing in a refugee camp in Malaysia. Of particular interest were four femurs (two right and two left), each measuring somewhere in the vicinity of 45+ cm (the distal ends were damaged or missing so no accurate measurement could be obtained). Certainly 45 cm is not the proportions of a giant by any means — the femurs of Trotter and Gleser's sample of white males in the military averaged 46.9 cm — but it is not exclusive of American servicemen by any means, and by contrast it is somewhat longer than the average Vietnamese, Laotian, or Cambodian femur commonly encountered at CILHI. Closer examination, however (and it did not require too close an examination), revealed that the femurs had in fact been altered. In fact, eight femoral shafts had been cut transversely — four approximately two-thirds down the shaft and four approximately three-fourths down the shaft — and then reconstructed into four "longer" femurs. The new femurs were held together by the insertion of a metal re-bar into the medullary cavity, and a mortar "disk" measuring about 1 cm in thickness was used to secure the metal rod and to "caulk" the joint. The femurs were then covered with a reddish clay slip to camouflage the joint. The result was four longer femurs that apparently were more "Western" in appearance (Figure 1A, B). Further analysis suggested that all of these remains were Southeast Asian Mongoloid in origin.

Certainly, altering the length of femurs represents one of the more ambitious attempts to modify human remains, but it by no means is an isolated phenomenon. Other examples of human alteration are common. The use of human remains, especially those purported to be of Americans, in folk medicines is not a rumor. Human bones are bartered and sold in a manner little different from tiger's teeth and monkey skulls. The receipt at CILHI of human remains from Southeast Asian sources that have been cut, sawed, drilled, and snapped occurs

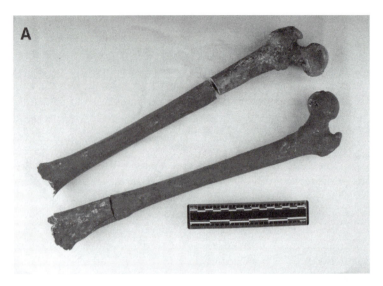

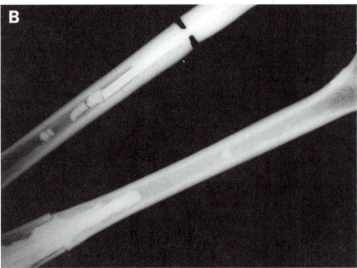

**Figure 1**   (A) Photograph of femurs altered to increase their lengths, thus making them appear more "Western." (B) Radiograph of same femurs. Note metal rod and cement filler.

with staggering frequency, as bone merchants ply their trade on the unwary. For example, a common scenario might be: a bone trader approaches a local peasant known to be somewhat disgruntled and informs him, in a friendly manner, that he has heard that the U.S. government will reward highly for the return of U.S. remains (or, even better, will relocate the peasant in the U.S. if he has some remains). The poor unsuspecting villager laments that, alas, he has no such remains. "You're in luck," the bone merchant informs him, "because I do" (or heard more commonly, "I have a friend who has a cousin who has an in-law who does") and "for only x number of dollars (or Dong, Kip, Riel, etc.) I can be persuaded to part with them" (or "I can convince my friend to convince his cousin..."). After the villager has rounded up every penny his extended family has, the bone merchant will supply a bundle of bones (which our analysis invariably shows to be Southeast Asian mongoloid), or, once again more commonly, will supply a small fragment of bone, perhaps 2 cm in diameter, freshly cut or snapped from his "store." The undiagnostic fragment, along with an occasional paper rubbing of a U.S. dog tag, ultimately finds its way to CILHI. In fact, it is not uncommon for CILHI to receive a

**Figure 2**   Bone fragments purportedly from multiple individuals. Note the uniform size of the fragments. All indicators suggest that these specimens originated from a single skull.

package (via some government or nongovernment agency) with several dog-tag rubbings, each with an associated tooth and bone fragment. Analysis often suggests that the teeth, purported to represent several individuals, originated in one mouth, and the bone fragments, all of uniform size and exhibiting fresh cut marks, originated from a single skull (Figure 2). Like a dope dealer "stepping" on his product, a bone dealer can make a single skull go a long way. Almost always, these types of accessions prove to be indigenous Southeast Asian mongoloids.

Occasionally, the opposite has occurred, and rather than receiving a small bone chip, CILHI has received a relatively intact set of skeletal remains, usually via a unilateral turnover by some Southeast Asian government, that subsequently could be identified through dental and anthropological analyses. Closer examination, however, revealed postmortem damage to minor elements (e.g., ribs, metatarsals) consistent with having been caused by a knife, side-cutters, or saw. (Some cases have even displayed "score-and-snap" breaks of the type so well known to zooarchaeologists.) Thus alerted to the possibility that this set of remains was being parceled out by bone traders, the CILHI staff could search through the laboratory's previous accessions of small, undiagnostic fragments. In several cases, fragments of small, otherwise nondescript, bone that found their way to CILHI by entirely different sources at entirely different times could be matched up to these identified remains (Figure 3).

**Figure 3**   Bone fragments received at CILHI via different sources at different times. The articulating fragments underscore the manner in which bone fragments are bought and sold.

**Figure 4**   Human remains repatriated to the United States as those of a missing U.S. serviceman. Note that the name written on the bones does not correspond to any unaccounted-for American from the Vietnam War.

In addition to cut marks, some of these bone fragments are labeled. If it is remembered that many of these fragments are being bartered or sold on the assumption that the United States will provide monetary rewards or arrange resettlement in the U.S., then it follows that individuals would want to ensure their proprietary interest by attaching their name. Sometimes the bones are labeled with the province where they were obtained, and sometimes they may be labeled with the name of the individual that the bones purportedly represent. CILHI has one case, for example, where a tibia is labeled in bright purple paint with the name "Mossakowski" (Figure 4); other bones in the accession are labeled with either an "A" or a "M" (the Vietnamese government indicated that these remains were those of an American named "Alphonse Mossakowski"). This name association might be a valuable piece of circumstantial evidence were it not for the fact that Mr. Mossakowski is not an unaccounted for U.S. serviceman.

It should be noted, however, that Southeast Asians are not the only ones labeling bones. Though not a routine practice, CILHI scientists sometimes label bones in noncritical areas to facilitate analysis, thus adding to the postmortem alteration process. The North Koreans apparently do likewise. Many of the skeletal remains recently received from the North Korean government that purportedly were dug up in late 1993 bear early 1960s dates neatly pen-and-inked on them. Other skeletal elements exhibit suspicious, recent-looking, abrasion marks over faint ink stains, suggesting that an attempt to remove the dates by sanding was made prior to their repatriation to the United States. Fortunately, thanks to a few less-than-conscientious North Korean workers, we now have a better idea of how long these remains have been out of the ground.

The lucrative bone market of Southeast Asia, superimposed over an agrarian peasant economy, leads to predictable ends. Crash sites of U.S. aircraft have literally been mined for their rich yield of scrap metal, personal effects, and human remains. An example of this was documented by a CILHI search and recovery team excavating a purported grave site in Southeast Asia. A local villager provided the location of a grave that he claimed contained the remains of an American pilot whose airplane crashed in the immediate area. Upon arrival at the site, the search and recovery team noted what appeared to be evidence of the site having been excavated previously. The team anthropologist noted a marked depression with probable shovel marks present in the side wall. Immediately adjacent was a small hummock seemingly formed by backfill. Controlled excavation of both the depression and the hummock yielded human remains and fragments of a flight suit. The remains, subsequently identified as the downed flyer, were very sparse, and it was the team anthropologist's opinion that the grave had in fact been excavated previously, possibly in response to the assumption that the remains

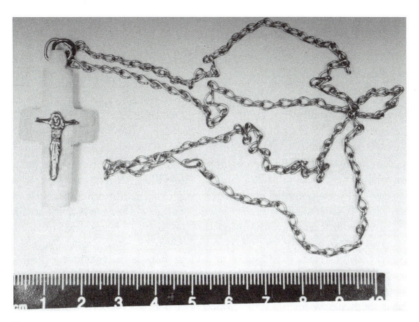

**Figure 5**   Possible human bone fashioned into a religious icon. The small size and polished nature of the bone rendered it unidentifiable.

included a "mouth full of gold fillings." The few bits and fragments of clothing and human remains were all that remained from this earlier, clandestine, exhumation.

When the American bone vein goes dry, the miners turn to indigenous cemeteries in their belief that "bones are bones." Partly in response to this, the U.S. government adopted a policy of not paying for remains in the hope that it will somewhat dampen this market.

Of course Asian peasants are not the only ones to fall victim to the seductive tale of the bone merchant. Recently, a well-meaning American visited Vietnam and was approached by an identification-tag dealer (yet another surprising mercantile niche that is exploited with some frequency). The dealer told the woman that he had information on the whereabouts of U.S. remains. The woman ended up buying some human remains (ultimately determined to be Southeast Asian mongoloid) in addition to 1444 U.S. dog tags in the sincere belief that she was aiding the cause. Unfortunately, not one of the tags represents an American who died or is unaccounted for in Southeast Asia.

And then, of course, there is the 1985 case involving a 2.5-×-4-cm polished-bone cross to which was attached a silver crucified Jesus. The cross, suspended from a long silver chain, was received at CILHI with the name association of an individual whose partial remains were identified through the Da Nang mortuary in 1967. Due to the small size and highly polished nature of the cross, it was impossible to definitively determine whether the bone was human or nonhuman, and subsequently the item was dealt with as a nonassociable portion (Figure 5).

## Incompetence or Intent

Remains unilaterally repatriated to the United States by the Democratic People's Republic of [North] Korea — all remains received from North Korea are unilateral since CILHI Recovery Teams have not had access to that country — show an interesting pattern of postmortem events. A high percentage (over 90 percent of the earlier accessions) of the remains are missing the bones of the face. A cranial vault generally is present, and sometimes the loose and fragmented maxilla and mandible are present as well, though it usually is impossible to demonstrate that these fragments originated from the same individual. Since the face typically is the most racially diagnostic area, attempts to identify these damaged remains are hampered significantly. In addition, identifiable dental fragments often cannot be linked to the remaining skeletal elements because of the high rate of commingling seen among the Korean War remains.

The pattern of postmortem damage was so uniform as to raise questions as to intent. Were the North Koreans intentionally damaging the crania to preclude identifications? It certainly seemed a possibility, though the intent remained elusive.

In late 1993 the North Korean government repatriated over 100 sets of skeletal remains. In contrast to earlier turnovers, the condition of the remains showed some improvement. Though commingling remained a significant problem, fewer of the faces were damaged. The answer became clear a few months later. In early 1994 CILHI representatives met with North Korean officials to discuss potential joint recoveries, and at that time met with a North Korean archaeologist who had been detailed by his government to oversee the North Korean recovery of U.S. remains. The archaeological protocols that the North Korean scientist was employing, while somewhat dated by modern U.S. standards, were having a noticeable effect on the condition of recovered remains. It now became clear that the damaged faces previously seen probably were the result of incompetent recovery techniques. Because the face commonly is the skeletal region closest to the surface of the ground (in supine inhumations), it also is the region first encountered by the blade of a shovel or bulldozer. It is very probable that gangs of poorly motivated, skim-shovelling North Korean soldiers, prior to adequate supervision, had simply sliced the faces off of the skulls before they even realized that they had encountered bone.

The remains returned from North Korea show some other interesting postmortem alterations. A small minority of skeletons exhibit circular holes in certain bones. The holes vary in diameter, from approximately 1 cm to 1 mm. All of the perforations are round, or oval, and are smooth edged. Certainly they give the appearance of probe holes not unlike those resulting from "pot-hunting" activities at archaeological sites in the United States. It is not unreasonable to speculate that the North Koreans used probes to locate buried U.S. remains.

But in at least one case, the pattern of perforations is telling. Upon initial examination the damage appeared to be random "probing" by an instrument slightly smaller in diameter than a clothes hanger. When the skeleton was thoroughly examined, however, the pattern was resolved. Perforations were located, not on surfaces that would ordinarily be exposed to probing, but on articular surfaces. Furthermore, perforations of adjacent elements (e.g., the distal humerus and the proximal ulna) were aligned (Figure 6). Many of the other elements were missing their articular ends. The most parsimonious explanation is that this skeleton had been disinterred for some time and that the bones were wired together, most probably for use as a teaching or display specimen. Analysis of other skeletons repatriated at the same time as this one revealed similarly damaged articular ends. In one case, the distal fibula tip was broken and abraded through a perforation. It is possible that, like the abraded bones discussed above, the articular ends of these long bones were intentionally removed to eliminate evidence of articulation which would of course be a volatile political issue.

## Conclusions

We now have some of the answers to our questions. Why do CILHI recovery teams often recover so few bones of individuals lost in combat? Where are the other remains? Why so few at crash sites as opposed to ground losses?

Time is the enemy of any researcher who deals with biological remains. Taphonomic processes conspire to erase the proof of any organism's existence. Human beings are not immune; in fact, human agents are themselves among the most potent in the taphonomic process. The Vietnam War was waged in one of the most beautiful, and yet most inhospitable, locations in the world. The high year-round temperature, the amazing variety of insect life,

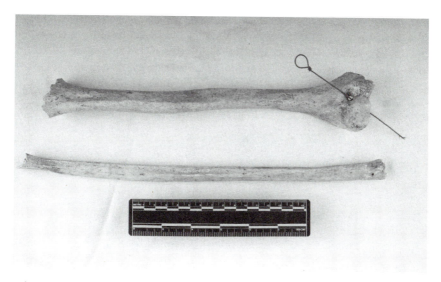

**Figure 6**   Holes drilled near the articular ends of bones. The pattern and placement of the holes suggests that these were used to articulate the remains.

the constant unrelenting high humidity, and the acidic jungle soils and abundant vegetation of Southeast Asia savage organic remains. Factor two to three decades into the equation and it is a wonder that anything identifiable can be recovered. But the bones of American service-men are particularly vulnerable because they are particularly valuable.

The attachment of monetary or other value to human remains is not new, nor is it restricted to the Vietnamese or the North Koreans, as any visit to a major American anthro-pology museum will illustrate. (In fact, CILHI recently took possession of a mongoloid "trophy skull" in the possession of an American Vietnam veteran.) The difference may be that the bones of U.S. servicemen have become, for some countries, a type of political tender or script. They are not war trophies, as such, but are human scrap to be collected, sorted, weighed, bartered, traded, and sold.

## Acknowledgments

This paper would not have been possible without the hard work of past CILHI scientists. Early drafts of this paper were read and commented on by William Grant, Scotty Law, William Mayhew, and Johnie Webb, Jr. The views expressed are those of the authors and should not be construed to represent the U.S. government.

## References

McKern, T.W., and T.D. Stewart
  1957   *Skeletal Age Changes in Young American Males.* Quartermaster Research and Devel-opment Center, U.S. Army, Natick, MA.
Trotter, M.
  1970   Estimation of Stature from Intact Long Limb Bones. In *Personal Identification in Mass Disasters,* edited by T.D. Stewart, pp. 71–83. Smithsonian Institution, Washington, D.C.

Trotter, M., and G.C. Gleser

1952  Estimation of Stature from Long Bones of American Whites and Negroes. *American Journal of Physical Anthropology* 10:463–514.

1958  A Re-evaluation of Estimation of Stature Based on Measurements of Stature Taken during Life and of Long Bones after Death. *American Journal of Physical Anthropology* 16:79–123.

# Fire Modification of Bone: A Review of the Literature

# 18

PAMELA M. MAYNE CORREIA

## Introduction

Fire is arguably one of the most destructive forces in our society from a forensic perspective, but what do we really know about the nature of its effect on bone? When cremated remains (intentionally or accidentally burned human tissues) are located, they may be charred, or they may be partially, incompletely, or completely cremated (see Table 1). Charred remains do not pose as difficult a job for analysis, as serology and visual identification often can be completed. When only portions of the individual's extremities are modified, there are fewer problems in the identification than if the remaining tissue consists of an amorphous mass containing the torso, organs, and bony tissue, a partial cremation. The incomplete cremation presents the greatest taphonomic problem because the bone fragments, discolors, and shrinks and may become unrecognizable, thereby complicating the analysis of the number of individuals represented, age and sex ratios, living stature, race, perimortem condition, nutritional status, and trauma (Krogman 1943a, 1943b; Wells 1960).

Table 1   Terminology for Cremated Remains

| Type of Cremation | Tissue Survival |
|---|---|
| Charred | Internal organs |
| Partial | Soft tissue |
| Incomplete | Bone pieces |
| Complete | Ashes only |

After Eckert et al. 1988.

The search for an understanding of cremated bone has resulted in the application of a wide range of research techniques in various experiments, usually producing incomparable results. Inconsistency in terminology and experimentation with a variety of skeletal materials have also produced disparate conclusions. Demographic methodology developed on noncremated bone is used for the analysis of cremated bone, although there is little information on the reliability of the results.

Descriptions of the characteristics of cremated bone and the methodologies used for its analysis come from a variety of sources, including the anthropological and medicolegal communities. This review is focused on the interpretation of cremated bone and does not include literature from archaeological sites or cremation practices of the distant past. Issues to be addressed include the interpretation of gross and histological characteristics, and the methodological techniques used by the anthropological and medicolegal communities in supporting such interpretations.

The majority of cremated bone research is based in North America and northern and central Europe. The emphasis in the European research is on modern human remains, although some work on nonhuman and archaeological human remains has been done. The

European research concentrates on understanding the effects of heat on the ability to interpret age, sex, stature, and ancestry (cf. Böhmer 1932; Bonucci and Graziani 1975; Classen 1991; Dijkstra 1938; Dokládal 1962, 1969, 1970, 1971; Dufková 1985; Gejvall 1969; Grimm and Theis 1952; Grupe and Herrmann 1983; Herrmann 1970, 1972, 1973, 1976, 1977a, 1977b, 1980; Hummel and Schutkowski 1986a, 1986b; Kühl 1986; Lepkowski and Wachholtz 1903; Malinowski and Porawski 1969; Müller 1964; Piontek 1975; Rösing 1977; Schutkowski and Hummel 1987; Van Vark 1970, 1975; Wahl 1982, 1983; and Wahl and Henke 1980). In contrast, North American work stresses descriptive analysis of bone tissue when exposed to heat, particularly with nonhuman or archaeological bones (cf. Baby 1954; Binford 1963; Buikstra and Swegle 1989; Forbes 1941; Shipman et al. 1984; Spence 1967; Thurman and Willmore 1980; Webb and Snow 1945; and Wells 1960). In recent years, there has been a change in the emphasis of the research (cf. Bradtmiller and Buikstra 1984; Holland 1989, Mayne 1990) to include questions of methodology. The medicolegal community has been able to provide additional insights into the accuracy of current methodology through practical application to modern populations (cf. Bass 1984; Burns 1988; Clark 1986; Dokládal 1969; Dunlop 1978; Eckert et al. 1988; Gebhardt 1923; Heglar 1984; Johanson and Saldeen 1969; Krogman 1943b; Maples 1988; Merkel 1932; Richards 1977; and Wilson and Massey 1987).

Cremation research can be organized into three general categories: analysis of visual characteristics, analysis of histological characteristics, and the demographic analysis of cremated remains including age, sex, stature, and ancestry determination. A fourth source of information is the data that comes from forensic cases reported by the medicolegal community. The following review is organized to consider each of these categories.

# Visual Characteristics

## Color Change

Cremated bone fragments exhibit a variety of colors ranging from brown to gray-blue, black, gray, gray-white, and chalk white (Shipman et al. 1984). Other colors less frequently noted are green, yellow, pink, and red (Dunlop 1978). The concensus is that these colors may be attributed to the temperature attained by the bone and the length of time exposed to heat (Bonucci and Graziani 1975; Heglar 1984; Shipman et al. 1984) and are also a reflection of the organic and inorganic material associated with the body as it responds to these increased temperatures. Brown coloration is associated with hemoglobin and/or soil discoloration (Gejvall 1969; Lisowski 1968), while black results from carbonization of the bone burned in an oxygen-starved state (Herrmann 1970). Gray-blue and gray result as the organic components of bone are pyrolized (Dokládal 1969, 1970; Shipman et al. 1984), while white represents the final stage of calcination where the china-like texture of the bone represents a complete loss of the organic portion and the fusion of bone salts. The latter group of colors (green, yellow, pink, and red) have been attributed to the presence of copper, bronze, or iron in the surrounding environment, zinc in coffin linings, systemic copper, and the madder plant, respectively (Dunlop 1978; Gejvall 1969; Lisowski 1968).

Little has been done with these observations other than to suggest the type of cremation practice which may have been utilized (cf. Gejvall 1969; Lisowski 1968; Schwartz 1993) and the temperatures which may have been achieved (Bonucci and Graziani 1975; Shipman et al. 1984). It should be noted that a variety of colors may be present on a single bone fragment (Mayne 1990), and that the entire range of colors may exist in a single cremation. Any interpretation of fire temperature based on the color of the bone must explain the range of colors usually present in a single cremation. The studies discussed above do not address directly the implications of finding a combination of colors on a single bone fragment. Recently, Schwartz (1993) suggested that the differential coloring resulted from the intentional breaking of bones either by moving bone into the hotter area of the fire or spreading them out to cool; however, this was not tested directly.

## Shrinkage and Deformation

Reduction in bone length and width occur during cremation. Researchers have attempted to quantify the amount of change in spongy and compact bone, since any shrinkage may influence conclusions regarding the age, sex, or stature of an individual. In an early study by Malinowski and Porawski (1969), the measurements of human skulls and long bones taken before cremation were compared with those taken afterwards. The differences were recorded in millimeters. For example, the diameter of the radius decreased 0.7 mm, while the head of the radius decreased 1.2 mm. (1969:396).

Dokládal (1971) cremated one half of each of five cadavers in a gas oven with a temperature range of 600 to 1,000°C. From measurements taken on the preserved unburned half compared to the cremated half of the same individual, he established shrinkage rates of between 5 to 12%. A similar rate of shrinkage, 6 to 13%, was described by Strzalko et al. (1974).

By heating 20-mm × 5-mm femoral sections of compact bone at temperatures ranging from 150 to 1200°C, Herrmann (1976, 1977a, 1977b) recognized three phases of shrinkage. The first, from 150 to 300°C and the second, from 750 to 800°C, resulted in 1 to 2% shrinkage. The third phase occurred between 1000 to 1200°C, and 14 to 18% total shrinkage was observed. He concluded that the shrinkage was dependent upon four criteria: (1) distribution of bone types (compacta, spongiosa, and lamellar), (2) temperature of exposure, (3) mineral content of bone, and (4) aspects of the mineral content of bone tissue. He found a relationship between sex and the amount of shrinkage present: males had a higher percentage of bone mineral and therefore, more shrinkage. The observation that male bones shrink proportionally more suggests that there may be an increased tendency to sex some males incorrectly as females; however, the 1 to 2% shrinkage expected up to 800°C should minimally effect sex determination in lower temperature situations.

In a further study using spongy bone, Grupe and Herrmann (1983) record a 12% reduction in various measurements. In compact bone, Bradtmiller and Buikstra (1984) observed a 5% shrinkage up to 600°C, and Buikstra and Swegle (1989) suggest a correction factor of 0 to 10%. Nelson (1992) found that a 16.7% shrinkage occurred in osteon diameters in femoral midshafts cremated at temperatures of 538 to 816°C. In another study, Hummel and Schutkowski (1986b), using temperatures up to 1000°C, record a 5% shrinkage in the proximo-distal length of compact bone, but a 27% reduction in the cross-sectional diameter. Methods of sex determination based upon robusticity or bone diameter (Garn et al. 1972; Iscan and Miller-Shaivitz 1984) may be adversely affected by this amount of shrinkage. Further work by Holland (1989) claimed that the cranial base is expected to shrink by 1 to 2.25%; but he noted that above 800°C this figure may be an underestimate, as measurements were more difficult to make on the severely calcined bone.

The above studies generally agree that the expected shrinkage in cremated bone up to temperatures of 800°C is not significant in the interpretation of the bone, and that more research is required for cancellous bone or diploë.

Even if shrinkage is of little significance, warpage and deformation will affect the visual appearance. Kühl (1986) has recognized deformation resulting from weight (stress) applied to the bone tissue while it is experiencing plastic deformation. While stress is the force which changes the bone, strain is a description of the change (Rogers 1982). As the stress increases, so does the strain until this strain produces in the bone a point of yielding which ultimately results in failure or fracture of the bone. The fracture is a mechanical failure of the bone tissue, which occurs at the failure point (Johnson 1985). Before the bone reaches the yield point, it may return to its original condition, if the stress is removed; this development is known as elastic deformation. However, once the bone enters the stage of plastic deformation, it can no longer recover; and may fail if stress continues. The deformation described by Kühl does not occur during life and is not pathological, but may appear, for example, in the vertebral arches or in the head of the joints in cremated bone. Identification of plastic deformation in cremated bone is vital to understanding the existence of perimortem trauma (Mayne 1990).

This is not to say that pathology may not be present and identifiable; on the contrary, many have noted the presence of dental pathology, arthritic change, healed fractures, periostitis, and growth lines in cremated bones (Baby 1954; Herrmann 1970; Kühl 1980; Lisowski 1968; Malinowski and Porowski 1969; Merbs 1967; and Rösing 1977). The recognition of pathological features by forensic anthropologists is valuable in establishing the identification for modern cremated remains (Dowling and Beattie 1988; Murray et al. 1991).

## Fragment Survival

In skeletal analyses, it is customary to determine whether the cremated bone is animal or human in origin, and the number of individuals represented; and to provide a description of the surviving fragments. These tasks must be done prior to any analyses of age, sex, stature, and ancestry (Gejvall 1969; Lisowski 1968; Malinowski and Porawski 1969; Stewart 1979; and Wells 1960).

It is noted by Gejvall (1969) that experience in handling cremated bone will lead to the identification of more and more fragments. Spongy bone, while shrinking, will generally retain its shape, whereas compact bone will shatter into small pieces. Unerupted teeth and roots protected by bone tissue survive, while the exposed crowns fall apart. In archaeologically derived urn cremations, Spence (1967) found that vault edges with suture lines always survive, and to a lesser degree (91%) the vault proper. Maxilla and mandibular fragments, petrous portion of the temporal bone, phalanges, and femoral and humeral fragments are present in 50 to 68% of the cremations he recorded. Dokládel (1971) supports these observations and includes the external occipital protuberance, acetabulum, and the pubic symphysis. Gejvall notes "the articular heads of thigh bones and upper arm bones, complete vertebrae, and various bones of the middle hand and middle foot are among the normal finds" (1969:471).

Least likely to survive the extremely high temperatures, according to Spence (1967), are the zygomatics and frontal bone (13.6%); sacral vertebrae, clavicles, and carpals (18.2%). Dokládal (1969), Spence (1967), and Wells (1960) supply extensive lists of skeletal parts which have survived most frequently in archaeological urn burials and in modern crematory studies. From these works it is apparent that the denser bones and those well embedded in muscle tissue are found more frequently.

## Fracture Patterns

Much attention has been given to heat-induced fractures. Controversy surrounds the appearance of heat-induced fractures in bone which is burned fleshed, defleshed (green), or dry (degreased). Early observations by Krogman (1943b:13) describe heat-induced fractures in a case of possible amputation:

> Wherever soft tissue surrounding a bone is scant or thin, the bone shows sharp, clear-cut heat fractures (looking somewhat like the patina of age on an old painting), charring, calcination and splintering; where the bone is deeply embedded in muscle...the action of heat on a bone is to produce a molten condition, characteristic of fusion by heat.

He applied this theory again in 1945 for W.M. Webb and C.E. Snow on archaeological cremated bone from the Adena and Hopewellian cultures. In this case, he was asked to determine if the individuals were burned in the flesh or after skeletonization. "Patina" cracks were used to indicate defleshed bone, whereas the presence of endosteum suggested bone burned with flesh attached. He found it difficult to distinguish bone in these two categories, a problem recognized by other researchers (cf. Binford 1963; Buikstra and Swegle 1989).

Baby (1954) concluded that cremated dry bone does not have any warping, but shows superficial checking, longitudinal fractures, and transverse splintering. Binford (1963) supported Baby's assertions; and he observed the presence of straight transverse cracks in dry bone, vs. curved, transverse cracking in fleshed bone. The latter cracks represented the so-called thumbnail fractures often observed on long bones. In the experiments on human, bovid, and canine bone, Buikstra and Swegle (1989) did not support the previous conclusions, since they found warping in both fleshed and dry bone. "The presence of deep transverse cracks clearly is not sufficient evidence for identifying fleshed cremations" (Buikstra and Swegle 1989:256).

The differentiation of fleshed and defleshed bone has been even more problematic as demonstrated by Thurman and Willmore (1980). In their attempt to distinguish fleshed human humeri from defleshed (green) human humeri, they concluded that fleshed cremations characteristically had serrated, transverse fractures and diagonal cracking and warping, while green bone had serrated fractures at the epiphyses only, parallel-sided fractures in the shaft, and less pronounced warping. The serrated transverse fracture noted by them in fleshed cremations is contradictory to the curved transverse fractures noted by Binford (1963). Obviously, the discrepancies evident in this research warrant more attention, as the determination of the pre-cremation condition of the bone is often of great significance in establishing the events prior to the cremation.

Lisowski (1968) has described fractures observed on cremated bone; but he does not indicate the pre-cremation condition. He noted the cracking of teeth, the splitting of the compact bone along a straight or elliptical trajectory, the twisting or bending of bone, and the separation of the internal and external tables in cranial bone.

White (1992) identifies the problem of distinguishing heated, cooked, and burned bone from weathered bone in an archaeological sample. He emphasizes the lack of standardized methodology for isolating heat-treated bone from bone fractured from weathering.

There is no satisfactory method available, based on visual observation of fractures, to differentiate the condition of bone prior to cremation. The various descriptions presented above are contradictory and lack any clear standardization.

## Histological Characteristics

Forbes' (1941) is the earliest work located which attempts to describe the histological changes found in cremated bone. His study was the result of a medicolegal case in which he was asked to determine whether a sample of burned material was bone. He supplied a description of compact and cancellous tissue exposed to the heat of a bunsen burner. General observations were made on decalcified thin sections under normal light microscopy. For compact bone, he described an initial prominence of the canaliculi which disappeared as the lamellae became coarse and granular. The lacunae were described as changing from flat and distorted to mere hazy outlines. The lamellae gradually disappeared, leaving a uniformly granular matrix with Haversian canals throughout. Haversian systems decreased in size, but the Haversian canals increased in diameter and filled with debris. Cracks, irregular in width, travelled along the periphery of the Haversian system to join with other cracks. Regarding the origin of the cracks, he stated:

> It is difficult to be certain whether these fissures are entirely due to the action of heat (Forbes 1941:59).

The cancellous bone underwent similar changes, with the exception of those noted for the Haversian systems. Lacunae and lamellar structures eventually disappeared, and only a granular matrix remained.

The observations made by Forbes were simplistic, but the basics were described, as studies in the last fifteen years have confirmed his initial insights. Various technical approaches have enhanced Forbes' ideas. For instance, thermogravimetry has provided a description of the process of water and carbonate removal from the tissue, and X-ray diffraction provides data about the conformational changes within the nonorganic crystalline matrix. Microradiography allows us to view the shrinkage of the osteons, and scanning electron microscopy has provided an intense magnification (e.g., ~1,000 to 1,500×) of the bone tissue surfaces.

## Thermogravimetry

Thermogravimetry research provides evidence for the weight changes experienced by bone tissue, as it increases in temperature. Bonucci and Graziani (1975) have identified three phases which relate to the loss of water, pyrolysis of organic components, and the loss of carbonates and crystal fusion (Bonucci and Graziani 1975; Civjan et al. 1971; Holager 1970; Rootare and Craig 1977). The first phase begins at 105°C, and is constant until 300°C. Water removed at this phase is adsorbed or physisorbed water (Rootare and Craig 1977). This is water that is loosely attracted to the crystal surface and is most easily removed. This phase is completed at approximately 500 to 600°C (Civjan et al. 1971).

In the latter part of the first phase, the loss of organic material begins. The organic substances (mucopolysaccharides, amino acids, collagen, etc.) are pyrolized by the time a temperature of 600°C is reached (Bonucci and Graziani 1975; Civjan et al. 1971). This loss introduces the second phase of weight reduction. The removal of collagen can be identified at 500 to 600°C, because at this point the bone tissue becomes isotropic; the collagen loses its birefringence in polarized light (Herrmann 1972). Schultz (1986) argues that birefringence of the bone tissue is still observed at 750 to 800°C.

The remaining components of bone, the carbonates and mineral salts, are important participants in the third phase. During this phase, the carbonates ($CaCO_3$) disappear, and there is some decomposition (release) of magnesium. Civjan et al. (1971) identified this weight loss at 700 to 900°C, but Bonucci and Graziani (1975) place it between 600 to 900°C. It is interesting that Holager (1970) identified a similar weight loss at 700 and 713°C for dentin and enamel, respectively. Hydroxyapatite (HAP) is also affected in the third phase. Bonucci and Graziani (1975) claim that the HAP crystals increase in size, and the ultrastructural change of hydroxyapatite to β tricalcium phosphate produces the weight loss. Civjan et al. (1971) support this suggestion; but, in contrast, Shipman et al. (1984) see no evidence that the crystals undergo a chemical conversion, only an increase in crystal size.

## X-Ray Diffraction

Newesely (1988), through X-ray diffraction, supported the conclusion that the hydroxyapatite (HAP) is altered in structure between 700 to 1,000°C to resemble β tricalcium phosphate. He attributed this alteration to a coalescence of the crystals.

This process of water loss, carbonate loss, and mineral sintering is compared by Shipman et al. (1984) to the changes associated with the production of ceramics. It is worthwhile discussing this idea, which, in this review, will be referred to as the DDIF process, named for the stages in the process of bone cremation, as it provides terminology which fits with this study. The first stage, dehydration, refers to the breaking of the hydroxyl bonds, and the removal of both loosely bound water (physisorbed) and bonded water (chemisorbed) from the apatite mineral. The second stage is decomposition, and correlates to the pyrolysis of organic materials. Inversion, the third stage, is identified by the loss of carbonates and crystal

**Table 2   Stages in the Process of Cremation**

| Stage | Histological Changes | Approximate Temperature Range (°C) |
|---|---|---|
| Dehydration | Water removal (physisorbed and chemisorbed) | 105–600 |
| Decomposition | Removal of organic components | 500–800 |
| Inversion | Removal of carbonates | 700–1100 |
| | Conversion of HAP → β tricalcium phosphate | |
| Fusion | Melting of crystals | 1,600+ |

conversion. The final stage, fusion, correlates with the melting of the crystals. Table 2 summarizes these points.

## Microradiography

Herrmann (1977b) stated that while bone remains below 700°C, it is incompletely cremated, because organic matter is still present. Shrinkage is estimated at only 1 to 2%. As major shrinkage of the bone does not occur until 700 to 800°C, microradiographs may still be useful in observing bone structure (Bradtmiller and Buikstra 1984). Herrmann refers to bones exposed to temperatures exceeding 700 to 800°C as complete cremations. The 700 to 800°C limit appears to be the "critical point" (Herrmann 1977b), after which microstructural and ultrastructural changes are extreme.

## Scanning Electron Microscopy

The final method of viewing burned bone involves the scanning electron microscope. SEM research describes the bone tissue surface at different temperatures and in this way, the weight loss changes identified by thermogravimetry can be explained by structural changes.

Viewed with the SEM, the first stage of the DDIF process is identified by bubbles in the external lamellae (Hunger and Leopold 1978:31), and the bone begins to crack (Hunger and Leopold 1978:31; Susini et al. 1988). The fine structure of the cortical bone remains visible (Bonucci and Graziani 1975), with the lacunae expanding and becoming closely packed (Schultz 1986). Shipman et al. (1984) describe the surface as "rough" up to the 285°C mark, and then as "glassy and smooth". Evans (1973:44) notes that the increase in temperature and the decrease in water content cause an increase in microhardness; this decrease in the energy-absorbing capability of the bone ultimately results in the formation of a brittle material.

During the decompositional stage, gross bone structure is still identifiable (Bonucci and Graziani 1975); but the crystals have increased in size to ~80Å in diameter (Bonucci and Graziani 1975; Susini et al. 1988). The lacunae are larger, and the edges of the Haversian canals have roughened (Schultz 1986). Hunger and Leopold (1978:78) identify large diagonal and reticular cracks, and the bubbles have deepened. The smooth glassy surface described by Shipman et al. (1984) has become "frothy and fleecy" in appearance.

In the third stage (inversion), cracks widen; and lamellae are lost as the matrix becomes homogeneous (Hunger and Leopold 1978:31; Schultz 1986). It is only at this point where Schultz (1986) observes fissures. The crystals have lost their characteristic hexagonal appearance, and have been replaced by irregular polygonal crystals (Bonucci and Graziani 1975). Once fusion begins at 800°C+, osteons appear to infold (Schultz 1986); and blisters or large oval openings are observed (Hunger and Leopold 1978:32; Schultz 1986; Shipman et al. 1984). The etiology of these blisters is not clear. The lacunae, according to Schultz (1986), are still visible; but gradually disappear by 1100°C. The cracks have crossed between osteons to produce large fissures. The crystals appear large (0.2 to 0.3 μm) and irregular (Susini et al.

1988). As this stage ends there is a decrease in the rate of shrinkage (Herrmann 1977b; Schultz 1986). After this point, there are no observable changes until the bone begins to melt around 1600°C (Schultz 1986).

It would appear that although the researchers have described the picture in their own vernacular, they are describing the DDIF process in much the same manner. It is interesting to reflect back on Forbes' (1941) observations, and to see how accurate he was with observation only of thin sections with normal light microscopy.

Observations of the nature of heat-induced fractures at a microscopic level do little to increase our understanding of the origin and propagation of the fracture. Baud et al. (1986) described cracks perpendicular to the periosteal surface and Haversian systems. This description was later expanded by Susini et al. (1988), who felt the fissures originated on the surfaces of canals and/or lacunae, and radiated at right angles to the collagen fibers, but would not extend beyond the ray of the osteon. Beyond these observations, we know nothing of the route of the fracture in the early stages; for example, does it follow the collagen fibers or lamellae? Are the cement lines important? At what stage does the material act brittle and does this development change the movement of the fracture front?

# Demographic Methodology

## Age Estimation

Age estimation of cremated remains has followed the development of aging techniques on noncremated bones. In the 1934 archaeological urn grave analysis, based on size comparisons of bones, Krumbein was unable to break down age categories into more than "mature" and "infant."

Cranial sutures have been used most consistently to estimate age, although as early as 1968 they were considered unreliable by those studying cremated bone (Lisowski 1968). Most early researchers suggest that ecto- or endocranial suture closure may be used (Dzierzykray-Rogalski 1967; Gejvall 1969; Malinowski and Porawski 1969; Merbs 1967; Müller 1964; Schäfer 1961; Wells 1960), but others (Buikstra and Goldstein 1973; Dokládal 1969; Hummel and Schutkowski 1986a,b; Lisowski 1968; Piontek 1975; Rösing 1977) see a limited use of sutures for age estimation of cremated bone.

More reliable estimates of age may be achieved by observing a combination of epiphyseal fusion, tooth eruption and abrasion (Dokládal 1969; Classen 1991), long bone length, pubic symphyseal changes, rib end changes, cranial bone thickness, tooth density (Dufková 1985), osteon remodeling, and degenerative diseases (Bradtmiller and Buikstra 1984; Malinowski and Porawski 1969; Piontek 1975; Rösing 1977; Nelson 1992). Herrmann (1970) noted that observations made upon cremated bone were dependent on the amount of shrinkage and/or warpage of the bone.

Once a methodology for estimating age is determined, there is still a problem in determining the number of reliable age categories. As few as two (Krumbein 1934) and as many as eleven categories (Herrmann 1970) have been used to categorize the age of the individual. The majority of researchers, however, use six categories (e.g., infant I, infant II, juvenile, adult, mature, and senile).

The accuracy of the age estimation is dependent upon the precision of the method, and the degree of bone destruction and distortion. Dokládal (1969) felt that he had a 60%+ correct estimation of age on a control group; his worst group was the 45 to 65 year olds (adult). He used a combination of epiphyses, sutures, marrow cavity size, porosity and pathological deterioration on which to base his conclusion. In an archaeological sample, using epiphyseal fusion, suture closure and dental eruption, Merbs (1967) was able to estimate age on only 36% of the adults; he gave no estimate of the percentage on nonadults.

## Sex Estimation

As with age estimation, sex estimation of cremated bone has progressed as the methodology on noncremated bone has developed. Morphological and metric analyses have all been tried. Some researchers were apparently unaware of the possible inaccuracies arising due to deformation of the bone exposed to high temperatures (cf. Dzierzykray-Rogalski 1967; Grimm and Theis 1952; Krumbein 1934; Schäfer 1961).

The use of morphological characteristics of the cranium and mandible have predominated in sex estimation methods, with the female skull perceived as more gracile than the male, and therefore several features may be compared. The degree of muscle attachment development, size of mastoid process, the shape of the supraorbital margin, the size of the external occipital protuberance, the thickness of cranial bones, the mandibular angle, and the shape of the mental protuberance are all characteristics, used in combination when possible, to establish the sex of the individual(s) (Dzierzykray-Rogalski 1967; Lisowski 1968; Merbs 1967; Müller 1964; Piontek 1975; Thieme 1970).

The analysis of these traits is dependent upon two main factors: (1) survival and (2) degree of shrinkage. Dokládal (1962, 1970) noted that the skull fragmented into many components when exposed to high temperatures. Facial bones rarely survived intact; but fortunately the denser portions, such as the pars petrosa, occipital ridge, supraorbital margin, portions of the mandible, and parts of the flat bones (parietal, frontal, and occipital) may survive. The interpretation of nonmetric sex indicators is subjective, and the researcher requires some knowledge about the normal variation expected in the expression of the traits within that particular population under study. As mentioned earlier, shrinkage may result in the misclassification of some males as females (Herrmann 1976, 1977a).

Morphological analyses of postcranial remains is more complex. Although the pelvis is considered the best area to estimate sex (Stewart 1979:104), it is frequently fragmented by fire (Dokládal 1969). The degree of destruction is dependent upon the temperature of the fire and will determine the value of the pelvis for interpretation. When present, the greater sciatic notch, ilium, and possibly pelvic shape may be used to suggest sex. The cortical thickness of the long bones has been used more frequently (Müller 1964; Schäfer 1961; Thieme 1970). The size of the femoral, humeral, and radial heads has been used; but the degree of shrinkage experienced by the spongy bone exposed to intense heat (up to 12%: Grupe and Herrmann 1983) makes these estimates extremely uncertain.

Another approach to sex determination is through discriminant analysis. Van Vark (1970) claimed that cremation does not reduce the validity of metric observations of bone. He felt that the discriminatory values need only be lowered slightly. Rösing (1977) suggested that a greater percentage of remains may be sexed, if discriminant analyses are used.

The pars petrosa has been examined by Wahl and Henke (1980) and Schutkowski (1983) to establish its value in sex discrimination. Wahl and Henke used five variables and two discriminant functions. One function uses three variables and the second uses five. They found that a shrinkage of 10% had little effect on the interpretations. A study completed by Holland (1989) suggested that the cranial base does not shrink more than 2.25% in temperatures under 800°C. He felt that this amount of shrinkage did not hinder metric analyses.

Duffy et al. (1991), through experimentation on pig and human tooth pulp, ascertained that sex chromatin could be used until the temperature in the pulp chamber exceeded 100°C.

Gender-related grave goods can also be used to determine the sex of an individual (Lisowski 1968; Müller 1964; Wells 1960). This is an important factor for juvenile or child graves.

Clearly, sex determination is reliant upon the researchers' knowledge of various methods used in noncremated bone analyses. It is necessary to be aware of the expected heat shrinkage for each bone type (compact and cancellous), and to know the effects of warpage upon the trait.

## Stature Estimation

The ability to reconstruct an individual's live stature from fragmentary remains is fraught with problems. If reconstruction of the long bone(s) can be done, then measurements can be taken and used in a stature regression such as those designed by Trotter and Gleser (1952); however, if fragmentation is extreme, and only small portions of the long bone can be reconstructed, it is necessary to use other methods (Holland 1992; Müller 1935; Müller 1958; Steele and McKern 1969; Steele 1970; and Strzalko et al. 1972). These methods have been used conservatively by researchers working with cremated remains (cf. Lisowski 1968; Malinowski and Porawski 1969; Piontek 1975; and Rösing 1977). The methods proposed by Müller (1958) and Strzalko et al. (1972) rely upon the diameter of the radial, humeral, or femoral head. The estimations must account for the shrinkage of the spongy bone (~12%) located in the epiphyses.

There seems to be no satisfactory answer to the issue of stature estimation. The use of vertebrae for estimation is not feasible, as survival of vertebrae is poor (Dokládal 1969). If a long bone has been protected by a muscle mass (e.g., femur), there is a greater chance of obtaining a near complete bone for analysis. Considering the error potential using fragmentary remains Holland (1992) estimated 50 to 100% accuracy, and compounding that with error introduced by shrinkage and warpage, it is obvious that any estimates of stature using cremated bone must be broad.

## Ancestral Estimation

Another aspect of individualization which presents a challenge is the estimation of ancestry (Lisowski 1968; Malinowski and Porawski 1969; Müller 1964; Schäfer 1961; Rösing 1977). Gladykowska-Rzeczycka (1965) attempted to reconstruct the orbit and to observe the shape of the orbit for ancestry estimation. Relying on a single characteristic for ancestry estimation is questionable. The estimation of ancestry should only be considered in instances, in which there is substantial facial or cranial material and/or complete long bones.

# Methodology of Medicolegal Community

The forensic community has the potential to provide valuable information about the reliability of the demographic methodology and the interpretation of visual characteristics for cremation analysis. In many instances, although an identity is established and circumstances surrounding the death are clarified, no record of the identification techniques used is published, and there is only a minimal discussion of the reliability of age, sex, or stature techniques when published.

Early forensic case reports have emphasized the use of the dentition to establish an identification. Early on Böhmer (1932) discussed the important role of dentition in five forensic cases. In one case, the examination of soft and hard tissues established that the victim was a female aged 15 to 30 years. From the remaining soft tissue, the cause of death was attributed to strangulation, and not to the fire. The size, shape, and eruption status of the teeth aided in the age and sex determination of this individual.

Merkel (1932) examined several instances of charred remains where cause of death was also interpreted. The examination of carbon monoxide in the body was advocated in order to determine the state of the individual before death. He also described the presence of trauma to calcined cranial bones; however, he realized that these may have been heat-induced fractures.

It was not until 1943 that a review of the evidence used in the analysis of bony cremated remains was completed. In one case, Krogman (1943a, 1949:74) was called upon to analyze charred human remains from a forest fire. Examination of skull shape, pelvic traits, teeth, sutures, and the radius (all suggesting a male, caucasian, aged 45 to 50) was possible due to the completeness of the individual. The particular individual was not identified at that time, so the analysis could not be verified. In a second case Krogman (1943b) established that a leg bone was shortened by fire, and not amputated. By observing the molten state of the compact bone and by providing no evidence for atrophy, he was able to conclude the leg burned away.

Johanson and Saldeen (1969) presented three cases in which dental and skeletal evidence, together with the cooperation of various agencies, resulted in positive identifications. By comparison of ante- and postmortem records, the identifications were verified. This is one of the earliest instances which records the use of bony tissue reconstruction for analysis. The left femur and an ulna were used to estimate age and sex in one case. In another case, skeletal pathology and X-ray comparison were used to support the identification.

From incinerated remains recovered in a garbage pit, Heglar (1984) was able to determine that the remains included a juvenile, two adults, and an infant. Multiple representation of parts, cranial sutures, epiphyseal fusion, muscularity, size, orbital margins, mandibular shape, tooth root and type (deciduous or permanent) were used to estimate age, sex, and number of individuals represented. The identities were verified using antemortem X-rays. Heglar also used the pubic symphysis and long bone cortical thickness to determine the age of one charred individual. The accused confessed to the murders and disposal of the bodies.

The use of X-rays for positive identification was also used by Dufková (1985). In this case, the body of a severely burned individual was recovered and estimated to be that of a female, aged 12 to 16 years (<20), using evidence from the pelvis, teeth (eruption and density), and epiphyses. No stature estimation was done, but comparison of tibial and fibular bone with antemortem X-rays provided twelve points of comparison. Also an X-ray of the left elbow showed evidence of a healed fracture.

A more recent case involved the identification of ten individuals in a railway disaster outside of Hinton, Alberta (Foisey 1986). This civil disaster resulted when a freight train carrying sulfur, grain, and culvert piping collided with a VIA Rail passenger train. The collision resulted in a fire fueled for more than 48 hours by grain, diesel fuel, and sulfur. As a result of this intense heat, the victims demonstrated a range of cremation, from charred to incomplete incineration. Pubic symphyseal changes, tooth eruption, epiphyseal fusion, and degenerative changes were used for age determination. Sex determination was based on a combination of ischial size, shape of the sciatic notch, cranial bone thickness, and bone size. Other factors used to distinguish the victims were genetic anomalies and association with soft tissue remains (Beattie 1986).

Another study by Eckert (1988) and his colleagues involved the disposal of the victim in a crematory oven. The bony remains and dried blood were sufficient to establish the identity of a caucasian female in her early thirties. DNA testing proved the blood belonged to the victim. Unfortunately, there is no mention of the methodology used by the physical anthropologist to establish age, sex, and ancestry. Problems arising from improper mortuary cremation practices have resulted in an increasing need to identify commingled individuals (Murad 1991; Kennedy 1991). In commercial cremations, the remains are also pulverized, complicating the forensic analysis.

The precise methods used by forensic scientists to establish the identity of cremated remains are often not provided in the literature. It is usually unclear whether there is due consideration of the effects of shrinkage on the bone and its implications in the interpretation of radiographs and bone characteristics. Since positive identifications are frequently based on comparison with antemortem radiographs, it is often considered unnecessary to record the methods used to obtain the initial physical description. This shortcoming in the medicolegal reporting could be remedied by adding a few explanatory notes. With the collection of several cremation cases and a critical approach to discussing the methodology, age, sex, stature, and ancestry estimation protocols could be tested and standardized for cremation analysis. The database available to the medicolegal community is immense and can be used effectively to corroborate experimental research on nonhuman materials.

## Conclusion

Cremation research has not followed an orderly path. The careful study of visual characteristics (e.g., color, shrinkage, fracture patterns, histology) has led to a better understanding of bone tissue and how heat affects it. Unfortunately, there is a paucity of research on methods for interpreting demographic information. Instead, researchers have apparently used the same methods as for noncremated bone. The caveat, "there is no significant influence on the results" often accompanies any conclusions. Methods used to interpret cremated bone should be designed or at least tested on cremated bone to establish reliability.

    The color of cremated bone appears to demonstrate the state of decomposition of the bone, as opposed to the temperature of the fire. It is difficult to extrapolate the specific temperature of the fire from bone fragments, but an interpretation of the body's position (or at least the bone's position) within the fire may be possible.

    Research on the fracture patterns found in cremated bone has emphasized the condition of the bone prior to cremation. Attempts have been made to distinguish fleshed, defleshed, or dry bone, but there is considerable controversy over the characteristics of the fracture patterns. There are problems in the use of nonstandardized terminology, and the results are highly variable. A standardization of terminology is essential before the value of fractures can be realized. Only recently (e.g., Mayne 1990) has an attempt been made to interpret the fractures in order to suggest other factors, such as the presence of trauma prior to cremation.

    Histological analysis of cremated bone has supported the phased model of decomposition throughout the cremation process. And although there is still controversy regarding the conversion of hydroxyapatite, there is an agreement that the bone changes from a plastic to a brittle material. By recognizing cremated bone as a brittle material, the evidence of trauma, age, sex, and ancestry may be better understood.

    Current methods available for age, sex, stature and ancestry determination for cremated remains, including both bone and teeth, are unsatisfactory. Methods not tested for their reliability on cremated bone are regularly used for demographic interpretation. In many instances, it is unclear if the researcher is aware of the error introduced by cremation, particularly differential shrinkage. Cooperation between research and applied fields is necessary to test techniques, standardize terminology, and develop new methods for working with cremated bone.

    It is clear that there is still much to be learned about cremated bone. Many of the ideas presented in the early part of the century need to be verified through experimental research and direct application in forensic situations. Since research in North America has focused on the visual interpretation of cremated bone in contrast to the European emphasis on methodology, cooperation between these communities is fundamental to the advancement of our understanding of cremated bone material.

## Acknowledgments

The author would like to express her appreciation to the Department of Anthropology, University of Alberta for the financial support required to complete this review. Also the author is indebted to Dr. Owen Beattie (Department of Anthropology, University of Alberta) and to Dr. William Haglund (King County Medical Examiner Division, Seattle) for their continuing encouragement and advice. Special thanks go to Dr. A. Galloway for her editorial comments.

# References

Baby, R.S.

 1954   Hopewell Cremation Practices. *Papers In Archaeology* 1:1–7. Ohio Historical Society, Columbus.

Bass, W.M.

 1984   Is It Possible to Consume a Body Completely in a Fire? In *Human Identification: Case Studies in Forensic Anthropology*, edited by T. Rathbun and J.E. Buikstra, pp. 159–167. Charles C Thomas, Springfield, IL.

Baud, C.A., A. Susini, and A. Wetz

 1986   Microstructural Alterations in Burned Bones from a Neolithic Tomb, *VI European Meeting of the Paleoanthropology Association*, pp. 61–66. Madrid.

Beattie, O.B.

 1986   Descriptions of Identifications Made on Human Skeletal Remains from the Hinton/Via Rail Train Disaster of February 8, 1986. Report on file, Office of the Chief Medical Examiner, Edmonton.

Binford, L.R.

 1963   An Analysis of Cremations from Three Michigan Sites. *Wisconsin Archaeology* 44(2):98–110.

Böhmer, K.

 1932   Identifikation nach Verbrennung. *Deutsche Zeitschrift fur die gesamte gerichtliche Medizin* 18:250–263.

Bonucci, E., and G. Graziani

 1975   Comparative Thermogravimetric, X-ray Diffraction and Electron Microscope Investigations of Burnt Bones from Recent, Ancient and Prehistoric Age. *Atti Memorie Accademia Nazionale die Lincei Scienze, Fisiche, Matematiche Naturali*, Ser. 8, Sec. 2A (Roma) 59:517–534.

Bradtmiller, B., and J.E. Buikstra

 1984   Effects of Burning on Human Bone Microstructure: A Preliminary Study. *Journal of Forensic Sciences* 29:535–540.

Buikstra, J.E., and L. Goldstein

 1973   *The Perrins Lodge Crematory*. Illinois State Museum Reports of Investigation 28, Illinois Valley Archaeological Program Research Papers, 8, Illinois State Museum, Springfield, IL.

Buikstra, J.E., and M. Swegle

 1989   Bone Modification Due to Burning: Experimental Evidence. In *Bone Modification*, edited by R. Bonnichsen and M.H. Sorg, pp. 247–258. Center for the Study of the First Americans, University of Maine, Orono, ME.

Burns, K.R.

 1988   Linear Effects of Drying and Burning on Human Bones and Teeth. In *Abstracts of the 40th Annual Meeting of the American Academy of Forensic Sciences*, p. 106. American Academy of Forensic Sciences, Colorado Springs, CO.

Civjan, S., W.J. Selting, L.B. de Simon, G.C. Battistone, and M.F. Grower

 1971   Characterization of Osseous Tissues by Thermogravimetric and Physical Techniques. *Journal of Dental Research* 51:539–542.

Clark, D.H.

 1986   Dental Identification Problems in the Abu Dhabi Air Accident. *American Journal of Forensic Medicine and Pathology* 7:317–321.

Classen, H.
    1991  Methoden zur Lebensaltersbestimmung am Menschlichen Skelett, Dargestellt am
    Beispiel von Hallstattzeitlichen Körper-und Brandbestattungen. *Zeitschrift für Gerontologie* 24:316–318.

Dijkstra, D.K.S.
    1938  Die Skelettreste aus dem Kreisgrabenfriedhof von Sleen, Provinz, Drente, Neiderlande. *Mannus* 30:546–567.

Dokládal, M.
    1962  Über die Möglichkeiten der Identifikation von Knochen aus Leichenbränden. *Mitteilungen der Arbeitsgruppe Anthropologie der biologischen Gesellschaft in der DDR.* (Berlin)
    6:15.
    1969  Über die Heutigen Möglichkeiten der Personenidentifikation auf Grund von Verbrannten Knochen. In *Aktuelle Kriminologie*, pp. 223–246. Kriminolog Verlag, Hamburg.
    1970  Ergebnisse Experimenteller Verbrennungen zur Feststellung von Form- und Grössenveränderungen von Menschenknochen Unter dem Einfluss von Hohen Temperaturen.
    *Anthropologie* 8(2):3–17.
    1971  A Further Contribution to the Morphology of Burned Bones. In *Proceedings of the
    Anthropological Congress Dedicated to Ales Hrdlicka,* edited by N. Novotny, pp. 561–568.
    Czechoslavak Academy of Sciences, Prague.

Dowling, G., and O.B. Beattie
    1988  Autopsy Report 7841–8–88. Report on file, Office of the Chief Medical Examiner,
    Edmonton.

Duffy, J.B., J.D. Waterfield, and M.F. Skinner
    1991  Isolation of Tooth Pulp Cells for Sex Chromatin Studies in Experimental Dehydrated
    and Cremated Remains. *Forensic Science International* 49:127–141.

Dufková, J.
    1985  Beitrag zur Identifizierung von Leichen/Skeletteilen unter Berucksichtigung von
    Brandleichen. I and II. *Beitrage zur gerichtlichen Medizin* 43:233–248.

Dunlop, J.
    1978  Traffic Light Discoloration in Cremated Bones. *Medicine, Science and the Law*
    18:163–173.

Dzierzykray-Rogalski, T.
    1967  New Methods of Investigation of Bone Remains from Cremation Graves. *Anthropologie* (Brno) 4:41–45.

Eckert, W.G., S. James, and S. Katchis
    1988  Investigation of Cremations and Severely Burned Bodies. *American Journal of Medicine and Pathology* 9:188–200.

Evans, F.G.
    1973  *Mechanical Properties of Bone.* Charles C Thomas, Springfield, IL.

Foisey, R.P.
    1986  Commission Of Inquiry Hinton Train Collision. Report of the Commissioner, The
    Honourable Mr. Justice René P. Foisey, Canadian Government Publishing Center, Ottawa.

Forbes, G.
    1941  The Effects of Heat on the Histological Structure of Bone. *Police Journal* 14(1):50–60.

Garn, S.M., J.M. Nagy, and S.T. Sandusky
    1972  Differential Sexual Dimorphism in Bone Diameters of Subjects of European and
    African Ancestry. *American Journal of Physical Anthropology* 37:127–129.

Gebhardt, H.
1923 Verbrennungserscheinungen an Zähnen und Zahnersatz und Ihre Gerichtsärztliche Bedeutung für die Identifizierung Verbrannter Leichen. *Deutsche Zeitschrift für die gesamte gerichtliche Medizin* 2:191–209.

Gejvall, N.G.
1969 Cremations. In *Science in Archaeology*. 2nd ed., edited by D. Brothwell and E. Higgs, pp. 468–479. Praeger, New York.

Gladykowska-Rzeczycka, J.
1965 A Trial of Reconstructing the Entrance to the Orbit from Bone Remnants from Crematory Graves. *Folia Morphologica* 24:280–283.

Grimm, H.
1961 Der gegenwärtige Stand der Leichenbranduntersuchungen. *Ausgrabungen und Funde* 6:299–306.

Grimm, H., and G. Theis
1952 Anthropologische Untersuchungen am Leichenbrand-Inhalt von Urnen der Frühen Eisenzeit aus Berlin-Britz. *Wissenschaftliche Zeitschrift der Humbolt-Universität zu Berlin Mathematische-Naturwissenschaftliche Reihe* 2(3/4):85–87.

Grupe, G., and B. Herrmann
1983 Über das Schrumpfungsverhalten Experimentell Verbrannter Spongiöser Knochen am Beispiel des Caput Femoris. *Zeitschrift für Morphologie und Anthropologie* 74(2):121–127.

Heglar, R.
1984 Burned Remains. In *Human Identification: Case Studies in Forensic Anthropology*, edited by T. Rathbun and J.E. Buikstra, pp. 148–158. Charles C Thomas, Springfield, IL.

Herrmann, B.
1970 Anthropologische Bearbeitung der Leichenbränden von Berlin-Rudow. *Ausgrabungen in Berlin* 1:61–71.
1972 Zur Beurteilung von Kohlenstoffverfärbungen bei Leichenbränden. *Ausgrabungen und Funde* 17(6):275–277.
1973 Möglichkeiten und Grenzen der Anthropologischen Bearbeitung von Leichenbränden. *Mitteilungen der Berliner Gesellschaft für Anthropologie, Ethnologie, und Urgeschichte* 2:53–55.
1976 Neuere Ergebnisse zur Beurteilung menschlicher Brandknochen. *Zeitschrift für Rechtsmedizin* 77:191–200.
1977a Über die Abhängigkeit der Schrumpfung vom Mineralgehalt bei Experimentell Verbrannten Knochen. *Anthropologische Anzeiger* 36:7–12.
1977b On Histological Investigations of Cremated Human Remains. *Journal Human Evolution* 6:101–103.
1980 Kleine Geschichte der Leichenbranduntersuchungen. *Fornvännen* 75:20–29.

Holager, J.
1970 Thermogravimetric Examination on Enamel and Dentin. *Journal of Dental Research* 49:546–548.

Holland, T.D.
1989 Use of the Cranial Base in the Identification of Fire Victims. *Journal of Forensic Sciences* 34:458–460.
1992 Estimation of Adult Stature from Fragmentary Tibias. *Journal of Forensic Sciences* 37:1223–1229.

Hummel, S., and H. Schutkowski

1986a Neue Ansätze in der Leichenbranduntersuchungen. In *Innovative Trends in der Pra-historischen Archaeologie*, edited by B. Herrmann, pp. 141–146, Mitteilungen der Berliner Gesellschaft für Anthropologie, Ethnologie und Urgeschichte 7. Berlin.

1986b Das Verhalten von Knochengewebe unter dem Einfluss höherer Temperaturen, Bedeutungen für die Leichenbranddiagnose. *Zeitschrift fur Morphologische Anthropologie* 77(1):1–9.

Hunger, H., and D. Leopold

1978  *Identifikation*. Springer, New York.

Iscan, M.Y., and P. Miller-Shaivitz

1984  Determination of Sex from the Tibia. *American Journal of Physical Anthropology* 64:53–58.

Johanson, G., and T. Saldeen

1969  Identification of Burnt Victims with the Aid of Tooth and Bone Fragments. *Journal of Forensic Medicine* 16:16–25.

Johnson, E.

1985  Current Developments in Bone Technology. In *Advances in Archaeological Method and Theory*, Vol. 8, edited by M.B. Schiffer, pp. 157–235. Academic Press, New York.

Kennedy, K.A.R.

1991  The Wrong Urn: Commingling of Cremains in Mortuary Practices. In *Abstracts of the American Academy of Forensic Sciences 43rd Annual Meeting*, p. 153. American Academy of Forensic Sciences, Colorado Springs, CO.

Krogman, W.M.

1943a Role of the Physical Anthropologist in the Identification of Human Skeletal Remains, I. *FBI Law Enforcement Bulletin* 12(4):17–40.

1943b Role of the Physical Anthropologist in the Identification of Human Skeletal Remains, II. *FBI Law Enforcement Bulletin* 12(5):12–28

1949  The Human Skeleton in Legal Medicine. In *Symposium on Medicolegal Problems*, Series Two, edited by S.A. Levinson, pp. 1–92. J.B. Lippincott, Philadelphia.

Krumbein, C.N.

1934  Anthropologische Untersuchungen und urgeschichtlichen Leichenbränden. *Forschungen und Fortschritte* 10:411–412.

Kühl, I.

1980  Harris's Lines and Their Occurences Also in Bones of Prehistoric Cremations. *Ossa* 7:129–171.

1986  Hinweise auf Belastungsdeformationen an Skelettresten aus prähistorischen Brandbestattungen. *Zeitschrift fur Rechtsmedizin*. 97:227–238.

Lepkowski, V., and L. Wachholtz

1903  Über Veränderung Naturlicher und Kunstlicher Gebisse Durch Extreme Temperatur und Fäulnis. *Artzliche Sachverstandigenzeitung* 6:119–121.

Lisowski, F.P.

1968  The Investigation of Human Cremated Remains. *Anthropologie und Humangenetik* 4:76–83.

Malinowski, A., and R. Porawski

1969  Identifikationsmöglichkeiten Menschlicher Brandknochen mit Besonderer Berücksichtigung Ihres Gewichts. *Zacchia*, 5 Ser. 3(3):1–19. Archivio di Medicina Legale, Sociale Criminologica, Roma.

Maples, W.R.

1988 Identification of the Cremated Remains in the Meek/Jennings Case. In *Abstracts of the American Academy of Forensic Sciences 40th Annual Meeting*, p. 105. American Academy of Forensic Sciences, Colorado Springs, CO.

Mayne, P.M.

1990 The Identification of Precremation Trauma in Cremated Remains. Unpublished Master's thesis, University of Alberta, Edmonton.

Merbs, C.F.

1967 Cremated Human Remains from Point of Pines, Arizona: A New Approach. *American Antiquity* 32:498–506.

Merkel, H.

1932 Diagnostische Feststellungsmöglichkeiten bei Verbrannten und Verkohlten Menschlichen Leichen. *Deutsche Zeitschrift für Gesamte Gerichtliche Medizin* 18:232–249.

Müller, G.

1958 Schätzung der Körperhöhe bei Funden von Leichenbränden. *Ausgrabungen und Funde* 4:52.

1964 Methodisch-kritische Betrachtungen zur Anthropologischen Untersuchung von Leichenbränden. *Prähistorische Zeitschrift* 42:1–29.

Müller, G.

1935 Zur Bestimmung der Länge Beschädigter Extremitäten-knochen. *Anthropologische Anzeiger* 12(1):70–72.

Murad, T.A.

1991 A Case Involving the Inappropriate Disposal of Cremains. In *Abstracts of the 43rd Annual Meeting of the American Academy of Forensic Sciences*, p. 153. American Academy of Forensic Sciences, Colorado Springs, CO.

Murray, E.A., H.J. Bonnell, and A.J. Perzigian

1991 Cremation in a Chicken Coop: Self-incineration or Fowl Play? In *Abstracts of the 43rd Annual Meeting of the American Academy of Forensic Sciences*, p. 152. American Academy of Forensic Sciences, Colorado Springs, CO.

Nelson, R.

1992 A Microscopic Comparison of Fresh and Burned Bone. *Journal of Forensic Sciences* 37:1055–1060.

Newesely, H.

1988 Chemical Stability of Hydroxyapatite under Different Conditions. In *Trace Elements in Environmental History*, edited by G. Grupe and B. Herrmann, pp. 1–16, Springer-Verlag, Berlin.

Piontek, J.

1975 Polish Method and Results of Investigations of Cremated Bones from Prehistoric Cemeteries. *Glasnik Anthropoloskog Drustva Jugoslavise* Sveska 12:23–34.

Richards, N.F.

1977 Fire Investigation — Destruction of Corpses. *Medicine, Science and the Law* 17:79–82.

Rogers, L.F.

1982 Skeletal Biomechanics. In *Radiology of Skeletal Trauma*, Vol. 1, edited by L.F. Rogers, pp. 15–22. Churchill Livingstone, New York.

Rootare, H.M., and R.G. Craig

1977 Vapor Phase Adsorption of Water on Hydroxyapatite. *Journal of Dental Research* 56:1437–1448.

Rösing, F.W.
  1977  Methoden und Aussagemöglichkeiten der Anthropologischen Leichenbrandbearbe-
  itung. *Archaeologie und Naturwissenschaften* 1:53–80.

Schäfer, U.
  1961  Grenzen und Möglichkeiten der anthropologischen Untersuchung von Leichenbränden. Berliner Vertrag International Kongress für Vor- und Frühgeschichte, Hamburg,
  1958, pp. 717–724. Hamburg.

Schultz, M.
  1986  Hitzeiduzierte Veränderungen des Knochens. *Die mikroskopische Untersuchung
  Prähistorischer Skeletfunde*. Archaeologie und Museum 1:116–129.

Schutkowski, H.
  1983  Über den Diagnostischen Wert der Pars Petrosa Ossis Temporalis für Geschlechts-
  bestimmung. *Zeitschrift fur Morphologische Anthropologie* 74:129–144.

Schutkowski, H., and S. Hummel
  1987  Variabilitätsvergleich von Wandstärken für die Geschlechtszuweisung an Leichenbränden. *Anthropologische Anzeiger* 45(1):43–47.

Schwartz, J.H.
  1993  *What the Bones Tell Us*. Henry Holt, New York.

Shipman, P., G. Foster, and M. Schoeninger
  1984  Burnt Bones and Teeth: An Experimental Study of Color, Morphology, Crystal
  Structure and Shrinkage. *Journal of Archaeological Science* 2:307–325.

Spence, T.F.
  1967  The Anatomical Study of Cremated Fragments from Archaeological Sites. *Proceedings of the Prehistoric Society* 5:70–83.

Steele, D.G.
  1970  Estimation of Stature from Fragments of Long Limb Bones. In *Personal Identification
  in Mass Disasters*, edited by T.D. Stewart, pp. 85–97. National Museum of Natural History,
  Washington, D.C.

Steele, D.G., and T.W. McKern
  1969  A Method for the Assessment of Maximum Long Bone Length and Living Stature
  from Fragmentary Long Bones. *American Journal of Physical Anthropolology* 31:215–28.

Stewart, T.D.
  1979  *Essentials of Forensic Anthropology*. Charles C Thomas, Springfield, IL.

Strzalko, J., J. Piontek, and A. Malinowski
  1972  Problem Rekonstrukcji Wzrostu na Podstawie Kasci Zachowanych we Fragmentach
  lub Spalonych [Problem of the reconstruction of stature on ground of bones preserved
  in fragments or burnt.] *Przeglad Antropologiczny* 38:277–287.

Susini, A., C.A. Baud, and H.J. Tochon-Danguy
  1988  Identification d'un Traitement Thermique des os Prehistoriques Humain. *Actes des
  3 Journees Anthropologiques, Notes et Monographies Techniques* 24:43–67.

Thieme, U.
  1970  Über Leichenbranduntersuchungen Methoden und Untersuchungsergebnisse aus
  den Jahren 1935 bis 1941, ein Beitrag zur Geschichte der Leichenbranduntersuchungen.
  *Neue Ausgrabungen und Forschung in Niedersachsen* 5:253–286.

Thurman, M.D., and L.J. Wilmore
  1980  Replicative Cremation Experiment. *North American Archaeology* 2:275–283.

Trotter, M., and G.C. Gleser
    1952   Estimation of Stature from Long Bones of American Whites and Negroes. *American Journal of Physical Anthropology* 10:463–514.

Van Vark, G.N.
    1970   Some Statistical Procedures for the Investigation of Prehistoric Skeletal Material. Master's thesis, Gröningen, Netherlands.
    1975   The Investigation of Human Cremated Skeletal Material by Multivariate Statistical Methods II. Measures. *Ossa* 2:47–68.

Wahl, J.
    1982   Leichenbranduntersuchungen. *Prähistorische Zeitschrift* (Berlin) 57:1–125.
    1983   Zur metrischen Alterbestimmung von Kindlichen und Jungendlichen Leichen-bränden. *Homo* 34(1):48–54.

Wahl, J., and W. Henke
    1980   Die Pars petrosa als Diagnostikum für die multivariat-biometrische Geschlechts-betimmung von Leichenbrandmaterial. *Zeitschrift für Morphologische Anthropologie* 70:258–268.

Webb, W., and C.E. Snow
    1945   *The Adena People.* Reports in Anthropology and Archaeology, no. 6, pp. 59–81, 166–199. University of Kentucky, Lexington.

Wells, C.
    1960   A Study of Cremations. *Antiquity* 34:29–37.

White, T.D.
    1992   *Prehistoric Cannibalism at Mancos 5MTUMR-2346.* Princeton University, Princeton, NJ.

Wilson, D.F., and W. Massey
    1987   Scanning Electron Microscopy of Incinerated Teeth. *American Journal of Medicine and Pathology* 8:32–38.

# Human Bone Mineral Densities and Survival of Bone Elements: A Contemporary Sample

# 19

ALISON GALLOWAY
P. WILLEY
LYNN SNYDER

## Introduction

The preservation of human remains has attracted considerable interest in both physical and forensic anthropology and archaeology. Preservational concerns are particularly critical because of the multitude of factors which must be assessed to reconstruct the depositional and excavational impact on human remains (Henderson 1987). These interacting and overlapping factors include soil compaction, carnivore damage and transport, rodent gnawing, leaching of mineral components, trampling, water transport, exposure to sunlight, and alternating moisture/dryness phases. Bone elements will be altered by these factors to differing extents depending upon the intrinsic qualities of their composition, including the size, mass, shape, structure, and density. Similarly, influential in bone survival are changes in bone structure due to pathological, traumatic, or taphonomic influences. The processes of excavation, recovery, cleaning, and curation may also result in loss or degradation of material. Of all the intrinsic variables, bone mineral density of the element and density distribution within the element may have the single most important influence on survival.

Although bone density values are available for several ungulate species (Binford and Bertram 1977; Brain 1967; Lyman 1982, 1984), there are few density values for humans which are applicable to taphonomic questions. Boaz and Behrensmeyer (1976) measured the bone density of 35 portions of unprovenienced human bone, but their data are of limited utility because the measurements are based on one example of each element or element portion and address the combined effects of shape and density in fluvial transport. On the other hand, large clinical samples have been measured (Favus 1993; Stini et al. 1992; USDHHS 1986; Wasnich et al. 1985), but these measurements have been limited to a few locations of clinical, rather than taphonomic, importance.

This study was motivated by the need to obtain a standardized and relatively accurate measure of bone mineral density at a variety of sites in humans. The six major limb bones (humerus, radius, ulna, femur, tibia, and fibula) were measured with a single photon absorptiometer at consistent locations along the shaft, metaphyses, and epiphyses. Significant differences were found between males and females, but few consistent differences due to side were noted. Age changes were found at all locations, although not all reach a level of statistical significance.

## Materials and Methods: Age, Sex, and Racial Composition

The contemporary sample was drawn from 41 modern human specimens whose skeletal remains were donated to the University of Tennessee, Knoxville, or from forensic cases curated by the Department of Anthropology, UTK, between 1981 and 1990. Skeletonization was accomplished through long-term exposure above ground, with persistently adhering tissues being removed through boiling. The series includes 16 females and 25 males, ranging in age from infant to 87 years (Table 1). Only adults (over age 15 years), including 15 females and 23 males of known age, race, and sex, were incorporated into the sample (Table 1). Most of the individuals were caucasoids, although there were a few African-Americans. Because there were so few of the latter group and, more important, because members of African populations tend to have bone densities which are greater than Europeans, Asians, or Native Americans (Cohn et al. 1977; Nelson et al. 1991), they were omitted from further analysis in this study, bringing the total number of individuals included in the study to 32 (10 females and 22 males). Because the number of skeletal elements available at each site varied, as well as suitability of the scan site for measurement, the maximum number of females measured at each scan location was 9 (minimum 6) and the maximum number of males was 22 (minimum 15).

Whenever possible, limb bones from both sides of the body were scanned. Information on the handedness of the individuals in the study was not available. No attempt was made to assess handedness from skeletal characteristics since these methods have not been proven reliable.

**Table 1   Mean Age (standard deviation in parentheses) and Sex Distribution of Known Individuals from Contemporary Series**

|  | Females | | | Males | | |
|---|---|---|---|---|---|---|
|  | Mean | Age | Number | Mean | Age | Number |
| Caucasoid | 49 | (22) | 10 | 56.7 | (18) | 22 |
| Negroid | 42 | (22) | 5 | 43 |  | 1 |

## Specimen Preparation and Comparabiity

The number of individuals scanned varied, depending on the element, side, and location of the scan. Bones were not scanned at specific sites if these locations were damaged. Materials with gross pathological conditions were also excluded; however, histological changes which may have affected bone mineral content could not be excluded. No preservatives or consolidants had been used on the modern bone in this analysis.

The processing of the contemporary material may have had an effect on bone mineral density. Some elements or individuals, for instance, may have required more exposure or cooking than others to produce clean bone. MacDonald (1991) has shown that maceration and prolonged boiling techniques cause loss of as much as 10% in bone mineral density, and such effects may have had an influence on the results of this paper.

## Bone Scan Procedures and Their Assumptions

Long bones of studied individuals were analyzed using the Norland Cameron Model 2780 Single Photon Absorptiometer (SPA). This equipment uses a monochromatic radionuclide source, iodine-125, to determine the density of substances in the path of the highly collimated photon beam (Cameron and Sorenson 1963). A scintillation detector counts and converts the transmission of photons into an estimation of bone mineral content and density based on comparisons with ashed samples. This equipment was chosen, since it was relatively inexpensive, available, met the requirements for replicability of results, and has been used in other studies of bone density and taphonomy.

Single photon absorptiometry measures "slices" through bone, so that bone mineral density is assumed to be evenly distributed throughout the cross section. In fact, long bones have medullary cavities, which means that bone is compacted into much denser cortical bone than predicted by the scan results. The integrity of the trabeculae and their contribution to overall density cannot be calculated. It is important to note that the algorithm used in converting its scan result

$$T_b = [\log_e(I_o^*/I)]/(m_b\, r_b - m_m\, r_m)$$

assumes an approximately cylindrical shape to the bone being scanned (Cameron and Sorenson 1963). In essence, the machine measures the difference between the photon beam as it passes through a baseline material ($I_o^*$) and the intensity of the beam as it passes through the bone and baseline (I). The amount of mineral present in the bone ($T_b$) is calculated from the differences in the photon streams and mass absorption coefficients of bone mineral ($m_b$) and of tissue ($m_m$), with $r_b$ and $r_m$ being the microscopic density of bone and soft tissue, respectively, in g/cm³. The measure I is taken at closely spaced intervals across the bone, allowing reconstruction of a cross-section. The technique has been found to be highly accurate for the bone mineral content as determined by bone ash weight and precise in its replicability when close to these ideal conditions are met. For irregularly shaped bone, however, the results can be expected to be less accurate. The equipment must assume a roughly circular shape to the bone in order to calculate the thickness of bone present and distribute the amount of mineral measured over the area assumed. In living subjects, the inclusion of fatty marrow inside the bone and variations in the baseline material may distort the readings. Other technical causes of reading errors include beam hardening, photon beam size, and scattered radiation. Despite these problems, accuracy has been reported at 1 to 4% and precision at 2 to 4% (U.S. Department of Health and Human Services 1986).

Clinical assessment has focused on a limited number of locations where close to ideal conditions are met, such as the midshaft of the radius. Exact placement of dry bone is far easier than in living subjects, allowing for precise measurements. Normally, a baseline reading alongside the bone is made to calibrate the subsequent bone scan. Without the surrounding soft tissue, however, the difference between the unobstructed photon beam and that passing through the bone is too great to allow the equipment to monitor any changes in density within the bone itself. Therefore, some substitute material must be provided to produce a baseline. Options are a water bath, a soft tissue equivalent such as dialysis tubing filled with water, or Plexiglas sheets. These serve to lower the baseline levels.

In addition to the need to lower the baseline, we are also faced with the problem of "zero counts," those areas in which the bone or bone and baseline combination are so dense that the photon beam is completely occluded. Excess numbers of zero counts will impair the ability of the machine to monitor extremely dense bones. Essentially, the machine fails to read any density above the maximum of its capacity. Therefore, for each scan location, the thickness of the baseline material may need to be adjusted to maximize the readable area while, at the same time, retaining a useable baseline.

In this study, four scans were taken at each site and the results were averaged. Because a water bath could potentially produce unnecessary additional damage to the skeletal material, up to six sheets of ¼-in. Plexiglas were placed beneath the bone. These sheets were added in order to maintain a baseline below 6,800 photon counts. Sheets were adjusted to minimize the number of zero counts at each scan site. The actual number of sheets reflected the best compromise between these opposing requirements. Repeat scans of the same bone were made during the course of the study to check replicability of the methodology which was found to be within the acceptable range.

Total or diaphyseal length was used to determine the scan sites on the six major long bones of the human body: humerus, radius, ulna, femora, tibia, and fibula (see Figure 1). On

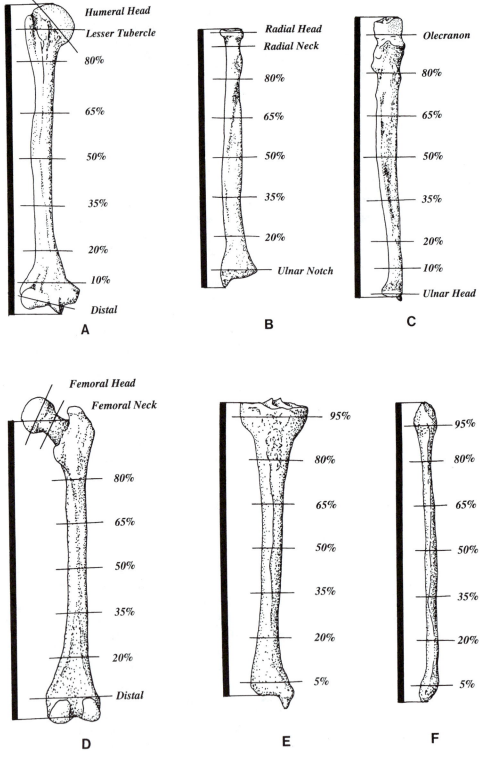

**Figure 1**   Scan locations of the long bones from the modern skeletal series used in this study: humerus (A), radius (B), ulna (C), femur (D), tibia (E), and fibula (F).

each bone, sites at 20-, 35-, 50-, 65-, and 80% of the length, measuring from the distal end, were included. In addition, sites at the distal and proximal ends which conformed to major morphological landmarks were also defined.

At each scan site, the thickness of the bone was measured with sliding calipers. Thickness here is defined as the distance between the top and bottom of the bone as placed during the bone scan. Width of the bone was machine measured during the bone scan. Circumference was taken with a linen tape at the site of each scan. The tape was placed to take minimum circumference and did not adhere to the concave contours of the bone.

The scan locations and positioning in the bone scanner differed, depending on the element. The humerus, radius, ulna were scanned with the anterior surface uppermost. The humeral head was measured through the proximal articular surface near the anatomical neck, with the humeral shaft rotated so the scan included the maximum amount of the head (Figure 1A). The distal end was measured through the distal articular surface (capitulum-trochlea) avoiding the epicondyles; the humerus was angled to maximize this distal measurement. The rest of the measurements were taken perpendicular to the long axis of the humerus shaft. The lesser tubercle was scanned through the midpoint of the tubercle. The other humeral locations were percentages of the maximum length (Martin 1957:532, measurement 1) at the standard points (20-, 35-, 50-, 65-, 80%) with the addition of a 10% site.

For the radius, all scans were taken perpendicular to the long axis of the bone (Figure 1B). The head was scanned through the proximal articular circumference, avoiding the superior articular fovea. The neck was scanned through the narrowest diameter of the neck. And the ulnar articulation was scanned through the midpoint of the height of the ulna articulation. All of the other scan locations were standard proportions based on the maximum length (Martin 1957:535–536, measurement 1).

All ulnar scans were perpendicular to the long axis of the bone (Figure 1C). The olecranon was scanned through the semilunar (trochlear) notch immediately superior to the nonarticular rugosity. The head was scanned through the distal articular circumference. All other scan locations were standard proportions of the physiological length (Martin 1957:539, measurement 2).

The femur was scanned with the posterior surface up except for the distal location. The head was scanned through the proximal articular surface of the head near the neck; the femoral shaft was rotated to expose the maximum of the head (Figure 1D). The neck was scanned through the narrowest diameter of the neck with the shaft angled. The distal end was scanned with the lateral side up, with the scan location immediately superior to the superior margins of the condyle articular surfaces. All other scan locations were standard. Percentages were proportions of the shaft length measured from the most inferior point on the superior margin of the neck to the most superior point on the inferior patellar surface margin.

The tibia, except for the proximal end, was scanned with the posterior surface up. The proximal end was scanned with the lateral surface up. All scan locations were perpendicular to the long axis of the bone at standard locations with the addition of 5% and 95% sites (Figure 1E). Percentages are of physiological length (inferior articular surface to lateral condyle).

The fibula was scanned perpendicular to the long axis with the lateral side up. Scan locations included 5% and 95% locations in addition to the standard sites and were based on the maximum length (Martin 1957:576, measurement 1) (Figure 1F).

## Bone Density Calculations

The machine scan provided results in (1) bone mineral content (BMC): expressed as grams per centimeter; (2) bone width (BW): the width of the bone in centimeters; and (3) bone mineral density (BMD): a calculation of bone mineral density in $g/cm^2$. BMC is calculated assuming a cylindrical bone, which is then size corrected by dividing by the machine-calculated width. This produces the areal density, BMD.

The bone scan sites used in this study are frequently of irregular cross-sectional shape: tall and narrow or wide but thin. The basic machine-generated algorithm assumes perfect cylindrical shape, and bone irregularities could substantially distort the calculated BMD. To cope with this problem, several additional measures have been used:

> **Volume density (VD)** — bone thickness was taken to provide the volume density, a measure already in common use in taphonomic studies in zooarchaeology (viz., Lyman 1982). This measure further divides the density by the thickness of the bone to provide results in grams per cubic centimeter.
>
> **Bone density** by circumference (BMDc) — bone circumference was measured and the BMC was divided by a diameter calculated from the circumference (circumference/3.14).

None of these measures will accurately reflect the distribution of mineral within the bone since they all presume a solid form rather than a hollow cylinder with the possible addition of trabeculae. The relative efficiencies of these different measures in estimating bone mineral density will be discussed below.

Statistical analysis was conducted using SPSS. Basic descriptive statistics, including means and standard deviations, were produced for the overall sample of modern material and then male and female subgroups. Correlations between these various measures of density are expected to be high, since they are derived from the same database. A nonparametric analysis (Mann-Whitney U Test) was conducted to test the significance of differences between sexes, and paired t-tests were used to compare measurements from opposite sides of each individual (Thomas 1986). Correlations and regressions were calculated between age and bone mineral density.

## Results

Tables 2 and 3 provide summary information for the bone mineral density from the modern human samples by the scan locations. The density values are presented by bone, scan location, and side for males and females. The numbers of individuals used at each scan location are also presented. In general, the bones show higher density readings along the diaphysis, particularly in the area of the midshaft. The more proximal and distal diaphyseal sites frequently show some decrease in density. Bone mineral densities of the most distal and proximal portions tend to vary depending upon the morphology of the bone and whether or not articular regions were included within the scan section. Differences related to sex, side, and age are discussed below by bone element. Table 4 presents the significance levels of bone mineral density differences by sex and side.

While bone normally increases or stabilizes during young adult life, bone mass is lost in the later years. Table 5 presents correlations between age and density along with significance levels. Figure 2 presents a scatterplot of the slope and intercept of the regression between BMCc and age where denser bones will have a higher intercept, while those bones showing the greatest loss of bone mineral with age will have a more negative slope value.

The study revealed major differences in the accuracy of estimates of bone mineral density depending on variations in elements' cross-sectional shape (Table 6). For circular bones, both BMD and BMDc provide accurate representations of the cross-sectional area. However, when the bone is oval in cross section, the area derived by BMD and VD calcuations may deviate considerably from the actual area, while the BMDc is approximately equal to this measurement.

**Table 2 Mean Bone Mineral Density Measurements (standard deviation in parentheses) for Upper Limb Bones of Modern Caucasoid Females and Males**

| | Humerus | | | | | | | | |
|---|---|---|---|---|---|---|---|---|---|
| | Distal | 10% | 20% | 35% | 50% | 65% | 80% | Lesser Tubercule | Head |
| **Modern Caucasoid Males** | | | | | | | | | |
| **Right** | | | | | | | | | |
| Number | 22 | 22 | 22 | 22 | 22 | 22 | 22 | 21 | 21 |
| BMD | 0.88 (.15) | 0.78 (.18) | 1.26 (.25) | 1.46 (.31) | 1.36 (.31) | 1.23 (.25) | 0.95 (.17) | 0.76 (.17) | 0.94 (.17) |
| BMDc | 0.94 (.17) | 1.02 (.25) | 1.40 (.26) | 1.37 (.29) | 1.34 (.31) | 1.19 (.26) | 0.92 (.18) | 0.77 (.17) | 0.90 (.15) |
| VD | 0.29 (.05) | 0.38 (.10) | 0.64 (.13) | 0.66 (.14) | 0.59 (.14) | 0.51 (.12) | 0.37 (.09) | 0.14 (.03) | 0.21 (.04) |
| **Left** | | | | | | | | | |
| Number | 21 | 21 | 21 | 21 | 21 | 21 | 21 | 20 | 20 |
| BMD | 0.85 (.16) | 0.77 (.17) | 1.23 (.24) | 1.41 (.29) | 1.31 (.36) | 1.29 (.24) | 0.94 (.17) | 0.74 (.17) | 0.91 (.16) |
| BMDc | 0.91 (.17) | 0.98 (.22) | 1.36 (.25) | 1.34 (.27) | 1.33 (.30) | 1.21 (.24) | 0.92 (.17) | 0.75 (.17) | 0.89 (.15) |
| VD | 0.27 (.05) | 0.37 (.10) | 0.64 (.12) | 0.65 (.14) | 0.57 (.16) | 0.55 (.10) | 0.38 (.08) | 0.14 (.03) | 0.20 (.04) |
| **Modern Caucasoid Females** | | | | | | | | | |
| **Right** | | | | | | | | | |
| Number | 8 | 8 | 8 | 8 | 8 | 8 | 8 | 8 | 8 |
| BMD | 0.67 (.15) | 0.59 (.12) | 0.93 (.18) | 1.05 (.21) | 0.99 (.22) | 0.90 (.22) | 0.75 (.15) | 0.59 (.13) | 0.69 (.13) |
| BMDc | 0.71 (.14) | 0.74 (.16) | 1.01 (.19) | 1.00 (.20) | 0.98 (.23) | 0.89 (.21) | 0.74 (.15) | 0.60 (.13) | 0.66 (.11) |
| VD | 0.25 (.06) | 0.33 (.06) | 0.58 (.13) | 0.61 (.17) | 0.54 (.18) | 0.49 (.16) | 0.40 (.13) | 0.14 (.03) | 0.19 (.04) |
| **Left** | | | | | | | | | |
| Number | 8 | 8 | 8 | 8 | 8 | 8 | 8 | 8 | 8 |
| BMD | 0.64 (.12) | 0.58 (.12) | 0.90 (.14) | 1.03 (.18) | 0.96 (.21) | 0.88 (.22) | 0.75 (.14) | 0.59 (.13) | 0.72 (.12) |
| BMDc | 0.67 (.13) | 0.73 (.16) | 0.96 (.16) | 0.97 (.20) | 0.96 (.21) | 0.88 (.21) | 0.74 (.15) | 0.60 (.13) | 0.67 (.11) |
| VD | 0.20 (.08) | 0.32 (.06) | 0.57 (.11) | 0.58 (.12) | 0.51 (.12) | 0.47 (.13) | 0.40 (.11) | 0.14 (.03) | 0.19 (.03) |

**Table 2 (continued)  Mean Bone Mineral Density Measurements (standard deviation in parentheses) for Upper Limb Bones of Modern Caucasoid Females and Males**

| | | | | Radii | | | | |
|---|---|---|---|---|---|---|---|---|
| | Ulnar Notch | 20% | 35% | 50% | 65% | 80% | Radial Neck | Head |
| **Modern Caucasoid Males** | | | | | | | | |
| Right | | | | | | | | |
| Number | 21 | 22 | 22 | 22 | 22 | 22 | 22 | 21 |
| BMD | 0.59 (.10) | 0.74 (.13) | 0.94 (.14) | 0.95 (.15) | 0.86 (.15) | 0.89 (.20) | 0.66 (.13) | 0.82 (.25) |
| BMDc | 0.61 (.12) | 0.80 (.13) | 0.97 (.14) | 0.99 (.14) | 0.92 (.15) | 0.84 (.18) | 0.63 (.12) | 0.77 (.23) |
| VD | 0.24 (.04) | 0.58 (.11) | 0.77 (.13) | 0.72 (.12) | 0.66 (.12) | 0.60 (.14) | 0.44 (.09) | 0.34 (.10) |
| Left | | | | | | | | |
| Number | 19 | 21 | 21 | 21 | 21 | 21 | 21 | 19 |
| BMD | 0.57 (.10) | 0.73 (.13) | 0.92 (.15) | 0.94 (.15) | 0.86 (.17) | 0.88 (.21) | 0.64 (.13) | 0.81 (.21) |
| BMDc | 0.60 (.11) | 0.79 (.14) | 0.94 (.16) | 0.96 (.16) | 0.90 (.17) | 0.83 (.20) | 0.61 (.12) | 0.75 (.19) |
| VD | 0.24 (.04) | 0.59 (.13) | 0.76 (.13) | 0.73 (.12) | 0.68 (.15) | 0.61 (.16) | 0.41 (.11) | 0.33 (.08) |
| | Ulnar notch | 20% | 35% | 50% | 65% | 80% | Radial Neck | Head |
| **Modern Caucasoid Females** | | | | | | | | |
| Right | | | | | | | | |
| Number | 8 | 8 | 8 | 8 | 8 | 8 | 8 | 8 |
| BMD | 0.45 (.13) | 0.57 (.09) | 0.71 (.11) | 0.72 (.13) | 0.67 (.13) | 0.68 (.16) | 0.52 (.15) | 0.68 (.17) |
| BMDc | 0.47 (.14) | 0.62 (.10) | 0.74 (.15) | 0.76 (.14) | 0.72 (.15) | 0.66 (.16) | 0.50 (.15) | 0.61 (.15) |
| VD | 0.22 (.07) | 0.55 (.10) | 0.72 (.14) | 0.69 (.12) | 0.60 (.12) | 0.52 (.12) | 0.41 (.11) | 0.34 (.08) |
| Left | | | | | | | | |
| Number | 9 | 9 | 9 | 9 | 9 | 9 | 9 | 6 |
| BMD | 0.43 (.10) | 0.57 (.09) | 0.71 (.12) | 0.71 (.12) | 0.65 (.11) | 0.66 (.15) | 0.52 (.12) | 0.68 (.21) |
| BMDc | 0.43 (.10) | 0.63 (.10) | 0.74 (.12) | 0.74 (.12) | 0.71 (.14) | 0.64 (.14) | 0.49 (.12) | 0.62 (.20) |
| VD | 0.21 (.05) | 0.57 (.12) | 0.76 (.15) | 0.72 (.13) | 0.65 (.13) | 0.54 (.12) | 0.41 (.08) | 0.35 (.13) |

Ulnae

## Modern Caucasoid Males

| | Ulnar head | 10% | 20% | 35% | 50% | 65% | 80% | Olecranon |
|---|---|---|---|---|---|---|---|---|
| **Right** | | | | | | | | |
| Number | 22 | 22 | 22 | 22 | 22 | 22 | 22 | 22 |
| BMD | 0.53 (.10) | 0.55 (.12) | 0.77 (.15) | 1.04 (.17) | 1.15 (.19) | 1.14 (.16) | 1.10 (.22) | 0.77 (.13) |
| BMDc | 0.46 (.07) | 0.46 (.09) | 0.72 (.13) | 0.89 (.13) | 0.98 (.12) | 1.08 (.14) | 1.04 (.21) | 0.77 (.16) |
| VD | 0.28 (.05) | 0.37 (.09) | 0.58 (.12) | 0.68 (.11) | 0.67 (.12) | 0.71 (.10) | 0.51 (.12) | 0.37 (.06) |
| **Left** | | | | | | | | |
| Number | 18 | 18 | 19 | 19 | 18 | 19 | 19 | 20 |
| BMD | 0.51 (.07) | 0.53 (.10) | 0.74 (.13) | 1.01 (.14) | 1.10 (.14) | 1.14 (.16) | 1.11 (.20) | 0.73 (.15) |
| BMDc | 0.45 (.07) | 0.45 (.09) | 0.69 (.12) | 0.90 (.12) | 0.97 (.13) | 1.06 (.13) | 1.05 (.17) | 0.73 (.19) |
| VD | 0.26 (.04) | 0.36 (.07) | 0.59 (.10) | 0.68 (.09) | 0.67 (.12) | 0.71 (.11) | 0.51 (.10) | 0.35 (.07) |

## Modern Caucasoid Females

| | Ulnar head | 5% | 20% | 35% | 50% | 65% | 80% | Olecranon |
|---|---|---|---|---|---|---|---|---|
| **Right** | | | | | | | | |
| Number | 6 | 6 | 6 | 6 | 6 | 6 | 6 | 6 |
| BMD | 0.37 (.06) | 0.39 (.10) | 0.54 (.12) | 0.78 (.12) | 0.86 (.13) | 0.82 (.08) | 0.79 (.15) | 0.52 (.10) |
| BMDc | 0.30 (.05) | 0.32 (.09) | 0.51 (.10) | 0.64 (.11) | 0.68 (.12) | 0.78 (.10) | 0.75 (.16) | 0.51 (.09) |
| VD | 0.24 (.06) | 0.29 (.08) | 0.53 (.14) | 0.62 (.12) | 0.58 (.12) | 0.62 (.10) | 0.49 (.15) | 0.31 (.05) |
| **Left** | | | | | | | | |
| Number | 8 | 8 | 8 | 8 | 8 | 8 | 8 | 8 |
| BMD | 0.37 (.07) | 0.41 (.10) | 0.57 (.11) | 0.78 (.13) | 0.87 (.12) | 0.83 (.08) | 0.83 (.15) | 0.58 (.14) |
| BMDc | 0.32 (.07) | 0.35 (.09) | 0.53 (.10) | 0.64 (.12) | 0.68 (.11) | 0.76 (.09) | 0.81 (.15) | 0.57 (.13) |
| VD | 0.23 (.04) | 0.32 (.10) | 0.61 (.15) | 0.66 (.14) | 0.61 (.12) | 0.65 (.09) | 0.48 (.12) | 0.35 (.09) |

**Table 3   Mean Bone Mineral Density Measurements (standard deviation in parentheses) for Lower Limb Bones of Modern Adult Caucasoid Females and Males**

| | Femora | | | | | | | |
|---|---|---|---|---|---|---|---|---|
| | Distal | 20% | 35% | 50% | 65% | 80% | Neck | Head |
| **Modern Caucasoid Males** | | | | | | | | |
| **Right** | | | | | | | | |
| Number | 18 | 20 | 20 | 20 | 20 | 20 | 18 | 18 |
| BMD | 1.33 (.24) | 1.19 (.24) | 1.63 (.29) | 1.90 (.29) | 1.94 (.30) | 1.66 (.32) | 0.94 (.21) | 1.15 (.23) |
| BMDc | 1.09 (.28) | 1.24 (.26) | 1.60 (.28) | 1.79 (.29) | 1.87 (.30) | 1.68 (.34) | 0.95 (.22) | 1.13 (.22) |
| VD | 0.17 (.03) | 0.37 (.07) | 0.53 (.10) | 0.61 (.10) | 0.63 (.10) | 0.54 (.11) | 0.32 (.07) | 0.24 (.04) |
| **Left** | | | | | | | | |
| Number | 17 | 18 | 18 | 18 | 18 | 18 | 18 | 15 |
| BMD | 1.35 (.24) | 1.23 (.21) | 1.68 (.22) | 1.95 (.23) | 1.97 (.26) | 1.70 (.31) | 0.92 (.22) | 1.18 (.21) |
| BMDc | 1.11 (.22) | 1.27 (.22) | 1.64 (.24) | 1.85 (.23) | 1.94 (.25) | 1.74 (.32) | 0.94 (.22) | 1.16 (.21) |
| VD | 0.18 (.03) | 0.38 (.06) | 0.55 (.07) | 0.63 (.08) | 0.65 (.09) | 0.56 (.11) | 0.32 (.08) | 0.24 (.04) |
| | Distal | 20% | 35% | 50% | 65% | 80% | Neck | Head |
| **Modern Caucasoid Females** | | | | | | | | |
| **Right** | | | | | | | | |
| Number | 7 | 7 | 7 | 7 | 7 | 7 | 6 | 7 |
| BMD | 1.06 (.21) | 0.88 (.17) | 1.28 (.26) | 1.60 (.30) | 1.66 (.29) | 1.46 (.27) | 0.77 (.19) | 0.93 (.18) |
| BMDc | 0.84 (.20) | 0.96 (.21) | 1.24 (.23) | 1.46 (.26) | 1.57 (.27) | 1.45 (.28) | 0.78 (.19) | 0.91 (.18) |
| VD | 0.17 (.04) | 0.31 (.07) | 0.46 (.10) | 0.58 (.12) | 0.62 (.11) | 0.57 (.13) | 0.32 (.09) | 0.23 (.05) |
| **Left** | | | | | | | | |
| Number | 6 | 7 | 6 | 7 | 7 | 7 | 6 | 6 |
| BMD | 1.00 (.21) | 0.88 (.19) | 1.24 (.29) | 1.58 (.33) | 1.66 (.33) | 1.43 (.33) | 0.78 (.21) | 1.00 (.17) |
| BMDc | 0.81 (.19) | 0.92 (.20) | 1.19 (.27) | 1.43 (.30) | 1.55 (.30) | 1.42 (.33) | 0.79 (.22) | 0.98 (.17) |
| VD | 0.15 (.04) | 0.31 (.08) | 0.46 (.12) | 0.57 (.13) | 0.63 (.13) | 0.57 (.14) | 0.32 (.11) | 0.25 (.04) |

Tibiae

| | 5% | 20% | 35% | 50% | 65% | 80% | 95% |
|---|---|---|---|---|---|---|---|
| **Modern Caucasoid Males** | | | | | | | |
| **Right** | | | | | | | |
| Number | 21 | 20 | 21 | 21 | 21 | 21 | 19 |
| BMD | 0.89 (.19) | 1.15 (.25) | 1.69 (.29) | 1.76 (.30) | 1.68 (.33) | 1.42 (.37) | 1.22 (.33) |
| BMDc | 0.89 (.21) | 1.12 (.23) | 1.44 (.22) | 1.48 (.24) | 1.39 (.26) | 1.15 (.27) | 0.94 (.23) |
| VD | 0.24 (.05) | 0.47 (.11) | 0.62 (.09) | 0.58 (.08) | 0.49 (.09) | 0.34 (.08) | 0.17 (.05) |
| **Left** | | | | | | | |
| Number | 20 | 21 | 21 | 21 | 21 | 20 | 20 |
| BMD | 0.90 (.18) | 1.17 (.25) | 1.71 (.26) | 1.81 (.27) | 1.71 (.28) | 1.44 (.31) | 1.16 (.25) |
| BMDc | 0.91 (.22) | 1.13 (.23) | 1.46 (.20) | 1.49 (.20) | 1.39 (.22) | 1.15 (.24) | 0.94 (.20) |
| VD | 0.24 (.05) | 0.47 (.11) | 0.63 (.10) | 0.58 (.09) | 0.48 (.08) | 0.35 (.08) | 0.16 (.03) |
| **Modern Caucasoid Females** | | | | | | | |
| **Right** | | | | | | | |
| Number | 6 | 7 | 7 | 7 | 7 | 7 | 7 |
| BMD | 0.65 (.18) | 0.86 (.17) | 1.34 (.20) | 1.46 (.22) | 1.37 (.26) | 1.06 (.29) | 0.89 (.27) |
| BMDc | 0.68 (.21) | 0.84 (.17) | 1.16 (.18) | 1.26 (.19) | 1.16 (.23) | 0.88 (.26) | 0.70 (.20) |
| VD | 0.20 (.05) | 0.39 (.08) | 0.59 (.08) | 0.56 (.09) | 0.47 (.10) | 0.30 (.09) | 0.14 (.04) |
| **Left** | | | | | | | |
| Number | 8 | 8 | 8 | 8 | 8 | 8 | 8 |
| BMD | 0.68 (.16) | 0.88 (.17) | 1.37 (.21) | 1.47 (.27) | 1.40 (.29) | 1.04 (.27) | 1.00 (.40) |
| BMDc | 0.66 (.17) | 0.85 (.17) | 1.19 (.20) | 1.24 (.22) | 1.14 (.23) | 0.89 (.26) | 0.74 (.18) |
| VD | 0.21 (.05) | 0.39 (.07) | 0.55 (.10) | 0.56 (.09) | 0.47 (.09) | 0.29 (.08) | 0.16 (.07) |

**Table 3 (continued)  Mean Bone Mineral Density Measurements (standard deviation in parentheses) for Lower Limb Bones of Modern Adult Caucasoid Females and Males**

Fibulae

| | 5% | 20% | 35% | 50% | 65% | 80% | 95% |
|---|---|---|---|---|---|---|---|
| Modern Caucasoid Males | | | | | | | |
| Right | | | | | | | |
| Number | 19 | 19 | 19 | 19 | 19 | 19 | 15 |
| BMD | 0.56 (.09) | 0.70 (.14) | 0.79 (.12) | 0.79 (.15) | 0.78 (.17) | 0.69 (.18) | 0.44 (.11) |
| BMDc | 0.60 (.11) | 0.73 (.13) | 0.81 (.17) | 0.78 (.20) | 0.78 (.21) | 0.63 (.16) | 0.42 (.13) |
| VD | 0.28 (.05) | 0.66 (.22) | 0.66 (.11) | 0.62 (.12) | 0.68 (.15) | 0.63 (.17) | 0.18 (.05) |
| Left | | | | | | | |
| Number | 19 | 20 | 20 | 20 | 20 | 20 | 18 |
| BMD | 0.53 (.10) | 0.66 (.12) | 0.77 (.12) | 0.76 (.16) | 0.75 (.16) | 0.65 (.14) | 0.38 (.10) |
| BMDc | 0.55 (.10) | 0.70 (.12) | 0.78 (.12) | 0.76 (.20) | 0.73 (.15) | 0.50 (.13) | 0.35 (.11) |
| VD | 0.27 (.05) | 0.65 (.13) | 0.68 (.14) | 0.61 (.14) | 0.64 (.15) | 0.60 (.18) | 0.17 (.05) |
| Modern Caucasoid Females | | | | | | | |
| Right | | | | | | | |
| Number | 6 | 7 | 7 | 7 | 7 | 7 | 7 |
| BMD | 0.44 (.12) | 0.55 (.20) | 0.66 (.15) | 0.64 (.15) | 0.58 (.14) | 0.51 (.15) | 0.30 (.09) |
| BMDc | 0.46 (.11) | 0.54 (.13) | 0.65 (.12) | 0.64 (.13) | 0.60 (.15) | 0.51 (.15) | 0.30 (.08) |
| VD | 0.25 (.06) | 0.58 (.17) | 0.67 (.17) | 0.58 (.15) | 0.56 (.14) | 0.58 (.24) | 0.16 (.05) |
| Left | | | | | | | |
| Number | 6 | 7 | 7 | 7 | 7 | 7 | 6 |
| BMD | 0.38 (.07) | 0.49 (.12) | 0.61 (.12) | 0.61 (.15) | 0.58 (.16) | 0.51 (.16) | 0.31 (.08) |
| BMDc | 0.42 (.08) | 0.53 (.14) | 0.60 (.12) | 0.61 (.14) | 0.59 (.16) | 0.51 (.17) | 0.32 (.08) |
| VD | 0.23 (.05) | 0.58 (.19) | 0.67 (.15) | 0.60 (.17) | 0.59 (.18) | 0.62 (.22) | 0.16 (.05) |

**Table 4 Comparisons of Bone Mineral Density Side Differences by Sex and Sex Differences by Side**

| | Sex Differences | | | Side Differences | | |
|---|---|---|---|---|---|---|
| | BMD | BMDc | VD | BMD | BMDc | VD |
| **Humerus** | | | | | | |
| Distal | ** | ** | * | ns | ns | ns |
| 10% | ** | ** | * | ns | * | * |
| 20% | ** | ** | * | ns | * | ns |
| 35% | ** | ** | * | * | * | ns |
| 50% | ** | ** | * | ns | ns | ns |
| 65% | ** | ** | ns | ns | ns | ns |
| 80% | ** | ** | ns | ns | ns | ns |
| Lesser tubercle | * | * | ns | ns | ns | ns |
| Humeral head | ** | ** | ns | ns | ns | ns |
| **Radius** | | | | | | |
| Ulnar notch | ** | ** | * | ns | ns | ns |
| 20% | ** | ** | ns | ns | ns | ns |
| 35% | ** | ** | ns | ns | ns | ns |
| 50% | ** | ** | ns | ns | ns | ns |
| 65% | ** | ** | ns | ns | ns | * |
| 80% | ** | ** | ns | ns | ns | ns |
| Radial neck | * | * | ns | ns | ns | ns |
| Radial head | * | * | ns | ns | ns | ns |
| **Ulna** | | | | | | |
| Ulnar head | ** | ** | * | ns | ns | ns |
| 10% | ** | ** | * | ns | ns | ns |
| 20% | ** | ** | ns | * | * | ns |
| 35% | ** | ** | ns | * | ns | ns |
| 50% | ** | ** | ns | * | * | ns |
| 65% | ** | ** | ns | ns | * | ns |
| 80% | ** | ** | * | ns | ns | ns |
| Olecranon | ** | ** | * | * | ns | ns |
| **Femur** | | | | | | |
| Distal | ** | * | ns | ns | ns | ns |
| 20% | ** | ** | * | ns | ns | ns |
| 35% | ** | ** | * | ns | ns | * |
| 50% | ** | ** | ns | ns | ns | ns |
| 65% | ** | ** | ns | ns | ns | ns |
| 80% | * | * | ns | ns | ns | ns |
| Femoral neck | ns | ns | ns | ns | ns | ns |
| Femoral head | * | * | ns | ns | ns | ns |
| **Tibia** | | | | | | |
| 5% | ** | ** | ns | ns | ns | ns |
| 20% | ** | ** | * | ns | ns | ns |
| 35% | ** | ** | ns | ns | ns | ns |
| 50% | ** | ** | ns | ns | ns | ns |
| 65% | ** | ** | ns | ns | ns | ns |
| 80% | ** | ** | ns | ns | ns | ns |
| 95% | * | * | ns | ns | ns | ns |
| **Fibula** | | | | | | |
| 5% | ** | ** | ns | ns | ns | ns |
| 20% | ** | ** | ns | ns | ns | ns |
| 35% | ** | ** | ns | ns | ns | ns |
| 50% | ** | * | ns | ns | ns | ns |
| 65% | ** | * | ns | ns | ns | ns |
| 80% | * | ns | ns | ns | ns | ns |
| 95% | * | ns | ns | ns | ns | ns |

*Note:* T scores are paired Ts. Side differences are left-right values, and sex differences are female-male values. Probabilities are two-tailed (* <.05, **<.001).

**Table 5**   Correlation Coefficients and Significance Levels of Density Measurements with Age ($*<.05$, $**<.001$)

| | BMD | BMDc | VD | | BMD | BMDc | VD |
|---|---|---|---|---|---|---|---|
| Humerus | | | | Femur | | | |
| Distal | ns | −.242* | −.347* | Distal | −.399* | −.282* | −.482** |
| 10% | −.372* | −.369* | −.456** | 20% | −.415* | −.400* | −.473** |
| 20% | −.350* | −.344* | −.512** | | | | |
| 35% | −.385** | −.381* | −.585** | 35% | −.398* | −.423** | −.447** |
| 50% | −.472** | −.450** | −.640** | 50% | −.339* | −.275* | −.494** |
| 65% | −.366* | −.478** | −.629** | 65% | −.517* | −.453** | −.540** |
| 80% | −.473** | −.506** | −.661** | 80% | −.377* | −.393* | −.630** |
| Lesser tubercule | −.537** | −.525** | −.672** | Femoral neck | −.609** | −.519** | −.627** |
| Humeral head | −.302* | −.356* | −.448** | Femoral head | −.472** | −.474** | −.536** |
| | | | | | | | |
| Radius | | | | Tibia | | | |
| Ulnar notch | ns | ns | −.378* | 5% | −.301* | −.373* | −.426** |
| 20% | −.391** | −.354* | −.548** | 20% | −.456** | −.476** | −.568** |
| 35% | −.367* | −.324* | −.605** | 35% | −.318* | −.374* | −.431** |
| 50% | −.375** | −.358* | −.634** | 50% | −.357* | −.411** | −.479** |
| 65% | −.370* | −.379** | −.541** | 65% | −.404** | −.500** | −.596** |
| 80% | −.342* | −.369* | −.464** | 80% | −.464** | −.552** | −.636** |
| Radial neck | −.436** | −.458** | −.576** | 95% | −.388* | −.368* | −.463** |
| Radial head | ns | ns | ns | | | | |
| | | | | | | | |
| Ulna | | | | Fibula | | | |
| Ulnar head | ns | ns | −.325* | | | | |
| 10% | −.375* | −.361* | −.611** | 5% | ns | ns | −.384* |
| 20% | −.349* | −.356* | −.551** | 20% | −.452** | −.474** | −.507** |
| 35% | −.322* | −.343* | −.605** | 35% | −.464** | −.377* | −.508** |
| 50% | −.264* | −.253* | −.510** | 50% | −.477** | −.364* | −.549** |
| 65% | ns | ns | −.487** | 65% | −.498** | −.472** | −.606** |
| 80% | −.294* | −.298* | −.501** | 80% | −.491** | −.552** | −.645** |
| Olecranon | ns | ns | −.278* | | −.304* | −.355* | −.460** |

When the bone cross section is triangular, all three measures fail to represent the density per cross-sectional area, although that produced by BMDc is most consistent with the actual value.

In the following section, summaries of the the sex, side, and age comparisons are discussed for each bone. Tables 2 and 3 provide mean values and standard deviations; Tables 4 and 5 refer to the side and age relationships.

## Humerus

Mann-Whitney U-tests show that there are significant differences in bone mineral densities by sex at a majority of sites in the humerus. The least difference is seen with VD in that no significant differences are apparent at the 65%, 80%, lesser tubercle, and humeral head sites. When looking at either BMD and BMDc, however, significant sex differences are observed throughout the bone.

Right and left density readings are highly correlated. Paired t-tests show that, although the mean measures of the left side were consistently lower than the right, there were few statistically significant differences in the density by side. The more distal portions of the humerus do suggest some sidedness, with statistically significant differences at the 10% site (VD and BMDc), the 20% site (BMDc), and the 35% site (BMD and BMDc). This is probably a product of relatively greater thickness and circumference in the distal portion of the left humeri. This would increase the differences in the relative density readings in these areas by distributing the bone mineral over a larger area while compacting the mineral in the right humerus.

Significant age-dependent changes in density are seen at all scan sites in the humerus, with the exception of the most distal, articular site, where there is a nonsignificant trend toward decreased bone density with the BMD measure. The width, thickness, and circumference measures show significant increases with age at the diaphyseal sites. This suggests either that bone mineral content is stable but being utilized to form an increasingly wider bone, or that bone size is increasing as bone mineral content is decreasing.

## Radius

Sex differences in the radius occur at all sites in the BMD or BMDc density measures. The VD measure produced no significant differences between the sexes except at the most distal site, adjacent to the ulnar notch.

Paired t-tests of side differences in mean bone mineral densities revealed little evidence of density differences. The only statistically significant difference was produced with the VD at the 65% site ($p < .01$). As with the humerus, strong correlations exist between paired elements' density readings at each site.

Age-dependent changes appear throughout the diaphysis of the radius. At the articular ends (ulnar notch and radial head), age differences are not evident, with the exception of some suggestion at the distal end with the VD measurement. As with the humerus, bone thickness and circumference show a significant positive correlation with age. The bone width is also positively and significantly correlated at most of the diaphyseal sites, increasing with older ages, with the exception of the 80% site.

## Ulna

With both BMD and BMDc measures, ulnae show sexual dimorphism in density at all sites. In contrast, VD shows no evident dimorphism in most of the diaphyseal sites, although significant differences by sex are seen at the ulnar head, 5% and 80% sites, and olecranon.

As with the other bones of the upper limb, there are few statistically significant differences by side in the ulna. Both BMD and BMDc show some statistically significant diaphyseal differences, and the olecranon is different when measured as BMD.

Decreases in bone density correlate with age at most sites; however, the correlation coefficients tend to be weaker than those in the humerus and radius. No changes are seen at the ulnar head using the areal measures, BMD or BMDc. Similarly, no change is seen at the olecranon process and the 65% site using either of these two values. None of the bone size measures show any increase at the olecranon, but both thickness and circumference increase with age at all other sites. Bone width also increases with age along most of the element, including the distal end.

## Femur

BMD and BMDc reveal statistically significant differences by sex at the 5% through 80% diaphyseal and femoral head sites. In contrast, neither measure shows any statistically significant difference at the femoral neck. The VD values are only significantly different between males and females at the 20% and 35% sites.

Side differences are not evident in paired t-tests of this material. The only value reaching statistical significance is the VD measure at the 35% site. Right and left values are highly correlated, as is expected.

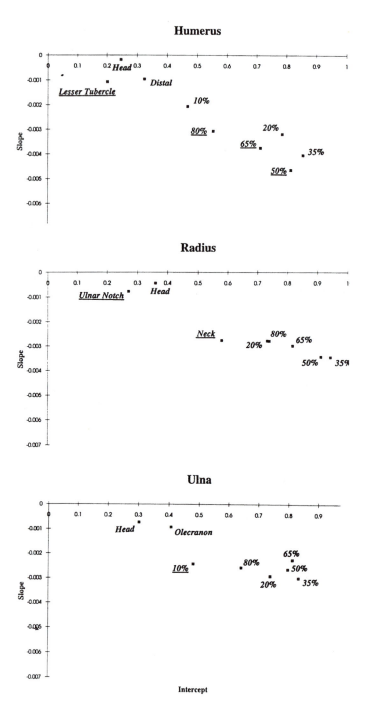

**Figure 2** Plot of the slope and intercept from the correlation of BMDc with age in the modern skeletal series. Statistical significance of correlation indicated by underline.

All three density measures show significant changes with age. By contrast, no significant increases occur in bone width, thickness, or circumference with age. This indicates that bone mineral density decreases in the older adult are primarily due to simple losses in bone mineral content through endosteal resorption without subperiosteal expansion.

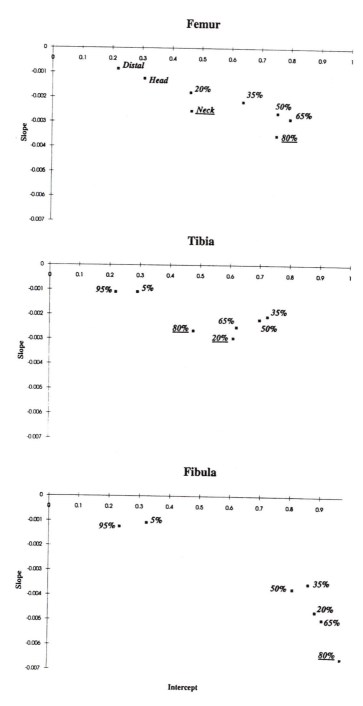

**Figure 2 (continued)**

## Tibia

The BMD and BMDc values show statistically significant differences between males and females at all sites. The VD value at the 20% site is significantly different, although the other sites do not differ in this measure.

**Table 6  Schematic Representation of Area Discrepancies Depending Upon the Cross-sectional Shape of the Bone When Calculating Bone Mineral Density by BMD, VD, and BMCc given a BMC = 1.5 gm/cm**

| Bone Shape | Dimension | Real | BMD | VD | BMDc |
|---|---|---|---|---|---|
| ⬭ (circle) | Width | 1.25 | 1.25 | 1.25 | 1.25 |
| | Thickness | 1.25 | 1.25 | 1.25 | 1.25 |
| | Diameter | 1.25 | 1.25 | 1.56 | 1.25 |
| | Bone Density | 1.20 | 1.20 | 0.96 | 1.20 |
| | **% of Actual** | | **100%** | **80%** | **100%** |
| ⬭ (wide ellipse) | Width | 1.25 | 1.25 | 1.25 | 0.93 |
| | Thickness | 0.60 | 1.25 | 0.60 | 0.93 |
| | Diameter | 0.93 | 1.25 | 0.75 | 0.93 |
| | Bone Density | 1.61 | 1.20 | 2.00 | 1.61 |
| | **% of Actual** | | **74%** | **124%** | **100%** |
| ⬭ (tall ellipse) | Width | 0.60 | 0.60 | 0.60 | 0.93 |
| | Thickness | 1.25 | 0.60 | 1.25 | 0.93 |
| | Diameter | 0.93 | 0.60 | 0.75 | 0.93 |
| | Bone Density | 1.61 | 2.50 | 2.00 | 1.61 |
| | **% of Actual** | | **155%** | **124%** | **100%** |
| △ (triangle) | Width | 1.25 | 1.25 | 1.25 | 0.95 |
| | Thickness | 0.60 | 1.25 | 0.60 | 0.95 |
| | Diameter | 0.97 | 1.25 | 0.75 | 0.95 |
| | Bone Density | 1.54 | 1.20 | 2.00 | 1.58 |
| | **% of Actual** | | **78%** | **130%** | **102%** |

No side differences are apparent in this sample in any of the three density values tested. Right and left side density values are highly correlated.

All three measurements at all the tibial sites display age-dependent decreases in bone density at statistically significant levels. Neither bone thickness nor bone width shows any significant increase with age. Only increase in bone circumference at the 5% site reaches statistical significance among the size measurements.

## Fibula

The distal portions differ significantly between the sexes on both BMD and BMDc measures through the 65% site. The proximal portions of the fibula are significantly different using the BMD, but not for the BMDc. None of the VD values reveal any notable difference between males and females.

Side differences for the fibula are not statistically significant. With one exception, density readings for the fibula show statistically significant negative correlations with age. The only exception is at the the most distal site, where BMD or BMDc reflect no change. The changes in bone size associated with age noted in the upper limb are again evident in the fibula, where statistically significant increases in thickness, width and circumference are seen. These changes are irregular throughout the bone, with bone width only increasing in the distal half, circumference increasing in all but the midshaft site, and thickness increasing at the 5, 35, 65, and 80% sites.

## Discussion

Studies on contemporary human populations, although primarily limited to those bone regions of clinical importance, can be used to validate the data produced in this project. The BMDs, when compared by sex and element side, are generally comparable to the results of other studies. Sumner (1984) measured the femora from the Grasshopper Pueblo site using both single-photon absorptiometry and computed tomography. He found a BMD range of 0.76 to 1.33 at the this 20% site, 0.97 to 1.62 at the 35% site, 1.11 to 1.74 at the 50% site, 1.14 to 1.66 at the 65% site, 1.01 to 1.47 at the 80% site, and 0.62 to 1.11 at the femoral neck for combined sexes. The results of the present study suggest that the midshaft regions of our study collection have substantially higher bone densities than the Grasshopper sample, while the proximal and distal ends are similar. In part this may be due to differences in measurement technique, particularly in the locations of the scan sites. Favus (1993) reports density measures of the proximal femur ranging from 0.633 to 0.995 g/cm$^2$ for females aged 20 to 60, and 0.699 to 1.089 for males of the same age range. These overlap well with our results for the femoral neck.

Some differences among results of different studies are to be expected, given variation in skeletal series and methodology. Side differences (Tables 2 and 3) in the upper limbs have greater BMDs on the right than the left, while the side differences of the lower limb are mixed. Similar results have been found in individuals who do not partake in heavy physical activity, where differences of up to 2 to 7% are found (Smith and Gilligan 1989). Unfortunately, handedness data were not available on the present study sample.

As in other studies (National Institutes of Health 1984), statistically significant sex differences in BMDs exist. The pattern seen in clinical studies of females is one in which bone mass is accumulated during adolescence and early adulthood, peaking in the mid-thirties, slightly earlier than is found in males (Stini 1990). Even at peak values, however, the mean values for females are significantly lower than males. Following the menopause, there is a period of 8 to 10 years in which women lose an additional 2 to 3%/yr of their cortical bone and up to 8%/yr of their trabecular bone (Riggs and Melton 1986).

### Forensic and Archaeological Implications

The major contribution of this paper is that it provides density values at a number of points along the long bones which may be applied to the differential survival with both forensic material (Galloway et al. 1991) and archaeological material (Willey et al. in prep.). However, there are multiple factors which must be considered in applying these values to a skeletal series. These can be roughly divided into intrinsic and extrinsic factors: those inherent to the bone and bone structure, and those due to environmental factors (Table 7). Among the intrinsic factors, other studies have demonstrated that density is but one factor affecting bone survival. Also important are mass, shape, and composition (e.g., cortical:trabecular ratio). Environmental factors such as exposure, transport, carnivore damage, and burial degradation interact with these to result in differential bone survival.

Boaz and Behrensmeyer's study (1976) utilized wet weight of various skeletal elements, calculating density from weight in air and water. Element portions were then tested for movement in a controlled stream flow. In the six long bone portions tested, there is little correlation between density and movement. Morden (1991) in her study on water transport of human remains concluded that the effects of density and mass differ. Bones weighing less than 10 g are almost always transported by water, while only in those over 10 g does density become an important factor. In heavier specimens, shape is important in determining transport. Spherical bones move easily while slender (long) bones are less likely to be moved.

**Table 7    Extrinsic and Intrinsic Factors Involved in Degradation of Skeletal Material**

| Intrinsic Factors | Extrinsic Factors |
|---|---|
| Bone density | Exposure to sunlight |
| Overall morphology | Water transportation |
| Bone mass | Humidity fluctuations |
| Trabecular/cortical components | Soil compaction |
| Bone microanatomy | Acidity/alkalinity of soil |
| Trace element composition | Percolation of liquids |
| Pathological defects | Insect activity |
| Traumatic defects | Carnivore damage |
| | Rodent damage |
| | Trampling |
| | Vegetation and fungal invasion |
| | Excavation damage |
| | Cleaning damage |
| | Curation damage |
| | Analysis damage |

Cylindrical bones do not align with water and move slowly in the water. Bone size is important in differential destruction by carnivores, while density is less important than absolute size. The present study also suggests that density may be important for determining those long bone segments which will be recovered, since the combination of dense bone within a cylindrical form apparently restricts water transport.

This study highlights the need to recognize variation due to other factors including sex, handedness, and age. While density is an important factor in bone transport and survival, within any skeletal assemblage those bones belonging to individuals with lesser mineral accumulation will be most prone to loss.

These intrinsic factors will also interact with the environmental factors which have been documented as affecting bone survival. Haglund (Haglund et al. 1989; Haglund 1991) proposed a sequence of carnivore consumption/disarticulation for scavenged human remains begining with the visceral cavities, followed by removal of the lower limbs and the attached pelvic girdle. Finally, there is disarticulation of the entire skeleton with the exception of the vertebral column. The bones then are more widely scattered. Of the skeletonized and dispersed remains from forensic cases, he reports the most frequent recovered long bones are the femora (61%), followed by the tibiae (50%), fibulae (50%), humeri (42%), radii (38%), and ulnae (25%).

Midshaft densities, in the present study sample rank the elements from the most to least dense as femora, tibiae, humeri, radii, ulnae, and fibulae. This roughly parallels the findings of Haglund, but with a striking anomaly in the recovery of fibulae. The similar forensic recovery of the lower leg elements suggests that these bones act as a unit through at least a portion of the taphonomic processing. The strong ligaments linking these bones and the distance of the proximal tibiofibular joint from the knee may provide resistance to detachment. Observations by Snyder in studies of wolves devouring deer carcasses show that these bones are treated as one, with the majority of gnawing occurring at the joints. This argument is supported by consistent recovery of both tibiae and fibulae in other stages of disarticulation as reported by Haglund (1991), suggesting that carnivores most probably attack the knee joint and are thus able to detach the lower leg as a unit. The two bones will only become separate at such time as dermestid or other insect activity degrades the ligamentous attachments.

Density also plays a role in survival of buried bones. Most often noted in excavated burial remains is the low recovery of the smaller or thinner bones (Waldron 1987). Even relatively dense bones, however, may be well below expected recovery levels. Fungal invasions of bones have been recorded (Hackett 1981), resulting in early demineralization of the bone. Leaching of mineral and infiltration of the bone with soil components are also a constant occurrence once burial has occurred (Garland 1987). The relative effect of these on subsequent survival needs to be assessed.

The ultimate goal of inquiries into survivorship of skeletal material is ability to reconstruct the events and develop an understanding of the people who constitute the skeletal series. In mass graves or cemetery series remains are no longer segregated within discrete individual graves, which complicates the problem of determining the size of the series. When multiple, commingled human remains are recovered, determination of the minimum number of individuals (MNI) depends upon selection of the appropriate element for assessment. The present study suggests that the effect of age within the adult population must be considered in the choice of location for element counts in determining MNI. Determination of MNI is of particular importance to forensic and physical anthropologists and mortuary archaeologists. In contrast to the minimum number of elements (MNE), which is useful in reconstructing food consumption patterns from faunal remains, MNI provides the basis for preliminary identification as well as demographic reconstructions (mortality and survivorship curves, life tables, and population size).

Some portions of long bones are relatively dense but, with increasing age, experience rapid loss of bone mass. In those skeletal series in which a large number of elderly individuals are represented, it is possible that a portion of the older individuals will be excluded in the minimal number count due to disproportionate loss of these bone segments. Age biases in burial populations previously have been attributed to differences in calcification. Walker et al. (1988) noted that not only were immature individuals minimally preserved in a cemetery series, but that the elderly also were poorly preserved. The results of the present study provide a quantitatively based model with which to assess whether this can be attributed to density alone or other changes in bone structure.

## Conclusion

This study presents data which can be tested against forensic and archaeological skeletal collections. Patterns of damage due to exposure, transport, carnivores, and burial, as well as recovery, may interact with intrinsic factors such as density. While other intrinsic factors may play a role in bone survival, the present study provides a baseline density series from which we can begin to assess the impact of these factors.

## Acknowledgments

The contemporary skeletal material was collected and made available through the kindness of Dr. William M. Bass. Funds for the densitometer and radioactive source were provided by the Wenner-Gren Foundation for Anthropological Research (Grant No. 5251), and Ms. Pam Poe, University of Tennessee, Knoxville, oversaw their administration. Funds to aid manuscript preparation were provided to Willey through the Summer Scholars program by the CSUC University Foundation. We would like to thank Diane Gifford-Gonzalez, Judith Habicht-Mauche, Richard L. Jantz, and Charles Miksicek for editorial assistance.

## References

Binford, L.R., and J.B. Bertram
   1977    Bone Frequencies and Attritional Processes. In *Theory Building in Archaeology*, edited by L.R. Binford, pp. 77–153. Academic Press, New York.

Boaz, N.J., and A.K. Behrensmeyer
1976   Hominid Taphonomy: Transport of Human Skeletal Parts in an Artificial Fluvial Environment. *American Journal of Physical Anthropology* 45:53–60.

Brain, C.K.
1967   Hottentot Food Remains and Their Bearing on the Interpretation of Fossil Bone Assemblages. *Scientific Papers of the Namib Desert Research Station* 32:1–11.

Cameron, J.R., and J. Sorenson
1963   Measurement of Bone Mineral *In Vivo*: An Improved Method. *Science* 142:230–232.

Cohn, S.H., C. Abesamis, S. Yasumura, J.F. Aloia, I. Zanzi, and K.J. Ellis
1977   Comparative Skeletal Mass and Radial Bone Mineral Content in Black and White Women. *Metabolism, Clinical and Experimental* 26:171–178.

Favus, M.J.
1993   Bone Density Reference Data. In *Primer on the Metabolic Bone Diseases and Disorders of Mineral Metabolism*, 2nd ed., edited by M.J. Favus, pp. 426–430. Raven Press, New York.

Galloway, A., P. Willey, and L. Snyder
1991   Bone Density Determinants of Carnivore Scavenging and Bone Survival. Paper presented at the 43rd Annual Meeting of the American Academy of Forensic Sciences, Anaheim, CA.

Garland, A.N.
1987   A Histological Study of Archaeological Bone Decomposition. In *Death, Decay and Reconstruction: Approaches to Archaeology and Forensic Science,* edited by A. Boddington, A.N. Garland, and R.C. Janaway, pp.109–126. Manchester University Press, Manchester, U.K.

Hackett, C.J.
1981   Microscopical Focal Destruction (Tunnels) in Exhumed Human Bones. *Medicine, Science and the Law* 21(4):243–265.

Haglund, W.D.
1991   *Applications of Taphonomic Models to Forensic Investigations.* Ph.D. dissertation, Department of Anthropology, University of Washington, Seattle. University Microfilms, Ann Arbor, MI.

Haglund, W.D., D.T. Reay, and D.R. Swindler
1989   Canid Scavenging/Disarticulation Sequence of Human Remains in the Pacific Northwest. *Journal of Forensic Sciences* 34:587–606.

Henderson, J.
1987   Factors Determining the State of Preservation of Human Remains. In *Death, Decay and Reconstruction: Approaches to Archaeology and Forensic Science,* edited by A. Boddington, A.N. Garland, and R.C. Janaway, pp.43–54. Manchester University Press, Manchester, U.K.

Lyman, R.L.
1982   *The Taphonomy of Vertebrate Archaeofaunas: Bone Density and Differential Survival of Fossil Classes.* Ph.D. dissertation, Department of Anthropology, University of Washington, Seattle. University Microfilms, Ann Arbor, MI.
1984   Bone Density and Differential Survivorship of Fossil Classes. *Journal of Anthropological Archaeology* 3:259–299.

Martin, R.
1957   *Lehrbuch der Anthropologie*, Vol. 3. 3rd ed. Gustav Fischer, Stuttgart.

MacDonald, R.
1991   *Quantitative Effects of Skeletonizing Processes on Bone Density.* Master's thesis, University of Tennessee, Knoxville.

Morden, J.L.
1991 *Hominid Taphonomy: Density, Fluvial Transport, and Carnivore Consumption of Human Remains with Application to Three Plio/Pleistocene Hominid Sites.* Ph.D. dissertation, State University of New Jersey, Rutgers. University Microfilms, Ann Arbor, MI.

National Institutes of Health
1984 Osteoporosis. *NIH Concensus Dev/Conf. Stat.* No. 5. Washington, D.C.

Nelson, D.A., M. Feingold, F. Bolin, and A.M. Parfitt
1991 Principal Components Analysis of Regional Bone Density in Black and White Women: Relationship to Body Size and Composition. *American Journal of Physical Anthropology* 86:507–514.

Riggs, B.L., and L.J. Melton
1986 Involutional Osteoporosis. *New England Journal of Medicine* 314:1676–1686.

Smith, E.L., and C. Gilligan
1989 Mechanical Forces and Bone. *Bone and Mineral Research* 6:139–173.

Stini, W.A.
1990 "Osteoporosis": Etiologies, Prevention, and Treatment. *Yearbook of Physical Anthropology* 33:151–194.

Stini, W., P. Stein, and Z. Chen
1992 Bone Remodeling in Old Age: Longitudinal Monitoring in Arizona. *American Journal of Human Biology* 4(1):47–55.

Sumner, D.R.
1984 *Size, Shape and Bone Mineral Content of the Human Femur in Growth and Aging.* Ph.D. dissertation, University of Arizona, Tucson. University Microfilms, Ann Arbor, MI.

Thomas, D.H.
1986 *Refiguring Anthropology: First Principles of Probability and Statistics.* Holt, Rhinehart & Winston, New York.

U.S. Department of Health and Human Services, Public Health Service
1986 Single Photon Absorptiometry for Measuring Bone Mineral Density. *Health Technology Assessment Reports*, No. 7. Washington, D.C.

Waldron, T.
1987 The Relative Survival of the Human Skeleton: Implications for Palaeopathology. In *Death, Decay and Reconstruction: Approaches to Archaeology and Forensic Science* edited by A. Boddington, A.N. Garland, and R.C. Janaway, pp. 55–64. Manchester University Press, Manchester, U.K.

Walker, P.L., J.R. Johnson, and P.M. Lambert
1988 Age and Sex Biases in the Preservation of Human Skeletal Remains. *American Journal of Physical Anthropology* 76:183–188.

Wasnich, R.D., P.D. Ross, L.K. Heilbrun, and J.M. Vogel
1985 Prediction of Postmenopausal Fracture Risk with Use of Bone Mineral Measurements. *American Journal of Obstetrics and Gynecology* 153:745–751.

Willey, P., A. Galloway, and L. Snyder
In preparation   Human Bone Mineral Densities and Survival of Bone Elements. Part II: The Crow Creek Massacre Victims. Ms. in possession of authors.

# Cranial Bone Displacement as a Taphonomic Process in Potential Child Abuse Cases

20

THOMAS A.J. CRIST
ARTHUR WASHBURN
HYDOW PARK
IAN HOOD
MOLLY A. HICKEY

## Introduction

Since 1962, when the term "battered child" was first used, pathologists have been interested in the correlation between skull fracture characteristics and head injury mechanisms (Child Accident Prevention Foundation of Australia 1983; Dudley et al. 1993; Duhaine et al. 1987; Harwood-Nash et al. 1971; Hobbs 1984). This research has focused solely on antemortem and perimortem head trauma and has not explored the effects of the postmortem environment on the bones of the immature cranium. The extent to which the effects of taphonomic processes are misidentified as antemortem or perimortem trauma to the head has been generally unrecognized. Through their experience and familiarity with skeletonized human remains, forensic physical anthropologists can provide significant contributions to understanding cranial injuries in children and infants, particularly diagnostic criteria to distinguish antemortem trauma from normal skeletal variants and postmortem lesions.

The analysis of historic and prehistoric burials often yields information on human skeletal biology that is directly applicable to osteological materials recovered from forensic contexts. The literature on human skeletal paleopathology is especially relevant. Physical anthropologists and bioarchaeologists who study ancient human remains deal with the results of taphonomic processes frequently, and recognize many of the effects that postmortem interactions can exert on human remains of medicolegal significance.

While the number of child abuse cases reported in the United States continues to increase, the skeletal remains of children comprise the smallest percentage of forensic cases with which physical anthropologists are involved. Stewart (1979) and Krogman and Işcan (1986) have both commented on the paucity of forensic cases involving children. Subadults also constitute a relatively small proportion of the remains recovered from archaeological sites, since children are often buried in separate graveyards or in selected areas set aside for them in cemeteries and family plots. Subadult remains are also more susceptible to postinterment deterioration and rodent disturbance and scattering (Haglund 1992). Consequently, the effects of taphonomic processes acting on subadult remains have not been thoroughly documented. It is likely that these processes vary in terms of type, degree, and appearance when compared to changes observed in adult remains. As with the remains of adults, gross taphonomic changes of skeletal material from children may masquerade as perimortem trauma, thus potentially yielding false conclusions about the cause and manner of death.

Despite the small number of subadult remains from forensic contexts available for analysis, physical anthropologists can draw on the relatively larger number of subadult crania that have been disinterred from historic and prehistoric burial grounds to document the full range of taphonomic effects found in most necroenvironments. Archaeological specimens manifest the additional advantage of diachronicity or time depth; once the dates of the interments in a cemetery assemblage are established, the long-term results of different taphonomic processes can be assessed across a variety of postmortem temporal stages.

The most common factors on which forensic taphonomic studies have been based include manner of body preparation, coffin and casket types, locational aspects of deposition, season of death, and environmental conditions (Berryman et al. 1991; Cotton et al. 1987; Galloway et al. 1989; Mann et al. 1990; Micozzi 1986). These studies have typically been limited to the remains of adults. However, archaeological assemblages provide opportunities to document the differential effects of the same taphonomic processes on the remains of both adults and children.

This chapter illustrates the application of information gathered from the osteological analysis of subadults from archaeological sites to account for distortions observed in the crania of children recovered from crime scenes. We view the phenomenon of cranial bone displacement as a taphonomic process that affects immature remains due to environmental factors, and present two cases where the effects of these processes could have been misidentified as the result of perimortem trauma to the head.

## Development of the Immature Cranium and Pseudotrauma

The variety of taphonomic processes that affect human remains often results in a number of different modifications to the fresh and dry hard tissues of the same individual. While the constitution of human bone is generally constant, different skeletal elements vary in their internal architecture, reflecting the assorted functions they serve. This structural variability results in a considerable range of resistance to the array of possible taphonomic forces to which bones may be subjected. The primary factor which seems to determine the durability of skeletal elements is the amount of bony tissue per unit volume (Gifford 1981); for instance, cortical or compact bone appears to resist localized stress better than cancellous or trabecular bone, and by extension, thicker compact bone is more resistant to damage than is thin compact bone. Thus, different skeletal elements from the same body, and sometimes different segments of the same bone, present dissimilar postmortem transformations (Brain 1967, 1976; Nordin and Frankel 1989). This differential resistance to taphonomic change is even more marked when adult skeletal remains are compared to those from immature individuals, due to the significantly lower percentage of calcified bone in infants and children.

Fetal osteology has emerged as a separate subfield of study based on the recognition that the bones of the fetus exhibit different morphological features from those of infants and young children (Fazekas and Kósa 1978; Kósa 1986). In the skull, bones develop either by direct ossification in mesenchymal tissues or indirectly in cartilage. In humans, the roof and sides of the neurocranium (cranial vault) arise from membranes of mesenchyme, while the base is developed from cartilage (Moss 1955; Moss et al. 1956). The neurocranium appears at about the 30th day *in utero*, and consists of curved plates of mesenchyme which extend superiorly as development progresses. As illustrated in a very rare case of bilateral absence, these plates may not appear even as the frontal, temporals, and occipital develop normally (Dunn et al. 1991). Chondrification of the base of the cranium begins in the second fetal month. Growth of the cranial bones occurs at the sutures through biochemical tissue interactions rather than biomechanical forces, since the presence of dura mater is essential for suture patency but not for initial suture formation (Opperman et al. 1993). Thus, the presence of dura mater is necessary for the sutures to resist ossification and allow functional movement during birth and early brain development.

The skull of the full term fetus contains the same individual bones as the adult, although the proportions and articulations differ significantly. For instance, in the fetal cranium the ratio of the neurocranium to the viscerocranium (the cranial portions of the respiratory and digestive tracts) is 8:1, but is only 3:1 in the adult (Berkovitz and Moxham 1989). This is because the brain grows to 50% of its adult weight in the first 6 months of life and then expands rapidly, so that by the 3rd year the brain reaches 80% of adult weight. Between the ages of 5 to 8 years, the brain grows to 90% of the adult size (Enlow 1990; Martin 1989). The structures of the dentition and associated muscles are responsible for the remainder of cranial growth, which takes place through remodeling and displacement until age 13 in females and into early adulthood in males (Enlow 1990; McKern and Stewart 1957; Steele and Bramblett 1988). About 90% of adult facial height and 84% of bizygomatic width are typically reached by 5 years of age (Lowe 1952).

At birth, many of the bones of the cranial vault are fully formed but incomplete. Approximately 110 ossification centers are present in the fetal skull, which reduce to 45 separate bones by birth (Marshall 1979). Hence, ossification defects and sutures not present in the adult cranium may be mistaken for fractures (Kósa 1986). For instance, the occipital bone in a newborn consists of four portions: the squama, basioccipital, and two exoccipitals that fuse together between the 2nd and 6th years of life. The squama and basioccipital exhibit different growth parameters (Olivier 1975), and the line of union (sutura mendosa) between the upper and lower portions of the squama, present at birth, may be misinterpreted as an antemortem cranial fracture (Sorg and Sweeney 1993). The longitudinal fissure present in the superior portion of the squama occipitalis at birth may also be misidentified as a fracture by those not familiar with the morphology of the immature occiput.

Sutures in other undeveloped neurocranial bones may also be misclassified. Occasionally, these sutures persist into adulthood and may be misinterpreted both grossly and in radiographs as fractures in various states of healing. The frontal, which at birth consists of two halves articulated by the sutura interfrontalis, may persist as two bones through adulthood, articulated superior to the nasals along the midline by the metopic suture. This persistent suture, which can occur in up to 11 to 16% of Europeans and Asian Indians and at lower frequencies among East Asians and Africans, is occasionally misclassified as a traumatic lesion in cranial specimens (Hauser and DeStefano 1989). Although prevalent in much lower frequencies, several other persistent sutures may occur in immature and adult crania, which may be misidentified as the result of trauma. With a frequency of less than 1%, os parietale partitum or divided parietal bone may result from either a horizontal suture that connects the lambdoid and coronal sutures or a vertical suture that traverses the bone from the sagittal suture to the squamosal suture at the temporal (Hauser and DeStefano 1989). Bipartite temporal squama, also found in very low frequencies, results when an approximately horizontal or very rarely a vertical suture (sutura squamosa) divides the temporal squama partially or completely (Hauser and DeStefano 1989). Representing incomplete fusion of the three ossification centers of the temporal, this epigenetic trait is found in both sexes and at all ages, and has been associated with the occurrence of wormian bones in the lambdoid suture.

Sutures and fissures unique to fetal and juvenile crania represent normal skeletal features that are predominantly under genetic control. Together with epigenetic anomalous traits, these features represent one category of morphological characteristics that can be easily misidentified as the result of head trauma in suspected child abuse cases. Another category, postmortem lesions, can similarly be misidentified since they are often influenced by the structure of the developing cranial bones and the physical properties associated with the architecture of the neurocranium.

In the newborn, the bones of the calvaria are separated by six membranous fontanelles, which typically reduce to sutures by the 18th month (Enlow 1990). The sutures of the fetal cranium are relatively nonjagged, and become more serrated as adolescence and adulthood are attained. The fibrous joints (synarthroses) of the cranium include serrated, denticulate, squamous, and plane sutures, all of which provide the head a high degree of resistance to shearing and torsional forces (Marshall 1979). Serrated sutures like the sagittal and coronal exhibit edges similar to the teeth of a saw and are notched superiorly and inferiorly at the junctions. Denticulate sutures are characterized by small, toothlike projections that widen toward their free ends. This type of suture, an example of which is the lambdoid, is similar to a dovetail joint and provides a stronger and more effective union than does a serrated suture (Williams et al. 1989). Joined by sutural ligament and periosteum, these sutures are almost completely immobile. Squamous sutures, like those that articulate the temporals and parietals, join two reciprocally beveled bones that overlap, allowing for some degree of movement. The beveled edges may be ridged or serrated (limbous sutures) and are also practically immovable. Plane sutures include those that are joined along contiguous irregular surfaces, which, even though not serrated, provide stability and strength when combined with sutural ligament. Examples of plane sutures are those that join the nasals, palatines, and maxillae as well as the sutures of the hard palate.

The cortices of the immature cranium are thin and comprise only a single layer, lacking a diplöe. By the 6th year, the structure of the cranial bones constitutes a "sandwich" in which hemopoietic red bone marrow fills the trabecular space between internal and external tables of compact bone. Red marrow, which is found throughout the skeleton at birth and is gradually replaced in the long bones by yellow adipose marrow, is essential for the development of red blood cells and the synthesis of hemoglobin (Williams et al. 1989). The walls of the cranium vary in thickness but tend to be thinner where covered by muscles. The inner table is thin and relatively brittle, while the outer table is more dense and maintains a greater resiliency to biomechanical and traumatic forces.

While the processes that affect subadult remains are no doubt variable and complex, we believe that the immature neurocranium exhibits a consistent response to at least two different taphonomic forces: solar exposure and fluctuations in ambient temperature and humidity. This response, cranial bone displacement, is a process closely related to the structure of the developing bones of the vault, which are thin in relation to their large surface areas and are therefore easily altered by various external forces (Kósa 1986). Since the sutures in the skull do not begin to fuse until adolescence, trauma to the head usually results in a separation of the cranial bones along the suture lines, rather than a fracture (Snow and Luke 1970). In cases involving a blow to the head, the impacted bone is depressed and lies below the plane of its adjacent bones. Conversely, in cranial bone displacement the affected bone is separated along its sutures but is elevated above the plane of the cranial surface, as if forced outward from internal pressure. This appearance may be misinterpreted as acute brain swelling or the result of a coup–contrecoup response to blunt force trauma.

In this chapter two cases are described in which the process of bone displacement was observed in subadult crania from forensic contexts. In both cases the observed alterations were inconsistent with lesions expected as a result of antemortem or perimortem trauma. Comparisons made with subadult crania recovered from archaeological sites suggested that the observed neurocranial alterations were caused by taphonomic processes, specifically from postmortem warping. The cases are similar in that both involved suspected homicides, and therefore shared a common manner of death. In each case the gross taphonomic changes of the cranium could have been mistaken for perimortem trauma, but recognition of the taphonomic processes involved avoided misclassification of the respective causes of death.

# Case Histories

## Case 1

Cranial bone displacement in subadult skeletal remains was first described by Snow and Luke (1970) in their report on the Oklahoma City Child Disappearances of 1967. The partial remains of a 6-year-old girl were recovered from a shallow depression under thick underbrush on an abandoned farm outside Oklahoma City. The girl had disappeared on August 3, 1967, and her remains were recovered almost 4 months later, near the end of November. Snow and Luke observed an elevation of the left parietal with associated separations of the sagittal and left coronal sutures. The separation of the coronal suture was 6 mm wide at bregma, while the sagittal separation was 4 mm in width. The left squamous suture was also separated and the left parietal was displaced 3 mm superiorly on the temporal. The inner table of the left parietal was elevated to the same level as the outer table of the frontal. The complicated spurs of the unfused sutures were intact. No other evidence of trauma was observed.

The left side of the cranium was more bleached than the right, indicating that the left side had been exposed to direct sunlight during the interval between deposition and discovery. No soft tissue or putrefactive odors were present at recovery, and numerous pupae cases and loose sand and seeds were found within the cranial cavity. The body had been concealed near the end of the summer, and Snow and Luke reasoned that the thin bone of the cranium had warped due to drying from sun exposure and heat. Although trauma to the head in children typically results in separations along the sutures, Snow and Luke concluded that the observed parietal displacement was the result of taphonomic processes acting on the remains. Based on this conclusion, head trauma was ruled out as the immediate cause of death. The case currently remains unsolved (Clyde C. Snow, personal communication 1994).

## Case 2

The skeletonized remains of a child were recovered from a large garbage can in the basement of an abandoned rowhouse in Philadelphia 10 months after deposition. The child had been clothed, and the remains were protected from direct exposure to the elements. The child had been reported missing in July of the previous year, and suspicion had fallen on the child's father, who had custody of the child and his 8-year-old brother. The missing child was a male of Hispanic ancestry who was 5 years and 11 months old at the time of his disappearance. The father reported that his youngest son had moved to Georgia to live with relatives, yet his son's public assistance checks continued to be cashed in Philadelphia for 8 months following his disappearance. Social services discovered the fraud, and when they could not locate the child they contacted the police. In the course of questioning the father stated that his son had suffered a seizure in the bathtub, that he had placed the child in bed, and later discovered the child had died. The father claimed that he was fearful police would suspect him of killing his son, so he disposed of the body in the rowhouse basement. The child's older brother reported that on the night he last saw his brother alive, he heard splashing and his brother's scream, and saw his father coming out of the upstairs bathroom. Upon entering the bathroom he saw his brother lying unconscious in the bathtub, which was filled with water. He last saw his younger brother clothed on their bed.

The remains were generally complete and exhibited extensive rodent gnawing and numerous pupae cases in the cranial orifices. After having been identified, the remains were examined for evidence of antemortem and perimortem trauma. Healed fractures were present on the posterior and lateral aspects of the eighth and ninth left ribs and the seventh, ninth, and twelfth right ribs. Rib fractures are common in child abuse cases, the result of both direct

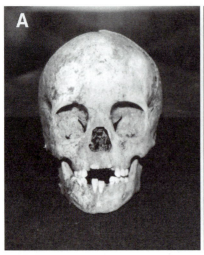
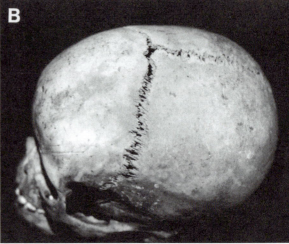

**Figure 1**   Philadelphia MEO forensic case, aged 5 years, 11 months. (A) Superior and lateral displacement of left parietal along coronal suture; (B) Separation of left coronal and anterior sagittal sutures with intact sutural serrations.

blows and, in cases involving small children, grasping around the chest, often in conjunction with violent shaking (Caffey 1972; Duhaine et al. 1987; Ludwig and Warman 1984). The lateral end of the left clavicle was also remodeled, suggesting additional antemortem trauma and possible child abuse. The child had not received medical attention for these injuries.

The skull provided the most enigmatic evidence in the case. The left coronal suture was widely separated and the left parietal projected several millimeters above the plane of the frontal and right parietal, especially at bregma and along the open anterior sagittal suture (Figure 1A, B). Although widely spaced anteriorly, the gap between the parietals narrowed posteriorly, appearing normal above lambda. The base of the skull and the delicate bones of the face were not damaged, and the complicated, interdigitated spurs of the cranial sutures were completely intact. In addition, the left zygomaticotemporal suture was open, while the right one was closed. A rib, shreds of clothing, and rodent droppings were recovered from inside the cranial cavity, the result of rodent nesting. The ectocranial surfaces of the skull were consistent in color, indicating that no exposure to sunlight had occurred.

The evidence of physical abuse was compelling. The rib fractures indicated that the child had been subjected to trauma for which he had not been treated, but, having healed, the fractures were not associated with the cause of death. Likewise, the remodeled left clavicle suggested abuse, but was not related to the child's death. The cranium, however, was initially thought to present evidence that could be related to the child's death in the bathtub. Original speculation focused on the displaced left parietal as a possible consequence of blunt trauma to the head. Brain swelling was also considered as a possible reason for the projecting parietal, but could not account for the asymmetry of the lesion. The initial assumption that the cranial lesions represented perimortem trauma taken in conjunction with the testimony provided by the older brother could have formed the basis of an indictment against the father on charges of first-degree murder.

However, even though the sutures were separated, their edges were not damaged and all of the fragile bones of the skull were completely intact. This suggested that the cranial changes had occurred postmortem, not as a result of trauma to the head. The most probable cause for the cranial alterations was warping of the thin parietal due to the heat and humidity of the summer when the remains of the boy were deposited in the rowhouse basement. A secondary factor may have been a cycle of moistening and drying from continued rodent micturition.

We concluded that the observed lesions represented postmortem damage rather than perimortem trauma. In our opinion, the damage to the skull was not credible evidence for the cause of death, and could not be used to support a case of first-degree murder against the father. Based primarily on the information provided by the older brother's testimony and aided by the evidence of prior physical abuse, the father was arrested and indicted on murder and child abuse charges. The case was pleaded out and the father was convicted of third-degree murder. The father has not given any further statements regarding the events that led to the death of his son.

## Archaeological Examples

Examples of cranial deformation in archaeological skeletal specimens are ubiquitous among burial sites from all time periods and locations. The depth of the burial is not always the determining factor in whether skeletal remains are deformed or fragmented, as causes other than soil weight affect the decomposition of skeletal remains (Micozzi 1991). A dramatic example of differential preservation among an archaeological skeletal series is provided by the remains recovered from the African Burial Ground in Manhattan, where human remains were interred during the 18th century (Harrington 1993; Parrington 1995). Found between 20 and 30 ft. below grade underneath the foundations of several multistory buildings, most of the approximately 390 sets of remains were crushed and flattened, the result of pressure, soil perturbation, and vibration. Yet, when excavated, close to one-quarter of the crania were sufficiently intact for metric analyses. While fewer than 10 of the intact crania were those of children, these burials demonstrated the remarkable ability of skeletal tissues to resist the effects of extreme taphonomic stressors.

In order to document the warping response of subadult crania to various taphonomic forces, the crania of children from the Tenth Street First African Baptist Church Cemetery site were evaluated for degree of fragmentation and deformation. A total of 89 individuals were recovered in 1990 from the historic cemetery, which was in use between 1810 and 1822 (Crist et al. 1995). Of these, 33 interments contained the remains of newborns, infants, and children. Preservation of the series ranged from good to excellent because the unmarked cemetery had been sealed under a series of rowhouses, paved courts, and later the lanes of a large street almost immediately after its closing. For instance, 46% of the adult crania presented little or no deformation, while most of the unfused infant cranial bones were completely intact. Four of the articulated subadult crania recovered at the site exhibited deformation that ranged from slight to moderate with mild to extensive fragmentation. Two crania that represented children with ages at death close to those of the children comprising the two forensic cases presented in this chapter were chosen for comparison. Additionally, two other crania that illustrate the results of taphonomic process on buried subadult remains were included in this comparative analysis.

Burial 54 from the Tenth Street Cemetery was between 4 to 5 years old at death and presented bowing of the upper limbs, probably the result of rickets (vitamin D deficiency) or a chronic intestinal disorder. Most likely a male, the remains did not indicate a specific cause of death. The cranial vault of this child displayed both fragmentation and deformation, particularly along the right coronal suture where the posterior and lateral portions of the frontal were depressed below the plane of the adjacent right parietal (Figure 2). The frontal presented three separate cracks that extended posteriorly from the superciliary tori and terminated at the coronal suture. The frontal also displayed significant deformation along its right side, with the outer table of the frontal depressed 53 mm medial to the outer table of the right parietal. The right parietal exhibited no deformation, but was fragmented along its anterior border, with concomitant separation of the right side of the coronal suture. These postmortem lesions suggest continual slow-rate loading that resulted in the deformation of

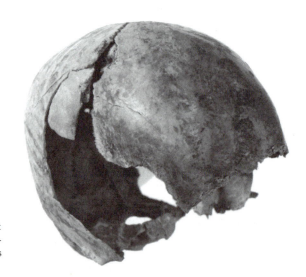

**Figure 2**  Fragmentation of right parietal and extensive medial deformation of frontal, Burial 54, 4 to 5 years old.

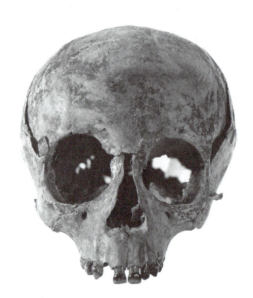

**Figure 3**  Lateral warping of both parietals with associated coronal suture separation, Burial 55, 4.5 to 5.5 years old.

the frontal along with separation of the serrated coronal suture and subsequent fracturing of the right parietal.

Burial 55 was probably a female who died between the ages of 4.5 and 5.5 years. The remains exhibited no evidence of pathology, and the cause of death could not be determined. The cranium of this child expressed minimal fragmentation and slight deformation, but clearly demonstrated lateral expansion of both parietals at pterion (Figure 3). Both sides of the coronal suture were separated inferior to the complicatae, with the right parietal extended 3 mm laterally and the left parietal 5 mm laterally from the outer table of the frontal. The greater wings of the sphenoid on both sides were absent, although the anterior portions of the squamous sutures of the temporals were completely intact. This cranium presented mild parietal displacement, the result of external as well as internal pressure from soil compaction.

Burial 57 was a female aged 14 to 15 at death. The remains of this individual displayed no pathology and gave no indication regarding the cause of death. The frontal of this individual was fragmented and deformed along its right side, but neither parietal had been

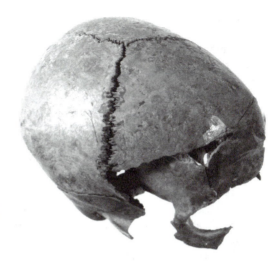

**Figure 4** Fragmentation and deformation of frontal with separation of right coronal and anterior sagittal sutures, Burial 57, aged 14 to 15 years.

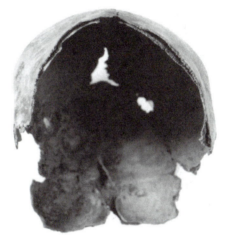

**Figure 5** Bilateral separation of parietal precursor diploic space, Burial 74, aged 20 to 28 months.

damaged. Fractures of the frontal were oriented transversely across the forehead just superior to the orbits and terminated at the coronal suture. Sutural separation had occurred along the entire right side of the coronal suture, at bregma, and along the anterior portion of the sagittal suture for 37 mm posterior to bregma (Figure 4). The coronal separation averaged 5 mm in width along the outer table, while the sagittal was 2 mm apart just posterior to bregma. All of the serrations along the open edges of both sutures were completely intact, even at complicata superior to pterion. These lesions were the result of slow-rate loading and subsequent deformation and fracture of the frontal along with consequent separation of the coronal and serrated portion of the sagittal sutures.

Burial 74 was an infant aged 20 to 28 months at death whose remains presented no evidence of disease. The cranial bones of this individual were unfused and the sutures were generally smooth and unserrated, although initial formation of the serrations along the coronal suture had occurred. While deformation of the parietals and frontal was minimal, the inner and outer tables of both parietals were split along the anterior edges of the bones (Figure 5). Superiorly, the outer tables of both parietals extended away from the inner tables, which curled slightly medially and inferiorly. The gap created in this precursor of the diplöic space measured 6 mm on the left side and 4 mm on the right. A similar degree of table separation was also present along the coronal edge of the frontal. This "peeling" of the outer cranial table did not occur along the other suture lines.

## Discussion

Head wounds are the second most common cause of death during childhood (Cohen 1993). However, little research has been conducted to link specific head injuries with particular causes (Dudley et al. 1993). This is due in large part to the poor correlation between the results of cranial trauma in living children with those of animal or cadaver models. Given the obvious importance and ramifications of distinguishing between accidental cranial trauma and that resulting from child abuse, it is crucial that the characteristics of both types of trauma are well-defined and clearly identifiable. Research that relies on radiologic and computer tomography (CT) techniques has been instrumental in defining the types and locations of cranial fractures common in child abuse (e.g., Merten and Osborne 1983; Merten et al. 1984; Pickett et al. 1983; Saulsbury and Alford 1982). Some studies have been successful in identifying specific patterns in the characteristics of cranial fractures from abuse as opposed to those observed in association with accidents (Dudley et al. 1993; Hobbs 1984). Abuse cases usually include multiple depressed fractures that involve more than one bone, stellate-shaped and complex lesions, subdural hematomae, and a predilection for fractures on most cranial bones except the parietals. Accidental fractures typically result in single, narrow, linear lesions that often involve the parietals. The results of the study conducted by Dudley et al. (1993) indicated that forces impacting the frontal and occipital tended to cause vertical fractures, while fractures of the parietals and temporals were usually horizontal. They also noted that CT scans and magnetic resonance imaging (MRI) films often do not indicate the presence of cranial fractures, especially those located on the cranial base, and recommend the use of plain film radiographs to determine the true extent of injury and verify its occurrence as reported. However, all of these studies and many more share a similar focus on the identification of abuse in living children and fresh remains. They do not address the osteological signatures of abuse in the decomposed and dry remains of children, and it in this area that forensic anthropologists can contribute important diagnostic information based on their knowledge of skeletal biology and biomechanics and their experience with human remains from archaeological contexts.

The crania of both children and adults recovered from archaeological sites often present postmortem damage related to interment. Usually these lesions occur from pressure, as the weight of overlying soil and subsequent structures presses down onto the burial shaft. However, other factors can also account for postmortem alterations. Soil perturbations, frost and root wedging, mineral expansion, vibrations, water table fluctuations, and animal and insect intervention all combine to affect human remains interred in the earth (Micozzi 1991; Murray and Tedrow 1975). While modern burials are protected from many of the these necroenvironmental factors through the use of concrete burial vaults and sealed caskets, historic period interments were typically made in simple wooden coffins which decomposed naturally over time. Consequently, these containers did not afford a great deal of protection to their human contents. Prehistoric populations generally did not use burial containers, so interred human remains were directly exposed to the subterranean environment throughout all phases of decomposition.

The most common cranial modifications observed in human remains from archaeological contexts are fragmentation and deformation. Fragmentation results from fractures of the cranial bones following decomposition of the soft tissue and the subsequent drying and mineralization of the skeletal tissues. When recovered, a fragmented bone can be restored to its original shape at the fracture lines because of its brittleness, having exhibited little deformation before failure. Deformation (a change in dimensions) occurs as an external force or load is applied to the bone. Depending on the amount of the load and the rate at which it is applied, the acquiring bone will either return to its original shape after the load is removed (the bone is elastic) or will yield to the force and become permanently deformed (the force exceeds the bone's elastic region and the bone exhibits plastic behavior). If the force continues and is progressively increased, the structure of the bone fails and a fracture results (Nordin and Frankel 1989). These processes also affect human remains from forensic contexts, even those that were not interred prior to recovery.

The viscoelastic nature of bones makes them rate-dependent to the effects of loading (Rockwood and Green 1984). That is, slow loading allows the bone to yield to the applied force and stretch prior to fracture, the result of which is deformation (Smith et al. 1993). This type of bone response is typical of manually applied blunt force trauma and crushing and pressure mechanisms, the latter of which are associated with burial. With faster loading, as in gunshot wounds and impacts from high velocity projectiles, the viscous element of the bone does not have time to yield to the force and the resultant fractures resemble shattered brittle materials with little to no plastic deformation (Rogers 1982; Smith et al. 1993). Reconstruction of deformed crania is difficult, since the warped fragments will not join at all margins.

The initial stages of decomposition after burial in a coffin probably do not involve cranial deformation or fragmentation, since the weight of the aerated overlying soil can most likely be supported by a new coffin. However, as the coffin wood decomposes and the soil becomes progressively more dense through time, the weight of the soil increases as the strength of the coffin decreases. Since most historic burials were interred at a depth of 6 feet and typical coffins were 2 feet in height, an average of 4 feet of soil was present in the typical burial shaft. Most shafts average 6 feet in length and 3 feet in width, so an average total of 72 cubic feet (2.81 cubic yards) of fill typically overlays most historic coffin burials. One cubic foot of soil *in situ* weighs between 75 and 100 pounds, depending upon the degree of compaction (Murray and Tedrow 1975). Therefore, a typical burial shaft contains 5400 to 7200 pounds of soil, or 2.7 to 3.6 tons. Such weight, which is often increased through compaction if structures are built over the cemetery, gradually leads to the failure of the coffin. The lid collapses inward and the sideboards split open, allowing soil to penetrate the coffin and compress the human remains inside.

As the bone within a coffin or burial shaft becomes packed within the dynamic soil matrix, it may fracture from shearing, where the load is applied differentially parallel to the surface of the bone, or from bending, which is a combination of tension and compression. Whenever a bone surface is subjected to tensile or compressive loading, shear stress is produced. Bending occurs when tensile stresses act on one side of a neutral axis and compressive forces act on the other side. When a long bone is subjected to tensile stresses on its superior side, resultant compressive stresses act on the inferior surface so that the stresses are highest at the periphery of the bone and lowest at its neutral axis. If loading continues beyond the yield point of the bone, the bone will break at the point of application of the middle force, usually located near the axis of the two tensile forces.

In four-point loading, two force couples produce two equal moments on the bone. The force couple is formed when two parallel forces of equal magnitude but opposite direction are applied to the bone surface. Because the magnitude of the bending moment is the same between the two force couples, the bone breaks at its weakest point. With long bones this fracture usually occurs at the area of the diaphysis with the smallest diameter, where the cross-sectional area is least. The tubular shape of the long bones confers a greater resistance to bending motions because much of the bone tissue is distributed at the epiphyseal ends, away from the neutral axis. In living bone, compression stresses cause the bone to shorten and widen. At the microscopic level the failure mechanism for the bone tissue is the oblique cracking of the osteons (Nordin and Frankel 1989). In decomposed and dry bone discontinuities in the periosteal and endosteal surfaces from breakdown of the osteon system decrease the bone's ability to resist loads, particularly in torsion. Torsion tests conducted on *in vitro* human tibiae indicated that an open section defect, caused by cutting out a slot of bone from the cortex, reduced the load to failure by as much as 90% and the deformation to failure by 70% (Frankel and Burstein 1970). Other studies demonstrate comparable failure rates for bone as it becomes decalcified and loses its organic matrix through decomposition (Lindahl 1976).

Bone exhibits brittle or ductile behavior depending on its architecture and age, its geometry, the loading mode applied, and the rate and frequency at which the load is applied. Living bone is typically more brittle in individuals of older age and in response to higher loading rates. For instance, while long bone samples from both younger and older individuals resisted the same levels of stress, the older bone sample could withstand only half the strain of the younger sample (Burstein et al. 1976). However, bone is stiffer and maintains a higher load to failure when loads are applied at higher rates. Thus, the loading rate directly influences the fracture pattern and the amount of stored energy the bone releases at failure. At a low loading rate, typical of forces encountered by prehistoric and historic burials subjected to soil compression, the energy can dissipate through a single crack, while high-energy fractures result in comminution of the bone and the production and displacement of numerous fragments. When loading is frequent or constant, the decomposed bone progressively loses its ability to store energy, and transverse cracks occur on the tensile side while oblique fractures occur on the compressive side. Additionally, growing bone has different structural characteristics than does adult skeletal material, as the haversian canals occupy a greater proportion of the bones in children. The more porous nature of the younger bone results in its failing under stresses of both compression and tension, while adult bone fails only in tension (Porter 1989). Children are also less likely to have displaced fractures since their periosteum is much stronger and less easily torn than that of an adult.

In tension and compression, the load to failure and stiffness of a bone are proportional to the cross-sectional area of the bone (Nordin and Frankel 1989). Since cranial bones are flat, their cross-sectional areas are very small, and hence the stiffness of these bones is reduced. Flat cranial bones deform very little before failing, usually resulting in radial cracks or fractures that emanate from the point of impact. Secondary concentric cracks branch out from the radial cracks and connect two or more radial cracks. Antemortem fractures in cranial bones of the living often continue along the suture lines, which redirect the force traveling along the radial cracks. These fractures typically cross suture lines as well, continuing onto the adjacent bone. In postmortem cranial fractures, which occur when the bone is dry, the radial cracks usually continue from the point of impact to the nearest suture line, where they terminate.

Postmortem fractures can also be distinguished from those that occurred antemortem or perimortem (i.e., when the bone was fleshed) by differences in the color of the edges exposed by the fracture and the sharpness of the breaks (Mann and Murphy 1990). When a fracture occurs antemortem, its edges become less acute and smoother as the body decomposes and soil movement abrades the fringes of the fracture. Additionally, the exposed internal bone surfaces absorb the minerals and other contaminants from the surrounding soil matrix at the same rate as the external bone surfaces, the result of which is a consistent color throughout the bone, including the fractured surfaces. Had the fracture occurred postmortem, the rate of weathering of the fractured edges and exposed internal surfaces would be different from that of the external surfaces, these areas thus appearing lighter in color than the surrounding intact outer layer. Antemortem fractures tend to be sharp and beveled, with the small splinters and spalls of bone associated with the break adhering to the larger broken segments. Characteristics of postmortem fractures include breaks that are irregular to jagged with blunt edges and little beveling, few or no radiating fractures, and missing fragments of bone that were completely destroyed and lost as the fracture occurred (Mann and Murphy 1990; Rockwood and Green 1984).

The comparison of subadult crania from the early 19th century site of the Tenth Street First African Baptist Church Cemetery with those from two forensic contexts indicated that the bones of the immature cranium respond to several different kinds of taphonomic processes in a consistent manner. This response is dependent on the rate of the applied force and exposure to particular environmental conditions, especially fluctuations in temperature and humidity. The crania from the historic cemetery exhibited deformation and fragmentation with separations predominantly along the coronal and anterior portion of the sagittal sutures, which are serrated rather than denticulate, the stronger of the two types. These postmortem alterations resulted from soil compaction and vibration as well as from the weight of structures subsequently built over the burials. At least one historic period cranium displayed lateral expansion of the parietals along the inferior borders of the coronal suture, while a second presented sutural separations from mechanical stress with no associated damage to the serrations of the sutures.

The crania in the forensic cases both presented displacement of the parietals along the coronal and sagittal sutures; however, these lesions did not result from applied force, but rather from deformation caused by biochemical and mechanical alterations associated with temperature and humidity fluctuations. In neither case were the sutural serrations damaged, and no other evidence of perimortem trauma was present. Behrensmeyer (1978) notes that progressive weathering and amino acid racemization was enhanced by fluctuations in heat and humidity, and that weathering proceeds along lines of structural weakness in the bone. The dynamics of subadult cranial bone displacement are very likely related to these principles. Based on the similarities between the crania from the two forensic cases and those recovered from archaeological sites, examples of which were taken from the First African Baptist Church skeletal series, the anthropologists involved with both cases could confidently exclude blunt force trauma and acute brain swelling as the causes underlying the observed lesions and correctly assign both causes of death as indeterminate based on the cranial remains.

## Conclusions

The effects of taphonomic processes on subadult bone have not been adequately documented due to the paucity of these types of remains in forensic and archaeological contexts. Because the conditions of each case are unique, broad generalizations about the actions and results of taphonomic processes should not be made without caution. However, if regularities occur in the ways that surviving skeletal elements interact with postmortem processes, these responses should be reflected in patterns observable in samples of similar types (Gifford 1981). Although the two forensic cases and archaeological examples reported here do not constitute an adequate statistical sample, the similarity of observations in each case suggests that the immature skull responds to several taphonomic processes in a consistent manner. It is important to distinguish this response to postmortem forces from similar responses to perimortem trauma in order to accurately reconstruct the circumstances surrounding an undocumented death.

Analogous to statements concerning taphonomy and the fossil record (Gifford 1981), the search for regular linkages between static attributes of recovered skeletal elements and their dynamic causes is the key to understanding the forensic evidence provided by the bones. First, the interactions between skeletal remains and the taphonomic processes that operate on them must be clarified. We must specify which processes are responsible for the observed alterations to the bones, as well as those which are unrelated to such changes. As suggested by the two cases reported here, it appears that the immature cranium responds to sunlight and heat through separation along its open sutures and displacement of the thin broad bones of the vault. The dynamics of this warping response are related to the internal structure of the parietals and frontal as well as to the architecture of the sutures that articulate these bones. The case from Philadelphia demonstrates that direct exposure to sunlight is not necessary for the bones of the vault to warp, and that the activity associated with rodent nesting may contribute to the gross changes observed due to heat and humidity.

Second, the response must appear in a group of skeletal elements sharing the same architectural characteristics recovered from similar contexts. It is at this stage that we currently find ourselves. Consistent with any actualistic research scheme, we have first documented the observed phenomenon through description and measurement, and now seek to establish the range of variation in the occurrence of the response. This stage will require the testing of the proposed causal relationship between several taphonomic processes and the final appearance of the subadult crania described here. It will also require additional information yielded by the recovery of other subadult remains from a variety of contexts. The archaeological examples suggest that the crania of subadults often warp without fracturing, the result of external forces rather than acute brain swelling or blunt force trauma.

It is clear that the structure of a particular bone is a major determinant of its survival. When fresh bone is exposed to the elements, particularly sunlight, its surface deteriorates at the same rate that its organic component decays, and starts a process of weathering that is dependent on both temperature and humidity (White 1991:360). The response of human bone to these environmental factors has not been well documented; Micozzi (1991) does not address these aspects of postmortem change at all, and Ubelaker (1989) mentions only bleaching and an increase in brittleness due to solar exposure. While a substantial literature exists concerning the response of mammalian bone to various types of stress, previous studies have primarily focused on long bones and carnivore damage, while few references are made to cranial materials, particularly those from subadult individuals.

An understanding of taphonomy can provide forensic scientists with information about the spatial, temporal, and biological factors involved in the formation of evidence presented by recovered skeletal remains. Clarifying the actions of various taphonomic processes on human remains can establish a statistical basis for particular inferences drawn from a given set of evidence. The actualistic nature of taphonomic studies can supply forensic science with information about the meaning of patterns observed in recovered skeletal remains, and can be extended to other types of evidence. As illustrated by the two cases reported here, caution must be applied when ascribing manner or cause of death based on gross changes to the skeleton. In cases of potential child abuse, the fragile nature of the osteological material and lack of experience with immature remains may lead to misidentification of bone modifications as perimortem trauma when in fact they can be attributed to other noncriminal factors. Since the forensic pathologist must recognize a broad range of child fatalities for which an adult must appropriately bear criminal responsibility, it is critical that the effects of postmortem processes be considered when the remains of a child are the subject of an autopsy. The inclusion of a forensic anthropologist in such cases enhances the ability of the autopsy team to correctly identify evidence of child abuse and, of equal importance, significantly reduces the likelihood that a normal skeletal variant or taphonomic response will be misclassified as an indication of battered child syndrome.

## Acknowledgments

The authors would like to thank Dr. Haresh G. Mirchandani, Chief Medical Examiner of Philadelphia, for his support and encouragement. We also appreciate the constructive comments regarding this research provided by Dr. Ted A. Rathbun and Dr. Clyde C. Snow.

## References Cited

Behrensmeyer, A.K.
1978 Taphonomic and Ecologic Information from Bone Weathering. *Paleobiology* 4:150–162.

Berkovitz, B.K.B., and B.J. Moxham
1989 *A Colour Atlas of the Skull.* Wolfe Medical Publications, London.

Berryman, H.E., W.M Bass, S.A. Symes, and O.C. Smith
   1991   Recognition of Cemetery Remains in the Forensic Setting. *Journal of Forensic Sciences* 36:230–237.

Brain, C.K.
   1967   Bone Weathering and the Problem of Bone Pseudo-tools. *South African Journal of Science* 63:97–99.
   1976   Some Principles in the Interpretation of Bone Accumulations Associated with Man. In *Human Origins: Louis Leakey and the East African Evidence*, edited by G. Isaac and E. McGown, pp. 97–106. Benjamin, New York.

Burstein, A.H., D.T. Reilly, and M. Martens
   1976   Aging of Bone Tissue: Mechanical Properties. *Journal of Bone Joint Surgery* 58A:82–86.

Caffey, J.
   1972   On the Theory and Practice of Shaking Infants. *American Journal of Diseases of Children* 124(2):161–169.

Child Accident Prevention Foundation of Australia
   1983   *Accidents to Children — Their Incidence, Causes and Effects*. Child Accident Prevention Foundation of Australia, Melbourne.

Cohen, D.
   1993   Accidental Injury in Childhood. In *The Pathology of Trauma*, edited by J.K. Mason, pp. 150–162. Edward Arnold, London.

Cotton, G., A. Aufderheide, and V. Goldschmidt
   1987   Preservation of Human Tissue Immersed for Five Years in Fresh Water of Known Temperature. *Journal of Forensic Sciences* 32:1125–1130.

Crist, T.A.J., R.H. Pitts, A. Washburn, J.P. McCarthy, and D.G. Roberts
   1995   *"…A Distinct Church of Lord Jesus": The History, Archaeology, and Physical Anthropology of the Tenth Street First African Baptist Church Cemetery*. Prepared for Gaudet & O'Brien Associates/Urban Engineers Inc. and the Pennsylvania Department of Transportation. John Milner Associates, Inc., Philadelphia.

Dudley, M.H., K.J. Griest, S.J. Cambron, M.C. Pozzi, and R.E. Zumwalt
   1993   Skull Fractures in Children Under the Age of Two Years, Accident vs. Child Abuse. Paper presented at the 45th Annual Meeting of the American Academy of Forensic Sciences, Boston.

Duhaine, A.C., P.A. Gennarelli, L.E. Thibault, D.A. Bruce, and R. Wiser
   1987   The Shaken Baby Syndrome: A Clinical, Pathological, and Biomechanical Study. *Journal of Neurosurgery* 66:409–415.

Dunn, R., S.D. Stout, and J. Dix
   1991   A Unique Case of Congenital Bilateral Absence of Parietal Bones in a Neonate. *Journal of Forensic Sciences* 36:593–598.

Enlow, D.H.
   1990   *Facial Growth*. W.B. Saunders, Philadelphia.

Fazekas, I.Gy., and F. Kósa
   1978   *Forensic Fetal Osteology*. Akadémiai Kiado, Budapest.

Frankel, V.H., and A.H. Burstein
   1970   *Orthopaedic Biomechanics*. Lea & Febiger, Philadelphia.

Galloway, A., W.H. Birkby, A.M. Jones, T.E. Henry, and B.O. Parks
   1989   Decay Rates of Human Remains in an Arid Environment. *Journal of Forensic Sciences* 34:607–616.

Gifford, D.P.
  1981   Taphonomy and Paleoecology: A Critical Review of Archaeology's Sister Disciplines.
    In *Advances in Archaeological Method and Theory*, Vol. 4, edited by M.B. Schiffer, pp.
    365–438. Academic Press, New York.

Haglund, W.
  1992   Contribution of Rodents to Postmortem Artifacts of Bone and Soft Tissue. *Journal
    of Forensic Sciences* 37:1459–1465.

Harrington, S.P.M.
  1993   Bones and Bureaucrats: New York's Great Cemetery Imbroglio. *Archaeology* 46(2):
    28–38.

Harwood-Nash, D.C., E.B. Hendrick, and A.R. Hudson
  1971   The Significance of Skull Fractures in Children. *Pediatric Radiology* 101:151–156.

Hauser, G., and G.F. DeStefano
  1989   *Epigenetic Variants of the Human Skull.* E. Schweizerbart'sche Verlasbuchhandlung,
    Stuttgart.

Hobbs, C.J.
  1984   Skull Fracture and the Diagnosis of Child Abuse. *Archives of Disease in Childhood*
    59(3):246–52.

Kósa, F.
  1986   Age Estimation from the Fetal Skeleton. In *Age Markers in the Human Skeleton*,
    edited by M.Y. Isçan, pp. 21–54. Charles C Thomas, Springfield, IL.

Krogman, W.M., and M.Y. Iscan
  1986   *The Human Skeleton in Forensic Medicine.* Charles C Thomas, Springfield, IL.

Lindahl, O.
  1976   Mechanical Properties of Dried Defatted Spongy Bone. *Acta Orthopaedica Scandi-
    navica* 47:11–19.

Lowe, A.A.
  1952   *Growth of Children.* Aberdeen University Press, Aberdeen, Scotland.

Ludwig, S., and M. Warman
  1984   Shaken Baby Syndrome: A Review of 20 Cases. *Annals of Emergency Medicine*
    13(2):104–107.

Mann, R.W., and S.P. Murphy
  1990   *Regional Atlas of Bone Disease.* Charles C Thomas, Springfield, IL.

Mann, R.W., W.M. Bass, and L. Meadows
  1990   Time Since Death and Decomposition of the Human Body: Variables and Obser-
    vations in Case and Experimental Field Studies. *Journal of Forensic Sciences* 35:103–111.

Marshall, D.
  1979   Engineering of a Human Skull II: Relationship of Parts in Formation of Skull. *Dental
    Radiography and Photography* 52(3):49–61.

Martin, T.
  1989   Normal Development of Movement and Function: Neonate, Infant, and Toddler.
    In *Physical Therapy*, edited by R.M. Scully and M.R. Barnes, pp. 63–82. J.B. Lippincott,
    Philadelphia.

McKern T.W., and T.D. Stewart
  1957   Skeletal Age Changes in Young American Males: Analyzed from the Standpoint of
    Age Identification. Technical Report EP-45. Environmental Protection Research Division,
    U.S. Army Quartermaster Research and Development Center, Natick, MA.

Merten, D.F., and D.R. Osborne
  1983 Craniocerebral Trauma in the Child Abuse Syndrome. *Pediatric Annals* 12:882–887.

Merten, D.F., D.R. Osborne, M.A. Radkowski, and J.C. Leonidas
  1984 Craniocerebral Trauma in the Child Abuse Syndrome: Radiological Observations. *Pediatric Radiology* 14:272–277.

Micozzi, M.S.
  1991 *Postmortem Change in Human and Animal Remains: A Systematic Approach.* Charles C Thomas, Springfield, IL.
  1986 Experimental Study of Postmortem Change Under Field Conditions: Effects of Freezing, Thawing, and Mechanical Injury. *Journal of Forensic Sciences* 31:953–961.

Moss, M.L.
  1955 Relative Growth of the Human Fetal Skeleton, Cranial and Postcranial. *Annals of the New York Academy of Sciences* 63:528–536.

Moss, M.L., C.R. Noback, and G.G. Robertson
  1956 Growth of Certain Human Fetal Cranial Bones. *American Journal of Anatomy* 48:191–204.

Murray, R.C., and J.C.F. Tedrow
  1975 *Forensic Geology: Earth Sciences and Criminal Investigation.* Rutgers University Press, New Brunswick.

Nordin, M., and V.H. Frankel
  1989 Biomechanics of Bone. In *Basic Biomechanics of the Musculoskeletal System,* edited by M. Nordin and V.H. Frankel, pp. 3–29. Lea and Febiger, Philadelphia.

Olivier, G.
  1975 Biometry of the Human Occipital Bone. *Journal of Anatomy* 120:507–518.

Opperman, L.A., T.M. Sweeney, J. Redmon, J.A. Persing, and R.C. Ogle
  1993 Tissue Interactions with Underlying Dura Mater Inhibit Osseous Obliteration of Developing Cranial Sutures. *Developmental Dynamics* 198(4):312–322.

Parrington, M.
  1995 The African Burial Ground: An Adventure in Urban Anthropology. *Transforming Anthropology.*

Pickett, W.J., E.J. Faleski, A. Chacko, and R.V. Jarrett
  1983 Comparison of Radiographic and Radionuclide Skeletal Surveys in Battered Children. *Southern Medical Journal* 76(2):207–212.

Porter, R.E.
  1989 Normal Development of Movement and Function: Child and Adolescent. In *Physical Therapy,* edited by R.M. Scully and M.R. Barnes, pp. 83–98. J.B. Lippincott, Philadelphia.

Rockwood, C.A., and D.P. Green
  1984 *Fractures in Adults.* J.B. Lippincott, Philadelphia.

Rogers, L.F.
  1982 *Radiology of Skeletal Trauma,* Vol. 1. Churchill Livingstone, New York.

Saulsbury, F.T., and B.A. Alford
  1982 Intracranial Bleeding from Child Abuse: The Value of Skull Radiographs. *Pediatric Radiology* 12:175–178.

Smith, O.C., H.E. Berryman, S.A. Symes, J.T. Francisco, and V. Hrdlicka
  1993 Atypical Gunshot Exit Defects to the Cranial Vault. *Journal of Forensic Sciences* 38:339–343.

Snow, C.C., and J.L. Luke

    1970    The Oklahoma City Child Disappearances of 1967: Forensic Anthropology in the Identification of Skeletal Remains. *Journal of Forensic Sciences* 15:125–153.

Sorg, M.H., and K.G. Sweeney

    1993    Discriminating Developmental Variants from Perimortem Trauma in the Infant Cranium: Forensic Case Study. Paper presented at the 9th Annual Meeting of the Northeastern Forensic Anthropology Association, York, PA.

Steele, D.G., and C.A. Bramblett

    1988    *The Anatomy and Biology of the Human Skeleton.* Texas A&M University Press, College Station, TX.

Stewart, T.D.

    1979    *Essentials of Forensic Anthropology, Especially as Developed in the United States.* Charles C Thomas, Springfield, IL.

Ubelaker, D.H.

    1989    *Human Skeletal Remains: Excavation, Analysis, Interpretation.* Taraxacum, Washington, D.C.

White, T.D.

    1991    *Human Osteology.* Academic Press, San Diego.

Williams, P.L., R. Warwick, M. Dyson, and L.H. Bannister

    1989    *Gray's Anatomy.* 37th ed. Churchill Livingstone, Edinburgh.

# Biodegradation of Hairs and Fibers

# 21

WALTER F. ROWE

## The Role of Trace Evidence

Hairs and fibers constitute important categories of trace evidence. "Trace evidence" is the term used by forensic scientists to describe the minute particles of soil, glass, paint, hairs, textile fibers, arson accelerants, and explosive residues that may be found at the scene of a crime, on the body of a crime victim, or on the person of the perpetrator of a crime. Trace evidence is frequently exchanged between the crime scene, the victim, and the perpetrator of the crime; it therefore provides circumstantial evidence that may associate a suspect in a criminal investigation with a victim or with a crime scene. The exchange of trace evidence is governed by the Locard Exchange Principle. Named for French forensic scientist Edmond Locard, this principle states that when two surfaces come into contact, there will be an exchange of material between them. Because so many crimes involve contact between the perpetrator and the crime scene (including the person of the victim) some kind of trace evidence should be recoverable in virtually all crimes. The use of trace evidence in criminal investigations and subsequent prosecutions depends on its recognition and preservation at the scene of the crime and its identification and comparison with exemplars in the forensic science laboratory (DeForest et al. 1983).

This discussion will focus on the biodeterioration of physical evidence, specifically hairs and fibers. It is therefore important to understand at the outset what is meant by the term biodeterioration. Huek (1965, 1968) has defined biodeterioration as "any undesirable change in the properties of a material caused by the vital activities of organisms." The deterioration of biological materials by agents other than living organisms does not fall within the limits of this definition of biodeterioration. Nevertheless, the deterioration of biological materials is commonly included under the term "biodeterioration." "Biodegradation" is a term that is often used in conjunction with the term "biodeterioration." As commonly used, biodegradation means the use of the ability of organisms to break down materials to convert waste material into a more useful or acceptable form. (Allsop and Seal 1986) No restrictions are placed on the size or nature of the organisms involved in biodeterioration and biodegradation. Microorganisms, given their ubiquity and versatility, are obviously significant agents of biodeterioration and biodegradation. However, higher organisms such as insects, mice, rats, and human beings are also major biodeteriogens.

Biodeterioration becomes an issue in a criminal investigation when it either prevents the identification of a piece of physical evidence or prevents that evidence from being meaningfully compared with an exemplar. As will be seen in the subsequent discussion, the most common effect of biodeterioration on hairs and fibers is to produce morphological changes. If these are severe enough, meaningful comparisons with exemplar materials may be precluded. If the biodeterioration of an item of evidence is severe enough to prevent its identification, the evidence will probably not be recognized and preserved at the scene of the crime. Occasionally,

0-8493-9434-1/97/$0.00+$.50
© 1997 by CRC Press, Inc.

biodeterioration of evidence can produce health hazards. For example, clothing can be contaminated with a variety of microorganisms. Mold-contaminated clothing can cause severe allergic reactions among police and laboratory personnel unless appropriate safety precautions are taken.

## Hair as Forensic Evidence

Animal hairs are proteinaceous shafts with circular or elliptical cross sections. Each hair is comprised of three morphologically distinct regions: the medulla, the cortex, and the cuticle. The medulla is a group of specialized cells running approximately through the center of the hair shaft. If these cells shrink, the resulting cavities become filled with air or, less commonly, with fluid. The air-filled cavities refract and reflect light so that the medulla appears as a dark irregular band or a cluster of dark globules when the hair is viewed with a transmitted light microscope. When the cavities are filled with fluid, the medulla appears as a bright band or a cluster of glassy globules. Some hairs exhibit dark and light medullas in different regions of the hair shaft (Bisbing 1982; Hicks 1977; Seta et al. 1988).

The cortex comprises the layer of cells surrounding the medulla. In human hair, the cortex makes up the bulk of the hair shaft. Within the cortex are found the pigment granules that give hair its color, spindle cells, ovoid bodies (dark, oval inclusions), and occasionally cortical fusi (air-filled vacuoles). These structures, located within the cortex, play a crucial role in the microscopic comparison of hairs (Bisbing 1982; Hicks 1977; Seta et al. 1988).

The cuticle is the surface of the hair. It is a layer of cells from one to ten cells thick. At the surface of the hair, the cuticular cells resemble overlapping scales with irregular edges. The free edges of the scales point toward the distal or tip end of the hair. The cuticular scales on the surface of a hair interlock with cells lining the hair follicle. This prevents the hair falling out until the follicular tissue shrinks away from the hair shaft in the telogen phase of hair growth. The cuticular scale pattern of a hair is used to help identify the species of animal that the hair came from (Bisbing 1982; Hicks 1977; Seta et al. 1988).

The forensic identification of hairs is carried out primarily with transmitted light microscopy. Scanning electron microscopy (SEM) may occasionally be used to examine cuticular scale patterns. Otherwise, the value of SEM for hair examinations is limited because most of the morphological features used to identify the species of animal from which the hair originated and used to compare evidentiary and exemplar hairs are within the hair, not on its surface.

Evidentiary hairs are examined first to determine whether they are human. The following features are used to make this determination: diameter, diameter variation, texture, cuticular scale pattern, the diameter of the medulla, the nature of the medulla, and the distribution of pigment granules. The diameters of human hairs lie between those of animal down hairs and animal guard hairs. The diameter of the medullas in human hair is less than one third of the overall diameter of the hair, while many animal hairs have medullas whose diameters exceed one half the diameter of the hair. If human hairs have a medulla, it is either fragmentary or interrupted. Many animal hairs have continuous periodic medullas; other animal hairs have lattice medullas (Bisbing 1982; Hicks 1977; Seta et al. 1988).

Once hairs have been determined to be human hairs, they must be examined to determine the somatic origin of the hairs. The texture and cross section of the hairs are particularly significant for this determination. Head hairs may be straight with circular cross sections or curly with oval cross sections. Pubic hairs are flattened and ribbon-like; they display characteristic buckling. Beard hairs are coarse, with triangular cross sections. Beard hairs frequently have multiple medullas (Bisbing 1982; Hicks 1977; Seta et al. 1988).

The population ancestry of the person from whom the hair came can frequently be determined from its microscopic features. Caucasoid head hair is straight or somewhat wavy with a circular or oval cross section; it also has fine pigment granules. Negroid head hairs are very curly with oval cross sections; their pigmentation is dense and coarsely clumped. Mongoloid head hair is straight with a circular cross section; its pigmentation is moderately coarse. Mongoloid hair has a distinct auburn cast when viewed with transmitted light. It is very important to keep in mind that because of natural variations within the human population and because of the existence of individuals with mixed racial ancestries, the estimation of population ancestry from human hairs may be erroneous (Bisbing 1982; Hicks 1977; Seta et al. 1988).

Once an evidentiary hair has been found to be human and its somatic origin has been determined, the hair may be compared with known hairs having the same somatic origin. The comparisons are conducted with a comparison microscope. The following features of the hairs are compared: diameter, diameter variation, cuticle thickness, cuticle thickness variation, color, color variation, size and distribution of pigment granules, medulla morphology, and the presence or absence of less common features such as ovoid bodies and cortical fusi. In order for the evidentiary hair to be said to match the known hair sample, at least one known hair must have the same microscopic features as the evidentiary hair. Because the microscopic features of a hair change from root to tip, corresponding regions of the known and evidentiary hairs must match: that is, the roots must match, the midshaft regions must match, and the tips must also match (Bisbing 1982; Hicks 1977).

Meaningful microscopic comparisons cannot be made if the evidentiary and exemplar hairs come from different parts of the body. Nor can meaningful comparisons be made if either the evidentiary hair or the exemplar hairs have been significantly altered from their natural state. For example, if hairs have been chemically bleached (as indicated by such features as abrupt color changes along the hair shaft, lifted cuticular scale edges and a brassy, greenish color) they cannot be compared.

The forensic hair examiner can render one of three opinions based on his microscopic comparisons of evidentiary and exemplar hairs. If the hairs match, then they could have had a common origin. If the hairs have both similarities and dissimilarities, the results of the comparison are inconclusive. If the evidentiary and exemplar hairs are dissimilar, they did not have a common origin. The confidence with which this exclusionary conclusion can be stated is dependent on the adequacy of the exemplar hair sample. An exemplar hair sample should contain 50 to 100 randomly selected hairs from a particular region of the body.

The forensic hair examiner may have to examine human hairs that have been exposed to a variety of environmental conditions. For example, a hair may have been exposed to wind, rain, and sunlight for months or years before being collected as evidence. Alternatively, the hair may have been buried or immersed in water for an extended period of time. Although some research has examined the effects of hair cosmetic treatments on the forensically important microscopic features of hairs, very little is known about how environmental conditions may alter hair morphology. A number of studies have described the growth of microorganisms on hairs (Daniels 1953; Deshmukh and Agrawal 1982; English 1963, 1965, 1969, 1976; Page 1950; Vanbreuseghem 1952); however, only a few studies have considered the effect of microbial attack on the identification and comparison of hairs (Hawks and Rowe 1988; Kundrat and Rowe 1989; Kupferschmid et al. 1994; Serowik 1987; Serowik and Rowe 1987).

In the studies reported by Serowik and Rowe (1987) and by Kundrat and Rowe (1989), human hair samples were buried in soil for periods of up to 6 months. Both studies reported tunneling of the shafts of the hairs, presumably by fungal hyphae (microorganisms were rarely found *in situ* on the hairs). The tunneling of hairs by keratinolytic microorganisms has been reported by a number of other workers (Daniels 1953; English 1963, 1965, 1969, 1976; Page

**Table 1   Biodeterioration of Human Hair Buried in Well-Watered Garden Soil**

| | |
|---|---|
| Month 1 | All hair samples show fungal tunneling. |
| Month 2 | All hair samples show fungal tunneling. Half of the samples have vesicles with the cortex or medulla. |
| Month 3 | Fungal tunnels and vesicles present. Damage to cuticle layer observed in 80% of hair samples. |
| Month 4 | Half of hair samples show fragmentation of hair shaft. Tunnels, vesicles, and cuticular damage observed in all samples. |
| Month 5 | 30% of hair samples too severely deteriorated to recover. Remaining hair samples display all types of biodeterioration artifacts: tunneling, vesicles, cuticular damage, and fragmentation. |
| Month 6 | Hair samples too severely deteriorated to recover. |

From Serowik, J.M. Biodeterioration of Hair in a Soil Environment, Master's thesis, George Washington University, Washington, D.C.

1950; Vanbreuseghem 1952). Serowik and Rowe (1987) also observed the development of small cavities or vesicles in both the medulla and the cortex of the buried hairs. These latter changes are those most likely to cause problems for forensic hair examiners, because the vesicles in the cortex might be mistaken for cortical fusi. The tunnels, on the other hand, would be immediately recognized as being the result of biodeterioration. Serowik and Rowe (1987) and Kundrat and Rowe (1989) observed the appearance of darkened "necked" regions on the shafts of buried hairs. The darkening of the hairs in these areas is an artifact resulting from the etching of the surfaces of the shafts of the hairs as they are progressively destroyed by microorganisms. Kundrat and Rowe (1989) have reported that some of their exhumed hair specimens exhibited transverse fractures that closely resembled the ends of hairs that have been cut with scissors. Deadman (1990) has reported both transverse fractures and darkened regions on hairs from putrefied remains; the darkened regions were, however, confined to the root of the hair shaft. Table 1 shows the succession of the different types of damage observed in buried hair samples (Serowik 1987).

The study of the biodeterioration of hair by airborne microorganisms conducted by Hawks and Rowe (1988) was primarily concerned with the effects of microorganisms on museum specimens exposed to high relative humidities. However, one observation in this study is relevant to the forensic examination of human and animal hairs. White dog hair samples exposed to high relative humidity for 96 days developed a distinct yellow-orange coloration. This color change was associated with the growth of brown fungal hyphae and spores on the surfaces of the hairs. Washing of the hairs with a phosphate detergent removed some of the surface hyphae, but left colored hyphae within the shafts of the hairs. The color change of the hairs may be due solely to the microorganism and its waste products or to the accelerated oxidation of fatty acids on the hair surfaces when they are exposed to high relative humidity.

DeGaetano et al. (1992) have reported fungal tunnels in the head hair from a buried body. In this instance, the body of a murder victim had been buried 3 weeks in a coffin before being exhumed to obtain hair samples to further the ongoing homicide investigation. Although no fungal hyphae were found on the surfaces of the hairs, the examined hairs had numerous transverse tunnels. The tunnels most closely resembled those produced *in vitro* by *Curvularia ramosa* and *Alternaria sp.* Examination of the hair surfaces with a scanning electron microscope revealed that the tunneling hyphae had no preference in the site of penetration: some had entered under the free edge of the cuticular scales, while others had tunneled directly through the scale surface.

Figure 1A–D are scanning electron micrographs showing the effect of burial in well-watered soil on the cuticular scales of human hairs. Figure 1A shows the condition of the sample hairs before they were buried. Figure 1B–D shows the effect of burial for 2, 4, and 6 weeks, respectively. After 4 weeks of burial, fungal hyphae are evident on the surface of the

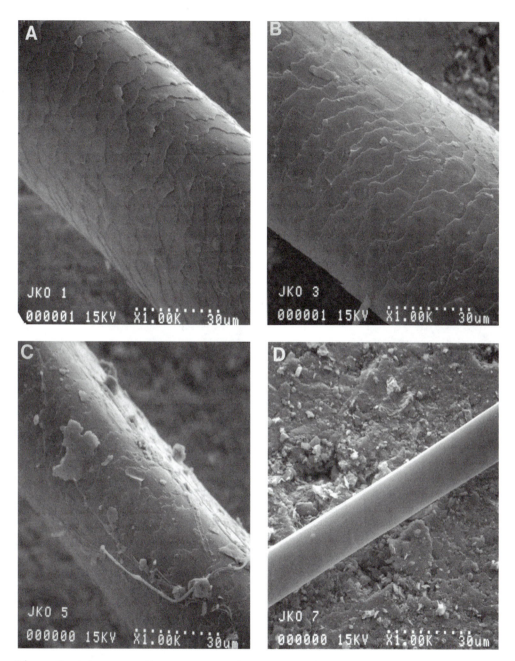

**Figure 1** (A) Scanning electron micrograph of a human head hair; (B) buried for 2 weeks; (C) buried for 4 weeks, showing presence of fungal hyphae on the cuticular scales; and (D) buried for 6 weeks, showing absence of cuticular scales.

hair; after 6 weeks the cuticular scales have completely vanished. Kupferschmid et al. (1994) have reported similar results, not only for buried specimens but also for hairs that were immersed in water.

Figures 2 and 3 show some of the different stages in the fungal attack on hairs. Figure 2A shows the fungal hyphae wrapped tightly about the hair. As may be seen in Figures 2B through 2E, fungal hyphae may not be found on the surface of hairs even when they have clearly been attacked by fungi. The fungal hyphae may be stained with Trypan blue stain (0.4 gm Trypan

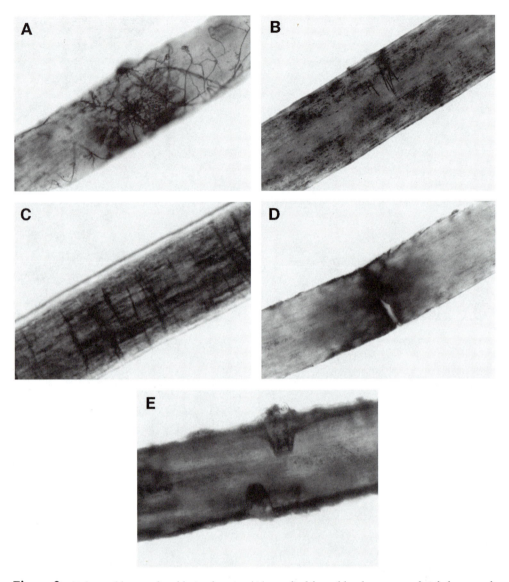

**Figure 2** Exhumed human head hair, showing (A) attached fungal hyphae wrapped tightly around the shaft; (B) early stages of fungal tunneling with a few tunnels extending through the cuticle into the cortex; (C) extensive fungal tunneling; (D) transverse fracture and surface etching due to fungal attack; and (E) conical fungal tunnels.

blue in 55:45 distilled water:acetic acid). Figures 2B through 2E show various stages in the fungal tunneling of hair. Figure 2B shows a solitary tunnel extending through the cuticle into the cortex. Figure 2C shows tunnels beginning to branch and extend parallel to the axis of the hair shaft. These tunnels resemble those produced by *Curvularia ramosa* (English 1963) and *Alternaria sp.* (English 1965) in *in vitro* studies of fungal attack on hair. Other fungi produce tunnels with different characteristics, as shown in Figure 3.

Hairs may also be attacked by a variety of insects. Many moths and beetles use keratin as a nutrient source (Allsop and Seal 1986). The debris in birds' nests is the common source of keratin in nature for these insects. However, many moths and beetles have adapted to living with human beings and feeding off human detritus. Moth larvae are a common source of damage to woolen textiles. The most common moth pests are the common clothes moth (*Tineola bissiella*), the tapestry moth (*Trichophaga tapetzella*), the case-bearing clothes moth

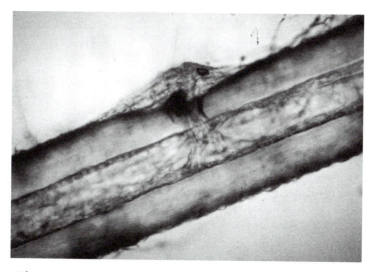

**Figure 3**   Dog hair showing invasion of medulla by fungal hyphae.

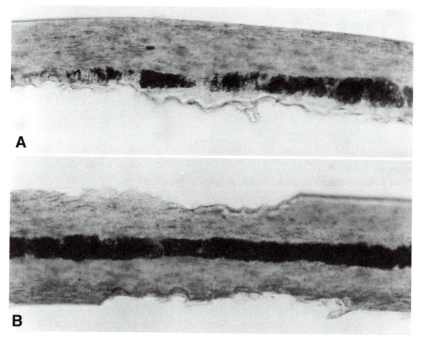

**Figure 4**   Human pubic hair showing insect damage following 3-week exposure on surface of clothing.

(*Tinea pellionella*), and the brown house moth (*Hofmannophila pseudospretella*). The larvae of many members of the family Dermestidae also consume hair. The major dermestid beetle pests that attack hair are museum beetles (*Anthrenus* spp.), the fur beetle (*Attagenus pellio*), and *Dermestes maculatus*. Figure 4 shows pubic hair samples that have been subjects of insect attack. In this particular case, the hair samples were recovered from the clothing of a rape suspect. The clothing had lain on the floor of the suspect's bathroom for 3 weeks before it was collected as evidence by police. The hairs were successfully matched microscopically to known pubic hair samples from the rape victim.

## Textile Fibers as Trace Evidence

Textile fibers are classified as either natural or man-made. Natural fibers include proteinaceous fibers such as wool or silk, cellulosic fibers such as cotton and flax, and inorganic fibers such as asbestos. Man-made fibers are further classified according to the source of the polymer comprising the fiber. Regenerated fibers are produced either by breaking down and reforming a natural polymer or by modifying the pendant groups on a naturally occurring polymer. Rayon is produced by breaking down cellulose into its constituent glucose moieties and then reforming a polymer chain of glucose molecules. Cellulose acetate, on the other hand, is a regenerated fiber that is produced by acetylating the hydroxyl groups on cellulose. In contrast to regenerated fibers, wholly synthetic fibers are ultimately derived from petrochemicals. Polyamides (nylons), polyesters, acrylics, and modacrylics (modified acrylics) are common synthetic fibers. The textile industry has also begun to introduce bicomponent fibers, i.e., fibers in which different types of polymer are blended together or in which different regions of the fiber are composed of different polymers (David and Pailthorpe 1992).

Forensic science laboratories may use a variety of analytical techniques to identify and compare textile fibers. Natural fibers are commonly identified microscopically. Microscopy is also a useful tool for the identification and comparison of man-made fibers. Because man-made fibers generally lack internal morphological features, they are identified microscopically by such optical properties as refractive index, birefringence, and dispersion staining colors. Microscopy is particularly useful in forensic case work because it is nondestructive. The following features of man-made fibers are commonly compared microscopically: diameter, cross section, birefringence, degree of delustering, color, and color variation (Carroll 1992; Gaudette 1988).

Man-made fibers may also be placed in generic categories according to their solubilities in selected solvents. Solubility tests, because of their destructive nature, are normally reserved for identification of exemplar fibers in garments and other textiles, rather than individual fibers. Several protocols with differing levels of discrimination are available (Engel et al. 1981; Federal Bureau of Investigation 1978).

Man-made fibers may also be identified using instrumental methods of analysis. One of the most powerful and widely used instrumental methods is infrared spectroscopy. When a molecule absorbs infrared radiation, its internal vibrational energy changes. The vibrational energy levels are determined by the masses of the atoms composing the molecule and the strengths of the chemical bonds between them. Because of the intimate relationship between the chemical structure of a molecule and its vibrational energy levels, infrared spectra can be thought of as "molecular fingerprints." In the case of polymers, the infrared spectrum is that of the constituent monomeric units, so that the chemical makeup of the polymer may readily be determined (Kirkbride 1992).

Another instrumental method of analysis that has proven to be useful for identifying man-made fiber is capillary pyrolysis–gas liquid chromatography. In this technique, a small fiber sample is pyrolyzed (thermally decomposed) in the injection port of a capillary gas chromatograph. The pyrolysis products are then separated by gas chromatography, resulting in a chromatogram of the pyrolysis products, which is termed a pyrogram. Pyrolytic analyses commonly use "fingerprint" identification, in which a questioned sample is identified by a peak-for-peak comparison of its pyrogram with the pyrogram of a known standard. Because capillary pyrolysis–gas liquid chromatography detects subtle differences in polymer formulations, it is extremely useful for comparing questioned and known fibers (Challinor 1992).

The biodeterioration of textile fibers has been studied with respect to how environmental conditions affect the durability of fabrics. However, the forensic scientist is more interested in how biodeterioration affects the ability to identify textile fibers and match them to a particular source. Morse et al. (1983) carried out the first detailed study of the deterioration of natural and man-made textiles, in an attempt to refine estimates of postmortem interval based on the degree of deterioration of death scene materials. Fabric samples were exposed

**Table 2   Deterioration of Man-Made Fibers Buried in Well-Watered Soil**

| Fiber Type | Month[a] | | | | | | | | |
|---|---|---|---|---|---|---|---|---|---|
| | 1 | 2 | 3 | 4 | 5 | 6 | 7 | 8 | 9 |
| Rayon | N | SL | SL | DF | DF | DF | DF | SD | SD |
| Acetate | N | SL | SD | SD | SD | SD | SD | — | — |
| Triacetate | N | N | N | N | N | N | N | N | N |
| Nylon | N | N | N | N | N | N | N | N | N |
| Polyester | N | N | N | N | N | N | N | N | N |
| Acrylic | N | N | N | N | N | N | N | N | N |

*Note:*  N = no deterioration; SL = slight deterioration; some microscopic pitting or splitting of fibers; textile basically intact; DF = definite deterioration; extensive pitting and splitting of fibers; textile basically intact; SD = severe deterioration; extensive fragmentation of fibers; textile disintegrating; — = textile completely decomposed; not recoverable.

[a]  Earliest appearance of deterioration.

Compiled from Northrop and Rowe 1987; Singer and Rowe 1989; Singer et al. 1990.

on the ground surface or buried in trenches in a variety of different types of soil found in south Georgia and northern and central Florida. The fabric samples consisted of cotton, a cotton/polyester blend, silk, wool, rayon, cellulose acetate, cellulose triacetate, nylon, and acrylic. Deterioration of the textile materials was monitored by light microscopy, scanning electron microscopy, tensile strength testing, and chemical tests. Unfortunately, the common instrumental methods of analysis such as infrared spectroscopy and pyrolysis–gas liquid chromatography were not used. Moreover, no attempt was made in this study to describe in detail the changes in microscopic appearance of the textile fibers or their solubility behavior.

Northrop and Rowe (1987), Singer and Rowe (1989), and Singer et al. (1990) have examined the effects of burial in various types of soil on common man-made fibers (cellulose acetate, cellulose triacetate, rayon, acrylic, nylon, and polyester). The exhumed fibers were subjected to a number of analytical procedures, including solubility tests, polarized light microscopy, dispersion staining microscopy, pyrolysis–gas liquid chromatography, and infrared spectrophotometry. Only the rayon and cellulose acetates showed significant deterioration in these studies. Table 2 summarizes the progression of deterioration of man-made fibers observed in these studies (Northrop 1986; Singer 1989). The microscopic appearances of these fibers were substantially altered (Figure 5). In addition, Northrop and Rowe (1987) reported changes in the solubility behavior and optical properties of deteriorated cellulose acetate fibers. Samples of these deteriorated cellulose acetate fibers were subsequently analyzed using an FTIR spectrometer equipped with an infrared microscope (Singer et al. 1990). The infrared spectra of individual deteriorated cellulose acetate fibers buried for 9 months showed loss of intensity for the characteristic ester absorption bands at 1747, 1370, and 1236 cm$^{-1}$. Singer et al. (1990) interpreted these changes as being the result of the loss of some acetate groups through partial hydrolysis of the cellulose acetate polymer. Singer et al. (1990) also discussed the examination of cellulose triacetate fibers recovered from an archaeological dig site near Johnstown, PA. These fibers showed anomalous solubility behavior, and a comparison of the FTIR spectrum of a sample fiber with that of standard cellulose acetate was consistent with partial hydrolysis of the acetate groups in the cellulose triacetate polymer.

In considering the results of the burial studies cited above, it should be pointed out that these studies do not replicate the conditions likely to be encountered if such evidence were interred with a corpse or in a landfill. Rodriguez and Bass (1985) have noted that autolytic and putrefactive changes in the human body produce a considerable amount of heat (to the

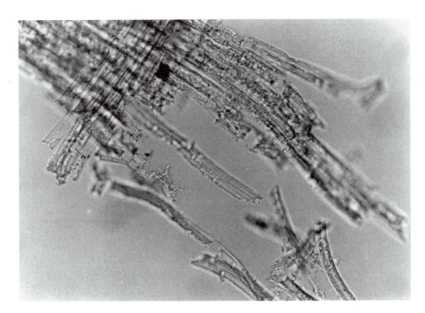

**Figure 5**   Exhumed cellulose acetate fibers, showing fragmentation and surface etching.

extent that remains exhumed in winter may be observed to steam). Likewise, decay in landfills also generates substantial amounts of heat. The elevated temperatures of graves and landfills will accelerate the degradation of hairs and textile fibers. Where the deterioration of the natural or man-made fibers is due to the activities of microorganisms, the presence of other sources of carbon (in the form of human tissue or decaying garbage) may actually reduce the biodeterioration of hairs and textile fibers.

The rapid biodeterioration of regenerated cellulose fibers and the lack of biodeterioration of wholly synthetic fibers (polyamide, polyester, acrylics, and the like) in the burial studies cited above are consistent with what is known about the biodeterioration of polymers in general. Terrestrial microorganisms have evolved enzyme systems to break down naturally occurring polymers. In the case of cellulose, they can do this with spectacular efficiency. The ease with which microorganisms break down natural polymers is also related to the fact that these polymers are very hydrophilic. The microbial enzymes require an aqueous medium in order to function, and the wetting of a natural polymer also facilitates access to reactive linkages within the polymer chains. Regenerated cellulose polymers (i.e., rayon and cellulose acetate) are hydrophilic and contain chemical bonds that are readily attacked by microbial enzyme systems. Many studies have shown that these polymers are highly susceptible to microbial degradation. On the other hand, a variety of studies have shown that polyamides, polyesters, and polyacrylics are less susceptible to attack. This is due partly to the hydrophobic nature of these synthetic polymers. Also, some synthetic polymers do not contain chemical bonds that can be readily broken by microbial enzymes (Allsop and Seal 1986).

It is important to keep clearly in mind that the biodeterioration of man-made fibers is a surface phenomenon. The polymer structure can only be attacked at the fiber surface where it is accessible to the environment. Consequently, biodeterioration will be manifested as surface etching. Severe etching can obscure the original cross-sectional shape of the fiber and make a microscopic comparison of the deteriorated fiber with an exemplar questionable. Because the degradation of the polymers comprising the fibers takes place in a shallow surface zone, methods of identification that depend on surface properties are the most likely to be adversely effected by biodeterioration. For example, measurements of refractive index by the Becke line or oblique illumination methods may be erroneous; dispersion staining colors may be anomalous. On the other hand, methods that analyze both the surface and the interior of

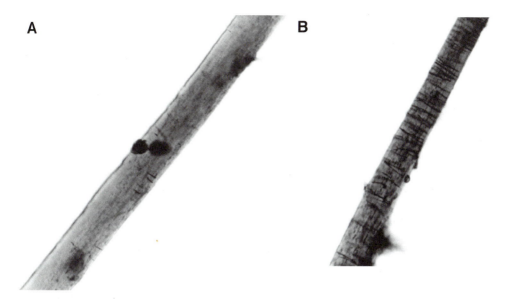

**Figure 6** (A) Human head hair from lead coffin, St. Mary's City, MD, showing (A) attached fungal spores, and (B) showing fungal tunneling.

the fiber will be less likely to give incorrect results. The birefringence of the fibers should not be much affected by biodeterioration. The infrared absorption spectra should also be unaffected except in cases where groups with very strong absorption bands (e.g., carbonyls) are being created or destroyed. The major peaks in the pyrograms of the fibers will not be affected by biodeterioration; however, the pattern of minor peaks (which is used to detect subtle differences in polymer formulation) may be significantly altered. In summary, the research on the biodeterioration of man-made fibers shows that deteriorated fibers can be correctly identified; they may not be suitable for comparative examinations.

## Three Case Studies

### Case 1

Project Lead Coffins was a multidisciplinary effort to examine the contents of three lead coffins uncovered during archaeological excavations at St. Mary's City, the site of the first colonial capitol of Maryland. It was initially hoped that the coffins would contain samples of 17th century air. Unfortunately, the coffins proved not to be hermetically sealed. They did contain skeletalized human remains later determined to be those of Philip Calvert, the fourth Royal Governor of the Colony of Maryland, his wife Ann Wolseley Calvert, and an infant child of Calvert. A large number of archaeologically significant artifacts were also found in the coffins. Insect remains and pollen found in the coffins indicated that the interments had taken place in the early autumn.

Light brown or blond human head hairs were recovered from one of the coffins. Microscopic examination of these hairs revealed that in some areas they had lost their cuticular scales. Fungal spores were observed on the surfaces of the hairs (Figure 6A). No fungal hyphae were seen on the hairs; these may have been disturbed when the hairs were removed from the coffin. There were, however, numerous fungal tunnels through the hair shafts in many areas (Figure 6B). These tunnels closely resemble those previously reported by DeGaetano et al. (1992). The presence of the tunnels is consistent with the burial taking place at a time of the year when it was warm enough and there was sufficient moisture available for the growth of fungi.

## Case 2

The second case concerns textile specimens recovered from a young murder victim whose body had been interred for approximately 8 years in a state park north of Baltimore, MD. When buried, the body had been fully clothed in cotton briefs, cotton/polyester corduroy trousers, a polyester shirt, and a cotton jacket with nylon cuffs and tab (the strip down the front containing the button holes). The cotton briefs had completely decayed except for the waistband (made of synthetic elastomer). The shell of the jacket had likewise decomposed, leaving only the synthetic cuffs and tab. Most of the cotton fibers in the trousers had also vanished. However, a triangular segment of the original fabric adjacent to the fly had survived. The survival of the fabric in this particular area may have been due to the brass zipper. Archaeologists have noted that buried natural fibers may be preserved if they are closely associated with copper artifacts. Copper corrosion products in the soil presumably exert a bacteriocidal and fungicidal effect (Boddington et al. 1987).

Microscopic examination of the fibers comprising the surviving fragment of the trousers disclosed that the polyester fibers had not undergone significant biodeterioration. The FTIR spectrum of the polyester fibers matched that of standard polyester fibers in the Collaborative Testing Service fiber collection. The FTIR spectrum of the cotton fibers matched that of standard cotton fibers, except for a small peak at 1735 cm$^{-1}$. Photochemical oxidation of cotton fibers is known to introduce carboxylic acid groups into the cellulose structure (Yang and Freeman 1991). In the present case, this peak is most likely due to exposure of the cloth to sunlight during normal wear. It is unlikely that oxidation occurred after burial because a grave filled with decaying organic matter is a highly reducing environment.

## Case 3

In 1943, two U.S. Coast Guard submarine chasers sank in a hurricane off the coast of Florida. Fifty years later a sports diver recovered three fragments of clothing from one of the sunken vessels. Although items of clothing have been recovered from marine and riverine environments, there apparently have not been any published studies of the microscopic changes in textile fibers brought about by prolonged submersion.

A visual examination of the textile fragments revealed that the largest was the yoke (upper back panel) of a shirt, jacket, or jumper. The remaining fragments could not be associated with any particular type of garment; their similarity of appearance suggested that these smaller fragments were part of the same item. The initial microscopic examinations of the fibers in the fabric fragments revealed that they were composed exclusively of wool. These preliminary microscopic examinations were carried out on wet-mounted samples in distilled water. Permanent mounts were made after dehydration of the fibers. Two dehydration methods were employed. In the first, sample yarns approximately 10 mm in length were immersed in a succession of ethanol solutions with increasing alcohol concentrations. The yarns were immersed for one day each in 1-ml aliquots of 70%, 90%, 95%, and 100% (v/v) ethanol solutions. In the second dehydration method, sample yarns approximately 10 mm in length were immersed for a day in 1-ml aliquots of glacial acetic acid. The dehydrated yarns were transferred to 1-ml aliquots of cedarwood oil for a day. Finally, the yarns were carefully teased apart into their component fibers and the fibers mounted in Permount. Comparisons of the wet-mounted fibers and the dehydrated fibers indicated that neither dehydration method caused additional damage to the fibers.

Although the wool fibers were basically intact, they did display some interesting anomalies. Some fibers had lost patches of cuticular scales (Figure 7A). In a few it appeared that half of the cortex had been lost (Figure 7B). One hypothesis that would explain this strange observation is that protein binding together the cells of the ortho cortex in some of the wool fibers had been completely hydrolyzed and the freed cortical cells had dispersed into the

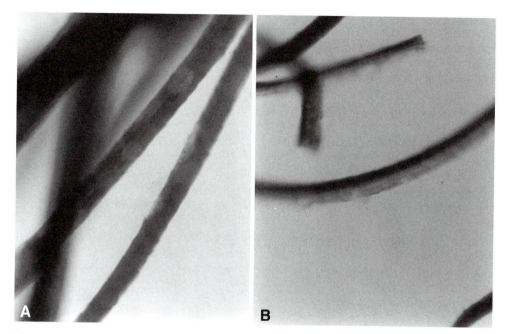

**Figure 7** Wool fibers from sunken U.S. Coast Guard submarine chaser, showing (A) missing cuticular scales, and (B) loss of half of fiber.

surrounding water. An attempt was made to test this hypothesis by refluxing wool fibers in distilled water for several weeks. Unfortunately, none of the refluxed fibers showed this peculiar feature. The cause of this feature remains a mystery.

## Acknowledgments

The author would like to thank Jennifer Kay Owens and Elizabeth Jane Rowe for helping prepare some of the photomicrographs used to illustrate this article. He would also like to thank Project Lead Coffins for providing access to the hair samples from St. Mary's City.

## References

Allsop, D., and K.J. Seal
  1986  *Introduction to Biodeterioration.* Edward Arnold, London.
Bisbing, R.E.
  1982  The Forensic Identification and Association of Human Hair. In *Forensic Science Handbook*, edited by Richard Saferstein, pp. 184–221. Prentice-Hall, Englewood Cliffs.
Boddington, A., A.N. Garland, and R.C. Janaway
  1987  *Death, Decay and Reconstruction: Approaches to Archaeology and Forensic Science.* University of Manchester Press, Manchester, U.K.
Carroll, G.R.
  1992  Forensic Fibre Microscopy. In *Forensic Examination of Fibres*, edited by J. Robertson, pp. 99–126. Ellis Horwood, Chichester, U.K.
Challinor, J.M.
  1992  Fibre identification by Pyrolysis Techniques. In *Forensic Examination of Fibres*, edited by J. Robertson, pp. 219–238. Ellis Horwood, Chichester, U.K.

Daniels, G.
 1953  The Digestion of Human Hair Keratin by *Microsporum Canis* Bodin. *Journal of General Microbiology* 8:289–294.

David, S.K., and M.T. Pailthorpe
 1992  Classification of Textile Fibers: Production, Structure and Properties. In *Forensic Examination of Fibres*, edited by J. Robertson, pp. 1–40. Ellis Horwood, Chichester, U.K.

Deadman, H.
 1990  Hair Analysis in the Helle Crafts Murder Trial — The Woodchipper Case. Paper presented at the Annual Meeting of the Mid-Atlantic Association of Forensic Scientists, Fredericksburg, MD.

DeForest, P.R., R.E. Gaensslen, and H.C. Lee
 1983  *Forensic Science: An Introduction to Criminalistics.* McGraw-Hill, New York.

DeGaetano, D.H., J.B. Kempton, and W.F. Rowe
 1992  Fungal Tunneling of Hair from a Buried Body. *Journal of Forensic Sciences* 37:1048–1054.

Deshmukh, S.K., and S.C. Agrawal
 1982  *In Vitro* Degradation of Human Hair by Some Keratinophilic Fungi. *Mykosen* 25:454–458.

Engel, L., H. Klingele, G.W. Ehrenstein, and H. Schaper
 1981  *An Atlas of Polymer Damage.* Prentice-Hall, Englewood Cliffs.

English, M.P.
 1963  The Saprophytic Growth of Karatinophilic Fungi on Keratin. *Sabouradia* 2:115–130
 1965  The Saprophytic Growth of Non-Keratinophilic Fungi on Keratinized Substrata, and a Comparison with Keratinophilic Fungi. *Transactions of the British Mycological Society* 48:219–235.
 1969  The Destruction of Hair by *Chrysosporium keratinophilum*. *Transactions of the British Mycological Society* 52:247–255.
 1976  Destruction of Hair by Two Species of *Chrysosporium*. *Transactions of the British Mycological Society* 66:357–358.

Federal Bureau of Investigation
 1978  *Solubility Schemes by Generic Class.* Federal Bureau of Investigation, Washington, D.C.

Gaudette, B.D.
 1988  The Forensic Aspects of Textile Fiber Examination. In *Forensic Science Handbook*, Vol. 2, edited by R. Saferstein, pp. 209–272. Prentice-Hall, Englewood Cliffs, NJ.

Hawks, C.A., and W.F. Rowe
 1988  Deterioration of Hair by Airborne Microorganisms: Implications for Museum Biological Collections. In *Biodeterioration 7*, edited by D.R. Houghton, R.N. Smith, and H.O.W. Eggins, pp. 461–465. Elsevier Science, New York.

Hicks, J.W.
 1977  *Microscopy of Hair: A Practical Guide and Manual.* Federal Bureau of Investigation, Washington, D.C.

Huek, H.J.
 1965  The Biodeterioration of Materials as a Part of Hylobiology. *Material und Organismen* 1:5–34.
 1968  The Biodeterioration of Materials — An Appraisal. In *Biodeterioration of Materials*, pp. 6–12. Elsevier Science, London.

Kirkbride, K.P.
 1992  The Application of Infrared Microspectroscopy to the Analysis of Single Fibres. In *Forensic Examination of Fibres*, edited by J. Robertson, pp. 181–218. Ellis Horwood, Chichester, U.K.

Kundrat, J.A., and W.F. Rowe
   1989   A Study of Hair Degradation in Agricultural Soil. In *Biodeterioration Research 2: General Biodeterioration, Degradation, Mycotoxins, Biotins, and Wood Decay*, edited by G.C. Llewellyn and C.E. O'Rear, pp. 91–98. Plenum Press, New York.

Kupferschmid, T.D., R. Van Dyke, and W.F. Rowe
   1994   Scanning Electron Microscope Studies of the Biodeterioration of Human Hair Buried in Soil and Immersed in Water. In *Biodeterioration Research 4*, edited by G.C. Llewellyn, W.V. Dashek, and C.E. O'Rear, pp. 479–492. Plenum Press, New York.

Morse, D., J.W. Duncan, and J. Stoutmeyer
   1983   *Handbook of Forensic Archaeology and Anthropology*. Rose Printing, Tallahassee.

Northrop, D.M.
   1986   Biodeterioration of Man-Made Textiles and Analysis by Pyrolysis-Gas Liquid Chromatography. Masters thesis, George Washington University, Washington, D.C.

Northrop, D.M., and W.F. Rowe
   1987   Effect of the Soil Environment on the Biodeterioration of Man-Made Textiles. In *Biodeterioration 1*, edited by G.C. Llewellyn and C.E. O'Rear, pp. 7–16. Plenum Press, New York.

Page, R.M.
   1950   Observations in Keratin Digestion by *Microsporum gypseum. Mycologia* 42:591–602.

Rodriguez, W., and W. Bass
   1985   Decomposition of Bodies and Methods That May Aid in Their Location. *Journal of Forensic Sciences* 30:836–852.

Serowik, J.M.
   1987   Biodeterioration of Hair in a Soil Environment. Master's thesis, Department of Forensic Sciences, George Washington University, Washington, D.C.

Serowik, J.M., and W.F. Rowe
   1987   Biodeterioration of Hair in a Soil Environment. In *Biodeterioration Research 1*, edited by G.C. Llewellyn and C.E. O'Rear, pp. 87–93. Plenum Press, New York.

Seta, S., H. Sato, and B. Miyake
   1988   Forensic Hair Investigation. In *Forensic Science Progress*, edited by A. Maehly and R.L. Williams, pp. 47–166. Springer, Berlin.

Singer, S.M.
   1989   Biodeterioration of Man-Made Textile Fibers in Various Soil Environments. Master's thesis, George Washington University, Washington, D.C.

Singer, S.M., D.M. Northrop, M.W. Tungol, and W.F. Rowe
   1990   The Infrared Spectra of Buried Acetate and Rayon Fibers. In *Biodeterioration Research 3: General Biodeterioration, Degradation, Mycotoxins, Biotins, and Wood Decay*, edited by G.C. Llewellyn and C.E. O'Rear, pp. 577–587. Plenum Press, New York.

Singer, S.M., and W.F. Rowe
   1989   Biodeterioration of Man-Made Textiles in Various Soil Environments. In *Biodeterioration Research 2: General Biodeterioration, Degradation, Mycotoxins, Biotins, and Wood Decay*, edited by G.C. Llewellyn and C.E. O'Rear, pp. 81–89. Plenum Press, New York.

Vanbreuseghem, R.
   1952   Keratin Digestion by Dermatophytes: A Specific Diagnostic Method. *Mycologia* 44:289–294.

Yang, C.Q., and J.M. Freeman
   1991   Photo-Oxidation of Cotton Cellulose Studied by FT-IR Photoacoustic Spectroscopy. *Applied Spectroscopy* 45:1695–1698.

# Forensic Botany

# 22

DAVID W. HALL

## Introduction

Forensic botany is the study of plants related to the law. Botany, while widely known as a science, lacks professionally trained botanists. In proportion to the numbers of students trained in other disciplines, botanists are but a tiny fraction. Those who teach botany at any level have perhaps only a course or two, or often only a portion of a course in botany. With this low level of exposure it is no wonder that so little school training is devoted to plants.

Law enforcement officers and attorneys are no more informed, on average, than the general population; therefore, important plant evidence is frequently overlooked in forensic cases. Sometimes this evidence can place a person or object at or away from a crime scene, or help determine time of death or the time of a crime, or the cause of death or illness.

To be of value, evidence usually has to be interpreted by a botanist trained in systematics, anatomy, and ecology. Not all botanists have such training. Some botanists are physiologists (chemists) and others work with only a single group of plants. The initial analysis of botanical material should be done by a botanist with well-rounded training and experience. The material can then be referred to an appropriate specialist, such as a plant physiologist, if needed.

## Evidence

Any plant part touching or buried with human remains can be valuable. Frequently time of death, time of year, or prior locations can be indicated. If a botanist is not on site, color photographs and preservation of all associated plant material are crucial. Footprints on plant material and branches which have been broken, as well as all the material directly under, on, or buried with the remains can be valuable. Some evidence concerning time of death will need to be evaluated at the scene by a trained botanist. Color photographs can be used to check with a botanist to determine if such a visit is warranted.

When someone digs a hole to bury remains they usually disturb and damage associated plants to some extent. Dirt from the hole is usually returned to cover the remains. Raking or shoveling the dirt into the hole damages additional plants. Often thousands of plant fragments will be buried with remains. All fragments should be saved. This can be time consuming and greatly slow the progress of remains recovery. Screening is usually the best means of finding the fragments.

Clothing and hair are obvious places to search for evidence. Everything exposed to plant material should be carefully examined. Pockets, cuffs, and seams can conceal evidence. Shoe laces and shoe seams are obvious focal points for hard-to-see evidence. Bruised or broken surfaces of plants can leak sap which, if sticky, can enable plant parts to stick to a smooth surface. Natural glandular secretions from leaves, fruits, seeds, and other plant parts serve to help plants naturally move from place to place. These characteristics provide a means of attachment to many surfaces. Spines and thorns can pierce skin and many other substances. Hundreds of kinds of hairs are found on plants. Hairs enable plant pieces to adhere to clothing and other rough surfaces. Most suspects overlook plant evidence and have no knowledge of its possible importance. If possible, to reduce the chances of missed evidence, a systematic botanist should recheck all evidence because his eye is trained to see small plant parts (Hall 1988).

Perennial plants such as trees which grow for several to many years often contain seasonal and/or yearly rings which can be used to show that the remains at a minimum are older than the interval shown. Other perennial and even annual species can be used similarly in certain situations.

Roots can be equally valuable. Some species of plants produce annual rings, but most do not. Even so, roots can still be used to show relative time intervals. Roots should be photographed when encountered. If roots are to be cut, try to cut the roots at some distance from the remains to preserve the internal structure at the point of contact. Many species of plants are difficult to identify from roots alone. At the scene it is important to try to follow the roots to the plant and preserve a sample of that plant for help with identification. Roots of many species frequently intermingle, thus following the root to its source is often futile. Identification may or may not affect the value of the root evidence (Willey and Heilman 1987).

Roots, on occasion, etch bones. The depth of etching may be helpful in suggesting time intervals, but no research has been produced which shows the time interval necessary for the roots of various species of plants to etch bones (Lyman 1994:375–377).

## Plant Characteristics

Plants are combinations of various structures such as roots, stems, branches, leaves, and flowers. These structures are composed of various kinds of cells. Obviously, a tree has different stem cells than does a water lily. A plant anatomist (one who studies cells) can often determine to what structure certain cells belong. Sometimes a plant anatomist can determine a genus or even the species when examining a plant fragment which has distinctive cells (Stern 1988).

Closely related species may only differ in a single characteristic which may be on a part of the plant not present. If the crucial character needed to determine a species is not present, the plant cannot be named. It may be possible to determine a broader relationship such as a genus or family which can still yield useful information.

Many plants have unique parts which can be used by a systematic botanist (one who studies plant names) to determine the name. Different kinds (species) of plants have leaves of various shapes and colors as well as unique tips, bases and margins. Leaves can be arranged in distinct patterns and may or may not have stalks. Stems and branching patterns vary. Root systems vary tremendously. Flowers and fruits are the principal means by which we separate plant species. Flowers and fruits, obviously, are not always found on a body or at a scene. Many other characteristics can be used for identification, but usually identification is more difficult and can be less certain. Many characters such as hairs and scales on leaves are microscopic. Microscopic as well as macroscopic characteristics may or may not be useful.

The usefulness of the name of the plant should be self-evident. The name of the plant is the index to all information concerning that plant! It is the key that unlocks the door. Practical experience and the library are the two best resources available for information about plants but they both are dependent on the plant name.

The two most important thoughts concerning plant characteristics are: have a qualified botanist name the plant and have a qualified botanist interpret the evidence.

# Ecology

Plants grow with other plants in associations. The habitats in which they grow are governed by soil, temperature, wind, moisture, altitude, latitude, and longitude. Hardwood forests and swamps are two easily recognized plant associations. Some plant associations are widespread, such as the northern coniferous forest. Other associations are narrowly limited, such as the scrub found in central Florida. Obviously, finding plant evidence from a habitat which is rare can be extremely valuable to a case.

All habitats are dominated by certain species. This domination can be by numbers of individuals of that species or by the size of the species. In grass prairies the dominant species usually is indicated by the vast numbers of certain grasses. In a cypress swamp the dominant plant is the very large cypress tree, although there may be fewer cypress trees than other kinds of plants present.

Most plant associations have been investigated and described. Identifying any particular plant known to be an element of the particular habitat can indicate other species in the association. Much additional information can be gained from a plant ecologist (one who studies plants and their relationship to the environment) based on relationships among plants. Determination of even a single plant can be of great help in placing a person or object at a location.

# Lack of Habitat

Many species of plants can occur in several different habitats, i.e., various weeds that grow in any cultivated or otherwise disturbed area. This may mean that a specific habitat cannot be indicated. Still, some kinds of information can be useful even if a specific plant association is not indicated. For instance, one might be able to determine if it is a wet or dry area, or at least if the plant material is from a different area than that in which the body was found.

An example would be that of creeping beggar-weed seeds found on something in a pine woods. Creeping beggar-weed occurs in almost every open or disturbed habitat in its range. Since pine woods are open woods with light to medium shade, this plant could have been growing near or at the scene or almost anywhere except wet habitats. If these seeds had been taken as evidence from a burial scene in a wet area they would prove an encounter with drier habitat.

# Plant Dispersal

Plants have both simple and complex ways of moving seeds and vegetative reproductive pieces. Some fruits and seeds are edible so that animals ingest and/or carry them to new spots. Many seeds are light and have hairs and/or papery wings or are very tiny so that winds provide transport. Seeds and fruits with air spaces are moved by water. Flowers, fruits, seeds, and other pieces of plants can have hooks, hairs, spines, sticky secretions, and break-away parts. These stick to passing animals including humans. Our pets often show proof of this. In the case of humans, the reproductive parts usually stick to clothing, but sandspurs can penetrate the skin.

Many seeds and other plant propagules are tiny. Some are no more than a tenth of a millimeter in length or diameter. Pollen can be smaller. To see such small objects takes a careful examination and skill and experience. Without magnification, much plant evidence can be missed.

## Naming Plants

Should a case go to court, it is crucial to have a systematic botanist involved in identification. Plant identification can be difficult. The number of vascular plant species in the world exceeds 250,000. Usually the smaller the area, the fewer the species. Local areas can have few to several hundreds of species. In addition to large numbers of species that exist, an inadequate sample can make identification difficult. It is crucial to have a botanist who is familiar with the local vegetation assisting with identification. He may readily put names on the plants, regardless of their condition, due to his familiarity with them. This procedure can save time and effort and therefore money.

The botanist may recognize the plant from the macroscopic characteristics or may need to check for distinctive microscopic characteristics. If the material is not recognized, then it must be identified by the use of botanical keys. Botanical keys provide a process of elimination. Some keys are published and readily available, others are made up by the botanists for their own use. An initial examination usually can rule out many species. For example, is it a herbaceous plant or a woody tree? There are many fewer trees than there are herbaceous plants. Is the leaf arrangement opposite or alternate? Fewer plants have opposite leaves. Obviously, the more plants from which you have to choose, the slower and more difficult the process.

Even with excellent material not all plants can be named. In the United States there are few unnamed species. Other areas of the world are still somewhat unexplored botanically and have many unidentified species. Also, plants have not been compiled into inclusive treatments in various parts of the world. The South American tropics fall into such a category. Identification of a plant from the Amazon Basin would require several specialists and have only a 50% chance of success, even with excellent material. Still, knowing that the plant is tropical can indicate a trip out of the United States.

## Time

Plants can give an indication of time. Many plants are annuals, such as warm season crops like corn and soybeans. Some annuals are quite short-lived, completing their life cycles in a matter of days or weeks. These short-lived annuals may germinate as soon as the ground is warm enough and die as the weather becomes hot. Annual plants at high altitudes commonly are quite short-lived. Thus, if a short-lived plant is present, the person or object would have been where that plant grew during its growing season.

Other characteristics also indicate seasonality and therefore can be of help. Plants that lose their leaves for the winter or in dry seasons also will then regain leaves in warmer or wetter times. The timing of these events can be of great use. Flowering, fruiting, shoot or branch growth, etc. timing can be very valuable.

When regular leaf fall occurs the layers of leaves can indicate longer periods of time. Colder climates and very dry climates will normally accumulate several layers of leaves because the leaves take several years to decompose. In warm to hot climates, leaves decompose very rapidly and can, when use is possible, only be used for time intervals of a few weeks or months. Leaves falling into standing water or buried in certain soil types will accumulate and are very slow to deteriorate due to the lack of oxygen.

## Stomach Contents

Plants within stomachs can be identified by means of their anatomy. A book by Bock et al. (1988) details identification of plant food cells in gastric contents. Surprising deductions can occasionally be made on the basis of ingested food. In one case an analysis of stomach contents of two murdered women led to the assumption that a serial killer was responsible. Sometimes the contents can lead investigators to the place of a last meal (Bock et al. 1988; Lane et al. 1990).

## Pollen

Pollen is the microscopic male propagule of plants. It is moved by air currents, water, insects, and larger animals including humans. Hundreds of millions of pollen grains can be released by a single plant in a single season. Due to similarities within related groups, pollen analysis can be quite difficult. Frequently, identification to only a family or genus is possible. Identification will need to be done by an expert in a very clean environment to avoid contamination from ever-present grains in the air.

Wind-blown pollen can be extremely valuable for geographical location. Pollen can fill the air in the vicinity of the plant releasing it. Any person who is in the vicinity will have this pollen. Most likely the pollen will be in hair, clothing, nostrils, ears, body, or possibly lungs. Many pollen grains are ornamented with various microscopic characteristics which roughen the exterior, enabling them to become entangled with hairs or to easily stick to other suitable surfaces. Due to its microscopic size pollen is often overlooked and difficult to identify but can be of great value in determining location and time of year (Stanley 1991).

## Fungi

Fungi are nonphotosynthetic organisms in the plant kingdom and are most commonly thought of as mushrooms. Mushrooms are but one of the groups of fungi. Reproduction is commonly by spores. The bodies are usually filamentous and are the agents responsible for much of the disintegration of organic matter. Many fungi have both underground and above-ground parts. The spores of fungi, like pollen, are microscopic and move by air currents, water, insects, and larger animals. Spores and the filaments of fungi can be of help to determine time of death and prior locations of the body.

## Algae

Algae are nonvascular plants which typically possess chlorophyll and are photosynthetic. Algae can present distinctive opportunities for linking a suspect to a location. An alga can be unique in a particular habitat, or an assemblage of algae can be just as characteristic. Often particular combinations of algae can define a body of water. One case linked several suspects to the scene of an attack by the combination of algae found in their clothing and shoes. Some algae have very resistant coverings (diatoms) and are extremely resistant to decay, lasting thousands of years. Such long-lasting evidence can be of importance, but will need to be handled by an expert just as other trace evidence should be (Silver et al. 1994).

## DNA

DNA is an extremely valuable new tool in the arsenal of the forensic investigator. To determine if any fragment was part of a suspected parent plant, just as with human DNA, the DNA of both can be compared. To determine the absolute relationship, statistics must be employed. Unfortunately, no database exists for any plant species. A database would have to be created before any comparison could be made. To be valid, the population of the species would have to be sampled throughout its range. This would be very time consuming and expensive. Eventually, data for common species will be compiled.

Although an exact match cannot be made, sometimes a simpler test can be used to determine that the sample is matched to a certain species. This method of identification utilizes laboratory procedures in the hands of an expert and is good only to the level of species, not to match a specific plant. To be able to make a comparison for identification, a selection of suspected species will be needed. Obviously, a random selection of species could entail hundreds of possibilities.

## Evidence Collection

Plants retain nearly all of their characteristics after drying. Colors can change and shapes of fleshy parts such as fruits often change. Colors, shapes, and other characteristics that change after drying can be measured and recorded. Material does not have to be "green" to be useful. The best method to preserve evidence is in paper, between sheets of newsprint, or a telephone book, catalog, etc. Paper bags can be used, but there is a risk of shattering dried plant parts if they are smashed. Pasteboard boxes are excellent for larger pieces.

Since the evidence is collected in paper, the necessary information can be written directly on it. In addition to color, shape, and size it is mandatory to record the name of the collector, a unique sample number, the date and time of collection, exactly where found, and chain of custody. Include some indication of location with reference to a major road, lake, or other landmark easily found on a map just as is usually done when recording the location of the crime scene.

Plant material contains moisture and sugars. Both of these elements are attractive to bacteria and fungi. The higher the sugar and/or moisture content the faster the degradation. If heat is present, rotting can be complete within 2 to 3 days, but many of the distinguishing characteristics will disappear within a few hours. It is crucial not to collect plant material in plastic bags or any nonporous container. However, if plant material is stuck to a body part or soaked in fluids, it may be collected in plastic and refrigerated. Coolers with ice can be used for temporary storage in the field. The plant material should not be placed directly on the ice to avoid freezing it. It is important not to freeze the material as the cells will disintegrate, destroying important identification characteristics. The evidence should be placed in a refrigerator a soon as is practicable. Refrigerated plant material should be examined as quickly as possible because deterioration under refrigeration will be slower, but still present.

To help with evaluation by a botanist, plants surrounding the scene need to be sampled by the investigator. The same information as noted above should be recorded. Smaller plants need to be collected in their entirety. The whole plant including roots should be removed from the ground with a shovel, soil knocked off, and be placed in paper. If the plant is too large for the paper or container it can be folded. Folding should be in a zigzag fashion like an accordion. If the plant cannot be folded, it can be cut into sections. Each section should be put into separate paper. All sections of the same plant should have the same number. Each section should be noted as top, middle, bottom, or other.

Larger plants need only have a piece of the plant collected. For instance a 12- to 18-inch portion of a branch or vine with its accompanying leaves should be satisfactory. To trim these pieces requires sharp pruners or a sharp knife. Dull tools sometimes cause much damage to the sample.

Very small fragments or seeds can best be put into a packet made from a folded piece of paper. Thick roots, branches, stems, bark, etc. can be split so that they conveniently fit into the paper or box. It is very important to look under and around the collected plant for fallen leaves, fruits, flowers, or other parts. Always try to collect a plant with fruits or flowers. All plants (even if they are the same kind) do not necessarily flower at the same time. By looking around the scene for flowers or fruits on identical plants you will greatly enhance the chances for identification.

Watery, succulent samples or juicy fruits, such as an orange, should either be sliced thin enough to place into newsprint or placed whole into a pasteboard box. In either case the sample should have waxed paper placed on both sides or around the sample. The waxed paper will keep the sample from sticking to the paper or container and still permit it to dry. Sugar-filled and excessively wet samples almost always will stick to unwaxed paper. If stuck to the paper, determination and analysis may be impossible.

Many, if not all, scenes have plants present, at least in the immediate vicinity. Homes have flower arrangements and/or potted plants inside. Most buildings have ornamental plants outside, including lawns and lawn weeds. Weeds, so often overlooked in nature, are likewise frequently ignored in forensics. Weeds, because of their adaptations for seed transport, can be extremely valuable in an investigation. Pollen can be everywhere.

A handy plant collection device, called a field press, can easily be made using cardboard or light weight boards. Two pieces of cardboard or board are cut to the size of a once-folded page of newspaper. Newspaper can then be folded to this size (newspapers are frequently delivered once folded). When all samples are in newspaper they should be stacked. One piece of the wood or cardboard is placed on each side of the stacked samples. Any two or more pieces of rope, webbing, belting, etc. can be used to tighten the stack. This bundle is easily carried.

When the plants are bound tightly together they should be taken immediately to a botanist for separation, drying, and analysis. This procedure will prevent rotting.

# Placing People or Objects at Scenes

## Case 1

A woman who was sexually attacked was able to find the scene of the attack. It was outside a city in a wet area. The examination of the spot revealed thousands of seeds and broken flowering parts. These seeds and flower parts were sampled and collected. The surrounding vegetation was also sampled so that the scene could be documented.

Upon arrest of a suspect, a blanket described by the victim as being used in the attack was found. The blanket was covered with plant material. Upon examination thousands of seeds and flower parts were found. Seven different species of plants were represented. Four of the species were widespread weeds found in most lawns and open disturbed areas. These four species were represented by only a few samples among the thousands on the blanket. The remaining thousands of seeds, flower parts, and fragments were the same species as those found at the scene of the attack which was previously examined.

The suspect said he had used the blanket for picnics with his family on his lawn and at two local lakes. These areas were checked for evidence of the three plants. One of the species was found as a weed in the lawns. It has light, hairy, wind-blown seeds and frequently occurs in lawns, but is killed by mowing long before it would mature and produce flowers and fruits.

At the trial the three kinds of plants on the blanket were described as matching those at the scene. It was also explained that the plants grew in moist to wet areas and would not be found growing to maturity in lawns. The defense maintained that the seeds and other fragments could have blown into those lawn areas near lakes where the blanket was said to have been used. It was pointed out that two of the species did not have seeds that could be carried by the wind. There were three clinching facts: (1) the plants have to be mature and are 3 to

9 feet tall when flowering and fruiting, which would not happen in a mowed lawn; (2) the thousands of seeds and fragments would not be found in a lawn where the mature plants did not grow; (3) these seeds and fragments matched those at the scene of the attack. The defendant was convicted and is serving a long sentence.

## Case 2

This case involved a lady returning to her apartment to find a man waiting who had a pillowcase over his head. She immediately escaped and the man ran out and left. The man was observed to have picked up a motorcycle helmet from beneath a bush. A motorcyclist was stopped nearby minutes later; he had a leaf fragment beneath his visor.

The leaf fragment had enough characteristics present so that it could be identified. It was the same kind of plant as that growing at the scene. Unfortunately, the fragment did not show any cut or broken surface in common with the plant at the scene. Some intermediate piece was probably lost along the way. Unfortunately for the suspect, the plant at the scene was unusual in that it is seldom grown as an outdoor plant in that area. The area is subject to freezing temperatures and this plant easily freezes. It could only grow outdoors in a spot protected from freezing. This plant was in a protected spot and its size indicated that it had grown outdoors for several years.

This unusual situation provided strong circumstantial evidence linking the suspect to the scene. The suspect was convicted and sentenced.

## Case 3

This case involved a murder victim found in his barn. He had been killed with a shotgun. A young next-door neighbor was immediately a suspect because of a recent heated argument. A shotgun in the suspect's house had been recently fired. Also, muddy footprints led from the barn to the suspect's house and a pair of the suspect's shoes were muddy.

Upon arrest the suspect confessed, but recanted when advised by a lawyer. The district attorney now was faced with the need for additional evidence.

The butt of the gun had several small plant fragments attached. These plant fragments were determined to all be one grass. Grasses are particularly difficult to determine from fragments. Luckily, one fragment was of a portion of a leaf with a distinguishing hair characteristic. The grass was a common species used for forage, hay, or lawns, and found in most disturbed habitats.

The fragments, when found shortly after the shooting, were already dried, so had not been stuck to the gun while green, i.e., pulled from a growing plant. In the several county area around the murder this grass is seldom used for forage, hay, or lawns. The murdered farmer had used the grass for hay and had placed a pile of it beneath the outside of the window through which he was shot. The killer had put the gun down in the hay. This strong circumstantial evidence helped lead to a conviction and sentence.

## Case 4

This case involves an intact skeleton found at an airplane crash site. The circumstances were such that the remains could not have been part of the crash. The skeleton was completely clean except for a small patch of skin behind an ear against the ground. The patch of skin had human hairs and a few plant fragments stuck to it. The plant fragments luckily had one portion of a grass seedhead from which an identification could be made. This grass is used for forage and is not very common. All the grasses nearby were different, including those in an adjacent pasture. This evidence indicated the skeleton had been moved after deterioration.

## Case 5

Often circumstantial botanical evidence does not help a case. A body of a murder victim was found in a forested area. The victim's car was found in another state. When found, an extensive examination of the vehicle yielded a single fingerprint and numerous plant fragments.

The person to whom the fingerprint belonged admitted stealing the car, but said that he had found it elsewhere. The plant fragments matched the vegetation at the scene. During the deposition the defense attorney, who had a degree in forestry, was able to show that the evidence not only could have come from the scene but also could have been from anywhere along a thousand mile track of identical woods. This circumstantial evidence was of little help in solving the crime.

# Determining Time of Death

## Case 1

A skeleton found in woods was beyond the normal means for determining time of death. The majority of the skeleton had been moved before the botanist visited the scene. Plant evidence beneath the skeleton was no longer useful. Two bones had not been recovered at the scene, a jaw bone and a leg bone. After an intensive search, the bones were discovered, both at some distance from the original scene. The bones were not disturbed until after an analysis by the botanist. The jaw bone was in a patch of sand and yielded no botanical evidence. The leg bone was on a fully grown leaf of a seedling of a deciduous (leaves falling in winter) tree. Under the leg bone, the chlorophyll had been shaded and killed, leaving a brown band the width of the bone. Chlorophyll in this tree takes several weeks to die. The period of weeks during which the shaded chlorophyll died was used as a time window. The leaf of the seedling was full grown. The tip of the leaf was not distorted, which indicated that the bone had been put on the leaf after full expansion. Residents in the area gave an estimate of when spring occurred and the tree had likely budded out. The time necessary for the leaf to grow to maturity yielded a second time window.

Tooth marks on the bone indicated that it had been moved by a dog. A dog cannot rip a bone from a body until it is well deteriorated. To determine how long this deterioration would take, experienced medical examiners who worked in this area of the state were consulted. They provided an average time interval for such deterioration. The local weather service records indicated that the winter, during which the decomposition occurred, was unusually cold. The lower temperatures would slow the process. Extra time was added to the average that provided the third time interval.

These three time windows were added and then subtracted from the time of discovery. A search through files for people missing near the postulated time of death produced a match. The disappearance of the person was during the week prior to the time of death estimate.

## Case 2

Growth patterns and biology of nonwoody plants can also be of value. A quite deteriorated body was found lying on the top of a bent-over plant which is a common agricultural weed. The chlorophyll was dead and the plant was beginning to rot. Time windows were again useful.

Experience has shown that a certain period of shading will kill the top. The time necessary to kill the top provided the first time window.

A shoot was growing from the base of the plant. Research on this agricultural weed has shown shoot initiation will occur within a certain interval after the top is cut. Since the body killed the plant top, this served the same function as cutting the top. The time from top death until shoot initiation was the second time window.

The third time window was the estimated time for the shoot to reach the length found on the plant at the scene. These three time windows — top death, time for resprouting, shoot regrowth — were added. The time of death estimated from the plant evidence corresponded to that determined from other evidence by the medical examiner.

## Case 3

A portion of a skeleton was found in a ditch. Plants had grown around and through the portion. Although several types of plants could be used for evidence of time of death, a vine was growing through the skeleton. This type of vine produces annual growth rings which were easily interpreted. A minimum time of deposition for this partial skeleton could be accurately given the medical examiner.

## Case 4

A body was found under a common species of low growing palm. Good color photographs were taken as the body was removed. Plants found on and in the skeleton were of little use as the area in which the body was found flooded intermittently. Soil washed over and was deposited on the skeleton. Since the time of soil depositions was impossible to track, the best evidence for time of death was the growth of the adjacent palms. The palms had been burned and the skeleton had not. The skeleton must have been deposited after the fire. Fire records are very accurate, but this fire was not recorded. The number of fronds which had grown since the fire were counted. Research indicated an average number of fronds per year. By dividing the total number of fronds by the average, a minimum time since body deposition could be determined.

## Case 5

Various pieces of plants were included when a body was buried. One of the species was identified as a common turf grass. The grass showed discoloration indicating death of chlorophyll due to loss of light, which could indicate the time of the burial. Similar pieces of grass were buried and removed at selected intervals. By matching the color of the evidence grass to the color of the experimental samples, a time of burial of the grass could be estimated to within a few hours. Of course, the burial of the plant samples could have occurred after the body had been placed.

## Conclusion

Plants and parts of plants are useful evidence in forensic cases in reconstructing details about past events, determining time since death, sequences of events, and placing people or objects at scenes. Collection and identification methods are critical to the quality and comparability of the evidence. The involvement of a professional botanist is frequently necessary in order to correctly process and interpret botanical information acquired during scene investigations or discovered in the forensic laboratory.

## References

Bock, J.H., M.A. Lane, and D.O. Norris
    1988  Identifying Plant Food Cells in Gastric Contents for Use in Forensic Investigations: A Laboratory Manual. National Institute of Justice, U.S. Department of Justice, Washington, D.C.

Hall, D.W.
   1988   The Contributions of the Forensic Botanist to Crime Scene Investigations. *The Prosecutor* 22(1):35–38.

Lane, M.A., L.C. Anderson, T.M. Barkley, J.H. Bock, E.M. Gifford, D.W. Hall, D.O. Norris, T.L. Rost, and W.L. Stern
   1990   Forensic Botany. Plants, Perpetrators, Pests, Poisons, and Pot. *BioScience* 40:34–39.

Lyman, R.L.
   1994   *Vertebrate Taphonomy.* Cambridge University Press, Cambridge, MA.

Silver, P.A., W.D. Lord, and D.J. McCarthy
   1994   Forensic Limnology: The Use of Freshwater Algal Community Ecology to Link Suspects to an Aquatic Crime Scene in Southern New England. *Journal of Forensic Sciences* 39:847–853.

Stanley, E.A.
   1991   Forensic Palynology. Paper presented at the 1991 International Symposium on the Forensic Aspects of Trace Evidence, FBI Laboratory, Quantico, VA.

Stern, W.L.
   1988   Wood in the Courtroom. *World of Wood* 41(9):6–9.

Willey, P., and A. Heilman
   1987   Estimating Time Since Death Using Plant Roots and Stems. *Journal of Forensic Sciences* 32:1264–1270.

# SECTION III

## Scavenged Remains

- *Carnivore Scavenged Remains*
- *Rodent Scavenged Remains*
- *Scavenged by Insects*
- *Scavenging by Water Organisms*

# Dogs and Coyotes: Postmortem Involvement with Human Remains

# 23

## WILLIAM D. HAGLUND

## Introduction

Dogs and coyotes are the most frequently reported canids responsible for scavenging human remains (Bass 1984; Haglund 1991; Haglund et al. 1988, 1989; Rodriguez 1987; Rossi et al. 1994). Their scavenging results in soft tissue modification and consumption, disarticulation, modification of bone, and scattering of remains. The significance of scavenging to forensic investigations is its potential to: (1) destroy or scatter body parts; (2) alter or destroy indications of the cause and manner of death; and (3) create postmortem artifacts. Additionally, carnivores can alter the scene and evidence, such as clothing, so as to complicate its interpretation.

A fuller understanding of animal scavenging can prove invaluable in forensic investigations (Haglund et al. 1988, 1989; Rodriguez 1987; Sorg 1986). This is true relative to: (1) locating and recovering dispersed skeletal elements (Haglund 1991; Haglund et al. 1989; Morse et al. 1983); (2) interpreting the relative times that scavenging took place during the postmortem interval; and (3) in distinguishing animal artifacts from other modifications of soft tissue and bone. Some authors have suggested that investigation of scattering and damage to skeletons by animals may aid in establishing the postmortem interval (Haglund et al. 1988; Morse et al. 1983), and may reflect the ecological and environmental conditions under which disarticulation occurred (Hill 1979; Rhine et al. 1988).

Three reports, surveying scavenged human remains from the Pacific Northwest, as well as subsequent cases in which the author participated, are used as a basis for the following summary (Haglund 1991; Haglund et al. 1988, 1989). The discussion is structured topically as: (1) disarticulation and soft tissue consumption; (2) damage to bone and frequencies of skeletal element recovery; and (3) movement of scavenged remains by dogs and coyotes. Variables affecting scavenging are presented, and the conclusion discusses applications of this information to forensic investigations.

## Disarticulation and Soft Tissue Consumption

Disarticulation exposes bones to other types of damage, for instance, weathering, and reduces the remains into smaller, more easily dispersed units.

In a report of 53 canid-scavenged human remains recovered from the Pacific Northwest, disarticulation stages for canid-scavenged human remains are described (Haglund 1991) (Table 1) using the proposed model for stages of canid-scavenged disarticulation complement stages described by Hill (1979) and Haynes (1980, 1982). These observations suggest that coyote and dog disarticulation/dismemberment of human remains takes place in a relatively consistent sequence. This is especially true for bodies which are scavenged prior to modification from other processes such as advanced decomposition and insect activity.

0-8493-9434-1/97/$0.00+$.50
© 1997 by CRC Press, Inc.

**Table 1   Stages of Canid-Assisted Scavenging (N = 37)**

| Stage | Condition of Remains | Range of Observed Postmortem Interval |
|---|---|---|
| 0 | Early scavenging of soft tissue with no body unit removal | 4 hours to 14 days |
| 1 | Destruction of the ventral thorax accompanied by evisceration and removal of one or both upper extremities including scapulae and partial or complete clavicles | 22 days to 2.5 months |
| 2 | Lower extremities fully or partially removed | 2 to 4.5 months |
| 3 | All skeletal elements disarticulated except for segments of the vertebral column | 2 to 11 months |
| 4 | Total disarticulation with only cranium and other assorted skeletal elements or fragments recovered | 5 to 52 months |

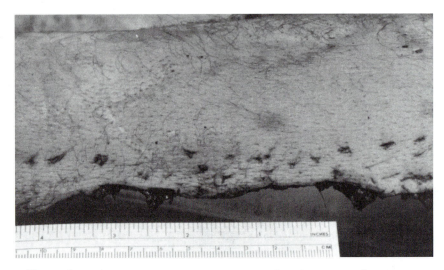

**Figure 1**   Tooth damage to skin margin; note V-shaped canine tooth punctures.

Removal of skin and muscle from the face and neck, accompanied by removal of neck organs, is routinely the first action of scavengers (stage 0). At this point there may be minor damage to thin bones of the orbits, caused by canine punctures. Margins of the nasal aperture may evidence chewed edges with adherent tags of fractured bone. Neck structures, including the hyoid, are usually consumed.

A typical case involved a 22-year-old male who came to his death as a result of a suicide from a drug overdose. He died in the last part of August and was discovered 5 days later in early September. He was found in a suburban, wooded area with dense undergrowth of blackberry bushes. Upon discovery he was clothed in a shirt, quilted winter coat, jeans, socks, and shoes. Upper portions of the coat, including the collar, had been torn by animals. The skin, muscles including the tongue, and vascular structures were removed from the left side of the neck to the level of the shoulder. Absence of skin and underlying tissue was noted in the right frontal scalp area ranging to the lower aspect of the neck on the left side. The right eye had been removed. Destruction extended into the thoracic inlet to residual ends of vessels emanating from the arch of the aorta. Areas of damaged skin were circumscribed by chewed, irregular margins which exhibited a serrated appearance. Sometimes the V-shaped defects from canid punctures were evident along the margins of uneaten skin or muscle (Figure 1).

In stage 1, feeding activity progresses to the thoracic inlet and is followed by evisceration and destruction of bony structures of the ventral thorax, including the sternum, proximal

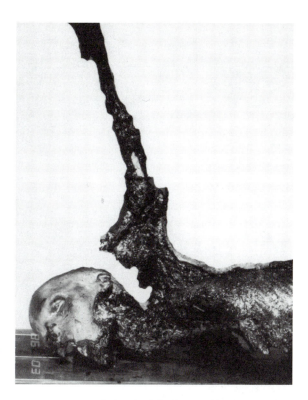

**Figure 2** Stage 1 disarticulation, 22 days postmortem interval, near detachment of left upper extremity.

clavicles, and sternal ends of the ribs. A consequence of the clavicles being detached at their sternal–clavicular articulation is that this leaves the pectoral girdle attached to the thorax by muscle, thus easily detached with the upper extremity (Figure 2). Overlapping, or subsequent to, consumption of viscera, one or both upper extremities are removed. Once disarticulated, upper extremities are usually transported away from the remains as a unit. By the end of stage 1, most major muscle masses have been eaten from the thorax and pelvic region as well as the thighs.

Stage 1 scavenging is typified by a middle-aged male whose death was attributed to stab wounds. He had been deposited in a rural area of chaparral an estimated 2 to 5 weeks previously. The remains were recovered in February as two separate units (Figure 3A). One unit consisted of an articulated skull, the complete vertebral column, pelvic girdle, and lower extremities. The lower extremities were clothed in jeans and shoes. The second unit consisted of an articulated left upper extremity, including the scapula, clavicle, and first rib. The right upper extremity was not recovered.

Except for portions of the posterior parietal and occipital scalp, the soft tissues of the cranium and mandible were missing. The complete viscera and majority of soft tissue of the neck, thorax, and pelvis were missing. Articulations were maintained by ligamentous tissue. Residual muscle tissue was frayed and stringy in character. Distal aspects of the ribs had splintered margins, some with greenstick fractures Figure 3C). Anterior aspects of several vertebral centra were chewed with cancellous bone exposed. The pelvis was intact with tissue around the obturator foramen still adherent. The lower extremities were fleshed to the level of the proximal femora. Skin of the damaged margin was ragged, irregular, and undermined (Figure 3B).

The left upper extremity retained muscle and skin of the fingers, hand, and the distal aspect of the forearm (Figure 3D). There was intermembranous tissue between the radius and ulna. The humerus, scapula, and clavicles were articulated but denuded of soft tissue. The proximal aspect of the clavicle showed canid damage (Figure 3E). The attached first left rib had splintered edges on its inferior proximal margin. The scapula had chewing damage to its vertebral border and there was a perforating defect along the axillary margin.

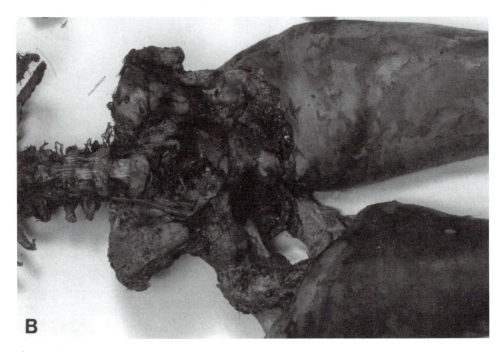

**Figure 3**   Stage 1 disarticulation/consumption in the fall of the year, unknown postmortem interval. (A) Overview of two body units recovered. (B) Skin margins areas illustrating irregular margins, and undermining of muscle. (C) Damage to thorax. (D) Left upper extremity. (E) Closeup of pectoral girdle, showing damage to vertebral border of scapula, proximal clavicle, and attached first rib.

During stage 2 the lower limbs are detached from the body. Lower limbs may be detached from the body from various points (stage 2). Lower legs may be removed by gnawing through the distal femoral condyles. This appears to be an occurrence more frequent in winter. Lower extremities can also be removed in association with the complete pelvic girdle and various sequences of lumbar and thoracic vertebrae.

In an illustrative case, a 19-year-old woman was reported missing in late December and her remains were discovered in mid-February in a wooded area 18 m off a main road, partially beneath some fallen trees. The mandible was found approximately 6 m from the rest of the body. The skull and entire axial skeleton were present and articulated. Only the coccyx was absent. Ribs were extensively gnawed at their sternal ends. Both upper extremities were missing, including both clavicles and scapulae. Lower extremities were missing from below the distal condyles of the femur, which had also been gnawed through. Gnawing damage was present at the subpubic angle, although the superior pelvic rim was intact. Wet ligament and muscle tissue was present along the entire spinal column and pelvic region. At the time of autopsy the remains weighed 7.3 kg; in life the deceased weighed 54.5 kg.

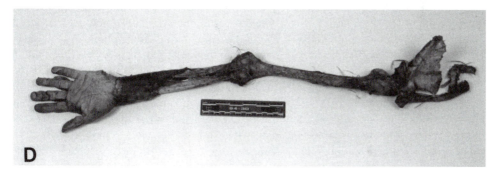

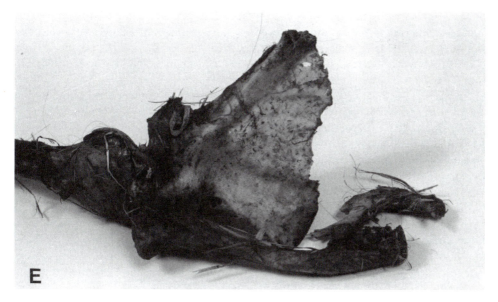

**Figure 3 (continued)**

At stage 3, major segments of the axial skeleton may still be articulated, but are usually scattered, and long bones have been disarticulated and damaged at both ends. This was illustrated in the case of a 49-year-old male who was known to be alive in late August and was discovered the following April, having been exposed for a period of slightly over 6 months. He was discovered in a rural area at the fringe of dense evergreen forest. Death was due to a gunshot wound to the head. Two sections of vertebral column remained articulated: the sacrum with ten associated vertebrae and thoracic vertebrae one through seven. The latter segment had one rib fragment attached. All transverse processes and one spinous process showed damage typical of carnivore gnawing. All remaining skeletal elements were disarticulated and scattered. The skull and mandible were not damaged. Both first ribs, both innominates, and the left femur were extensively damaged by gnawing. Skeletal elements were scattered over approximately 183 m.

In the final stage, stage 4, all recovered bones are disarticulated, extensively gnawed, and scattered. Typical of stage 4, was a 19-year-old female deposited in September and discovered over 2½ years later in a densely forested area. The remains were recovered from three general locations. The skull, mandible, and both femur shafts were within 6 m of each other. Bones of the right upper extremity consisting of the scapula and shafts of the humerus, radius, and ulna were approximately 9 m in one direction, while the same bones left of the upper extremity were 86 m in the opposite direction.

Anatomy has a great deal to do with the ease or difficulty at which certain bones or body units can be removed by scavengers. For example, the hyoid is consumed along with soft tissues of the neck. The amount of soft tissue surrounding a bone or joint, and its ease of removal, are also factors enumerated as affecting whether an underlying bone is damaged or removed (Haynes 1982). The patellae are examples. In their relatively exposed positions, they are easily removed in the course of consumption of the quadriceps and its ligament of insertion, which detaches them proximally, and destruction of the ligament of the patella distally.

The bony architecture of a joint and its ligamentous attachments also contribute to relative resistance to scavenger-assisted disarticulation. The head of the femur, protected by the acetabulum, is not readily accessible to gnawing while articulated. Its compact shaft serves as a deterrent to disarticulation, often leaving only the greater trochanter damaged. This may be why smaller carnivores, such as coyotes, may damage only the distal extremity at the softer, distal femoral condyles. If the femur were detached at the hip joint, one might expect damage to the acetabular rim. In many cases observed in this study, disarticulated femora showed no damage at the rim of the acetabulum; even so, the proximal end of the femur had been completely destroyed. This suggests that the disarticulation occurred after the remains were in a stage of advanced decomposition, at a time when the femur could have been easily pulled from the socket.

In warmer weather, scavenger-assisted disarticulation is in "competition" with disarticulating influences such as decomposition and insect activity, augmented by amounts and types of soft tissue available. Depending upon the state of skeletonization at the time of scavenging, these other phenomena might contribute to considerable modification of the expected sequence of disarticulation by the scavenger. Skeletons scavenged when in advanced stages of decomposition may be discovered in relative anatomical position. In such cases bones which are missing or damaged may have been removed after they disarticulated.

The typical scavenging sequence is subject to modification when portions of the body are in sheltered circumstances or positions which protect the body from scavengers. Some of the special circumstances which may alter expected sequences include when the body has been heavily clothed, partially buried or submerged, wrapped in plastic or a sleeping bag, frozen in snow, or in a mixed water/terrestrial environment (see Table 2). Figure 4 illustrates scavenging skewed from expected scavenging sequences. Other exceptions are observed when there are areas of open trauma to which animals are attracted or areas soiled by feces or urine. In such cases, scavengers may be drawn to these locations to initiate feeding.

**Table 2  Summary of Scavenged Remains Exposed to Special Circumstances**

| Case | Postmortem Interval (days) | Protective Circumstances |
|------|------|------|
| 16 | 330 | Heavily clothed |
| 20 | 252 | Heavily clothed |
| 23 | 730 | Swamp, partially submerged |
| 25 | 270 | Partial burial |
| 27 | 960 | Partial burial |
| 22 | 1,020 | Wrapped in plastic |
| 55 | 120 | Heavily clothed, positioned, partially buried by snow |
| 66 | — | Heavily clothed |
| 69 | — | In water and partially disarticulated before scavenging |
| 70 | 385 | Submerged in cold water of mountain stream before scavenging |
| 71 | — | Heavily clothed plus boots |

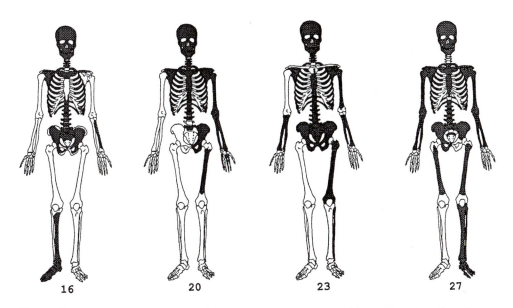

16  20  23  27

**Figure 4**  Remains exposed to special circumstances, exposure and loss of bone for selected cases summarized in Table 2. (Shading = present, no shading = absent.)

## Damage to Bone

Figure 5 illustrates the dental formula of the family Canidae, adapted for a carnivorous diet:

$$I\frac{3}{3}\ C\frac{1}{1}\ P\frac{4}{4}\ M\frac{2}{3}$$

The prominent canines are distinguished by their triangular cross section, which produces V-shaped marks in soft tissue (Figure 1). A distinctive feature of canids which they share with other carnivores is development of the upper fourth premolar and lower first molar or carnassial teeth. These teeth are blade-like and shear against each other to cut through meat and skin. Other molars have broad, occlusal surfaces for crushing. Powerfully developed jaw muscles, in combination with pulling motions and the use of their own body weight, aid

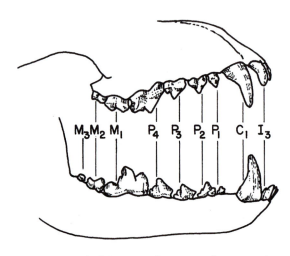

**Figure 5**   The canid dental battery.

canids in stripping integumentary tissue away from underlying muscle masses. Consumption of the muscle in these areas is responsible for undermining of the skin, frequently seen in canid-scavenged remains.

Haynes (1980) and Binford (1981) recognized four types of carnivore tooth marks in bone: (1) punctures; (2) pits; (3) scoring; and (4) furrows. Punctures are produced when bone collapses under a tooth and most often appear as perforations in thin portions of bones such as the scapula or in cancellous ends of long bones (Bonnichsen 1973). Both canine and carnassial teeth produce punctures. Pits are indentations caused by the tips of teeth as the animal bites down, and occur when there is insufficient strength to penetrate the surface. Scoring is produced when teeth slip and drag over compact bone. Shafts of long bone are the most likely areas of these linear, often parallel scratches which are oriented transverse to the long axis of the bone. Such marks generally follow the contours of bones (Eickhoff and Herrmann 1985). Furrows are channels in bone produced by cusps of cheek teeth which extend from the ends of long bones longitudinally into the marrow cavity (Haynes 1980).

Crania are found for nearly all canid-scavenged remains. They are usually undamaged except for canine punctures of the mastoid processes, perforations of the thin bones of the orbits and maxillae, or chewed margins of the nasal aperture. More drastic destruction is encountered in subadult crania or crania subjected to previous blunt force trauma or high velocity gunshot wounds with comminuted fractures. Severe damage to the mandible may leave only features of the body from the third molar forward.

The axis and atlas are frequently undamaged and often found in association with disarticulated crania. Severe scavenging often leaves transverse and spinous vertebral processes chewed away, with only crushed, splintered margins surviving. Similar features are noted on proximal remnants of ribs. All margins of the sacrum are frequently destroyed, leaving only the promontory. Primary areas of damage to slightly gnawed innominate bones are the iliac crest, ischial tuberosities, and pubic symphysis. The acetabular rim is the most persistent area of the innominate bone to survive prolonged scavenging.

Minor damage to the scapula removes the vertebral margin, leaving crenulated, chewed, and crushed edges. Depressed fractures, associated with splintering, pits, and punctures, are also noted extending onto areas of the scapular blade. Heavy gnawing damage destroys all but the glenoid region and neck. The most likely site of initial destruction to the humerus is the head and greater tuberosity. In early stages of gnawing, both the capitulum and trochlea are also involved. Destruction of the ulna is initiated at the olecranon process. The radius and ulna, in many instances, show spiral fractures. Spiral fractures are also noted in the fibulae. Lightly gnawed femora were attacked at the greater trochanter and, with moderate gnawing, the head and neck are destroyed and both condyles removed. Scooping out of cancellous bone is frequently noted in long bones and recovered long bone shafts frequently show scoring marks and furrows.

Carnivore damage to long bones is generally consistent with observations from traditional taphonomic studies (Brain 1981). Damage is more frequent in less dense, articular ends. Once articular surfaces of long bones are removed, there is progressive reduction of shaft length until the bone is totally destroyed. This usually results from progressive furrowing up the length of the shaft. Punctures and pits, which often cause depressed fractures with shattered and crushed margins, are commonly found short distances from the edges of damages. Pits and scoring are most often noted on surfaces near the ends of larger compact bones.

Bones retrieved from areas inhabited by dogs in the author's surveys, were significantly more gnawed and pitted than those found in areas of coyote scavenging. The increased gnawing damage produced by dogs is also a finding observed by Binford (1981). He suggested "boredom" of yard-confined dogs to be a factor of increased gnawing activity, a rationale he also noted for bones found in the vicinity of wolves.

Yet another artifact that may be encountered in canid scavenged remains are those due to digestion. Fragments may be eaten only later to be regurgitated or deposited by defecation (Sutcliff 1970; Murad, this volume). These have been reported for smaller prey of coyotes (Rensberger and Krantz 1988).

## Survivorship and Recovery Frequencies of Skeletal Elements

Inferences that can be made about the survivability of individual bones are limited by the thoroughness and the success of the recovery effort. For those untrained in osteology, the recognition value of various bones differs. The most noted example is the high recognition of the human cranium which usually triggers the subsequent report of a human skeletal find. Therefore, the apparent survival rate of the cranium might be an artifact of discovery and recognition. Other influences on the high rate of crania recovery could be related to the crucial nature of the cranium and mandible for identification purposes, which adds additional impetus for their recovery. It very well may be that other skeletal elements often go unnoticed or are missed by a cursory search.

Overall recovery frequencies in 53 cases of scavenged remains from the Pacific Northwest reveal that bones of the upper extremities, including the scapula and clavicles, are recovered less frequently than those of the lower extremities. Recovery rates for bones of the upper extremities ranged from a high of 50% for the scapula to a low of 25% for the clavicle, while those of the lower extremity, including both innominates, ranged from a high of 65% for the femur with a low of 42% for the tibia. This largely reflects the sequence of animal scavenger-assisted disarticulation of human remains (Haglund et al. 1989). It is not uncommon for the elements of one upper limb or lower limb to be found associated in one location and elements of the other associated in a different location. This is because an upper limb is often removed as unit. A unique case of upper extremity transport was recently encountered where both upper limbs, were moved as one unit because they had been handcuffed together at the wrists.

With the exception of the cranium and mandible, bones of the axial skeleton were recovered between 73% and 61% of the time. Axial skeletal elements were usually found scattered about the original site of discovery. Appendicular elements, once disarticulated from the body, can be removed as a unit, and fairly easily transported. Hands and feet are often not recovered for the same reason, although they are also more often overlooked in the recovery effort. Figure 6 summarizes recovery frequency ranges for skeletal units in all 53 scavenged remains. Table 3 summarizes relative abundance of skeletal elements recovered by stage and for those remains exposed to special circumstances.

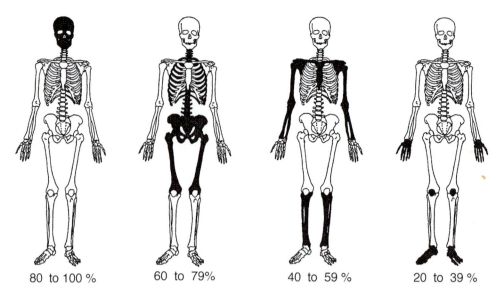

80 to 100 %          60 to 79%          40 to 59 %          20 to 39 %

**Figure 6**   Frequency ranges for the recovery of skeletal units from all cases in the sample of scavenged remains (N = 53).

**Table 3   Relative Abundance of Skeletal Elements Recovered for Scavenging Stages 0–4 and Atypical Cases**

| Skeletal Elements | Stage 0 N = 5 | Stage 1 N = 4 | Stage 2 N = 4 | Stage 3 N = 4 | Stage 4 N = 18 | Atypical N = 17 |
|---|---|---|---|---|---|---|
| Crania | 100.0 | 100.0 | 100.0 | 100.0 | 100.0 | 94.0 |
| Mandibles | 100.0 | 100.0 | 100.0 | 75.0 | 83.0 | 82.4 |
| Hyoids | 100.0 | 0.0 | 0.0 | 0.0 | 16.0 | 29.4 |
| Atlases | 100.0 | 100.0 | 100.0 | 50.0 | 72.2 | 64.7 |
| Axes | 100.0 | 100.0 | 100.0 | 25.0 | 55.5 | 88.2 |
| Cervical vertebrae 2–7 | 100.0 | 100.0 | 100.0 | 35.0 | 48.8 | 74.1 |
| Thoracic vertebrae | 100.0 | 100.0 | 100.0 | 62.5 | 98.1 | 74.5 |
| Lumbar vertebrae | 100.0 | 100.0 | 100.0 | 65.0 | 60.0 | 44.7 |
| Sacra | 100.0 | 75.0 | 100.0 | 50.0 | 66.6 | 70.5 |
| Coccyges | 100.0 | 100.0 | 50.0 | 25.0 | 33.3 | 88.2 |
| Sterna | 100.0 | 25.0 | 75.0 | 25.0 | 38.8 | 82.3 |
| Ribs | 100.0 | 100.0 | 93.7 | 25.0 | 52.7 | 41.6 |
| Clavicles | 100.0 | 12.5 | 62.5 | 25.0 | 47.2 | 76.4 |
| Scapulae | 100.0 | 12.5 | 50.0 | 25.0 | 47.2 | 82.3 |
| Humeri | 100.0 | 12.5 | 50.0 | 25.0 | 41.6 | 73.5 |
| Ulnae | 100.0 | 12.5 | 25.0 | 25.0 | 25.0 | 64.7 |
| Radii | 100.0 | 12.5 | 25.0 | 12.4 | 38.0 | 64.7 |
| Carpals | 100.0 | 25.0 | 0.0 | 0.0 | 13.8 | 32.3 |
| Hand elements | 100.0 | 25.0 | 90.0 | 0.0 | 10.9 | 29.7 |
| Innominates | 100.0 | 100.0 | 87.5 | 50.0 | 58.3 | 85.2 |
| Femora | 100.0 | 100.0 | 87.5 | 62.5 | 61.1 | 67.6 |
| Patellae | 100.0 | 100.0 | 25.0 | 0.0 | 8.3 | 32.3 |
| Tibiae | 100.0 | 100.0 | 50.0 | 25.0 | 50.0 | 64.7 |
| Fibulae | 100.0 | 100.0 | 50.0 | 25.0 | 50.0 | 64.7 |
| Tali | 100.0 | 100.0 | 0.0 | 0.0 | 16.6 | 41.1 |
| Calcanea | 100.0 | 100.0 | 0.0 | 0.0 | 16.6 | 38.2 |
| Tarsals | 100.0 | 100.0 | 0.0 | 0.0 | 7.1 | 31.9 |
| Foot elements | 100.0 | 100.0 | 0.0 | 0.0 | 10.9 | 30.8 |

## Movement of Remains by Canids

Ability to move a carcass is interdependent upon the relative size and strength of the scavenger(s) vs. the weight and size of the remains. Coyotes are medium-sized canids ranging from 13 to 18 kg (Beckhoff and Wells 1980). Breeds of domestic dogs can range from small to medium to large and vary considerably in their ability to move remains. Although complete remains may be moved by canids, the potential movability of a carcass will increase as scavenging progresses and more muscle mass is removed. Movement is also affected by topography, partial burial, or vegetation that may serve to inhibit movement of the remains. The author has observed limitations to movement of remains for bodies crammed into tight spaces, covered for concealment, and enclosed by structures or natural barriers such as water, cliffs, or dense vegetation. Contrary to a frequently touted myth, canids do move bones or body units uphill.

Establishing the original site of the remains is crucial to a forensic investigation. It is at the original site of deposition that a high potential for evidence recovery exists (Haglund this volume). That a body has been moved by animals can be inferred by drag marks or disturbed ground cover. A sprawled attitude of the body may often be in evidence. Previous resting places of a body may be marked by discoloration areas from body fluid leakage, the presence of scavenging insect remains, or strong odor at the site of such leakage. This was true in a case where "grease spots" marked multiple locations the remains had occupied in route to its final resting place. In cases where death is due to suicide by gunshot, the deceased's location at the time of death is marked by the weapon. In one such case, coyotes were responsible for movement of the entire thorax. In another case, scavenging coyotes had moved the body about, but had not flipped it over as attested by undamaged skin on the back, preserving stab wounds that had caused the death.

Distances that bones can be transported are dependent upon the strength, size, and range of the transporting species. For example, coyotes in open landscapes may have ranges up to a 16.1 km radius, while those in forested areas may have ranges extending up to a 3.2 km radius (Beckhoff and Wells 1980). Most skeletal elements recovered in cases participated in by the author have been within a 100 m radius of where the body had been deposited. One exception was a mandible found in a residential yard 402 m from the site where the rest of the skeleton was located. It had been transported by a domestic dog. In another example, elements of one upper extremity, consisting of the shafts of the humerus, radius, and ulna, were discovered over 180 m from where the skull, mandible, and tibial shafts were discovered.

## Variables that Affect Scavenging of Human Remains

Several variables can affect the extent and type of damage to soft tissue and bone. The sequence in which body units or skeletal elements are disarticulated, scattered, or survive depends upon factors dictated by the remains, the scavenger, climate, and environment.

Variables of scavenging dictated by the remains include the architecture of the bone, relative cortical thickness, and ratio or amount of compact bone to cancellous bone. Age affects the size of the individual and the state of epiphyseal fusion. Anatomical position of skeletal elements determines their susceptibility to damage and disarticulation. Binford (1981) points out that the amount of soft tissue plays a role in damage to underlying bone. Another factor according to Haynes (1980) is the amount of soft tissue and ease with which it is stripped from the bone. Relative freshness of soft tissue may also affect its "desirability" and alteration by animals. For instance, "wintered over," or saponified remains appear to provide less interest to canids. The present study did not give any indications as to whether freezing of tissue affected scavenging. Position of the body, especially for smaller canids, dictates what parts of the body they can access. Rigor mortis may also limit access to the body (Burgett

1990). Freezing of the body could have a similar limiting effect (Micozzi 1986) on access to various parts of the body.

The manner in which bones are altered by carnivores varies with the carnivore species, their tooth morphology, jaw mechanics, and their strength relative to the bone. Scavenger size and number of animals feeding have been cited as factors affecting carcass destruction (Hill 1979). Common sense would suggest that scavenger competition, hunger, and the number of feeding bouts affect scavenging (Haglund 1991; Haglund et al. 1989). For coyotes, the seasonal nature of food sources influences their social behavior and eating. In summer, when coyotes sustain themselves on rodents, they are less social than in winter when greater food sources are available to support larger group sizes (Beckhoff and Wells 1980).

Position of the body or covering of the remains can protect it from animal scavenging. Such circumstances may be due to partial burial or burial in a shallow grave, covering by snow or rockslides, and heavy clothing or various wrappings such as plastic, blankets, or tarps (Table 2 and Figure 4). With partial protection from exposure, damage or absence of bones on the unprotected side of the body is to be expected.

Human population density has also been correlated with presence or absence of animal scavenging (Haglund 1991, Haglund et al. 1989). There are relatively fewer scavenged human skeletons found in areas of higher human population density. This is consistent with the likelihood there are fewer animals and smaller animal group sizes in inhabited areas. Human remains are more likely to be discovered sooner in more populated areas.

Season of the year affects the amount of clothing worn by the deceased, ground cover of the area in which the body is deposited, rate of decomposition, and behavior of the potential scavengers. Protection offered by heavy clothing may provide a considerable barrier to scavengers; however, remains in this study did not necessarily reflect expected seasonal garb, because many "dumped" bodies were deposited with little or no clothing, regardless of season.

## Conclusions

The most common questions asked of the forensic anthropologist when animal scavenging is involved are:

1. How can scattered remains be located in order to maximize their recovery?
2. Is it possible to distinguish scavenger-induced damage to bone from other death or injury-related trauma?
3. Can scavenging assist in estimation of the postmortem interval?

### Locating Remains

The most likely sites of recovery of skeletal material from surface scattered remains are in the immediate vicinity of the initial body location and along animal trails accessing the area. Rodriguez (1987; also see Chapter 29 of this volume) suggests disarticulated bones have a propensity to roll down inclines and be moved by sedimentation, sheetwash, or by rains. Isolated teeth can be recovered by screening areas considered to be the original resting place of the body and areas between the original site and the location where the mandible and cranium were recovered. Some smaller elements of hands and feet are occasionally recovered from rodent burrows during the screening process. One femur shaft was found in a hollowed-out portion of a tree trunk. Depending on the scavenging species and their behavior, teeth and bone fragments may be recovered from scat deposits in latrine areas or near den entrances. Some scavengers cache food, which may involve shallow burial in soil or brush debris. No reliable information was available on caching by coyotes.

## Distinguishing Animal-Induced Artifacts

Artifacts of soft tissue induced by medium-sized canids consist of punctures from canine teeth, scratches on skin beyond the areas of soft tissue destruction, and undermining of the integument at the margins of tissue of destruction. Carnivore tooth damage, with its characteristic locations and constellation of pits, punctures, scoring, and furrows, usually allows ready distinction from other artifacts to bone. Cut marks, unlike scoring which follows contours of bones, usually follow a straight, rigid course. The linear lines from sediment abrasion tend to be fine and have a smoothing effect on sharp features of bone. The filigree-like lines caused by etching of roots on bone are often associated with the causative root mass and are usually more intricate and multidirectional than scoring marks. Pits, not associated with the usual suite of carnivore gnawing marks, are most problematic and may not be readily distinguished with certainty. Gnawing by rodents such as mice, can be distinguished from that of carnivores (Haglund, this volume). A characteristic of rodent-gnawed margins of bone is their relatively uniform pitch extending from outer to inner tables of bone. Margins of carnivore damage tend to be less regular, often rounded, with no uniform pitch from inner to outer surface.

## Estimation of the Postmortem Interval

This study suggests that scavenging by coyotes in the Pacific Northwest may produce a fully skeletonized body with both upper extremities missing in as little as 28 days. Disarticulation and scattering of all bones, except for segments of vertebral column, can be expected in as little as 2 months. For elapsed times of exposure beyond 1 year, coyote-scavenged human remains are fully disarticulated and may be widely scattered, resulting in many bones not being recovered.

Elapsed times for various stages of disarticulation are subject to wide and overlapping intervals (see Table 1). As pointed out by Murad and Bayham (1990), the predicted postmortem intervals based on canid-scavenging stages are extremely variable. Any assessment of postmortem interval is extremely area dependent and does not depend on a single criterion. Knowledge of the species of scavenger is critical to any estimation of postmortem interval.

## Acknowledgments

To dog handler, Andy Rebmann, Connecticut State Police, retired, for his comments.

## References

Binford, L.
  1981  *Bones: Ancient Men and Modern Myths*. Academic Press, New York.

Bass, W.M.
  1984  Will the Forensic Anthropologist Please Help: A Case of a Woman Eaten by Dogs. Paper presented at the 36th Annual Meeting of the American Academy of Forensic Sciences, Anaheim, CA.

Beckhoff, M., and M.C. Wells
  1980  The Social Ecology of Coyotes. *Scientific American* 242:130–148.

Bonnichsen, R.
  1973  Some Operational Aspects of Human and Animal Bone Alteration. In *Mammalian Osteo-Archaeology: North America*, edited by M. Gilbert, pp. 9–25. Missouri Archaeological Society, Columbia.

Brain, C.K.
1981 *The Hunters or the Hunted? An Introduction to African Cave Taphonomy.* University of Chicago Press, Chicago.

Burgett, G.R.
1990 The Bones of the Beast: Resolving Questions of Faunal Assemblage Formation Processes Through Actualistic Research. Unpublished Ph.D. dissertation, University of New Mexico, Albuquerque.

Eickhoff, S., and B. Herrmann
1985 Surface Marks on Bones from Neolithic Collective Grave (Odagsen, Saxony): A Study on Differential Diagnostics. *Journal of Human Evolution* 14:263–274.

Haglund, W.D.
1991 *Applications of Taphonomic Models to Forensic Investigations,* Ph.D. dissertation, Department of Anthropology, University of Washington, Seattle. University Microfilms, Ann Arbor, MI.

Haglund, W.D., D.Y. Reay, and D.R. Swindler
1988 Tooth Artifacts and Survival of Bones in Animal-Scavenged Human Skeletons. *Journal of Forensic Sciences* 33:985–997.
1989 Canid Scavenging/Disarticulation Sequence of Humans in the Pacific Northwest, *Journal of Forensic Sciences* 34:587–606.

Haynes, G.
1980 Prey Bones and Predators: Potential Ecologic Information from Analysis of Bone Sites. *Ossa* 7:75–97.
1982 Utilization and Skeletal Disturbances of North American Prey Carcasses. *Arctic* 35:226–281.

Hill, A.P.
1979 Disarticulation and Scattering of Mammal Skeletons. *Paleobiology* 5:261–274.

Micozzi, M.S.
1986 Experimental Study of Postmortem Change Under Field Conditions: Effects of Freezing, Thawing, and Mechanical Injury. *Journal of Forensic Sciences* 32:953–961.

Morse, D., J. Duncan, and J.W. Stoutamire (editors)
1983 *Handbook of Forensic Archaeology.* Rose Printing, Tallahassee.

Murad, T., and F.E. Bayham
1990 Northern California Examples of the Effects of Animal Scavenging on the Estimation of the Postmortem Interval. Paper presented at the 42nd Annual Meeting of the American Academy of Forensic Sciences, Cincinnati.

Rhine, S., B. Curran, S. Boydstun, S. Churchill, P. Ivey, and M. Oglivie
1988 Skeletonization Rates in the Desert. Paper presented at the 40th Annual Meeting of the American Academy of Forensic Sciences, Philadelphia.

Rensberger, J.M., and H.B. Krantz
1988 Effects of Predator Digestion on the Microsurface of Teeth and Bone. *Scanning Microscopy* 2:1541–1551.

Rodriguez, W.C.
1987 Postmortem Animal Activity: Recognition and Interpretation. Paper presented at the 39th Annual Meeting of the American Academy of Forensic Sciences, San Diego.

Rossi, M.L, A.W. Shahrom, and R.C. Chapman
1994 Postmortem Injury by Indoor Pets. *American Journal of Forensic Medicine and Pathology* 15(2):105–109.

Sorg, M.H.
  1986  Scavenger Modifications of Human Skeletal Remains in Forensic Anthropology. Paper presented at the 38th Annual Meeting of the American Academy of Forensic Sciences, New Orleans.

Sutcliff, A.J.
  1970  Spotted Hyena: Crusher, Gnawer, Digester and Collector of Bones. *Nature* 227:110–1113.

# Scattered Skeletal Human Remains: Search Strategy Considerations for Locating Missing Teeth

# 24

WILLIAM D. HAGLUND

## Introduction

Positive identifications, in cases where the body is skeletonized, are resolved by dental means in the majority of cases (Haglund et al. 1987; Rothwell et al. 1989). Therefore, it is essential that recovery of teeth be maximized. Antemortem facial trauma and taphonomic processes of the postmortem interval, such as decomposition, scavenging, and dispersion of remains by animals, can serve to confound recovery of teeth. With the disappearance of the surrounding soft tissue and the periodontal ligament, teeth commonly become disassociated from their alveoli (Rothwell et al. 1989; Sperber 1986) (Figure 1). This is true for single-rooted teeth such as incisors and canines, but also holds for immature molars and premolars, and when the roots of multirooted teeth are not sufficiently splayed to lock them into their sockets. As decomposition progresses, the mandible becomes detached from the cranium, and the cranium, in turn, is disassociated from the rest of the body. This has been reported to occur early in the disarticulation sequence of animals (Toots 1965; Micozzi 1985) and humans (Haglund et al. 1990; Skinner and Lazenby 1983:13). Teeth may also be lost when either the mandible or cranium is moved. Such movement is most commonly mediated by scavengers and can occur when the body is fresh, in various stages of decomposition, or after it is completely skeletonized.

At the time a scene is processed, searchers generally do not know which teeth will be documented in antemortem records. A further complication to dental identification is that dental charting and dental radiographs may be available for only a few select teeth.

In the following six case examples, teeth were missing postmortem and not readily located at the time the body was initially discovered. These cases are analyzed in terms of decomposition, disarticulation, and dispersion. Search strategies are suggested for efficient, maximum recovery of dental remains.

## Case Examples

### Case 1

This 39-year-old suicidal male disappeared in July of 1986, in a rural county of Washington State. His skeletal remains were discovered in a remote wooded area in March of 1991, after a postmortem interval of 45 months. At the scene of discovery, bones and clothing, partially covered by seasonal debris, rested on the ground immediately beneath a tree limb from which hung a partially rotted rope. Skeletal elements were completely disarticulated and no soft tissue was present. The noose-end of the rope was recovered from among the jumble of bones

0-8493-9434-1/97/$0.00+$.50
© 1997 by CRC Press, Inc.

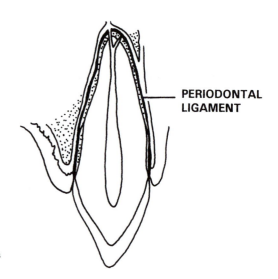

**Figure 1**   The periodontal ligament binds the tooth in its alveolus.

and clothing. There was no scattering of the remains, and skeletal elements revealed no evidence of animal scavenging. Scene processing and recovery were done by local law enforcement investigators. The manner and cause of death was determined to be suicide by hanging.

The skeletal remains, sawn-off branch and ligature, along with antemortem dental records of a missing individual, were sent to the author for analysis and identification. Upon examination of the maxilla and mandible, 14 teeth were missing postmortem. Where were the missing teeth?

As indicated by the presence of skeletal remains, clothing, the noose end of the rope, and the rope hanging from the tree, the original site where the remains were discovered was the location of death, decomposition, and disarticulation. Because there was no scavenging or scattering of skeletal elements, the teeth should have been recovered from among the bones and clothing, or from screening of the soil and seasonal debris, where they were collected.

## Case 2

The cranium of this 14-year-old female was discovered in an evergreen forest by a pine cone hunter. The postmortem interval was 1 year. Nine maxillary teeth were missing. These included the four incisors, both canines, two premolars, and an immature left third molar (teeth 5 to 12, and 16). An initial survey of the area by police investigators and the author revealed fully disarticulated and scavenged skeletal elements, devoid of all soft tissue, and scattered over an area of approximately 300 by 150 feet (76.9 by 38.5 meters) (Figure 2A). The majority of ribs and vertebrae were clustered in anatomical disarray (Figure 2B). Associated with this area was the fully skeletonized right wrist and hand which rested in relative anatomical order. The head hair mass was located at the periphery of this cluster (Figure 2B). Where were the missing teeth?

Presence of the majority of the vertebrae and ribs, plus finding the right wrist and hand in relative anatomical order, supports the hypothesis that this location was where the body originally rested (Figure 2B). Association of the mandible with this grouping of skeletal elements indicates that the disarticulation of cranium and mandible occurred here, and that this was the main decomposition site. Based on these observations, the most likely pattern of scatter radiates from this decomposition site (Figure 2B.) The cranium was initially moved to the site where the hair mass was found and where further decomposition took place. Eventually, the cranium had been moved to the location of its discovery. Note that bones away from the location of primary decomposition are widely scattered and are not found associated with other skeletal elements to which they normally articulate. This indicates that they were

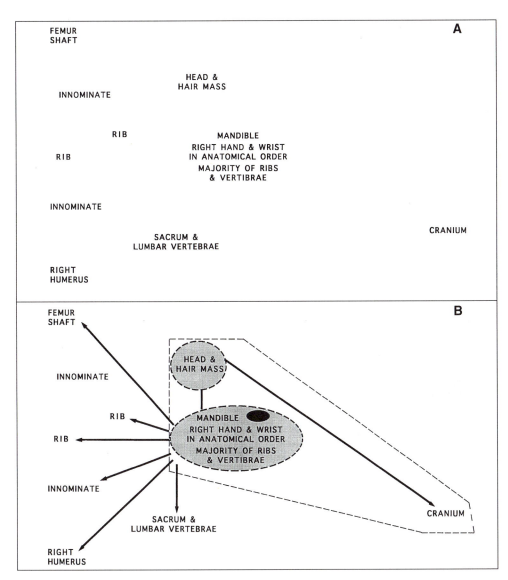

**Figure 2**   Case 2. (A) Associations and relative distribution of remains without interpretation. (B) Inferred scatter pattern. Shaded areas indicate primary deposition/decomposition sites. Trajectories of dispersal are indicated by arrows. Maximum potential location of disassociated teeth is indicated by dashed perimeter. Darkly shaded location indicates site where teeth were recovered.

moved from the site of decomposition **after** soft tissue had decomposed and disarticulation had occurred.

The area where the teeth are most likely located is between the site where the mandible and head–hair–mass rested. Because disarticulation had advanced enough to detach the mandible, screening for the missing maxillary teeth was initiated at the mandible's location, and that is where the teeth were located. Failure to find teeth in this area would have necessitated screening at the location of the hair mass and then the area between it and the mandible.

## Case 3

This 21-year-old female's skeletal remains were found when her cranium was discovered by a moss hunter. Subsequent to her identification, it was learned she had been missing 7 years.

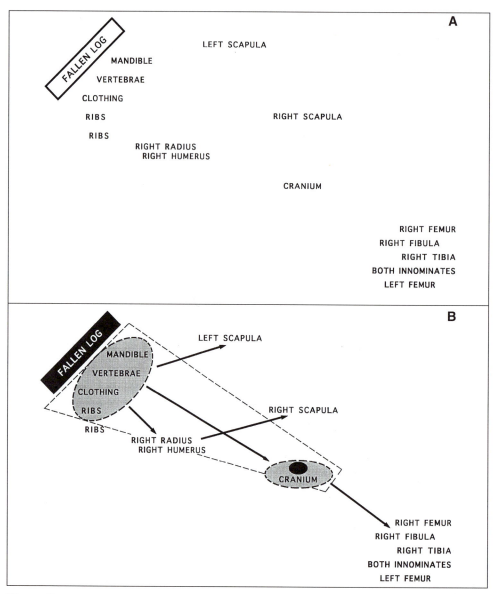

**Figure 3**  Case 3. (A) Associations and relative distribution of remains without interpretation. (B) Inferred scatter pattern. Shaded areas indicate primary deposition/decomposition sites. Trajectories of dispersal are indicated by arrows. Maximum potential location of disassociated teeth is indicated by dashed perimeter. Darkly shaded location indicates site where teeth were recovered.

The location of discovery was in a rural area of evergreen forest. The cranium rested in a depression created by pine needles that had fallen around it. Seven maxillary teeth including the right first, second, and third molars (teeth 1 to 3), the right lateral and central incisors, and the left central incisor (teeth 7, 8, and 9), and the left first molar (tooth 14) were missing. An initial survey of the vicinity by police investigators and the author revealed scavenged skeletal remains scattered in an east–west direction for approximately 200 feet (51.3 m) (Figure 3A). Clothing, the mandible, and the majority of ribs and vertebrae were located adjacent to a turn-around area at the westerly extreme of the scatter pattern. The cranium was located approximately at the midpoint of this scatter pattern. Along the path of scatter, and associated, were bone shafts of the right arm. At the most easterly end of the scatter was a loosely associated cluster representing shafts of the major elements of the both lower limbs

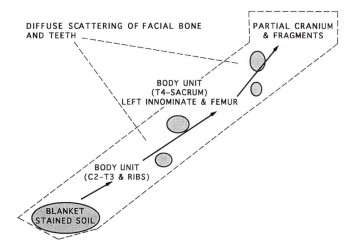

**Figure 4**   Case 4. Location of human remains in a case where there was extreme antemortem blunt trauma to the skull. Cranial fragments and disassociated teeth (darkly shaded areas) were dispersed along the trajectory (arrows).

including the right and left femurs, right tibia and fibula, and both innominate bones. Where were the missing teeth?

The original site of the body deposition was considered to be where clothing and major bones of the thorax were located. Dispersion of the remains took place from this location (Figure 3B). Scatter occurred before disappearance of soft tissue was complete. This can be inferred because scattered clusters of associated skeletal elements represented anatomically related bones. As observed in Figure 3B, major elements of the right arm (including shafts of the radius, humerus, and the scapula) were strewn along a trajectory, and the pelvic girdle accompanied by major bones of both lower extremities (both innominate, femora, tibiae, and fibulae) were located at the furthest extreme of scatter. The right arm plus its girdle and the lower portion of the body were initially moved as units of articulated sequences of bone. In this example it was considered most likely that the cranium was moved with the teeth still in anatomical position. Therefore, the search and screening efforts for maxillary teeth concentrated first at the location of the cranium's discovery. All were found at this location. If this strategy had failed to yield the missing teeth, the original deposition site, and then the path between it and the location of the cranium, would have been screened.

## Case 4

This 22-year-old female homicide victim's remains were discovered in April, in a rural area of woods and thick underbrush, 2 months following her disappearance. Her killer had severely beaten her about the face and head. Blood and a maxillary left central and lateral incisor were found in the trunk of the suspect's vehicle. By the time the remains were discovered, much soft tissue decomposition had occurred and the remains had been scavenged and scattered by coyotes (Figure 4). The original body deposition site was marked by a blanket, clothing, and darkly stained, odor-laden soil. The extremes of scatter were marked by the decomposition site at one end and at the other end by a partial cranial vault that was absent the face from below the superior orbital margins. Two major articulated body units were present. The first body unit included the partially skeletonized and scavenged upper trunk inclusive of the second cervical vertebrae through the third thoracic vertebrae. The second body unit section included the remainder of the trunk inclusive of the fourth thoracic vertebrae through the sacrum, left innominate, and femur. All remains were located along a 240-foot (61.5 m) linear trajectory. Numerous cranial fragments were littered along this path. Where were the missing teeth?

A special circumstance complicates this case. There was extensive antemortem fragmentation of facial bones and teeth due to impact trauma to the face. Because of this and the fact that scatter took place while decomposition was in progress, cranial bone fragments, including teeth and tooth-bearing bones, were potentially scattered between the extremes from where the body was deposited and where the mandible and farthest portion of the cranium were found. Indeed, in the weeks following the initial scene processing, further searches of the area were made separately by medical examiner and law enforcement personnel and family members. All teeth were eventually recovered along the path where they had fallen away from mandible and cranium as they were moved. Careful screening of path between the original site where the body had rested to the section of cranial vault, at the time of initial scene processing, would have saved considerable time and embarrassment for law enforcement as well as unnecessary distress to surviving family members.

## Case 5

This 37-year-old female was discovered approximately 120 feet (30.7 m) over the side of a steep embankment off a remote mountain road. The remains had been placed within two plastic trash bags which had apparently been disrupted when they were rolled over the embankment. The majority of viscera and muscle was absent due to insect activity and decomposition. There was exposure of the majority of bones of the skeleton, although they remained articulated by dried ligaments and skin. Integument of the head and face was mummified and relatively intact (Figure 5A, head and soft tissue). Five anterior teeth were missing from their sockets. Inspection of the oral cavity and posterior pharynx did not disclose the missing teeth, and detectives were advised to screen the area beneath the head end of the body where the teeth were presumed to have fallen. Four hours of meticulous sifting failed to yield the missing teeth. Where were the missing teeth?

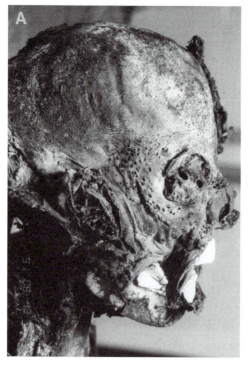 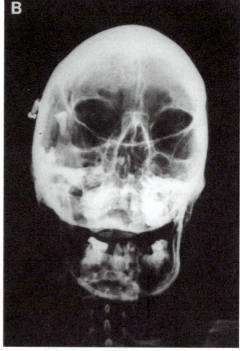

**Figure 5**    Case 5. (A) Desiccated soft tissue covering the majority of the head and face. (B) Postmortem radiograph showing teeth entrapped between cranium and scalp.

Since the majority of the remains were articulated and there was no scattering or traumatic damage to dentition bearing bones, it is unlikely that teeth would be anywhere but near the area of the head end of the body. Screening of this general area failed to yield the missing teeth. At time of autopsy, routine X-rays of the skull revealed the missing teeth entrapped between the scalp and the right posterior parietal bone (Figure 5B). Absence of the disassociated teeth in the oral cavity and pharynx had misled the author to suggest that missing teeth had dropped from the oral cavity to the ground. Instead, the missing teeth had fallen onto the internal surface of the cheek and then, as decomposition advanced and the scalp loosened from the skull, continued to drift into that space to finally settle in the dependent location from which they were recovered.

When the soft tissue of the oral cavity and face is intact and the rear of the oral cavity is in a dependent position, loosened teeth routinely fall back into the mouth and pharynx. Contrarily, when the mouth opening is dependent, the teeth may fall out of the oral cavity and to the ground. The position of the remains is crucial to such evaluations. Case 6 suggests that investigators should be aware that teeth may also be entrapped between soft tissue and the cranium in other locations. Therefore, it is important to assess the final and potential positions of the body in such cases.

## Case 6

The cranium of this 37-year-old female was discovered by a mushroom hunter in April. She had been missing since March of the previous year. The location was adjacent to a major highway that ran through an evergreen forest. An initial survey of the area indicated several groupings of scattered skeletal elements were located along the fringe of a swamp. Scattered clusters of associated bones included: (1) the cranium and first through third cervical vertebrae; (2) a loose association of clothing, mandible, and major bones of the trunk; (3) long bone shafts of the right arm; and (4) long bone shafts of the lower extremities (Figure 6A). Much of the area was littered with downed tree trunks and growth of brush. The two central maxillary incisors were missing and four incisors were missing from the mandible. Where were the missing teeth?

The remains were fully skeletonized and scattered. Body units had been moved before complete disarticulation had taken place. At a minimum, the cranium and the three cervical vertebrae, the majority of the right arm, and the pelvis and lower extremities were moved as discrete body units. Enough disarticulation had occurred before the movement of the cranium that the mandible had already detached from the cranium. The location where the body originally rested and from which it was scattered is at the association of bones of the trunk, the mandible, and where the clothing was found. Because there is evidence that some disarticulation had occurred before disarticulation was complete, it is not possible to limit the potential area of the missing maxillary incisors any further than the area between the group of bone containing elements of the trunk and mandible and the site of the cervical vertebrae and the cranium. Sifting of this area produced the missing central incisors. Mandibular teeth were near the mandible.

## Discussion

Crime scene investigators often labor under manpower, financial, and time constraints (Skinner and Lazenby 1983). It behooves them to achieve efficient scene processing, with an eye towards maximizing efforts for complete recovery of evidence and remains. This begins with an overall survey of the area to assess the locations of bones and/or other remains, associations with each other, likely scatter patterns, and location(s) where decomposition has taken place.

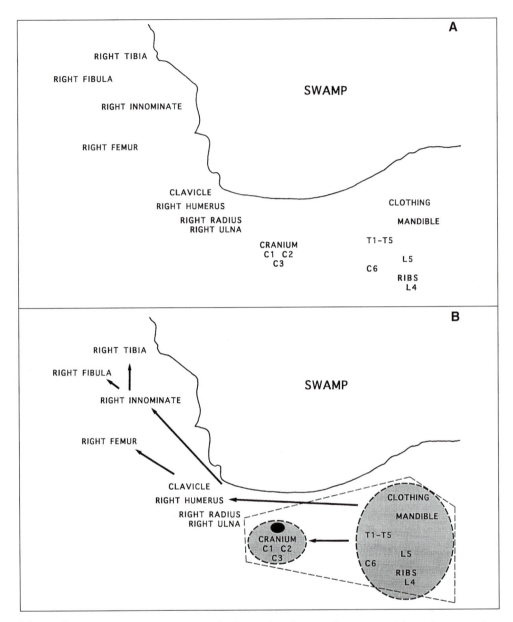

**Figure 6** Case 6. (A) Associations and relative distribution of remains without interpretation. (B) Inferred scatter pattern. Shaded areas indicate primary deposition/decomposition sites. Trajectories of dispersal are indicated by arrows. Maximum potential location of disassociated teeth is indicated by dashed perimeter. Darkly shaded location indicates site where teeth were recovered.

In the above cases, recovery of missing teeth was maximized by establishing a search strategy based on answers to the following questions:

1. Are the remains scattered?
2. From where was the body scattered?
3. What is the skeletal element composition of the scattered groupings of bones?
4. What were the most likely trajectories and dispersion?
5. Are there any special circumstances that might affect disassociation of teeth or their scatter?

Considerations for answering these questions are as follows:

### Are the remains scattered?

If the remains are *not* scattered (cases 1 and 5), inspection of the remains themselves or the immediate area where the remains rest is the logical location where the teeth should be found. When teeth are missing postmortem and the soft tissue of the oral cavity or face is relatively intact, with the rear of the oral cavity in a dependent position, loosened teeth routinely fall back into the mouth and pharynx. (This is also a likely area to find teeth of charred remains resting in the supine position.) Contrarily, when the mouth opening is dependent, the teeth may fall out of the oral cavity and to the ground. Case 6 suggests that investigators should be aware that teeth can also be entrapped between soft tissue and the skull in other locations.

If the remains are scattered, an initial survey of the scene will give an overview of the locations of scattered bones and artifacts. If dentition-bearing bones are scattered away from other skeletal elements or from each other (cases 2, 3, 4, and 6) it is important to establish: the time relative to the decomposition and disarticulation that the scatter took place and the location from which scattering took place (see questions 2 and 3 below).

### Where was the body scattered from?

Suicide weapons, such as the rope in case 1, may mark the obvious place of death. The location of death for gunshot suicides is often marked with the location where the firearm is found. Visual signs may indicate location(s) where the remains decomposed. These include discolored areas of substrate marked by odor or discoloration from body fluid leakage, presence of insect puparium, and yellowish discoloration of low, overhanging deciduous foliage (Rodriguez 1989). Some bones are more likely to be found at the original site of decomposition than others. One survey of 23 surface-scattered remains conducted by the author suggests that associations of bones commonly located at the primary deposition include: ribs (88.2%); thoracic vertebrae (82%); lumbar vertebrae (71%); and cervical vertebrae 2 to 7 (59%) (Haglund 1991).

It should be cautioned that the site where the majority of decomposition takes place may or may not be the original site of the body's deposition. Remains, especially of subadults or nearly complete portions of adults, can be moved by medium-sized canids. This can occur more easily in open terrain, but the author is aware of an adult torso of a gunshot suicide victim being moved approximately 40 feet (10.3 m), in a swampy area of dense underbrush, by coyotes. The location of the victims backpack and the suicide weapon marked the site of death. Of course, larger carnivores such as bears (*Ursa sp.*) and cougars (*Felis concolor*) would be capable of moving complete, adult human remains.

There may be secondary sites of decomposition when a body unit with soft tissue attached is moved to another area. The head–hair mass often indicates the site where soft tissue of the scalp decomposed and may be a likely location where teeth became loosened and separated from the alveoli.

### For scattered remains, what is the skeletal element composition of the scattered groupings of bones?

Are anatomically related bones associated within scattered clusters, or are anatomically unrelated bones found singly or together? The answer to this question helps to infer at what time, relative to decomposition and disarticulation, that scatter most likely took place. Parts may be removed and scattered from fresh, decomposing, or completely disarticulated remains.

Each of these states dictates potential body units that can be easily detached from the remains. Case 4 presents an obvious example of remains that were scattered while decomposition was in progress, because scattered body units remain connected by soft tissue. For fully skeletonized and scattered remains, examine the skeletal elements which compose the scattered groupings of skeletal elements. (A **group** of skeletal elements is defined as a discrete cluster of bones or bones strung along a short span of trajectory.)

For the majority of groupings, if bones were still connected by soft tissue, or represent bones of the same anatomical region, such as upper arm or forearm and hand (case 3 and 6), they were more likely transported as connected body units. These associations indicate transport took place before disarticulation was complete and that bones were connected to each other at the time of movement. Predictable body units, such as complete arms and their respective partial girdles, are commonly removed from fresh remains by medium-sized canids (Haglund et al. 1989). It is also common for major sections of lower limbs including parts of the pelvic girdle to be moved as body units (cases 4, 6, and 7). When transport takes place after decomposition/disarticulation is complete, individual bones are moved, and the resulting scatter pattern may consist of single bones or a mix of bones representing different anatomical regions. Case 3 fits this latter category.

### What were the most likely trajectories of dispersion?

Between the original resting place of the remains and locations of dispersed body units or skeletal elements are the most likely paths along which skeletal elements parts traveled. This may not be a straight line. A secondary decomposition site(s) may need to be considered as in case 2. Trajectories of scattered bones (case 3) and/or artifacts may conform to animal trails or terrains (case 6) and may guide the investigator in establishing the most likely trajectories. Primary, secondary, and even tertiary resting sites may be identified and need to be taken into consideration when determining pattern of dispersion.

### Are there any special circumstances that might affect disassociation of teeth or scatter?

Circumstances such as preexisting facial trauma, terrain, or purposeful dismemberment and dispersion may serve to bias the forgoing considerations. For instance, extensive impact trauma to the face in case 4 knocked out teeth, loosened others, and fractured dentition-bearing bones into many pieces. This situation complicated the mechanism of tooth loss and extended potential areas from which they might be recovered. Terrain, such as the swamp in case 6, defined a perimeter for potential search because the scavenging animals skirted the margins of the swamp and limited their trail along downed tree trunks which served as high ground to the surrounding bog. Location of teeth for purposefully dismembered and dispersed human remains is not predictable by the above means (Haglund and Reay 1993).

The above search strategy assumes surface scattering of human remains by medium-sized canids. When teeth are consumed, carried into burrows by rodents or birds, or moved by environmental factors such as water, the suggested search strategy may not apply.

## Conclusion

In cases of scattered human remains, complete dentition is frequently not recovered because teeth separate from their sockets early in the decomposition process and are overlooked during scene processing. Available antemortem dental records may document only a limited number of teeth. These factors can combine to limit the information available for dental comparisons. Because identification by dental means is routine for skeletonized human remains, it is important that as many teeth as possible be recovered.

Attention to sound scene processing often yields evidence and human remains that would otherwise be overlooked. Six cases that involve fully to partially skeletonized surface remains for which teeth, not recovered at the time of the body's original discovery, are analyzed. Search strategies to locate postmortem missing teeth in outdoor, surface-scattered skeletal remains are presented. Considerations for recovery of teeth include analysis of factors such as: the status of articulation of the remains; presence or absence of scattering; associations of skeletal elements in scattered clusters of bones; determination of the primary site of disposition/decomposition; the most likely trajectory of scattering; and considerations of special circumstances such as existence of facial trauma, terrain, or purposeful dismemberment.

## Acknowledgments

For case examples the author is indebted to the following Washington State agencies and individuals: San Juan County Sheriff's Department; Pierce County Medical Examiner Emanual Luxscina, M.D.; Chief Medical Examiner of Snohomish County, Eric Kiesel, M.D.; Detectives of the King County Public Safety Department; and the King County Chief Medical Examiner, Donald T. Reay M.D.

## References

Haglund, W.D.
  1991 *Applications of Taphonomic Models to Forensic Investigations.* Ph.D. dissertation, Department of Anthropology, University of Washington, Seattle. University Microfilms, Ann Arbor, MI.

Haglund, W.D., and D.T. Reay
  1993 Problems of Recovering Human Remains at Different Times and Locations: Concerns for Death Investigators. *Journal of Forensic Sciences* 38:69–80.

Haglund, W.D., D.T. Reay, and C.C. Snow
  1987 Identification of Serial Homicide Victims in the "Green River Murder" Investigation. *Journal of Forensic Science*s 32:1666–1675.

Haglund, W.D., D.T. Reay, and D.R. Swindler
  1989 Canid Scavenging/Disarticulation Sequence of Humans in the Pacific Northwest. *Journal of Forensic Sciences* 34:587–606.

Haglund, W.D., D.O. Reichert, and D.T. Reay
  1990 Recovery of Decomposed and Skeletal Human Remains in the Green River Murder Investigation: Implications for Medical Examiner/Coroner and Police. *American Journal of Forensic Medicine and Pathology* 11:35–43.

Miccozi, M.S.
  1985 Experimental Study of Postmortem Change Under Field Conditions: Effects of Freezing, Thawing and Mechanical Injury. *Journal of Forensic Sciences* 31:953–961.

Rodriguez, W.C.
  1989 Irregular Decomposition and Postmortem Pathology. Paper presented at the 41st Annual Meeting of the American Academy of Forensic Sciences, Las Vegas.

Rothwell, B.R., W.D. Haglund, and T.H. Morton
  1989 Dental Identification in Serial Homicides: The Green River Murders. *Journal of the American Dental Association* 119:373–379.

Skinner, M., and R.A. Lazenby
  1983 *Found Human Remains: A Field Manual for the Recovery of Recent Human Skeletons.* Simon Frazer University, Archaeology Press, Burnaby, Australia.

Sperber, S.

    1986  The Forensic Dental Examination and Identification. In *CAP Handbook for Postmortem Examination of Unidentified Remains: Developing Identification of Well-Preserved, Decomposed, Burned, and Special Remains,* edited by M.F. Fierro, pp. 121–139. College of American Pathologists, Skokie, IL.

Toots, H.

    1965  Sequence of Disarticulation in Mammalian Skeletons. *University of Wyoming Contributions in Geology* 4:37–39.

# The Utilization of Faunal Evidence in the Recovery of Human Remains

# 25

## TURHON A. MURAD

## Introduction

In 1984 Warren discussed the recovery of human remains as the weakest link in the chain of forensic evidence. As many have detailed (DeForest et al. 1983; Fisher 1992; Geberth 1990), the recovery of evidence is the most basic and important aspect of a forensic investigation. Certainly, in the absence of raw data, there can be neither an analysis nor a conclusion.

## Case Examples

In "Will the Forensic Anthropologist Please Help: A Case of a Women Eaten by Dogs" Bass (1984) detailed an unusual request by concerned insurance authorities. He was asked to attempt the recovery of a valuable diamond ring, believed to have been worn by a woman at the time of her demise. The deceased's remains were recovered from within her home, along with several pounds of dog feces (Figure 1). It seems the decedent's house pets ate a large portion of her, following her death. After Bass had agreed to help the authorities his graduate assistant began to search through the recovered scats by first washing them through a screen and later by scanning them under an X-ray machine. In addition to enhancing the assistant's morale, the latter scat-scan technique not only allowed a larger amount of the excrement to be searched in less time, but yielded immediate positive results. Various metal fragments, one of the deceased's teeth, and other possible significant detritus were noticed in the X-rays (Figure 2). In spite of optimism on the part of the insurance agents and scat-scanners, Bass reported that the valuable piece of jewelry was not recovered (1984).

As part of the taphonomic environment, that particular faunae may account for the destruction and/or reduction of human remains through gnawing, breaking, and consumption of both osseous materials (Binford 1981; Bonnichsen and Sorg 1989) and soft tissues has been documented (Haglund at al. 1989; Murad and Bayham 1990; Willey and Snyder 1989). Although there is a need for caution in making such a suggestion, the degree of destruction to a carcass has been said to assist in estimating the postmortem interval (Haglund et al. 1989; Murad and Bayham 1990; Willey and Snyder 1989). The abundance of predator/scavenger species, the time of the year, and the behavior of the specific species may each account for the condition of the remains and/or their transport from the area of first encounter, as might the interaction of such variables. That the consideration of such factors could contribute greatly to the success or failure of an investigation is apparent. The value of animal scats in defining the potential search area and in explaining the condition of both the scene and the recovered evidence was addressed in a case reported by Murad and Boddy (1987).

Specifically, Murad and Boddy (1987) reported a 1985 case from northern California in which the remains of a 46-year-old male were recovered down an embankment beside a logging road in midsummer. The automobile of the decreased was discovered on the road at

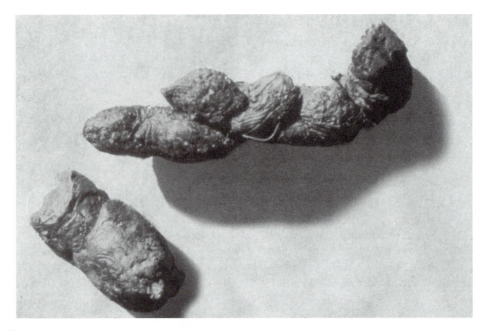

**Figure 1**   One of several dog (*Canis familiaris*) scats recovered from within a house where the decedent was found consumed by her pets. (Courtesy of William Bass.)

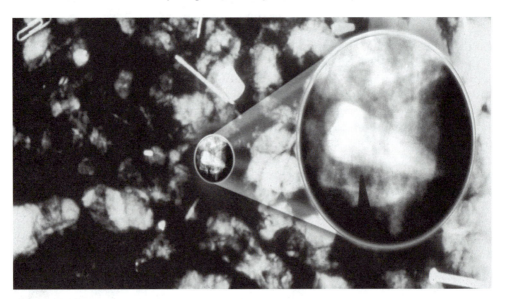

**Figure 2**   X-ray of several dog feces containing detritus ranging from metal to a human tooth. (Courtesy of William Bass.)

an elevation of approximately 1600 m. Various material culture and biological evidence was found distributed over a radius of nearly 57 m from the auto. In addition to the destruction of both the exterior and interior of the vehicle, dried muddy bear tracks were encountered on the automobile and around the scene. Dried feces was also recovered. It was determined that the scat was that of an omnivore, since it contained both vegetable and animal tissue, and, moreover, that it was most likely produced by a bear (*Ursus americanus*). Among the scat, the still-articulated left index finger of the victim was recovered. Of particular note, the fingernail was still attached to the terminal phalanx (Figure 3). The combination of when the deceased was last seen alive, the date the missing person's report was filed, and other circumstantial

**Figure 3**   Dried bear *(Ursus americanus)* feces which contains a decedent's articulated left index finger with the attached nail (highlighted in the right photo).

evidence, including the wintering behavior of bears, was used to suggest that bears were not responsible for the victim's death. However, knowledge of bear feeding behavior, variation in seasonal and daily activities and distribution, as well as their defecation practices, played an important role in defining the search area and accounting for the condition of the recovered evidence. For example, all the appendicular elements possessed large spiral fractures or were so drastically reduced from their original size that, given the context, it was likely they had been altered by the scavenging reported to occur among large animals (Binford 1981) (see Figure 4A). Except for the nearly complete mandible (Figure 4C), the decedent's face was represented by only six relatively small fragments, three of which were lone teeth (Figure 4B). While there was no direct evidence to suggest that the smaller facial fragments had passed though a bear's gut, these fragments are believed to have been capable of doing so.

The predation on domestic animals and fatal attacks on humans by mountain lions *(Felis concolor)* have received recent attention throughout California (i.e., in northern and central California, *Enterprise Record,* April 26, 1994; *San Francisco Chronicle,* May 2, 1994; Williams 1994; in southern California, *Enterprise Record,* December 11, 1994), and Colorado (Gerhardt 1994). While ten fatal mountain lion attacks were recorded between 1890 and 1990 in Canada and the United States (Rollins 1995), two such attacks have occurred in California recently. One occurred in April 1994 in El Dorado County, which is in the Sierra Nevada mountain range east of Sacramento, while the other occurred in December 1994 in San Diego County. The victim in the El Dorado County incident was a 40-year-old female who stood 173 cm tall and weighed 264.5 kg. She was an avid jogger and marathoner and was discovered near a path in a remote area of the Sierra Nevada where she had frequently jogged. The bite mark and claw mark evidence combined with the conditions encountered at the scene document a struggle between the victim and the mountain lion. Further, there is evidence to suggest that the jogger was initially attacked from the rear. Specific knowledge identifying a mountain lion as the perpetrator (i.e., bitemarks, method of attack, tracks, etc.) was addressed by Rollins (1995), who autopsied the victim and Rollins and Spencer (1995).

The decedent's body was found covered by leaves and vegetation the day after she had been reported missing. The fact that the deceased was covered with such debris is consistent with what is known about mountain lions hiding their prey only to return at a later time to continue feeding (William Clark, Wild Life Division of the California Department of Fish and Game, personal communication, February 27, 1995).

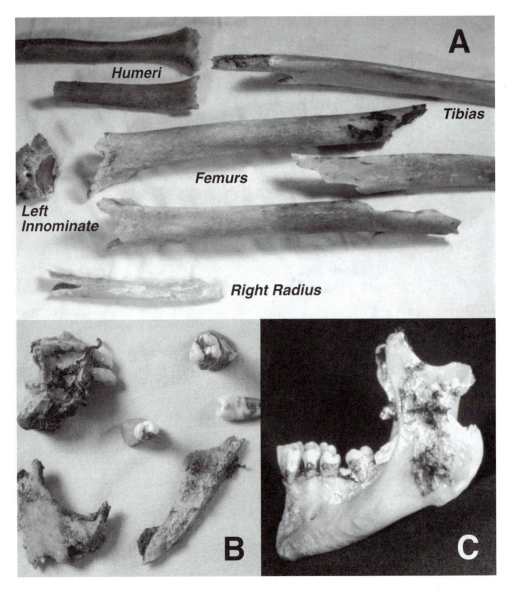

**Figure 4**   The remains of a 46-year-old male who had been partially eaten by a bear *(Ursus americanus)*.

It took 8 additional days to capture the offending animal, and during the search, trackers encountered bear feces. The bear scat contained both deer tissue and vegetable fiber. Mountain lion scat was not encountered until the same day the animal was dispatched. The day the lion was shot and killed, fresh lion feces, also containing deer flesh, was discovered. While mountain lions prey on animals which range in size from bighorn sheep and domestic cows to mice, it is well known that deer make up a large portion of their diet (Macgregor 1975). Indeed, the autopsy of the offending lion revealed deer flesh in its digestive tract. Although the animal's dentition was determined to match bite marks in the victim (Rollins 1995), the most compelling evidence that the dispatched mountain lion was responsible for the attack came from trace evidence of the jogger's tissue around the quick of the lion's claws (William Clark, personal communication, February 27, 1995).

The identification of a mountain lion as the predator in this case combined with general knowledge of mountain lions, their territory, stalking behavior, and feeding habits, played an important role in not only capturing the offending animal, but also in understanding the scene and the condition of the victim's remains.

That the identification of the species responsible for preying on humans or scavenging their remains can play an important role in understanding the conditions encountered at a scene is illustrated by the mountain lion case in San Diego County. In that particular case, the victim was again a female. It is believed her body was discovered within an hour of her death. Except for wearing her bra, she was found nude, with much of her clothing pulled down around her legs but above her boots. She was discovered lying prone over a log. Indeed, when first discovered by hikers and later observed by the initial investigators, she was believed to have been a victim of a savage rape/homicide. Only after a more careful analysis of the scene was it suggested that she had been attacked by a mountain lion. The fact that she had been pulled through the brush by her scalp was used to explain the dislocation of her clothing.

Following the removal of the body, authorities from Fish and Game then baited the area with a recently killed deer tagged with a radio transmitter. Within moments of leaving the bait the trackers received a signal that the deer was on the move. Because of the timing of the events it is believed the mountain lion may have been stalking the hunters at the time the bait was set. The lion was dispatched within 12 hours of the victim's discovery (Mark Super, Forensic Pathologist, San Diego Medical Examiner's Office, personal communication, February, 14, 1995).

It is clearly not uncommon for death investigators working at outdoor scenes in rural areas to be confronted with cases involving animal scavenging. However, as the Bass case suggests, evidence of similar activity can be encountered even within a residence.

In addition to mountain lions (*Felis concolor*), and bears (*Ursus americanus*) the species involved in California cases have included: domestic cats and dogs (Felidae and Canidae), rodents (woodrats or packrats — *Neotoma* sp.), coyotes (*Canis latrans*), and others. In spite of the recent mountain lion attacks, experience clearly suggests that the Canidae, such as dogs or coyotes, account for much of the scavenging of human remains throughout California (Murad and Sonek 1991). Regional work addressing the distribution and daily movements of coyotes in Arkansas (Gipson and Sealander 1972), Nebraska (Andelt and Gipson 1979), and Michigan (Ozoga and Harger 1966), have assisted in defining the potential search area for human remains in cases from California. One can suggest that the basic feeding and scavenging behavior of coyotes is not regionally specific and that the application of such information could be usefully applied almost anywhere (Bekoff 1978).

Haglund (personal communication, August 3, 1992) reports that in 1989 on the Olympic Peninsula, in addition to an armless torso, the scavenged remains of a 48-year-old Native American female were recovered. The remains were found scattered in a remote area, approximately 33 m to 44 m from an animal trail. Classic signs of canid activity were encountered, and coyotes were specifically suspected. Following the decedent's positive identification, based upon the discovery of her dentures and two surgical screws discovered at the site of a previous ankle injury, it was determined that the deceased was last seen alive 37 days earlier. Interestingly, distributed along the animal trail for approximately 60 m were portions of the woman's sweater and other clothing as well as two cervical vertebrae (C2 and C3). Of note, scats (believed to be those of coyotes) were found in the same area. Pink knit fabric found within the scat was matched to that from the decedent's sweater (Figure 5). Not only did the remains and the conditions encountered at the scene suggest canid scavenging, but now, so did the recovered excrement. Cause of death was blunt trauma to the head and the manner was homicide. Distribution and condition of the remains was attributed to the scavenging canids (W. D. Haglund, Medical Examiner Division of Seattle/King County Department of Public Health, WA, personal communication, August 3, 1992).

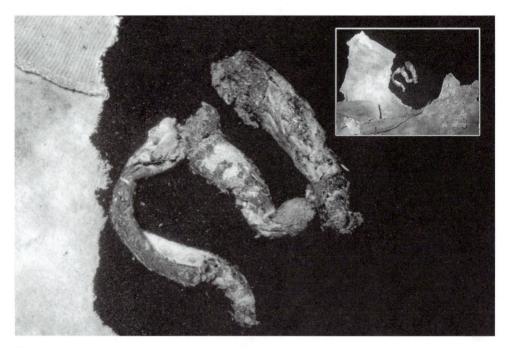

**Figure 5**   Coyote *(Canis latrans)* feces containing a portion of a deceased woman's sweater (the inset depicts the feces within that portion of the sweater which was devoured). (Courtesy of William Bass.)

## Discussion

Binford (1981:272) writes that:

> Animals consume at the kill (site) and at least some destruction takes place there. The destruction may be minimal at the kill proper where mainly meat is consumed, whereas bones that are gnawed and subjected to heavy destruction are generally dragged away from the kill proper.

The condition of the human remains as well as the general appearance of the scene in the northwest offered by Haglund, in addition to many of those encountered throughout California (Murad and Bayham 1990; Murad and Sonek 1991; Murad and Boddy 1987) generally support Binford's suggestion.

The value of an examination of excrement has been recognized for over 170 years.* Callen and Cameron (1960) provided a breakthrough in archaeologically recovered coprolites by noting that a 0.5% solution of trisodium phosphate could be used to rehydrate dried feces without damaging its constituents (e.g., delicate plant tissues, parasite eggs, cysts, and other fragile detritus). Martin and Sharrock (1964) recognized that by noting pollen contained in a recovered coprolite, speculation as to the time of year for its production could be offered. In a forensic context, discovery of such detritus could, for example, assist in suggesting a postmortem interval.

Identification of the species that produced a scat could be applied to defining the search area. Bryant and Trevor-Deutsch (1980) report that while it is difficult to identify the species that produced a scat, an appropriate suggestion can frequently be offered after noting: the

---

* G.A. Mantell reported on fish feces (probably shark) in *The Fossils of South Downs: Or Illustration of the Geology of Sussex* in 1822.

initial shape of the feces, the various characteristics of the trisodium phosphate solution after at least 3 days of rehydration, and the kind of detritus recovered from within the scat. To illustrate their point, the authors state, "Fecal pellets from certain types of rodents, such as mice, pack rats, gophers, and moles, and from many herbivores such as elk, deer, antelope, sheep, and horses, can easily be recognized by their shapes," (Bryant and Trevor-Deutsch 1980:294). Further, they report that the scat of large carnivores is typically characterized by a hard dried coating of lubricant secreted in the gut, while the fecal matter passes through the intestine (Figures 1 and 5). The lubricant, which appears shiny when dried, is suggested to aid against perforation of the intestinal wall by bits of bone (1980:294). It is common knowledge among dog owners that adult bird bone can be dangerous when eaten by their pets.

Rodriguez (personal communication, July 18, 1993) reports that a rancher from a western state filed suit against the armed forces after the rancher's dog had gotten into a crash site created from a downed military jet. Following recovery attempts, the rancher's dog was noticed to be scavenging in the area. The dog later became ill and died and while it was suspected that the dog may have ingested toxic fuel, an autopsy revealed that the dog died from gastritis. Based upon the autopsy, the dog's owner claimed it had died from complications due to a perforation of the gut caused by the ingestion of human bone. Indeed, two small fragments of alleged human bone were recovered from the animal's bowel. However, the histomorphology of the fragments was not accepted as consistent with that of human bone. The case was reconciled when the government paid the veterinarian's bill and reimbursed the rancher for the loss of his dog (W. C. Rodriguez, Armed Forces Institute of Pathology, Washington, D.C., personal communication, July 18, 1993).

Interestingly, the case reported by Rodriguez speaks to the point that bone retrieved from canid feces can be examined histomorphologically. Such an analysis could be of value in a forensic investigation by not only assisting the determination of whether the digested bone was human, as was attempted in this case, but, after employing techniques like those pioneered by Kerley (1965), could be used to suggest the represented decedent's age at death.

Although a coprolite's shape can be important in suggesting its producer, critical variables such as the postdefecation interval, exposure to the weather, and other variables may dramatically alter its otherwise tell-tale shape. In such instances, the observation of other characteristics may offer an opportunity to identify a scat's producer. Although the theory is controversial (Fry 1977; Reinhard 1985,1988), Callen (1967) suggested that after rehydrating a coprolite for at least 72 hr, the presence of surface scum as well as other gross visible features such as the color and transparency of the trisodium phosphate solution frequently allows an identification of the scat's producer to be narrowed. If the solution possesses a thin layer of surface scum, is clear, and either pale- to yellow-brown, it is likely the scat was produced by a carnivore. If the solution lacks the scum and varies from pale yellow to light brown in color, a herbivore producer is suggested. Among omnivores such as humans and bears, the solution is opaque, its color varies from dark brown to black, and a distinctive odor is present (Callen 1967).

A meaningful contribution to identifying a scat's origin also involves the careful examination of the detritus recovered from within. Exclusive plant and vegetable fibers such as grasses, leaves, twigs, etc., suggest a herbivore origin, while exclusive animal tissues such as hair, fur, bone, feathers, scales, insect skeletons, etc. suggest a carnivore producer. Among omnivores, as one might expect, both vegetable fibers and the remains of animal tissues are frequently encountered (Bryant and Trevor-Deutsch 1980:294).

One need note that coyotes, although they are carnivorous, consume a varied a diet which includes rabbits, rodents, birds, amphibians, reptiles, fish, and all sorts of vegetable matter (Bueler 1973; Johnson and Hansen 1979). Pet dogs would be at a loss, as would be their owners, if it were not for the fact that they eat cereals laced with animal fat and protein (which accounts for the scum on the surface of the trisodium phosphate solution).

Although there is value in noting the initial shape of feces, the color of the trisodium phosphate solution, and a scat's contents to suggest a producer, recent work involving the recovery of DNA from scat appears very promising. For example, Constable et al. (1995) reports that she has recovered a baboon's nuclear DNA from its feces, while others have reported the recovery of mitochondral DNA from chimpanzee scat (Hoss et al. 1992). In the future, such analyses will undoubtedly play an important role in identifying the species that produced a particular scat. However, the need for a gross inspection is likely to continue, for only at the gross level could one expect to recover jewelry, bone, fabric, and other possibly significant detritus that may assist in a forensic investigation.

In conclusion, while the recovery of evidence is important to any investigation, one can suggest that knowledge of faunal activity may have a positive impact on understanding a forensic scene, i.e., the size of the potential area to be searched and the condition of the remains encountered. Additionally, age, heritage, stature, and any uniqueness which can contribute to identification or prescribing because anthropologists are trained in a holistic approach and are oftentimes not afraid to get their hands dirty, they frequently have much more to offer than an analysis of bone, which may include knowledge of how to analyze scat.

# References

Andelt, W.F., and P.S. Gipson
   1979  Home Range, Activity, and Daily Movements of Coyotes. *Journal of Wildlife Management* 43:944–951.

Bass, W.M.
   1984  Will the Forensic Anthropologist Please Help: A Case of a Women Eaten by Dogs. Paper presented at the 36th Annual Meeting of the American Academy of Forensic Sciences, Anaheim, CA.

Bekoff, M. (editor)
   1978  *Coyotes: Biology, Behavior, and Management.* Academic Press, New York.

Binford, L.R.
   1981  *Bones: Ancient Men and Modern Myths.* Academic Press, New York.

Bonnichsen, R., and M.H. Sorg (editors)
   1989  *Bone Modification.* Center for Study of the First Americans, University of Maine, Orono, ME.

Bryant, V.M., Jr., and B. Trevor-Deutsch
   1980  Analysis of Feces and Hair Suspected to Be of Sasquatch Origin. In *Manlike Monsters on Trial,* edited by M. Halpen and M.M. Ames, pp. 291–300. University of British Columbia Press, Vancouver.

Bueler, L.E.
   1973  *Wild Dogs of the World.* Stein and Day, New York.

Callen, E.O.
   1967  Analysis of Tehuacan Coprolites. In *The Prehistory of the Tehuacan Valley:* Vol. 1, *Environment and Subsistence.* pp. 261–289. University of Texas Press, Austin.

Callen, E.O., and T.W.M. Cameron
   1960  A Prehistoric Diet Revealed in Coprolites. *New Scientist* 90:35–40.

Constable, J., C. Packet, D.A. Collins, and A.E. Pusey
   1995  Nuclear DNA from Primate Dung. *Nature* 373:193.

DeForest, P.R., R.E. Gaensslen, and H.C. Lee
   1983  *Forensic Science: An Introduction to Criminalistics.* McGraw Hill, New York.

*Enterprise Record*
   1994  Lion May have Killed Jogging Woman. April 26:B2. Chico, CA.

1994   Body in San Diego Park May be Cougar Victim. December 11:A1. Chico, CA.

Fisher, B.A.J.
1992   *Techniques of Crime Scene Investigation.* CRC Press, Boca Raton, FL.

Fry, G.F.
1977   *Analysis of Prehistoric Coprolites from Utah.* University of Utah Anthropological Papers, No. 97, University of Utah Press, Salt Lake City.

Geberth, V.J.
1990   *Practical Homicide Investigation.* Elsevier Science, New York.

Gerhardt, G.
1994   Woman Tells What She Recalls of Attack by Mountain Lion. *Enterprise Record* December 16:B3. Chico, CA.

Gipson, P.S., and J.A. Sealander
1972   Home Range and Activity of Coyote (*Canis latrans frustor*) in Arkansas. *Proceedings of the Annual Conference of the Southeastern Game and Fish Commission* 26:82–95.

Haglund, W.D., D.T. Reay, and D.R. Swindler
1989   Canid Scavenging/Disarticulation Sequence of Human Remains in the Pacific Northwest. *Journal of Forensic Sciences* 34:587–606.

Hoss M., M. Kohn, and S. Paabo
1992   Excrement Analysis by PCR. *Nature* 359:199.

Johnson, M.K., and R.M. Hansen
1979   Coyote Food Habits on the Idaho National Engineering Laboratory. *Journal of Wildlife Management* 43:951–956.

Kerley, E.R.
1965   The Microscopic Determination of Age in Human Bone. *American Journal of Physical Anthropology* 23:149–163.

MacGregor, W.
1975   *Big Game of California.* Revised by W.P. Dasmann. Department of Fish and Game, Sacramento.

Martin, P.S., and F.W. Sharrock
1964   Pollen Analysis of Prehistoric Human Feces: A New Approach to Ethnobotany. *American Antiquity* 30:168–180.

Murad, T.A., and F.E. Bayham
1990   Northern California Examples of the Effect of Animal Scavenging on the Estimation of the Postmortem Interval. Paper presented at the 42nd Annual Meeting of the American Academy of Forensic Sciences, Cincinnati.

Murad, T.A., and M.A. Boddy
1987   A Case with Bear Facts. *Journal of Forensic Sciences* 32:1819–1826.

Murad, T.A., and A. Sonek
1991   Animal Scats as Taphonomic Factors in the Recovery of Human Remains. Paper presented at the 45th Annual Meeting of the American Academy of Forensic Sciences, Boston.

Ozoga, J.J., and E.M. Harger
1966   Winter Activities and Feeding Habits of Northern Michigan Coyotes. *Journal of Wildlife Management* 30:809–818.

Reinhard, K.J.

    1985   Recovery of Helminths from Prehistoric Feces: The Cultural Ecology of Ancient Parasitism. Master's thesis, Department of Biology, Northern Arizona University, Flagstaff.

    1988   Cultural Ecology of Prehistoric Parasitism on the Colorado Plateau as Evidenced by Coprology. *American Journal of Physical Anthropology* 82:355–366.

Rollins, C.E.

    1995   Bite Mark Analysis and Profile: A Fatality and the American Mountain Lion. *Proceedings of the Annual Meeting of the American Academy of Forensic Sciences* 1:120.

Rollins, C.E., and D.E. Spencer

    1995   A Fatality and the American Mountain Lion: Bite Mark Analysis and Profile of the Offending Lion. *Journal of Forensic Sciences* 40: 486–489.

*San Francisco Chronicle*

    1994   Trackers Shoot Cougar They Think Killed Jogger. May 2:A15. San Francisco, CA.

Warren, C.

    1984   The Recovery of Human Remains: The Weakest Link in the Chain of Forensic Evidence. Paper presented at the 36th Annual Meeting of the American Academy of Forensic Sciences, Anaheim, CA.

Willey, P.S., and L.M. Snyder

    1989   Canid Modification of Human Remains: Implications for Time-Since-Death. *Journal of Forensic Sciences* 34:894–901.

Williams, J.

    1994   Mountain Lion: We Must Protect Wildlife. *Reno Gazette-Journal* 19 June:B5.

# Rodents and Human Remains *

# 26

WILLIAM D. HAGLUND

## Introduction

Archaeologists and paleontologists who study taphonomic phenomena have focused on the part rodents play in bone accumulation (Binford 1981:207; Brain 1981; Mcquire et al. 1980), and tooth mark modification to bone (Miller 1969; Morse 1983). The most noted accumulators of bone are porcupines (*Hysterix africaeustralis*) (Brain 1981). Woodrats or packrats (*Neotoma* sp.) of the American southwest often hoard "treasures" that include bone (VanDevender et al. 1984; Wells 1976). Rodents cited as gnawers of bone include the African porcupine (*H. africaeustralis*) (Brain 1981), gerbil (*Desmodillus* sp.) (Brain 1980, 1987), mouse (*Peromyscus manaculatus*) (Krogman and Iscan 1986:23), and various squirrels, and rats (Brain 1970; Hill 1979; Morse 1983).

Brain (1981) attributes gnawing on bones by rodents to their need to provide attrition to their continuously growing incisors to keep them at a "usable" length. Rodent tooth marks on bone surfaces have been variously described as channels or striae (Bonnichsen 1979; Sorg 1985), windows (Johnson 1985), straight parallel grooves (Johnson 1985), and flat-bottomed grooves (Shipman and Rose 1982).

The characteristic specialization of rodents is their ability to gnaw (Moore 1981:177). Gnawing is a type of incisive movement capable of reducing hard fibrous substances in which the separated material is not always digested. Second incisors and canine teeth are absent in the rodents, and the central incisors are separated from the cheek teeth by a long diastema. The cheek teeth generally consist of three to four teeth with some species having fewer. The rodents possess a relatively uncommon feature in that the lower jaw is loosely joined at the symphysial region, allowing a considerable range of motion. The biting action consists of the upper incisors being pressed into the object being gnawed, to hold the head steady (Moore 1981) (Figure 1). This may leave readily identifiable marks (Hillson 1986:57). The lower jaw is free to move up and down, gouging in the pointed, chisel-like lower incisors. During gnawing, the lower incisors are moved forward and upward several times instead of in a single stroke.

The expected distinct parallel stria indicative of rodent gnawing are not always found. In cancellous bone or skeletal elements of smaller long bones such as metacarpals, metatarsals, and phalanges where the shaft cortex is extremely thin, telltale parallel stria may be absent. Patterns produced by suites of rodent gnaw marks vary depending on chewing behavior, number of chewing bouts, over-chewing, and character of the bone being modified, i.e., whether it is fresh, weathered and degreased, cancellous or compact. Multiple gnawing may present as a series of parallel marks, fan-shaped patterns, or totally disorganized striae overlying each other (Shipman and Rose 1988). A common site of damage to subadult skeletons gnawed by rodents is the epiphyseal cartilages and adjacent areas of long bones. This leaves a thin stem of gnawed bone connecting the articulating ends to the shaft (Haglund et al. 1988) (Figure 2).

* Adapted for reprint courtesy of *Journal of Forensic Sciences, Vol. 37*, 1459–1465, 1992.

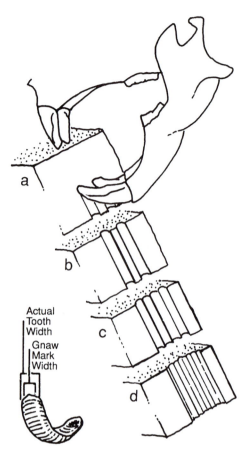

**Figure 1** Biting action of rodents and resulting artifacts (adapted from Moore 1981; Shipman and Rose 1983). (a) The upper incisors being pressed into the object and lower incisors moving up and down, gouging in the pointed, chisel like lower incisors. (b) The effects of repeated gnawing showing two gnaw marks made by one stroke. (c) The second gnawing action, displaced slightly to one side of the first. (d) Area of repeated gnawing, containing linear striations that are remnants of earlier marks. Lower left: lower incisor diagram demonstrating that the incisor may produce a mark narrower than the incisor width because the tip is rounded, and that the cutting edge may be thinner than the actual incisor.

Miller (1975) cautions that the incisors of canids such as coyotes (*C. latrans*) and wolves (*C. lupus*) can cause hollow grooves which may mimic the gnawing marks of rodents. This occurs when canids gnaw with their incisors transverse to the longitudinal axis of long bones. A characteristic of gnawed cross sections of long bone shafts is their uniform pitch, extending from the outer to inner surfaces. In contrast, damage from carnivores is less regular and often rounded with no uniform pitch from the inner to outer surface (Haglund et al. 1988).

Some authors writing about ancient bones suggest that rodents favor bones that are somewhat weathered and free from fat and sinew (Brain 1981; Gifford 1981). This view may reflect the limited experience of these authors with remains that retain soft tissue. It may also, in part, reflect the arid climatic regimes from which such observations have been made. Other authors suggest rodents prefer spongy portions of fresh bones (Eikhoff and Herrmann 1985). Rodent damage to soft tissue has received mention in the forensic literature (Adelson 1974:88, 633; Haglund 1992; Patel and Path 1994). Crenulated edges delineating margins of damage to soft tissue have been noted (Knight 1991:68). The potential for confusing antemortem, ulcerated skin lesions with gnawing by mice and rats has also been discussed (Fisher 1980).

Forensic investigators, in contrast to paleontologists and archaeologists, have the abililty to routinely observe the immediate postmortem interval ranging from minutes, hours, and days, and hence to extend taphonomic observations into the realm of fresh soft tissue. Three cases presented by Haglund (1992) demonstrate a spectrum of postmortem rodent activities with human remains ranging from fresh and mummified soft tissue to dry and fresh bone, as well as the use of human remains utilized for nesting purposes. Rodents were also noted to be vectors of bone transport. The following case examples illustrate these observations.

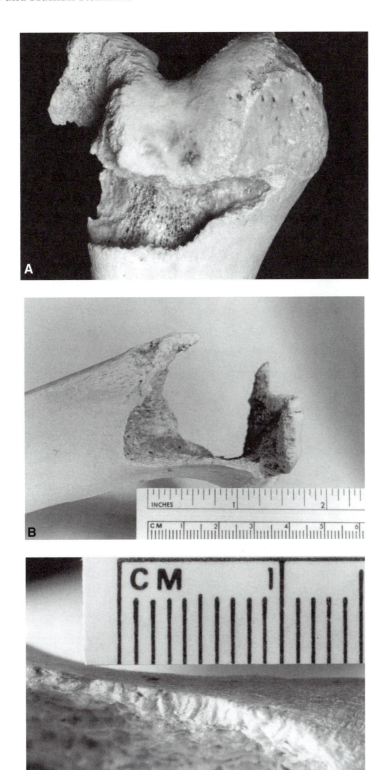

**Figure 2**  Pedestal phenomena resulting from rodent gnawing of subadult femur (A) and tibia (B). Inset (C) demonstrates the uniform pitch and parallel damage of typical rodent gnawing across the relatively thick cortex.

## Case Examples

### Case 1

Twenty years following discovery and identification of the postcranial remains of a homicide victim, a cranium suspected to be that of the victim was discovered. Lack of antemortem skeletal or dental records reduced identification efforts to superimposition. Rodent damage to the supraorbital margin and destruction to other areas such as the zygomatic arch compromised superimposition efforts (Figure 3).

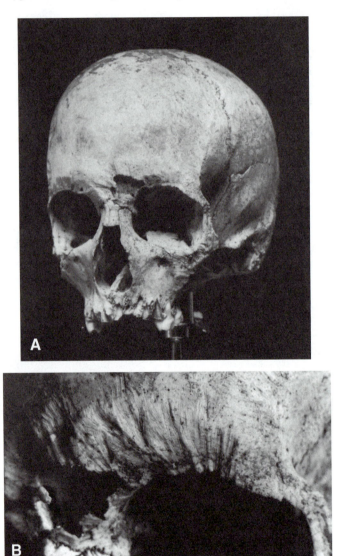

**Figure 3**    Case 1. (A) Typical pattern of rodent damage to crania. (B) Left supraorbital margin of a weathered cranium with parallel pattern of stria (close-up).

### Case 2

This 33-year-old victim of a suicide by hanging was discovered in a secluded, wooded area 7.4 months following his death. The deceased was fully clothed in winter apparel and suspended by a rope from a tree limb with knees bent and feet touching the ground. Two adult rats were observed leaving the body at the scene. When the body was undressed, a nest composed of pine needles, newspaper, and down and fibers from the deceased's clothing was found occupying the entire thoracic cavity. Nine live, juvenile common rats (*Rattus norvegicus*), were extracted from the nest.

The anterior chest was nearly completely skeletonized. Tissue of the face was mummified, with rodent damage to the nasal aperture (Figure 4A), the trachea was damaged (Figure 4B), and chewed edges of dried muscles were frayed (Figure 4C). The right forearm and hand were completely skeletonized. Distal phalanges of the second through fifth fingers were absent. Remaining skin and soft tissues were mummified. Margins of damage to skin were finely scalloped. Tightly circumscribed circular defects were present in areas covered by integument, and a tunnel from the posterior aspect of the left shoulder connected the right axilla to the nest in the thoracic area.

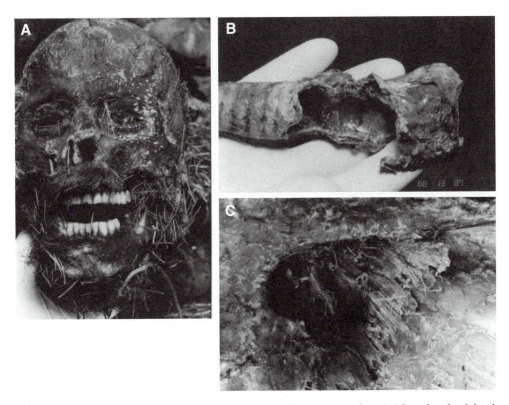

**Figure 4**   Case 2. (A) Damage to mummified face; (B) damage to trachea; (C) frayed ends of dried muscle fibers.

### Case 3

A 27-year-old male was discovered approximately 3 days following his death in a dilapidated wooden shack. The deceased was fully clothed. His head and thorax were inside a plastic garbage sack that was tucked into his belt. Both upper extremities were entrapped inside the plastic bag. Nestled in the deceased's left arm was a small propane tank with the valve in the "on" position. At the time of discovery, the plastic bag had been torn open by rodents, allowing them access to the upper portion of the body. There were rat droppings on the chest and inside the bag. Rodent hairs adhered to exposed muscle tissues.

All soft tissue of the face and neck was absent. Also absent were both eyes and the soft tissue of the left temporal, frontal, and parietal areas. Both forearms were completely skeletonized. The metacarpals of the right hand were completely exposed and the majority of digits were absent (Figure 5A). The bones of the left hand were completely absent. Damage to the thin cortical layers of bone of the fingers demonstrated no telltale parallel stria. Margins between rodent damaged areas and non-affected areas of soft tissue of the forearm exhibited scalloped edges, giving a finely serrated appearance. Damage to soft tissue took place in a layered fashion with distinct, differential destruction to the skin, and including underlying adipose tissue and muscle (Figure 5B).

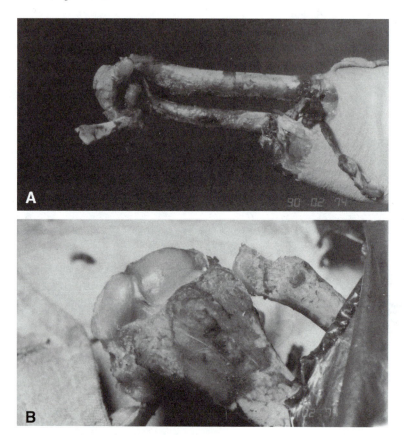

**Figure 5**  Case 3. (A) Removal of soft tissue from face and mandible by rats; (B) layered rodent damage to soft tissue.

## Case 4

This 95-year-old man was found dead in his house, having died of probable arteriosclerotic cardiovascular disease. He was last known to be alive 5 days earlier. The body was in bed, clad in long johns, and partially covered by a blanket. Decomposition was characterized by skin slippage with drying in some areas, as well as early abdominal bloating and discoloration. Rat gnawing damage was noted on the face (Figure 6A) and left hand (Figure 6B).

## Case 5

A 16-year-old female homicide victim was recovered from a suburban Seattle park in February, 1988. She was last known to be alive approximately 1 week previously.

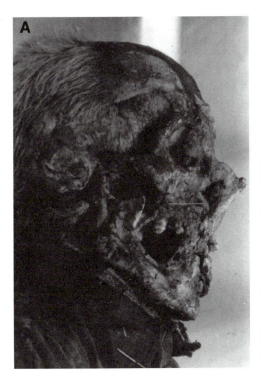
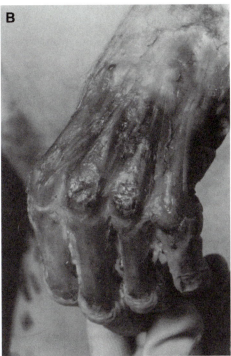

**Figure 6**   Case 4. (A) Rat gnawing damage to the face of a 95-year-old man; (B) damage to the hand.

Upon discovery, the body was nude and had received multiple gunshot wounds to the head (Figure 7A). Rat scavenging damage consisted of a 12.7- by 13.34-cm defect over the left shoulder, exposing muscles, the lateral aspect of the scapula, and the joint capsule of the humerus. There was minimal gnawing damage to the scapular spine. Scat rested on the exposed muscle (Figure 7B). A second defect over the left hip measured 15.2 by 19.1 cm and was approximately 3.8 cm in depth.

## Discussion

The preceding cases demonstrate a spectrum of rodent damage to human tissue that includes fresh and mummified soft tissue, as well as fresh and dry bone, and shows rodents as agents of bone transport. Occasionally rodents may utilize human remains for nesting purposes. Recent gnawing activity on bony surfaces previously discolored from long exposure may also enable investigators to make inferences relative to the postmortem exposure interval.

Bone gnawing by rodents can often be distinguished from that of carnivores by a characteristic parallel series of furrows created by the incisors. Table 1 compares soft tissue damage by rodents to that caused by carnivores. Rodent damage to soft tissue is illustrated by layered destruction of tissue layers. Case 3 (Figure 5) exhibits margins that are marked by a series of crenulations and an absence of scratch marks beyond damaged areas. By contrast, canid damage to soft tissue is often accompanied by claw-induced, linear, scratch-type abrasions or puncture marks from canine teeth beyond consumed margins. These marks are frequently V-shaped. Margins of carnivore-damaged soft tissue tend to be relatively more ragged (Haglund 1991).

Dispersal of skeletal elements by rodents was not observed in the above examples, but has been observed in other cases by the author. Small bones of the hands and feet have been found in rodent burrows. In another case, two lumbar vertebrae were found in a length of PCV pipe.

**Figure 7**   Case 5. (A) Decomposed body of a young homicide victim scavenged by rats; (B) inset of scat deposited on the damaged area.

**Table 1    Features Distinguishing Soft Tissue Damage by Rodents from Carnivore Scavenging**

| Characteristic | Rodent | Carnivore |
|---|---|---|
| Defect shape | Tight, circumscribed | Irregular |
| Defect margin | Relatively smooth or crenelated | Irregular |
| Undamaged area beyond margin | No damage | Scratched or bruised |

**Table 2    Widths of Occlusal Surfaces of Commonly Encountered Rodent Upper Incisors**

| Size | Rodent Genus (example) |
|---|---|
| Very small — less than 1 mm | Voles |
|  | Mice |
|  | Lemmings |
| Small — 1 mm to 1.5 mm | Rats |
| Medium — 1.5 to 2 mm | Squirrels |
| Large — 2 mm to 5 mm | Marmots |
| Very large — more than 5 mm | Beaver |
|  | Porcupine |

*Note:*   Some genera are variable and fall into more than one category; some genera have grooved buccal incisor surfaces; (Gerbillus — gerbil).

Adapted from Hillson 1986: 59.

Table 2 presents the widths of occlusal surfaces of commonly encountered rodent upper incisors. Similar surveys of commonly encountered rodents of the anthropologist's area of practice are encouraged. It is the lower incisor's dimension that produces the "furrows;" however, the depth and consequently the width of marks produced is partly due to the jaw strength of the rodent and hardness of the object being gnawed. Although determination of specific rodent species from dimensions of gnaw marks in bone may be unreliable, these measurements can be corroborated by identification of associated scat or hair which may be found in the nearby vicinity or deposited on exposed tissue. Rodents have a fairly high metabolic rate and defecate frequently.

It is not surprising that the ubiquitous "chisel-toothed" mammals, the rodents, rank among the most common scavengers of human remains. Their activities can affect skeletal element recovery, human identification, and interpretation of antemortem artifacts. Investigators should be aware of specific rodent species inhabiting regions which they investigate. Consultation with a local mammalogist is also advised. Rodent species identification and knowledge of seasonal behaviors may assist investigators in determining the season of rodent-induced damage, particularly in instances of hibernating species.

# References

Adelson, L.
  1974  *The Pathology of Homicide.* Charles C Thomas, Springfield, IL.

Binford, L.
  1981  *Bones: Ancient Men and Modern Myths.* Academic Press, New York.

Bonnichsen, R.
  1979  *Pleistocene Bone Technology in the Beringian Refugium.* Archaeologal Survey of Canada Paper No. 89, Mercury Series. National Museum of Man, Ottawa.

Brain, C.K.
  1970  New Finds at the Swartkrans Australopithecine Site. *Nature* 225:1112–1119.
  1980  Some Criteria for the Recognition of Bone-Collecting Agencies in African Caves. In *Fossils in the Making*, edited by A.K. Behrensmeyer and A.P. Hill, pp. 107–129. University of Chicago Press, Chicago.
  1981  *The Hunters or the Hunted? An Introduction to African Cave Taphonomy.* Chicago University Press, Chicago.
  1987  Hottentot Food Remains and Their Bearing on the Interpretation of Fossil Bone Assemblages. *Scientific Papers Namib Research Station* 32:1–11.

Eickhoff, S., and B. Herrmann
  1985  Surface Marks on Bones from Neolithic Collective Grave (Odagsen, Saxony): A Study on Differential Diagnostics. *Journal of Human Evolution* 14:263–274.

Fisher, R.S.
  1980  Time of Death and Changes After Death. In *Medicolegal Investigation of Death*, edited by W.U. Spitz and R.S. Fisher, p. 30. Charles C Thomas, Springfield, IL.

Gifford, D.
  1981  Taphonomy and Paleoecology: A Critical Review of Archaeology's Sister Disciplines. In *Advances in Archaeological Method and Theory*, Vol. 4, edited by M.B. Schiffer, pp. 65–438. Academic Press, New York.

Haglund, W.D.
  1991  *Application of Taphonomic Models to Forensic Investigations.* Ph.D. dissertation, Department of Anthropology, University of Washington, Seattle. University Microfilms, Ann Arbor, MI.
  1992  Contributions of Rodents to Postmortem Artifacts of Bone and Soft Tissue. *Journal of Forensic Sciences* 37:1459–1465.

Haglund, W.D., D.T. Reay, and D.R. Swindler
  1988  Tooth Artifacts and Survival of Bones in Animal-Scavenged Human Skeletons. *Journal of Forensic Sciences* 33:985–997.

Hill, A.P.
1979 Disarticulation and Scattering of Mammal Skeletons. *Paleobiology* 5:261–274.

Hillson, S.
1986 *Teeth.* Cambridge University Press, New York.

Johnson, E.
1985 Current Developments in Bone Technology. In *Advances in Archaeological Method and Theory,* Vol. 8, edited by M.B. Schiffer, pp. 157–235. Academic Press, New York.

Knight, B.
1991 *Forensic Pathology.* Oxford University Press, New York.

Krogman, W.M., and M.Y. Iscan
1986 *The Human Skeleton in Forensic Medicine.* Charles C Thomas, Springfield, IL.

Mcquire, J.M., D. Pemberton, and N.H. Collett
1980 The Makapansgat Limeworks Gray Brecca: Hominids, Hyaenas, Histricids or Hillwash. *Paleontology Africa* 23:75–98.

Miller, G.J.
1969 A Study of Cuts, Grooves, and Other Marks on Recent and Fossil Bones, I: Animal Tooth Marks. *Tebiwa* 12:9–19.
1975 A Study of Cuts, Grooves, and Other Marks on Recent and Fossil Bones, II: Weathering Cracks, Fractures, Splinters, and Other Similar Natural Phenomena. In *Lithic Technology,* edited by E. Swanson, pp. 212–226. Mouton, The Hague.

Moore, W.J.
1981 *The Mammalian Skull.* Cambridge University Press, New York.

Morse, D.
1983 The Skeletal Pathology of Trauma. In *Handbook of Forensic Archaeology,* edited by D. Morse, J. Duncan, and J.W. Stoutmire, pp. 145–185. Rose Printing, Tallahassee.

Patel, F., and M.R.C. Path
1994 Artifact in Forensic Medicine: Postmortem Rodent Activity. *Journal of Forensic Sciences* 39:257–260.

Shipman, P., and J. Rose
1982 Early Hominid Hunting, Butchering, and Carcass-Processing Behaviors: Approaches to the Fossil Record. *Journal of Anthropological Archaeology,* 2:47–98.

Sorg, M.H.
1985 Scavenger Modification of Human Remains. *Current Research in the Pleistocene* 2:37–38.

VanDevender, T.R., J.L. Batencourt, and M. Wimberly
1984 Biogeographic Implications of Packrat Midden Sequence from Sacramento Mountains, South-Central New Mexico. *Quaternary Research* 22:344–460.

Wells, P.V.
1976 Macrofossil Analysis of Wood Rat (Neotoma) Middens as a Key To the Quaternary Vegetational History of Arid America. *Quaternary Research* 6:223–248.

# On the Body: Insects' Life Stage Presence and Their Postmortem Artifacts

# 27

NEAL H. HASKELL
ROBERT D. HALL
VALERIE J. CERVENKA
MICHAEL A. CLARK

## Introduction

Often, when human remains are found, artifacts such as soft tissue destruction and trauma to the internal organs or skeleton are discovered. These artifacts can be seen on remains of extremely short postmortem interval (PMI) or cases of extended PMI (greater than one month) duration. Of great importance is the determination of the origin and time of occurrence of these artifacts, and whether or not they occurred antemortem (possibly by an assailant) or postmortem (by other means). In many cases, what appears to be antemortem trauma to soft tissue may actually be feeding patterns of omnivorous or sarcosaprophagous insects. Insects that may be responsible for causing soft tissue trauma during the early period are: cockroaches (Dictyoptera), body lice (Phthiraptera), ants, bees, wasps (Hymenoptera), mites (Acari), and even dipterous larvae. A knowledge of these insects' feeding patterns and of situations where they may be encountered can be extremely important in assessment of human death cases. For the longer postmortem interval cases, insects causing postmortem artifacts can include: dipterous larvae, Dermestidae adults and larvae, and larvae or adults of several scavenger beetle families. The presence of insect life stages and their longevity at a scene, whether in the soil or within enclosures, may be of great benefit when interpreting scenes. Larval cast skins (either Diptera or Coleoptera), Diptera puparia, and adult insect exoskeletal parts (elytra, sternites, tergites, head, or mouth parts) all may be important in making proper determinations regarding time of death, location of death, and other factors surrounding the investigation.

## Background

Insects comprise the most important group of living organisms found to colonize decomposing animal carrion with respect to the speed and completeness with which soft tissue of dead animals is removed. The typical death-scene investigator learns quickly that maggots and corpses go together. For many years, the "worms" crawling in the eyes, nose, and other orifices and wounds on dead bodies were considered just another disgusting element of decay — something to be rinsed away as soon as the body was placed on the table for autopsy.

Animal carcasses have been observed being skeletonized within 96 hours of death (Haskell 1989), due exclusively to high numbers of voraciously feeding fly larvae and corresponding high environmental temperatures. Insects are part of a very specific ecological system that is initiated immediately upon death of most vertebrate animals and ends finally with the animal's bleached white bones. These include necrophagous species, predators and parasites of the carrion feeders, omnivorous species, adventive species, and accidental species (Smith 1986). These organisms are usually the first to find the dead animal, with many colonizing species feeding specifically and universally on decomposing animal tissue.

In addition to the insects, associated with this tightly serried ecosystem are bacteria, fungi, molds, and several additional groups of arthropods. Small (e.g., rodents and scavenging mammals) or large vertebrate scavengers or carnivores (e.g., dogs, coyotes, and bears) may also aid in extensive soft tissue clearing and significant postmortem artifacts and damage to the remains.

This ecosystem is confined and in a closely packed area, usually limited to the remains itself, until the advanced stages of the process, when the physical dimensions expand somewhat. But the expansion is still within a few meters of the originating carcass, thus maintaining a compact and specifically denoted area; this is an important factor when attempting to identify and locate insect specimens for analysis to use during a death investigation. Any one of these organisms potentially adds to the taphonomic understanding of the remains.

The broad title "forensic entomology" applies to any involvement of arthropods (insects and some close relatives such as spiders, ticks, and mites) with legal matters. For convenience, it has been divided into three major areas (Lord and Stevenson 1986): urban entomology (the study of insects affecting structures and other elements of the human environment, including such forensically important aspects as termite damage and control, spider bites, and so forth), stored products entomology (insects and insect residue in food and other stored commodities), and medicolegal entomology. The latter field has been known as "forensic medical entomology" or more simply "forensic entomology," but is perhaps best termed "medicocriminal entomology" because of its close association with criminology and, consequently, violent crime (Hall 1990). Forensic entomology is concerned with arthropods as they relate to (1) determination of the time and sites of human death, (2) possible sudden death cases, (3) traffic accidents of unknown etiology, and (4) possible misuse of arthropods as instruments of crime (Leclercq 1969). The present discussion focuses strictly on medicocriminal entomology, with the term forensic entomology being used throughout the rest of the text to signify this focus.

The principal role of forensic entomology today is to provide biological inferences regarding the circumstances surrounding and the length of time since human death — based upon examination of arthropods (mainly insects) collected from or near corpses. Two main approaches exist: (1) analysis of the pattern of corpse colonization by successive "waves" of arthropods, or (2) determination of the life stage of insects, usually flies, collected in, on, or near the body. Specialists can collect, rear, and identify the insects involved, and analyze and interpret the evidence thus obtained. In particular, the role of the forensic entomologist is to identify the arthropods associated with such cases. The forensic entomologist, an entomologist specifically trained in insect identification, behavior, biology, physiology, and proper specimen procurement of the carrion insects, will provide additional dimensions to conclusions derived from a death scene.

## History and Background of Forensic Entomology

The first documentation of Western applications of forensic entomology in death investigations came in 1855 when Bergeret (1855), in France, used insect sequences or succession to solve a case. By the mid-1880s, J. P. Megnin, also in France, published several articles dealing with forensic entomology. The most noted of these, *La Faune des Cadavres: Application de Tomologie a la Medicin Legale* (Megnin 1894), served in large part to make the medical and legal professions aware that entomological data could prove useful in death investigations.

ʏThe recognition by Megnin of a sequence and progression of decomposition of a corpse was recorded in this work. In association with this decomposition progression, he observed changes in the insect assemblages as the corpse aged. This brought about the˟expansion of the successional insect wave concept used earlier by Bergeret (1855).

In the United States, Fowler (1888) studied insects associated with human remains. Later, Motter (1898) tabulated the insect fauna from 150 grave disinterments from the Washington, D.C. area. A considerable number of fauna identified were a result of colonization of the remains prior to burial, a result of embalming techniques not being as thorough as what is recommended today.

Inaccuracy in insect species identification due to taxonomic keys not being available in the early part of the 20th century greatly restricted species-specific data analysis of carrion-colonizing insects. Species identification of the most important fly groups, Calliphoridae (blowflies) and Sarcophagidae (flesh flies), used in forensic cases could not be done until Aldrich's (1916) monograph on the Sarcophagidae made use of distinctive male genitalia of adult flies to identify specimens from this important family. This technique has been applied with similar success to the forensically important blowflies (Hall and Haskell 1995).

Twenty years later, Knipling (1936a) published descriptions and keys to many common early (1st instar) maggots of flesh flies and *Lucilia* larvae (1936b), and considerable work had been done on the blowfly fauna of North America (Knipling 1939) prompting elegant pioneering research on blowfly ecology and distribution within habitat type (Parish and Cushing 1938).

It was not until publication of *The Blowflies of North America* (Hall 1948) that the North American adult calliphorid fauna could be identified with assurance. This publication also made possible accurate identification of mature larvae of most species of the calliphorids as well. It should be noted that Hall's monograph was the direct result of requests by law enforcement agencies (FBI and others) for entomological support in homicide investigations (Hall and Townsend 1977).

Wardle (1921) conducted studies on what type of foods were best for attracting calliphorids. By using different domestic animal and food products (liver, kidneys, meats from a variety of domestic animals, and fish) in raw, preserved, and cooked states, Wardle compiled a list of those products least and most attractive to calliphorids. Lodge (1916) observed that fresh or putrefied blood seemed unattractive to female blowflies. Smith and Dear (1978) studied fish as an attractant for calliphorids. These studies prompted work on blowfly distribution within habitat type and on blowfly ecology (Green 1951; James 1947; Parish and Cushing 1938; Wardle 1930). Davidson (1944) showed that blowfly developmental time intervals are affected by temperature, and other studies addressing the effects of temperatures on developmental time of calliphorid species life cycles have been conducted (Greenberg 1991; Kamal 1958; Muller 1975; Nuorteva 1971; Reiter and Wollenek 1983; Vinogradova and Marchenko 1984).

Although very few new North American calliphorid species have been described recently, efforts have been devoted to accumulate improved distribution information (Goddard and Lago 1983; Hall 1979; Hall and Townsend 1977).

The North American calliphorid and sarcophagid fly fauna is now fairly well understood, although entomologists are aware that introduced species may affect medicocriminal cases (Baumgartner 1986; Gagne 1981; Richard and Ahrens 1983). Presently, four species of Old World blowflies have been confirmed from South or North America (Baumgartner and Greenberg 1984; Gagne 1981; Greenberg 1988). These include *Chrysomya rufifacies* (Macquart), *C. albiceps* (Wiedemann), *C. megacephala* (F.), and *C. putoria* (Wiedemann). The effect that these species may have on te succession of indigenous North American Diptera on carrion is not known and will require detailed study (Baumgartner 1993; vonZuben et al. 1993; Wells and Greenberg 1992). Such introduced species have already figured in medicocriminal cases from the southern U.S. (Hall and Haskell 1995).

Regional studies on blowfly distribution have been conducted for California (James 1955), Hawaii (Hardy 1981), Mississippi (Goddard and Lago 1983), Missouri (Hall 1979), and Virginia (Hall and Townsend 1977), and springtime urban species have been surveyed in Chicago, IL (Baumgartner 1988). Catalogues on Diptera include *A Catalogue of the Diptera of America North of Mexico* (Stone et al. 1965), which lists all known species of Diptera for this given geographic area as well as the above-mentioned work by Hall (1948) for North American calliphorids. For South America, a work by James (1970) should be consulted. Taxonomic research on the blowflies has focused on intraspecific variation (James 1953; James 1967), changes in the genital structure of males postmating (Gagne and Peterson 1982), and the identification of immature stages (Erzinclioglu 1985; Ishijima 1967; Kano and Sato 1951a, 1951b, and 1952; Liu and Greenberg 1989; Reiter and Wollenek 1983, 1985). Because fly development is a temperature-driven event (Davidson 1944) and varies according to species, accurate data are fundamental to medicocriminal estimates. Some recent studies on the effect of temperature on carrion fly development include those of Marchenko (1985), Nuorteva (1971), and Vinogradova and Marchenko (1984); Norris (1965) provided a valuable review of blowfly bionomics; and the use of these insects as forensic indicators has been summarized (Greenberg 1985; Hall and Haskell 1995).

The study of insects potentially important to forensic entomology has been conducted mainly through the use of nonhuman animal models. A variety of different animals have been used, including: dogs (Reed 1958), cats (Early and Goff 1986), squirrels (Johnson 1975), foxes (Smith 1975), pigs (Payne 1965), seals (Lord and Burger 1984), and other small animals (Goddard and Lago 1985; Lane 1975). The only research on insect faunal succession conducted on human corpses was in Tennessee (Catts and Haskell 1990; Rodriguez and Bass 1983, 1985).

At present, 1st instar blowfly larvae (the stage that hatches directly from the egg) are generally not identifiable as to species, and second instars (the next maggot stage) can be identified accurately only on occasion. The situation is somewhat better with respect to third instar or prepupal larvae (the largest maggot stage, and that most commonly observed), but only if such specimens are preserved properly. Even so, a significant number of indigenous blowflies cannot be identified at present as immatures. This is currently an area of active research, and to this end the relatively new technique of scanning electron microscopy is being applied (Liu and Greenberg 1989).

Because of the forensic entomology requirement for reliable data on rates of larval development, considerable effort has been expended to measure such intervals. Anecdotal information on blowflies contained in earlier works was largely supplanted by Hall's (1948) rearing data, and the latter has been refined for some forensically important species to degree-hour status (Greenberg 1985). Because insects are cold-blooded animals, their rate of development is more or less dependent on ambient temperature. Research has shown that for each species there is generally a threshold temperature below which no development takes place. As temperature rises above this threshold, a certain amount of time is required for the insect to attain defined stages of development (for instance, from the newly laid egg through the second instar maggot). Because this heat is accumulated as "thermal units," it can be calibrated and described as "degree-days" or "degree-hours," depending on the accuracy of temperature readings and time period involved. However, most laboratory rearings (upon which the degree-hour data are developed) have been done at constant temperature, so additional research will be necessary to establish correlation between these data, typical fluctuating field temperatures (warmer during the day and cooler at night), and the average daily measurements frequently reported from weather stations. Retrospective weather records from the nearest weather-recording station (such as an airport) are those most often used in medicocriminal evaluations.

Biologically, there is theoretical similarity between the process of carrion decomposition and the decomposition of other organic materials such as dung. In the latter case, the decomposition of bovine excreta ("cow pats") has been studied thoroughly in Europe, the United

States, and Australia, especially in relation to the flies associated therewith, because of the importance of this phenomenon to range land ecology. Many techniques used in such studies can be applied to medicocriminal entomology and the two fields share fundamental ecological principles (Hall and Haskell 1995).

The documentation of the case histories using forensic entomology has been considerable in Europe and expanding for cases in the United States. Case studies constitute the type of literature most easily documented during this part of the science's development and comprise the most fascinating and glamorous aspect of medicocriminal entomology. Nuorteva published a series of case studies from Finland (Nuorteva et al. 1967, 1974; Nuorteva 1974, 1987). In Smith (1986), 19 case studies from Europe are discussed in detail. Case studies relating to the United States include one case from California (Webb et al. 1983), three cases from Illinois (Greenberg 1985), three cases from Hawaii (Goff and Odom 1987), two dealing with cases from aquatic environments in Indiana (Hawley et al. 1989), 26 from across the U.S. by Lord (1990), and four additional new cases from the Midwest (Hall and Haskell 1995).

The literature on forensic entomology has been complemented by three recent bibliographies (Catts and Goff 1992; Meek et al. 1983; Vincent et al. 1985). Procedures and information concerning entomological protocol for death scene investigations were published by Lord and Burger (1983) and Leclercq and Brahy (1985). An overview of the applications of entomology in criminal investigations is found in a publication by Keh (1985). The first textbook dealing exclusively with forensic entomology, *A Manual of Forensic Entomology*, by K.G.V. Smith (1986), contains many literature citations, summarizes most of the case histories and research conducted in the field, and gives detailed information on insect groups and species identifications. The first field manual, *Entomology and Death: A Procedural Guide* (Catts and Haskell 1990), for death scene investigators, medical examiners, and the forensic science community on processing death scenes for entomological evidence has been used internationally in death investigations. Guidelines for the legal and medical community concerning applications, techniques, responsibilities, and qualifications of the forensic entomology expert were provided in a book chapter by Hall and Haskell (1995).

## Contributions of Entomology to the Death Scene Investigation

Evaluation and interpretation of entomological evidence at a crime scene can address many confounding and complicated issues, including: time of death, season of death, geographic location of death, movement or storage of the remains following death, specific sites of trauma on the body, sexual molestation, and use of drugs. These findings can then inform several stages of the criminal justice process: the initial scene investigation, the subsequent follow-up investigative process when evaluating suspects and witnesses, and the criminal trial. It is during two of the above-mentioned periods when the entomologist can provide the greatest benefit to the case: first, during the initial scene investigation and processing, and later, during the trial.

### Time Since Death

When remains have gone undiscovered for days, weeks, or even months, it is the natural biological fauna and flora that can provide more accurate estimates of intervals between when the remains were discovered and when the person died. The most prominent group of organisms to aid in this estimate are from the Arthropod group. Insects, and more specifically Diptera (flies), will generally be on the scene within a matter of minutes (with adequate temperatures for activity present), eagerly awaiting the chance to colonize the decedent. The ability of flies from the family Calliphoridae (blowflies) to detect and oviposit (lay eggs) on a corpse shortly after death is a major reason underlying the utility of such evidence (Hall and Haskell 1995).

## Season of Death

Bodies that have been dead a long time (months or years) may still be amenable to entomological analysis, inasmuch as the puparia (pupa cases) left by developing flies do not deteriorate rapidly. As in the case where the death of ancient corpses was dated seasonally (Gilbert and Bass 1967), the presence of empty fly puparia and the species collected can be valuable in making such determinations. Several forensic case studies have been concluded using the empty fly puparia that remained behind months or years after the individual died and the living, newly emerged adult flies flew off to propagate another generation. Additionally, the hardened exoskeletons (outside shell) of many beetles persist in arid soils for decades and are present in association with burials (Haskell, unpublished data). These parts can be extremely small (1 to 2 mm) and when broken into the elementary segments (elytra, legs, head, thorax, sternites), may not resemble insects at all to the untrained examiner.

## Geographic Origin of Remains

Entomologists studying blowfly biology have through the years been impressed by the predictable presence of certain species in either urban or rural habitats. Despite the fact that some common species are relatively ubiquitous, the presence of others on a corpse suggests that oviposition occurred in a relatively definable environment. Taking such evidence into account may permit inferences that the body was moved after death; for example, that the decedent was killed downtown (where oviposition by an urban-type species occurred) and subsequently transported to a rural site for disposal. In an analogous manner, although most species of North American sarcosaprophagous flies evidence a fairly broad geographic distribution, some are confined regionally or temporally by certain biological limitations, principally their ability to survive inimical temperatures. The effect of this is that some species range only through certain areas, and their presence on a body found outside such a region is evidence of postmortem transportation (Hall and Haskell 1995).

## Movement or Storage of Remains Following Death

Multiple movements of remains can be identified in some cases by successive and intermittent broods of flies or other groups being found on the body. If, for instance, a person was murdered (with insect colonization occurring initially) and 3 days later buried, the determination of the surface exposure interval would be possible due to the age of maggots when the remains were recovered from the grave. There would be a successive number of life stages, all of differing ages and sizes, and containing few or none of the insect fauna known to arrive later as decomposition progresses.

As with the burial example, interrupted stages, breaks in the normal succession, or exclusion of commonly known colonizers should trigger a response by the forensic entomologist that something out of the normal chain of entomological events is occurring. A sequence of bodies being left for colonization, then placed in some environment where physical barriers to colonization have excluded certain groups of insects, and later, being located in an environment where colonization can resume, can be potentially identified by the knowledgable and experienced forensic entomologist.

## Evidence of Trauma

For adult human corpses, the only access into the underlying soft tissues of the body is through the nine natural body orifices. Of first preference are those opening on the face: the nose, mouth, and eyes. The nose and mouth, the two sites from which odors emanate that attract carrion flies, are the first on the body where colonization occurs. The eyes will be used, in many instances, due to the high moisture presence and the protection afforded by the deepened eye corners and small spaces around and under the lids. Later, the hair, folds in clothing, and the body/ground interface will serve as major sites of egg deposition once high numbers of flies find the remains. All of this can occur within a few hours of death if environmental conditions are favorable.

On nude human remains, the vaginal or anal openings and penis (the pelvic area in general) will attract a sizable number of flies with moderate colonization with eggs and larvae. In research observations with many dead pigs and human remains (Haskell, unpublished data) it has been observed that there appears to be a delay in colonization of this area by the flies. These sites will eventually generate significant numbers of larvae, but they will be of a younger age than when compared to those of the colony of the head or face. There can be as much as 12 to 36 hours of difference in their ages. In certain case studies, however, it was found that specimens collected from specific independent sites of the face and vagina were of the same age; or the vaginal colony was actually older; or the vaginal site was the sole colony (but massive) on the remains, even when the face was exposed (Haskell, unpublished data; Introna et al. 1990; Lord, personal communication). The above-mentioned cases involving dead females were cases where it was known or suspected that each had been sexually molested, and they tend to show earlier and greater fly colonization in the vaginal area. Coroner's officials in Canada have accepted this vaginal colonization occurrence as evidence of trauma for several years (Blenkinsop, personal communication).

Other inferences of trauma can be supported by locations where insect colonization is found. When a mass of maggots is found on the face or on the abdominal wall, there is most likely some opening in the surface of the abdomen that attracted the female flies, probably a break in the skin. Most often these colonies are the result of gunshot wounds, stabbing, or blunt force trauma that tears open the skin and exposes underlying soft tissue. The palms of the hands are another site infrequently affected by initial blowfly infestation; a corpse with maggots feeding on the palms might suggest a knife attack, wherein the decedent attempted with his hands to fend off an assailant. Subsequent examination of the bones will often reveal additional evidence of such attack (Hall and Haskell 1995).

## Presence of Drugs

In some cases it has been possible to establish the presence of drug residues from a corpse by analysis of its entomological life stages, even though the human tissue itself was too badly decomposed for work-up. Drug residue is ingested by the fly larvae and is then deposited into fat bodies and the exoskeletal material of the insect known as chitin. These ingested drugs are "locked" into the chitin and remain in the specimen for an extended period of time. In a recent case study, it was found that cocaine remained in empty puparia (the pupal stage of flies) 4 years after the feeding maggots had crawled off the drug-overdosed victim, completed their development to adult flies and flown off (Lord, personal communication). A number of compounds have been isolated from the exoskeleton of fly larvae (Beyer et al. 1980; Gunatilake and Goff 1988; Introna et al. 1990; Kintz et al. 1990).

## Other Types of Entomological Determinations

The predilection of fly species for ovipositing in direct sunlight, shade, or during hours of darkness have figured in various medicocriminal cases. A widely held view is that *P. sericata* is active only during daylight and will oviposit only on corpses in direct sunlight (Cragg 1956; Hall 1948). As with most animal species, there are few absolutes in blowfly behavior: a study on the south side of Chicago found that *P. sericata* oviposited in small numbers on rat carcasses exposed nocturnally near sodium vapor lamps where the light intensity varied from 0.2 to 0.5 lux (Greenberg 1990). A 2-year study in rural northwestern Indiana failed to detect nocturnal oviposition (Haskell, unpublished data). Most references relating to these habits of

*P. sericata* have originated from studies and observations in northern Europe. In 1993, this author trapped blowflies in Hamburg, Germany during the summer. When it was overcast, only bluebottle flies were attracted to the bait. However, when the clouds parted and direct sunlight shown upon the bait, greenbottle flies were collected. Similar studies in the United States did not show this specificity for these blue and green bottlefly species. These observations may be true for northern Europe, but these species may exhibit different behavior in North America or elsewhere. The behavior of such species is likely best understood in terms of probabilities, with concomitantly greater likelihood that oviposition will be restricted to daylight hours and will be greater under higher intensities of illumination (Hall and Haskell 1995).

Although the foregoing constitutes the typical manner in which entomological evidence figures into medicocriminal cases, other examples of insects' utility to jurisprudence can be documented. In one murder case, unusual "hairs" were found in a blood spot on a bank note in the possession of a suspect. These were identified as beetle or bee setae, and a search turned up the fragments of a bumblebee in the desk where the decedent kept his money (Howden 1964). In another well-known case, the feeding lesions of a chigger were used to link a suspect to a victim (Hall and Haskell 1995; Webb et al. 1983).

# The Insects Most Commonly Encountered at Death Scenes

A number of insect groups commonly colonize decomposing remains. This insect colonization persists throughout the progression of decomposition from within the first few minutes after death until the bones are approaching the bleached white stage. Insects from the orders Diptera (flies) and Coleoptera (beetles) are by far the most frequent in numbers of species and individuals. In certain areas of the country and within particular habitats, Hymenoptera (bees, wasps, ants), Dictyoptera (cockroaches, crickets, grasshoppers), and Arthropoda of the class Acari (mites) may be found in high numbers during specific periods of decomposition.

## The Common Fly Species

Of the approximately 17,000 species from 107 families of Diptera (flies) in North America north of Mexico (Borror et al. 1976), there are approximately 18 families of flies representing more than a hundred species associated with decomposing carrion. At present, the most utilized family of flies is the family Calliphoridae (blowflies). The blowflies are the bright metallic blue and green "bottle" flies recognized by almost everyone as the flies seen flying around garbage cans in the summer or swarming around dead animals at the side of the road. The species found in North America are most conveniently divided into four major groups or tribes represented by: the "bluebottle" flies which tend to be large, robust species adapted to cooler climates and found during spring and fall in temperate areas; the "greenbottles" which are smaller, agile flies encountered during midsummer; the "screwworm flies" which are tropical in distribution, found in the lower latitudes of the United States, and needing higher overall temperatures for their development; the "black blowflies" which are dark blue to olive green in color, smaller than the bluebottles and found when moderate temperature persists (Hall and Haskell 1995).

Greenbottle flies, comprising the tribe Luciliini, figure prominently in U.S. forensic entomology cases. *Lucilia* species, typified by *L. illustris* (Meigen) in North America, are often described as "woodland and meadow" flies, and are often collected in rural environments (Hall 1948). The opposite is true of *Phaenicia* ( = *Lucilia*) *cuprina* (Weidemann), a species that in the United States is strongly associated with urban areas. *Phaenicia sericata* (Meigen) figures prominently in U.S. cases and has been collected in various habitats. While found occasionally on remains from rural areas (in combination with *L. illustris*, *P. regina*, *C.*

*macellaria*, or others), it is strongly associated, however, with cases of urban origin. A species of greenbottle fly which is found to dominate carrion studies from nonurban environments in the midwestern states is *Phaenicia coeruleiviridis* (Macquart). In most case studies and research, these species of calliphorids are found to be seasonally distributed during the warmer months (e.g., April through October in the midstates region). Other species of *Phaenicia*, especially *P. cluvia* (Walker), *P. eximia* (Weidemann), and *P. mexicana* (Macquart) are confined to southern regions in North America (Hall and Haskell 1995).

The Tribe Phormiini contains the most commonly encountered blowfly in U.S. forensic entomology cases, that being the species *Phormia regina* (Meigen). This widespread species is extremely flexible in its geographic distribution, occurring during most times of the year when temperatures are above 16°C. Diurnal studies (Hall and Doisy 1993; Haskell 1989, 1993, and unpublished data) have shown that *P. regina* shows a tendency to delay 12 to 24 hours before coming to carrion under temperature regimes between 16° and 29°C and less of a delay with temperatures over 32°C. This species is found to occur in more rural habitats but may be found in combination with flies of urban distribution during certain times of the year. Its northern counterpart is *Protophormia* (= *Phormia*) *terraenovae* (Robineau-Desvoidy). *Protophormia terraenovae* is quite common in cases from Alaska and the Pacific Northwest during cooler times of the year, and found to occur at higher elevations in the Rocky Mountains and across Canada.

Species of Calliphorini, the tribe containing the bluebottle flies, are found commonly in northern latitudes of the United States and appear farther south during the spring and fall season; therefore, they exhibit a "bimodal" population distribution in most of the United States. The "blues" are commonly found on remains during the early to midspringtime in the midwest. They then drop out of the species assemblage during the warmer months of the year, but return to dominate the carrion species assemblage by mid- to late autumn. The species in this group are very large in size as both adults and larvae, producing what some death scene investigators have termed "king maggots," due to their length, approaching almost an inch (22 mm). Common species in the genus *Calliphora* include *C. livida* (Hall), *C. vicina* (Robineau-Desvoidy), and *C. vomitoria* (L.). *Cynomyopsis* ( = *Cynomya*) *cadaverina* (Robineau-Desvoidy) is very widespread, although *Cynomya mortuorum* (L.) and *Cyanus elongatus* (Hough) are apparently restricted to the Arctic and sub-Arctic (Hall and Haskell 1995).

Within the tribe Chrysomyini (screwworms), the secondary screwworm, *Cochliomyia macellaria* (F.), is strongly attracted to carrion and is confined temporally to midsummer activity throughout most of the central and northern parts of the country. Hall and Doisy (1993) demonstrated that there appears to be a delay of 18 to 48 h in this species' appearance at carrion, thus confirming Haskell's observations of this species in carrion studies in Indiana during 1990 and 1991.

This species' delay is somewhat longer than that shown for *P. regina* as mentioned above. *Cochliomyia macellaria* favors warmer temperatures and suffers high mortality when temperatures approach freezing. It will not survive the winters in the northern regions of the United States and, depending on the severity of the winter, is killed back to southern latitudes in varying degrees. Once spring arrives, it will progress north again through migration and successive generations. As an example, *C. macellaria* will not normally be found in the Chicago area before mid- to late June. In past years it has been the dominant calliphorid species in Florida, the Gulf States, south Texas, and across New Mexico, Arizona, and southern California.

Within the past 10 years, two new species of flies from the Chrysomyini group have been identified from the southern states. As mentioned above, four species of Old World blowflies have been recently confirmed from South or North America (Baumgartner and Greenberg 1984; Gagne 1981; Greenberg 1988). Two of these species are becoming established as the dominant species in the regions where *C. macellaria* was established. *Chrysomya rufifacies* (Macquart) and *C. megacephala* (F.) have been recovered as specimens in ever-increasing numbers, with *C. macellaria* declining in its presence on corpses. This has been observed from a number of cases and specific research studies in Florida and Texas. This has prompted an interest in research regarding the growth, development, and behavior of these new species (Byrd 1994; Wells and Greenberg 1992, 1994b).

As is evident from the previous discussion, there are specific areas of the country where insect species are found to be distributed. It is through this geographic distribution of the insects that evidence is possible to support theories of body transfer and movement of remains. When dealing with certain species (some of the aquatic species), it is possible to identify a location of origin for a set of remains to within only a few miles.

## The Dipteran Life Cycle and Its Development

At present, establishing the PMI (postmortem interval) is the primary reason for evaluating entomological evidence from a death scene. This time of death estimate is accomplished using two entomological methodologies: a specific species' known development and insect successional evaluations.

The first, and most precise, is to use a known insect species life cycle (specifically the blowflies) where developmental rates have been previously established under differing temperature regimes in laboratory and field studies. Precision by using this method is extremely good when temperatures at the scene are known and accurate species identification can be obtained. There is the potential to be within 12 hours or less of the actual time of death when remains have been out in excess of 15 to 20 days. Key to these estimates are knowledge and understanding of the behavior of the species involved and the ability of the species to find carrion, then deposit their eggs or larvae (Hall and Haskell 1995).

Figure 1 depicts a generalized blowfly life cycle. While the sizes vary from species to species, this generalized life cycle will conform to Diptera species from most families within the "higher flies" group, Cyclorrhapha. Adult fly females generally lay eggs in close proximity to, or on, the food source. There must be adequate moisture available and deposition sites most often are protected from direct solar radiation. Inside the nasal passages, inside the mouth (not deeply into the mouth, however) or corners thereof, in folds of clothing close to the face or wound, in the hair along the ground line or on the ground line where shelter and seclusion is created by the body's contours, are all locations where eggs can be deposited.

Within a few hours, dependent on species (see Table 1 for variability of development among species developing at approximately identical temperatures) and ambient temperature, the eggs will hatch, giving rise to the 1st of three stages (instars) of larvae. This stage is often the hardest to see when conducting a search for entomological evidence, much less evident than the eggs themselves. In mass, because they are usually less than 2 mm in length with a darkened hue, they will appear as a darkening or "dirty" discoloration in the nose or mouth corners, feeding on the moist areas of the mucosa in the nose, mouth, or eyes. Upon close study, they can be seen to be moving ever so slightly.

The second instar larvae are derived from molting (shedding of the old exoskeleton) of the 1st instars. This stage is usually the shortest duration of any of the life stages for the blowflies, lasting sometimes no more than 8 to 12 hours at moderate temperatures. During this stage, the larvae will begin to feed more heavily, partially due to the fact that they are larger than first instars (up to 4 to 6 mm for late second instar). Chemical composition of the soft tissues are changing by this time (acid to alkaline), also facilitating increased digestion of connective tissues and muscle (Hobson 1932).

Once the second instars molt, third instar larvae continue to feed but increase their voracity to a point where, in the huge "maggot mass," it is possible to observe soft tissues disappearing from the bodies. The larvae will consume tremendous amounts of tissue in a very short time, with their growth equaling the decline in tissue. This is an example of the ultimate in biomass conversion. During this heavy feeding, the maggots are laying down stored fat bodies of energy units to facilitate the period when they experience metamorphosis. Once

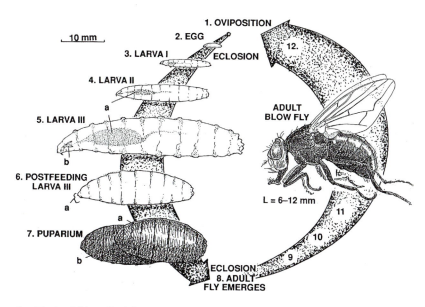

**Figure 1**   Typical blowfly life cycle. (1) Oviposition: eggs white to yellow. (2) Eclosion: maggot emerges. (3) Larva I: length about 10 mm. (4) Larva II: length 20 mm, (a) food in crop (internal). (5) Larva II: length 45 mm, (a) blood in crop (internal); (b) internal skeleton for feeding. (6) Postfeeding larva III: (a) internal features obscured. (7) Puparium: changes color with age from off-white to red, brown and black; (a) early stage; (b) late stage. (8) Eclosion: adult fly emerges. (9) After hardening for a few hours, adult male and female flies seek mates (they may meet at carrion). (10) Following copulation, female completes egg development (she may need a protein meal prior to oviposition). (11) Female lays egg mass (oviposits) on carrion/corpse at moist sites. (12) Female may lay several egg masses in her adult life (1 to 3 weeks).

**Table 1   Common Calliphorid Species' Total Developmental Times under Constant Rearing Temperatures**

| Common Blowfly Species | Total Days to Complete |
| --- | :---: |
| Tropical species[a] | |
| *Chrysomyia megacephala* | 9 |
| *Chrysomyia rufifacies* | 10 |
| Summer species[b] | |
| *Phormia regina* | 13 |
| *Phaenicia* | 14 |
| Cool weather species[b] | |
| *Cynomyopsis cadaverina* | 18 |
| *Calliphora vicina* | 21 |
| *Calliphora vomitoria* | 35 |

[a]  Rearings at 28°C; M.L. Goff, personal communication.
[b]  Rearings at 26.5°C; Kamal 1958.

adequate amounts of fat bodies are accumulated, the larvae cease feeding and migrate off and away from the food source.

It is during this third instar period that the phenomenon known as "maggot mass heating" is prevalent. Recorded temperatures from the "maggot mass" have been measured to exceed 25°C above the surrounding air temperature (Catts and Haskell 1990; Greenberg 1991; Haskell

1993). What the larvae have done is to create their own constant temperature environment, where little influence then prevails with lower ambient temperatures. During case studies where bodies have been in coolers (3°C) for periods of from 30 to 48 hours, measured maggot mass temperatures have been in the range of from 27 to 35°C. The impact of this is that the cooler does not retard or stop the feeding activity. If remains are held over for a weekend, by Monday morning, the maggots may have eaten away much of the physical evidence on the body. It is our recommendation that bodies exhibiting large maggot masses be autopsied as soon as possible.

The period where migration occurs is known as the postfeeding larvae, prepupae, wandering, or migration (all synonymous) stage. As the larvae move away from the body, they are attempting to find a location of seclusion where they will be protected from predators or the elements while making the radical physical change of their body from a headless, legless organism to the very mobile sexually reproductive winged adult. Generally the larvae will burrow down into soft soil or crawl into leaf litter. It is in these media where great scrutiny must be employed to ensure that this stage is not missed. In enclosed structures, they will move to outer edges of the room and attempt to crawl under the carpet or any other substrate that is lying on the floor. The investigator must also remember to search in the deep pile of carpeting or the nap of blankets. Larvae have been known to migrate up to 150 feet from the food source. In one study with humans in Tennessee, migrating larvae were observed crawling up surrounding trees shortly after a drenching downpour of rain (Haskell 1993).

As the larvae near the end of the migration stage, their body form begins to shorten and their breadth increases. Generally, their mobility is reduced, eventually ending in little or no noticeable movement and attaining an oval, blunt-ended football shape. At this point, they still appear whitish in color but have finally reached the beginning of the pupal stage.

It is the exoskeleton of the third stage larva that forms the outer hardened casing known as the puparium (puparia is the plural) of the pupal stage. It is within this structure that the pupa is formed. This is the stage, similar to the chrysalis of butterflies or the cocoon of the moth, where the metamorphosis of the species occurs. As time passes, the puparium hardens and changes color in quite a dramatic fashion, beginning with the white color of the prepupa darkening through reddish to maroon, to dark brown, and eventually to almost black. This color assessment is one of the techniques used to age puparia. For most species found indigenous to northern latitudes, the pupal stage is used for overwintering. There are some individuals, however, that will overwinter as males or sexually mature, gravid (full of viable eggs) females.

Several days will pass until the adult fly finally emerges. The transformed adult inside of the puparium inflates a structure in the area of what we would call the forehead, thus expanding within the puparium, forcing the anterior end of the puparium to fracture and break open. The newly formed adult then pushes out between the fractured segments and pulls itself free from the remaining puparium. Its thin legs, underdeveloped wings and abdomen, and its fast crawling movement are deceptive to the causal observer. Individual newly hatched flies such as these have been mistaken for spiders at death scenes and not collected, thus missing opportunities to attain greater precision on the time of death. It will be a few minutes to an hour before the fly pumps blood into its wings and other body structures. At this point the flies will appear colorless, with an opaque or frosted appearing exoskeleton. It will require several minutes to a few hours, dependent on temperature, for the adults to attain their brilliant metallic blue or green color. In another 3 to 5 days (again dependent on temperature), after taking both carbohydrate and protein meals, the adults will be sexually mature and ready for mating.

Puparium and the eclosed (empty) puparium are often overlooked or misidentified at the death scene (Figures 2 and 3). On several occasions this author has been asked by attending death scene investigators, "Why are there so many rat droppings around the body?" Figure 4

**Figure 2** Multiple puperia.

**Figure 3** Magnified eclosed and uneclosed puperia.

shows a comparison of rat droppings and bluebottle fly puparia, which are quite large. Species of flies that are smaller may have their puparia mistaken for mouse droppings. The unhatched or hatched puparia can be of great importance when establishing the PMI. They may be present in literal handfuls or it may take diligent searching to find their presence, depending on season of year and accessibility of the corpse to flies. This search is critical in cases of extended PMI, where several months to several years have passed. Species identification may be possible, but not guaranteed, by using the empty puparia (due to this being the 3rd larval exoskeleton), and season of the year or even the month when death occurred may be estimated (Gilbert and Bass 1967; Haskell 1989).

Unhatched puparia taken back to the forensic entomological laboratory from the scene may hold yet another possibility for increasing the precision of estimating extended PMI periods due to their being parasitized. There are also a number of parasitic wasps that will parasitize fly puparia. Wasps that parasitize blowfly or other fly puparia are generally known. Life cycles are also generally known for many of these species. Therefore, when emergence of the tiny parasites is noted, additional time can be calculated into the development of the blowfly, and an overall time interval can be estimated.

## Other Fly Groups at the Death Scene

The group Diptera contains additional species not previously mentioned. In addition to the calliphorids arriving first at the scene, often large flies with gray/black checkered abdomens

**Figure 4**  Comparison of rat droppings (left) and blowfly puperia (right).

having a red tip at the posterior end and stripes on their thorax will also be seen. These are from the family Sarcophagidae (flesh flies). This particular group, unlike most of the other Diptera, larvaposits, that is, they deposit 1st instar living larvae on the corpse instead of the traditional egg. This enhances the chances of acquiring a food source prior to other competitors. Species in this group are strong fliers.

Many "gnat" like flies will be observed in corpses of older PMI. These can be from several families, such as Phoridae (the humpbacked fly), within which is found a species which has keyed its life cycle to actually entering buried coffins. *Conicera tibialis* (Schmitz) (the coffin fly) is thought to either lay eggs on the soil surface with the succeeding hatched larvae moving down to depths as much as 4 ft and entering into a coffin, or the adult females actually conducting the migration through the soil. Multiple generations have been observed in exhumed remains. Sepsidae (black scavenger flies), Sphaeroceridae (small dung flies), Ephydridae (shore flies), Drosophilidae (fruit flies), Milichiidae (milchid flies), Heleomyzidae (heleaomyzid flies), and Piophilidae (skipper flies) would be included among the most common. In the family Piophilidae is found a larvae very common in advanced decomposing bodies. These are the small maggots that, when disturbed, jump all over the place. *Piophila casei* (L.) (the cheese-skipper) coils itself into a circle, then flings itself as far as 20 in. This is a protective measure enabling it to escape predators. This species is found when caseic fermentation is occurring (Smith 1986).

Larger flies found with the body and their associated larvae include Stratiomyidae (the soldier flies), of which one species *Hermetia illucens* (L.) (the black soldier fly) is found with advanced decomposing remains. Lord et al. (1994) cited several cases from the United States where this species was used to assist in determining the PMI. Larvae of *H. illucens* are quite large and dark brown to gray in color. They have been found to occur as far north as southern Illinois and Indiana, but are common across the south, usually associated with chicken manure pits. The adults look like wasps in flight and at rest and exhibit similar flight orientation, as do the Hymenoptera (bees, wasps, and ants).

Muscidae (muscid flies) include the housefly, *Musca domestica* (L.), which may be found on advanced PMI bodies, but generally, this species is found on food sources related to fecal material or urine. *Musca domestica* has been used in cases for proving abuse and child neglect. Within the muscid family is found a common fly, somewhat smaller than the housefly and shiny black in color. This is the dump fly, *Ophyra leucostoma* (Wiedemann). This fly is usually found where older tissues are present, but in a recent study in Florida (Haskell, unpublished data), adults of the species comprised a large proportion of the early adult fauna (arriving within the first 2 to 3 days). The species *Mucina stabalans* (Fallen) is reported to be one of the few species that can access buried remains. This behavior was observed on a case from northwest Indiana in 1993 (Haskell, unpublished data).

**Figure 5** Silphid beetle. (Photograph courtesy of K. Perkins.)

## Beetles at the Death Scene

The order Coleoptera (over 300,000 species worldwide) provides nearly as many species and families that appear on carrion as do the Diptera. However, the role of the beetles is somewhat different from that of the flies. The flies are primarily feeders on the carrion, while the beetles are primarily predacious on the eggs and larvae of the flies. However, there are some beetle groups such as the silphids (carrion beetles), dermestids (hide beetles), nitidulids (sap beetles), and individual species of clerids (checker beetles) which feed directly upon the decomposing carrion.

Early in the decomposition process, beetle species from the families Staphylinidae (rove beetles), Silphidae (carrion beetles) (Figure 5), Histeridae (hister beetles), and Hydrophilidae (hydrophilid beetles) will be found on the corpse within 1 to 2 days following death under warm temperature regimes. Most species in these families are predacious on fly eggs and larvae. If populations of these beetles are high, they may play a part in reducing the fly population on the carcasses.

It is possible to utilize some of the beetle species' life cycles to extend PMI estimates once the flies have completed their life cycles and departed the corpse. Their life cycle is a complete metamorphosis life cycle similar to the flies but may include additional stages of larvae. In the dermestids, for instance, if the individuals are stressed due to food shortage, they can limit their number of instars from 5 to 7, while under normal conditions they may require as many as 9 instars for completion to pupa. Therefore, estimates of the PMI would become less precise as compared to the flies, necessitating a wider PMI "window" for the estimate. Even with the widening of the time estimate, increased accuracy of the time of death is provided when compared to any other method of PMI estimation.

The beetles appear at the corpse somewhat later than do the flies. In addition, many of the beetle species have longer life cycles than the flies. While there is less known regarding precise timing of development of most beetles, general estimates of a beetle species' life cycle may aid in adding additional days to known estimates from the flies giving an overall greater precision to an estimate for a corpse.

The beetles constitute some of the last insect species to colonize the bits of remaining dried soft and cartilaginous tissues on the bones. The ptinids (spider beetles), some species of dermestids (hide beetles), trogids (skin beetles), tenebrionids (darkling beetles), and the red-legged ham beetle (*Necrobia rufipes* [DeGeer]), a clerid beetle, are generally found when the remains are nearing complete skeletonization. Larvae or adults of the darkling beetles, spider beetles, red-legged ham beetle and others will be found immediately under the bones in soil or carpeting or within the clothing associated with the skeletal remains. In addition, adults and larvae of the red-legged ham beetles and larvae of the cheese skipper (Diptera) may be found in the marrow cavity of long bones when fracturing has occurred. Always examine these cavities (including sinus or cranial cavities) for the presence of dried larval cast skins, pupa, or even dead adults. Once all soft tissue is removed and only bones remain, if the remains are on soil and depending on temperate and season, the soil insect fauna will return to normal within approximately 2 years after death in the temperate regions of North America. This does not preclude the possibilities of carrion insect residues (e.g., eclosed puparia, cast skins, peritrophic membrane, or dead adults) remaining for many years after the death of the human.

This is especially helpful when dealing with extended PMI and the beetle groups which will be found to colonize at that time. It may be possible to utilize development of the clerid, dermestid, and tenebrionid immatures to assist in estimating the PMI in this way. However, additional research that deals specifically with beetle growth and development on carrion is needed. It is unfortunate that more information is not readily available for immature stages of the common species of carrion-frequenting beetles.

## Other Arthropods Found at the Death Scene

Other orders of insects known to frequent decomposing carrion include the Hymenoptera (bees, wasps, ants), Lepidoptera (butterflies and moths), Hemiptera (true bugs), Dictyoptera (cockroaches), and Acari (mites) of the class Arachnida (spiders, ticks and mites). Of these groups, species in Hymenoptera are the most common. Wasps (hornets and yellow jackets) and ants (of great importance is the fire ant) are major predators of fly eggs and larvae, while bees feed periodically on fluids. Hornets have been observed capturing adult flies while on the wing, flying to adjacent vegetation, stinging the captured fly until motionless, and returning to the nest to provide food for young hornet larvae. Wells and Greenberg (1994a) observed fire ants so numerous on animal carcasses in Texas that it took 2 to 3 days for the flies to actually lay enough eggs for hatching to out-pace the ants' removal of the eggs.

The cockroaches (order Dictyoptera) are commonly found to cause superficial feeding artifacts on the surface of the skin of the corpse. They also may be responsible for chewing off the eyebrows and eyelashes. Generally, these artifacts are found in conjunction with bodies in dwellings where potentially large numbers of the insects live. There are occasions where cockroach feeding is seen in bodies outdoors, but in most cases those lesions are caused by ants feeding on the remains instead of cockroaches.

Butterflies and moths have been observed to feed off of seepage from the carcasses, while bugs have been seen probing into the carrion, feeding in the underlying tissues. With the exception of clothes moths (family Tineidae), found in cases where there are extended PMIs involved, neither of these groups (Lepidoptera and Hemiptera) play a major roll in forensic entomology evaluations.

In the order Acari, certain mite species are found to be associated with decomposing human remains. The problem with mites is that they are so very small that, most often, they are overlooked as evidence because they are not readily seen. These arthropods appear when remains are in advanced decay and drying. They will aggregate in very large numbers and appear to be mold or piles of sawdust. The color of these piles will range from a dark brown to light tan or yellow. If one were to place a small sample of the material under a microscope or hand lens, immediate recognition of the mites is obvious. The whole mass is nothing but waving, moving legs and globular bodies. General estimates of their development, and hence additions to the PMI, are possible if species determination can be made.

# Using the Fly Life Cycle in PMI Estimations

It is well known that most of the blowflies used for the forensic entomology estimates arrive (if they can find access and environmental conditions are favorable) at a corpse very shortly after death. In recent field studies with pigs in Indiana, Florida, Illinois, and Tennessee (Haskell 1989, unpublished data), adult blowflies have been observed on carcasses within seconds of death. Egg deposition by these flies followed within 1 to 2 hours. In a few documented cases, infestation occurred prior to death with eggs or larvae being laid on living tissues; this type of infestation is called *myiasis* (James 1947; Hall and Haskell 1995).

The application of a fly species life cycle (see Figure 1) in establishing the PMI from a conceptual basis is as follows. Flies, in common with other invertebrates, are poikilothermic ("cold-blooded"); that is, their temperature is greatly influenced by the temperature of their macro- and microenvironment. Within the general bounds of acceptable temperature regimens (above which it is too hot, and below which it is too cold — with both extremes essentially inhibiting development), the growth patterns of most insects follow an S-shaped curve that is for all practicality linear in typically encountered temperature ranges. Thus, for a variety of chemical and physiological reasons (enzyme kinetics), development of insects (flies in particular) proceeds at a predictably more rapid rate as temperature increases. This rate of development has been measured numerous times at various temperatures for most fly species of forensic interest. Therefore, as mentioned previously, the approach is to identify the species collected from a corpse of unknown PMI, note the stage of development, retrospectively obtain weather records for the area in question, and calculate the amount of time that would have been required to "drive" that insect species from the egg (or first instar larva, as appropriate) to the stage collected.

The retrospective temperatures may be available on an hourly basis, or in the majority of cases as daily maximums and minimums, generally obtained from meteorological equipment located at the nearest airport. Most current estimates of fly development are made by calculation of accumulated degree-hours (ADH) or degree-days (ADD), a concept that has solid footing in both field biology and in engineering estimates of heating or cooling requirements of buildings. Degree-days can be calculated according to several formulae, the most common of which approximates a sine-wave fluctuation of temperature above and below an average; however, all methods produce similar results. Usually these data incorporate lower thresholds below which temperatures are noninfluential. After the forensic entomologist has calculated the degree-hours or degree-days available, this information can be applied to the template of known development of the species in question at a temperature regime similar to that recorded from the field. The result will give an estimate of the time required for that fly to progress from the stage produced by the female (and deposited on the corpse) to the stage collected. This, then, is the minimum PMI — all else being equal, the corpse must have been *in situ* for at least that period; otherwise, the developing flies would not have been able to get to the noted point of maturity. Such estimates can be bolstered if several different fly species can be collected from a single corpse and each analyzed independently (Hall and Haskell 1995). In some cases, the presence of empty puparia has been used to gauge the season of death (Gilbert and Bass 1967).

## Accessibility of the Corpse

Corpses are not always conveniently exposed to the open air. While some homicide victims are left where they drop and others are dumped carelessly, some are carefully concealed. At one extreme, what happens when a murderer dismembers his victim and puts the remains into plastic trash bags? If the job is well done, there will be little odor and certainly flies will be unable to access the dead tissue. A similar phenomenon results when a body is concealed within the well-fitted trunk of an automobile, or when it is within a closed building. Bodies outdoors during winter may freeze; this and the lack of adult flies combine to allow such bodies to age unaffected by flies until the spring thaw. There are many additional permutations. In these cases, availability of ancillary data will be mandatory if the entomologist is to fit the biological estimate within the context of the facts as they become known. Additional research is needed into possible effects of fire (such as gasoline fire) on subsequent colonization of bodies by insects. Likewise, few replicated entomological data are available on the insect fauna of buried bodies or of bodies submerged in water (Hall and Haskell 1995).

## Insect Postmortem Artifacts

Death investigators occasionally discover unknown substances and artifacts or unusual physical trauma sites from remains in varied states of decomposition. These materials and artifacts are thought to be substances other than what they truly are, such as: red carpet fibers (Hawley et al. 1989), sawdust (Haskell, unpublished data), mold and funguses (Haskell, unpublished data), rat droppings (Catts and Haskell 1990), seeds from plants, antemortem or postmortem injuries of abuse (Hawley, unpublished data), or gunshot wounds. In actuality, any of the above-mentioned artifacts and trauma sites can be the result of insect feeding activity, insect life stages, or products of an insect's behavior or biology.

### Artifacts of Maggots on the Body and at the Scene

Since most fly larvae cannot penetrate human adult skin, they must have access to underlying tissues through some opening. This access can be a small needle puncture, a cut, a deep abrasion, or extensive trauma such as a shotgun blast to the abdomen. However, once the skin has begun to soften due to putrefaction, fly larvae may have an opportunity to penetrate at localized areas creating a series of small holes to move into and out of the underlying food source. There was a case in which an aggregation of small holes located in the back of the victim was thought to be shotgun pellet entry wounds (similar to Figure 6). It did not occur to the examining physician (a pathologist who was not a forensic pathologist) that there was no corresponding lead shot in the underlying areas of the body. Later, these holes were identified as larval bore holes.

Sizable maggot masses on remains can devour tremendous amounts of soft tissue in an incredibly short period of time with high temperature and humidity. Maggots, when in this mass, are able to move relatively sizable objects considerable distances from the remains. This author has observed on numerous occasions the maggot mass moving bones from pig carcasses. The larvae will actually work under the bone needing removal, position it so that it will be on top of the mass, and then simply work it along the top of the mass until it is passed beyond their perimeter. In a study in Tennessee at the Anthropological Research Facility with human remains, dentures were seen being moved by the maggot mass in the manner described above and found to be an incredible 25 cm. This movement was solely due to the action of the maggot mass. If the potential for this phenomenon is not recognized, inaccurate conclusions may be drawn in cases of extended PMI after all the maggots are gone and the physical evidence is found out of place.

The life stage of maggot migration or postfeeding larvae is equally important for collecting the subsequent puparia. Study of this migration suggests that there may be solar influence on the direction of travel during different parts of the day. This migration most often occurs with the maggots leaving together in a long line, although in some circumstances the dispersion is in a 360° radius. Usually the later ones leaving will follow the earlier ones, with the migration comprising tens of thousands of individuals from some carcasses. The maggots

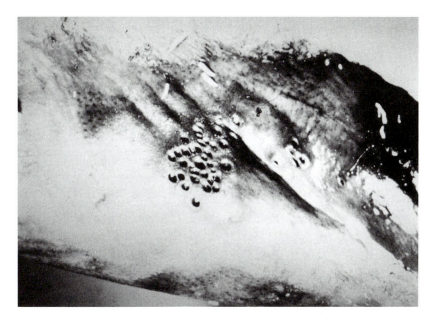

**Figure 6** Entry holes in skin made by maggots.

leave the wet, aqueous mixture of decompositional fluids, retaining some of this fluid on their bodies.

In a case study from southern Tennessee, a body was found between a cluster of evergreen trees in a suburban neighborhood. There was an obvious path worn over time where cars had periodically driven past the dump site. The location of the body was several yards up an incline from the car path. In addition, there were obvious parallel marks, appearing to be drag marks leading from the car path up to the body. Therefore, the police investigators reconstructing the crime formulated that the murderers drove their car into the area using the commonly known car path. They parked their car at the bottom of the incline and dragged the body up the hill where they placed it on the ground among the trees.

Several days later, when other investigators were canvassing the neighborhood for witnesses, they came across an elderly lady who lived immediately behind the clump of trees at a distance of about 50 yards. She had observed a car pull around on her side of the trees one evening several days prior. She had seen two occupants of the car remove something from the trunk and carry it over to the trees and disappear in the foliage. A few minutes later she saw them leave. This story completely mystified the investigators because there were obvious drag marks up the hill going directly to the body (Figure 7). Luckily, a noted forensic anthropologist from Tennessee with experience in entomological evidence recovery was called to view the scene. After studying the scene for only a few moments he walked down a few feet from the body along the drag marks, dug into the soil a few inches in the drag mark itself, and pulled out several blowfly puparia. The puzzle had been solved. These were not drag marks of the body being brought up the hill. They were migration trails (two roughly in parallel) of the maggots leaving the corpse. The neighbor lady had been accurate in her observations of the assailants bringing the body in for disposal (Lehran, personal communication).

## Prevalence of Beetle Peritrophic Membrane

A case from the Midwest in 1987 provided the forensic science team (a forensic pathologist, anthropologist, and entomologist) with a considerable challenge where a previously unknown (to the investigative forensic team) tough, stringy material was found in association with two mummified human remains located inside a home in an affluent neighborhood in the suburbs.

**Figure 7**    Pseudo "drag" marks. (Photograph courtesy of C. Lehren.)

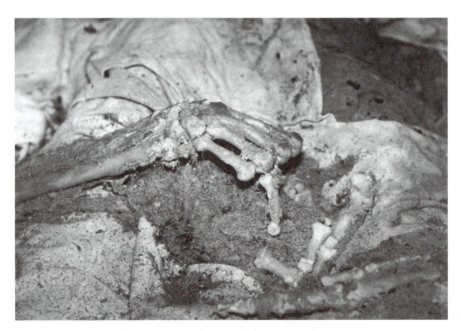

**Figure 8**    Dermestid beetle peritrophic membrane found in association with skeletal remains.

After a few hours of studying the material and consulting the entomological literature, the forensic entomologist was able to determine that the material was peritrophic membrane (Figure 8), a protective covering over fecal material as it passes through the gut of beetle (Coleoptera) larvae of the family Dermestidae; *Dermestes lardarius* (L.). The peritrophic membrane was associated with the soft tissues of two mummified bodies and was literally present by the cupful. This was the first documentation of this substance being found in the

**Table 2  Cases Involving the Presence of *Dermestes* sp. Larvae Peritrophic Membrane with Known PMI**

| Location | Year | PMI (in years) |
|---|---|---|
| Denmark[a] | 1962 | 1.5 |
| Indiana[a] | 1987 | 10.0 |
| Wisconsin[a] | 1990 | 2.0 |
| Minnesota[a] | 1990 | 6.0 |
| Minnesota[a] | 1991 | 0.3 |
| Indiana[a] | 1992 | 3.0 |
| Illinois[b] | 1993 | Unknown |
| Florida[c] | 1994 | 1.0 |

[a]  Haskell et al. 1993a.
[b]  Haskell unpublished data.
[c]  Haskell unpublished data.

U.S. (Lord 1990). Previously, this material had been discovered on a mummified body from a case in Denmark in 1962, where the corpse had been kept in a closet for more than a year and a half (Voigt 1965). In addition to the above-mentioned dermestid species, two other species were found: *Attagenus unicolor* (Brahm = *Attagenus piceus* Oliv.) and *Anthrenus museorum* (L.). These latter two species were collected after body recovery from the scene on the window ledges and sills behind closed blinds in the rooms where the remains were discovered. Most of the dermestids prefer and utilize dry natural materials for their food source such as: hair, feathers, skin, dried beef, natural fabrics, and others (Metcalf et al. 1962). These are the same critters that destroy mounted trophy heads hanging on the wall, or destroy nice butterfly collections. Several species of this family will normally be found associated with decomposed and mummified human remains.

Since the 1987 discovery in Indiana, forensic entomologists have been instructing investigators to be alert for this material in cases of mummification and extended PMI. The dissemination of the diagnostic characteristic of the peritrophic membrane has led to its recognition from several cases around the U.S.

An illustrative case involving beetle peritrophic membrane was investigated in Minnesota. On September 21, 1991 the body of a 55-year-old man was discovered in his pickup truck near a composting site in central Minnesota. The person had last been seen on May 29, 1991. His truck had apparently gone off the road; its front end was smashed, and there was a large hole in the windshield. It had gone undetected because it was wedged between two embankments and was hidden by brush and leaves until the leaves began to drop in late September. When discovered, the remains were dried, but most of the skin was intact and well preserved, except for a large laceration on the forehead. Numerous eclosed *P. regina* puparia were found with the remains, as well as puparia of *P. casei*. and the stable fly, *Stomoxys calcitrans* (L.) (Diptera: Muscidae). Many live mites were associated with the empty puparia. In some cases, large aggregations of mites have been mistaken for fine sawdust or mold. Live adult *Necrobia rufipes* (DeGeer) (Coleoptera: Cleridae) were collected from the remains, as well as the living larvae of both *Dermestes maculatus* DeGeer and *D. ater* DeGeer. This case represents the shortest PMI where peritrophic membrane has been found to date (see Table 2).

The presence of peritrophic membrane of beetles, and their cast skins suggests certain likely conditions through the course of the remains' decomposition. The PMI will be for an extended period (months to years). The remains will have been sheltered (e.g., in a house, car, truck, or other physical structure) in some fashion from the elements where degradation of the peritrophic membrane and delicate beetle larval cast skins is minimized. Drying and mummification of the soft tissues of the remains will have taken place without fly larvae dominating the soft tissue clearing. All of these points can be important when investigating a case.

## Other Insect Artifacts on Human Remains

Artifacts on bodies which resemble antemortem wounds can actually be postmortem artifacts created by multiple species of insects from at least three major groups (orders). These artifacts can be very confussing when they have had the opportunity to age, dry, and darken. These lesions can resemble human bite marks, scratches, burns, or other types of superficial lesions on the skin and mucous membranes of the nose, mouth, and genitals. Discriminating postmortem insect artifacts from ante- or perimortem trauma requires considerable experience on the part of the forensic entomologist or pathologist. Some generalized observations regarding size and orientation of the lesions and habitat where the remains were found may aid in this determination.

Ant feeding is generally found on remains located outdoors. The area of disrupted skin where feeding is located is small (but there may be many excavations on the skin), superficial, oriented in some type of linear fashion, and found where there is exposed, uncovered skin. This is contrasted with cockroach feeding excavating larger areas of skin tissue and in many cases being spread over a considerable portion of the body. While cockroach feeding is not limited to bodies in indoor environments, the preponderance of cockroach cases are found to occur inside.

In a case from the northwest on the lower slopes of the Cascade Mountains, a body of a female was found to have petechial hemorrhages arranged in clustered patterns on exposed portions of the thighs. The area where the body was found was in a wet low swampy type habitat which was heavily forested and contained thousands of mosquitoes. The decedent, clad in a swim suit, was placed under a log with brush covering most of the remains except for portions of the legs. The petechial hemorrhages on the thighs were inconsistent with circumstances surrounding the death, for which the forensic pathologist had no explanation. Once the participating forensic entomologist studied the body and the habitat, he concluded that these "hemorrhages" were actually multiple probing marks on the uncovered, exposed skin caused by the mosquito's mouth parts (proboscis) as the female mosquito was attempting to find blood pressure on the still warm but dead body. When probing into the skin with their proboscis, the mosquitoes were unable to bring up blood due to lack of blood pressure in the decedent. The female mosquitoes would then move to an adjacent site and probe again, thus repeating their probes many times creating the clusters of "petechial hemorrhages." The high number of mosquitoes at the scene was additional support for this conclusion. When the assailant was finally apprehended, he confessed to having placed the body there shortly after he had killed her (Catts, personal communication).

In an unusual case from Seattle, considerable confusion was created when blood spatters were trailing in the wrong direction from where the decedent was found. In addition, blood was found beneath the exposed page of a calendar hanging on the wall (Figure 9), but none on the exposed page. Later, after the removal of the remains, the investigator, working on additional evidence in the room, glanced up and observed a big, fat cockroach walking out from under an upper kitchen cabinet, cross the counter and walk through a large pool of blood on the counter. The insect then proceeded to cross a white piece of paper and leave blood "spatters" identical to what was found on the calendar. This chance observation answered the perplexing question of the blood spatters, which were really cockroach foot prints (Haglund, personal communication).

## Entomological Procedures

The procedures used for proper collection of entomological specimen evidence at a death scene are generally standard procedures employed by most trained entomologists making routine specimen collections anywhere in the world. Likewise, documenting recovery of physical evidence at a death scene by trained crime scene technicians is generally no different

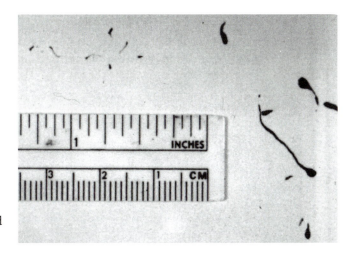

**Figure 9** Pseudo blood "spatter" on calendar.

from data recorded by entomologists when engaged in their normal specimen collecting. There are, however, specific techniques and methods which have been modified especially for use in a forensic context which will enhance the ultimate evaluation of the insect evidence. Therefore, through correct identification of the specimens, accurate assessment of the corresponding climatological data, and critical evaluation of behavior and biology of the properly identified specimens relative to the environmental factors driving these organisms, extremely accurate inferences can be achieved. Procedures used in entomological evaluations at death scenes have been described by Catts and Haskell (1990) and are summarized here.

## Visual Observations and Notations of the Scene

The observations and notes of the forensic entomologist may provide valuable information for the overall death scene investigation and important substantiating data for the entomological evidence evaluated from the scene. These include:

1. Entering basic case data, such as: case number, date, geographic location, investigators, their phone numbers and departments, etc.
2. Approximating the number and kinds of flying and crawling insects.
3. Noting locations of major insect infestations associated with the body or surrounding areas. These infestations may be eggs, larval, pupal, or adult stages alone or in any combination.
4. Noting immature stages of particular adult insects observed. These stages can include eggs, larvae, pupae, empty (eclosed) pupal cases, cast larval skins, fecal material, and exit holes or feeding marks on the remains.
5. Noting any insect predation such as beetles (e.g., silphids, staphylinids), ants and wasps (e.g., formicids, vespids), or insect parasites (e.g., ichneumonid and chalcid wasps).
6. Noting the exact position of the body, including the compass direction of the main axis, position of extremities, and position of the head and face; noting which body parts are in contact with substrate; noting where there would be sunlight and shade in the immediate area during a normal daylight cycle.
7. Noting insect activity within 10 to 20 feet (3 to 6 m) of the body. Observing flying, resting, or crawling insect adults and larvae or pupae within this proximity to the body.
8. Noting any unusual naturally occurring, manmade, or scavenger-caused phenomenon which could alter the environmental effects on the body (e.g., trauma or mutilation of the body, burning, covering or enclosing of the body, burial, movement, or dismemberment).

## Climatological and Temperature Data

Gaining a reasonable grasp of the temperature regimes to which the insects have been subjected during their growth and development can be accomplished by obtaining temperature readings from the scene. These include:

1. Ambient air temperature can be evaluated by taking readings at 1 ft and 4 ft (0.3 to 1.3 m) heights in close proximity to the body.
2. Ground surface temperatures can be obtained by placing the thermometer on the ground immediately above any surface ground cover.
3. Body surface temperatures should be obtained by placing the thermometer on the skin surface.
4. Under-body interface temperatures can be obtained by sliding the thermometer between the body and the ground surface.
5. Maggot mass temperatures can be obtained by inserting the thermometer into the center of the maggot mass.
6. Soil temperatures should be taken immediately following body removal at a ground point which was under the corpse mass. Also, take soil temperatures at a second point 3′ to 6′ (1 to 2 m) from where the body lay. These should be recorded from 3 levels: directly under any ground cover (grass, leaves, etc.); at a soil depth of 4 in. (10 cm); and at a soil depth of 8 in. (20 cm).

**Note:** The direct rays of the sun should not be allowed to shine on the thermometer sensing element. Radiant heat from the sun will cause readings far in excess of the true environmental temperatures.

Estimate the duration of exposure of the corpse to direct sunlight, broken sunlight, and shade for the total daylight hours. If there is any question as to this relationship, observation of the site periodically throughout a sunny day will provide additional information. With direct sunlight on the body, the external temperature and some internal temperatures of the body close to the surface will be higher than when the corpse is shaded. These higher temperatures will be recorded even if the thermometer bulb is shaded and will reflect accurate temperature readings for the body.

Weather data for the time period in question should be obtained by contacting the nearest National Weather Service (NWS) station or other climatological data gathering agency. These offices have records of data collection sites in each state and can indicate which station is in closest proximity to the death scene. Some NWS stations (including forest service fire towers and airport facilities) can give extensive weather data including hourly temperatures, humidity, extent of cloud cover, precipitation, and wind speed and direction. In addition, soil temperatures, water temperatures, river stages, tidal swings, soil moisture conditions, and evaporation rates may also be obtained from the first-order NWS stations. All data are eventually sent to NOAA, National Climatic Data Center, Asheville, NC, 28801-2696, and can be obtained in the form of published, recorded material for court documentation. Other stations will have only daily maximum, minimum temperatures and total precipitation, but these data may be all that are necessary.

It is of the greatest necessity to properly recognize, collect, preserve, label, and record pertinent data for entomological data to be accurately evaluated. Accurate entomological data are essential when entering this evidence into the court record at the time when the case is tried. There can be three or more opportunities for entomological evidence to be observed and collected in the course of a death investigation. If present, insect evidence will be found at the time the remains are discovered at the scene. Second, insect evidence will remain for a period of time (some stages may remain for months or even years at the scene) following the removal of remains. Third, the entomologist may be allowed to thoroughly search the body for insect evidence during autopsy.

## Acquisition and Preservation of Entomological Evidence at the Scene

If flying insects are present over the body, the aerial sweep net technique for collecting can be employed for collecting fast flying and fast crawling adult insects. Flying insects associated with carrion are strong, fast fliers; thus, netting of specimens requires some experience and practice. It is important to obtain permission to be the first to directly access the remains following a period of time when the corpse has gone undisturbed. This will ensure that fast flying insects previously chased away will most likely have returned to the corpse for feeding or ovipositing. The netting technique uses several rapid, back and forth sweeping motions of the net (6 to 10 sweeps) with reversal of the opening of the net 180° on each pass. On the last pass, the opened portion of the net is brought up to about chest level with rotation of the opening 180°. This causes the netting material to be folded over the top edge of the large net ring opening, thus trapping the insects in the net bag. The net then can be placed on the ground so that two hands can be used to trap and confine the specimens in the tailing end of the net. The end of the net, with insects inside, can then be placed into a wide-mouth killing jar, which is then capped. The killing jar should contain a few cottonballs soaked with fresh ethyl acetate. This will kill the insects after a few minutes (2 to 5 minutes is usually adequate). Following immobilization, the insects can be transferred into screw-cap vials of 75% ETOH by placing a small funnel into the vial and carefully dumping the contents of the net into the funnel. Some of the specimens may be placed into a dry vial for direct pinning. If stored in this dry condition, however, the insects must be processed in a few hours because excessive moisture on the insects (condensation arising from within the closed vial) can promote mold growth which will quickly damage or destroy the specimens. Aerial netting procedures should be repeated three to four times to ensure a representative sample of all of the flying insects present. Ground-crawling adults can be collected with forceps or fingers. Preservation should be conducted in the same manner as with the adult flying insects.

The aerial netting technique described above also can be used to sample insects from vegetation in the area surrounding the body. Many of the Diptera (flies) associated with carrion rest on nearby plants or grasses. By sweeping the vegetation within 10 to 20 feet (4 to 6 m) of the corpse, some of these adult insects may be collected.

It is extremely important that nothing be moved or taken from the corpse except insects which are on the surface and clearly visible. Do not disturb any portion of the clothing, the immediate area around the body, or the body itself. Collect only those stages of insects which can be seen readily on the body, and use extreme caution when using forceps or other tools for collecting. Postmortem artifacts inflicted inadvertently while collecting specimens may be misleading and can cause needless questions to be asked. A thorough examination of the clothing and body bag (some insects may crawl off the body during transportation) can be conducted at the time of the autopsy for insects not collected at the scene. The body bag, too, must be examined for previous insect infestations before the remains are placed inside. Some agencies require new body bags for each case to eliminate the question of residual evidence from previous cases, but others may not.

Eggs and a mixed size sample of larvae (several hundred) should be collected and preserved. The largest larvae observed should be collected and, if numbers permit, several dozen of these should be placed into vials containing solution. A second portion (2 to 3 dozen) of these large larvae should be placed alive into plastic specimen cups containing some damp paper toweling. This procedure should be repeated for some smaller larvae or eggs, placing a portion of the specimens into the preservative solution and saving a portion alive for rearing.

Areas where concentrated insect activity most likely will be encountered during the earlier stages of insect infestation are the nasal openings, ears, mouth, eyes, and traumatized areas of the body (cuts, gunshot wounds, and blunt force injuries where the skin is broken). Skin creases of the neck also may contain egg masses. Egg masses will also be found along the hair line close to the natural body openings. Wounds may have both egg masses and larvae associated with them, and exposed genital and anal areas may contain egg masses and larvae, especially if these areas were traumatized prior to or after death.

In cases where bodies are outdoors and heavily infested, many insect adults, larvae, and pupae as well as other arthropods will remain on the ground after the body is removed. The procedures described above should be followed for each of the different insect stages seen following removal of the body. A number of specimens of each immature stage should be collected and preserved, while a second sample should be collected alive for rearing.

Litter samples (e.g., leaves, grass, bark, humus) or any material on the ground surface close to or under the corpse should be collected and labeled. Many of the carrion-feeding insects will shelter or hide in this material close to the body; therefore, this too can be examined for faunal evidence. Collect handfuls of the litter down to the exposed soil, particularly litter very close to the ground surface. This material can be placed into 2-quart cardboard or plastic containers for subsequent examination in the laboratory.

Soil samples should include a 4-in. cube or core (100 cc) of material from areas associated with different body regions (head, torso, extremities). Soil samples of this size fit well into 2-pint (1 liter) or slightly larger cardboard (cylindrical ice cream type) or plastic containers. Soil samples (about six in all) should be taken from under, adjacent to, and up to 3 ft (1 m) from the body, noting the origin of each sample in reference to the position of the body. These samples should be labeled as were the insect vials.

## Acquisition and Preservation of Entomological Evidence at Autopsy

Many times remains are stored for some time in coolers or refrigeration units prior to autopsy from several hours to several days. Notation should be made of both the total time the body was cooling and the temperature of the chamber along with any other temperature information regarding the transport of the body to the morgue (e.g., monitoring temperatures of the body compartment periodically on long drives). Also, the temperature of the maggot mass should be recorded when the body is removed from the cooler. There may be little or no effect of the lower temperatures on insect development if the maggot mass was well established prior to the body being placed in the cooler. Maggot mass temperatures may be in the 100° F (27 to 37°C) range, even if the temperatures in the cooler are in the 30s Fahrenheit (2 to 4°C).

After the corpse has been taken from the body bag and placed on the autopsy table, an external examination is made. The entomologist and the pathologist can assist one another in their collection of evidence at this stage. A complete and detailed examination of clothing is essential and may yield a variety of stages and kinds of insects. Folds in clothing where eggs, larvae, pupae, or adults may be sheltering should be gently opened. Moist patches on clothing are good areas to search; fly eggs are often laid in these moist areas. The collection of seeds and other plant materials should be conducted at this time for analysis by a forensic botanist. Certain live stages of insects may be found in stems or seeds of plants which may give clues as to habitat, time, or geographic aspects.

After the clothing has been examined and removed, the areas of the body where concentrations of insect activity are found should be noted and photographed with a macro lens to show the extent and insect composition. Collection of representative samples from each major concentration should be performed using techniques described earlier. If fly larvae are present, some should be kept alive and some preserved.

Very small arthropods such as fleas, ticks, mites, lice, or nits may be present. These small insects may attempt to leave the body as the temperature drops, and can be found in the clothing, or may even hitch a ride on the examiner. Small ectoparasites may be present on the corpse itself; thus, it is important to examine the hair close to the scalp for the presence of nits (lice eggs). The eye lashes or sebaceous gland areas of the face may harbor follicle mites, *Demodex* sp. (Acari: Demodicidae). A few lashes are typically plucked and examined microscopically if the presence of this mite is suspected. Estimation of time intervals may be based on whether or not these arthropods are still alive.

Once surgical entry into the torso and skull has begun, other possible sites of insect activity can be explored. These may include the skull, natural body openings, hair and scalp, respiratory tract (including inner nasal passages), esophagus, genital and rectal areas, and antemortem wound sites, as well as the chest cavity, pelvic area under desiccated skin, or areas under desiccated skin of the limbs. Insects collected from any of these body areas should be labeled, preserved, and their location noted.

## Identification of Specimens

The ultimate purpose for proper collection, handling, labeling, and processing techniques is to ensure that specimens are maintained and preserved in as pristine a condition as possible. This is to enable the insect taxonomic expert to arrive at species specific determinations by use of morphological characteristics. Many characteristics are very subtle and may be damaged or obliterated if specimens are not processed carefully.

Species identification can be an extremely time-consuming and tedious task, and may require extensive study of specimens under the microscope. In some cases, however, experts may be able to identify a species with superficial examination of the specimen. While it is possible to provide species determinations with one specimen, it is beneficial to have a series of specimens to enhance the certainty of the identification if morphological variations exist. This is one reason for collecting multiple specimens from specific locations.

## Qualifications of Forensic Entomologists

When entomological evidence is discovered in association with a death scene, it is essential that a qualified forensic entomologist be used for evaluation and conclusions drawn from that evidence. There are several thousand entomologists found in universities and private industry across the United States, but very few would have the training, experience, or taxonomic (insect identification) knowledge to fulfill the needs of a criminal investigation that may result in a capital murder trial.

Participating entomologists should hold a Ph.D. in entomology (the very minimum is a master of science in entomology). Their area of study should emphasize the fields of insect ecology, taxonomy, medical entomology, insect behavior, or Dipteran research. They must have published and presented research related to carrion field studies or carrion insects in professional journals dealing with either entomology or forensic science. Additional qualifications might include: studying in an academic program under a nationally recognized forensic entomologist; participation in seminars and symposia related to forensic entomology with other recognized forensic entomologists; membership in the American Academy of Forensic Sciences; membership in the Entomological Society of America; and above all, board certification by the American Board of Forensic Entomology (ABFE); and case experience which demonstrates the ability to produce court quality reports and findings.

When a case progresses from the initial death scene through the lengthy police investigation and ultimately to a costly trial, it is critical that the entomologist involved be qualified.

It is the entomological evidence that will support, corroborate, and confirm or refute many other elements of physical or testimonial evidence. The reasonable doubt the jury may have often may be removed by the unbiased, quantitative scientific evidence of the forensic entomologist. In the end, the qualified and properly trained forensic entomologist can help achieve the justice and the ultimate truth which we all seek.

# References

Aldrich, J.M.
  1916  *Sarcophaga and Allies.* Thomas Say Foundation, Lafayette, IN.

Baumgartner, D.L.
  1986  The Hairy Maggot Blowfly, *Chrysomya rufifacies* (Macquart), Confirmed in Arizona. *Journal of Entomological Science* 21:130–132.
  1988  Spring Season Survey of the Urban Blowflies (Diptera: Calliphoridae) of Chicago, Illinois. *Great Lakes Entomologist* 21:119–121.
  1993  Review of *Chrysomya rufifacies* (Diptera: Calliphoridae). *Journal of Medical Entomology* 30:338–352.

Baumgartner, D.L., and B. Greenberg
  1984  The Genus *Chrysomya* (Diptera: Calliphoridae) in the New World. *Journal of Medical Entomology* 21:105–113.

Bergeret, M.
  1855  Infanticide, Mumification du Cadavre. Decouverte du Cadavre d'un Enfant Nouveau-Ne dan une Cheminee ou Il S'etait Momife. Determination de L'epoque de la Naissance par la Presence de Nymphes et de Larves D'insectes dans le Cadavre et par L'etude de Leurs Metamorphoses. *Annals d'Hygiène et Médecine Légale* 4:442–452.

Beyer, J.C., W.F. Enos, and M. Stajic
  1980  Drug Identification through Analysis of Maggots. *Journal of Forensic Sciences* 25:411–412.

Borror, D.J., D.M. DeLong, and C.A. Triplehorn
  1976  *An Introduction to the Study of Insects.* 4th ed. Holt, Rinehart and Winston, New York.

Byrd, J.
  1994  Temperature Preferences of Some Forensically Important Tropical Flies. Paper presented at the Annual Meeting of the Entomological Society of America, Dallas.

Catts, E.P., and M.L. Goff
  1992  Forensic Entomology in Criminal Investigations. *Annual Review of Entomology* 37:253–272.

Catts, E.P., and N.H. Haskell
  1990  *Entomology and Death: A Procedural Guide.* Joyce's Print Shop, Clemson, SC.

Cragg, J.B.
  1956  The Olfactory Behavior of *Lucilia* Species (Diptera) under Natural Conditions. *Annals of Applied Biology* 44:467–477.

Davidson, J.
  1944  On the Relationship between Temperature and Rate of Development of Insects at Constant Temperatures. *Journal of Animal Ecology* 13:26–38.

Early, M., and M.L. Goff
  1986  Arthropod Succession Patterns in Exposed Carrion on the Island of O'ahu, Hawaiian Islands, U.S.A. *Journal of Medical Entomology* 23:520–531.

Erzinclioglu, Y.Z.
1985 Immature Stages of British *Calliphora* and *Cynomya* with a Re-evaluation of the Taxonomic Characters of Larval Calliphoridae (Diptera). *Journal of Natural History* 19:69–96.

Fowler, W.W.
1888 The Worm (?) That Devoureth. *Entomology Monthly Magazine* 24:276–277.

Gagne, R.J.
1981 *Chrysomya* sp., Old World Blowflies (Diptera: Calliphoridae), Recently Established in the Americas. *Bulletin of the Entomological Society of America* 27:21–22.

Gagne, R.J., and R.D. Peterson, II.
1982 Physical Changes in the Genitalia of Males of the Screwworm, *Cochliomyia hominivorax* (Diptera: Calliphoridae), Caused by Mating. *Annals of the Entomological Society of America* 75:574–578.

Gilbert, B.M., and W.M. Bass
1967 Seasonal Dating of Burials from the Presence of Fly Pupae. *American Antiquity* 32:534–535.

Goddard, J., and P.K. Lago
1983 An Annotated List of the Calliphoridae (Diptera) of Mississippi. *Journal of the Georgia Entomological Society* 18:481–484.
1985 Notes on Blowfly (Diptera: Calliphoridae) Succession on Carrion in Northern Mississippi. *Journal of Entomological Science* 20:312–317.

Goff, M.L., and C.B. Odom
1987 Forensic Entomology in the Hawaiian Islands: Three Case Studies. *American Journal of Forensic Medicine and Pathology* 8:45–50.

Green, A.A.
1951 The Control of Blowflies Infesting Slaughterhouses. 1. Field Observations on the Habits of Blowflies. *Annals of Applied Biology* 38:475–494.

Greenberg, B.
1985 Forensic Entomology: Case Studies. *Bulletin of the Entomological Society of America* 31:25–28.
1988 *Chrysomya megacephala* (F.) (Diptera: Calliphoridae) Collected in North America and Notes on *Chrysomya* Species Present in the New World. *Journal of Medical Entomology* 25:199–200.
1990 Nocturnal Oviposition Behavior of Blowflies (Diptera: Calliphoridae). *Journal of Medical Entomology* 27:807–810.
1991 Flies as Forensic Indicators. *Journal of Medical Entomology* 28:565–577.

Gunatilake, K., and M.L. Goff
1988 Detection of Organophosphate Poisoning in a Putrefying body Analyzing Arthropod Larvae. Paper presented at the 40th Annual Meeting of the American Academy of Forensic Sciences, Philadelphia.

Hall, D.G.
1948 *The Blowflies of North America.* Thomas Say Foundation, Lafayette, IN.

Hall, R.D.
1979 The Blowflies of Missouri: An Annotated Checklist (Diptera: Calliphoridae). *Transcripts of the Missouri Academy of Sciences* 13:33–36.
1990 Introduction. In *Entomology and Death: A Procedural Guide*, edited by E.P. Catts and N.H. Haskell, pp. 1–8. Joyce's Print Shop, Clemson, SC.

Hall, R.D., and K.E. Doisy

1993   Length of Time After Death: Effect on Attraction and Oviposition or Larviposition of Midsummer Blowflies (Diptera: Calliphoridae) and Flesh Flies (Diptera: Sarcophagidae) of Medicolegal Importance in Missouri. *Annals of the Entomological Society of America* 86:589–593.

Hall, R.D., and N.H. Haskell

1995   Forensic Entomology — Applications in Medicolegal Investigations. In *Forensic Sciences*, edited by C. Wecht. Matthew Bender, New York.

Hall, R.D., and L.H. Townsend, Jr.

1977   The Blowflies of Virginia (Diptera: Calliphoridae). *Insects of Virginia No. 11*, Virginia Polytechnical Institute State University Research Bulletin No. 123.

Hardy, D.E.

1981   *Insects of Hawaii*, Vol. 14. *Diptera: Cyclorrhapha IV.* University of Hawaii Press, Honolulu.

Haskell, N.H.

1989   Calliphoridae of Pig Carrion in Northwest Indiana: A Seasonal Comparative Study. Master's thesis, Purdue University, West Lafayette, IN.

1993   Factors Affecting Diurnal Flight and Oviposition Periods of Blowflies (Diptera: Calliphoridae) in Indiana. Ph.D. dissertation, Purdue University, West Lafayette, IN.

Hawley, D.A., N.H. Haskell, D.G. McShaffrey, R.E. Williams, and J.E. Pless

1989   Identification of Red "Fiber": Chironomid Larvae. *Journal of Forensic Sciences* 34:617–621.

Hobson, R.P.

1932   Studies on the Nutrition of Blow-fly Larvae. III. The Liquefaction of Muscle. *Journal of Experimental Biology* 9:359–365.

Howden, H.F.

1964   The Mercure Trial: A Sideline of Entomology. *Canadian Entomologist* 96:121.

Introna, F. Jr., C. Lo Dico, Y.H. Caplan, and J.E. Smialek

1990   Opiate Analysis in Cadaveric Blowfly Larvae as an Indicator of Narcotic Intoxication. *Journal of Forensic Sciences* 35:118–122.

Ishijima, H.

1967   Revision of the Third Instar Larvae of Synanthropic Flies of Japan (Diptera: Anthymyiidae, Muscidae, Calliphoridae, and Sarcophagidae). *Japanese Journal of Sanitary Zoology* 18:47–100.

James, M.T.

1947   The Flies That Cause Myiasis in Man. *Miscellaneous Publications of the United States Department of Agriculture* 631: 1–175.

1953   Notes on the Distribution, Systematic Position, and Variation of Some Calliphorinae, with Particular Reference to the Species of Western North America. *Proceedings of Entomological Society of Washington* 55:143–148.

1955   The Blowflies of California (Diptera: Calliphoridae). *Bulletin California Insect Survey* 4:1–34.

1967   Variation in Chaetotaxy in *Phaenicia sericata* (Diptera: Calliphoridae). *Annals of the Entomological Society of America* 60: 706.

1970   Family Calliphoridae. In *A Catalog of the Diptera of the Americas South of the United States,* fasc.102. Zoological Museum, University of Sao Paulo, Brasil.

Johnson, M.D.

1975   Seasonal and Microseral Variations in the Insect Population on Carrion. *American Midland Naturalist* 93:79–90.

Kamal, A.S.
1958 Comparative Study of Thirteen Species of Sarcosaprophagous Calliphoridae and Sarcophagidae (Diptera). 1. Bionomics. *Annals of the Entomological Society of America* 51:261–271.

Kano, R., and K. Sato
1951a Notes on the Flies of Medical Importance in Japan. 2. The Larvae of *Sarcophaga* Known in Japan. *Japanese Journal of Experimental Medicine* 21:115–131.
1951b Notes on the Flies of Medical Importance in Japan. 3. Larvae of Calliphorinae in Japan. *Japanese Journal of Experimental Medicine* 21:133–140.
1952 Notes on the Flies of Medical Importance in Japan. 6. Larvae of Luciliini in Japan. *Japanese Journal of Experimental Medicine* 22:33–42.

Keh, B.
1985 Scope and Applications of Forensic Entomology. *Annual Review of Entomology* 30:137–154.

Kintz, P., B. Godelar, A.Tracqui, P. Mangin, A. Lugnier, and A.J. Chaumont
1990 Fly Larvae: A New Toxicological Method of Investigation in Forensic Medicine. *Journal of Forensic Sciences* 35:204–207.

Knipling, E.F.
1936a A Comparative Study of the First Instar Larvae of the Genus *Sarcophaga*, with notes on the Biology. *Journal of Parasitology* 22:417–454.
1936b Some Specific Taxonomic Characters of Common *Lucilia* Larvae — Calliphorinae — Diptera. *Iowa State College Journal of Science* 10:275–293.
1939 A Key for Blowfly Larvae Concerned in Wound and Cutaneous Myiasis. *Annals of the Entomological Society of America* 32:376–383.

Lane, R.P.
1975 An Investigation into Blowfly (Diptera: Calliphoridae) Succession on Corpses. *Journal of Natural History* 9:581–588.

Leclercq, M.
1969 Entomology and Legal Medicine. In *Entomological Parasitology: The Relations between Entomology and the Medical Sciences*, edited by M. Leclercq, pp. 128–142. Pergamon Press, Oxford, U.K.

Leclercq, M., and G. Brahy
1985 Entomologie et Medecine Legale: Datation de la Mort. *Journal de Médecine Légale* 28:271–278.

Liu, D., and B. Greenberg
1989 Immature Stages of Some Flies of Forensic Importance. *Annals of the Entomological Society of America* 82:80–93.

Lodge, O.C.
1916 Fly Investigations Reports. IV. Some Inquiry into the Question of Baits and Poisons for Flies, Being a Report on the Experimental Work Carried Out during 1915 for the Zoological Society of London. *Proceedings of the Zoological Society of London* 1916:481–518.

Lord, W.D.
1990 Case Histories of the Use of Insects in Investigations. In *Entomology and Death: A Procedural Guide*, edited by E.P. Catts and N.H. Haskell. Joyce's Print Shop, Clemson, SC.

Lord, W.D., and J.F. Burger
1983 Collection and Preservation of Forensically Important Entomological Materials. *Journal of Forensic Sciences* 28:936–944.

1984  Arthropods Associated with Harbor Seal (*Phoca vitulina*) Carcasses Stranded on Islands along the New England Coast. *International Journal of Entomology* 26:282–285.

Lord, W.D., M.L. Goff, T.R. Adkins, and N.H. Haskell
1994  The Black Soldier Fly *Hermetia Illucens* (Diptera: Stratiomyidae) as a Potential Measure of Human Postmortem Interval: Observations and Case Histories. *Journal of Forensic Sciences* 39:215–222.

Lord, W.D., and J.R. Stevenson
1986  *Directory of Forensic Entomologists.* 2nd ed. Defense Pest Management Information Analysis Center, Walter Reed Army Medical Center, Washington, D.C.

Marchenko, M.I.
1985  Features of the Development of the Fly *Cyrosomya albiceps* (Diptera: Calliphoridae). *Entomol. Obozr.* 64:79–84.

Meek, C.L., M.D. Andis, and C.S. Andrews
1983  Role of the Entomologist in Forensic Pathology, Including a Selected Bibliography. *Bibliography of the Entomological Society of America* 1:1–10.

Megnin, J.P.
1894  *La Fauna des Cadavres: Application de la Entomologie a la Mededin Legale. Encyclopedie Scientifique des Aide-Memoires.* Masson et Gauthiers, Villars, Paris.

Metcalf, C.L., W.P. Flint, and R.L. Metcalf
1962  *Destructive and Useful Insects.* 4th ed. Mcgraw-Hill, New York.

Motter, M.G.
1898  A Contribution to the Study of the Fauna of the Grave. A Study of One Hundred and Fifty Disinternments with some Additional Experimental Observations. *Journal of the New York Entomological Society* 6:201–231.

Muller, B.
1975  *Gerichtliche Medizin*, 2nd ed. Springer-Verlag, Berlin.

Norris, K.R.
1965  The Bionomics of Blowflies. *Annual Review of Entomology* 10:47–68.

Nuorteva, P.
1971  Duration of Development of *Calliphora alpina* (Zett.) (Diptera: Calliphoridae) in Subarctic Northern Finland. *Annales Entomologici Fennici* 37:209.
1974  Age Determination of a Blood Stain in a Decaying Shirt by Entomological Means. *Forensic Science* 3:89–94.
1987  Empty Puparia of *Phormia terraenovae* R.-D. (Diptera: Calliphoridae) as Forensic Indicators. *Annales Entomologici Fennici* 53:53–56.

Nuorteva, P., M. Isokoski, and K. Laiho
1967  Studies on the Possibilities of Using Blowflies (Diptera) as Medico-Legal Indicators in Finland. *Annales Entomologici Fennici* 33:217–225.

Nourteva, P., H. Schuman, M. Isokoski, and K. Laiho
1974  Studies on the Possibilities of Using Blowflies (Diptera) as Medico-Legal Indicators in Finland. 2. Four Cases Where Species Identification was Performed from Larvae. *Annales Entomologici Fennici* 40:70–74.

Parish, H.E., and E.C. Cushing
1938  Location for Blowfly Traps: Abundance and Activity of Blowflies and Other Flies in Menard County, Texas. *Journal of Economic Entomology* 31:750–763.

Payne, J.A.
1965  A Summer Carrion Study of the Baby Pig, *Sus scrofa* Linnaeus. *Ecology* 46:592–602.

Reed, H.B.
  1958  A Study of Dog Carcass Communities in Tennessee, with Special Reference to the Insects. *American Midland Naturalist* 59:213–245.

Reiter, C., and G. Wollenek
  1983  On the Determination of Maggots of Forensically Important Blowflies. *Zeitschrift für Rechtsmedizin* 90:309–316.
  1985  Disintegration Durability and Forensic Information from Empty Fly Pupa Cases. *Archaeologische Kriminologie* 175:47–56.

Richard, R.D., and E.H. Ahrens
  1983  New Distribution Record for the Recently Introduced Blowfly, *Chrysomya rufifacies* (Macquart) in North America. *Southwestern Entomologist* 8:216–218.

Rodriguez, W.C., and W.M. Bass
  1983  Insect Activity and Its Relationship to Decay Rates of Human Cadavers in East Tennessee. *Journal of Forensic Sciences* 28:423–432.
  1985  Decomposition of Buried Bodies and Methods That May Aid in Their location. *Journal of Forensic Sciences* 30:836–852.

Smith, K.G.V.
  1975  The Faunal Succession of Insects and Other Invertebrates on a Dead Fox. *Entomologist's Gazette* 26:277–287.
  1986  *A Manual of Forensic Entomology.* Comstock University Press, Ithaca, NY.

Smith, K.G.V., and J.P. Dear
  1978  National Fish Skin Week. *Antenna* 2:125–126.

Spitz, W.U. (editor)
  1993  *Spitz and Fisher's Medicolegal Investigation of Death.* 3rd ed. Charles C Thomas, Springfield, IL.

Stone, A., C.W. Sabrosky, W.W. Wirth, R.H. Foote, and J.R. Coulson (editors)
  1965  *A Catalog of the Diptera of America North of Mexico.* Agricultural Handbook No. 276, Agriculture Research Service, U.S. Department of Agriculture, Washington, D.C.

Tantawi, T.I., and B. Greenberg
  1993  The Effect of Killing and Preservative Solutions on Estimates of Maggot Age in Forensic Cases. *Journal of Forensic Sciences* 38:702–707.

Vincent, C., D.K. McEvan, M. Leclercq, and C.L. Meek
  1985  A Bibliography of Forensic Entomology. *Journal of Medical Entomology* 22:212–219.

Vinogradova, E.B., and M. I. Marchenko
  1984  Use of Temperature Parameters of Fly Development in Legal-Medical Practice. *Sudebno-Meditsinskaya Ekspertiza* 1: 16–19.

Voigt, J.
  1965  Specific Postmortem Changes Produced by Larder Beetles. *Journal of Forensic Medicine* 12:76–80.

von Zuben, C.J., S.F. Dos Reis, J.B. do Val, W.A. Godoy, and O.B. Ribeiro
  1993  Dynamics of a Mathematical Model of *Chrysomya megacephala* (Diptera: Calliphoridae). *Journal of Medical Entomology* 30:443–448.

Wardle, R.A.
  1921  The Protection of Meat Commodities Against Blowflies. *Annals of Applied Biology* 8:1–9.
  1930  Significant Variables in the Blowfly Environment. *Annals of Applied Biology* 17:554–574.

Webb, J.P., Jr., R.B. Loomis, M.B. Madon, S.G. Bennett, and G. E. Green

1983   The Chigger Species *Eutrombicula belkini* Gould (Acari: Trombiculidae) as a Forensic Tool in a Homicide Investigation in Ventura County, California. *Bulletin of the Society of Vector Ecology* 8:141–146.

Wells, J.D., and B. Greenberg

1992   Interaction between *Chrysomya rufifacies* and *Cochliomyia macellaria* (Diptera: Calliphoridae): The Possible Consequences of an Invasion. *Bulletin of Entomological Research* 82:133–137.

1994   Effect of the Red Imported Fire Ant (Hymenoptera: Formicidae) and Carcass Type on the Daily Occurrence of Postfeeding Carrion-Fly Larvae (Diptera: Calliphoridae, Sarcophagidae). *Journal of Medical Entomology* 31:171–174.

1994   Resource Use by an Introduced and Native Carrion Flies. *Oecologia* 99:181–187.

# Human Remains Recovered from a Shark's Stomach in South Carolina*

# 28

TED A. RATHBUN
BABETTE C. RATHBUN

## Introduction

The involvement of physical anthropologists in forensic science identification has increased in recent years; documentation of the range of circumstances and types of cases has merited inclusion in the professional literature (Bass and Driscoll 1983; Snow 1982; Stewart 1979). Individual case reports frequently appear in the media and are of special interest at the annual academy meetings. Besides their intrinsic interest and importance, each case usually has a unique aspect and serves as a continuing test of the theories, methods, and data available for accurate analysis. Since many of the quantitative methods available for human identification depend on complete bones for analysis, fragmentary human remains provide a particular challenge to interpretation.

## Background

In May 1982, a fisherman in Port Royal, SC caught a 243-cm (8-ft) tiger shark off Daws Island in the Broad River, an estuary near Beaufort, SC. While the fisherman was waiting for the purchaser of the 59-kg (130-lb) shark to arrive, the stomach contents were examined and bone was noticed. He called the county coroner, who confirmed that the remains were human. Little hope was given for personal identification. The coroner speculated that the remains could be from recent plane crashes in the area, from which not all bodies were recovered. Since I had identified other remains for the coroner, he called to see if I would be interested in the material as a curiosity or for teaching purposes, since it was not considered a forensic science problem.

## Material

The remains arrived at my laboratory late in June 1982. In a plastic bag were the proximal fourth of the left tibia and fibula, the complete patella, and two distal fragments of the femur. Connective tissue and bits of flesh and skin surrounded the bone. Initial inspection suggested a petite adult individual. The material was photographed, adherent hairs embedded in the bone and sticking to the tissues were removed, and the skin shreds were preserved. Some connective tissue was removed manually and the remaining material was soaked in enzyme detergent and later in a dilute solution of sodium hypochloride. Even though the case was not a pressing legal one, the specimens were processed as completely and systematically as possible.

* Adapted for publication courtesy of *Journal of Forensic Sciences, Vol. 29, 269–276, 1984.*

## Tiger Sharks

As forensic scientists, we are continually aware of the importance of staying within our own areas of expertise. Since I am not a marine biologist, I contacted a renowned shark authority, Dr. Perry Gilbert of the Mote Marine Laboratories in Sarasota, FL. He provided information on shark attacks, reports of human remains recovered from shark stomachs, and suggestions for a literature search of topics relevant to this case (Gilbert 1982).

The tiger shark, *Galeocerdo cuvieri*, is a member of the largest of all the shark families, the *Carcharhinidae*, sometimes called the typical sharks. It is named not for its ferocious reputation, but for the vertical brown stripes on the backs of the younger specimens (Ellis 1975; Leneaweaver and Backus 1970). It ranges the world over, primarily in warm coastal waters, and is often found close to the shore in very shallow water (Bigelow and Schroeder 1948). It is known and feared for its ferocity from Australia to the West Indies. The tiger shark is common in South Carolina waters; attacks have been reported fairly frequently. The average size of the adult fish is 300 cm (10 ft) and 180 to 225 kg (400 to 500 lb). It is believed to grow as long as 550 cm (18 ft) and to surpass 900 kg (2000 lb). The all-tackle record tiger shark was taken at Cherry Grove, SC in 1964. It was 438 cm (13' 10") long and weighed 801 kg (1780 lb) (Leneaweaver and Backus 1970).

Although the distinguishing stripes fade with maturity, the tiger's appearance makes it quite easy to identify. It has a very broad head with a short snout and an upper tail lobe that is long and pointed. The teeth are unique and quite recognizable. They are broad with an outward bending tip. The inner edge is convex and the outer is deeply notched. The serrations are coarse at the base, becoming progressively finer at the tip. The serrations may themselves be serrated (Applegate 1967; Leneaweaver and Backus 1970).

This shark is known to eat virtually anything. It is one of the very few species that has given the sharks the reputation of scavengers. This reputation may be because many of the stomachs examined were from sharks caught in harbors or shipping lanes, where there is a variety of garbage (Springer 1967). The shark catcher in this case reported that he has found rocks, sea gulls, turtles, shellfish, and rats in sharks he caught locally. Among the items found in the stomachs of tiger sharks in other areas are large conches, horseshoe crabs, pieces of large sea turtles, porpoise, sea birds, large fish, garbage, and various items such as copper wire, clothing, nuts and bolts (Leneaweaver and Backus 1970), and an unopened can of salmon (Ellis 1975). There are also several accounts of human remains found in the stomachs of tiger sharks (Coppleson 1958; Llano 1957).

Numerous instances of tiger shark attacks on humans have been reported worldwide. In some cases the sharks have later been caught and killed and the stomach contents examined. Body parts could sometimes be identified as coming from persons known to have been attacked. Means of identification have been scars, fingerprints, and in at least one famous case, a tattoo (Ellis 1975). In some cases, the remains seem to be identified simply by the knowledge that a certain person had a leg bitten off by a shark in the vicinity of the capture.

Sharks swallow their food whole and digestion does not begin until the food enters the stomach (Sullivan 1907). At that point, they can apparently store food undigested for long periods of time. Since it is impossible to know when the shark swallows the food in the wild, it is also impossible to determine the exact length of time that the food remains in the stomach. However, sharks captured and held in captivity until their death have provided some information on this point. Sir Edward Hallstrom reported an episode of a tiger shark held in the zoo in Sydney, Australia. The only food given to it was horse meat, which it repeatedly regurgitated. It died after 21 days and was autopsied. The stomach contents included two perfectly preserved dolphins. Not only had it failed to begin digestion of the dolphins in 3 weeks time, it had also vomited the horsemeat while somehow retaining the dolphins (Coppleson 1958). According to Coppleson, human remains also appear to remain undigested in shark stomachs for days or even weeks. He has recorded several examples of body parts found in various stages of decomposition. In some cases they were the victims of known shark attacks on swimmers or divers. In other cases, they were the result of sharks mutilating already dead bodies (Coppleson 1958).

The famous "shark arm" mystery of 1935 in Australia is a good example of a tiger shark retaining human remains for a long period of time. This shark was being held in an aquarium for public viewing, when it regurgitated an entire human arm, complete with tattoo. The investigation showed that the arm had not been bitten off by the shark and a case was eventually made that the victim had been murdered and his body dismembered and thrown into the water (Coppleson 1958). The tattoo and fingerprints were used to identify the victim. Although a thorough search was made, the rest of the body was never found. The Australian Supreme Court ruled that a single limb could not be a murder victim, so the case was never prosecuted (Ellis 1975). But it was clear that the shark had swallowed the arm sometime between the last sighting of the victim and when it was captured. The shark was in captivity for 8 days before it regurgitated the arm, which was held in its stomach undigested for at least 8 days and possibly for as long as 18 days (Coppleson 1958).

## Circumstances and Time Since Death

Judgments of time since death from wholly or partially skeletalized material have been shown to be highly variable and dependent on local circumstances and environments (Bass 1984; Stewart 1979). As mentioned above, human remains have been documented to remain undigested from 8 to 21 days in sharks' stomachs. The sketchily known digestive process of tiger sharks precludes accurate estimates of time since death. No shark attacks had been reported in the preceeding month along the South Carolina coast, but a plane crashed in May 1982 near Savannah, GA, which is within the range of movement of the species (up to 48 km [30 miles] a day). To date, only miscellaneous portions of the crash victims, including one foot and three hands, have been recovered.

The location and nature of the bite is inconclusive concerning the circumstances of ingestion. The wounds of a tiger shark bite are usually crescent-shaped and a deep bite produces scratches and occasionally tooth fragments lodged along the edge of the wound. The most common areas bitten are the legs and buttocks (Llano 1957). The angle of the bite mark in the bone suggests that the leg was bent when attacked. However, somewhat similar wounds were sustained by a South Carolina native sitting in shallow water (Burton 1935). At any rate, the knee area was severed from the rest of the body with a bite to the vertical axis of the leg. The wound showed very little tearing but the bite force has been determined to be approximately 294 mPa (30 kgf/mm$^2$) for each tooth (Snodgrass and Gilbert 1967).

## Race

The bone portions themselves were not diagnostic of racial ancestry. The shreds of skin adhering to the bone were the best evidence. Putrefaction had darkened some of the soft tissue, but sufficient dermal and epidermal material was present for evaluation. Some consideration was given to bleaching from hydrochloric acid in the gastric juices and prolonged exposure to seawater, but the most probable diagnosis of race was white.

## Sex

All of the bones appeared small, and the morphology suggested that they came from a female. Such subjective evaluations can be important, but quantitative methods add credence to evaluation. A number of morphological and quantitative techniques have been developed for the

**Table 1    Sex Determination from Proximal Width of Tibia**

| Source | Male Mean (mm) | Standard Deviation (mm) | Sectioning Point (mm) | Female Mean (mm) | Standard Deviation (mm) |
|---|---|---|---|---|---|
| Iscan and Shaivitz (1982) | 77.33 | 3.59 | 73.5 | 69.72 | 3.39 |
| Symes (1982) | 79.15 | 3.06 | 74.56 | 69.97 | 3.19 |
| Olivier (1969) | 76.00[a] | — | — | 74.00[a] | — |
| Present case | — | — | 62 | — | — |

[a]  Olivier's data are not given as male and female means, but as minimum male and maximum female widths.

**Table 2    Sex Determination from Patella Measurements**

| Parameter | Male Mean (mm) | Standard Deviation (mm) | Present Case (mm) | Female Mean (mm) | Standard Deviation (mm) |
|---|---|---|---|---|---|
| Maximum height | 50.7 | 3.59 | 35.0 | 46.17 | 2.58 |
| Maximum width | 50.3 | 2.58 | 36.0 | 45.12 | 2.16 |

diagnosis of sex from the postcranial skeleton. Multivariate analysis of multiple long bones (Giles 1970) and femora of different samples (DiBennardo and Taylor 1982; Taylor and DiBennardo 1982) produce accurate results with complete bones. The specimens in this case were too fragmentary to even apply the circumference measurements for univariate analysis of the femur (Black 1978; DiBennardo and Taylor 1979). Even Olivier's (1969) femur distal epiphyseal breadth could not be used, since a segment of the intertrochanteric area was missing.

The tibia was also too incomplete for multivariate analysis. Only the proximal tibial breadth could be established with reasonable certainty (see Table 1). Olivier (1969) indirectly provided quantitative information on this dimension by equating the tibial breadth to be redundant to the distal femoral breadth in French samples. Data on the American white and black samples of the Terry collection were available from a discriminant function analysis (Iscan and Shaivitz 1982); protohistoric Arikara (Symes 1982) values also had a very good discriminating efficiency. All of these studies support a diagnosis of female for the specimen in question. Another study of the Terry collection of white tibiae (Symes and Jantz 1983) places it well within the female range.

Although the size and shape of the patella informally have been considered as supportive information for sex determination, a search of the osteological as well as forensic science literature revealed little substantiated data. Volumes of over 15 cm$^3$ for males and less than 11 cm$^3$ for females with a percentage error of 3% have been suggested (El-Najjar and McWilliams 1978). A volume of 9 cm$^3$ was established for the patella from the shark by using a water displacement method. Because of the scant quantitative data available, measurements on living white males and females (ten each) were collected (Taylor 1982). Maximum heights and widths and tissue thicknesses at each location were determined and then probable bone dimensions tabulated. As can be seen in Table 2, the size of the unknown specimen falls well below the female mean. This information is supportive, but further work with dried specimens of known sex is needed.

# Age

The unknown specimen was an adult, as indicated by epiphyseal union. Although the articular surfaces were porous beneath the cartilage, the epiphyses were fully united, as indicated by

**Table 3   Maximum Lengths of Long Bones from Bone Segments**

| Bone | Maximum Length (cm) | Range (cm) |
|---|---|---|
| Tibia | | |
| Segment I (2.6 cm) | 34.45 ± 2.15 | 32.3–36.6 |
| Segment 2 (5.6 cm) | 34.65 ± 1.75 | 32.9–36.4 |
| Segments 1 and 2 | 34.05 ± 1.74 | 32.3–35.8 |
| Femur | | |
| Segment 4 (3.7 cm) | 43.28 ± 2.49 | 40.79–45.77 |

**Table 4   Estimate of Stature from Long Bones**

| Long Bone | Stature Estimate (cm) | Range, cm (ft) |
|---|---|---|
| Femur and tibia | 160.69 ± 3.55 | 157.14–164.24 (5' 2" to 5' 5") |
| Tibia | 160.275 ± 3.66 | 156.6–163.93 (5' 2" to 5' 4½") |
| Femur | 161.0 ± 3.72 | 157.3–164.7 (5' 2" to 5' 5") |

gross observation and radiography. No indications of degenerative joint disease were noted. Macroscopic evaluation of age in this instance was very imprecise.

The fibula was submitted to Dr. Ellis Kerley of the University of Maryland for microscopic evaluation. His analysis, based on microscopic structures used in age determination (Kerley 1965) suggested an age of 33 years with a range of 28 to 38 and an accuracy of 87% in comparison with samples of known age fibulas.

# Stature

Estimations of stature from complete long bones is a well-established and accurate procedure (Trotter and Gleser 1958). Regression formulas and estimation of maximum bone length from segments (Steele 1970) developed from the Terry collection are somewhat less accepted, because of difficulties in locating some of the landmarks. Estimates of bone length from the distal femur fragment and the superior two segments of the tibia were congruent enough to indicate probable accuracy in this case (see Table 3). Steele's formulas for estimating total living stature could not be applied, since the right combinations of segments were not present. The long bone length estimates were applied initially to both sexes and whites and blacks. Considerable harmony of results was attained. After the age estimate and the sex and race diagnoses were complete, the Trotter and Gleser (1958) formulas for white females were applied, with the resultant range of 157.5 to 165 cm (5' 2" to 5' 5") for individual bones as well as combinations (see Table 4 and Figure 1).

# Hairs

It initially was hoped that the hair imbedded in the bone and adhering to some of the soft tissue could contribute to the diagnosis of sex and race. Examination of the hair by Dr. Walter Birkby of the University of Arizona indicated that the specimens were not from a human. The individual hairs were tapered and had not been cut. The heavy pigment and the medullary form were outside the human range. Exact origin was not determined. In a subsequent interview with the fisherman, it was found that the remains had been deposited in the back

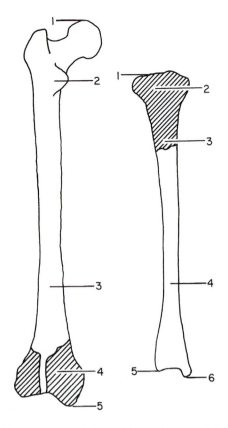

**Figure 1**   Shaded portions indicate femur and tibia elements from shark stomach for estimation of long bone length. Adapted from Steele (1970:87).

of his pickup truck and hence contamination could have occurred there. Although he could not remember what, if anything else, was in the shark's stomach, he reported that he had caught other sharks with rats as part of the stomach contents.

## Summary

The final evaluation of all the data indicated that the human remains retrieved from the shark's stomach were those of a white female, age 28 to 38 with a most likely age of 33, whose stature was between 157.5 and 165 cm (5' 2" and 5' 5"). The circumstances of death could not be determined, but the shark bite was along the vertical axis of the leg. The literature review indicated that sharks can retain human remains undigested for up to 21 days, so time since death could not be accurately determined. Positive identification has not yet been established.

Besides the unusual circumstances of discovery of the human remains, this case was illustrative of the utility of many of the techniques that have been developed through the years in physical anthropology. Although many of the methods were developed without a definite forensic science orientation, the range of data allowed application in a forensic science setting. The areas of uncertainty centered around the fragmentary nature of the remains and the inapplicability of some of the quantitative multivariate statistical analyses. As is so often the case, the analysis in this instance highlighted gaps in our repertoire and indicated areas for further research. Racial determination would have been impossible without the shreds of skin. The other identifying characters were reasonably accurate, given the fragmentary nature of the remains.

# Acknowledgments

Special thanks for participation in various aspects of this case are extended to Curt Copeland, Randall McCoy, Ellis Kerley, Walter Birkby, Perry Gilbert, and Kathryn Propst. M. Y. Iscan, P. M. Shaivitz, and Steve Symes kindly provided prepublication data for tibia breadth analysis.

# References

Applegate, S.P.
    1967   A Survey of Shark Hard Parts. In *Sharks, Skates,* and *Rays,* edited by P.W. Gilbert, R.F. Mathewson, and D.P. Rall, pp. 37–67. Johns Hopkins Press, Baltimore.

Bass, W.M.
    1984   Time Interval Since Death: A Difficult Decision. In *Human Identification: Case Studies in Forensic Physical Anthropology,* edited by T.A. Rathbun and J.E. Buikstra, pp. 136–147. Charles C Thomas, Springfield, IL.

Bass, W.M., and P.A. Driscoll
    1983   Summary of Skeletal Identification in Tennessee: 1971–1981. *Journal of Forensic Sciences* 28:159–168.

Bigelow, H.B., and W.C. Schroeder
    1948   Sharks. In *Fishes of the Western North Atlantic,* pp. 266–276. Memoir No. I, Part One. Sears Foundation for Marine Research, Yale University, New Haven, CT.

Black, T.K., III
    1978   A New Method for Assessing the Sex of Fragmentary Skeletal Remains: Femoral Shaft Circumference. *American Journal of Physical Anthropology* 48:227–321.

Burton, E.M.
    1935   Shark Attacks Along the South Carolina Coast. *Scientific Monthly* 40:279–283.

Coppleson, V.M.
    1958   *Shark Attack.* Angus and Robertson, Sydney, Australia.

DiBennardo, R., and J.V. Taylor
    1979   Sex Assessment of the Femur: A Test of a New Method. *American Journal of Physical Anthropology* 50:635–637.
    1982   Classification and Misclassification in Sexing the Black Femur by Discriminant Function Analysis. *American Journal of Physical Anthropology* 58:145–151.

El-Najjar, M.Y., and K.R. McWilliams
    1978   *Forensic Anthropology.* Charles C Thomas, Springfield, IL.

Ellis, R.
    1975   *The Book of Sharks.* Grosset and Dunlap, New York.

Giles, E.
    1970   Discriminant Function Sexing of the Human Skeleton. In *Personal Identification in Mass Disasters,* edited by T.D. Stewart, pp. 99–109. National Museum of Natural History, Washington, D.C.

Iscan, M.Y., and P.M. Shaivitz
    1982   Sexual Dimorphism in the Epiphyseal Breadth of the Femur and Tibia. Paper presented at the 51st Annual Meeting of the American Association of Physical Anthropologists, Eugene, OR.

Kerley, E.R.
    1965   The Microscopic Determination of Age in Human Bone. *American Journal of Physical Anthropology* 23:149–163.

Leneaweaver, T.H., and R.H. Backus
　　1970　*The Natural History of Sharks.* J. B. Lippincott, Philadelphia.

Llano, G.A.
　　1957　Sharks vs. Men. *Scientific American* 196(6):54–61.

Olivier, G.
　　1969　*Practical Anthropology.* Charles C Thomas, Springfield, IL.

Snodgrass, J.M., and P.W. Gilbert
　　1967　A Shark-Bite Meter. In *Sharks, Skates* and *Rays*, edited by P.W. Gilbert, R.F. Mathewson, and D.P. Rall, pp. 331–337. Johns Hopkins Press, Baltimore.

Snow, C.C.
　　1982　Forensic Anthropology. *Annual Review of Anthropology* 11:97–131.

Springer, S.
　　1967　Social Organization of Shark Populations. In *Sharks, Skates* and *Rays*, edited by P.W. Gilbert, R.F. Mathewson, and D.P. Rall, pp. 149–174. Johns Hopkins Press, Baltimore.

Steele, D.G.
　　1970　Estimation of Stature from Fragments of Long Limb Bones. In *Personal Identification in Mass Disasters*, edited by T.D. Stewart, pp. 85–97. National Museum of Natural History, Washington, D.C.

Stewart, T.D.
　　1979　*Essentials of Forensic Anthropology.* Charles C Thomas, Springfield, IL.

Sullivan, M.X.
　　1907　The Physiology of the Digestive Tract of Elasmobranchs. *Contributions from the Biological Laboratory of the Bureau of Fisheries at Woods Hole, Mass., Bulletin of the Bureau of Fisheries*, Document 625, 27:1–27.

Symes, S.A.
　　1982　Sex Assessment of the Tibia by Discriminant Function Analysis. Manuscript on file at the Department of Anthropology, University of Tennessee, Knoxville.

Symes, S.A., and R.L. Jantz
　　1983　Discriminant Function Sexing of the Tibia. In *Abstracts of the 35th Annual Meeting of the American Academy of Forensic Sciences*, p. 76. American Academy of Forensic Sciences, Colorado Springs, CO.

Taylor, K.
　　1982　Patella Size and Shape in Relation to Sex. Ms. on file, Department of Anthropology, University of South Carolina, Columbia.

Taylor, J.V., and R. DiBennardo
　　1982　Determination of Sex of White Femora by Discriminant Function Analysis: Forensic Science Applications. *Journal of Forensic Sciences* 27:417–423.

Trotter, M., and G. Gleser
　　1958　A Reevaluation of Stature Based on Measurements Taken during Life and of Long Bones after Death. *American Journal of Physical Anthropology* 16:79–123.

# SECTION IV

*Buried and Protected Remains*

# Decomposition of Buried and Submerged Bodies

# 29

WILLIAM C. RODRIGUEZ, III

## Decomposition of Buried and Submerged Bodies

In death investigation, the forensic scientist will certainly encounter his or her share of cases involving a decomposed body or remains. A substantial number of these cases will involve buried bodies or those recovered from an aquatic environment. Such cases require careful consideration in determining the postmortem interval based on decompositional change, as the rate of decomposition is slower than that which occurs in air. When not specified otherwise, case observations are those from the authors' case experience.

The reduced rate of decomposition of a buried corpse, which in general proceeds at a rate eight times slower than above ground, can be attributed to two major factors. The first factor is that of limitation of carrion insect and animal activity. Burial of a corpse either limits or totally prevents access to the body by carrion insects and animals; thus breakdown of the tissues is primarily the result of autolysis and bacterial putrefaction (Clark this volume). The degree of access is directly related to the burial depth and soil compactness. Studies and numerous field observations have shown that carrion depredation is primarily restricted to burial depths of a foot or less (Rodriguez and Bass 1985).

At burial depths less than a foot, decompositional odors given off by a corpse easily penetrate the soil, reaching above ground, thus attracting insects and other animals. Carrion-frequenting mammals, primarily carnivores, will dig up and expose portions of, or all of a corpse buried at depths less than a foot in order to feed on the soft tissues and bones. Carrion insects, such as adult blowflies, gain access to a shallow burial by migration through small cracks and crevices in the soil created by bloating of the body. Upon reaching the corpse, the adult females will ovideposit on the tissues. It has also been observed that after a period of rain or in the presence of moist soil conditions and concentrated decompositional odors, adult females will ovideposit on the soil surface (Rodriguez and Bass 1983). Upon emergence from the eggs, the fly larvae migrate down to the corpse to feed and develop. For treatments of forensic entomology see Catts and Haskell (1990), Smith (1986), and Haskell et al. this volume.

The second major factor responsible for reduced decompositional rates below ground is the soil environment. Soil provides an efficient barrier to solar radiation, and therefore both temperatures and temperature fluctuation decrease with soil depth. As temperature decreases with soil depth so does the rate of decomposition by cooling of the body. At depths of less than a foot or so, one can expect temperatures to be close to those above ground and to fluctuate daily (Rodriguez and Bass 1985).

Thermal stabilization in soil, in general occurs at depths greater than 2 feet, with no significant temperature fluctuations other than by season. Deep burials of approximately 4 feet or greater, by maintenance of cool temperatures and inhibition of depredation, provide an extremely reduced rate of decomposition. A corpse buried at such depths will remain virtually intact, with minimal tissue loss for a period of at least 1 year.

Two other aspects of the soil environment affecting the decompositional rate are moisture content and the presence of soil organisms, both plant and animal. The presence of ground water, or clay type soils which retain moisture, in most cases produces an environment conducive for adipocere formation. A body recovered from a burial site which contains significant amounts of clay soil typically exhibits advanced adipocere formation, whereas a body recovered from dry or well-drained soil lacks significant adipocere formation. Wet soil environments are commonly associated with deep burials, and therefore bodies recovered from such sites tend to exhibit adipocere formation over most of the body surface. At greater soil depth there is typically more moisture due to lesser degree of evaporation, due to the soil barrier, and resulting from being more approximate to the water table.

At shallow depths, a buried body is subjected to temperatures which approximate those above ground and undergoes increased degradation by plants and soil organisms. Plant roots grow towards a decaying corpse, seeking the rich organic nutrients produced by decomposition. The release of organic nutrients by decomposition results in increased and differential plant growth at the burial site (Rodriguez and Bass 1985). This observation may permit the rapid location of a buried body in large fields where changes in soil compaction may be difficult to spot. Once in contact with the body, the roots will begin to degrade the clothing, skin, and finally the skeletal remains during the later stage of decomposition. Many skeletal remains recovered from shallow burials exhibit obvious root damage. This damage appears as irregular multichanneled grooving of the outer bone cortex. In many instances, skeletal material will be recovered with adhering roots which have grown into the bone trabeculae or completely through the bone. Skeletal or clothing remains which have been penetrated by roots should be handled with care so as to not disturb the context of the roots. Root growth associated with remains can be useful in estimations of the postmortem interval, especially in cases involving remains approximately 1 year to a few years in age (Willey and Heilman 1987). Such material should be taken to an experienced botanist for identification of the plant species and time required for present stage of root growth.

Soil-dwelling insects and bacteria, like plant roots, are most prolific at shallow depths due to the enriched upper soil, and therefore contribute to the more rapid decompositional process associated with shallow burials. The criminal disposal of a corpse in a deep grave tends to produce a retardation of surface plant growth, as primary root structures are destroyed and there is surface redeposition of nonnutritive soil by the digging. A lack of, or disruption of plant growth at a burial site is one sign which fortunately provides evidence of a grave. Also it is fortunate that no matter how carefully a grave site is filled, resettling of the soil will occur, producing an outlined depression of the grave site which can be referred to as a "primary grave depression" (Morse 1983). With the passage of time, the depth of the depression will increase until the soil finally settles. As a general rule, the presence of a deep primary depression usually indicates a deep burial. A corpse buried during warm weather and at depths of 2 feet or less, in general, undergoes decomposition in which there is significant bloating of the chest and abdomen by decompositional gases. As bloating occurs, the soil covering the body is pushed upwards followed by resettling of the soil into the chest cavity as it collapses in the latter stage of decomposition. This filling in of the chest area by soil creates what can be referred to as a "secondary grave depression".

Mummification of a corpse is commonly encountered in cases involving a shallow burial during winter months, after which the body is recovered in the late spring or summer. The cold temperatures greatly retard or practically halt the decompositional process. As environmental temperatures slowly warm in the spring, the body begins to desiccate similar to the effect of freeze-drying, thus producing mummification of the corpse (Rodriguez and Bass 1985).

Experimental studies conducted on the decay rate of buried cadavers in Tennessee (Rodriguez and Bass 1983, 1985) and observations on cases in the Northeast have shown that in general, complete skeletonization of a buried corpse at depths of approximately 4 feet or greater takes approximately 2 to 3 years. Complete skeletonization of a body buried at a shallow depth of approximately a foot takes approximately 6 months to a year or more. This is true for most latitudes in North America. The time required for complete degradation of buried skeletal and dental remains is extremely lengthy, with breakdown taking anywhere from several years to hundreds, as demonstrated by the survivability of archaeological specimens. The two most significant factors responsible for the degradation of skeletal remains are soil pH and moisture. Skeletal remains subjected to very wet burial environments can degrade rapidly and be destroyed within a few years. The same is true for skeletal remains if the soil pH is too alkaline or too acidic.

Decomposition of a body submerged in an aquatic environment occurs at a rate roughly half that of decomposition in air. The reduced rate of decomposition in water, like that of buried bodies, results primarily from cooler temperatures and inhibition of insect activity. As in the case of drowning, the victim will proceed to sink downward in the water as air escapes the lungs. The depth and rate at which the victim descends is quite variable and is dependent on a number of factors. With the expulsion of most of the air in the lungs, the decedent will sink to the bottom of the lake, river, or other aquatic body (Donoghue and Minnigerode 1977; Sorg et al. Section V this volume). Once reaching the bottom, the early changes associated with death occur, followed by active decomposition. With the accumulation of decompositional gases in the gastrointestinal tract and lungs, the body will begin to ascend to the surface. Once at the surface, the body will float with the head and limbs hanging down beneath the surface. This position in the water results in the head and limbs exhibiting more lividity than observed on the trunk. At the surface, the body continues to undergo decomposition and therefore attracts carrion insects such as the blowflies which feed and reproduce on the tissues exposed above the surface. Entomological analysis of developing fly larvae on a body which has resurfaced may prove useful in the determination of time at which the body resurfaced.

The time required for the body to resurface is primarily dependent on the water temperature, which typically decreases with depth. With fairly warm water temperatures, a body can be expected to surface within a few days, whereas with cold or near-freezing water temperatures, resurfacing of the body can be delayed for several weeks to several months (Cotton et al. 1987). Other factors which affect the rate of decomposition in water include bacterial content and salinity. A corpse submerged in a stagnant swamp, for example, or a water source polluted with organic wastes, will decompose much more rapidly than a corpse in a relatively clean lake that has a lower bacterial content. Decomposition of a body in the ocean or other salt water sources, undergoes a slower decomposition than would a corpse submerged in fresh water, due to the reduction of bacterial action by the salt concentration. The presence of aquatic animal life may also alter the rate of decomposition and surfacing time by tissue removal, thus providing additional portals of entry for bacteria, or reducing torso body weight.

Adipocere formation is typically observed in bodies submerged for lengthy periods of time. Advanced adipocere formation in submerged bodies will provide some preservation of tissues. There are many documented cases of bodies recovered in relatively good condition after being submerged for months to a few years. One case of particular note involved an elderly male who committed suicide by jumping off a high bridge into a river. The remains of the deceased were not recovered until some 3 years later in northern Louisiana, when they were spotted along the banks of the Red River, at a time when the water level of the river had dropped to a record low due to a drought.

Examination of the remains, which consisted of the lower torso, legs and feet, found them to have undergone advanced adipocere formation followed by complete desiccation. The subject made his fatal jump during cool weather, when his body became permanently entangled in the branches of a large and deeply submerged tree. At the time of recovery, the river level had dropped well below the tree, allowing the adipocere-engulfed remains to mummify, high in the branches of the tree. Positive identification of the decedent was accomplished by radiographic comparison of an antemortem pelvic film.

# Anomalies of Decomposition and Artifactual Preservation

With the multitude of factors affecting the rate of decomposition, it seems only reasonable that anomalies exist, such as cases involving extended preservation or irregular decomposition. Recognition of variations in the decompositional sequence is of extreme importance to the forensic scientist and death investigator, as it may provide clues to circumstances at death.

The first anomaly can be termed "irregular or disproportional decomposition." Irregular decomposition can be defined as the premature or disproportional decomposition of tissues in an area or areas of a body. There are three mechanisms responsible for irregular decomposition (Rodriguez and Bass 1983).

1.  Antemortem or postmortem injury in an area of the body which results in the exposure of blood and underlying tissues, thus providing a portal of entry for carrion insects and bacteria (Rodriguez and Bass 1983).
2.  Exposure of a specific area of the body to physical or chemical agents such as heat or corrosive acids.
3.  Prior local bacterial infection, such as an abscess or cellulitis (Willey and Heilman 1987).

Of these three, the first (antemortem or postmortem injury) is the one most commonly encountered. Cases involving irregular decomposition should be subjected to detailed investigation, as many of these cases are homicides. An excellent example involved the death of a young white adult female whose body was discovered approximately 12 days after her disappearance (Rodriguez and McCormick 1987a). The decedent was reported missing several hours after her failure to return from an evening walk in her neighborhood. Law enforcement officers along with local neighbors conducted extensive and numerous searches for the missing girl.

Twelve days later, her body was discovered in a partially wooded field near the interstate. At the scene, the body was found to be in a fairly advanced state of decomposition with extensive infestation of blowfly larvae. An autopsy was performed although no significant organ material was present. The findings of the autopsy and what little toxicology could be preformed provided no answers as to cause or manner of death.

Approximately 2½ years later, the case was being reviewed by a police detective who questioned whether or not the decedent may have been abducted and held for some period of time and then later killed. A forensic anthropologist was consulted by the case detective concerning an estimate as to the time since death of the decedent. Upon review of scene photographs and environmental data, it was found that the time period for which the decedent had been missing appeared consistent with the state of decomposition. However, it was noted that there appeared to be "irregularities" of the decompositional state which indicated antemortem or postmortem injury to the body. The most notable irregularity observed in the photographs consisted of extensive tissue destruction in the chest and upper abdominal area along with heavy maggot infestation. Also noted was the comparatively large amount of remaining tissue on the skull and the decomposition and maggot infestation in the palms of both hands. Other areas of the decedent's body were noted to be in relatively fair condition. The markedly advanced state of decomposition appeared at first to be the result of carnivore activity. Closer inspection of the scene photos revealed the exposed ribs and costal cartilages to be intact; thus it was unlikely that carnivores were responsible. As for the palmar surfaces of the hands, large scavengers were also ruled out as most of the tendons were undamaged. It was concluded that a strong possibility existed that the decedent had been stabbed in the chest and had suffered defense cuts on the hands. The wounds to the chest and hands provided a portal of entry for bacteria and insects, resulting in areas of premature decomposition. At this point, it was suggested that the body be exhumed. Approximately a year later, the body was exhumed and a detailed examination of skeletal elements in question was conducted. Each of the exposed skeletal elements was carefully removed by hand, as only minor dissection by scalpel was required due to the decomposed state of the surrounding tissues. The elements removed were then wrapped in burlap cloth and carefully cleaned of adhering soft tissue by boiling. Inspection of the cleaned bones revealed several cut marks consistent with knife wounds, on the manubrium and sternebrae, as well as on the palmar surfaces of a few of the metacarpals. Also discovered was a cut mark on the inferior edge of the right second rib. Dark staining was observed along the cut marks, suggesting the injuries to have occurred perimortem. In view of these findings, the cause and manner of death were changed from unknown to death resulting from multiple stab wounds to the chest, and manner of death — homicide.

Cases involving a badly decomposed corpse tend not to be thoroughly examined due to the lack of recognizable soft tissues, the presence of maggot masses, and offensive decompositional odors. Many injuries, such as the ones in the previously discussed case, may not be readily visible on direct visual or radiographic examination, as they are masked by the decompositional debris and repositioned skeletal structures. However, recognition of "irregular decomposition," along with a thorough and detailed examination of the remaining tissues and bones, will many times provide more answers than one might think.

The second decompositional anomaly to be discussed is that which is termed "artifactual preservation." Artifactual preservation refers to the preservation of a body or body tissues by chemical substances, or by destruction of decompositional bacteria. Artifactual preservation may provide a false impression of a relatively short postmortem interval. One example is the tanning of body tissues by tannic acids, such as found in the remarkably preserved bodies from the ancient peat bogs of Denmark. Similar cases of body and tissue preservation have been documented in the forensic literature as the result of the corpse being placed in contact with plant materials such as tree bark, pine needles, decomposing leaves, or leather containing preservative compounds. Naturally occurring tannins leach out from the plant material under moist conditions, and in sufficient concentrations, tan and preserve the body tissues. Leaching of preservative compounds from leather goods in close contact with the body after death, such as tight boots or a leather jacket, may produce preservation of the tissues (Zugibe et al. 1987).

Other examples of artifactual preservation include bodies that have been placed in environments that inhibit bacterial action. One noteworthy case involved a homicide victim whose body had been wrapped in several layers of carpet and plastic sheeting. The body had been hidden in a concrete rental garage and not discovered by authorities until some 3 years later. Unwrapping of the body revealed it to be in excellent preservation, with only moderate skin shrinkage and discoloration. Not only was there remarkable external preservation, but there was also good preservation of the internal organs including the lungs. Other forensic scientists have encountered similar cases in which there has been remarkable preservation of the body or portions thereof which have been tightly covered by plastic or finely woven synthetic fabric.

To better understand this phenomenon, an experiment was conducted which involved the wrapping of body portions in plastic bags (Rodriguez and Bass 1986). Two intact unembalmed cadavers used in this experiment were buried in shallow graves following wrapping. One of the subjects had his left foot wrapped tightly inside two plastic bags, the other subject had his head, lower right arm, and leg wrapped inside doubled plastic bags.

After a period of 9 months and 6 months, respectively, the cadavers were exhumed and examined for gross decomposition changes. It was observed that the tightly wrapped plastic produced marked preservation of the covered tissues in comparison to those areas which were uncovered. Other field and case observations led to the conclusion that the observed preservation resulted from the buildup of bacterial by-products in an enclosed system. Initially, the bacteria acting to degrade the tissues multiply rapidly; however, as their by-products such as ammonia and alcohol increase, along with the pH within the closed system the bacterial action is suppressed. Additionally, oxygen depletion by aerobic bacteria may further retard bacterial life.

Another type of artifactual preservation by suppression of bacterial action is that which has been reported for the recovery of embalmed bodies (Berryman et al., this volume), in particular those buried in historic type caskets made of lead or iron (see Owsley, this volume). In cases involving historic remains, it is believed that in addition to the embalming compounds, the airtight sealing of these caskets by welding with the release of oxidized metals in the form of gases may produce a highly bacterio-static environment. A classic example of a case involving such preservation is that of a Civil War army Colonel (see Bass, this volume).

## Injuries Due to Insect and Terrestrial or Aquatic Animal Life

An exposed body that is not immediately discovered at death becomes increasingly subject to animal depredation with the progression of the postmortem period. Depredation of the corpse by various animals produces a wide array of postmortem injuries that may be easily misinterpreted by the unfamiliar death investigator as being antemortem injuries resulting from human action (Rodriguez and McCormick 1987b). There are five primary animal groups that have been associated with the postmortem depredation of a human corpse. They are insects, birds, rodents, aquatic animals, and mammalian carnivores.

Insects commonly responsible for postmortem injuries include the blowflies, roaches, and ants (Rodriguez and Bass 1983; Spitz 1993:44–47). Blowflies are the first insects to arrive at the corpse. The blowfly larvae upon emerging from their eggs, begin their ravenous feeding on the tissues of the corpse, and in large numbers are capable of tremendous tissue damage. Damage by the larvae is exhibited as small cylindrical bore holes which range from one to several millimeters in size, and mimic wounds produced by an ice pick or a small caliber bullet. An antemortem injury, for example a knife or bullet wound, in many instances will be distorted, enlarged, or made unrecognizable by feeding of the larvae at the injury site. Roaches and ants, like flies, can be commonly found indoors as well as outdoors. Depredation by ants and roaches appears as small erosions on the skin that may give the impression of antemortem abrasions. Drying of these postmortem bites gives the impression of brush type abrasions. In most cases, one can distinguish ant bites from roach bites, as the feeding pattern of ants is less confined, with small linear trails bordering the primary erosion points.

A corpse exposed outdoors is subject to depredation by various types of birds, most commonly vultures and crows. Vultures and crows typically feed on the corpse in the latter stages of decomposition. Injuries to the tissue from crows appear as small triangular shaped punctures resulting from pecking with the beak. The pecking and tearing action used in feeding by buzzards and vultures produces small strips of adherent tissue which has a sinewy type appearance. Smaller birds such as the common sparrow or blackbird will remove head hair, once it has sloughed from the body, for use as building and insulation material for their nests. This may account for the lack of head hair at scenes involving a decomposing body. Locating and searching birds nests near the death scene may be useful in securing the deceased's hair.

Rodents are another group of animals responsible for postmortem depredation of human remains (Haglund et al. 1988, 1989, also this volume; Rossi et al. 1994; Sorg 1985). Bodies exposed indoors in substandard housing are subject to attack by rodents such as mice and rats. Mice and rats are known to feed on a body within the first days following death, producing injuries that resemble antemortem ulcerated skin lesions. The areas of the body typically attacked include the face, scalp, and finger tips. In cases involving skeletal remains, rodents such as mice, rats, squirrels, and rabbits, will gnaw on bones for their mineral content. Common sites for gnawing include along the foramen magnum, eye orbits, mandible, and maxilla of the skull, as well as the long bones. Gnaw marks on bone closely resemble cutmarks by a knife or other sharp-bladed instrument, and may initially appear suspicious when observed on the cervical vertebrae of the neck. Rodent gnaw marks can be distinguished from cut marks by the double-channeled grooving produced by the rodent's incisor teeth. Field mice in particular are infamous for their removal of small bones of the hands and feet, as well as teeth and small jewelry items, which are taken to their burrows. In the case of missing small skeletal elements or teeth at a death scene, it may be well worth the time and trouble to locate nearby rodent burrows and check them for the missing remains.

In addition to destruction due to their gnawing, mice are known to construct burrows inside the mummified remains or skull of a corpse. Aquatic animals, which include sharks (Rathbun and Rathbun 1984, this volume), fish, turtles, and crabs are commonly responsible for postmortem injuries observed on corpses recovered from ponds, lakes, rivers, and oceans (Spitz 1993:44–47). Depredation by small fish is primarily observed on exposed fingers and toes and along the lips and ears, and appears as small erosions of the tissue. Turtles and crabs, on the other hand, produce significant tissue damage during their feeding on the corpse. Most tissue injury produced by turtles is exhibited as large scalloped pits on exposed areas of the body. The size of the pitting will vary with the size of the turtle. Large turtle species such as the alligator snapping turtle are capable of producing crushing injuries to facial bones. Crabs found in bodies of fresh- and saltwater feed on most exposed areas of the body. Crab depredation can in some instances be mistaken for cutting injuries due to the "clean edge" appearance around the denuded feeding site. Depending on the feeding area, one might see small slits in the tissue adjacent to the denuded area which result from the pinchers used to grasp and move along the feeding site.

With the exception of carrion insects, mammalian carnivores are responsible for most cases of postmortem injury by depredation. Small carnivores like raccoons, skunks, and opossums, typically frequent an exposed corpse during the early part of the postmortem period. Areas of the body most commonly attacked are the hands, feet, and upper chest. The injuries produced by their feeding is typical of most carnivores as exhibited by tearing of the tissues, with multiple puncture marks produced by the canines, and linear scratches and tears by the claws. A corpse exposed indoors is subject to depredation by pet cats and dogs. Such cases of pet depredation are commonly seen among the elderly who live alone. One case of particular interest involved an elderly woman who for the most part had been totally consumed by her five dogs. Positive identification of the woman was established through dental comparisons of teeth which were recovered from the fecal remains of the dogs. The presence of urine or fecal material on the deceased, such as in the case of an individual who died while defecating, is commonly responsible for injury specifically to the genitals or buttocks by pet canines.

Larger carnivores, primarily wolves, coyotes, and domestic dogs are known to attack the corpse throughout the postmortem period, including skeletonization. Postmortem injury by these larger carnivores in most cases is quite extensive. Canid carnivores are also responsible in large part for the scattering and removal of bones commonly encountered in cases involving skeletonized remains. Scattering and removal of skeletal elements by coyotes and wolves tend be less than scattering by domestic dogs. Domestic dogs are known to scatter skeletal remains over quite a large area.

Recently a number of studies concerning canid depredation and scavenging of human remains have provided valuable information on the types of bone injury and dispersal patterns (Haglund et al. 1988, 1989; Rodriguez and McCormick 1987b). One study that was reported involved the injuries commonly observed along the eye orbits, maxilla, and occipital area of the skull. These postmortem injuries which appear as fracture and puncture marks, may be misinterpreted as the result of a sharp pointed instrument such as an ice pick. The specific occurrence of these injuries to the facial area of the skull was found to be the result of the skull being transported in the jaws of the canid.

In conclusion, one cannot emphasize enough the importance of possessing a good understanding of postmortem changes. These changes do not merely represent physical alterations to the body, but serve as important clues to answering a number of crucial questions common to death investigation such as: the estimation of the postmortem interval, determination of environmental conditions at and after death, and identification of antemortem injury vs. postmortem artifact.

## References

Catts, E. P., and N.H. Haskell (editors)
    1990 *Entomology and Death: A Procedural Guide.* Joyce's Print Shop, Clemson, SC.

Cotton, G.E., A.C. Aufderheide, and V.G. Goldschmidt
    1987 Preservation of Human Tissue Immersed for Five Years in Fresh Waters of Known Temperature. *Journal of Forensic Sciences* 2:1125–1130.

Donoghue, E.R., and S.C. Minnigerode
    1977 Human Body Buoyancy: A Study of 98 Men. *Journal of Forensic Sciences* 22:573–579.

Haglund, W.D., D.T. Reay, and D.R. Swindler
    1988 Tooth Artifacts and Survival of Bones in Animal-Scavenged Human Skeletons. *Journal of Forensic Sciences* 33:985–997.
    1989 Canid Scavenging/Disarticulation Sequence of Humans in the Pacific Northwest, *Journal of Forensic Sciences* 34:587–606.

Morse, D.
    1983 Time of Death. In *Handbook of Forensic Archaeology,* edited by D. Morse, J. Duncan, and J.W. Stoutamire, pp. 124–127, 148–153. Rose Printing, Tallahassee.

Rathbun, T.A., and B. Rathbun
    1984 Human Remains Recovered from a Shark's Stomach in South Carolina. *Journal of Forensic Sciences* 29:269–276; Chapter 28 in this volume.

Rodriguez, W.C., and W.M. Bass
    1983 Insect Activity and Its Relationship to Decay Rates of Human Cadavers in East Tennessee. *Journal of Forensic Sciences* 23:423–432.
    1985 Decomposition of Buried Bodies and Methods That May Aid in Their Location. *Journal of Forensic Sciences* 30:836–852.
    1986 The Effects of Plastic Bag Containment on the Decompositional Rates of Buried Bodies. Paper presented at the 33rd Annual Meeting of the American Academy of Forensic Sciences, New Orleans.

Rodriguez, W.C., and G.M. McCormick
    1987a Examination of Badly Decomposed Skeletonized Remains — Overlooked Evidence. Paper presented at the 39th Annual Meeting of the American Academy of Forensic Sciences, San Diego.
    1987b Postmortem Animal Activity: Recognition and Interpretation. Paper presented at the 39th Annual Meeting of the American Academy of Forensic Sciences, San Diego.

Rossi, M.L., A.W. Shahrom, R.C. Chapman, and P. Vanezis
    1994 Postmortem Injuries by Indoor Pets. *American Journal of Forensic Medicine and Pathology* 15(2):105–109.

Smith, G.V.
    1986 *A Manual of Forensic Entomology.* Cornell University Press, Ithaca, NY.

Sorg, M.H.
   1985   Scavenger Modification of Human Remains. *Current Research in the Pleistocene*
   2:37–38.

Spitz, W.U.
   1993   *Spitz and Fisher's Medicolegal Investigation of Death.* 3rd ed. Charles C Thomas,
   Springfield, IL.

Willey, P., and A. Heilman
   1987   Estimating Time Since Death Using Plant Roots and Stems. *Journal of Forensic
   Sciences* 32:1264–1270.

Zugibe, F.T., J.F. Costello, and M.K. Breghaupt
   1987   The Man in the Mask. *Journal of Forensic Sciences* 32:310.

# Decomposition Rates of Deliberate Burials: A Case Study of Preservation

# 30

## MARY H. MANHEIN

## Introduction

A fascination with postmortem modification of human remains in burial contexts extends back to ancient times when preliterate societies searched for explanations for natural phenomena associated with death and decay. The mysteries and attendant explanations surrounding variation in rates of decay of soft tissue and skeletonization have generated much speculation and many a hair-raising tale in both ancient and modern lore (Barber 1988; Evans 1963a, 1963b; Mant 1957, 1987; Micozzi 1991). In recent history, curiosity about the decomposition processes specific to buried human remains has received renewed attention from anthropologists. Researchers are striving to understand the processes impacting preservation of buried remains in both archaeological and forensic contexts (Galloway et al. 1989; Garland 1987; Mann et al. 1990; Mellen et al. 1993; Rodriguez and Bass 1985). An understanding of those processes can aid in more accurately assessing antiquity of ancient remains in bioarchaeological settings and postmortem interval for those forensic cases in which date of death is unknown.

By studying both ancient and recent burial preservation, the forensic anthropologist is in a better position to evaluate those natural processes at work universally and other forces at work that are specific to a particular case. Of special interest is whether or not predictive models may be established to assist in the estimate of time since death.

The first section of this chapter briefly summarizes the type of preservation documented over the last decade in burials from archaeological and forensic contexts in Louisiana. The second section of the chapter reports the results of a national survey of practicing forensic anthropologists who have encountered deliberate burials. This survey extends across broad geographical areas and has the potential to set the stage for further research on preservation of buried human remains.

## Preservation of Archaeological Burials in Louisiana

Soft tissue survival on prehistoric bodies is usually due to such factors as waterlogging, preservation in peat bogs, or desiccation in hot sands or tombs with good air circulation (Brothwell 1986). Most of these criteria are not met in Louisiana. Preservation of soft tissue in burials in prehistoric settings in Louisiana's subtropic climate is almost nonexistent. In fact, preservation of bones is usually poor, with prehistoric burials often consisting of fragmented tooth enamel and bone meal (Manhein 1985, 1992b; Ramenofsky and Mires 1985).

A typical example of this type of poor preservation comes from the Crooks Site in LaSalle Parish in central Louisiana. Works Progress Administration (WPA) excavations of the 1930s documented the fragmented bony outlines of more than 1000 human burials from this large

0-8493-9434-1/97/$0.00+$.50
© 1997 by CRC Press, Inc.

earthen mound site. Museum collections, however, contain the fragmented remains of fewer than 100 persons. Records and photographs from the excavations document the poor quality of bone preservation in this archaeological site from approximately 1500 years ago. Louisiana's climate and soil conditions are cited as major contributing factors to the poor preservation at this site (Ford and Willey 1940; Manhein 1985).

Some exceptions to the poor preservation in prehistoric sites in Louisiana include the Morton Shell Mound in Iberia Parish (Robbins 1976) and the Tchefuncte Site in St. Tammany Parish (Lewis 1993), where bone is well preserved and can be used to document the demographics and health of earlier Louisiana populations. The good preservation at these two sites is due in part to the neutralization of surrounding soils by leaching from *Rangia* (clam) shells found in the burial matrix.

Historic burials in Louisiana do not fare much better than prehistoric ones. They are usually discovered in a salvage archaeology context where urban renewal or vandalism has drawn attention to old public and private cemeteries which have faded from local memory. Representative of these types of burials (rarely buried deeper than 3 to 4 feet) are those from the American Civil War. Preservation is similar to the prehistoric burials and one typically finds only bone meal and fragmented teeth (Manhein and Whitmer 1989, 1992; Manhein et al. 1991).

An exception to this poor preservation in historic burials is in the cemeteries of New Orleans where soil with a high clay content provides conditions which facilitate preservation (Owsley et al. 1985, 1987). Other exceptions are scattered throughout the state in isolated metal coffin burials and/or above-ground vault burials that may or may not include embalmed bodies. Embalming procedures have been practiced in the U.S. for more than 100 years and might account for some tissue preservation in these historic burials. Such burials occasionally exhibit good bone preservation with hair, desiccated skin, and hardened brain tissue preserved. One example of this type of burial preservation is an above-ground vault burial of a young woman who died in 1859. Buried less than 5 miles away from the earlier-noted Civil War soldiers who had very little bone preserved, she had excellent bone preservation as well as good preservation of hair, desiccated tissue, and clothing (Manhein 1992a).

Rarer still are the few wooden coffin or noncoffin historic burials in Louisiana where some type of metal object, such as a button or safety pin, found near or on a body aids in preservation of an isolated tissue fragment and/or bone (Hunter et al. 1994; Manhein et al. 1991). However, even in recent historic burials, such as that of Dr. Carl Austin Weiss in 1935 (the alleged assassin of Huey Long), one finds poorly preserved soft tissue remains in a sealed-vault burial, most likely a result of Louisiana's moisture-laden climate (Starrs et al. 1992).

In these bioarchaeological settings, taphonomic studies which include those forces that impact tissue decomposition of both an anaerobic and aerobic nature assist in understanding the complexities for decomposition in more recent settings (Bethell and Carver 1988; Evans 1963a; Garland 1987; Henderson 1987; Mant 1987; Micozzi 1991; Payne 1965). Included among these are studies of diagenesis which assist in understanding how macro- and microenvironmental processes such as climate, soil pH, and access to ground water impact skeletal integrity once a body has been buried for a substantial period of time (Whitmer et al. 1987). These types of studies usually relate to those burials outside the realm of forensic anthropology (generally, cases older than 75 years), but they can be used in forensic anthropology as investigative models for understanding the role that environment and other factors play in the dynamics of preservation in a particular geographical area.

## Preservation of Forensic Burials in Louisiana

For those anthropologists working in the applied field of forensics, an estimate of time since death has become a routine element in the case profile. Rates of decay are valuable evidence for reconstructing past events and for determining time since death. In above-ground forensic cases, consultation with forensic entomologists often adds invaluable expertise in our determination of the interval since death. The entomologist can usually pinpoint the time since death, and that assistance is especially helpful when the person has been dead for a short period of time, or, specifically, before all soft tissue has completely decomposed (Goeff 1992; Mann et al. 1990; Meek and Andrews 1992; Reichs 1986; Stewart 1979). Buried bodies present a different challenge (Bass 1986).

On occasion, forensic anthropologists have the opportunity to assist in burial exhumations in a medicolegal context. These circumstances usually arise out of personal association with a local coroner or medical examiner who is well aware of the expertise which properly trained forensic anthropologists can bring to a criminal investigation. The buried bodies in these types of cases are usually discovered in one of two ways, by assistance from an informant or by accident (Levine et al. 1984; Morse 1983; Wolf 1986).

Only a few studies provide insight into the mysteries surrounding decay of buried bodies in recent times (Evans 1963a, 1963b; Mant 1957, 1987; Payne 1965; Rodriguez and Bass 1985). These include ongoing research at the University of Tennessee in Knoxville where anthropologists have documented both surface and subsurface decomposition (Mann et al. 1990). A few other studies have looked at decomposition in various depositional settings, including aquatic environments (Cotton et al. 1987; Haglund 1993; Mellen et al. 1993; Micozzi 1991) and dry climates (Galloway et al. 1989).

The following case histories from Louisiana are representative of the situations one encounters in trying to understand the impact of postmortem processes in the estimation of time since death. Since the known time of disappearance is available for these cases, the degree of preservation in their histories provides data for others who encounter similar burial contexts. They will also be compared to other cases from across the country.

## Case 1

An informant told authorities about a murder victim, an older white male, who was allegedly buried on the banks of a river between the river and the levee, less than 50 yards from the river's edge. The burial had taken place approximately 4½ years prior to the informant's confession. Retrieval efforts resulted in location of the body approximately 2½ feet below the surface.

The body was sealed in heavy plastic and was secured with tape. Initial examination at the scene indicated that the person was lying on his stomach. Extensive adipocere was present, with pink coloring visible in some muscle tissue, and an intense odor of putrefaction. The skull was in several pieces, but the rest of the body was somewhat intact with buttocks clearly visible. An autopsy confirmed multiple gun shot wounds to the head with additional high velocity trauma. Though dental identification was not possible (no available records for the few fragmented teeth), positive identification was made by using fingerprints from disarticulated fingers, after almost 5 years of burial. Further analysis of contents from the bag suggested that lime may have been placed with the remains.

## Case 2

A young, white female's skeleton was discovered accidentally in a grave less than 4 feet deep on the side of the house where she had once lived. She had been missing for approximately 8 years. She was wrapped in a polyester mattress cover and was wearing clothing. A large volume of adipocere was present as were multiple signs of perimortem trauma. Her grave had experienced periodic water seepage because it was in the direct path of drainage for a septic tank at the back of the house.

## Case 3

The body of a middle-aged white male was discovered accidentally in a shallow grave, less than 18 in. deep. Dental identification confirmed that he was a person who had been missing approximately 3½ months (winter months) when the body was found. He was clothed in a warm-up suit, bound, and wrapped in a vinyl tablecloth. Carnivore activity had partially uncovered the body and had allowed insect access for a minimum of 3 weeks prior to discovery. The left side of his body (shoulder and thoracic region) was closest to the surface and was skeletonized. The right side of his body, face, and lower extremities were well preserved and suitable for autopsy. Putrefactive tissue was present in those areas of the body exposed through animal activity.

## Case 4

The body of an older, white male was discovered in a concrete crawl space beneath the porch of a house. He had been missing for approximately 17 years. The crawl space was not unlike an above-ground tomb one might see throughout Louisiana except that it had a dirt floor (some of the tombs also have dirt floors). The bones were in excellent condition, and small amounts of desiccated tissue and adipocere were present. A few strands of hair were also present on his scalp. His overall appearance was similar to remains found in above-ground vault burials in Louisiana from the 1800s.

## Case 5

This case is somewhat different from the other four in that it is the case of a cat's burial. Although not a part of the survey data, the circumstances in this case warrant discussion. The cat was illegally buried in an above-ground vault. It was sealed in a plastic blanket storage bag. Authorities believe that the cat's owners convinced someone to open the vault and entomb their beloved cat in an already-occupied tomb. They then resealed the tomb. Seventeen years later (documented by notes in the bag), vandals broke into the tomb at night, discovered the bag, opened it, and fled. The odor arising from the bag was most foul, for the cat was still quite well preserved, after 17 years in a plastic bag.

# Discussion

These representative cases from Louisiana illustrate the importance of several variables which influence preservation in this subtropic environment (see Table 1). In a climate where a body left on the surface can be completely skeletonized in 2 weeks (especially during summer months), burial coverings and contexts offer startling contrasts. Multiple variables dramatically alter normal decomposition. In my work in Louisiana, I have found that the use of plastic and other synthetic products to cover bodies greatly retards decomposition. Some research has documented that coverings over recently buried bodies can impact preservation of soft tissue to varying degrees (Mann et al. 1990). Evans (1963a) and Mant (1957) have also noted this, but some of their major studies included burials which had taken place prior to the advent of wholesale production and use of synthetics and before these synthetics became a typical part of the burial artifact.

In cases such as these where decomposition is retarded, the formation of adipocere and its volume and retention vary greatly. Adipocere forms in both surface and subsurface depositions; yet, earlier researchers believed that adipocere did not form without the presence and persistence of moisture. Both Mant (1957, 1987) and Evans (1963b) found that this was not necessarily the case, with adipocere forming in fairly dry conditions in multiple cases. Though some water is required for the initial production of adipocere, that water source may simply

**Table 1    Preservation Factors in Louisiana Cases**

|  | Case 1 | Case 2 | Case 3 | Case 4 | Case 5 |
|---|---|---|---|---|---|
| Depth | 3 ft | 3 ft | 18 in | Surface | Surface |
| Context | River edge | Moist grave | Shallow grave | Covered porch | Vault |
| Time since death | 4.5 years | 8 years | 3 mo. | 17 years | 17 years |
| Adipocere | Large | Large | None | Small | None |
| Cover |  |  |  |  |  |
|   Natural fiber |  |  |  | X |  |
|   Synthetic | X | X | X |  | X |

be the body's own moisture. Other researchers had also suggested that adipocere may not be visible on the body until 2 months or more after death (Stewart 1979).

The range of variation of preservation factors in Louisiana cases suggested several areas of focus for a national survey of forensic cases. In particular, information was needed about types of covering, the presence of adipocere across broad geographical areas, and the influence of varied climates on preservation.

## Survey of Practicing Forensic Anthropologists

The purpose of the survey was to begin a data bank about preservation of buried bodies. The survey instrument (see Figure 1) includes the following variables: time since death, depth, covering, tissue preservation, bone preservation, presence or absence of adipocere, and weighted variables of greatest impact on preservation.

The survey was sent to members of the American Academy of Forensic Sciences under the Physical Anthropology Section (excluding students). Though these were mainly forensic anthropologists associated with academic institutions, they also included anthropologists working for coroners' offices, medical examiners' offices, and museums.

Almost 50% of those persons polled returned the survey form. Respondents included 12 anthropologists with no cases, those with a minimum of one case, and others whose case loads have included as many as 10 to 12 burials.

Cases were contributed from 17 states and 2 Canadian provinces (Figure 2). At least one response from each area was recorded as a response for that state or province. Some states, such as California, had multiple respondents.

All cases are presented as the burial data set in Table 2. Of the 87 sets 24 (or approximately 27.6%) were surface depositions.

Initially, the case data can have broad appeal. Of those 63 cases that were buried, 50 (79%) were recovered from depositions of 1 to 3 feet (Table 3) and only 12 (19%) were buried at depths greater than 3 feet. Of those 12 buried deeper than 3 feet, 11 were coffin burials, and only one (Case #46 from Louisiana) was a noncoffin burial.

Twenty-three burials from diverse geographical locations and from varying depths contained at least some evidence of adipocere (three of these were coffin burials). Results suggest that depth, if plotted alone, may play a reduced role in formation or retention of adipocere. However, when the variables of depth and covering are combined, the results are relevant. Of all noncoffin burial cases with adipocere, coverings were present in 17 of 20 cases (85%) (Table 4).

In this survey, 13 of 24 reported surface cases listed presence of adipocere in small to large quantities. Eleven (85%) of the 13 cases had some type of covering over the body. The number of surface cases with adipocere is interesting, but is a factor of selecting those surface cases to include in cases sent to me because something about them was deemed significant. Of greater relevance than the total number of surface cases with adipocere is the fact that a

```
Respondent:
Agency:

                              Case #:        Case #:        Case #:

Year Recovered:

Time Since Death:

Burial Depth
        Surface
        Less than 2'
        More than 2'
Burial Covering
        Blanket
        Sleeping Bag
        Plastic
        Other
Soft Tissue Preservation
        Poor
        Good
        Excellent
Bone Preservation
        Poor
        Good
        Excellent
Adipocere
        Pres/small qty
        Pres/lg. qty.
        Absent
Soil pH (if known)

Trauma for each case:

Variable with greatest impact on preservation (rate 1, 2, 3, 4, with "1"
being variable of greatest impact):

        Covering
        Climate
        Soil
        Preservative
        Other           _____        _____        _____

General Comments:
```

**Figure 1**  LSU burial case survey instrument.

major percentage of those with adipocere had coverings of some kind. More importantly, some of the surface cases exhibited discernable amounts of adipocere less than 2 months after death — two as recently as 2 to 3 weeks after death.

Since data from this survey suggest that evidence of adipocere formation can be seen early after death, these data can be used as a springboard for further controlled studies on adipocere. Such studies could confirm adipocere's detection at an early phase in the decomposition process and assist in assessment of postmortem interval.

The survey also confirms that adipocere can be retained in a burial for many years. Cases from Louisiana show large amounts of adipocere in burials that are 5 and 8 years old, respectively, but the survey indicates that adipocere can be present for as long as 122 years in one coffin burial and absent in an adjoining coffin of the same vintage. In those two cases (#75 and #76), volume of body fat may have played a major role (Pfeiffer 1993). Also, preservation in coffin cases may be impacted by embalming practices. One case from Louisiana (#50) was embalmed. This case had been buried for 8 years. Adipocere and soft tissue were present throughout the body, and water seepage into the casket had obviously taken place.

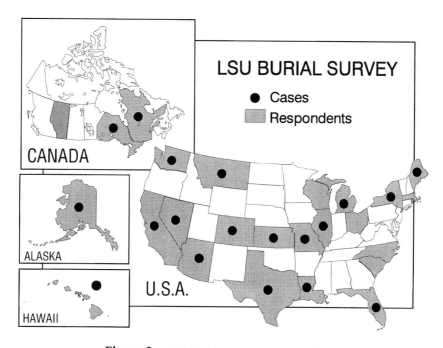

**Figure 2**     LSU burial case survey respondents.

**Table 2     Cases Reported in Burial Survey**

| Case No. | State | Death (years) | Depth (ft) | Covering | Adipocere | Climate Impact[a] |
|---|---|---|---|---|---|---|
| 1 | AK | 2.00 | 0 | Clothing | None | 2 |
| 2 | AZ | 1.08 | 1.5 | Plastic | Large | 2 |
| 3 | AZ | 14.00 | 2.5 | Plastic | None | — |
| 4 | CA | 2.00 | 0 | Brush | None | 1 |
| 5 | CA | 2.00 | 2.5 | Clothing | Small | 3 |
| 6 | CA | 0.25 | 1.5 | Clothing | Large | 2 |
| 7 | CA | 5.00 | 2.5 | Clothing | None | 1 |
| 8 | CA | 0.25 | 2.5 | Blanket, clothing | Large | 3 |
| 9 | CA | 0.08 | 2.5 | Clothing | Large | 3 |
| 10 | CA | 0.10 | 0 | Brush, clothing | Large | 1 |
| 11 | CA | 0.08 | 0 | Plastic bags | Large | 2 |
| 12 | CA | 3.00 | 2.5 | Blanket, clothing | Small | 3 |
| 13 | CA | 0.15 | 0 | Brush | Large | 1 |
| 14 | CA | 0.04 | 0 | Clothing, plastic | Large | 2 |
| 15 | CA | 0.04 | 0 | Blanket, clothing | Large | 2 |
| 16 | CA | 0.15 | 2.5 | Clothing | Small | 3 |
| 17 | CA | 0.33 | 0 | Sleeping bag | None | 2 |
| 18 | CA | 3.25 | 5 | Casket, crypt | None | — |
| 19 | CA | 1.00 | 1.5 | Clothing | None | 2 |
| 20 | CA | 1.00 | 1.5 | Clothing | None | 2 |
| 21 | CA | 1.08 | 0 | Clothing | Small | 1 |
| 22 | CO | 10.00 | 2.5 | None | None | 1 |
| 23 | CO | 10.00 | 2.5 | None | None | 1 |
| 24 | CO | 10.00 | 2.5 | None | None | 1 |
| 25 | CO | 4.00 | 2.5 | None | None | — |
| 26 | CO | 0.06 | 0 | None | Large | — |

**Table 2 (continued)   Cases Reported in Burial Survey**

| Case No. | State | Death (years) | Depth (ft) | Covering | Adipocere | Climate Impact[a] |
|---|---|---|---|---|---|---|
| 27 | FL | 0.03 | 1.5 | Clothing | None | 1 |
| 28 | FL | 1.08 | 2.5 | Clothing | None | 2 |
| 29 | FL | 0.04 | 0 | Clothing | None | 1 |
| 30 | FL | 7.00 | 1.5 | Clothing | None | 2 |
| 31 | FL | 7.00 | 1.5 | Clothing | None | — |
| 32 | FL | 7.00 | 1.5 | Clothing | None | — |
| 33 | FL | 1.00 | 2.5 | Sleeping bag | Large | 2 |
| 34 | FL | 3.00 | 1.5 | None | Large | 2 |
| 35 | FL | 3.00 | 1.5 | None | None | 2 |
| 36 | FL | 3.00 | 1.5 | None | None | 2 |
| 37 | FL | 2.00 | 2.5 | Plastic | — | 3 |
| 38 | HI | 2.00 | 0 | None | Small | 1 |
| 39 | IL | 0.33 | 1.5 | None | None | — |
| 40 | KS | 0.17 | 0 | Clothing | Large | 2 |
| 41 | KS | 0.17 | 0 | Clothing | None | 1 |
| 42 | KS | 0.54 | 1.5 | Clothing | — | — |
| 43 | LA | 8.00 | 3 | Clothing, mattress cover | Large | 3 |
| 44 | LA | 17.00 | 0 | Concrete vault | Small | 2 |
| 45 | LA | 4.00 | 1.5 | Sleeping bag | Large | 3 |
| 46 | LA | 4.00 | 4 | Blanket, clothing | Small | 3 |
| 47 | LA | 4.50 | 3 | Plastic | Large | 4 |
| 48 | LA | 4.50 | .5 | Clothing | None | 2 |
| 49 | LA | 0.25 | 1 | Clothing, vinyl | — | 2 |
| 50 | LA | 8.00 | 6 | Casket, clothing | Large | 4 |
| 51 | ME | 4.00 | 2.5 | Blanket, plastic, rug | None | 3 |
| 52 | MI | 11.00 | 1.5 | Clothing | None | — |
| 53 | MO | 2.00 | 1.5 | — | — | — |
| 54 | MO | 2.00 | 1.5 | — | — | — |
| 55 | MO | 2.00 | 1.5 | — | — | — |
| 56 | MO | 2.00 | 1.5 | — | Large | 2 |
| 57 | MO | 2.00 | 1.5 | — | Large | — |
| 58 | MO | 5.00 | 0 | Clothing | None | 1 |
| 59 | MT | 51.00 | 1.5 | Wood packing crate | None | 1 |
| 60 | MT | 1.50 | 1.5 | Rag, styrofoam chest | Small | 2 |
| 61 | MT | 1.00 | 0 | Clothing | Small | 1 |
| 62 | MT | 100.00 | 2.5 | None | None | 1 |
| 63 | NV | 90.00 | 6 | Coffin | None | 1 |
| 64 | NV | 90.00 | 6 | Wooden coffin | None | 1 |
| 65 | NV | 67.00 | 2 | Crypt–metal coffin | None | 1 |
| 66 | NV | 67.00 | 6 | Wooden coffin | None | — |
| 67 | NV | 101.00 | 6 | Wooden coffin | None | 1 |
| 68 | NV | 99.00 | 6 | Wooden coffin | None | 1 |
| 69 | NV | 92.00 | 6 | Wooden coffin | None | 1 |
| 70 | NY | 2.00 | 1.5 | Blanket | Large | — |
| 71 | NY | 1.00 | 2.5 | Clothing, plastic | Small | — |
| 72 | NY | 9.00 | 1.5 | Clothing | None | 1 |
| 73 | NY | 0.33 | 0 | Clothing | Large | 1 |
| 74 | ON | 1.83 | 1.5 | Cremated remains | — | — |
| 75 | ON | 122.00 | 4 | Coffin (double) | Large | — |
| 76 | ON | 121.00 | 4 | Coffin (double) | None | — |
| 77 | QU | 0.67 | 1.5 | Plastic | None | 2 |
| 78 | QU | 0.13 | 0 | Shoes | None | 2 |

**Table 2 (continued)   Cases Reported in Burial Survey**

| Case No. | State | Death (years) | Depth (ft) | Covering | Adipocere | Climate Impact[a] |
|---|---|---|---|---|---|---|
| 79 | QU | 4.00 | 0 | Boots, coat | None | 1 |
| 80 | TX | 0.42 | 0 | Blanket, plastic | Small | — |
| 81 | TX | 36.00 | 4 | Casket | Small | — |
| 82 | TX | 3.00 | 1 | Boulders | — | 1 |
| 83 | WA | 0.83 | 2.58 | Sleeping bag | Large | 2 |
| 84 | WA | 12.00 | 0 | Plastic | — | — |
| 85 | WA | 12.00 | 0 | Plastic | — | — |
| 86 | WA | 12.00 | 0 | Plastic | — | — |
| 87 | WA | 0.50 | 2.5 | Blanket, clothing | Large | — |

[a]   Compiled from survey instrument. Variable with greatest impact on preservation (rated 1, 2, 3, 4, with "1" being variable of greatest impact): choices are covering, climate, soil, preservative, other.

**Table 3   Depth of Cases Reported**

| Depth (ft) | Cases Reported Number | Cases Reported Percent |
|---|---|---|
| 0–1 | 27 | 31 |
| 1–2 | 27 | 31 |
| 2–3 | 21 | 24 |
| 3–4 | 4 | 5 |
| 4–5 | 1 | 1 |
| 5–6 | 7 | 8 |
| Total | 87 | 100 |

**Table 4   Presence of Adipocere in Non-Coffin-Buried Cases**

| Covering Present Depth < 2 ft. N | % | Depth > 2 ft. N | % | Covering Absent Depth < 2 ft. N | % | Depth > 2 ft. N | % | Total N | % |
|---|---|---|---|---|---|---|---|---|---|
| 5[a] | 25 | 12 | 60 | 3 | 15 | 0 | 0 | 20 | 100 |

[a]   Does not include 13 surface cases with adipocere.

Adipocere formation in cases with trauma has been another area of interest for those researchers examining preservation of buried bodies. Some of the burial cases in this survey had perimortem trauma, such as high velocity, blunt force, sharp instrument, or combinations of those; these also contained medium to large amounts of adipocere. Generally, trauma accelerates the decomposition process, but is its impact on the formation of adipocere under certain circumstances major or negligible? Evans (1963a) notes that time exposed to the environment after death and before burial can play a role in the formation of adipocere — the longer a body is exposed to the environment the more likely putrefactive organisms will begin their work and, therefore, reduce the opportunity for the formation of adipocere. Case #50 from Louisiana had experienced dramatic perimortem trauma to the skull, had been embalmed, and had large amounts of adipocere present. However, additional data must be collected before suggestions can be made about the role of trauma in adipocere formation and retention.

In addition to adipocere, preservation of soft tissue in burials is a critical variable. Of the burial cases in this survey, 17 exhibited soft tissue preservation. Cases similar to case study

#1 from Louisiana where tissue and adipocere were present contain information which can be vital to the identification process. If fingerprints can still be found after almost 5 years of burial in plastic coverings, the possibility that other identifying markers, such as tatoos, might also be preserved, is quite good. Law enforcement and others can be made aware of the potential for finding them.

Climate is another variable where its impact on preservation of buried bodies has not been well studied (Mann et al. 1990). This survey asked participants to rank four variables which had greatest impact on preservation (Figure 1). Climate was viewed as an important variable and often received a score of "2" or better on a scale of 1 to 4, with 1 being the variable of greatest impact. These rankings suggest that one future avenue for controlled studies regarding preservation should include climate as a major variable.

Finally, the concept of "burial" also includes cases that can be referred to as "urban burials," where bodies are covered in a variety of ways and dumped in abandoned buildings, garages, or other storage facilities. Though not traditional burials, their preservation is impacted by coverings and many other factors. Decomposition rates of these cases may be predictable if data are recorded over broad areas.

## Conclusion

This chapter has briefly outlined the wide variation found in preservation of buried bodies in Louisiana and reported preliminary results of a survey concerning buried forensic cases nationwide. The results, though intriguing in many areas, point to the need for further data collection. In addition, problems with collecting data arise from different interpretations of requested data. For example, the impact of climate in the preservation process was only examined in a cursory manner in this general survey. Respondents' comments indicated that more specific information in regard to recording such variables as climate was needed. To overcome such a problem, climatic conditions specific to each case's microenvironment need to be recorded in such a way as to be universally tabulated. As suggested by several contributors, input from other anthropologists on ways to make the survey instrument more comprehensive can lead to tighter control over these categories of information. Scattered data sets can then be more uniformly reported and can offer more reliable data for predicting expectations for preservation under certain circumstances.

Continued interest and participation in this project is encouraged, with further input on the data request form and additional burial case data being directed to me.

## Acknowledgments

I would like to thank the more than 40 people who contributed data to the original survey. I also thank Dr. Robert Tague for his editorial assistance.

## References

Barber, P.
  1988   *Vampires, Burial, and Death.* Yale University Press, New Haven, CT.

Bass, W.M.
  1986   Time Interval Since Death, A Difficult Decision. In *Human Identification: Case Studies in Forensic Anthropology,* edited by T.A. Rathbun and J.E. Buikstra, pp. 136–147. Charles C Thomas, Springfield, IL.

Bethell, P.H., and M.O.H. Carver
    1988   Detection and Enhancement of Decayed Inhumations at Sutton Hoo. In *Death, Decay, and Reconstruction: Approaches to Archaeology and Forensic Sciences*, edited by A. Boddington, A.N. Garland, and R.C. Janaway, pp. 10–21. Manchester University Press, Manchester, U.K.

Brothwell, D.R.
    1986   *The Bogman and the Archaeology of People*. British Museum, London.

Cotton, G.E., A.C. Aufderheide, and V.G. Goldschmidt
    1987   Preservation of Human Tissue Immersed for Five Years in Fresh Water of Known Temperature. *Journal of Forensic Sciences* 32:1125–1130.

Evans, W.E.
    1963a Adipocere Formation in a Relatively Dry Environment. *Medicine, Science, and the Law* 3:145–153.
    1963b *The Chemistry of Death*. Charles C Thomas, Springfield, IL.

Ford, J.A., and G. Willey
    1940   *Crooks Site, A Marksville Period Burial Mound in LaSalle Parish, Louisiana*. Anthropological Study No. 3. State of Louisiana Department of Conservation. Louisiana Geological Survey, New Orleans.

Galloway, A., W.H. Birkby, A. Jones, T.E. Henry, and B.O. Parks
    1989   Decay Rates of Human Remains in an Arid Environment. *Journal of Forensic Sciences* 34:606–616.

Garland, A.N.
    1987   A Histological Study of Archaeological Bone Decomposition. In *Death, Decay, and Reconstruction*, edited by A. Boddington, A.N. Garland, and R.C. Janaway, pp. 109–126. Manchester University Press, Manchester, U.K.

Goeff, M.L.
    1992   Problems in Estimation of Postmortem Interval Resulting from Wrapping of the Corpse: A Case Study from Hawaii. *Journal of Agriculture Entomology* 9:237–243.

Haglund, W.D.
    1993   Disappearance of Soft Tissue and the Disarticulation of Human Remains from Aqueous Environments. *Journal of Forensic Sciences* 38:806–815.

Henderson, J.
    1987   Factors Determining the State of Preservation of Human Remains. In *Death, Decay, and Reconstruction*, edited by A. Boddington, A.N. Garland, and R.C. Janaway, pp 43–54. Manchester University Press, Manchester, U.K.

Hunter, D.J., J.T. Kutruff, and M.H. Manhein
    1994   The Mound at Phillip Nick's Place (16AV4) (Avoyelles Parish, Louisiana). *Mississippi Archaeology* 29(1):17–82.

Levine, L.J., H.R. Campbell, Jr., and S. Rhine
    1984   Perpendicular Forensic Archaeology. In *Human Identification in Forensic Anthropology*, edited by T.A. Rathbun and J.E. Buikstra, pp. 87–95. Charles C Thomas, Springfield, IL.

Lewis, B.
    1993   Treponematosis and Lyme Borreliosis Connections: Explanation for Tchefuncte Disease Syndromes? *American Journal of Physical Anthropology* 93:455–475.

Manhein, M.H.
    1985   Louisiana's Human Skeletal Material: Anthropology's Responsibility to the Past. Master's thesis, Louisiana State University, Baton Rouge.

1992a A Witch Named Alice. Paper presented at the 44th Annual Meeting of the American Academy of Forensic Sciences Last Word Society, New Orleans.

1992b Preservation of Human Remains in the Deep South — the Human Variable. Paper presented at the 44th Annual Meeting of the American Academy of Forensic Sciences, New Orleans.

Manhein, M.H., and A.M. Whitmer

1989  *1988 Investigations of the Port Hudson Military and Civilian Cemeteries (16EF68).* Report submitted to the Division of Archaeology, Department of Culture, Recreation, and Tourism, State of Louisiana, Baton Rouge.

1992  *1991 Archaeological Investigations at the Port Hudson State Commemorative Area (16EF7) Steadman House and Burial Area 2.* Report submitted to the Division of Archaeology, Department of Culture, Recreation, and Tourism, State of Louisiana, Baton Rouge.

Manhein, M.H., A.M. Whitmer, and J.M. Mitchem

1991  *Archaeological Investigations at Four Localities within the Boundaries of the Port Hudson State Commemorative Area (16EF7).* Report submitted to the Division of Archaeology, Department of Culture, Recreation, and Tourism, State of Louisiana, Baton Rouge.

Mann, R.W., W.M. Bass, and L. Meadows

1990  Time since Death and Decomposition of the Human Body: Variables and Observations in Case and Experimental Field Studies. *Journal of Forensic Sciences* 35:103–111.

Mant, A.K.

1957  Adipocere — A Review. *Journal of Forensic Medicine* 4(1):18–35.

1987  Knowledge Acquired from Post-war Exhumations. In *Death, Decay, and Reconstruction,* edited by A. Boddington, A.N. Garland, and R.C. Janaway, pp. 65–78. Manchester University Press, Manchester, U.K.

Meek, C.L., and C.S. Andrews

1992  Standard Techniques and Procedures at the Death Scene. In *Entomology and Death: A Procedural Guide,* edited by E.P. Catts and N.H. Haskell, pp. 72–81. Joyce's Print Shop, Clemson, SC.

Mellen, P.F.M., M.A. Lowry, and M.S. Micozzi

1993  Experimental Observation on Adipocere Formation. *Journal of Forensic Sciences* 38:91–93.

Micozzi, M.S.

1991  *Postmortem Changes in Human and Animal Remains.* Charles C Thomas, Springfield, IL.

Morse, D., J. Duncan, and J. Stoutamire

1983  *Handbook of Forensic Archaeology.* Rose Printing, Tallahassee.

Owsley, D.W., M.H. Manhein, and M.K. Marks

1987  Burial Archaeology and Osteology of Charity Hospital/Cypress Grove II Cemetery, New Orleans. Report of Investigations (progress report I), submitted to the City of New Orleans, Federal Highway Administration, and Louisiana Department of Transportation and Development. Baton Rouge, LA.

Owsley, D.W., C.E. Orser, R. Montgomery, and C.C. Holland

1985  An Archaeological and Physical Anthropological Study of the First Cemetery in New Orleans, Louisiana. Unpublished report submitted to Louisiana Division of Archaeology, Office of Culture, Recreation, and Tourism, Baton Rouge.

Payne, J.A.

1965  A Summer Carrion Study of the Baby Pig *Sus scrofa* Linnaeus. *Ecology* 46:592–602.

Pfeiffer, S.
  1993   Factors Contributing to Adipocere Formation and its Effect on Bone Preservation. Paper presented at the 45th Annual Meeting of the American Academy of Forensic Sciences, Boston.

Ramenofsky, A.F., and A.M. Mires
  1985   *The Archaeology of Cowpen Slough, 16CT147.* Report submitted to the Division of Archaeology, Office of Culture, Recreation, and Tourism, State of Louisiana, Baton Rouge.

Reichs, C. (editor)
  1986   *Forensic Osteology: Advances in the Identification of Human Remains.* Charles C Thomas, Springfield, IL.

Robbins, L.M.
  1976   Analysis of Human Skeletal Material from Morton Shell Mound (16IB3), Iberia Parish, Louisiana. Report on file at Department of Geography and Anthropology, Louisiana State University, Baton Rouge.

Rodriguez, W.C., and W.M. Bass
  1985   Decomposition of Buried Bodies and Methods That May Aid in Their Location. *Journal of Forensic Sciences* 30:836–852.

Starrs, J.E., I.M. Sopher, D.H. Ubelaker, A. Poklis, and H.C. Haag
  1992   A Blaze of Bullets: a Scientific Investigation into the Deaths of Senator Huey P. Long and Dr. Carl Austin Weiss. Paper presented at the 44th Annual Meeting of the American Academy of Forensic Sciences, New Orleans.

Stewart, T.D.
  1979   *Essentials of Forensic Anthropology.* Charles C Thomas, Springfield, IL.

Whitmer, A.M., A.F. Ramenofsky, J. Thomas, L.J. Thibodeaux, S.D. Field, and B.J. Miller
  1987   Stability or Instability: The Role of Diffusion in Trace Element Studies. In *Archaeological Method and Theory*, Vol. 1, edited by M.B. Schiffer, pp. 205–273. University of Arizona Press, Tucson.

Wolf, D.J.
  1986   Forensic Anthropology Scene Investigations. In *Forensic Osteology: Advances in the Identification of Human Remains,* edited by K.J. Reichs, pp. 3–21. Charles C Thomas, Springfield, IL.

# Autopsied, Embalmed, and Preserved Human Remains: Distinguishing Features in Forensic and Historic Contexts

# 31

PAUL S. SLEDZIK
MARC S. MICOZZI

## Overview

Forensic anthropology has traditionally focused on the analysis of skeletal remains. In the past few decades, forensic anthropology has also proven valuable in the analysis of burned, mummified, decomposed, fragmented, and partially skeletonized remains. By analyzing skeletal remains and soft tissues that have been preserved by processes other than natural decomposition, the unique taphonomic processes leading to particular states of preservation can be illuminated (Garland and Janaway 1989; Micozzi 1991).

Preservation of soft tissues in nature is essentially a competition between decay and desiccation. Climatological factors such as temperature and humidity largely decide the outcome of this contest (Aufderheide 1980; Micozzi 1986). Geological factors which can enhance soft tissue preservation include immersion in water under certain conditions, freezing, and the actions of soil elements such as salts. Biological actions of microbiological organisms and plant products may also cause preservation of soft tissues. In modern cultural and forensic contexts, humans may also place remains in preservative environments intentionally or unintentionally.

Human actions have long affected the process of postmortem decomposition. Embalming and anatomical preparation leave distinct taphonomic characteristics. Evidence of postmortem and perimortem medical procedures (e.g., autopsy and surgery) are recognizable in skeletal and soft tissue remains. Intentional human actions resulting in "unnatural" postmortem preservation of soft tissues are documented in the forensic and anthropological literature (Berryman et al. 1991; Micozzi 1991; Sledzik and Ousley 1991).

## Natural Processes of Soft Tissue Preservation

### Desiccation and Mummification

Desiccation is the process of drying of soft tissues; mummification is the product of desiccation. Desiccation can affect the entire body or discrete portions of the body exposed to the proper environmental conditions. Postmortem disturbance can result in incomplete desiccation. Hot, dry climatological conditions are most favorable for desiccation because rapid drying of soft tissues prevents putrefaction by enteric microorganisms, soil bacteria, and other decay organisms.

Desiccatory climates are found in the coastal zones of Chile and Peru, the southwestern United States, and the desert areas of Australia and North Africa. Soft tissue preservation of prehistoric remains found in these areas has been sufficient to allow histologic and anatomic diagnosis of pathological conditions (Aufderheide 1980; El-Najjar and Mulinski 1980) and extraction of human and disease organism DNA (Rogan and Salvo 1990; Salo et al. 1994).

Desiccation can occur rapidly in the proper environment. Drying begins in areas of the body that contain little fluid, for example, fingers, toes, and scrotum (Perper 1992). The drying and shrinkage of the nail beds and surrounding tissues of these areas have led to incorrect assumptions that nails grow after death (Barber 1988). Internal organs are usually the last tissues to desiccate (if indeed they survive the postmortem decay process).

In the forensic literature, one author has noted that desiccated remains from temperate areas display poorly preserved or entirely decomposed internal organs (Perper 1992). This author also notes that complete mummification in temperate environments takes at least 3 months. Emson (1991) has reported on a case from Canada where a body was found 8 to 10 days after death in a dry, heated apartment. The skin was mummified, but the internal organs had decomposed before mummification was completed.

In a review of forensic cases in the eastern U.S., Mann et al. (1990) note that in hot, arid environments, a body can mummify in as little as 2 weeks. In a study of decomposition in the arid western United States, Galloway et al. (1989) reported that in open air partial mummification took place between 10 days and 1 month. Desiccation of soft tissues occurred as early as two months and as late as 18 months. In closed structures, mummification was documented in remains that had spent, on average, between 1 and 4 months in the structure. The authors also note that the microenvironment provided by a closed structure delayed the onset of desiccation.

## Sublimation

Sublimation, or freeze-drying, is prevalent in Arctic areas and dry, high-altitude locations. Sublimation has been documented in prehistoric remains from the Middle East permafrost zones (Artamonov 1965) and Siberia's Altai mountains (Rudenko 1970). The remains of Arctic explorer Charles Francis Hall, exhumed in 1968 in Thank-God-Harbour, Greenland, displayed good soft tissue preservation after 97 years (Horne 1980). Three bodies from Sir John Franklin's 1845–1848 Arctic expedition were exhumed and autopsied 136 years after death. The internal organs and eyes were well preserved, although brain tissue had liquified (Beattie and Geiger 1987).

Bodies left in open areas during the winter months in temperate areas can maintain a "fresh" appearance for long periods. In forensic contexts, sublimation may not be a practical consideration, given the length of time required to initiate and complete the process. Micozzi further discusses frozen remains elsewhere in this volume.

## Exposure to Mineral Salts

Due to their affinity for moisture and their desiccatory effects on soft tissue, mineral salts can preserve soft tissues. In North America, mummies preserved through the natural actions of mineral salts have been found in Mammoth Cave, Kentucky, the Lower Mimbres Valley in New Mexico, and several eastern U.S. sites (Maloney 1981). The forensic literature provides no cases of natural preservation from exposure to mineral salts.

## Remains in Water

In the rare situation when water creates an air-tight seal, soft tissues may become partially preserved. For example, prehistoric Native American remains discovered in a flooded sinkhole in southwest Florida, which dated from 12,000 to 6,000 B.P., displayed preserved brain tissues. Preservation of these tissues was attributed to the creation of an anaerobic environment by mineralized hard water and resettling of fine peat (Clausen et al. 1979; Doran et al. 1986).

## Adipocere

Adipocere was once thought to result from chemical saponification of organic fatty acids in the presence of alkali, such as lime or calcium carbonate. It is now known to consist primarily of fatty acids formed by the postmortem hydrolysis and hydrogenation of body fats (Mant and Furbank 1957). Initially, it was thought that adipocere formation required extraneous water, but this event has been observed in long-buried bodies from relatively dry climates (Evans 1963). Pre-inhumation conditions of warm weather, fog, or haze may contribute to the process (Evans 1963).

To study the frequency, time course, and factors affecting the formation and physical characteristics of adipocere, Mellen et al. (1993) placed human soft tissue in controlled environments. Adipocere formed frequently within 2 to 3 months in water at 60 to 70°F. In colder water (40°F), adipocere developed more slowly, taking on average 12 to 18 months to develop.

In a forensic context, presence of adipocere is an artifact of decomposition suggesting that a minimum length of time has passed since death, but it may not always be useful in determining the postmortem interval. Presence of adipocere also may reveal something about the depositional environment.

## Preservation in Peat Bogs

In peat bogs, the action of humic acid results in preservation of soft tissues. Although commonly found in northwest Europe, over 2,000 "bog bodies" have been found in other locations, such as Crete and western Russia (Fischer 1980). These bodies range in time from the Stone Age to the 16th century (Fischer 1980). Preservation in these cases is attributed to the actions of bog acids (which decalcify bone and tan skin), and to the maintenance of a high antibiotic and anaerobic environment. The skin of these bodies is better preserved than the internal organs, presumably due to the actions of intestinal anaerobic bacteria before the penetration of bog liquid into the viscera (Aufderheide 1981; Fischer 1980; Glob 1969). The temperature of the bog at the time of burial is important in preventing decomposition and the activity of intestinal flora. Extreme demineralization with decalcification of bone has also been seen in these remains (Stead et al. 1986). Mistaken initially as a recent murder, the Lindow Man proved to be an unique prehistoric case of ritual murder (Ross and Robins 1989).

## Preservation from Plant Products and Microbiologic Organisms

Aromatic spices and salts have antibacterial properties that can preserve fresh animal flesh and soft tissue, and disguise the foul flavor and smell of putrid meat. A combination of desiccation and the direct antibacterial action of these natural products can preserve soft tissues. Natural plant products with antibacterial action include honey, cinnamon, vanilla, anise, black pepper, garlic, hops, and red pepper. Foods with antibacterial action include mushrooms (*Agaricus bisporus*), cycads (nuts) (*Cycas* sp.), *Heliotropium,* sassafras (*Sassafras albidum*), and sesame seeds (*Sesamum indicum*). These plant products contain compounds that inhibit bacterial growth, especially when reacted under heat with amino acid and simple carbohydrates (Miller 1979). During artificial mummification, these conditions would be present. Preservation of this type has not been documented in the forensic literature.

# Human Actions Leading to Soft Tissue Preservation

Cultural practices resulting in soft tissue preservation may rely upon natural processes or on the direct actions of humans. These practices, which range from internment of remains in desiccatory environments to embalming, are part of the beliefs surrounding death, dying, burial, and handling of the dead of many cultures. Cultural characteristics of burial, cremation, embalming, entombment, interrment, mortuary practices, and public health influence the temporary and final disposition of human remains.

## Artificial and Intentional Mummification

The term "mummification" refers to all natural and artificial processes that cause preservation of the body or its parts. There are three principal types of mummification: (1) natural mummification, caused by several factors acting singly or in combination (e.g., dryness, heat, cold, or absence of air in the burial vault or grave); (2) intentional mummification, caused by intentional exploitation or deliberate enhancement of the natural processes listed above; and (3) artificial mummification, produced by a variety of techniques. These include evisceration, fire and smoke curing, and application of embalming substances (e.g., resins, oils, herbs, and other organic materials and chemicals).

The word "mummy" is derived from the Persian *mumeia* or *mum* meaning pitch or asphalt. In classical times, this substance was used in medical prescriptions. Medieval physicians introduced a refinement with preparations of pitch from Egyptian mummies. The first medical use of the word "mummy" dates to the early 15th century. As applied to a preserved body, however, the earliest record is 1615 in the *Oxford English Dictionary*.

Artificial mummification and other forms of soft tissue preservation have been practiced by various cultural groups around the world through time. The techniques of artificial mummification and preservation are most effective only in those regions in which climatological conditions favor natural preservation. In areas where long-term preservation of human tissues was precluded due to unfavorable environmental conditions, efforts at artificial mummification facilitated short-term preservation. Common features of artificial mummification include evisceration to prevent intrinsic decay processes due to enteric microorganisms, and desiccation through sun exposure, air drying, salt treatment, or smoking.

Artificial and intentional mummification has been practiced in Ancient Egypt, Greece, and Rome; by the ancient Hebrews, Babylonians, Persians, and Indians; in the islands of the Pacific, Torres Straits, and Australia; in Burma and Ceylon; on the southwest and west coasts of Africa and the Canary Islands; and in the New World by Native American and Alaskan groups, and by Incas in Argentina, Bolivia, Chile, and Peru.

## Preserved Remains from Forensic Contexts

Human skeletal remains recovered from forensic situations may, upon analysis, not be forensic in nature. These nonforensic remains can be divided into four categories: animal or other nonhuman remains; human remains that are modern but are not forensic in nature; prehistoric remains; and historic period remains. Because of the preservation encountered in them, this section will focus on modern nonforensic remains and historic period remains.

Several researchers have reported on modern skeletal remains that are not forensic in nature. Examples include biological supply material, trophy skulls, and remains from religious contexts such as *santeria* (Bass 1983; Sledzik and Ousley 1991; Taylor et al. 1984; Weinker et al. 1990; Welti and Martinez 1981). These remains show effects of handling, graffiti, painting, and other similar artifacts.

Human remains from biological supply companies or from medical school skeletons have been reported (Saul and Saul 1987; Weinker et al. 1990). These cases show particular postmortem changes: characteristic patina, bleaching, anatomical markings, preparation holes, varnishing, etc. Morphological analyses may also reveal that these remains are not forensic in nature.

Trophy or souvenir remains from war circumstances and serial homicide cases have also been documented. In most instances these remains have been altered in some manner to either preserve or decorate them. Among the souvenirs taken by serial murderers are heads, hands, skin, and skeletal remains (Ressler and Shachtman 1992).

In historic and modern times, trophies taken from enemies during and after battle have included skulls, ears, shrunken heads, and similar items. Distinguishing characteristics of trophy skulls include characteristic patina, postmortem breakage of fragile areas of the skull, postmortem loss of anterior teeth, graffiti, and evidence of burning (Sledzik and Ousley 1991).

The Jivaro Indians of the Upper Amazon River Basin of southeastern Ecuador prepared the well-known *tsanta* or "shrunken heads" into the 20th century (Stirling 1938). The process involved removal of the scalp, flaying of the soft tissue of the head, and removal of the bones of the skull. After shrinking to about one half the original size by air drying, the skin was then boiled in hinto juice (rich in natural tannins) and dried on a spear shaft. The head was then filled with hot sand, which was continually replaced as it cooled. The continual application of heated pebbles, vegetable oils, plant extracts, and powdered charcoal preserved the external surface of the skin. Despite the unfavorable climatological conditions for preservation in the Amazon Basin, this process resulted in remarkably well preserved skin.

Two "shrunken bodies" prepared in this fashion by a 19th century European physician are now in the collection of the National Museum of the American Indian (Alexander 1994). These remains of a European and a mulatto slave are scheduled for reburial in 1995.

Preserved historic remains have also been described in the forensic literature (Berryman et al. 1991). Such remains, which include embalmed and anatomically preserved remains, are sometimes difficult to differentiate from modern forensic remains because of their excellent preservation. For example, the case of Colonel William Mabry Shy reported by Bass (1984) showed remarkable soft tissue preservation after 113 years of internment.

# History of Embalming, Autopsy, and Anatomical Preparation

Familiarity with the practices of embalming and anatomical preparation from historic time periods helps in assessing historic remains (Berryman et al. 1991; also this volume). Chemical analyses of fluids and soft tissues may reveal the presence of embalming agents commonly used in historic periods (e.g., arsenic). Artifacts left by embalming procedures and anatomical preparations help to identify historic period remains. Distinguishing the effects of embalming from those of autopsy may also prove important, as both procedures leave similar marks. Unusual patterns of soft tissue preservation may also suggest that the remains have been anatomically prepared.

In the 17th century, the embalming procedure was similar in America and Europe. Philbert Guibert of Paris provided a general overview of the procedure (Guibert 1639). After removing the chest plate, the internal organs were removed, embalmed individually, placed in a barrel, and interred separately with the body. The skull was sectioned and brain removed for separate burial. Incisions were made along the arms and legs and cotton soaked with a vinegar and water solution, sometimes accompanied by balming powder, was placed in the void. Balming powders were comprised of salt, hoarie mints, wormwood, sage, rosemary, thyme, oregano, and olive oil. The incisions were sewn up and the body anointed with a mixture of oil of turpentine, oil of rose, and other spices. Once in the coffin, aromatic herbs such as marjoram, rue, wormwood, and thyme, were placed on the body.

The 17th century also saw the introduction of the injection technique. This method involved injection of certain distilled spirits (alcohol, wine, rum, turpentine) into the vascular system. This technique, however, was not widely practiced.

In the 18th century, the Hunter brothers applied variations of the injection technique for both anatomical preservation and embalming. William Hunter also placed bodies on beds of plaster of paris to hasten drying of tissues. The embalmed bodies produced by William Hunter were said to have had the appearance of a mummy (Johnson et al. 1990).

By the 19th century, materials such as zinc, arsenic, aluminum chloride, mercury, and alum became more popular for embalming. These chemicals are thought to have prevented bacterial decay of soft tissues long enough for preservation to occur (Berryman et al. 1991). Specifically, tissues embalmed with alum became preserved through a process of mummification. Extensive use of arsenic during this time has forced soil scientists to consider the effects of this preservative on the groundwater near large 19th century cemeteries in the Eastern United States (Konefes 1991).

The first book published in English on embalming, which also included information on anatomical preparation, was a translated version of Gannal's "History of Embalming and Preparations in Anatomy, Pathology, and Natural History" (Johnson et al. 1990). The text was first published in Paris in 1838 and in the United States in 1840. By the time of the U.S. Civil War, embalming was an accepted practice as embalmers such as Holmes and Cornelius applied their skills to the war dead (Habenstein and Lamers 1981; Johnson et al. 1990).

Following the war, embalming by arterial injection became less popular for both economic and health reasons. Temporary preservation by application of ice became more common (Strub and Frederick 1989).

Mendelsohn (1944) provided four reasons for the rise of modern arterial injection: (1) to withstand transportation over great distances; (2) to permit leisurely disposal despite adverse climatic conditions; (3) to insure prevention of communicable infections before or after burial; and (4) for cosmetic restoration of normal antemortem appearance.

Education and certification of embalmers resulted in standardization of most materials and methods of embalming. Hanzlick (1994) has examined the modern methods of embalming, body preparation, and burial. He notes the presence of certain soft tissue artifacts and material artifacts caused by embalming. Among soft tissue artifacts are incised sites for arterial injections seen usually near the axillary, brachial, carotid, external iliac, femoral, popliteal, and radial arteries and jugular vein. Material artifacts include trocar buttons; packing materials (e.g., cotton) placed in the body orifices; barbed wire or drill and wire for securing the mouth; mouth former for edentulous individuals; eye caps; and various creams, cosmetics, compounds, and tissue builders for use in topical cosmetic application or reconstructive work.

Modern embalming slows, but does not halt, the process of soft tissue decomposition. Mann et al. (1990) have noted that the decomposition pattern of an embalmed body differs from that of a fresh corpse. They report that the first evidence of decomposition in embalmed remains is usually observed in the buttocks and legs.

## Autopsies in Historic America

Coroner's inquests also took place in early America (Gordon 1949; Semmes 1970). Although the autopsy procedure is not described in detail, enough can be gleaned from historic records to show that chest cavities were opened and crania sectioned to determine the cause of death. These autopsies were not complete by modern standards. Autopsies were performed on victims of violence as well as those who died of natural and unnatural causes. Often, however, autopsies took place when there was some question regarding the manner of death.

Autopsies were performed on commoners, indentured servants, Native Americans, and aristocrats (Gordon 1949). The body of Governor Henry Sloughter of New York was autopsied in 1691 after it was suspected that his sudden death was the result of poisoning (Long 1962). The body of an infant was autopsied in 1642 in St. Mary's County, MD (Gordon 1949).

Modern autopsy technique requires opening of the chest cavity, and in some cases, sectioning of the cranium. These techniques will leave characteristic cuts on the ribs and skull, and possibly the sternum. Embalming of autopsied bodies requires additional procedures such as suturing and packing of removed areas of soft tissue, use of hardening compounds, and application of embalming powders (Hanzlick 1994).

## Anatomical Preparation

Because anatomical preparation was closely tied to embalming and dissection, anatomists and embalmers prepared anatomical specimens (Tompsett 1956). Unfortunately, information about the date of introduction of particular preparation techniques is scarce.

Before the publication of Gannal's text, information on anatomical preparation existed as treatises on embalming and from students educated by practitioners in 18th century Europe. Europeans who taught at American embalming schools in the late 18th and early 19th centuries introduced techniques of anatomical preparation common in Europe. The most common methods included injection of veins and arteries, drying of ligaments and tendons, and storage of remains in preservative fluids.

Injection techniques for anatomical purposes were outgrowths of injection embalming methods. Hardening compounds were added to injections to obtain the desired effect of preserved veins, arteries, and other anatomical systems.

The earliest use of solidifying injected masses dates from mid-17th century Europe (Tompsett 1956). The expense of jars and spirits in the 17th and 18th centuries led most preparers to produce dried and varnished specimens. Injected masses containing wax, resin, tallow, and turpentine, were also common during this time. As the cost of wet specimen preservation decreased, masses of starch, plaster of Paris, and gelatin were used.

In wax injections, the body was immersed in hot water while hot fluids were run through the vessels, so that the wax would not harden before it had been entirely injected. The bodies of young people were prized for arterial injections because of the elasticity of the arterial walls. Starch and plaster injection did not require heating of the body or the material. However, they formed brittle masses which crumbled upon handling.

### Case Study: Anatomically Preserved Remains in a Forensic Context

In July 1992, the preserved remains of a 35- to 45-year-old female were sent to the National Museum of Health and Medicine by Dr. James L. Frost, Deputy Chief Medical Examiner of West Virginia. The remains were found at the entrance to a Westover, WV, flea market before opening on August 20, 1989. The man suspected of depositing the remains was the owner of a nearby rival, and nonthriving, flea market. Following the death of this man in 1990, his associates and relatives provided information on the history of the remains.

Reportedly, the preserved body had been stored in a copper coffin in a Parsons, WV, funeral home for many years. After its sale, the building became a local hardware outlet, where the body had been placed in the rafters. As a young woman in 1939, a local historian remembered being held up to the rafters to view the remains.

Upon examination, the body was missing both arms and scapulae and the right clavicle. Dried preserved ligaments, tendons, and muscle tissues were evident in the legs, arms, and head (see Figure 1). The appearance of these tissues, however, was not similar to mummified remains. Internal organs, particularly the heart and large blood vessels, had been injected with red and white substances which had hardened inside the organ. The organ tissues were dried and paper-like in texture. Several smaller vessels on the skull and thorax had been injected with similar material, resulting in hard, brittle masses. Chemical analysis of the injected masses revealed two different compounds. The white material was a talc derivative comprised largely of carbonate. The red material was a red clay suspension in a paraffin base.

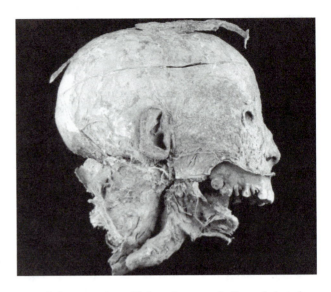

**Figure 1**  Photograph of preserved head from West Virginia.

The appearance of the soft tissues and the presence of injected organs indicated that the remains represented an anatomical preparation. These structures looked remarkably similar to the late 19th and early 20th century anatomical preparations of limbs and torsos in the collection of the National Museum of Health and Medicine.

## Case Study: Embalmed Remains in an Historic Context

In historic period remains, the evidence left on the body by embalming and autopsy may be similar, i.e., a sectioned cranial vault and cut sternum and ribs. This evidence was observed in the remains of Governor Lionel Copley and his wife Anne, who were buried in the churchyard of the Trinity Episcopal Church in St. Mary's City, MD and examined by Sledzik and Douglas Owsley in 1992.

The Copleys arrived in America from England in 1691. Anne, aged 33 years, died March 5, 1692, and Lionel died at the age of 45 on September 27, 1693. Their deaths were ascribed to "seasoning," the result of rapid changes in environment, diet, and disease exposure experienced by immigrants to the Chesapeake Bay region. The remains of the Copleys were placed in lead coffins and were interred in a brick-lined vault.

The remains of Mrs. Copley had been examined three times previously. The first and most remarkable examination took place in 1799, when medical students removed her coffin and opened it in a nearby shed (Sioussat 1922). They reported that the winding sheet and other material was "perfect and sound". The remains, although black in color, were perfectly preserved, but the eyes were shrunken in the sockets. The account also says that the "body was opened and the entrails removed and filled with gums and spice, and the coffin filled with the same". In passing, the account mentions that the skull of the Governor "was sawed through, the brain removed, and filled with embalment, but he was not so well done as the other...."

In the 1992 analysis, the skeletal remains from both coffins were in excellent condition. Hair and portions of dried soft tissues were present on both bodies and the eyes of the Governor were dried. A black stain, presumably from the embalming material and decompositional by-products, was evident in the areas surrounding both torsos and on portions of both skulls, ribs, and vertebrae.

In addition, the cranial vaults of both skulls had been sectioned. On the Governor's skull, the cuts extended through the external occipital protuberance, where a terminal snap was present. Cuts measuring 0. 6 mm were evident around the perimeter of the skull indicating several false starts. This skeleton also showed evidence of several postmortem rib fractures and a perimortem fracture of the superior portion of the sternum. No evidence of perimortem injury was observed.

The cuts on Anne Copley's skull were more crude. The internal edges of the cut vault had been broken in several places and the cuts were incomplete. The body of the sternum was cut longitudinally. As with the Governor, there was no evidence of perimortem trauma in the skeleton of Anne Copley.

In this case, the cuts on the skull vaults and the sternum may be interpreted as being the result of autopsy or embalming. That these remains were embalmed is evident: the preserved soft tissue and eyes, the black staining, and the 1799 account indicating embalming evidence provide proof of this fact. However, it is the cuts that are problematic. Embalming procedures and autopsy procedures from the late 17th century required sectioning of the vault and opening of the chest cavity (Waldron and Rogers 1988).

The evidence shows that these cuts were most likely made during embalming. The preserved soft tissue and eyes, the black staining, and the 1799 account indicating embalming are evidence that the Copleys were embalmed. In addition, autopsy can be ruled out because the Copleys did not die under questionable circumstances, the typical reason for conducting an autopsy in colonial times. Their deaths as a result of "seasoning" were common in colonial times. Therefore, we can probably rule out the possibility that the sectioned cranial vaults and sternum were due to autopsy.

## Case Study: The Hardin Cemetery Flood Disaster

During the severe 1993 floods in the central United States, over one half of the town cemetery located in Hardin, MO, was eroded away by flood waters. Over 800 remains were affected, dating from the mid-1800s to the present. A team of four forensic anthropologists was asked by the Federal Emergency Management Agency to provide expertise in identification of remains.

Given the time elapsed since burial and the effects of the flood waters, the remains from the Hardin cemetery were in various states of preservation. Some information on preservation of embalmed remains can be gleaned from the anthropological work in the Hardin disaster. Forensic anthropological efforts were focused on analyzing complete and partial human remains from two sources: (1) unopened vaults and coffins and (2) remains that were removed from coffins and vaults by the flood and recovered by search and rescue teams.

The forensic anthropology team examined the remains of 66 complete or partial bodies, 196 complete and partial crania, 105 fragmentary crania, and over 1,400 miscellaneous bones. In addition, over 2,000 additional skeletal elements were examined but did not offer usable anthropological information. The age and sex distributions of the remains examined fit with those expected in a modern, rural, community cemetery.

Complete and partial remains had a greater chance of being identified because information that could be obtained from them was greater than the information that could be collected for individual skeletal elements. In addition, complete and partial remains had been interred more recently, and as such, the availability of antemortem records for comparison was greater.

Preservation of remains was extremely variable. There appeared to be no relationship between the condition of remains (e.g., mummification, skeletonization, presence of soft tissue) and length of internment. Certainly, the flood actions, especially water mixing with the remains and the remains being exposed to air once recovered, contributed to the observed differential preservation.

Judging by the appearance of the coffins, a majority of the complete and partial remains dated from the early 1920s to the early 1960s. Several artifacts found inside the coffins, such as newspapers and burial goods, indicated dates of burial.

Of the 66 complete remains analyzed, one half were skeletonized. Ten bodies were completely mummified. The other remains had both skeletal material and soft tissues present. In two cases where the remains were interred in 1937 and 1950, the remains were mummified.

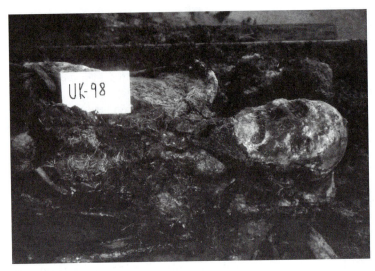

**Figure 2**   Mummified body interred in 1937 from Hardin Cemetery, Missouri.

(See Figure 2 of a mummified body interred in 1937.) In one case interred in 1954, the remains were skeletonized. This information shows that the degree of preservation of interred, embalmed remains is highly variable.

## Conclusion

The preservation of human soft tissues is reliant upon a variety of natural and cultural processes. Preservation by natural means involves climatological, geological, and geophysical processes, and results in bodies preserved by natural mummification, freezing, sublimation, salt, tannins, and exposure to an anaerobic environment. Cultural processes resulting in soft tissue preservation include artificial mummification, drying, tanning, the application of spices, oils, salts, and other desiccants, and chemical embalming. Certain plant products and the actions of selected bacteria may also result in preservation of soft tissues.

## Acknowledgments

We are indebted to Henry Miller, Timothy Riordan, and Douglas Owsley for helping coordinate the work on the Copley burials. For their perseverance in Hardin, MO, we acknowledge David Hunt, Allison Webb Willcox, Laurie Carroll, P. J. Schoebel, Gina Overshiner, Jennifer Smith, and Beth Goldstein.

## References

Alexander, C.
    1994   Little Men: A Mystery of No Small Significance. *Outside* 9(4):98–101.

Artamonov, M.L.
    1965   Frozen Tombs of the Scythians. *Scientific American* 212:101–109.

Aufderheide, A.C.
    1980   Soft Tissue Anatomic Findings in Three Basket-Maker Mummies. In *Abstracts of the Annual Meeting of the Paleopathology Association*. Niagara Falls, NY.

1981 Soft Tissue Paleopathology — An Emerging Subspeciality. *Human Pathology* 12:865–867.

Barber, P.
1988 *Vampires, Burial and Death: Folklore and Reality.* Yale University Press, New Haven, CT.

Bass, W.M.
1983 The Occurrence of Japanese Trophy Skulls in the United States. *Journal of Forensic Sciences* 28:800–803.
1984 Time Interval Since Death: A Difficult Decision. In *Human Identification: Case Studies in Forensic Anthropology*, edited by T.A. Rathbun and J.E. Buikstra, pp. 136–147. Charles C Thomas, Springfield, IL.

Beattie, O., and J. Geiger
1987 *Frozen in Time: Unlocking the Secrets of the Franklin Expedition.* E.P. Dutton, New York.

Berryman, H.E., W.M. Bass, S.A. Symes, and O.C. Smith
1991 Recognition of Cemetery Remains in the Forensic Setting. *Journal of Forensic Sciences* 36:230–237.

Clausen, C.J., A.D. Cohen, C. Emiliani, J.A. Holman, and J.J. Stipp
1979 Little Salt Spring, Florida: A Unique Underwater Site. *Science* 203:6.

Doran, G.H., D.N. Dickel, W.E. Ballinger Jr., O.F. Agee, P.J. Laipis, and W.W. Hauswirth
1986 Anatomical, Cellular and Molecular Analysis of 8000 year old Human Brain Tissue from the Windover Archaeological Site. *Nature* 323:803–806.

El-Najjar, M.Y., and T.M.J. Mulinski
1980 Mummies and Mummification Practices in the Southwestern and Southern United States. In *Mummies, Disease and Ancient Cultures*, edited by A. Cockburn and E. Cockburn, pp. 103–110. Cambridge University Press, New York.

Emson, H.E.
1991 The Case of the Empty Body. *American Journal of Forensic Medicine and Pathology* 124:332–333.

Evans, W.E.D.
1963 *The Chemistry of Death.* Charles C Thomas, Springfield, IL.

Fischer, C.
1980 Bog Bodies of Denmark. In *Mummies, Disease and Ancient Cultures*, edited by A. Cockburn and E. Cockburn, pp. 177–193. Cambridge University Press, New York.

Galloway, A., W.H. Birkby, A.M. Jones, T.E. Henry, and B.O. Parks
1989 Decay Rates of Human Remains in an Arid Environment. *Journal of Forensic Sciences* 34:607–616.

Garland, A.N., and R.C. Janaway
1989 The Taphonomy of Inhumation Burials. In *Burial Archaeology: Current Research, Methods, and Developments*, edited by C.A. Roberts and J. Bintliff, pp. 15–37. British Archaeological Reports International Series 211. Oxford, U.K.

Glob, P.V.
1969 *The Bog People.* Cornell University Press, New York.

Gordon, M.B.
1949 *Aesculapius Comes to the Colonies: The Story of the Early Days of Medicine in the Thirteen Original Colonies.* Ventnor Publishers, Ventnor, NJ.

Guibert, P.
1639 *The Charitable Physician.* Thomas Harper, London.

Habenstein, R.W., and W.M. Lamers
  1981  *The History of American Funeral Directing.* National Funeral Directors Association, Milwaukee.

Hanzlick, R.
  1994  Embalming, Body Preparation, and Disinterment: An Overview for Forensic Pathologists. *American Journal of Forensic Medicine and Pathology* 15:122–131.

Horne, P.
  1980  The Death of Charles Francis Hall, Arctic Explorer. In *Abstracts of the Annual Meeting of the Paleopathology Association.* Niagara Falls, NY.

Johnson, E.C., G.R. Johnson, and M.J. Williams
  1990  The Origin and History of Embalming. In *Embalming: History, Theory, and Practice,* edited by R.G. Mayer and G.S. Bigelow, pp. 23–57. Appleton and Lange, Norwalk, CT.

Konefes, J.
  1991  Ashes to Arsenic…Dust to Death. *Soils* November–December:36–41.

Long, E.R.
  1962  *A History of American Pathology.* Charles C Thomas, Springfield, IL.

Maloney, R.A.
  1981  Mummification Techniques Around the World. In *Selected Papers in Human Paleopathology,* edited by M.A. Kelley, pp. 1–20. University of Rhode Island, Kingston.

Mann, R.W., W.M. Bass, and L. Meadows
  1990  Time Since Death and Decomposition of the Human Body: Variables and Observations in Case and Experimental Field Studies. *Journal of Forensic Sciences* 35:103–111.

Mant, A.K., and R. Furbank
  1957  Adipocere — A Review. *Journal of Forensic Medicine* 4:18–35.

Mellen, P.F., M.A. Lowry, and M.S. Micozzi
  1993  Experimental Observations on Adipocere Formation. *Journal of Forensic Sciences* 38:91–93.

Mendelsohn, S.
  1944  Embalming From the Medieval Period to the Present Time. *Ciba Symposium* 6:1805–1812.

Micozzi, M.S.
  1986  Experimental Study of Post-mortem Changes Under Field Conditions: Effects of Freezing, Thawing, and Mechanical Injury. *Journal of Forensic Sciences* 35:953–961.
  1991  *Postmortem Changes in Human and Animal Remains.* Charles C Thomas, Springfield, IL.

Miller, J.A.
  1979  Chemistry: Spicing Up a Peppery Issue. *Science News* 115:265.

Perper, J.A.
  1992  Time of Death and Changes after Death. In *Medicolegal Investigation of Death,* edited by W.U. Spitz, pp. 14–49. Charles C Thomas, Springfield, IL.

Ressler, R.K., and T. Shachtman
  1992  *Whoever Fights Monsters.* St. Martin's Press, New York.

Rogan, P., and J. Salvo
  1990  Study of Nucleic Acids Isolated from Ancient Remains. *Yearbook of Physical Anthropology* 33:195–214.

Ross, A., and D. Robins
  1989  *The Life and Death of a Druid Prince.* Summit Books, New York.

Rudenko, S.I.
1970  *Frozen Tombs of Siberia*, edited and translated by M.W. Thompson. University of California Press, Berkeley, CA.

Salo, W.L., A.C. Aufderheide, J. Buikstra, and T.A. Holcomb
1994  Identification of *Mycobacterium tuberculosis* DNA in a Pre-Columbian Peruvian Mummy. *Proceedings of the National Academy of Science U.S.A.* 91:2091–2094.

Saul, F.P., and J.M. Saul
1987  An Osteobiographic Analysis of an Early Dissecting "Room" Population. *Anatomical Record* 218:1–120A.

Semmes, R.
1970  *Crime and Punishment in Early Maryland.* Patterson Smith, Montclair, NJ.

Sioussat, A.L.
1922  Lionel Copley, First Royal Governor of Maryland. *Maryland Historical Magazine* 17:163–177.

Sledzik, P.S., and S. Ousley
1991  Analysis of Six Vietnamese Trophy Skulls. *Journal of Forensic Sciences* 36:520–530.

Stead, I.M., J.B. Bourke, and D. Brothwell
1986  *Lindow Man: The Body in the Bog.* Cornell University Press, Ithaca, NY.

Stirling, M.W.
1938  *Historical and Ethnographical Material on the Jivaro Indians.* Bulletin 117. Bureau of American Ethnology, Smithsonian Institution, Washington, D.C.

Strub, C.G., and L.G. Frederick
1989  *The Principles and Practice of Embalming.* Professional Training Schools, Inc. and Robertine Frederick, Dallas.

Taylor, J.V., L. Roh, and A.D. Goldman
1984  Metropolitan Forensic Anthropology Team (MFAT) Case Studies in Identification: 2. Identification of a Vietnamese Trophy Skull. *Journal of Forensic Sciences* 29:1253–1259.

Tompsett, D.H.
1956  *Anatomical Techniques.* E. & S. Livingstone, London.

Waldron, T., and J. Rogers
1988  Iatrogenic Palaeopathology. *Journal of Palaeopathology* 1:117–129.

Weinker, C.S., J.E. Wood, and C.A. Diggs
1990  Independent Instances of "Souvenir" Asian Skulls from the Tampa Bay Area. *Journal of Forensic Sciences* 35:637–643.

Welti, C.V., and R. Martinez
1981  Forensic Sciences Aspects of Santeria, A Religious Cult of African Origin. *Journal of Forensic Sciences* 26:506–514.

# NecroSearch Revisited: Further Multidisciplinary Approaches to the Detection of Clandestine Graves

# 32

DIANE L. FRANCE
TOM J. GRIFFIN
JACK G. SWANBURG
JOHN W. LINDEMANN
G. CLARK DAVENPORT
VICKEY TRAMMELL
CECILIA T. TRAVIS
BORIS KONDRATIEFF
AL NELSON
KIM CASTELLANO
DICK HOPKINS
TOM ADAIR

## Introduction

NecroSearch International, Inc. is a nonprofit, volunteer organization dedicated to investigating the methods and technology involved in the location of clandestine graves and the recovery of the remains and evidence in and around the gravesite. To implement this investigation, the relationships between buried pig carcasses and their surroundings as well as the applicability of various techniques in quantifying the changes in the immediately environment surrounding are being studied. The primary purpose of this article is to update the scientific community on research conducted at the research site, and to cite successes and difficulties with techniques used at suspected and actual crime scenes. For additional information, please consult a previous article (France et al. 1992).

The project is an interdisciplinary one involving law enforcement agencies, private businesses, and academicians in an attempt to pool information traditionally obtained separately. The aim is NOT to state that a specific site is indeed the location of a buried body. Instead, a compilation of all of the techniques indicates a given spot or number of spots that would be the most likely to be the site of a clandestine grave. In addition, these techniques may also help determine time since burial and provide evidence that may tie a suspect to a burial site. As many as practical of the different techniques for site location are being attempted at the test area. Some of the techniques are suspected of being time-sensitive in that they may be of value only for a limited period of time. A specific sequence may be found to be needed (going from least destructive to most). Some of the results (both present and future) may prove to be unique to our altitude, soil, etc., so other groups are encouraged to try our approach for their environmental conditions.

Currently the NecroSearch team consists of experts in crime scene and laboratory analysis, aerial photography, thermal imagery, geology and pedology, geophysics, geochemistry, petrology, meteorology, botany, entomology, wildlife biology, criminal psychology, serology, photography, archaeology, forensic anthropology, and scent-detection dog handling.

## Background

Few studies in the literature concentrate on multidisciplinary methods used for the location of buried human remains. Studies by Boyd (1979), Imaiuzma (1974), McLaughlin (1974), and Bass and Birkby (1978, which also offers the rationale behind proper excavation techniques) offer overviews of some of the techniques also used in NecroSearch research. Killam (1990) offers a comprehensive survey in search techniques, and Hunter (1994) recently reviewed various techniques for the location of clandestine graves in the United Kingdom.

Although no group has undertaken a study of as many multidisciplinary techniques as presented in the NecroSearch research, many articles address individual methods for location of clandestine graves. Davenport et al. (1988, 1990) discuss the ways in which geoscientists work with law enforcement, while Hoving (1986) describes the use of a small ground-penetrating radar (GPR) unit for locating buried bodies. Infrared detection of decomposing remains has been tested by, among others, Dickinson (1977) and Rodriguez and Bass (1985).

Other studies have used pigs to research individual aspects of clandestine grave systems. Haglund et al. (1989, 1990, 1991) and Haskell (personal communication 1990) have studied the scavenging and scatter patterns of pig and human remains. Haskell, in addition, does research on decay processes.

The role of insects and other arthropods in the decay process of human remains has been reviewed by Nuorteva (1977) and Smith (1986). Studies using unembalmed cadavers or pigs have elucidated a specific succession of arthropods and the resulting decompositional process (Galloway et al. 1989; Payne et al. 1968; Rhine et al. 1988; Rodriguez and Bass 1983; Smith 1973; Schoenly et al. 1991; Shean et al. 1993). Rodriguez and Bass (1985) have addressed entomological methods and their relationship to depth of burial and local climatic conditions. Tolhurst and Reed (1984) present information in the training and use of dogs for locating shallow graves.

In an effort to enhance a multidisciplinary approach, many techniques for clandestine grave-site location are still being applied at the research area in Colorado, and additional locations involving different environmental conditions will be initiated in the summer of 1995. These techniques have also been utilized at dozens of crime scenes.

## Location

The primary research site is located on the Highlands Ranch Law Enforcement Training Facility in Douglas County, CO, approximately 29 km (18 miles) south of Denver. Other research facilities are planned for the mountains west of Denver. As part of a 0.47-km² (117 acre) law enforcement training facility, it offers an area of controlled access to the public, though officers in training have used the area occasionally for SWAT-type missions. The training facility occupies a west-flowing drainage that feeds Plum Creek, a major tributary of the South Platte River. Elevation at the site averages 1829 meters (6000 feet) above sea level. The research site is on undeveloped ranch land that borders the western edge of Daniels Park, one of the parks of the Denver Mountain Parks system. Topographically the country surrounding the training facility consists of gently rolling, brush-covered uplands that change into partially developed badlands and low mesa topography with increasing elevation. The upper slopes of the badlands/mesa country support stands of conifer.

To date, 18 gravesites (two do not contain pigs) have been studied at the research site. Pigs are currently being used for two reasons. At present, human cadavers are unavailable for studies of this kind in Colorado. Also, these pigs are similar to humans in their weight (70 kg or 154 lbs on average, though smaller pigs have been recently included to simulate human bodies of different sizes and ages), their fat-to-muscle ratio, and in the fact that their skin is not heavily haired. Pigs have been considered to be biochemically and physiologically similar enough to humans to be used in studies of patterns and rates of decay and scavenging. Of equal importance, dog handlers have traditionally maintained that if a dog can detect pig remains, it can also detect human remains.

## Methods

Prior to the burial of the first pig in September of 1988, baseline data consisting of black and white aerial photographs, geophysical measurements, and geological and botanical observations were acquired for the overall research site. Before the burial of each additional pig, baseline data in electromagnetics, ground penetrating radar, and surface botanical features are acquired.

Near-field and far-field data gathering were performed prior to and after burial. The definitions of "near-field" and "far-field" are dependent on the specific discipline, in that near-field refers to anything that is interacting within the burial system, while far-field is outside of the range of influence of the burial system. For example, measurements of soil gas may only be above background levels within a few centimeters of a burial, whereas arthropod activity related to a burial may cover a much broader area.

Far-field observations contemporaneous with burial for this study include botany, entomology, geology/pedology, aerial photography, geophysics, thermal imagery, soil gas, scavenging patterns, and the use of decomposition-scenting dogs (see Table 1). Near-field observations contemporaneous with and after burial include all of the above. A disturbance is a physical disruption associated with burial processes. A control site is undisturbed both at the surface and subsurface, and therefore is remote from the burial site. A calibration pit is a grave without an interred pig, while a grave contains a pig. Back dirt is excess soil deposited near the perimeter of the grave or calibration pit. It is understood that there are disturbances geographically close to the burial system but still identified as far-field in that they are not part of the burial process — for example roads, animal burrows, building foundations, etc.

### Aerial Photography

Aerial photography was performed far-field, in an attempt to identify near-field parameters from the air. Aerial photographic surveying was performed on a periodic basis, consisting of both visible spectrum color and black and white film. A turbo-charged Cessna 205 aircraft containing two Zeiss RMK/A 15023 aerial cameras and one KA-2½-inch aerial camera were used. Film types used are Kodak Aerocolor negative type 2445, Kodak infrared color film type 2443, and Kodak black and white XX film type 2405. This provides standard 9 in. × 9 in. stereophoto coverage.

### Geology

Geologic investigation at the "Project Pig" site determined the geologic character of the site, to relate this character to the individual burial sites, to establish site recognition and evaluation parameters, and to suggest lines of future geologic study and investigation.

**Table 1  Methods Used in the Detection of Clandestine Graves**

| Method | Advantage | Disadvantage |
| --- | --- | --- |
| Aerial photography | Least destructive<br>Provides great overall characterization of a site; access, culture, drainage, topography<br>Large area covered<br>Preburial photos may be available from a variety of sources | Best results with large film format (scale of readily available photography may be too small)<br>May need to be performed at different times of growing season<br>Natural (trees, etc) and man-made (power lines, etc) may interfere with interpretations<br>Requires trained personnel for interpretation<br>May be moisture dependant |
| Geology | Relatively nondestructive<br>Determination of site stratification through core samples<br>"Real time" on site information about ground surface | Intrusive if core samples taken<br>Entire search area should be viewed |
| Botany | Relatively nondestructive<br>Can be performed with photography and samples from area<br>Can be performed years later | Similar succession patterns for any disturbance within ecosystem not limited to burial |
| Entomology | Nondestructive<br>Aids in narrowing site location<br>Provides information about time since death | Requires limited area for searching<br>Best for relatively fresh grave<br>Different species for different geographical regions |
| Geophysics<br>Magnetics | Relatively nondestructive<br>Nonintrusive<br>Equipment easily obtained<br>Rapid coverage of large area<br>Works over snow, fresh/salt water | Only for ferrous materials<br>Target could be missed if search grid too large<br>Data not in "real time;" values must be plotted and should be contoured<br>Magnetic interferences (natural and man-made) confuse readings |
| Electromagnetics | Relatively nondestructive<br>Nonintrusive<br>Rapid coverage of large area<br>Equipment relatively easily obtained<br>For ferrous/nonferrous materials<br>Records conductivity<br>Works over/through snow | Subject to cultural (fences, etc) interferences<br>Target could be missed if search grid is too large<br>Difficult in rough terrain<br>Data not in "real time;" values must be plotted and should be contoured |

| Method | Advantages | Limitations/Disadvantages |
|---|---|---|
| Ground penetrating radar | Relatively nondestructive; Nonintrusive; Fairly rapid coverage of large area; "Real time" display; Works over/through snow, fresh water | Equipment relatively difficult to obtain; Most units require moderately smooth and level terrain |
| Self-potential | Relatively nondestructive; "Real-time" information | Intrusive; No worthwhile information from our research |
| Soil gas | Relatively nondestructive; "Real-time" information | Intrusive; Must be positioned relatively close to burial; Site soil, ground moisture, climate, depth of probe critical; Detection of decomposition product(s) time and temperature dependent |
| Metal detector | Relatively nondestructive; Nonintrusive; Equipment easily obtained | Limited depth capability, detects only metal (ferrous/nonferrous) objects, presumes metal objects on or with body; Field application often improperly conducted |
| Thermal imagery | Nondestructive; Can examine large area; Hand-held or attached to vehicle (land or aircraft); "Real-time" data; Videotaped for review | Requires little or no wind; Requires special equipment and knowledgable operators; Most effective when air, ground moist |
| Decomposition dogs | Relatively nondestructive; Documented effectiveness even 170 years after burial; Effective over water | Dog may be trained for other uses and not properly trained for this type of work; handler may overstate qualifications |
| Naturalists | Excellent for information concerning scavenging cases and outdoor information | Ability to recognize animal scavenging may be altered by climatic conditions; Tracking easiest in snow, mud, soft sand, or dust |
| Archaeology | Experienced in mapping, data collection, preservation of information from excavated materials, and is therefore extremely valuable for building court cases. | Both destructive and intrusive; Though data collection can be modified to meet most time demands, can be relatively slow |
| Forensic physical anthropologists | On-site interpretation of remains; Locations of skeletal/body elements | Not all forensic physical anthropologists are trained in excavation techniques |

Literature research and far-field studies were performed to establish the geologic character and stratigraphic setting of the project site. This involved definition of rock types, establishment of the age relationships among the rock types, and the evaluation of the effect of rock type on subsequent soil formation. Far-field studies also involved relating the physical character (geomorphology) of the project area to the distribution of underlying rock types (stratigraphy).

The near-field studies on the sites and the related far-field studies focused on the definition of soil profiles at specific burial sites, road cuts, and other excavations; the relationship of these soil profiles to the parent rock units; and how soil composition and character affect the recovery of a soil profile to a "normal" state. All burial sites have been and continue to be monitored and photographed to document the recovery of the soil profiles.

This program involved photographing of each burial site on a monthly basis. In addition, soil samples were collected to monitor soil disintegration as a reference to actual disturbance recovery at the burial sites.

## Botany

As part of the far-field study of vegetation, percent area cover for bare soil (back dirt), litter and herbaceous vegetation were estimated, and a total species list was prepared listing the plants found within the training facility.

Near-field study of vegetation included listing the plants growing on each grave, calibration pit, and back dirt area. For the near-field study, a 1-m by 0.5-m rectangle of PVC pipe was set at the approximate center of the test plot (grave, control pit, etc.) and vegetation was analyzed from within that test plot. Far-field study was tested in the same manner, with the 1-m by 0.5-m rectangle of PVC pipe set at various areas away from the test plots. The areas for far-field study are not the same for each test, but are taken approximately at random within the training facility in the general vicinity of the test plots. Frequency of species was determined by counting the number of rectangular plots on which a particular plant species was found. For example, wheat grass was found on four disturbed plots (either a grave or calibration pit) and on two undisturbed sites, while sunsedge was found on no disturbed sites and on three undisturbed sites.

After the pigs were scavenged from sites #1, 2, and 5, members of the team decided to cover the unscavenged grave sites with heavy chain link fencing to protect those graves from further scavenging. Although vegetation on the grave is potentially altered, some plant growth is allowed, and the fencing can be easily removed for near-field investigations such as geophysical surveying.

## Entomology

A control site was established to examine the airborne and surface insects. A BioQuip Malaise trap was erected to monitor aerial-dispersing insects, and was cleaned of all insects 1, 2, 4, 7, 12, 15, 25, and 30 days after pigs were buried. In addition, this type of trap was erected directly over burial site #1 and cleaned of all insects at the above schedule. Additionally, five pit traps were placed around the site to sample surface dispersing arthropods, and were monitored and cleaned at the above schedule. At "burials" 12 and 13 (surface deposits), insects were collected at the same intervals.

## Geophysics

Three specific geophysical methods were selected for evaluation at the Pig site: magnetics (MAG), electromagnetics (EM), and ground penetrating radar (GPR). The selection of these methods was based on the direct experience of one of the authors (Davenport) in implementing geophysical investigations on archaeological projects. The equipment utilized to date has included an EG&G Geometrics G-856-AX proton precession magnetometer with gradiometer attachment, Geonics EM-31 and EM 38 ground conductivity meters, and a Geophysical Survey Systems, Incorporated (GSSI) subsurface interfacing radar (SIR) Model SIR-3 with magnetic data recording and color display capabilities. The GPR system has been evaluated using 80, 300, 500, and 900 megahertz (MHz) antennae. Self potential (SP) surveying has also been utilized at the research site, but not as extensively as the other geophysical methods. The SG surveying was performed utilizing a Photovas 10570 portable gas chromotograph, while the SP surveying was done with a BBC high impedance voltmeter and Tinker and Rasor electrodes. Geophysical surveying was performed in either lineal or grid arrays, with data collection points spaced from 1 to 3 meters apart, except in the case of GPR surveying, which produces a continuous record of data collection. Geophysical arrays were arranged to provide data over undisturbed areas, buried pigs, and control pits.

## Thermal Imagery

The initial thermal imaging was performed using a Xedar Model XS-420 infrared camera system. Current surveys are conducted with FLIR (Forward Looking InfraRed) Systems, Inc., model #2000F with a truck mount, and ISI VideoTherm Model 94 and Model 96 portable handheld infrared cameras. Fair-field thermal imagery consisted of obtaining high quality thermal images of steady-state and dynamic scenes by panning the camera across the terrain of the research site, whereas near-field information was obtained by aiming the camera toward and fixing it on each grave and calibration pit.

## Soil Gas

Soil gas sampling of the far-field consisted of determining background levels of methane and other volatile organic compounds throughout research site. Near-field studies were performed by taking soil gas readings directly over graves and calibration pits.

## Decomposition Dogs

Standard far-field and near-field investigations become less defined for work with scent-detection dogs, as the dog defines those fields itself. The ability of the scent detection dogs to locate the buried pigs was tested using standard search techniques. The dog was controlled on a lead of usually 5 meters (15 feet) in length at all times, and "worked" on a zigzag pattern downwind of the suspected area. The zigzag pattern was maintained for the dog until it alerted to a scent, at which point the dog was allowed to work its own search pattern to the source.

## Scavenging Patterns

Naturalists trained in animal tracking and familiar with the habits of indigenous species were responsible for identifying scat and other animal sign. This information was used to develop scavenging patterns related to the burial sites. Patterns of bone modification related to scavenging were studied.

Standard far-field and near-field investigations also became blurred in studies of scavenging, as those terms are defined by where the scavenged remains, scat, and the agents of scavenging (coyotes, dogs, rodents, etc.) are found.

# Results

## Aerial Photography

Grave sites are revealed by a number of factors in the air photographs taken at the research site. These factors include changes in growth patterns and characteristics of near-field vegetation, anomalous soil marks associated with excavational boundaries, and settlement of snow within some grave surface depressions. Low sun angle oblique photographs tend to emphasize texture of the ground surface, and the associated long shadows can reveal minute topographic relief.

## Thermal Imagery

Aerial photography has been combined with infrared photography (forward-looking infrared, or FLIR) to search for buried bodies. While the FLIR system offers the best possible resolution and clarity, it requires a mount only offered by a helicopter or a specially equipped truck.

The use of infrared should not be limited to detecting those heat-related changes associated with decomposition. Infrared is a valuable tool in detecting compaction or density differences between the disturbed and undisturbed ground and so can be useful in detecting gravesites years after heat-generating decomposition has ceased.

## Geology

At the research site, short-term (less than 5 years) geological effects are enhanced by climatic conditions. The climatic conditions that typify Colorado's eastern plains offer extreme consequences affecting both the soil character and the rate and nature of soil recovery over the graves. Climatic conditions during late spring, summer, and fall, and often into early winter tend to be dry. The dry conditions are inhibiting plant reestablishment over the graves and retard breakdown of the disturbed clay rich host soil horizon. Lack of moisture largely neutralizes mechanical breakdown of fill material that is characteristic of periodic freeze/thaw conditions.

The moist climatic conditions of winter, spring, and early summer enhance rapid breakdown of clay soils. Excavation boundaries tend to become masked, fill material becomes generally more fine-grained, and the compaction of the fill material to the original surface grade is facilitated.

Excavations made during dry climatic conditions persist with little change throughout the dry season. Moisture enhances grave site recovery and plant establishment.

## Botany

The consequences of digging a grave and burying a body in a natural area are the same as any type of disturbance that destroys the existing vegetation: secondary succession is set into motion. After 5 years of following the regrowth of vegetation on pig graves, several general observations can be made. Undisturbed plots contained the greatest species diversity and supported both "weedy" plants as well as "wild flowers." After disturbance by digging, the plots supported a community with very little species diversity, often a monoculture of *Alyssum minus* (in this area of Colorado). Slowly, other species are invading from the surrounding undisturbed areas, but no plots had attained the original species mix by May of 1994. There is no difference in the revegetation pattern between the holes that still contain pigs and the holes that do not contain pigs.

The graves and calibration pits continue to revegetate, though the mix of plants on the disturbed areas is noticeably different than on the undisturbed areas. Vegetation on the disturbed areas depends on several factors, including which plants are nearby and supplying seeds to the disturbed ground and where in the landscape the digging was done (in drainage areas or on high ground). For example, the pig at Site 6 was placed on top of the ground in a drainage ditch, and dirt from another area was deposited over it. Even though the pig was taken by scavengers, the disturbed area is revegetating differently than the rest of the sites, both because the seeds in the foreign soil are different from the indigenous plants, and because the drainage ditch provides extra water for growth.

Although the percent cover for each site does not differ, the species covering each site are different. After 5 years the grave sites are revegetating similarly to the calibration pits, and, though it is commonly believed that the presence of a decaying body will provide nutrition to the plants covering a gravesite, at this point the presence of a decaying pig has not obviously affected plant growth, though decomposition dogs used in the research and on search scenes have "indicated" on some species of plants surrounding gravesites. (See section on decomposition dogs.) The warmth provided by a decaying pig has not been seen to affect the plant species which occupy a gravesite, though it is still hypothesized that this warmth exceeding the temperature of the adjacent ground may encourage plants to stay active for a longer period of time than the surrounding plant colonies during the period of heat-generating decay.

Vegetation analysis on the eight sites shows that:

1. Digging a grave will destroy existing vegetation and set succession in motion.
2. Pioneer or opportunistic plants will be the first to grow on the disturbed area. At the research site, the plants that have shown up on disturbed plots that have never shown up on undisturbed plots are thistle (*Carduus* spp.), annual sunflower (*Helianthus annuus*), and common purslane (*Portulaca oleracea*).
3. Vegetation changes as the grave progresses through the serial stages of succession.
4. Presumably, the climax vegetation for the area will eventually grow on the graves and calibration pits if they are not further disturbed. For lowland dry grass areas this includes blue grama grass (*Bouteloua gracilis*), other grasses, and many wild flowers. The disturbed area (grave or calibration pit) will look different from the surrounding area for many years (exceeding so far, the duration of this study).
5. Knowledge of the plants of an area can supply clues to the discovery of a grave, particularly where the vegetation is largely otherwise undisturbed.

## Entomology

There was no visible entomological indication of the buried pig, such as evidence of surface stains from saponification/liquification ca. 30 days after burial. The blowfly, *Calliphora vomitoria*, was trapped by the Malaise trap within 24 h of burial, and *Phormia regina* arrived 48 h after burial. By day 15, significant numbers ($p = <0.05$) of blowflies were trapped over the burial site as compared with control sites. No arthropods typically considered to be forensic indicators were trapped by the pit traps.

## Geophysics

The results of geophysical surveys applied to the location and delineation of clandestine graves have been encouraging. Once suspected target areas are defined by other techniques, geophysical surveys can be efficiently run using portable equipment. MAG and EM surveys data are gathered and presented in the field via use of a portable computer. These data can be presented in the form of contour maps or as individual profiles. The GPR data are acquired in real time format, i.e., the results are immediately available to investigators in the field. Work at the Pig site has demonstrated that SP surveying has very limited application in delineating clandestine graves. The field work is labor-intensive and the data interpretation is ambiguous. Of all of the methods applied at the Pig site, the most useful have been determined to be MAG, EM, and GPR.

MAG surveys were performed on some of the planned graves sites prior to interment of the pigs. Monitoring with MAG surveys after interment demonstrates that these surveys can be used at this site to detect areas of excavation, even when metallics are not present. This effect, a MAG anomaly, appears to be directly related to a reorientation of magnetic soil particles upon backfilling the graves. EM surveys have proven more useful than MAG, as the ground conductivity changes over graves due to the increased porosity of the backfill materials. EM surveys can be utilized to determine changes in ground conductivity and to detect the presence of ferrous and nonferrous metallics. When properly used and depending on the electrical properties of the soil, GPR surveys offer the investigator the most useful tool to delineate graves. Soil changes and excavation patterns can be readily identified by trained GPR operators. The addition of color monitoring to the normally black and white monitoring capabilities of the GPR systems allows investigators to easily identify changes in soil horizons over actual grave sites.

Perhaps the most important result of the geophysical surveying at the Pig site has been the realization of the importance of constructing a calibration site to test any geophysical method prior to application on an actual investigation. Any information concerning the type and/or construction of the disposal facility should be used to construct a similar, albeit empty, facility near the actual area to be investigated. The geophysicists can utilize this "calibration" site to determine the following:

1. Response of different geophysical methods
2. Type and characteristics of the geophysical signal
3. Profile and data station separation(s)

## Soil Gas

The soil gas surveying performed at the research site holds promise of providing a useful, albeit labor intensive, technique to locate graves. Organic gases were detected within 3 meters of two of the grave sites; however, the investigators had the privilege of knowing in advance the locations of these sites. Soil gas surveying is best in soils with a low clay content (so as not to clog the probes) and over unfrozen ground. Soil gas is not routinely utilized at crime scenes by the NecroSearch team.

## Decompostion Dogs

Based on experience with cases in this study and on opinions of other dog handlers, the successful use of dogs seems to be most significantly affected by weather conditions. There appears to be a decrease in the dog's scenting ability at temperatures above approximately 29°C (85°F). Excessive heat apparently causes some discomfort to the dog which seems to decrease its ability to locate a scent. When the temperature is extremely high, the dog may still locate the scent; however in most cases it will need to be within approximately 1 m of a buried source. Even if the temperature is high, the results will improve if the ground is moist. Extremely low temperatures also seem to limit the dog's ability to detect the scent from a distance, especially if the source is buried. If the source is buried in snow with temperatures allowing only minimal melting, the dog must be within 1 meter to locate the source. If the temperature is warm enough to allow for significant melting, the dog can locate the source from a greater distance. Additionally, if the source is buried in snow, or in the ground below snow, and the temperature is below freezing, the dog may not locate the source at all. The precise relationships between temperature, burial, and wind have not been tested.

Other factors which appear to affect the dog's work include air humidity, ground moisture, and wind speed. Humidity seems to intensify the dog's ability to detect the source at a distance. The ground should be moist, ideally to the depth of the source, or so dry that desiccation cracks intercept the source (Major Glenn Rimbey, New Mexico State Penitentiary, personal communication). Ultimately, if no wind is present, the dog will have difficulty detecting a scent except from an area within a meter of the source.

Based on experience at the research and other sites, the optimal conditions for the successful use of cadaver dogs include temperatures between approximately 4 and 16°C (40 to 60°F), 20% or higher humidity, moist or very moist ground, and wind speed of at least 8 km (5 mi) per hour (there is no upper limit to wind speed, though the scent cone becomes narrower with higher wind speeds). Additionally, it has been hypothesized, but not tested, that lower barometric pressure may increase the ability of the dogs to detect scents of all kinds arising from the soil.

Also based on experience at the research site and other sites (including actual cases), the trained decomposition dog will indicate the presence of decayed human scent when the source is human blood, feces, urine, and other human compounds, as well as other materials that have been handled or worn by humans, and so will give a seemingly "false positive" indication. Due to this discovery the dog handlers involved in this research have reclassified their dogs as "decomposition dogs" rather than "cadaver dogs" since a positive reaction from the dog may not specifically indicate a cadaver. Also, the dogs have "marked" on particular spots where decomposing scent had been present but had since been moved either accidently or purposely. Double-blind tests are being devised at present to rigorously test the dogs and handlers to determine under what additional conditions "false negatives" are possible (that is, when the dog does not indicate a body which is present).

Additional tests are being devised to determine the maximum time since death in which dogs can be useful. Some cadaver dogs have "indicated" on archaeological remains dated to around 1400 years before the present in an above-ground informal test. As expected, the dogs are less likely to "indicate" on those pig burial sites with a longer time since burial interval. In those situations, however, the dogs are more likely to "indicate" on certain plant species (particularly shrubs and trees) surrounding the grave site, and in some cases the dogs have actually tried to chew or bite at those shrubs close to the grave site (which is atypical behavior).

## Scavenging

Animal tracks or scat identified in the research area include domestic dog, coyote, fox, rabbit, deer, elk, skunk, raccoon, horse, cattle, porcupine, woodrat, and mouse.

Intensive, systematic searches within a 1 km radius of the site have recovered bones of deer, cattle, horses, canids, and rabbits. Many fresh bone chips, teeth, and hair had been found around several sites, indicating scavenging, but no large pig bones had been recovered within that search radius of the pig burials in the earlier stages of the research. The absence of large bones within the search radius suggested that the remains were carried a greater distance than the approximately 0.2 km maximum reported by Haglund et al. (1989), though as Haglund mentioned (personal communication), the ranges of coyotes vary considerably with differences in terrain and vegetation. Small VHF transmitters designed for wildlife radio tracking were recently attached to various areas of several new pig carcasses before burial to trace the location of the scavenged remains. The greatest distance to date for removal of portions of the pig remains has been 300 meters (burial 13), but remains may be moved as little as a few meters at each time, shallowly buried by the scavenger, and moved again later (as recorded with the aid of the transmitters).

Birds (various hawks, turkey vultures, and other birds) are often the first scavengers on the scene of shallow burials or surface deposits and will visit the remains many times throughout the scavenging process. Initial observations suggest that birds may take the epidermis of the pigs in sheets leaving straight surgical-like "cut marks" on the remaining tissue. In future experiments, this material will be preserved for microscopic examination and comparison with true cut tissue.

## Conclusions

Table 1 has been prepared based upon the experiences gained by both studies done at the known (pig) burial sites and field work on sites of suspected criminal burials.

# References

Bass, W.M., and W.H. Birkby
   1978   Exhumation: The Method Could Make the Difference. *FBI Law Enforcement Bulletin* July:6-11.

Boyd, R.M.
   1979   Buried Body Cases. *FBI Law Enforcement Bulletin* February:1–7.

Davenport, G.C., J.W. Lindemann, T.J. Griffin, and J.E. Borowski
   1988   Geotechnical Applications 3: Crime Scene Investigation Techniques. *Geophysics: The Leading Edge of Exploration* 7(8):64–66.

Davenport, G.C., T.J. Griffin, J.W. Lindemann, and D. Heimmer
   1990   Geoscientists and Law Enforcement Professionals Work Together in Colorado. *Geotimes* July:13–15.

Dickinson, D.J.
   1977   The Aerial Use of an Infra-Red Camera in a Police Search for the Body of a Missing Person in New Zealand. *Journal of the Forensic Science Society* 16:205–211.

France, D.L., T.J. Griffin, J.G. Swanburg, J.W. Lindemann, G.C. Davenport, V. Trammell, C.T. Travis, B. Kondratieff, A. Nelson, K. Castellano, and D. Hopkins
   1992   A Multidisciplinary Approach to the Detection of Clandestine Graves. *Journal of Forensic Sciences* 37:1445–1458.

Galloway, A., W.H. Birkby, A.M. Jones, T.E. Henry, and B.O. Parks
   1989   Decay Rates of Human Remains in an Arid Environment. *Journal of Forensic Sciences* 34:607–616.

Haglund, W.D.
   1991   *Applications of Taphonomic Models to Forensic Investigations.* Ph.D. dissertation, Department of Anthropology, University of Washington, Seattle. University Microfilms, Ann Arbor, MI.

Haglund, W.D., D.G. Reichert, and D.T. Reay
   1990   Recovery of Decomposed and Skeletal Human Remains in the Green River Murder Investigation: Implications for Medical Examiner/Coroner and Police. *American Journal of Forensic Medicine and Pathology* 11(1):35–43.

Haglund, W.D., D.T. Reay, and D.R. Swindler
   1989   Canid Scavenging/Disarticulation Sequence of Human Remains in the Pacific Northwest. *Journal of Forensic Sciences* 34:587–606.

Hoving, G.L.
   1986   Buried Body Search Technology. *Identification News* February:3, 15.

Hunter, J.R.
   1994   Forensic Archaeology in Britain. *Antiquity* 68:758–769.

Imaizumi, M.
   1974   Locating Buried Bodies. *FBI Law Enforcement Bulletin* August:2–5.

Killam, E.W.
   1990   *The Detection of Human Remains.* Charles C Thomas, Springfield, IL.

McLaughlin, J.E.
   1974   The Detection of Buried Bodies. Study of Andermac, 2626 Live Oak Hiway, Yuba City, CA 95991.

Nuorteva, P.
1977 Sarcophagous Insects as Forensic Indicators. In *Forensic Medicine: A Study in Trauma and Environmental Hazards*, edited by C.G. Tedeschi, W.G. Eckert, and L.G. Tedeschi, pp. 1072–1095. W.B. Saunders, Philadelphia.

Payne, J.D.
1965 A Summer Carrion Study of the Baby Pig, *Sus scrofa*. *Ecology* 46:592–602.

Payne, J.D., and E.W. King
1972 Insect Succession and Decomposition of Pig Carcasses in Water. *Journal of the Georgia Entomological Society* 7:153–162.

Payne, J.D., E.W. King, and G. Beinhart
1968 Arthropod Succession and Decomposition of Buried Pigs. *Nature* 180:1181.

Reed, H.B., Jr.
1958 A Study of Dog Carcass Communities in Tennessee, with Special Reference to the Insects. *American Midland Naturalist* 59:213–245.

Rhine, J.S., B. Curran, S. Boydstun, S. Churchill, P. Ivey, and M. Ogilvie
1988 Skeletonization Rates in the Desert. Paper presented at the 40th Annual Meeting of the American Academy of Forensic Sciences, Philadelphia.

Rodriguez, W.C., and W.M. Bass
1983 Insect Activity and Its Relationship to Decay Rates of Human Cadavers in East Tennessee. *Journal of Forensic Sciences* 28:423–432.
1985 Decomposition of Buried Bodies and Methods That May Aid in Their Location. *Journal of Forensic Sciences* 30:836–852.

Schoenly, K., K. Griest, and S. Rhine
1991 An Experimental Field Protocol for Investigating the Postmortem Interval Using Multidisciplinary Indicators. *Journal of Forensic Sciences* 36:1395–1415.

Shean, B.S., L. Messinger, and M. Papworth
1993 Observations of Differential Decomposition on Sun Exposed v. Shaded Pig Carrion in Coastal Washington State. *Journal of Forensic Sciences* 38:938–949.

Sheriff, Robert E. (editor)
1984 *Encyclopedic Dictionary of Exploration Geophysics.* 2nd ed. Society of Exploration Geophysicists, Tulsa, OK.

Smith, K.G.V.
1973 *Insects and Other Arthropods of Medical Importance.* British Museum of Natural History, London.
1986 *A Manual of Forensic Entomology.* British Museum (Natural History) and Cornell University Press, Ithaca, NY.

Tolhurst, W., and L. Reed
1984 *Manhunters! Hounds of the Big T.* Hound Dog Press, Puyallup, WA.

# Preservation in Late 19th Century Iron Coffin Burials

# 33

DOUGLAS W. OWSLEY
BERTITA E. COMPTON

## Introduction

Increasing interest and research in bioarchaeology reflect not only the need to derive as much information as possible from historic sites threatened by development or environmental conditions but the desire to establish continuity with the past and to develop a better understanding of the relationship between past and present physiological and sociocultural traits and trends. The greater the number of disciplines participating in such research — e.g., archaeology, physical anthropology, biochemistry, palynology, geology, burial practices, history — the more productive and meaningful the results. Thus the investigation of lead coffin burials from the early colonial era in Maryland was a broad cooperative effort merging the knowledge of experts in fields ranging from atmospheric trace constituents to embalming practices to costume analysis (Miller 1993).

The better preserved the human remains that are studied, the more detailed the data that can be obtained and the closer the feeling of identification and continuity with prior generations and their lifestyles, health, and traditions. Especially productive sources of such information are late 19th century cast iron coffin burials, although to date only a few have been studied in detail.

This chapter first briefly summarizes the evolution in the United States of the cast iron burial case and embalming techniques. Then, using examples from archival sources, personal communications, and research on such burials, it describes the range of preservation encountered. The findings of four detailed studies of cast iron coffin burials undertaken by the Department of Anthropology of the National Museum of Natural History, Smithsonian Institution, illustrate the diverse data that can result from the multidisciplinary investigation of such burials. The chapter concludes with a section on postmortem processes of deterioration of human remains and the ways that iron coffin burial impeded these natural processes.

## Background

### Development of the Cast Iron Burial Case

During the first centuries of occupation, settlers in the United States typically buried their dead in the earth, sometimes in a shroud (Lang 1984). Subsequently, the use of coffins became commonplace, but these were usually of wood (Habenstein and Lamers 1981). Preservation, depending on climate and the type and acidity of the soil, is often poor. Soft tissues are rarely preserved, and frequently bone is fragile and powdery, with the cortex exfoliating. The patenting and eventual mass production of an air-tight, cast iron burial case, beginning in the

0-8493-9434-1/97/$0.00+$.50
© 1997 by CRC Press, Inc.

mid-1800s, together with advances in embalming techniques, resulted in substantially better preservation. Both developments were stimulated to a large extent by the Civil War and the need to preserve remains for return to distant families.

The first metallic coffin to achieve widespread acceptance and use in the United States was the Fisk metallic burial case, patented in 1848 (Boffey 1980; Habenstein and Lamers 1981; Lang 1984). It consisted of two metal shells that would accommodate a reclining human body with arms folded over the chest. The early coffins were mummy-shaped, with designs that simulated the folds of drapery and ornamental scrolls and flowers. A glass plate with a metal cover allowed viewing of the face. Fisk permitted other companies to acquire the right to produce these burial cases, and by the late 1850s, Crane, Breed and Co. of Cincinnati, Ohio, had modified the original design, eliminating the mummy shape and simplifying the decorations. This company began mass production in 1858, thereby reducing cost and making such burial cases widely available. Public demand was enhanced by demonstrations of the preservation that could be achieved, together with such advantages as protection from water seepage, vermin, contagion, and grave robbers, and by the feasibility and ease of transfer of a body from a vault or temporary facility to a place of permanent interment (Boffey 1980; *The Sunnyside* 1906).

The first sheet metal caskets were introduced in the early 1870s and soon replaced the cast iron models because of the reduction in weight and the greater flexibility in shape and ornamentation that was possible (Lang 1984). Although use of metallic caskets continued to increase, and patents for caskets made of such materials as stone, glass, or even celluloid were obtained, wood continued to be the material most frequently used for burial receptacles until the mid 1900s (Habenstein and Lamers 1981).

The cast iron coffin was in use mainly from about 1850 to 1880, and its development paralleled a shift in emphasis from encasement of a body for immediate burial to its presentation and display (Lang 1984; Little et al. 1992; Owsley and Mann 1992). This trend was apparent in the change from a mummy shape to a hexagonal, octagonal, or rectangular one, greater attention to interior furnishings (e.g., lining, pillows) and ornamental exterior hardware (e.g., handles, thumb screws, escutcheons), and enlargement of the glass viewing panel.

## Development of Embalming

Embalming has been practiced since about 6,000 B.C., when the ancient Egyptians and Babylonians employed various methods of preservation of the dead, aided greatly by dry, hot climatic conditions (Strub and Frederick 1967). The principal purposes were and are disinfection and preservation. These goals are accomplished by inhibiting the enzymatic action that dissolves soft tissues after death. Such enzymes derive from the body tissues themselves, bacteria (most frequently those of the colon), and insects (Aufderheide and Aufderheide 1991; Clark et al., this volume; Gill-King, this volume). These enzymes are sensitive to environmental changes in temperature, acidity (pH), the presence of heavy metal ions (e.g., bismuth, lead, mercury), and, most crucial, moisture (i.e., they require a liquid medium in which to function). In embalming, various chemical agents applied to the interior and exterior tissues of a dead body inhibit the organisms and enzymes that would otherwise induce such processes as fermentation, decay, and putrefaction (Strub and Frederick 1967). Many techniques and many formulae (see Berryman et al. and Clark et al., this volume) have been employed over the years, sometimes in combination with various herbs, spices, and oils. Especially in the 19th century, arsenic was frequently employed in various forms (Williams and Konefes 1992), with some coffins having as much as 14 pounds of powdered arsenic placed around the body (M. Williams, personal communication 1990). In 1910, when the level of arsenic that could be employed in preservation of the dead was restricted (Williams and Konefes 1992), widespread use of formaldehyde for embalming began.

In the United States, the Civil War was the main impetus to the adoption and further development of embalming, which at that time, was performed by medical doctors. From the Civil War era to the end of the century, embalming evolved through a period of public resistance (in part religious) to chemical preservation, transition from a specialty of the medical practitioner to one of the pharmacist, undertaker, and wholesale chemical company, and finally to the establishment of schools of embalming (in 1882) and the subsequent emergence of a large-scale commercial embalming enterprise (Habenstein and Lamers 1981). As general acceptance of embalming and refinement of embalming procedures came about only gradually during the past century in the United States, studies of well-preserved soft tissues have been relatively rare, being associated principally with mummies of Native Americans and the few late 19th century iron coffin burials that have been subjected to detailed analysis.

## Cast Iron Coffin Burials: Incidence and Preservation

The discovery of a cast iron coffin is typically accidental, such as when road or sewer construction intrudes on an unmarked family cemetery, when an environmental occurrence such as a flood reveals unmarked burials, when a newly dug grave reveals an older unmarked burial, or when planned development necessitates the relocation of a cemetery. In most instances, reburial occurs relatively quickly without a comprehensive study of either the coffin or the body it contains, though in some instances the body has been placed in another receptacle for reburial and the coffin given to a funeral home museum for restoration and display.

In response to a published request for assistance (Owsley and Mann 1991), the Smithsonian has received information on about 70 cast iron coffin burials from personal communications, often including newspaper accounts. Thus far, the burials described occurred in the central and eastern United States (i.e., Wisconsin, Iowa, Missouri, Illinois, Ohio, New York, Pennsylvania, Maryland, Virginia, Tennessee, Kentucky, Alabama, and Louisiana). Among the nationally prominent persons whose burial in an iron coffin has been noted are Dolley Madison, Henry Clay, Daniel Webster, John C. Calhoun, Stephen A. Douglas, and Zachary Taylor. Members of regionally prominent or founding families (e.g., Nathaniel Burwell of Roanoke County, VA and Governor Lewin Winder of Somerset County, MD) were often buried in iron coffins, as noted either in newspaper accounts at the time of death or when such burials have been rediscovered when cemeteries are relocated or when new graves intrude on older unmarked ones. In addition, anecdotal accounts in local histories and correspondence sometimes mention iron coffin burials. One such example describes a child buried in a cast iron coffin that was discovered when a family cemetery near Alexandria, VA, had to be relocated in 1940 because of commercial development (Chapman 1987): "This infant had been buried seventy years but her little features were just as they were when laid to rest. The white muslin frock fresh and white…. There was a tiny white rose bud in the baby's hand." The description further indicates that the steam shovel used in excavation cracked the air-tight coffin, with decomposition of the remains beginning immediately.

One of the relatively few studies made of an iron coffin burial (Clements 1976) took place when construction near a school encroached on the site of a former cemetery in Beardstown, IL. Human remains, garments, burial case, and moist decay residue in the coffin were analyzed. Metals found in the coffin residue included iron (from coffin erosion), lead (a constituent of the sealant), calcium (associated with initial human decomposition), and silicon (from the surrounding sandy soil). The clothing — cotton shirt and separate collar, bow tie, cotton trousers, and long-sleeved, cotton, shroud-like garment — was machine-made and inexpensive. The coffin, however, was one of the early, expensive cast iron Fisk mummy cases. The body was in a good state of preservation and was that of a white male, 20 to 30 years of age at death, with an estimated height of 73 in and an estimated weight of 166 to 178 pounds. His thick red hair was neatly combed and parted on the right side, and his beard was trimmed to about 1 inch in length and covered the side of the face and rim of the mandible. The body was not embalmed. The skin was leathery and dark, and the internal organs had decayed. A number of teeth had silver amalgam fillings. Neither visual examination nor radiography revealed any trauma or bone disease, thus the cause of death was not determined, nor was the body identified.

Study of another iron coffin burial began as a forensic investigation, for the preservation was so remarkable that law enforcement personnel and forensic scientists initially thought the deceased was a recent murder victim stuffed into an older grave (Bass 1984; *Blue & Gray Magazine* 1993). A headless torso was found protruding from a grave disturbed by vandals searching for Civil War curios in a family cemetery in Tennessee. The coffin was cast iron, and the shattered skull and mandible, which must have separated from the trunk when the vandals pulled the body out, were also present. Pink tissue adhered to the bones, and the clothing was intact. The initial estimate of time elapsed since death was about a year.

Detailed analysis, after removal of the body to a laboratory, indicated that it had been embalmed before being placed in the tightly sealed cast iron coffin. The deceased was a white male, 25 to 28 years of age at death. The cause of death was a head wound; a projectile had entered the left frontal bone and exited through the back of the right parietal bone. No dental caries or fillings were present, but four teeth had been lost before death, with advanced alveolar bone resorption. The physical characteristics and head wound coincided with the description of Col. William Shy of the Army of Tennessee, killed by a point-blank shot to the forehead during the Union attack on Confederate positions on Shy's Hill in the Battle of Nashville. Thus Shy's body had been interred 113 years prior to its discovery, rather than about a year, as the remarkable state of preservation had at first suggested.

Another study took place when a construction worker saw what he thought was a doll fall from the back of a truck clearing debris at a construction site (Owsley and Mann 1992). It was the upper part of a human body. Shortly afterward, a second truck dumped the other half with another load of dirt. Examination by physical anthropologists showed that the body was that of an approximately 5-year-old boy clad in smock, undershirt, pants, socks, and nonsided shoes (i.e., left and right were the same). Skin and hair were well-preserved, and although the nostrils were packed with cotton, there was no other indication of embalming. The style of the clothing suggested that the child had lived about 100 years previously, in the late 1800s, yet the excellent preservation of body tissues was consistent with death only a few weeks or months prior to discovery. Rust stains on the clothing, together with the exceptional preservation, caused the investigators to suspect that burial might have been in an iron coffin, and the construction workers were asked to look for metal fragments. Subsequently, they found portions of the lid and side of a cast iron coffin at the site from which the body had come.

Five lead coffin burials dating from the 17th century that were discovered in St. Mary's City, the first capital of Maryland, provide additional examples of the range of preservation in human remains placed in metallic burial cases (Owsley and Sledzik 1993). Two of the burials, an adult male and female interred inside the former Great Brick Chapel, are thought to be Philip Calvert, Governor, then Chancellor, of the colony, and his first wife. The third burial at this site was that of an infant, as yet unidentified, possibly a child of Philip and his second wife. Another adult male and female in a nearby subterranean burial vault are the royal governor of the colony (from 1691 to 1693), Sir Lionel Copley and his wife.

Among the three presumed Calverts, preservation varied greatly. The adult male skeleton was incomplete, with only the leg bones and feet in excellent condition. Most of the skeleton had been replaced by brushite (a hydrated acid phosphate that forms from the breakdown of calcium phosphate and calcium carbonate in the presence of water). Small textile fragments adhered to the bones that were present, and there was much hair associated with the remains. In contrast, the adult female skeleton was nearly complete with scalp hair, some textiles, and silk ribbons bound about the wrists. The skeleton of the infant was in good to excellent condition and virtually complete. Even though the Copley vault had been previously opened and the skeletons examined on three known occasions, the earliest being by medical students of St. Mary's College in 1799, bone preservation was still good, with hair present, although no soft tissues or fabrics were preserved. The medical students had found a winding sheet and other fabrics. They reported that only the bones of Sir Lionel remained, but that his wife was perfectly preserved, her hair braided and piled on top of her head (Owsley and Sledzik 1993). In the recent exhumation, examination of the bones *in situ* showed that both bodies had been sectioned and embalmed, as the medical students had also noted. Rosemary, which was often used in preservation in that era, was found in the coffin of the Calvert female.

# Four Recent, Detailed Studies of Iron Coffin Burials

Recent studies at the Smithsonian of four iron coffin burials, three in which there was preservation of only bone and clothing and one in which there was soft tissue, show the range of preservation in such burials and provide examples of the diverse data that multidisciplinary analyses of these remains can yield.

## Louisiana Burial

In 1988, Smithsonian physical anthropologists excavated and studied an iron coffin burial that had first been discovered in a family cemetery near Baton Rouge in 1963 when a new grave was dug (Owsley and Mann 1992). At that time, the glass viewing plate showed the well-preserved remains of a man in a frock coat, white shirt, and bow tie. None of the family recognized him, and cemetery records showed no burial at that location. The coffin was reburied in another place in the cemetery where it remained until the study was initiated at the request of a family member in 1988.

Reburial in 1963 had been in shallower, damper soil. As a result, the coffin had rusted, allowing the entry of water and plant roots, and some deterioration of the human remains had occurred. The coffin and its contents were removed to the Smithsonian where an autopsy was conducted in cooperation with pathologists from the Armed Forces Institute of Pathology. Based on the osteological analysis, the deceased was a white male, about 50 years old at death, 5 feet 6 inches tall, of medium build, and weighing about 150 pounds. His face was long and narrow, with a strong jaw. No trauma or old fractures were apparent, but lytic resorptive areas and osteophytes on the first and third metatarsals of the right foot suggested that the man had suffered from degenerative arthritis and gout. His teeth showed moderate wear, indicating a diet of gritty material. Four teeth contained gold fillings, and two had been lost as a result of abscessing prior to death. Because of the advanced deterioration of the remains and an overgrowth of fungal elements and bacteria, planned histological studies were not possible, nor was it possible to distinguish definite blood vessels containing erythrocytes; thus immunocytochemical assays for blood typing antigens could not be performed.

Based on costume analysis, death probably occurred in the late 1860s. The narrow width of the bow tie, for example, indicated that death was after 1857 when that style was introduced, and the thickness of the heels of the shoes was consistent with the late 1860s or early 1870s (S. Foote, personal communication 1988). The black wool frock coat and trousers were custom made and typical of what a late 19th century gentleman would wear on a relatively formal occasion, such as attendance at church.

The coffin, which was 6 feet long, weighed 250 pounds, and was mummy shaped, and was identified as a variation of the Model #3 Fisk Patent Coffin marketed by Crane, Breed and Co. (M.J. Williams, personal communication 1988). The firm operated a showroom in New Orleans from 1866 to 1869, making such coffins readily available in South Louisiana.

To date, archival searches of cemetery, legal, and family records have not led to positive identification. A facial reconstruction (produced by S. Long, Laramie, WY) and sketches made

**Figure 1**   Crane, Breed and Company cast iron coffin from Manassas, VA, dating to 1870.

by the Federal Bureau of Investigation were compared with family pictures, including a faded daguerreotype of a male in-law who died at age 50 in 1867, to which a resemblance was apparent. Though the remains have been reinterred, the effort to establish identity continues.

## Virginia Burial

When the Weir family cemetery in Manassas, VA, was relocated in 1990 as a result of encroaching development and vandalism, the court order obtained by the family included provision for a study of the osteological remains and associated artifacts prior to reburial (Owsley and Mann 1992). Of the 24 burials involved, one was in a cast iron coffin (Figure 1). Only in this burial was there a virtually complete skeleton in an excellent state of preservation. The other burials, eight adult males, eight adult females, one adult of indeterminate sex, and six sub-adults, had been interred in yellow or white pine coffins, generally hexagonal, and all remains were in extremely poor condition. In some instances only tooth crowns remained. For most, no analysis of physical characteristics and bone pathology was possible, and identification was based on the information provided by grave markers.

The iron coffin burial was transferred to Washington and autopsy of the remains took place at the Armed Forces Institute of Pathology in April 1990. Although the coffin face plate had collapsed and ground water had filled the coffin, the skeleton, body hair, and clothing were well preserved (Figure 2). The skin, muscles and ligaments, and internal organs had deteriorated. Adipocere was present in the medullary cavity of a femur sampled for molecular research. Examination indicated that the body was that of a white male, 5 feet 10 inches in height, of medium build, and in his early 30s at the time of death. These data were consistent with the grave marker indicating that the grave was that of Walter Weir, who died in 1870 at age 31.

There was no evidence of degenerative joint disease, trauma, congenital or developmental abnormality, or infectious disease of the bone, but analysis of dentition showed one gold filling, two unfilled carious lesions, one molar lost several years before death, and active

**Figure 2**   Clothing and skeletal remains of Walter Weir, Manassas, VA.

periapical abscessing at the time of death that had caused the loss of one tooth and had spread to the next one. Sepsis from such an abscess could have spread to the brain or heart, causing the death of an otherwise healthy young man, who had survived 4 years of Confederate military service unscathed.

Samples of water from the coffin were analyzed but showed no organisms other than those normally occurring in the environment or in the flora of the human intestinal tract (T. Hadfield, personal communication 1989). No pathogenic species were identified.

Biochemical and molecular analyses included comparison of tissue samples collected and placed in liquid nitrogen immediately after field recovery of the remains and additional samples recovered some 6 months later during autopsy. This research employed a new technique, being developed by N. Tuross (Smithsonian Conservation Analytical Laboratory) for identification of proteins, especially immunoglobulins of the IgG class, found in archaeological samples of human bone. A wide range of proteins, with molecular weights corresponding to those in contemporary bone specimens, was preserved in the Weir skeleton, and immunoglobulins of the IgG class were isolated. Analysis of this burial provided data relevant to paleodisease diagnosis based on IgG reactivity to pathologic antigens. It also showed that for tissues in a wet environment, immediate sampling produces the best results, with less deterioration in protein content. Further tests for immunoglobulins are in progress. If these can be isolated, they will show the persistence through time of proteins and provide a record, preserved in bone, of pathogens to which the deceased was exposed. In addition, bone samples were requested by an investigator at University College, London, for use in research on the effects of postmortem events on skeletal remains, with application to forensic analyses.

Weir was clad in a black wool, quilted frock coat, matching trousers, a white cotton vest and white shirt with detachable collar, and black silk bow tie, typical attire of a middle to upper class male of the mid-19th century (S. Foote, personal communication 1990). On his feet were white knitted socks, with "W. Weir" marked in ink, but no shoes.

The rounded, hexagonal, iron coffin was cast in two pieces, was 6 feet 6 inches long and 2 feet wide at the point of maximum width, and weighed (empty) 228 pounds. A glass viewing plate in the lid was shaped like a church window and fitted with a metal overplate. Placement of the handles (at the head and foot, as well as along each side) were key in identifying the coffin as a Crane, Breed and Co. model that was manufactured after 1865 (M.J. Williams, personal communication). It was lined and padded and contained a straw-filled mat and pillow.

A facial reconstruction was developed (S. Long, Laramie, WY). Though the family had no pictures of Walter Weir, there were two photographs of his brothers, both of whom had unusually large noses, as Walter's nasal bones suggested that his was.

The family presented the coffin and clothing to the National Museum of Health and Medicine where they are now part of the permanent historical collection, available to scholars, Civil War reenactment groups, and others for study. Samples of coffin hardware from this and several other of the Weir family burials were added to the Smithsonian's reference collection to assist in dating other burials.

## Tennessee Burial

A road construction crew working near Nashville in 1992 struck a badly corroded iron coffin containing a skeleton. The burial was sent to the Smithsonian for anthropological examination to determine the individuals's age at death, race, sex, stature, evidence of trauma and disease, and other information that would assist in identifying the remains so that they could be returned to descendants for reburial. The lid and glass viewing plate had been broken prior to the delivery of the coffin to the Smithsonian, and there was much water and red mud inside as a result of the breakage. A team of scientists from the Armed Forces Institute of Pathology and the Smithsonian opened the coffin and examined the contents.

The skeleton was dark colored and virtually complete, with teeth and hair present, but no soft tissues remained. The body was clothed in a black suit, fragmentary material from a shirt, underclothing, socks, and shoes. The bones were discolored (black) but in an excellent state of preservation, except for the left side of the face and vault, which had been in contact with the floor of the coffin and, as a result, were eroded and in poor condition.

Characteristics of the pelvis, cranium, mandible, and long bones indicated that sex was male. Facial morphology and the shape of the skull, together with the presence of long, straight head hair, showed that race was white. From the maximum length of the left femur, living stature was calculated as approximately 5 feet 5 inches (Trotter 1970; Trotter and Gleser 1958). Osseous changes associated with degenerative disease, together with degree of cranial suture closure and dental traits, were consistent with an estimated age of 50 to 60 years. The presence of a malignant marrow disease not usually found in individuals less than 45 years old was also consistent with advanced age.

There was no osteological evidence of trauma, but the skeleton was permeated with resorptive lesions, primarily affecting the spine, sacrum, sternum, ribs, os coxae, scapulae, clavicles, humeri, femora, tibiae, basilar and vault portions of the cranium. The only bones free of lesions and grossly normal were the mandible, patellae, fibulae, and the hand and foot bones. The lesions occurred bilaterally and symmetrically, and their size ranged from 1 mm to 19 mm (in the left os coxa). The margins of the lesions were irregular and well defined. The bone most affected was the sternum, whose ventral surface was nearly completely resorbed. Next in severity were the vertebral bodies, which exhibited multiple, often confluent, lesions that originated in the spongiosa of the centra and progressed outward (Figure 3). Many of the neural arches also had resorptive lesions. The ribs had multiple, ovoid lesions along the shafts, most being within about 5 cm of the costal ends, though there were also a few in the middle portions and at the vertebral ends. The lesions tended to be larger on the inner (i.e., trabecular) surface, indicating progression of the disease from within the bone toward its surface. In the os coxae, lesions occurred along the margins of the iliac crests, symphysi pubis, ischia, and retroauricular areas, being largest on the external surfaces of the os coxae

**Figure 3**  Lytic lesions in the lumbar vertebrae of William Binns, caused by multiple myeloma.

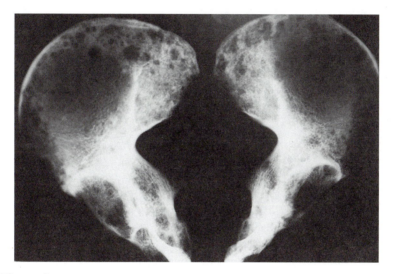

**Figure 4**   Radiograph showing multiple resorptive lesions in the innominates.

(Figure 4). Scattered resorptive lesions were also present in the scapulae, clavicles, and humeri, along the epiphyseal lines of the femoral heads and greater trochanters, and in the tibiae, although the latter were only visible radiographically. That the tibial lesions had not affected the outer cortex indicated that they originated within the medullary cavity. With time, they would have perforated the tibial diaphyses. In regard to the cranium, lesions occurred principally on the inner surface of the parietal bones and basilar portions of the occipital.

The gross and radiographic appearance of the lesions, as well as their occurrence in an older individual, supported a diagnosis of multiple myeloma, a malignant cancer of the bone marrow, as the likely cause of death.

The clothing (examined by S. Foote, National Museum of American History) consisted of a black, wool frock coat and trousers, ready-made rather than specially tailored and probably obtained from W. C. Browning & Co. of New York, as marked on the buttons. (Browning is listed in an 1860–1874 New York directory as a ready-made clothing establishment.) The coat sleeves were wide at the elbow and tapered to the wrist, a distinctive style characteristic of the 1870s. The trousers had a fly front (usual by the 1860s), buttons for the attachment of suspenders, and a buckle at the center back for adjusting waist size. The shirt disintegrated into a mass of fibers as soon as it was touched. However, seam lines apparent on initial viewing indicated a U-shaped bosom front and crease lines resulting from being worn close to the body and confined by the coat. Within the disintegrating mass of shirt and coat fibers were pieces of perforated leather. 19th century ads for chamois vests urged their use as a preventative health measure, and this individual, who would have suffered severely from his malignant disease, may have sought amelioration through wearing such a garment.

The shoes had leather soles but were topped with fabric containing five metal grommets on either side of the top front for laces. The toes were rounded, suggesting a date in the 1860s or early 1870s. (Prior to 1860 toes were square, and by the late 1870s, pointed toes were being adopted.) Further research on the design on the soles of the shoes may yield information on the date and place of manufacture.

The cast iron coffin appeared to be a version of the Fisk Model #3 Plain Case, introduced in 1854, modified in 1858, and subsequently mass produced. It had three plain handles on each side (two of which were missing). Maximum width was 20 in., and length was 74.5 in. Bolt holes around the flanges included two at the head, two at the foot, and ten along each side. The case was entirely plain; even the metal plate rotated to cover the glass viewing area was undecorated. Some sealant remained in the grooves of the flanges, and traces of white paint were evident on the badly eroded surface. The period of greatest use of such a coffin was from 1858 to 1870, after which the lighter, exactly rectangular (rather than tapered) sheet metal burial case began to be adopted.

Study of this burial yielded data useful in establishing, and subsequently corroborating, identification as William Alexander Burns, who died in 1867. Because of the extensive bone pathology, which makes this skeleton especially valuable for educational and research purposes, the descendant family has allowed it to remain at the Smithsonian.

## Maryland Burial

In Laurel, MD, during a construction project, a backhoe hit the foot end of a cast iron coffin in a 19th century family burial plot. The face plate had been previously broken and much dirt had fallen into the head end, but there was no water inside. Soil acids had pockmarked the exterior of the coffin. The coffin, which was lined with cotton material, was plain, with a tapered, rectangular shape, and weighed 300 pounds. Inside, resting on a pillow, was the body of an adult, white male. Soft tissues, bone, hair, and clothing were present. Large quantities of blue crystals (vivianite) and arsenic were around the body. At the request of the Maryland–National Capital Park and Planning Commission, Smithsonian physical anthropologists conducted a detailed analysis of this burial.

The body was supine, with hands resting on the lower abdomen and feet tied with cloth bands at the ankles and insteps. A chin strap extended over the top of the head and was tied under the chin and attached to the outer material of a shirt. Adipocere was present on the left side and top of the skull. Hair on the skull included scalp hair, eyelashes, mustache, and beard (Figure 5).

On the body was a white, shroud-like outer shirt, with wide, open sleeves with fold-back hems, and at the neck, open edges that folded back to form lapels. It was a typical commercial burial garment of the period. At the waist was a separate pleated band. In addition to this robe, the body was clad in a white cotton, long-sleeved, hip length dress shirt, cotton knit gloves and socks, and drawers. The tucked bosom of the shirt was of a finer quality material than the rest of the garment. A white glass button at the neck of the shirt would have been covered by a necktie, had one been present, and the other three shirt buttons were hidden beneath a fold of material (a hidden closure). The gloves were amazingly well-preserved and were knit in a radiating pattern that allowed the increase needed to cover the back of the hand. The socks were of a plain stockinette knit, with a top portion of rib knit. The drawers were of heavy wool knit, with ribbed leg openings and a white cotton Y-shaped yoke fastened

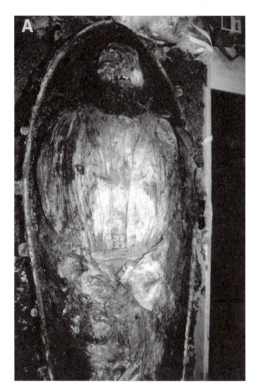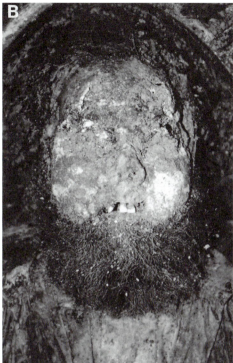

**Figure 5**   Preservation of the face, hair, and clothing of engineer John White, who was killed in a train accident in 1861. (A) View of body in coffin; (B) close-up of face.

with three large buttons. The lower edge of the leg openings was placed over the socks. The heaviness of the drawers suggested winter wear. (S. Foote, National Museum of American History, examined and described the clothing.)

In addition to these garments, beneath the drawers was a piece of seamed cotton fabric, probably cut from a piece of material such as a sheet. This cloth, wound about the loins, held in place a padding of cotton wool packed about the abdomen and pubic area.

Skull morphology was classic Caucasian, as was the texture of the head hair. Degree of cranial suture closure, the presence of slight arthritic changes on vertebrae and joints of long bones, and bone density indicated an estimated age of 40 to 50 years at death. Data on dentition (e.g., slight alveolar bone resorption, degree of dental wear, tooth loss) were also consistent with middle age. Estimated height, based on long bone measurements, was approximately 5 feet 6 inches (Trotter 1970; Trotter and Gleser 1958).

Skin on the chest and abdomen was moderately hairy, but there was little hair on the skin of the arms. Well preserved muscle tissue was present, as well as remnants of the collapsed lungs and pericardial sac. The right half of the diaphragm was ruptured with ragged edges, and several left and right ribs were fractured with intercostal hemorrhaging, all of which suggested a crushing injury.

The texture of the heart tissue was leathery, with minimal evidence of calcification of the tricuspid and mitral valves or narrowing of the left main coronary artery. The aorta was intact and in good condition. There was no evidence of heart disease. Tracheal rings had decalcified, the gall bladder showed no stones, and the appendix and kidneys were normal. The liver, however, showed damage, possibly postmortem. Parts of the penis and scrotal sacs were present. Cotton wool had been placed inside the pelvic cavity and in the rectum, with blood stains visible on the latter, and as previously indicated, the lower half of the trunk had been wrapped in cotton padding, with a sheet-like material forming a kind of bandage about the loins. The articulated thoracic spine showed pronounced antemortem lateral curvature (scoliosis) and convexity (kyphosis). There was no evidence of cranial trauma.

The cemetery in which this iron coffin burial occurred was that of the Aitcheson family. Through family records, the white male buried in an iron coffin has been identified as John White, an Englishman, who married Agnes Aitcheson in 1847. White was an engineer on the North Carolina Railroad from 1850 until his death on 4 January 1861. He was killed when the Raleigh-bound express was not delayed at Queries Turn Out and collided with the Charlotte-bound express (Creveling 1994). Both engines were smashed, and Engineer White was badly injured in the chest and abdomen and subsequently died. He was buried near the Aitcheson family home in Scotchtown (near Laurel), Maryland. Family records describe him as a hero whose reversal of his train in an effort to avert the collision saved the lives of his passengers though not his own.

Soft tissue preservation in this iron coffin burial was remarkably good, with skin, muscle, and organ tissue intact, permitting a detailed assessment of general health and the nature of the trauma that had resulted in death. Samples of soil, glass (from the coffin viewing plate), sealant, blue crystals (inside the coffin), and lining fabric were taken for analysis and further study, as were samples of tissue and scalp and beard hair. The body and coffin were reinterred.

## Taphonomic Processes in Iron Coffin Burials

### Normal Decomposition

During normal decomposition processes, body tissues produce enzymes that, following death, result in the self-digestion of these tissues. (Summary based on Strub and Fredrick 1967, and Aufderheide and Aufderheide 1991; see also Clark et al., Chapter 9 in this volume). One form of enzymatic decomposition is fermentation, the reduction of body carbohydrates, which can be initiated by bacteria, yeasts, and autolytic enzymes. Bacterial fermentation can be anaerobic or aerobic. Decay is another form of aerobic decomposition and involves the oxidation of proteins. Putrefaction, a third type of decomposition, is the step-by-step reduction of complex proteins to their components. It occurs in both air and water and continues after burial. Coliform organisms are the primary triggering agents. It is putrefaction that results in odoriferous gaseous emissions, color changes (e.g., blue/green, green/yellow, green/black, red/red brown), and liquefaction. Among the products of putrefaction are water, carbon dioxide, ammonia, hydrogen sulfide, hydrogen phosphide, and methane.

Immersion in water tends to slow putrefaction, but its progress is affected by temperature, water quality, and motion (i.e., it is more rapid in warm, polluted, fresh, and stagnant water). Saponification (formation of adipocere) is a modification of putrefaction in which fatty tissues are transformed into a waxy substance that is white to pale yellow and greasy in texture, with an odor like that of decayed cheese. It occurs in burials in moist soil or immersed in water (see Clark et al., this volume).

In air, a number of conditions affect the progress of putrefaction, including temperature, humidity, airborne bacteria, and characteristics of the deceased individual such as the cause and manner of death, nutrition, hydration, and sex specific diseases. In neonates, putrefaction is slower in stillborns than in those that have ingested nourishment.

### Preservation in Intact Iron Coffin Burials

Following burial, the rate of putrefaction is slower in soil than in air (as in a vault), but is affected by the depth of burial and type soil (e.g., porous sandy or clay, salty or acidic, dry or moist). Enclosure of a body in a casket tends to retard putrefaction, and in the case of a correctly sealed, cast iron coffin, delays the onset of fermentation, decay, and putrefaction for an extended period of time (i.e., several decades or more). Embalming, in addition to burial in an iron coffin, further inhibits processes of decomposition.

The key to preservation in a cast iron coffin, as early brochures, for example, those of the W. M. Raymond Company of New York and the Crane, Breed and Company of Cincinnati emphasized, was proper sealing (Boffey 1980). A cement made of ground white lead combined with boiled linseed oil, then mixed with dry red lead to a consistency like that of window putty, was placed in the groove running around the flange of the lower half of the coffin. A projection on the flange of the upper half was then pressed into this, and the two halves of the coffin were bolted together. Instructions for the preparation and use of the sealant were enclosed in each iron coffin sold to an undertaker, with the reminder that it was his responsibility to see that the coffin was correctly sealed. A properly sealed iron coffin would prevent the escape of any gases or odors from within and, more important, prevent the entry of air and water from the outside, thus suspending processes of decomposition for an extended period of time.

The coffin manufacturers encouraged embalming in addition to use of the cast iron burial case. For example, an 1854 pamphlet of Crane, Breed and Company states that: "We do not claim that these cases will preserve the body for all future time without some decay, unless properly prepared by injection into the arteries of an antiseptic fluid...." (*Sunnyside* 1906). The use of various preservative powders sprinkled within the coffin was also encouraged, one such mixture consisting of a pulverized mixture of alum, salt, and saltpeter, and until the early 1900s, large quantities of arsenic were often placed around a body in a coffin.

Coffin manufacturers' ads cited numerous letters attesting to the excellent preservation resulting from use of their metallic burial cases. For example, a pamphlet prepared by the Crane and Breed Manufacturing Company of Cincinnati on "Instructions for the Use of Patent Metallic Burial Cases and Caskets" (circa 1885) includes the following "extracts selected from hundreds of letters voluntarily written to us:"

St. Louis, MO: Body of lady removed after being buried. Body perfect in preservation, hair parted naturally and face entirely recognizable.

Memphis, TN: Body of child removed after 23 years' burial. A fine case of preservation. The golden hair curled over the forehead just as some loving hand had gently brushed it years before.

Louisville, KY: Body of child removed after 40 years. As natural as if in sleep. The cheeks had a "flesh" color, and the hair was fine and silky. The white robe was perfect, and a large yellow rose, pinned on the breast, was apparently as fresh as if just plucked from the bush.

Boffey (1980) describes a number of instances in which iron coffin burials were discovered when cemeteries were being relocated and excellent preservation was noted. For example, (Boffey 1980:45):

... in 1904, a cemetery near Cincinnati was sold...and the dead removed and reburied. Most of the original burials had been made in wooden coffins, and little remained but bones and rusty nails. But there were also Fisk cast-iron coffins, and they were found intact.... The bodies were described as in fine condition as viewed through the glass face plate ....

## Deterioration Following Coffin Damage

With the entry of air and often water into an incorrectly sealed or damaged iron coffin, the normal processes of decomposition promptly set in, with soft tissues, such as the parenchyma of organs, being first affected, then firm tissues, such as those of the muscles and stroma of organs, and last, hard tissue (cartilage and bone) (Strub and Frederick 1967). Especially when the body has not been embalmed, signs of decomposition — for example, color change, odor, gas in tissues, separation of epidermis from dermis — occur. In many instances, when an extended period of time has elapsed since burial, even though a coffin appears to be intact, the body is largely reduced to bone covered with desiccated, leathery skin and hair (Boffey 1980). Such coffins may have been imperfectly sealed, allowing the entry of air, thus airborne bacteria and mold. When water has seeped in also, as in the case of the Louisiana iron coffin burial, mold and a variety of bacteria flourish and speed the processes of decomposition. In the Virginia iron coffin burial, the following bacteria occurring naturally in the environment or in the normal human intestinal tract were found: *Cedecea davisae, Enterobacter amnigenus, Serratia marcescens, Enterobacter cloacae,* and *Serratia fonticola.* Four other organisms that were present could not be identified, other than that they were of the genus *Bacillus,* but none of these had the morphology of the pathogenic species *Bacillus anthracis* (T. Hadfield, personal communication 1989).

Most, though not all, iron coffin burials that have been viewed or studied have been dark colored, usually black. An exception was a burial transferred after 16 years from a family plot to Ivy Hill Cemetery, Laurel, MD, and described as "in a complete state of preservation and resembled white marble" (Brennan 1971). The usual dark coloration probably results from leaching of elements from an iron coffin, but as yet an analysis to determine the source of discoloration (e.g., manganese) has not been reported (in the sources checked when preparing this chapter).

Autolytic enzymes responsible for decomposition generally are highly specific in regard to the molecular structure of their substrate, as well as to temperature change, acidity, and heavy metal ions (Aufderheide and Aufderheide 1991). It is this enzymatic specificity (re substrate) that allows preservation through the action of substances that rearrange the molecular make-up of proteins, either by deliberate treatment with, for example, formaldehyde, or natural processes taking place in burials in swamps or peat bogs, in which tannic acid may be the agent responsible for preservation (Aufderheide and Aufderheide 1991).

# Conclusion

Past experience suggests that forensic anthropologists in some areas of the United States will encounter iron coffin burials from time to time, either as a result of vandalism or, more likely, because of disturbance of historic cemeteries through urban development. Investigators can anticipate excellent preservation of the skeleton and associated fabrics, especially silk and wool, even when adjacent remains buried in wood coffins are in extremely poor condition. Soft tissues may be well-preserved in correctly sealed, undamaged iron coffins, particularly when the body has been embalmed. If a coffin is inadvertently damaged and the seal has been broken on discovery, as frequently occurs when construction equipment intrudes on an unmarked family cemetery, renewed and rapid decomposition can be expected, with such accompanying problems as odor.

Because of the excellent state of preservation in many iron coffin burials, comparable in some instances to natural mummification, they offer a potentially rich source of data on life in the United States in the mid to late 19th century. Additional detailed studies of such burials would add to our knowledge of demography, pathology, diet and general health, sociocultural trends, burial practices, and the like in the immediate pre- and post-Civil War era. The thrust of future studies, however, should include levels of preservation in iron coffin burials, conditions affecting differential preservation, detailed biochemical analyses of samples from such soft tissues as are preserved, and comparisons with preservation in other types of burials, including mummies. The relatively few studies to date show the types of useful information that can result, as well as the need for greater emphasis in future research on bone taphonomy and processes of decomposition in iron coffin burials.

## Acknowledgments

We are especially grateful to the descendant families who not only permitted but encouraged this research: Mr. and Mrs. Drew Burk, Jean Beech, Jane Councill, and the Binns and Aitchensen families. Archaeological investigation of the Manassas cemetery was cosupervised by Barbara Little. Donald Creveling directed the recovery of the Maryland coffin burial. Cole and Garrett Funeral Home recovered the Tennessee coffin burial, and Nick Fielder, State Archaeologist for Tennessee, gave permission to transport it to the Smithsonian. Assisting in laboratory examinations and analyses were Glenn Wagner, Robert Zalme, Art Washburn, and Marc Micozzi (forensic pathology); Noreen Tuross (biochemistry); Ted Hadfield (microbiology); Shelly Foote (costume analysis); Douglas Harvey and Steven Rogers (archival research); Melissa Williams (evolution and design of the iron coffin); and Robert Mann, Karin Sandness, Paul Sledzik, Kim Lamphear, and Bernardo Arriaza (forensic anthropology). R. E. (Chip) Clark, Jr., and Jane Beck took the photographs used in this chapter. Support for this research was provided by the National Museum of Natural History, the Edgar Weir Family Foundation, the National Museum of Health and Medicine, the Manassas Museum, and the Louisiana State University.

## References

Aufderheide, A.C., and M.L. Aufderheide
   1991   Taphonomy of Spontaneous ("Natural") Mummification with Applications to the Mummies of Venzone, Italy. In *Human Paleopathology: Current Syntheses and Future Options,* edited by D.J. Aufderheide and A.C. Aufderheide, pp. 79–86. Smithsonian Institution Press, Washington, D.C.

Bass, W.M.
   1984   Time Interval Since Death. A Difficult Decision. In *Human Identification. Case Studies in Forensic Anthropology,* edited by T.A. Rathbun and J.E. Buikstra, pp. 136–147. Charles C Thomas, Springfield, IL.

Boffey, M.J.
   1980   The Fisk Metallic Coffin. *American Funeral Director* 104(4):43–45.

Brennan, J.C.
   1971   Notes on Laurel's Older Graveyards. *The News Leader* 16 September. Laurel, MD.

Chapman, M.F.
   1987   A History of Chapman and Alexander Families. Excerpted in *The Fireside Sentinel. The Alexandria Library, Lloyd House Newsletter* 1(8):58–59.

Clements, H.M., Jr.
   1976   *An Early Historic Burial from Beardstown, Illinois (CC 76:74).* Lincoln Land Community College, Springfield, IL.

Creveling, D.
   1994   A Melancholy Occurrence. *Passport to the Past* 5(1):1, 5–8.

Editors
    1993   That Cruel Hole in His Brow. The Death of Col. William Shy. *Blue & Gray Magazine* December:49.

Evolution of Metallic Caskets
    1906   *The Sunnyside* XXXVI(10):1, 14.

Habenstein, R.W., and W.M. Lamers
    1981   *The History of American Funeral Directing.* Bulfin Printers, Milwaukee.

Lang, K.A.
    1984   Coffins and Caskets: Their Contribution to the Archaeological Record. Masters thesis, University of Idaho, Moscow.

Little, B.J., K.M. Lanphear, and D.W. Owsley
    1992   Mortuary Display and Status in a 19th Century Anglo-American Cemetery in Manassas, Virginia. *American Antiquity* 57:397–418.

Miller, H.M.
    1993   *Project Lead Coffins: The Search for Maryland's Founders. Project Participants and Work Teams.* Historic St. Mary's City Commission, St. Mary's City, MD.

Owsley, D.W., and R.W. Mann
    1991   Smithsonian Needs Your Help. *The Director* July:66.
    1992   Multidisciplinary Investigation of Two Iron Coffin Burials. Paper presented at the Ist International Conference on Mummy Studies, Tenerife, Canary Islands.

Owsley, D.W., and P.S. Sledzik
    1993   *Osteological Examination of Five 17th Century Lead Coffin Burials from Historic St. Mary's City.* Report to Project Lead Coffins, Historic St. Mary's City Commission and on file Department of Anthropology, National Museum of Natural History, Smithsonian Institution, Washington, D.C.

Strub, C.G., and L.G. Frederick
    1967   *The Principles and Practice of Embalming.* 4th ed. L.G. Frederick, Dallas.

Trotter, M.
    1970   Estimation of Stature from Intact Limb Bones. In *Personal Identification in Mass Disasters,* edited by T.D. Stewart, pp. 71–83. Smithsonian Institution, Washington, D.C.

Trotter, M., and G.C. Gleser
    1958   A Re-Evaluation of Estimation Based on Measurements Taken During Life and of Long Bones After Death. *American Journal of Physical Anthropology* 16:79–123.

Williams, M.J., and J.L. Konefes
    1992   Environmental Concerns of Older Burial Sites. *The American Cemetery* February:22–24.

# SECTION V

## Remains in Water

- *Riverine Environments*
- *Lacustrine Environments*
- *Marine Environments*

# Fluvial Transport of Human Crania

**34**

STEPHEN P. NAWROCKI
JOHN E. PLESS
DEAN A. HAWLEY
SCOTT A. WAGNER

"Eventually, the river and its stories drain into the lake."

**Ted Leeson (1994)**
in *The Habit of Rivers*

## Introduction

Scientists employ a number of important and basic conceptual tools in their trade, including observation and description, theory construction, experimentation and hypothesis testing, and the use of analogy. Of these, the forensic anthropologist is generally most reliant on analogy. When creating a biological profile for an unidentified skeleton, the anthropologist examines features of the bones that have been proven (or are assumed) to be reliable indicators on skeletons with known vital statistics. For example, because females generally show certain characteristic traits of the pubic bones, the presence of these traits on the unknown individual becomes a proposed indicator of sex. In this case, an analogy is being drawn between the traits shared by the known and unknown individuals, with the underlying assumption that the same phenomenon (e.g., sexual dimorphism in circulating hormones during puberty) produced them both. An identical procedure is used when assessing race, age at death, stature, pathologies, postmortem interval, and circumstances of death. If and when the individual is positively identified, the case can serve as a test of the accuracy and appropriateness of the analogies that had been drawn.

In the same vein, the essence of taphonomy is analogy. When modifications are noted on bone surfaces, analogies are drawn with similar marks of known origin. The degree and pattern of soft tissue decomposition would be meaningless as an indicator of postmortem interval without a set of previously defined benchmarks. Dispersal patterns of bones at the scene may hint at the forces that moved them out of anatomical order, but only after we have an appropriate set of analogues for comparison. When analogies are made between present-day events and historic phenomena (which could not be directly observed), the term "actualism" is applied (Gifford 1981:367).

Our success rates in determining sex and postmortem interval clearly depend on the strength and appropriateness of the analogies we draw. Extensive observation and experimentation are the key to successful analogy construction (see Gifford 1981:393–396). In the realm of forensic taphonomy, however, numerous gaps in our knowledge still limit our ability to make inferences involving basic natural and cultural phenomena. This chapter addresses one such gap, that of fluvial transport of human crania. In the period between October 1991 and January 1995, we examined five cases of isolated crania recovered from freshwater riverine contexts in central Indiana. The resolution of these cases has been especially problematic because of our failure to recover additional bones and our inability to reliably estimate either the time since death or the transport distance involved. In other words, because little research has been done to establish the indicators and parameters of fluvial transport of skeletonized human remains, we had no basis from which to draw adequate or reliable analogies.

First we review the existing literature on the fluvial transport of cultural and biological materials. We then summarize the details of the Indiana cases and extract a number of specific postmortem modifications that appear to characterize transported crania. We finish by constructing a number of hypotheses that may be useful in guiding future forensic investigations. Four conclusions seem especially relevant (Nawrocki and Pless 1993). First, extensive hydrologic sorting, transport, burial, and reexposure must be considered in forensic cases recovered in fluvial settings. Second, fluvial transport of human remains depends in part on the degree and pattern of disarticulation of different body parts as well as soft tissue decomposition rates. Third, complete crania, when separated, can be transported a considerable distance, probably (but not necessarily) beyond other bones or body parts. Finally, crania transported in fluvial settings tend to show a pattern of damage that reflects their unique taphonomic histories.

## The Three Phases of Fluvial Transport

Water is an extremely important variable in the preservation and dispersal of human remains (Nawrocki 1995), with effects even reaching down to the molecular level (Von Endt and Ortner 1984). The scientific literature is laden with studies documenting the effects of fluvial transport of biological and cultural materials in the formation and modification of archaeological sites and bone assemblages. Many of these studies draw heavily from hydrologic theory as developed in physics and geology.

For the purposes of forensic research, it is useful to subdivide transport phenomena into three phases (Nawrocki and Pless 1993). Early in the transport sequence, before significant disarticulation has occurred, the body is the unit of transport. This phase could include traumatic perimortem events occurring during the body's entry into the water, which may affect the characteristics of subsequent transport as well as later analysis. The second phase of transport involves the movement and dispersal of disarticulated body parts (trunk, head, and limbs or portions thereof), which may react very differently to fluvial conditions than complete bodies. Patterns and rates of disarticulation are potentially important aspects of this phase. The third and final phase of transport is that of isolated bones, when damage can reach peak levels. The taphonomic literature on fluvial transport covers all three phases.

### Phase 1 Transport

As pointed out by the editors in the introduction to this volume, the more traditional paleontological and archaeological approaches to taphonomy have generally ignored soft tissue changes and their effects on bone preservation and assemblage formation. Traditional studies involving fluvial transport have usually been limited to examining the effects of water movement on animal bones (e.g., phase 3 transport) rather than on bodies or body parts. One exception is Weigelt (1989), who noted cases of fluvial transport of animal carcasses and briefly related the rate of sinking (and, by implication, the degree of transportation) to the mass and surface area as well as the general configuration of the body. Humans, however, were not specifically addressed. Some phase 1 studies in the forensic literature have reported transport in marine contexts (Boyle et al. 1993; Davis 1986; Ebbesmeyer and Haglund 1994; Giertsen and Morild 1989; London and Krolikowski 1994; Sorg et al. 1993, 1995; see also contributions in this volume), which may involve different dynamics than are seen in freshwater riverine or lacustrine contexts. They do, however, serve to underscore the vast distances that water can move remains (hundreds of miles in some cases) and the unpredictable circumstances of recovery. Other forensic studies (Copeland 1987; Davis 1986; Simonsen 1983) address cause and manner of death in freshwater contexts yet do not substantively address subsequent transport. Donoghue and Minnigerode (1977) examine circumstances under which bodies will float or sink in water, which may impact transport rates. They conclude that lung contents (air or water) are critical in the equation and that most people are buoyant with at least some air in their lungs.

Brief or anecdotal information on phase 1 transport in fresh water is occasionally mentioned (Brooks and Brooks 1984; Davis 1986; Haglund et al. 1990; O'Brien 1993). Haglund (1993) reports a few cases of complete or nearly complete body transport in both fresh and salt waters of the Pacific Northwest and New York City. Transport distances are not given for all cases, but postmortem intervals ranged from 1 to 36 months. Brooks and Brooks (this volume) describe the case of a body that may have traveled 40 to 50 miles downstream before recovery 8 months after death. Others have discussed failed attempts at locating bodies that are known to have been deposited by assailants. Williams (1995) reported on a extensive but unsuccessful search for a missing adolescent female along the Sheyenne River in North Dakota. A suspect had confessed to the killing and claimed to have tied cinder blocks to the body, dumping it from a bridge into the water a few weeks before a major flood.

The physics of movement of bodies in water, both horizontally (downstream) and vertically (to depths) are summarized by Dilen (1984). He describes four stages of motion of the body: sinking to the bottom, motion along the bottom, ascent to the surface, and drift at the surface. Sinking is governed by the body's density, specific gravity, and by Boyle's Law, which explains that as a body descends, the gases dissolved in the tissues and the air in the lungs compress, decreasing the buoyancy of the body and adding to its rate of descent. Bottom motion is affected not only by the characteristics of the river substrate (snags, etc.) but also by the sum of forces on the body — drag, friction, lift, and gravity. Apart from disturbances, ascent occurs when buoyancy changes, such as by gas production in putrefaction. As the body ascends, Boyle's Law takes effect once again, but this time in reverse: gas volume increases as the body rises, increasing buoyancy. Surface drift is moderated by currents, eddies and back-flows, wind, and snags. Currents at the surface flow downstream (primary currents) as well as perpendicular to the channel direction (secondary currents) and are governed by the characteristics of the channel itself (e.g., width, slope, shape, curvature, bank and bottom structure, etc.). Surface flow tends to be directly downstream in the middle of straight channels and towards the banks at the sides. Objects rounding sharp bends in the channel tend to flow to the outside corner. Below the surface, currents circulate in a complex spiraling fashion but generally decrease in velocity as one approaches the riverbed (see Behrensmeyer 1975:497). While not mentioned by Dilen, seasonal fluctuations in temperature may also affect surface and subsurface current patterns, particularly in large or deep rivers (see O'Brien, this volume). In addition, tides affect rivers emptying into oceans and large lakes, altering current patterns.

Dilen (1984) has conducted a controlled forensic study of phase 1 transport using two human manikins and 10-cm floating spheres dropped into the Chattahoochee River in Atlanta, GA. He found that (1) objects floating downstream tend to stay near the bank they originate at, and (2) bodies, once submerged, orient parallel with the direction of current flow and tend to resist downstream movement unless located in the very center of the river, where they may move slowly. However, the idiosyncrasies of the river surely affected the results. The segment of the Chattahoochee tested is relatively straight with a gentle slope and low banks. Dilen (1984:1036) warns that "Each river must be examined in its own case and the characteristics of these parameters defined for the area of interest." A swift, steep, cold mountain stream in floodstage will carry its victims differently than a slow, meandering Midwest river in late summer or a narrow, spring-fed limestone stream choked with watercress in central Pennsylvania.

## Phase 2 Transport

The same general principles of transport are likely to apply to disarticulated body parts as well, although some modifications may be necessary. For example, surface areas and densities vary in different regions of the body, and not all will react to the currents in the same way. Solid limbs will accumulate little bacterial gas in putrefaction compared to a hollow torso, affecting their buoyancy and thus their chances of resurfacing. As parts drop away, the torso will lose buoyancy and descend. Clothing may differentially affect transport or may tend to hold certain joints together (e.g., pants and shoes will hold hips and feet together). Ribcages may snag on obstructions more easily than heads and limbs.

Disarticulation sequences of animal bodies in water have been addressed on occasion by traditional taphonomists. Weigelt (1989:84–85) presents the "law of the lower jaw," noting that mandibles are especially susceptible to loss and dispersal from the body. Dodson (1973) charted the decomposition of a mouse, a frog, and a toad in an aquarium, and Payne and King (1972) utilized fetal pigs. Haglund (1993) is one of the few to have explicitly examined disarticulation sequences of human bodies in aquatic environments. Using observations of 11 forensic cases, he notes that the mandible, cranium, and hands tend to separate from the body first, followed by the remainder of the arms, neck, feet, and legs. The trunk, pelvic girdle, and thighs tend to stay articulated. These changes roughly parallel changes seen during decomposition on land, although since a body in water can move in three dimensions in response to wave and current action, the soft tissue connections between body parts and bones can weaken and disarticulate rapidly. Areas with thin overlying tissue and weak ligamentous connections become separated first. For example, synovial joints (e.g., the shoulder) fall apart before fibrous joints (intervertebral joints). Limbs disarticulate in sequence from distal to proximal ends — torsional forces created by currents will likely be greater at the ends of extremities compared to their attachment points with the trunk. Adipocere may hinder or otherwise alter disarticulation, although little research has been brought to bear on this question. O'Brien (1994, 1995) reports on experimental findings pertaining to adipocere formation on submerged human bodies.

Disarticulation in or near water creates the possibility of recovering body parts or bones of the same individual at widely separated times or locales. For example, Haglund and Reay (1993) record a case in which a foot and lower leg, held together by a sock and boot, were found 2 weeks before and 17 miles away from the rest of the body. A similar case was encountered in northwest Indiana in 1994, where a foot was found a month before and a few hundred yards downstream of the body (Matthew Williamson, personal communication, 1994). Skinner et al. (1988) describe the discovery of an isolated human mandible on the beach of Oak Bay in Victoria, British Columbia, in 1987. The decomposed body of the adult male had been recovered nearby two years previously. One case from the Missoula, MT area has stretched on for years (Randall Skelton, personal communication, 1995). The calotte (skullcap) and a few postcranial elements of a man who had drowned in late 1990 were discovered on the shore of Flathead Lake in March of 1991. Additional bones from the same individual were recovered in the same location in the springs of 1992 and 1994, during times when the lake level was at its seasonal low. The calotte had washed up on the surface of the beach at a distance of 8 m from the main cluster of bones, many of which were buried as deep as 20 cm in the sand and silt matrix.

After a corpse washes ashore and begins to decompose on land, body parts or bones may be retransported downstream at irregular intervals during flooding. Land decomposition is frequently accompanied by factors that are less likely to occur while the body is submerged, i.e., rapid tissue destruction by saprophagous insects, carnivore modifications, root damage, and a wider range of weathering scenarios (sunlight, freeze–thaw cycles, etc.). Adipocere formation may be hindered compared to the aqueous environment, while mummification becomes more likely. A body that is caught on a snag or floating high above the water line could theoretically decompose according to both aqueous and terrestrial patterns, as noted by Haglund (1993:811; see also Haskell et al. 1989).

## Phase 3 Transport

A rather large body of taphonomic literature exists regarding fluvial effects on artifacts and bones in archaeological and paleontological sites (see especially Behrensmeyer 1975; Dechant Boaz 1982; Gifford 1981; Hanson 1980; Korth 1979; Lyman 1994:171–185; Petraglia and Potts 1994; Schick 1986; Shipman 1981; also Behrensmeyer 1982; Dodson 1973; Gifford and Behrensmeyer 1977; Isaac 1967; Reinhardt 1993; Shotwell 1955; Turnbaugh 1978; Wolff 1973). This research can be divided into two categories: studies of object distribution and density within and between sites, and experimental flume studies. Distillation of this body of work leads to a number of broad generalizations concerning bone transport (some of which may also be relevant during phase 1 and 2 transport):

1. Flowing water is extremely important in site (and scene) formation and destruction, and can transport objects significant distances. In addition, water may disperse elements, making their distribution less concentrated, or may concentrate and sort elements into morphological classes.
2. Objects from temporally or geographically distinct sites or scenes can be mixed.
3. Object movement is correlated with time of surface exposure — more exposure permits further transport, whereas burial resists transportation.
4. Objects may be buried and later excavated and retransported. The probability of permanent burial increases as transport distance increases.
5. "Primary" or undisturbed assemblages can usually be distinguished from "secondary" assemblages that have been disturbed by water flow.
6. All else being equal, the shorter the transport distance, the more intact the assemblage or skeleton is likely to be.
7. Bones can be analyzed like any other sedimentary particle suspended in the fluid.
8. The size, density, and shape of an object greatly influence its transport distance and mode of transport (e.g., suspended, rolling or sliding on the bottom, bouncing off of obstructions, etc.). For example, spherical objects, with the least surface area for their mass, present the least resistance to flow and thus are transported most easily and at lower flow rates than nonspherical objects of equivalent density.
9. High energy contexts (e.g., fast currents in river channels) are more likely to disturb and remove (winnow) elements than low energy contexts (e.g., slow currents at lake margins).
10. Slow flow removes small or light objects more frequently than large or dense objects, while fast flow removes both small and large objects. Therefore, the presence of large or dense objects signifies deposition in high energy contexts, while small or light objects signify deposition in low energy contexts.
11. It takes more energy to overcome drag forces and move a resting object than to keep it flowing once it is moving, so deposition tends to occur at lower energies than are necessary for initially disturbing an object.
12. River bottom morphology and composition affect current flow and thus object movement. For example, for fine-grained, smooth bottoms, a thin low-velocity layer of water will lie in direct contact with the bottom, trapping small or flat objects until they are displaced by other forces.
13. Many objects tend to orient nonrandomly with the primary direction of flow. For example, long bones orient parallel with the direction of flow with the heaviest end downstream.
14. Roundness and abrasion of objects increase with transport distance and varies with the mode of transport.

These generalizations are potentially applicable in forensic settings, although one must alter the approach somewhat because the unit of analysis in a forensic case is usually not a complete archaeological site or multi-individual bone assemblage but rather a single individual or isolated portion(s) thereof. However, one can envision a scenario where a body and its associated personal effects are deposited at the head of an island or point bar and, upon decomposing, are washed across the land surface during periodic flooding. The distribution and orientations of bones and artifacts may then conform to the predictions of traditional fluvial studies, and a knowledge of these may assist in interpreting the pattern and, perhaps, in locating missing bones and evidence.

Special mention must be made of flume experiments that have utilized skeletal remains. Voorhies (1969:66–69) conducted what is now considered to be a classic study in vertebrate taphonomy. Dropping complete sheep, coyote, badger, rabbit, and human bones into a 4' × 45' artificial water channel (a flume), he observed their response to the current, transport distances, predominant modes of transport, and resting orientations. As a result of his experiments with sheep and coyotes, he divided the different bones into one of three loosely defined groups: a "transport" group that was immediately carried by the current, a "lag" group that sank and resisted transport, and an intermediate group that moved gradually. In general, ribs, vertebrae, the sacrum, and the sternum fell into the transport category, while the cranium and mandible fell into the lag group. Long bones, metapodia and phalanges, the pelvis, and scapulae fell into the intermediate category. These findings have significant implications for basic interpretation of deposits of fossil mammal bones: "The remarkable scarcity of ribs, vertebrae, sacra, etc. in some deposits … and their abundance in others … can be probably explained by their tendency to be removed very easily and swiftly by current action" (Voorhies 1969:68). In other words, differential fluvial transport of morphologically different bones produces sorted assemblages. Those comprised predominantly of lag group bones while missing ribs are more likely to be autochthonous, e.g., near the point of life and death of the organism. Conversely, those assemblages comprised predominantly of transport group bones are probably allochthonous, transported away from the origin point of the organisms.

Voorhies did not address the transportability of either weathered or fragmented bones or human crania. Boaz and Behrensmeyer (1976) later filled this void, subjecting human cranial and postcranial fragments as well as two complete crania to flume studies. Lag and transport groups were readily identifiable, although their compositions were somewhat different from Voorhies' groups. For example, a complete cranium was by far the fastest-moving specimen, while one with a fracture of the vault was the third fastest mover, right behind the sacrum. The intact cranium maintained an air bubble in the frontal region and floated, moving as fast as the current. Even filled with water, it rolled rapidly along the bottom. The fractured cranium sank but then rolled as quickly as the filled intact specimen. Cranial and mandibular fragments, on the other hand, showed no transport at all. The authors related transportability to a number of factors, including density, shape, condition, and the bottom substrate of the channel. They concluded that "Flat, low, well-braced, and dense skeletal parts tend to comprise the lag group. Rounded, higher, poorly braced, and less dense skeletal parts make up the transportable group" (Boaz and Behrensmeyer 1976:60).

## Case Studies

The analysis of isolated, transported crania is problematic for two main reasons. First, as can be surmised from the preceding discussion, the circumstances of death and subsequent postmortem events are generally unclear at best. Second, even assuming a well-preserved specimen, the biological profile generated from an isolated cranium will be incomplete, with no good estimation of stature and an uncertain estimate of age. The five Indiana cases described

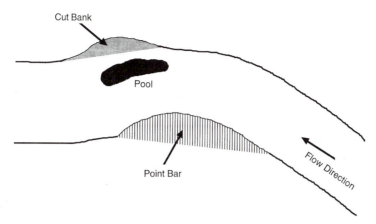

**Figure 1**   Basic features of a river meander (bend). The point bar forms on the low velocity inner side of the bend, and the cut bank forms on the high velocity outer side of the bend. A deep pool may be found adjacent to the cut bank.

below serve to illustrate these difficulties. At the time of writing, only two have been positively identified. One (case 4) was recovered in a fluvial context, but later proved to be terrestrial in origin. It is included here because it serves as an informative test case. Only a general description of each specimen is provided in this section, with details of postmortem alterations being addressed in the following section. The cases are listed in chronological order according to the dates that they were first reported to the authorities.

## Case 1

The first specimen (UI-01-91) was recovered in October 1991 by a farmer on an isolated stretch of the West Fork of the White River in northwest Johnson County, just south of Indianapolis in central Indiana. The cranium had come to rest on the surface of a wide "point bar" of sand and fine gravels. Point bars are generally located just downstream of the inside bank of a bend or meander in the river, representing areas covered by low energy eddy currents from which lighter particles in the flow can precipitate (Figure 1). Materials deposited by the flow will tend to be highly sorted and stratified by grain size and density. A "cut bank" of erosion (bank removal) will lie across from the point bar on the opposite side of the river, where quickly moving currents smash into the outside curvature of the bend (see Dechant Boaz 1982:82). Behrensmeyer (1982:214) notes that in systematic surveys, many more bones are found on point bars than at other areas of a channel. In case 1, extensive searching both upstream and downstream failed to produce additional human remains, although numerous animal bones were recovered on the point bar.

We searched the surrounding area of the point bar with a metal detector and then excavated and sifted the matrix beneath the cranium, producing no additional remains or artifacts. The matrix from the recovery site matched the sand and gravels extracted from the endocranial cavity of the specimen, supporting the recovery account given by the farmer.

In general, the specimen was very well preserved, and the facial skeleton and base were intact. All but three maxillary teeth (#s 7, 8, and 9) were present, and six had amalgam fillings. The malleus was retrieved from the middle ear on the left side. Slight to moderate sun bleaching had occurred during exposure on land, and fine roots had penetrated the larger orifices, although root etching of the bone surfaces was not yet present. There was no animal gnawing. Traces of dried adipocere were present inside the left zygomatic arch and in the left pterygomaxillary fissure. In addition, dried articular cartilage still adhered to the mandibular fossae. However, the fats in the bone had long since dissipated.

Discrete traits suggested that the individual was a white male, an assessment that was supported by craniometric discriminant analysis (e.g., Giles and Elliot 1962, 1963). Dental development indicated that the individual was fully adult, and a target age at death was estimated via cranial suture closure (Nawrocki 1996, Equation 8) at 33 years, with an upper limit of 49 years (+ 2 SE range).

Postmortem interval and transport distance could only be guessed at. The degree of sun bleaching indicated only a few months' exposure on the point bar (Behrensmeyer 1978), although the body could have entered and been preserved in the water for an extended period before disarticulation of the head and cranium. The good condition of the specimen suggested that it had not been transported very far, although again this hypothesis hinged on decomposition sequences. Recorded water flow volumes for the river's course in Indianapolis were obtained from the Indiana Department of Natural Resources for the previous few years. According to these data, the cranium had been recovered during the typical low-water season (100 to 800 cubic feet/second), attested to by the extensive surface exposure of the point bar at that time. Peak flows (>5500 cfs) tend to fall in the winter months, with secondary peaks (3900 to 4700 cfs) occurring in the spring. Since the cranium had been recovered approximately 25 m out from the water's edge (and 10 m down from the high water mark on the bank), it seems reasonable to assume that it had been deposited on the point bar during a heavy flow in the spring and left to bleach as the waters receded in the summer. Working backwards and allowing adequate time for decomposition and dispersal of the body, we speculated that the individual would have entered the water during the winter of 1990 to 1991 at the earliest, although probably not more than 2 or 3 years before the recovery of the cranium.

Shortly afterwards, the cranium was positively identified through dental records. The 42-year-old white male had been reported missing shortly after his disappearance in early February of 1990. At approximately the same time, passersby had witnessed an unidentified man commit suicide by jumping from a bridge into the White River in downtown Indianapolis. A search for the body, which entered the water at the height of the winter floodstage, had been unproductive. The cranium was eventually found approximately 14 miles downstream from the point of entry, with a postmortem interval of 1 year 8 months.

## Case 2

The second specimen (UI-04-92) was found in March 1992 by a fisherman in shallow water at the edge of a drainage pond in a suburban residential area of north Indianapolis, in Marion County. Spillways and culverts connect this pond to a series of additional ponds and drainage ditches in the immediate community, and numerous storm pipes drain into this system. The result is an extremely unstable fluvial environment in which bones could be washed back and forth between the ponds even after light rains. In addition, the White River, which runs immediately to the west, will overflow into the ponds during flood stages, adding to the instability of the area and (perhaps) acting as a source for the skeletal remains. A search of the recovery location was conducted, to no avail.

The vault and base of the specimen was intact, although the face was completely missing below the nasofrontal suture. Otherwise, the degree and pattern of abrasion and damage were similar to that seen in case 1. There was mild sun bleaching but no root damage, animal gnawing, dried soft tissues, or trapped fats within the bone.

Craniometric discriminant analysis using FORDISC 1.0 (Jantz and Ousley 1992) indicated that the individual was a black male. Target age at death as estimated from cranial suture closure (Equation 14 in Nawrocki 1996) was 47 years with a likely spread of 25 to 69 years (±2 SE range).

Based purely on the condition of case 1, the postmortem interval was judged to be between 1 and 3 years, although the transport circumstances are even less clear in case 2. Unfortunately, the individual remains unidentified, so these speculations cannot be confirmed.

## Case 3

The third case (UI-12-92) was recovered by a fisherman in October 1992 on the Big Vermillion River near Newport, in Vermillion County of west-central Indiana. The cranium was found on a sand bar at the head of an island, a few hundred yards upstream of a bridge. An extensive search of the island and riverbanks failed to produce additional remains.

This specimen displayed a state of preservation intermediate to that of cases 1 and 2. The vault and the base were intact. While the face was present, the alveolar borders of the maxillae had been heavily damaged (resulting in the loss of all teeth) and the more fragile bones of the mid-upper face (ethmoid, nasal conchae, vomer) were missing. There was mild sun bleaching but no root damage, animal gnawing, dried soft tissues, or trapped fats within the bone.

Craniometric discriminant analysis using FORDISC 1.0 (Jantz and Ousley 1992) indicates that the individual was a white male, an assessment that was also supported by discrete traits. Target age at death as estimated from cranial suture closure (Equation 8 in Nawrocki 1996) was 76 years with a likely spread of 54 to 98 years (±2 SE range).

Once again, reconstructing the postmortem interval and the transport distance is hampered by uncertainties concerning the timing of soft tissue decomposition. The sand bar at the head of the island, exposed by the low fall water levels, would not have held the specimen through another floodstage but probably allowed a season of surface exposure and weathering. This stretch of the Big Vermillion is similar to the White River in Indianapolis and is typical of the warm, meandering rivers of the flat Midwest. Thus it may be defensible to assume that the conditions and extent of transport in the two rivers would be broadly similar. If the abrasion and damage of case 1 is an accurate indicator, the third cranium appears to have been transported and exposed for a period of 1 to 3 years. Again, the individual remains unidentified.

## Case 4

The circumstances of the fourth case (UI-04-94) are rather unusual. In March 1994, children discovered a well-preserved cranium resting below the tracks in the rafters of a railroad trestle that crosses the Mississinewa River in the city of Marion, Grant County, in north-central Indiana. An underwater search in the vicinity of the bridge recovered numerous animal bones but no additional human bones. The origin of the specimen was a mystery from the beginning. Local authorities doubted that the water had reached a high enough level in recent years to have deposited the specimen in the rafters. In addition, it was extremely well preserved, with only minor damage to the thin bones of the midnasal region. It displayed few of the indicators of transport and abrasion that characterized the other cases (see below). There was mild sun bleaching but no root damage or animal gnawing. Small adhering fragments of dried, brittle skin, brain tissue, blood vessels, and trapped fats suggested a rather short postmortem interval. Without further information, however, no theories could be ruled out.

Craniometric discriminant analysis using FORDISC 1.0 (Jantz and Ousley 1992) indicated that the individual was a white female, an assessment that was also supported by discrete traits. Target age at death as estimated from cranial suture closure (Equation 7 in Nawrocki 1996) was 88 years with a likely spread of 72 to 104 years (±2 SE range). The individual once had a full upper denture, with complete resorption of all alveoli.

The mystery of case 4 was solved after the police obtained a lead that the cranium had been looted from a mausoleum in a local cemetery and later placed within the railroad trestle. In January 1996, the senior author accompanied authorities to the cemetery and removed the metal coffin and its contents from the vandalized crypt. The inscription and corresponding death certificate identified the individual as a white female who had died in 1929 at the age of 81. A full maxillary denture in the coffin fit the cranium perfectly, as did the mandible and first cervical vertebra. The cranium was returned to the coffin after its 2-year absence and resealed in the mausoleum. No fluvial transport had occurred in the interim.

## Case 5

The fifth specimen (UI-01-95) was brought to the senior author's lab at the University of Indianapolis by an amateur archaeologist in January 1995. It had reportedly passed through the hands of a number of private artifact collectors, who had apparently assumed that the cranium was of prehistoric Native American origin. However, it was immediately obvious that the specimen was a recent forensic case and had been recovered in a fluvial context. Unfortunately, investigations by the Indiana State Police have so far failed to trace the exact origin point or date of recovery of the specimen, although interviews with those involved suggest that it has been out of the water for a period of years.

The cranium was well-preserved and most closely resembled Case 1 in overall appearance. The face and base were intact. There was mild sun bleaching but no root damage, animal gnawing, or trapped fats within the bone. Traces of dried adipocere were present in some of the recesses of the cranial base.

Craniometric discriminant analysis using FORDISC 1.0 (Jantz and Ousley 1992) indicated that the individual was a white male, an assessment that is also supported by discrete traits. Target age at death as estimated from cranial suture closure (Equation 8 in Nawrocki 1996) was 61 years with a likely spread of 39 to 83 years (±2 SE range). The individual once had a full upper denture, with complete resorption of all alveoli. No identification has been made.

## Indicators of Fluvial Transport

Four of the five cases demonstrate a strikingly similar range of modifications that may be used to differentiate their riverine postmortem fate from terrestrial, lacustrine, or marine deposition (Nawrocki and Pless 1993). This section identifies and briefly discusses the "modal" condition of Cases 1, 2, 3, and 5. Not all specimens display each trait to the same degree, and some traits would not be uniquely diagnostic of fluvial transport when taken in isolation. Rather, it is the overall *pattern* or gestalt that reflects their unique taphonomic histories. A few of the traits (e.g., trait 12) are expressed only in one specimen but seem so clearly indicative of a fluvial origin that they are included as part of the suite. Twelve different traits are listed, subdivided into "abrasion and damage" and "general modifications" categories. Table 1 lists their occurrence by specimen.

### Abrasion and Damage

1. *Partial or complete destruction of the facial skeleton.*     The face is the least robust portion of the cranium and one of the first portions to break up in any environment. Rolling and tumbling of the cranium on the river bottom will do significant damage, dispersing the teeth in the process. Case 2 is completely missing its face, while case 3 displays significant destruction of the left inferior maxilla and all alveoli. The face is present and intact in case 1.

2. *Perforation of thin plates of bone.*     Many areas of the cranium are formed of single, thin layers of cortical bone and thus are differentially susceptible to abrasion and breakage. The maxillae, palate, pterygoid plates, cerebellar fossae, tympanic plates, and bones of the orbital cavity, for example, frequently demonstrated small perforations ranging in size from

**Table 1** **Characteristic Traits of Fluvial Transport as Expressed in Four Specimens from Indiana**

| Trait | Case 1 | Case 2 | Case 3 | Case 5 | Total Cases |
|---|---|---|---|---|---|
| 1. Destruction of the face | – | + | + | – | 2 |
| 2. Perforation of thin plates of bone | + | + | + | + | 4 |
| 3. Abrasion of exposed edges | + | + | + | + | 4 |
| 4. Pitting, scratching, and gouging | + | + | + | + | 4 |
| 5. Chipped enamel on anterior teeth | + | ? | ? | n/a | 1 |
| 6. Loss of articulating bones | + | + | + | + | 4 |
| 7. Loss of single-rooted teeth | + | ? | ? | n/a | 1 |
| 8. Algal staining | + | + | + | + | 4 |
| 9. Circumferential staining | + | + | + | + | 4 |
| 10. Silt "painting" | + | – | + | + | 3 |
| 11. Compaction of matrix in foramina | + | + | + | + | 4 |
| 12. Aquatic insect casings | – | – | – | + | 1 |
| TOTAL TRAITS | 10 | 8 | 9 | 9 | |

*Note:* "Total cases" is the total number of cases that expressed the trait in question. "Total traits" is the total number of traits expressed for the case in question. "+" = present; "-" = absent; "n/a" = not applicable.

pinpricks to openings a centimeter or more in diameter. Sometimes perforations were formed through enlargements of existing holes, such as the infraorbital foramina. Here we distinguish between holes created by simple mechanical damage and by erosion due to continued sand and silt abrasion. While the former are certainly common in both terrestrial and aquatic environments, the "sandblasted" appearance of the foramina created by fluvial processes should help to identify their origin. Similar if not identical perforations can be created by bones exposed to winds containing air-borne particles, such as on beaches or deserts. All four transport cases display trait 2.

**3. Abrasion or breakage of exposed edges or processes.** Projections of bone are especially prone to damage. Common sites of erosion include the mastoid processes (exposing the mastoid air cells), occipital condyles, the brows and margins of the orbits, the border of the foramen magnum, the zygomatic arches, nasal aperture, and alveolar margins. Interestingly, the zygomatic arches were worn but intact in cases 1, 3, and 5, and only partially missing in case 2, where the face had been completely removed. Less buttressed projections such as the styloid processes and hamuli of the sphenoid were generally fractured and missing, as is common in terrestrial cases. Once again the nature of the damage is as important as its location or presence, with abrasion being a primary cause. All four transport cases display trait 3.

**4. Pitting, scratching, and gouging.** Numerous "pockmarks" were distributed over the upper and lateral surfaces of the cranial vaults, undoubtedly formed from bouncing off of the river bottom or other objects. The scratching and gouging was generally randomly oriented and irregular in depth, following both straight and curving paths. Cross-sections of the deeper channels also varied in morphology, although most were broader than deep, U-shaped, and coarse-walled. None of these features extended into the diploe and thus all would be characterized as rather superficial. All four transport cases display trait 4.

**5. Chipped enamel on the anterior teeth.** Both canines and the remaining lateral incisor of case 1 showed irregular chipping and flaking along the incisal and labial edges. This flaking undoubtedly occurred as the cranium bounced or scraped against sand and gravel. Careful examination revealed that some of the chips had become secondarily abraded, although the pattern of wear was coarser and less regular than would be expected for intraoral, masticatory smoothing of antemortem chips. None of the teeth in case 1 were completely fractured, although the crowns showed many tiny longitudinal cracks in the enamel. Linear cracking is common in cases from many environments and is probably produced by alternating expansion and contraction during wet/dry cycles. Trait 5 was observable only for case 1.

## General Modifications

**6. *Loss of articulating bones and dentures.*** In all cases the mandible, hyoid, cervical vertebrae, and removable dentures were absent and could not be located at the recovery scene. This absence indicates that soft tissue decomposition occurred away from the final resting spot of the cranium, with these adjacent bones disarticulating and dispersing at some upstream point. The same would be expected in lacustrine settings where either vertical or horizontal transport can occur, as discussed previously (e.g., "the law of the lower jaw"). The aqueous pattern differs from that seen when a whole disarticulated head decomposes *in situ* in a terrestrial environment, even when significant horizontal dispersal of the body has occurred (Nawrocki and Clark 1994). The presence of the malleus in case 1 is undoubtedly due to the fortuitous filling of the external auditory meatus with sediment before the bone could fall out. No other auditory ossicles were recovered despite careful cleaning. All four transport cases display trait 6.

**7. *Loss and dispersal of single-rooted teeth.*** Incisors and canines are commonly missing in many environmental contexts, although in our experience their absence in terrestrial assemblages is usually due more to poor collection methods than to actual *dispersal* away from the body. The absence of one lateral and both central incisors in case 1 (the only case to have had teeth) is understandable, given the tumbling that the specimen likely encountered. This trait should be present in both lacustrine and riverine environments where decomposition and transport occurs.

**8. *Algal staining.*** All crania display at least some algal growth on the external bone surfaces. Colors range from dull green to dark brown or black, sometimes staining the bone with a dark patina. Being light-seeking, algae will grow on the surfaces exposed upwards to the sun, whether the specimen is fully submerged or not. Sunbleaching can occur on these same surfaces, creating a mosaic of colors. Cases 2 and 3 demonstrated abundant fine, wispy, gray or green filaments that at first glance could be mistaken for hair. These filaments are actually a form of water mold (phylum Oomyceta), a decomposer that commonly grows on dead algae and other organisms. While fine terrestrial plant roots were sometimes noted (case 1), no root etching of bone surfaces was present, which is common in terrestrial cases. The lack of root modification may have been due to the scarcity of vegetation on the point bars and/or to short surface exposure times. Algal staining has been noted in saltwater contexts (Skinner et al. 1988) and could also occur in terrestrial contexts with standing water. All four transport cases display trait 8.

**9. *Circumferential staining.*** Staining lines were present on the ectocranial and/or endocranial surfaces of the cranial vaults, generally arching in a mid- or parasagittal plane. This pattern can be used to verify the original (or most recent) resting orientation of the cranium on its substrate. All four of our transported cases came to rest on lateral sides of the vault. Ectocranial circumferential staining results from a combination of algal staining, sun bleaching, and sediment deposition on the upward-facing surface. The bottom-facing surface generally remains clean. Endocranial circumferential staining results from an influx of water and sediment into the cranial cavity or (perhaps) from a prolonged presence of the meninges or brain. Retransport may produce intersecting circumferential lines, reflecting the shifting orientation of the specimen. While circumferential staining is frequently noted in terrestrial cases, the presence of an algal patina and characteristic sediments (see below), when combined, typify the aquatic cases. All four transport cases display trait 9.

**10. *Silt "painting".*** Fine sediment suspended in the flow will slowly precipitate onto the ectocranial and endocranial surfaces of the cranium if the water is calm enough. As the water recedes or evaporates, the thin silt layer will dry and can become crust-like. The resulting effect looks as if someone had painted the sediment on with a fine brush. The appearance is frequently different from the rather clumpy nature of mud and dirt that adheres to terrestrial crania. In addition, water-borne sediments are likely to be well-sorted and thus very homogeneous in color, grain size, and texture. While an inverted cranium in the ground may display limited endocranial silt and mineral painting resulting from the slow percolation of groundwater through the grave, it would seem that ectocranial painting would be much more likely to occur in a fluvial context where water and sediments exist in abundant quantities. Cases 1, 3, and 5 display at least some silt painting, although the sediment appears to have been partially washed off from case 5 by collectors.

**11. *Compaction of matrix in foramina.*** Sand and small gravels invariably found their way into all foramina and orifices, usually tightly compacted or (in the case of pebbles) securely wedged in the smaller fissures. Loose sand and pebbles were usually present in the cranial cavity, although it is uncertain how much may have been removed during washing or rinsing at the recovery scene (case 1 was reportedly washed in the river by the finder immediately upon recovery, and case 5 has also probably been cleaned). No soil was mixed in with these larger-grained sediments, providing a comparison with specimens from many terrestrial environments. Samples of the extracted matrix should be saved for comparison with those found at the alleged recovery scene, to confirm the stories of the finders. All four transport cases display trait 11.

**12. *Aquatic insect casings.*** While terrestrial entomology has played an important role in the resolution of forensic cases (Catts and Haskell 1990), only a few publications have addressed the utility of aquatic insects (Haskell et al. 1989; Hawley et al. 1989). The floor of the nasal cavity of case 5 is covered with caddisfly casings, small "homes" made of tiny stones cemented together to encase the aquatic larval and pupal stages of this insect (Order Trichoptera). The casings are very solid and would survive much better than other forms of entomological evidence, especially as the cranium tumbled downstream. This particular type of caddisfly is classified as a "tube-case" maker (Superfamily Limnephiloidea — LaFontaine 1981) due to the elongated tube-shaped casings. They could easily be dismissed as clumps of matrix by the uninitiated eye. None of the other Indiana cases carried entomological evidence.

Other aquatic invertebrates might be encountered in aquatic cases. In 1995 the remains of two men were discovered in a submerged car in a northwest Indiana lake. The postmortem interval was 5 years, and by that time most of the soft tissues had either decayed, been eaten, or had been converted into adipocere, although the bones and much of the clothing were in excellent condition. Mixed into the assemblage were numerous crayfish, leeches, snails, bivalve mollusks, and an occasional fish bone. The molted exoskeletons of crayfish and tiny, immature mollusks were especially common, although both tended to decay into rather nondescript, brittle fragments that could have been misidentified in other contexts. These same organisms are abundant in freshwater rivers, and it is within the realm of possibility that they would be found on fluvial transport cases.

**Table 2    Distribution of Traits in Five Test Cases**

| Trait | Case 4 | Montana | Washington | Iceland 1 | Iceland 2 |
|---|---|---|---|---|---|
| 1. Destruction of the face | – | + | – | – | – |
| 2. Perforation of thin plates of bone | + | + | – | + | + |
| 3. Abrasion of exposed edges | – | + | – | + | – |
| 4. Pitting, scratching, and gouging | – | – | – | – | – |
| 5. Chipped enamel on anterior teeth | n/a | – | n/a | n/a | – |
| 6. Loss of articulating bones | + | + | + | + | + |
| 7. Loss of single-rooted teeth | n/a | + | + | + | + |
| 8. Algal staining | – | – | – | – | – |
| 9. Circumferential staining | + | + | – | + | – |
| 10. Silt "painting" | – | – | + | – | – |
| 11. Compaction of matrix in foramina | – | + | + | – | – |
| 12. Aquatic insect casings | – | ? | ? | – | – |
| TOTAL TRAITS | 3 | 7 | 4 | 5 | 3 |

*Note:*   Case 4 is from Indiana; data for "Montana" is provided courtesy of Dr. Randall Skeleton; data for "Washington" is provided courtesy of Dr. William Haglund; data for "Iceland" is provided courtesy of Dr. Eva Klonowski. See Table 1 for key.

## Trait Distribution and Test Cases

Table 1 summarizes the occurrence of the first 12 traits in the four transported Indiana specimens. A minimum of eight and a maximum of ten traits are expressed (cases 2 and 1, respectively). Seven of the traits are present in all four and would seem to be the most common results of fluvial transport. Traits involving the loss of the facial skeleton and dentition (traits 1, 5, and 7) are less well represented, probably because these phenomena occur quickly once initiated, and thus the window of opportunity for observation would be very narrow. Some traits, such as algal staining, circumferential staining, silt painting, compaction of matrix in foramina, and aquatic insect casings would be susceptible to loss during cleaning activities at the scene or in the lab. It is important for recovery personnel to be properly trained in the handling of such materials, in order to minimize the loss of evidence.

    Ideally, the postulated pattern of traits provided above should be tested against additional, known cases to verify their utility in distinguishing instances of fluvial transport. We offer five test cases for consideration: the terrestrial case (case 4) from Indiana, a lake transport case from Montana, a river transport case from Washington, and two cases from Iceland, one involving river transport and one an ocean recovery. The occurrence of all 12 traits is listed for each test case in Table 2.

**Case 4.**    This specimen displayed only three of the 12 traits: loss of articulating bones and circumferential staining. The loss of bones was due entirely to selective procurement by looters. The staining was clearly caused by decomposing soft tissues as the specimen rested within its coffin and thus is not analogous to the staining found on the other crania. While some of the thin bones of the nasal cavity were broken (trait 2), there were no abraded perforations.

**Montana.**    This case was mentioned previously and involves a calotte and postcranial bones that had washed up on the shore of Flathead Lake over a period of years (Randall Skelton, personal communication, 1995). The face and cranial base are missing, although portions of the maxilla, mandible, and teeth were found buried a few meters from the skullcap. A total of seven of the 12 traits are present, including three (traits 6, 7, and 9) that are attributable to aqueous decomposition: loss and dispersal of articulating bones and single-rooted teeth, and circumferential staining. The one anterior maxillary tooth that is still present (a right canine, tooth # 6) is not chipped or cracked. The sandy beach matrix may have contributed to the production of perforations and abrasion (traits 2 and 3). Notably absent are the pits and scratches of the vault that are so prominent in the riverine transport cases. The abrasion that is present on the Montana specimen is confined primarily to the bottom of the cranium. Some insect evidence is present but has not yet been identified as aquatic in origin.

**Washington.**   In 1990 a human cranium was recovered in a meandering river in the state of Washington (William Haglund, personal communication, 1992). An extensive search failed to recover any additional bones, but the individual (a 26-year-old white female) was eventually identified through dental evidence. She retained a deciduous maxillary right second molar, the only tooth to survive the journey. She had been missing for approximately 1 year prior to the recovery. The face and base of the cranium were intact, and very little damage was present. The river in question has a relatively muddy bottom, which undoubtedly cushioned the ride and protected the specimen from the types of erosion seen in the Indiana cases. As a result, only four of the twelve traits are scored as present.

Upon sectioning the calvarium, three concreted balls of mud were recovered, two of which were much larger than the foramen magnum. They had obviously formed as the cranium tumbled and rolled along, incorporating vegetation and insect debris into the matrix in the process. In rivers where the bottom substrate varies along its length or between its tributaries, such evidence may be of use in determining the origin point of the specimen. While endocranial mud balls are not present in the Indiana cases, their appearance in Washington serves to underscore the range of key transport indicators that may appear when different types of rivers are taken into account. It may be appropriate to add this as a 13th trait to the list.

**Iceland 1.**   This isolated cranium of a robust white adult male was recovered in October 1994 on the banks of the Olfusa River, near Reykjavik in south Iceland (Eva Klonowski, personal communication, 1995). The Olfusa is a "typical" Icelandic glacial river — very cold, fast, swollen, and full of sand and stones of volcanic origin. The specimen is well-preserved, with face and base intact. Only one tooth (the right first molar, tooth 3) survives, and it is unchipped. The only major damage is to the left maxilla, in which portions of the alveolar borders and the region of the infraorbital foramen are missing. The fragile bones of the medial orbital cavities are also broken out. No soft tissues are present but it still contains fats and presents an odor. The individual remains unidentified.

A total of five of the 12 traits are present on this specimen, fewer than would be expected on the basis of the Indiana cases. The intact face and lack of pits and scratches seems to stand in defiance of the potentially violent environment that the specimen emerged from. It is possible that extreme riverine conditions may have a counterintuitive effect on the remains. For example, fast and high flow levels may keep a cranium suspended high above the river bottom, shielding it from damage. Once again, without a knowledge of the time since death or the transport distance involved, it is difficult to place the range of modifications into a standardized frame of reference.

**Iceland 2.**   This isolated adult male cranium of possible Asian ancestry was fished from the sea in March 1994, just south of mainland Iceland near the island of Vestmanaeyja (Eva Klonowski, personal communication, 1995). The specimen is well-preserved, with face and base intact. Five teeth, all anterior maxillary (teeth 7 through 11), are missing antemortem. The only remaining anterior tooth (the right canine, tooth 6) is unchipped. The regions of the infraorbital foramina display large perforations and the bones of the medial orbital cavities are damaged. No soft tissues are present. The individual remains unidentified. Only three of the 12 traits are present on this specimen, two of which (traits 7 and 8) are to be expected for decomposition in aqueous environments.

These five test cases do not produce clearcut and obvious results that either strongly support or reject our trait characterization of fluvial transport cases. For example, all floating bodies — whether lacustrine, riverine, or marine — are influenced by a common set of taphonomic parameters that would tend to produce similar dispersal effects (traits 6 and 7). On the other hand, at least one trait — pitting and gouging — was only found in fluvial transport cases, although it was absent from the two riverine test cases.

In other words, it would seem that trait 4 is a *sufficient* but not a *necessary* criterion for indicating a riverine origin. There is also a hint that careful examination of perforations and erosional areas can aid in distinguishing between abrasive, high-energy aqueous environments on the one hand and muddy, nonabrasive, low-energy aqueous (or terrestrial) environments on the other hand — regardless of the specific aquatic context.

# Discussion

In 1981 Gifford (p. 418) noted that, "While a substantial amount of work has been done in the damaging effects of aqueous transport in invertebrate remains…very little parallel experimental work has been done in vertebrate taphonomy." Most have simply postulated a general relationship between transport distance and the degree of abrasion. However, in fluvial environments, abrasion and weathering can occur both within the water channel as well as on its banks, and so the association between transport distance and damage may not be particularly strong.

Abrasion can cause considerable problems for the skeletal analyst. Both naturalistic observations and experimentation have shown that edges, corners, crests, and projections can wear down quickly, removing important indicators of sex. Epiphyseal ends erode, precluding accurate estimates of stature. These problems will be exacerbated in sandy beach environments where wave actions can rapidly scour bone surfaces (see Skinner et al. 1988). Brooks and Brooks (1984, chapter 35 of this volume) illustrate a forensic case where the edges of perimortem cranial vault fractures were smoothed and polished by suspended silts in a river during transport. The soft tissues immediately surrounding the fractured area were removed by the same process. These alterations could obscure the true causal agents behind the fractures.

Abrasion will affect a bone's transport characteristics. Exposure of the trabecular bone or medullary cavity allows the entrance of water and sediments, increasing density and thus decreasing buoyancy. The decomposition and dispersal rate of any remaining soft tissues (e.g., marrow) would increase, as would molecular breakdown of the protein-mineral matrix in response to water exposure (Von Endt and Ortner 1984). The removal of crests and processes may increase sphericity and reduce drag, at the same time decreasing the number of projections that can catch on obstructions or lodge in the riverbed. Abrasion also weakens the bone, contributing to fracture formation.

Korth (1979) observed fracturing patterns of microvertebrate skeletons (including mice) that had been artificially abraded in tumbling experiments. The diaphyses of long bones did not fracture unless abrasion had first worn away a bony crest and perforated through into the medullary cavity, and fracturing at that point occurred only after the epiphyses had been worn off. In actual microvertebrate fossil bone assemblages from Nebraska, however, fractured diaphyses are common. Korth attributes this difference to the higher stream velocities in natural settings, and, perhaps, to carnivore action or terrestrial weathering before transport and burial. Periodic wetting and drying during beaching episodes can rapidly propagate fractures (Behrensmeyer 1978:154; Nawrocki 1995), which when combined with the potentially violent mixing of the bones with other objects and gravel in heavy flows, can result in much damage over even short periods of time.

The more robust bones of larger species, including humans, would seem to be less susceptible to fluvial fracturing. However, Voorhies (1969:18–20) observed rather high rates of fracturing in the fluvially transported long bones of Miocene Nebraskan *Merycodus* (a medium-sized hoofed herbivore, related to pronghorn antelopes). We speculate that the increased size of the long bones of large-bodied animals may actually contribute to fracture rates, offsetting the advantage of increased robusticity because of the greater leverage applied by passing currents or debris when one or both ends are fixed (e.g., it is easier to bend and break a 6-foot $2 \times 4$ than a 6-in. $2 \times 4$, even though the cross-sectional properties are identical). The more robust, squat *Merycodus* metapodials showed lower (but still high) rates of fracture.

In Korth's (1979) abrasion experiments, the thin areas of mouse cranial bones developed perforations like those observed on our modern forensic cases, and the maxillae readily fractured and separated from the skull. Separated maxillae are common for many mammalian assemblages in the paleontological record, and crania are generally highly fragmented (see Voorhies 1969:18). The crania of most nonprimate mammals are elongated and nonspherical, with braincases constructed of flattened plates that are easily fractured by postmortem processes. By contrast, the globular, arching shape of the human neurocranial vault, along with its thickened bone, increases its biomechanical integrity and contributes to its survivability in archaeological contexts (see Nawrocki 1991, 1992). This fact may explain why not one of our Indiana cases displayed significant upper vault fractures, even when damage in other areas was extensive. Of course, some self-selection may have produced a biased sample, since portions of fragmented cranial vault are less likely to be recognized and recovered than complete specimens and are more likely to be buried.

Missing faces and fractured cranial bases are common features in both fossil and recent human specimens because the bone of these areas, as in other animals, is generally quite thin compared to the upper vault (Nawrocki 1990, 1995). For example, the faces are missing from all of the dozen Ngandong fossil *Homo erectus* crania from Indonesia, as are most of the cranial bases. These specimens, excavated from the banks of the Solo River in Java, were accompanied by two tibiae and no other human bones. They clearly represent examples of fluvial transport and sorting, each cranium having reacted similarly to the currents in the volcanic mud stream that carried them (see Weidenreich 1943:190–191). As Santa Luca (1980:9) states:

> The combination of transport features and hydrodynamic sorting (only lag elements remaining) implies that the hominids were buried at some unknown distance from the site of death and that any previously associated skeletal remains had been removed. A further sign of transport is the maximization of the globular form of the hominid skull: that the face and zygomatic arches are missing could be a consequence of rolling …

Santa Luca misidentifies the crania as lag rather than transport elements, and it is likely that the crania were winnowed away from the postcranial elements rather than vice versa. However, his overall interpretation (which has not been universally accepted — see Bartstra et al. 1988) certainly makes sense in light of the modifications seen on the specimens. Portions of the cranial vaults are smooth and polished, conveying a water-worn appearance, and the pitting and gouging expected of fluvially transported specimens is clearly evident (G. Philip Rightmire, personal communication 1989). Before the critical eyes of taphonomic theory fell on paleoanthropology, most researchers believed that the missing faces and broken cranial bases were the result of cannibalism and intergroup warfare (Nawrocki 1990). Forensic investigators would be well advised to refrain from jumping to similar conclusions in modern cases.

While our forensic cases did not have broken cranial bases, the thin cortical bone surrounding the foramen magnum eroded quickly, sometimes exposing the softer spongy bone below. Case 2 had developed a postmortem fracture running from the posterior border of the foramen magnum upwards through the left cerebellar fossa. Given more time, these areas would undoubtedly have broken out completely, producing specimens similar to those found in the hominid fossil record.

Generally ignored by taphonomists is the potential for ice to abrade and fracture skeletal remains. Bones may be frozen and compressed within the ice, ground between block ice and gravel bars, or simply crushed between ice flows as they break up and pound together during the spring thaw (see Ambach and Katzgraber 1995). Morlan (1983:253–256) discusses the role of river ice in the production of spiral fractures on the long bones of large-bodied mammals, but in the end downplays its significance. O'Brien (1993, this volume) examines the effects of ice in a forensic case recovered from the shores of Lake Ontario.

## Conclusions

The taphonomic literature contains a number of studies that can potentially assist the forensic investigator when human remains are recovered from fluvial environments. "Traditional" taphonomists in the fields of archaeology, geology, and paleontology have emphasized phase 3 (individual bone) transport, generating and testing a number of hypotheses concerning the hydraulic behavior of bones and artifacts. Flume studies have been especially valuable, demonstrating through experimentation that bones tend to sort into lag and transport groups. These actualistic studies are the basis for forming analogies that explain the distributions of buried objects recovered in nature. Few forensic studies have been as rigorous, although their information on phase 1 (whole body) and phase 2 (body part) transport has begun to fill a gap in the traditional taphonomic literature.

Haglund et al. (1990:42) suggest that the investigator must ask some basic questions about the point and mode of entry of the body into the water. Is it possible that it could have floated from an upstream origin, perhaps miles away from the recovery site? Are there any barriers (such as dams) that would have prevented flotation beyond a certain point, thus limiting the scope of the search? Could the person have fallen or jumped in, or could the body have been thrown from a bank or bridge? Is the bank easily accessible? Are there any prominent natural or artificial features (such as sand bars, large rocks, or a dock) that the body may have come from or came into contact with? Could vegetation within the water or along the banks have impeded the downstream progress of the body or its parts?

Disarticulation contributes to the complexity of the case. One can view the transitions from phase 1 to phase 3 transport as processes of increasing information loss (see Nawrocki 1995), with analytically valuable portions of the remains dropping from the body and dispersing at variable rates and in different directions. The head and hands in particular are likely to disassociate from the body early during decomposition, the cranium losing the mandible and hyoid bone in the process. Separated parts may then come to rest in places that are subject to different environmental forces. Body parts resting at the bottom of a deep channel and covered with adipocere will disarticulate and abrade at different rates than, say, those sweeping downstream or drying out on land.

Given the wide variability in possible decomposition scenarios, when encountering defleshed bones in fluvial settings it may be more prudent to speak of an "exposure interval" describing the time period of exposure of the free bone surfaces to the elements, instead of the traditional "postmortem interval," which could be significantly underestimated if the decay of the soft tissues had been delayed by immersion in cold water. We have documented a known postmortem interval of 20 months (case 1), and the literature on fluvial transport of human remains gives known intervals ranging from less than a year (Brooks and Brooks, this volume;

Haglund 1993) to 6 years (Manhein 1994). These long periods of time would certainly allow for numerous unusual events that could significantly alter decomposition rates, stretching out or compressing the estimate of the postmortem interval. Even the exposure interval would be uncertain in cases where bones were allowed to weather at the surface between periodic episodes of transport and burial.

The unique morphology of the cranium predisposes it to rapid and extended transport, either floating like a cork or rolling near or along the bottom. Its recovery presents a situation that is quite unlike those normally encountered in terrestrial death investigations. The nature of the scene, characteristics of the river, and amount of manpower and time available to the investigator will determine the parameters and extent of the ensuing search. Unfortunately, in our experience it is unlikely that other bones will be located in or along the river. Knowing the proclivity of the skull for riding the waves, it is tempting to advise investigators to concentrate their efforts first in the immediate vicinity of the cranium, on adjacent point bars, and then upstream, recognizing that other bones would not have been transported as easily or as readily. However, this theory rests on the assumption that all bones entered the water as free units at the same origin point (as in flume studies). While Haglund (1993) has demonstrated that the head is the first part to dissociate from the body, this does not necessarily mean that it will rapidly outdistance the rest of the remains while the soft tissues are still attached. In fact, the head may sink or float ashore while the corpse travels past, with postcranial portions decaying and disseminating their bones miles downstream of the head and cranium (which may be transported later).

While it may seem a ridiculous hypothesis to the anthropologist, investigators should not interpret isolated crania as evidence of deliberate decapitation. Natural phenomena, including patterns of soft tissue decomposition and the effects of hydraulic transport, offer much more parsimonious explanations. We mention this only because those unaware of taphonomic processes in general have sometimes been quick to come to erroneous and even bizarre conclusions upon recovering skeletal remains.

Why, then, are the crania found first (or differentially), instead of other parts of the skeleton? The skull is more easily recognized as human by both laymen and forensic investigators than, say, isolated long bones or vertebrae. It is possible that human postcrania are encountered along rivers as or even more frequently than crania, but they are ignored as nonhuman or as sticks and stones. However, it is probably more likely that the majority of the postcranial bones, especially those belonging to the lag group, quickly sink and are buried by sediments, particularly if fractured. The test case from Montana illustrates this point for lacustrine environments as well. Many postcranial bones had become buried in the lake margin, whereas the calotte — the element first noticed by a passerby — remained on the surface. Because it floats, the cranium is exposed longer, permitting greater opportunity for discovery. Given the choice of one portion of a body to analyze, most anthropologists would pick the cranium, and so the optimist might view the skull's unique transport qualities as a significant and fortunate fact.

In any forensic case, it is the role of the investigator to verify the facts and circumstances of recovery, and the anthropologist can use the taphonomic evidence to support or deny the account given by the finder. Fluvial transport creates an identifiable pattern of abrasion and other modifications of the cranium that can be used to verify its status as a transported specimen. Case 4 from Indiana did not display the characteristic features of transported crania, and taking into account pertinent scene information, a fluvial origin scenario became questionable. By contrast, case 5 did not have a documented recovery, but the taphonomic clues provided a starting point for the investigation. This process illustrates what taphonomy is all about: utilizing observation and experimentation to construct hypotheses about unknown phenomena, i.e., to draw analogies between modern and past events.

It is worth noting again that the distinction between terrestrial and aquatic cases — and the corresponding taphonomic forces prevalent in each environment — is not necessarily clearcut. Terrestrial cases frequently encounter large concentrations of water on or in the ground or even from the decomposing soft tissues themselves. Fluvial cases commonly float ashore and are exposed to land-based variables, only to be washed into the current again during floodstages. Thus one should normally expect a varied mix of specific taphonomic indicators and, accordingly, attempt to identify the overall *pattern* of modifications rather than to focus on particular traits in isolation. This approach is identical to that used when determining the race, sex, or age of a skeleton. Because not all indicators are equally expressed in each individual or equally reliable, success or failure will depend on one's ability to weed through the "noise" and find the most parsimonious solution.

If the features of the river are known, the degree of damage may give a clue as to the possible transport distance and postmortem interval, although these relationships have yet to be quantified. Burial in sediment and periodic retransport adds to the difficulty. As Haglund (1993:811) states, these problems make "total assessment of the postmortem history speculative for a majority of cases." We hope that our discussion will give future investigators an appreciation of the complexity of the situation, as well as a starting point for informed speculation.

## Acknowledgments

A number of individuals offered expertise and experience that added in a significant fashion to the quality of the final product, including Bill Haglund, Eva Klonowski, Tyler O'Brien, Steve Ousley, Phil Rightmire, Randy Skelton, and Matt Williamson. We would like to thank the editors for inviting us to participate in the original AAFS symposium and for allowing us to contribute to this landmark volume.

## References

Ambach, E., and F. Katzgraber
    1995   Corpses Released from Glacier Ice (Tyrol, Western Austria). Paper presented at the 47th Meeting of the American Academy of Forensic Sciences, Seattle, WA.

Bartstra, G.A., S. Soegondho, and A. van der Wijk
    1988   Ngandong Man: Age and Artifacts. *Journal of Human Evolution* 17:325–337.

Behrensmeyer, A.K.
    1975   The Taphonomy and Paleoecology of Plio-Pleistocene Vertebrate Assemblages East of Lake Rudolf, Kenya. *Bulletin of the Museum of Comparative Zoology* 146:473–578.
    1978   Taphonomic and Ecologic Information from Bone Weathering. *Paleobiology* 4:150–162.
    1982   Time Resolution in Fluvial Vertebrate Assemblages. *Paleobiology* 8:211–227.

Boaz, N.T., and A.K. Behrensmeyer
    1976   Hominid Taphonomy: Transport of Human Skeletal Parts in an Artificial Fluviatile Environment. *American Journal of Physical Anthropology* 45:53–60.

Boyle, S., A. Galloway, and R.T. Mason
    1993   Taphonomy of Drowning Victims in the Monterey Bay Area. Paper presented at the 45th Meeting of the American Academy of Forensic Sciences, Boston.

Brooks, S., and R.H. Brooks
    1984   Effects on Bone of Abrasive Contents in Moving Water. Paper presented at the 1st International Conference on Bone Modification, Carson City, NV.

Catts, E.P., and N.H. Haskell
    1990   *Entomology and Death: A Procedural Guide.* Joyce's Print Shop, Clemson, SC.

Copeland, A.R.
   1987   Suicide by Drowning. *American Journal of Forensic Medicine and Pathology* 8:18–22.
Davis, J.H.
   1986   Bodies Found in the Water: an Investigative Approach. *American Journal of Forensic Medicine and Pathology* 7:291–297.
Dechant Boaz, D.
   1982   Modern Riverine Taphonomy: Its Relevance to the Interpretation of Plio-Pleistocene Hominid Paleoecology in the Omo Basin, Ethiopia. Ph.D. dissertation, Department of Anthropology, University of California, Berkeley, CA.
Dilen, D.R.
   1984   The Motion of Floating and Submerged Objects in the Chattahoochee River, Atlanta, GA. *Journal of Forensic Sciences* 29:1027–1037.
Dodson, P.
   1973   The Significance of Small Bones in Paleoecological Interpretation. *Contributions to Geology* 12(1):15–19.
Donoghue, E.R., and G.C. Minnigerode
   1977   Human Body Buoyancy: a Study of 98 Men. *Journal of Forensic Sciences* 22:573–579.
Ebbesmeyer, C.C., and W.D. Haglund
   1994   Drift Trajectories of a Floating Human Body Simulated in a Hydraulic Model of Puget Sound. *Journal of Forensic Sciences* 39(1):231–240.
Giertsen, J.C., and I. Morild
   1989.  Seafaring Bodies. *American Journal of Forensic Medicine and Pathology* 10(1):25–27.
Gifford, D.P.
   1981   Taphonomy and Paleoecology: A Critical Review of Archaeology's Sister Disciplines. In *Advances in Archaeological Method and Theory, Vol.* 4., edited by M.B. Schiffer, pp. 365–438. Academic Press, New York.
Gifford, D.P., and A.K. Behrensmeyer
   1977   Observed Formation and Burial of a Recent Human Occupation Site in Kenya. *Quaternary Research* 8:245–266.
Giles, E., and O. Elliot
   1962   Race Identification from Cranial Measurements. *Journal of Forensic Sciences* 7:147–157.
   1963   Sex Determination by Discriminant Function Analysis of Crania. *American Journal of Physical Anthropology* 21:53–68.
Haglund, W.D.
   1993   Disappearance of Soft Tissue and the Disarticulation of Human Remains from Aqueous Environments. *Journal of Forensic Sciences* 38:806–815.
Haglund, W.D., and D.T. Reay
   1993   Problems of Recovering Partial Human Remains at Different Times and Locations: Concerns for Death Investigators. *Journal of Forensic Sciences* 38:69–80.
Haglund, W.D., D.G. Reichert, and D.T. Reay
   1990   Recovery of Decomposed and Skeletal Human Remains in the "Green River Murder" Investigation. *American Journal of Forensic Medicine and Pathology* 11(1):35–43.
Hanson, C.B.
   1980   Fluvial Taphonomic Processes: Models and Experiments. In *Fossils in the Making: Vertebrate Taphonomy and Paleoecology*, edited by A.K. Behrensmeyer and A.P. Hill, pp. 156–181. University of Chicago Press, Chicago.

Haskell, N.H., D.G. McShaffrey, D.A. Hawley, R.E. Williams, and J.E. Pless
  1989 Use of Aquatic Insects in Determining Submersion Interval. *Journal of Forensic Sciences* 34(3):622–632.

Hawley, D.A., N.H. Haskell, D.G. McShaffrey, R.E. Williams, and J.E. Pless
  1989 Identification of a Red "Fiber": Chironomid Larvae. *Journal of Forensic Sciences* 34:617–621.

Isaac, G.L.
  1967 Towards the Interpretation of Occupation Debris: Some Experiments and Observations. *Papers of the Kroeber Anthropological Society* 37:31–57.

Jantz, R.L., and S.D. Ousley
  1992 FORDISC 1.0 Personal Computer Forensic Discriminant Functions. Department of Anthropology, University of Tennessee, Knoxville.

Korth, W.W.
  1979 Taphonomy of Microvertebrate Fossil Assemblages. *Annals of the Carnegie Museum* 48:235–285.

LaFontaine, G.
  1981 *Caddisflies.* Lyons & Burford, New York.

Leeson, T.
  1994 *The Habit of Rivers: Reflections on Trout Streams and Fly Fishing.* Lyons & Burford, New York.

London, M.R., and F.J. Krolikowski
  1994 The Return of the Native or Protocol for Handling Recovered Burials at Sea. Paper presented at the 46th Meeting of the American Academy of Forensic Sciences, San Antonio, TX.

Lyman, R.L.
  1994 *Vertebrate Taphonomy.* Cambridge University Press, Cambridge, MA.

Manhein, M.H.
  1994 When the Mississippi Takes Them, Where Do They Go: Case Studies in River Dynamics. Paper presented at the 46th Meeting of the American Academy of Forensic Sciences, San Antonio, TX.

Morlan, R.E.
  1983 Spiral Fractures on Limb Bones: Which Ones Are Artificial? In *Carnivores, Human Scavengers, and Predators: A Question of Bone Technology,* edited by G. LeMoine and A. MacEachern, pp. 241–269. University of Calgary Archaeological Association, Calgary.

Nawrocki, S.P.
  1990 Cranial Vault Thickness in Homo. Master's thesis, Department of Anthropology, University of New York, Binghamton.
  1991 A Biomechanical Model of Cranial Vault Thickness in Archaic Homo. Ph.D. dissertation, Department of Anthropology, University of New York, Binghamton.
  1992 Cranial Thickness and Skull Biomechanics in Archaic Homo. *American Journal of Physical Anthropology* Supplement 14:127.
  1995 Taphonomic Processes in Historic Cemeteries. In *Bodies of Evidence,* edited by A. Grauer, pp. 49–66. John Wiley & Sons, New York.
  1996 Regression Formulae for Estimating Age at Death from Cranial Suture Closure. In *Forensic Osteology,* edited by K. Reichs. Charles C Thomas, Springfield, IL.

Nawrocki, S.P., and M.A. Clark
    1994  Extreme Dispersal and Damage of Human Skeletal Remains by Farming Equipment. Paper presented at the 46th Meeting of the American Academy of Forensic Sciences, San Antonio, TX.

Nawrocki, S.P., and J.E. Pless
    1993  Transport of Human Remains in Fluvial Environments: A Review. Paper presented at the 45th Meeting of the American Academy of Forensic Sciences, Boston.

O'Brien, T.G.
    1993  Waxing Grave about Adipocere. Paper presented at the 45th Meeting of the American Academy of Forensic Sciences, Boston.
    1994  Human Soft-Tissue Decomposition in an Aquatic Environment and Its Transformation into Adipocere. Master's thesis, Department of Anthropology, University of Tennessee, Knoxville.
    1995  Human Soft Tissue Decomposition in an Aquatic Environment and Its Transformation into Adipocere. Paper presented at the 47th Meeting of the American Academy of Forensic Sciences, Seattle, WA.

Payne, J.A., and E.W. King
    1972  Insect Succession and Decomposition of Pig Carcasses in Water. *Journal of the Georgia Entomological Society* 7:153–162.

Petraglia, M.D., and R. Potts
    1994  Water Flow and the Formation of Early Pleistocene Artifacts Sites in Olduvai Gorge, Tanzania. *Journal of Anthropological Archaeology* 13:228–254.

Reinhardt, G.A.
    1993  Hydrologic Artifact Dispersals at Pingasagruk, North Coast, Alaska. *Geoarchaeology* 8(6):493–513.

Santa Luca, A.
    1980  *The Ngandong Fossil Hominids.* Yale University Publications in Anthropology No. 70, New Haven, CT.

Schick, K.D.
    1986  *Stone Age Sites in the Making: Experiments in the Formation and Transformation of Archaeological Occurrences.* BAR International Series 319, British Archaeological Reports, Oxford, U.K.

Shipman, P.
    1981  *Life History of a Fossil: An Introduction to Taphonomy and Paleoecology.* Harvard University Press, Cambridge, MA.

Shotwell, J.A.
    1955  An Approach to the Paleoecology of Mammals. *Ecology* 36:327–337.

Simonsen, J.
    1983  Injuries Sustained from High-Velocity Impact with Water after Jumps from High Bridges: A Preliminary Report of 10 Cases. *American Journal of Forensic Medicine and Pathology* 4(2):139–142.

Skinner, M.F., J. Duffy, and D.B. Symes
    1988  Repeat Identification of Skeletonized Human Remains: A Case Study. *Canadian Society of Forensic Science Journal* 21(3):138–141.

Sorg, M.H., H.F. Ryan, J.H. Dearborn, and E.I. Monahan
    1993  Forensic Taphonomy in Marine Contexts: Estimating Time since Death. Paper presented at the 45th Meeting of the American Academy of Forensic Sciences, Boston.

Sorg, M.H., J.H. Dearborn, K.G. Sweeney, H.F. Ryan, and W.C. Rodriguez
1995 Marine Taphonomy of a Case Submerged for 32 Years. Paper Presented at the 47th Meeting of the American Academy of Forensic Sciences, Seattle, WA.

Sorg, M.H., J.H. Dearbom, K.G. Sweeney, H.F. Ryan, and W.C. Rodriguez
1995 Marine Taphonomy of a Case Submerged for 32 Years. *Proceedings of the American Academy of Forensic Sciences,* Vol 1; 156-157.

Turnbaugh, W.A.
1978 Floods and Archaeology. *American Antiquity* 43:593–607.

Von Endt, D.W., and D.J. Ortner
1984 Experimental Effects of Bone Size and Temperature on Bone Diagenesis. *Journal of Archaeological Science* 11:247–253.

Voorhies, M.R.
1969 *Taphonomy and Population Dynamics of an Early Pliocene Vertebrate Fauna, Knox County, Nebraska.* Contributions to Geology, Special Paper No. 1. University of Wyoming, Laramie, WY.

Weidenreich, F.
1943 The Skull of Sinanthropus Pekinensis: A Comparative Study on a Primitive Hominid Skull. *Palaeontologia Sinica,* New Series D, No. 10.

Weigelt, J.
1989 [1927] *Recent Vertebrate Carcasses and Their Paleobiological Implications,* translated by J. Schaefer. University of Chicago Press, Chicago.

Williams, J.A.
1995 A Cemetery and a Missing Person. Paper delivered at the 2nd Annual Meeting of the Midwest Bioarchaeology and Forensic Anthropology Association, DeKalb, IL.

Wolf, R.G.
1973 Hydrodynamic Sorting and Ecology of a Pleistocene Mammalian Assemblage from California (U.S.A.). *Palaeogeography, Palaeoclimatology, Palaeoecology* 13:91–101.

# The Taphonomic Effects of Flood Waters on Bone

# 35

SHEILAGH BROOKS
RICHARD H. BROOKS

## Introduction

In mid-October the body of a young woman was found, trapped within a river log jam after flooding from the previous spring had subsided. The cranium had a large broken area in the left side, involving most of the temporal bone, some of the parietal, and a small area of the lateral occipital. About half of the temporal bone had been lost, presumably postmortem. During the identification process, a local orthodontist, whom the missing woman had seen, was asked to examine the antemortem dental work on the teeth and he recognized his own craftsmanship. The remains were positively identified by matching the dental X-rays of the missing woman with the dentition of the recovered cranium, despite the loss of the two central upper incisors, either peri- or postmortem. The missing woman was 19 years old at the time of her disappearance in mid-February.

The flooding river originates in a nearby mountain range, which had a heavy snow pack that year, and the spring run-off was unusually large, with an increased load of silt and debris. The log jam in which the body had been trapped was 40 to 50 miles downstream from where the missing woman was last seen alive. After the river dropped to normal level, the skull was found exposed on the ground, and separated from the body by about 9 feet. They were located about 20 feet above the normal river level. The body was caught in some timber debris accumulated at a bend in the river and was partially mummified, especially in the torso area. The skull, mandible, six cervical vertebrae, and some of the limb bones were partially or completely skeletalized.

According to the coroner's description, there was a rope tied around the right ankle and knotted, then wrapped around both wrists where it was knotted. This rope went around the right wrist once and looped twice around the left wrist where there was another knot. In the rope knotted about the wrists was a stick, with one end cut, apparently by a sharp instrument. No associated clothing was found.

From these remnants of rope on her wrists and ankles it was assumed they had been tied together in some fashion. As her body was carried downstream by the flooding river, probably it was snagged or struck by various objects also being washed downstream. With her hands tied, her head would have been unprotected, allowing for more injury to it than the rest of her body. Presumably her body was caught on different objects a number times while being carried downstream in the flooding waters, thus permitting further damage to her exposed head.

There was little or no soft tissue present on either the skull or the mandible, which were found together, with the atlas vertebra attached to the occipital area of the skull. According to the coroner's description (Report 0856-83-A-OAA) there is a "large, left sided defect in the skull … and a fracture which runs from the base of this into the left inferior bones of the skull and into the upper portion of the posterior maxilla…. Some more radiating fractures are noted on the posterior portion of the larger defect. One fracture radiates along the

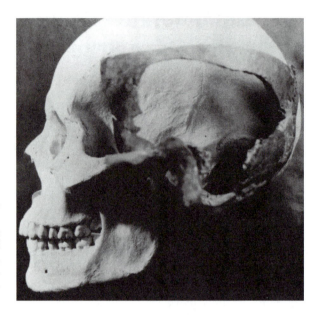

**Figure 1** Superimposition of the broken out section of the left frontal, parietal, temporal, and part of the occipital, placed over a photograph of the left lateral view of a skull (From White, T.D. *Human Osteology*. Academic Press, New York, With permission.)

posterior occipital bone and into the right inferior occipital bone. There is another radiating fracture into the left lambdoid suture" (Figure 1).

A forensic physical anthropologist was asked to assist in determining whether the broken area, with radiating fracture lines, in the left temporal region of the skull had occurred ante-, peri-, or postmortem. Could the broken lateral portion of the cranium have been caused by postmortem buffeting in the river, or was it the result of antemortem or perimortem trauma, or was there a possibility it could have been a surgical trephination. Additionally, could a head become almost skeletalized in such a short time period? During the forensic examination of the cranium no evidence of scavenger activity was noted.

Missing from the left temporal bone are the squamous portion, the area of the supramastoid crest and part of the mastoid, as well as the inferior part of the left parietal (Figures 1 and 2). Fracture lines extend across the left parietal to the sagittal suture and diagonally through the occipital. Although some of the edges of the posterior temporal break appeared smooth, almost polished, most of the bone surrounding the break and along the radiating fracture lines had sharp irregular edges (Figure 3). The left asterion area of the occipital was recovered separately, and one edge has a smoothed or polished appearance. It fits against a rather smoothed, almost polished appearing part of the occipital and both edges match, although they share somewhat polished surfaces (Figures 4 and 5).

In the nearly smooth section of the left lateral parietal, about 2.50 cm anterior to the lambdoid suture, the diploe was eroded more deeply than the compact bone of the outer and inner tables (Figure 6). When the almost smoothed and eroded section was examined under a dissecting microscope, the edges of this area were somewhat similar to an antemortem trephination cut where healing bone growth had begun.

Had the missing lateral cranial region been the result of trephination surgery, obviously no radiating fracture lines would occur, nor would a detached bone fragment be encountered which fitted the edge of a surgical cut. For such a large trephination a metal plate would have been wired into position to protect the brain, leaving evidence of holes for the wire in the adjacent cranial bones. No aspect of the skull observed during the forensic examination indicated this type of surgical procedure. Additionally the family doctor stated this young woman never had cranial surgery during her life.

The possibility of an accidental antemortem fall into the flooded river was not considered, since the remnants of rope around her wrists and ankle were evidence someone had tied her prior to her immersion in the river. In addition there was the question of whether she was

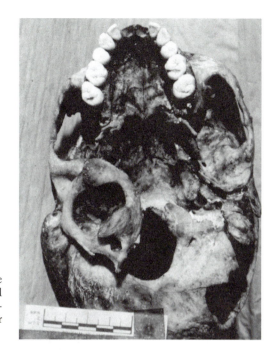

**Figure 2** Basal view of the cranium; note jagged edges of the break. The atlas is still attached to the cranium. The two upper central incisors may have been lost pre-, peri-, or postmortem.

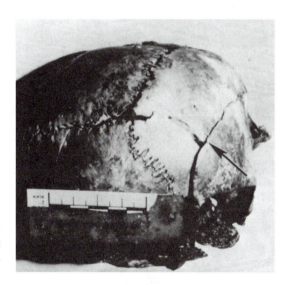

**Figure 3** Superior posterior view, illustrating the radiating fracture lines from the break, especially across the occipital, and a fracture line where the arrow points.

alive when put in the river and, if so, perhaps the break with fracture lines in the skull was the result of debris striking her unprotected head, eventually causing the skeletonization. This idea was discounted by the coroner. Postmortem damage through the subsequent actions of the river is suggested as a cause of the missing temporal and other bone pieces from the left lateral skull which apparently was broken perimortem.

## Discussion

During the questioning of a suspect (arrested and in jail on suspicion of another murder), the individual confessed to killing the young woman. According to his testimony he had struck her on the head with a piece of cement brick, tied her wrists and ankles, and threw her body

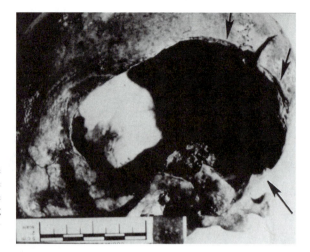

**Figure 4**  Overview of the left side of the cranium showing the extensive break with an arrow pointing to the broken edges and two arrows showing the location of the smoothed or polished areas.

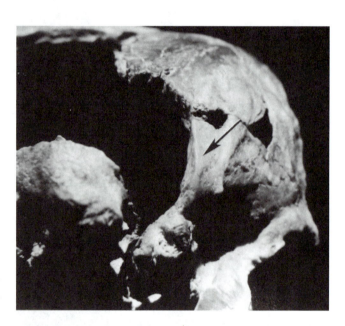

**Figure 5**  Close-up of the broken-off occipital area; arrow indicates the smoothing and extensive polish.

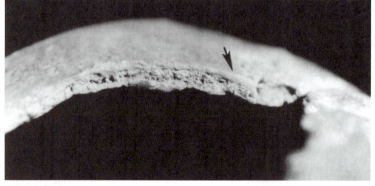

**Figure 6**  Close-up of a similar appearing section of the left parietal, with the compactum polished and the diploe depressed.

in the river. Information about the loss of the two central incisors was not mentioned. So whether the two central incisors were lost perimortem or postmortem is not known.

With the information provided by the suspect, this forensic case was well documented. The question of individual identification was resolved early through antemortem X-rays and forensic odontological information. Consequently, time since death is a known factor, 8 months. The body had been carried downstream between 40 and 50 miles to where it was eventually trapped in a log and debris jam. After the flood waters subsided, the remains were exposed on a bank above the normal river level. Photographs of the location of the log jam with the body entrapped and information on the height of the flood waters and the normal river level were recorded at the time of the recovery by the police.

The almost complete skeletonization of the cranium, after submergence in the river, apparently was the result of the taphonomic effects of the flood level waters containing a heavy silt load and other debris. The head would have been more exposed through the tying of her wrists and ankles, resulting in the loss of soft tissue from the cranium. Also the abrasive effects of the silt, in combination with the moving water, would macerate and erode away the flesh from the wound, exposing the damaged and fragmented bone. Several pieces of the broken temporal and adjacent bone probably worked free and were lost in the rapidly moving water. The body may have also been trapped several times by debris in the river and held firm while the moving water with its abrasive contents affected the now exposed edges of the bone break. The effects of moving or swirling water on bone are recognized paleontologically (Behrensmeyer et al. 1989; Brooks 1967; Driscoll 1967; Parsons and Brett 1991; Potts 1988; Shipman 1977) and described forensically here.

The smoothing of the fresh bone breaks, so that parts of them acquired an almost polished aspect, is attributed to the taphonomic effects of silt and debris in the rapidly moving river water (Figures 4, 5, and 6). As the body twisted and turned in the flooded river, finally to be caught in the log jam, various sections of the break would have been exposed to the abrasive action of the silt and flowing water. Significantly, these results occurred within a maximum period of 8 months, since this smoothing was effected prior to the drop in the river water level.

## Summary

After striking a young woman on the head with a cement brick, the perpetrator threw her body, with wrists and ankles tied, into a flooded river. After 8 months, her remains were recovered about 40 to 50 miles downstream. The skull was nearly skeletalized through the taphonomic effects of flood waters carrying abrasives, which is not unexpected. Also the two central upper incisors were lost, possibly postmortem. The body itself was partially mummified.

The smoothed and polished appearance of some of the broken edges of the wound, modified in such a relatively brief period, is unexpected. More than one section of the broken area was smoothed, including both sides of the fragmented left part of the occipital asterion region. Anterior to this is the portion of the break that had seemed similar to a healing trephination. More importantly, these smoothing and polishing effects occurred within a maximum time span of 8 months, as did the partial skeletonization of the head and some of the cervical vertebrae. The relatively short time in which environmental conditions, especially the results of moving water carrying silt and debris, can abrade away the soft tissues, is significant to both forensic researchers and law enforcement officers.

## Acknowledgments

Vernon O. McCarty, Washoe County Coroner, provided a copy of the "Record of Death and Autopsy Protocol" for this case. The data on water flow in the river during the months the body was caught in the log jam were supplied by the local sheriff's office, which sent copies of studies made on the river by the U.S. Department of Interior, Geological Survey, Water Resources Division. Several references were contributed through the courtesy of Dr. W.D. Haglund, Senior Forensic Consultant for the International Criminal Tribunal of the United Nations which have good descriptions of the taphonomic effects on bone, shell, or artifacts when carried by rapidly moving water containing abrasives.

## References

Behrensmeyer A.K., D. Gordon, and G.T. Yanagi
>    1989   Non-Human Bone Modification in Miocene Fossils from Pakistan. In *Bone Modification*, edited by R. Bonnichsen and M.H. Sorg, pp. 99–120. Center for the Study of the First Americans, University of Maine, Orono, ME.

Brooks, R.H.
>    1967   A Comparative Analysis of Bone from Locality 2 (C1-245) Tule Springs, Nevada. In *Pleistocene Studies in Southern Nevada*, edited by H.M. Wormington and D. Ellis, pp. 402–411. Nevada State Museum Anthropological Papers No. 13. Carson City.

Driscoll, E.G.
>    1967   Experimental Field Study of Shell Abrasion. *Journal of Sedimentary Petrology* 37:1117–1123.

Parsons, K.M., and C.E. Brett
>    1991   Taphonomic Processes and Biases in Modern Marine Environments: An Actualistic Perspective of Fossil Assemblage Preservation. In *The Processes of Fossilization*, edited by S.K. Donovan, pp. 22–65. Columbia University Press, New York.

Potts, R.
>    1988   *Early Hominid Activities at Olduvai*. Adine de Gruyter, New York.

Shipman, P.
>    1977   *Paleoecology, Taphonomic History and Population Dynamics of the Vertebrate Assemblage from the Middle Miocene of Fort Ternan, Kenya*. Ph.D. dissertation, New York University. University Microfilms, Ann Arbor, MI.

White, T.D.
>    1991   *Human Osteology*. Academic Press, NY.

# Movement of Bodies in Lake Ontario

# 36

TYLER G. O'BRIEN

## Introduction

This paper explores the use of information about the effects of wind, temperature, and the movement of lake water as it may affect human remains. One focus is to understand the potential for the movement of human bodies in a lake environment using limnological models. A second focus is on the environmental limits for the formation of adipocere in aquatic settings. By way of illustration, a case study is presented of an unidentified adipociferous body found on the shores of Lake Ontario for which the possibility of multiple taphonomic pathways limits the estimation of postmortem interval.

## Lake Effects

A typical lake passes through four phases which may be broken down into two distinct categories: the overturn cycle and the stratified cycle (Boyce et al. 1989, 1991; Hough 1958; Pickett 1977; Simons and Schertzer 1987).

In the spring, due to winds and the resultant current action, the water is in upheaval. In early spring, shallower water near shore warms more rapidly. This rise in temperature causes the warmer water to migrate away from shore, converge with colder offshore water, and sink. This overall turbidity is known as the "spring overturn."

After the convergence, the water becomes differentially warmed due to mixing (Boyce et al. 1989, 1991). The onshore water temperature increases above 4°C. and, due to its higher density, sinks, gradually increasing the overall lake temperature. In addition, the onshore/offshore pressure gradient pushes warm water offshore. The effect of mixing is countered by the earth's rotational force, known as the Coriolis effect. Coupled with the wind, the water tends to deflect the waves to the right of the wind, setting up a counterclockwise pattern of surface movement. A floating object within such a pattern would be affected by centrifugal force, causing it to move away from the center and toward shore (Boyce et al. 1989). Winds blowing across the center of the lake will additionally force the nearshore water along until it reaches the end of the lake, meets the currents from the other side, and they converge. Their direction now moves toward the center of the lake opposite the wind direction. This sets up a cycle where surface water warms and subsurface water cools to 4°C. The combined result of the Coriolis effect and wind provides enough force for upwelling to occur on one shore and downwelling on the opposite shore.

In Lake Ontario, the spring upwelling occurs on the northeast shore and the downwelling on the southeast (Simons and Schertzer 1987). The modifications of the upwelling and downwelling circulation depend on the lake's thermal stratification and basin geometry (Boyce et al. 1989).

The second phase of lake effects occurs in the summer when the water is stratified into an upper (epilimnion) layer and a lower (hypolimnion) layer (Hough 1958). A convection current from blowing winds moves surface water in a counterclockwise direction, due to the Coriolis effect. A thermocline continues to separate the warmer, low density water on top from the cooler, higher density water on the lake bottom (Boyce et al. 1989, 1991). Weather conditions are the major factor determining the depth of each layer.

Large-scale currents are restricted to the epilimnion, while the hypolimnion remains insulated from the atmosphere and the air–water interface. But, due to the circulation of the overlying layer, the shearing force against the cooler, lighter water moves it in a direction against the epilimnionic flow. Thus, the lower stratum maintains motion, while wind force from storm surges keeps the surface water circulating (Boyce et al. 1991).

By the end of summer, the shore water warms again, convection disrupts the thermal bar, and the "fall overturn" is produced (Hough 1958). The overturn is primarily due to destabilization of the water column. It is followed by the "winter stratification" phase, a pattern similar to that following the spring overturn.

Lake Ontario, the most easterly of the Great Lakes, has a long axis approximately parallel to prevailing winds. Its mean depth is about 86 m, and its maximum depth reaches 245 m (Boyce et al. 1989). A major influx of freshwater comes from the Niagara River located in the southeast corner of the lake. The mean monthly discharge of the Niagara River ranges from 3289 to 7590 m/s and furnishes about 83% of the total annual input (Aubert and Richards 1981). Particulate matter entering the lake will tend to be isolated into weight components, with the heavier, coarser particles settling to the bottom nearer the river (Boyce et al. 1991). Only forces such as storm surges produce enough power to resuspend these particles and flush them into the current.

## Adipocere Formation

The formation of adipocere in aqueous environments has been documented by Cotton et al. (1987), Dix (1987), Mant (1960), Mant and Furbank (1957), O'Brien (1994), Simonsen (1977), and Takatori and Yamaoka (1977). Complete transformation of all soft tissues to adipocere in water settings may occur in as little as 3 weeks, and has also been documented in cases up to 5 years after death (see Table 1).

**Table 1   Case Reports Citing Bodies Found with Adipocere**

| Author (Year) | Environment | Time Period | Condition |
|---|---|---|---|
| Cotton et al. (1987) | Water | 5 years | Complete |
| Mant and Furbank (1957) | Water | 1 year | Complete |
| Dix (1987) | Water | 10 months | Complete |
| Dix (1987) | Water | 6 months | Moderate |
| Takatori and Yamaoka (1977) | Water | 4.5 months | Complete |
| Dix (1987) | Water | 4 months | Slight |
| Mellen et al. (1993) | Water (lab) | 2.5 months | Complete |
| Dix (1987) | Water | 3 weeks | Minimal |
| Simonsen (1977) | Water | 3 weeks | Complete |
| Evans (1962) | Buried | 100–140 years | Complete |
| Rodriguez and Bass (1985) | Buried | 1 year | Complete |
| Rodriguez and Bass (1985) | Buried | 6 months | Moderate |
| Rodriguez and Bass (1985) | Buried | 3 months | Minimal |
| Rodriguez and Bass (1985) | Buried | 2.5 months | Slight |

Adipocere formation occurs within a limited temperature range, generally tied to the optimum growth temperature for the bacterium *Clostridium perfringens (welchii)* (Corry 1978; Cotton et al. 1987; Payne and King 1972; Tomita 1975). Tomita (1975) notes the lower limit is 21°C, Corry (1978) reports the optimum temperature is about 45°C, and Bryan et al. (1962) reports the optimum at 35 to 37°C. When the ambient temperature reaches a maximum or minimum, adipocere will not form due to a depression in the rate of bacterial action and enzymatic release.

The temperature range must be "just right," a requirement termed the "Goldilocks phenomenon" (O'Brien 1994). When the water is too warm the tissues liquefy easily and tend to macerate. Soft tissue cells autolyze, subcutaneous adipose deposits melt, and the leaking fluid adds to the liquefaction of all tissue. The soft tissue will decompose rapidly. If the water is too cold, decomposition slows, and, if the water is freezing, all bodily fluid will freeze and crystallization will commence (Zugibe and Costello 1993). When the temperature is moderate, the body will decompose and putrefaction will ensue. Bacteria will emerge from their intestinal and vascular lodging to penetrate the body's cellular network and destroy it. Subsequent release of the internal cell's mass will cause a chemical reaction (i.e., saponification) between the bacteria, the watery environment, and the cellular contents resulting in adipocere. Over time it accumulates, encasing the bacteria until they eventually die or until there is no more soft tissue to hydrolyze. The body can remain in this state of preservation for an indefinite interval (Bass 1984, Evans 1962). Even if brought to the surface, the adipocere will maintain its consistency. If allowed to dry, the transformed tissue will become a saponified, caseous mass of crumbling, chalky "soap."

## Adipocere Formation and Postmortem Interval

Gonzales and co-workers (1954), Spitz and Fisher (1980), and Taylor (1965) state that the complete adipocere transformation of soft tissue can occur in about 3 to 6 months. However, Simonsen (1977) has documented extensive adipocere formation appearing within only 22 days.

A study of adipocere formation in an aquatic environment was conducted by O'Brien (1994). Three human cadavers were immersed in excavated water-filled holes for three months in an outdoor setting. Observations were made of climatological and meteorological conditions, ambient air and water temperature, and gross morphological changes in the cadavers. Liquid and tissue samples extracted at intervals during the study were analyzed for fatty acid content and microbial composition. Not surprisingly, the study confirmed that a warm (21 to 45°C.), moist, virtually anaerobic environment is suitable for adipocere formation, and that 3 months is sufficient time. Less expected were the results that the two bodies which formed adipocere were also the ones that floated the entire time of the study. Thus, complete immersion was neither necessary nor sufficient. The progression of morphological change which occurred in these two bodies was as follows: float, bloat, insect activity, hatching, mummification/maceration, fungal growth, color loss, cutis anserina, and then adipocere formation.

## Case Description

On April 8, 1992, the Onondaga County Medical Examiner's Office in Syracuse, New York, recovered a body from a rocky shore of Lake Ontario behind the Alcan Aluminum Plant in Oswego. The partial body, found on the rocks in a supine position, with the head oriented to the east, was in an advanced state of decomposition with partial skeletonization of limbs and skull. No clothing was present except the elastic waistband from a pair of men's briefs positioned around the waist.

KEY ▨ = EROSION

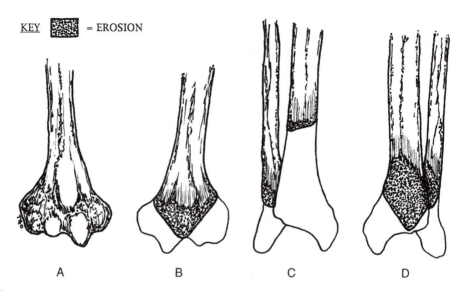

**Figure 1** (A) Posterior aspect of left humerus; (B) posterior aspect of distal right humerus; (C) anterior aspect of distal right tibia and fibula; (D) anterior aspect of distal left tibia and fibula. Unmarked areas represent portion which was missing; speckled areas represent sites of erosion.

Extensive abrasion was noted on the labial surface of the left maxillary canine, exposing dentin, on the nasal bones, the nasal aperture, the nasal spine, and the exposed frontal sinuses. The medial and lateral malleoli of the distal tibiae and fibulae were missing and the distal shafts eroded (see Figure 1). The right distal humerus showed a similar pattern; medial and lateral epicondyles were missing, probably due to erosion. Despite the distal humerus erosion, soft tissue kept the radius and ulna attached. Bones of the right hand and both feet were absent. Tissue comprising the cheeks, lower neck, thorax, abdomen, and upper legs had been transformed into adipocere; the abdominal cavity had been perforated, exposing internal organs. Although no external genitalia remained, the prostate was discernible at autopsy (Germaniuk 1992).

There are multiple fractures of all ribs; however, the lack of focal accumulation of blood in the surrounding soft tissue suggests they were sustained after death. A posterior occipital fracture which extends between the temporal bones could be peri- or postmortem, and may be due to impact on the rocks with the action of the waves or other causes.

An estimated postmortem interval was developed using a taphonomic approach, including the abrasion of long bones and face, meteorological data for the weeks prior to discovery of the body, models of lake water movement, and inferences regarding adipocere formation.

## Abrasion

The location and position of the body suggests the focal abrasion on the long bones and cranium may be a result of abrasion by rocks rather than water. The action of waves pushing the appendages back and forth against the rocks would have been sufficient to produce such localized soft tissue and bone loss. If the body had been trapped below the ice shelf or broken ice blocks it would have been subjected to damage due to solid abrasive matter contained within the ice itself (Boyce et al. 1989). Rock fragments, wood, silt, and sand may all be held within the ice layers (Fahnestock et al. 1973).

## Meteorological Data

Environmental data at the Alcan Aluminum Plant provided current meteorological information about air temperature, wind speed, and wind direction for the week prior to recovery.

Air temperature 9.1 m from shore ranged from 17.2 to 31.7°C, while lake temperatures ranged more narrowly from 19.4 to 21.8°C. Both high temperatures occurred the day before discovery. Weather reports stated conditions were "mostly sunny, breezy and cool" (Niagara Mohawk Power Corporation 1992).

## Multiple Taphonomic Pathways

The condition of the remains reported earlier suggests multiple taphonomic processes: abrasion due to sand-imbedded ice; skeletonization and disarticulation due to decomposition and water movement; and adipocere formation due to relatively warm, moist, anaerobic conditions. The timing and, to some extent, the sequence of these events is unknown, however.

Information about meteorological conditions and particularly lake effects suggests that the lake contains multiple depositional environments which vary according to depth, distance from shore, and season. Additional variation is added with consideration of weather and the proximity to the factory's effluent. Information from the literature about the formation of adipocere suggests it can form in as little as 3 weeks time, that its formation is temperature sensitive, and that it can form in bodies which float.

Examination of the context of discovery of the body suggests that the conditions at that location at that time of year are sufficient to explain the presence of localized and position-dependent bone abrasion as well as the presence of both wet and dried adipocere. The formation of the adipocere would probably have required a less aerobic microenvironment, and hence the body is hypothesized to have arrived at that location via lake current. Further, judging from the extent of the adipocere, the body most likely became located in a fairly stable, anaerobic setting, either floating or submerged, prior to extensive decomposition, and stayed there at least several weeks and probably longer.

Given the temperature-sensitive nature of adipocere formation as well as the fact that the off-shore hypolimnion tends to be quite cold during all seasons, if the body had been submerged at that depth, both decomposition and adipocere formation would have been delayed, suggesting a longer postmortem interval would be more likely, perhaps even years. Alternatively, adipocere could have formed more quickly in the warmer waters near the surface and near the shore, assuming the body was protected from predators and excessive aeration as it floated (or was caught and held in place at a shallow depth). In that case, the postmortem interval might have been shorter, perhaps months. In the absence of further data, however, one cannot choose between these two plausible scenarios.

## Summary

Lake Ontario provides a complex range of depositional environments for both floating and submerged remains. And, despite a number of studies of adipocere formation, many unknowns persist about this important postmortem process. Nevertheless, knowledge about the optimum conditions for adipocere formation, as well as documentation about its formation in floating remains, helped shape the taphonomic interpretation as well as the estimation of postmortem interval the case presented here. The limits of this interpretation point to a continuing need for systematic documentation of both the context of discovery and the condition of remains in future forensic cases in order to understand the range of variation of postmortem changes in aquatic settings, and ultimately increase of the accuracy of postmortem interval estimates.

# References

Aubert, E.J., and T.L. Richards
   1981  *IFYGL — The International Field Year for the Great Lakes.* U.S. Department of Commerce, National Oceanic and Atmospheric Administration, Great Lakes Environmental Research Laboratory, Ann Arbor, MI.

Bass, W.M.
   1984  Time Interval Since Death, A Difficult Decision. In *Human Identification: Case Studies in Forensic Anthropology,* edited by T.A. Rathbun and J.E. Buikstra, pp. 136–147. Charles C Thomas Publishing Company, Springfield, IL.

Boyce, F.M., M.A. Donelan, P.F. Hamblin, C.R. Murthy, and T.J. Simons
   1989  Thermal Structure and Circulation in the Great Lakes. *Atmosphere-Ocean* 27(4):607–642.

Boyce, F.M., W.M. Schertzer, P.F. Hamblin, and C.R. Murthy
   1991  Physical Behavior of Lake Ontario with Reference to Contaminant Pathways and Climate Change. *Canadian Journal of Fish and Aquatic Science* 48:1517–1528.

Bryan, A.H., C.A. Bryan, and C.G. Bryan
   1962  *Bacteriology: Principles and Practice.* Barnes and Noble Books, New York.

Corry, J.E.L.
   1978  Possible Sources of Ethanol Ante- and Postmortem: Its Relationship to the Biochemistry and Microbiology of Decomposition. *Journal of Applied Bacteriology* 44:1–56.

Cotton, G. E., A.C. Aufderheide, and V.G. Goldschmidt
   1987  Preservation of Human Tissue Immersed for Five Years in Fresh Water of Known Temperature. *Journal of Forensic Sciences* 32: 1125–1130.

Dix, J.D.
   1987  Missouri's Lakes and the Disposal of Homicide Victims. *Journal of Forensic Sciences* 32: 806–809.

Evans, W.E.
   1962  Adipocere Formation in a Relatively Dry Environment. *Medicine, Science, and Law* 3:145–153.

Fahnestock, R.R., D.J. Crowley, M. Wilson, and H. Schneider
   1973  Ice Volcanoes of the Lake Erie Shore Near Dunkirk, New York, U.S.A. *Journal of Glaciology* 12(64):93–99.

Germaniuk, H.D.
   1992  Autopsy Report for Unidentified Human Remains: Case No. 92-0199. Onondaga County Medical Examiner Office, Syracuse, NY.

Gonzales, T.A., M. Helpbern, M. Vance, and C.J. Umberger
   1954  *Legal Medicine.* Appleton-Century-Crofts, New York.

Hough, J.L.
   1958  *Geology of the Great Lakes.* University of Illinois Press, Urbana, IL.

Mant, A.K.
   1960  *Forensic Medicine: Observation and Interpretation.* Lloyd-Luke Ltd. London, England.

Mant, A.K., and R. Furbank
   1957  Adipocere — A Review. *Journal of Forensic Medicine* 4:18–35.

Mellen, P.F.M., M.A. Lowry, and M.S. Micozzi
　　1993　Experimental Observations on Adipocere Formation. *Journal of Forensic Sciences*
　　38:91–93.

Niagara Mohawk Power Corporation
　　1992　Nine Mile Point Weather Log Entries for 4/1/92-4/8/92. Oswego County, NY.

O'Brien, T.G.
　　1994　Human Soft-Tissue Decomposition in an Aquatic Environment and Its Transfor-
　　mation into Adipocere. Master of Arts Thesis, Department of Anthropology, University
　　of Tennessee, Knoxville.

Payne, J.A., and E.W. King
　　1972　Insect Succession and Decomposition of Pig Carcasses in Water. *Journal of the
　　Georgia Entomological Society* 7:153–162.

Pickett, R.L.
　　1977　The Observed Winter Circulation of Lake Ontario. *Journal of Physical Oceanography*
　　7(1):152–156.

Rodriguez, W.C., and W.M. Bass
　　1985　Decomposition of Buried Bodies and Methods That May Aid in Their Location.
　　*Journal of Forensic Sciences* 30:836–852.

Simons, T.J., and W.M. Schertzer
　　1987　Stratification, Currents, Upwelling in Lake Ontario, Summer 1982. *Canadian Jour-
　　nal of Fish and Aquatic Science* 44:2047–2058.

Simonsen, J.
　　1977　Early Formation of Adipocere in Temperate Climate. *Medicine, Science, and Law* 17:
　　53–55.

Spitz, W.U., and R.S. Fisher
　　1980　*Medicolegal Investigation of Death.* Charles C Thomas, Springfield, IL.

Takatori, T., and A. Yamaoka
　　1977　The Mechanism of Adipocere Formation. 1. Identification and Chemical Properties
　　of Hydroxy Fatty Acids in Adipocere. *Forensic Science* 9:63–73.

Taylor, A.S.
　　1965　Death and Postmortem Change. In *Principles and Practice of Medical Jurisprudence,*
　　12th edition, edited by K. Simpson, pp. 89–102. J. and A. Churchill Press, London.

Tomita, K.
　　1975　On Putrefactions and Flotations of Dead Bodies under Water. *Hiroshima Journal of
　　Medical Sciences* 24:117–152.

Zugibe, F.T., and J.T. Costello
　　1993　The Iceman Murder: One of a Series of Contract Murders. *Journal of Forensic Sciences*
　　38:1404–1408.

# Forensic Taphonomy in Marine Contexts

# 37

MARCELLA H. SORG
JOHN H. DEARBORN
ELIZABETH I. MONAHAN
HENRY F. RYAN
KRISTIN G. SWEENEY
EDWARD DAVID

## Introduction

Although the taphonomic literature includes research on marine taphonomy as it relates to ecological and paleontological issues (Donovan 1991; Schafer 1972), there have been few studies that focus on human remains in marine contexts. Nearly all these have been done as a byproduct of forensic casework (Boyle et al., this volume; Davis 1992; Ebbesmeyer and Haglund 1994, Giertsen and Morild 1989; Haglund 1993; Rathbun and Rathbun, this volume; Skinner et al. 1988; Sorg et al. 1995). Arnaud et al. (1978) report research on prehistoric remains. Other mention of prehistoric remains from marine settings has been mostly anecdotal. The dearth of research in marine taphonomy is due to two underlying factors. First, marine death assemblages that include terrestrial and especially human remains are very rare. Second, their recovery is even more rare.

The research reported here emerged from a growing need for information on this topic which could be used in forensic settings to interpret perimortem and postmortem modifications and to estimate time since death for remains recovered from the Northwestern Atlantic Ocean. A taphonomic approach seemed the best way to understand and interpret the wide range of ecological and geological data that constitute the depositional and recovery contexts for these remains.

In the first part of this paper we review in broad terms those aspects of the marine context which might relate to the accidental introduction of animal remains of terrestrial origin into the sea. We focus our discussion on the implications for modification of these remains over time and for the interpretation of time since death.

In the second part of the work, we present a series of forensic cases recovered from the Northwestern Atlantic Ocean, specifically the Gulf of Maine, for which time since death is known. The cases in this sample include only those with times since death of a month or more in which the body was submerged and skeletonization had already commenced. All remains were recovered accidentally by divers or from fishing vessels.

Because environmental contexts in the sea are different from those on land, separate models of decomposition and preservation are needed. The usual taphonomic goals of reconstructing depositional and preservation history are augmented by the forensic goals of determining individual identity, place of death, time since death, and cause of death. With these goals in mind, we will construct a very loose and preliminary model of decompositional changes for human remains in the Gulf of Maine, using a case series approach coupled with a theoretical understanding of marine ecology.

# The Marine Environment as a Forensic Taphonomic Context

Organic remains of terrestrial origin are important energy sources for marine organisms. These remains may be normal products of the ecosystem, such as allochthonous material carried to the sea by streams and rivers, or detritus from the normal decay cycle of marsh grasses and other vegetation.

Occurrences of terrestrial animal remains in the sea are, however, generally serendipitous events. A person may fall overboard far out at sea or a pilot may crash. The amount of animal biomass and timing of entry into the sea are largely due to chance and local circumstances. The carcass of a deer caught in river ice during the winter may subsequently be carried to the sea relatively intact; if fed upon by a variety of avian and mammalian scavengers during seaward passage, it may be deposited into a marine bay or off the open coast in disarticulated, greatly modified form. Under certain circumstances, even human remains originating inland may eventually be carried to the sea by moving freshwater. Over time, all such material moves downward through the water column and comes to rest on the sea floor, providing marine organisms with a source of energy and shelter.

Human remains reaching the sea floor serve several ecological functions. Depending on the nature of the specific resting site (e.g., depth, bathymetry, bottom types), degree of decomposition, and the nature of the local fauna, they may (1) become immediate or eventual sources of energy for a wide variety of scavenging fishes and invertebrates, (2) provide micro-habitat shelter for small, nonscavenging species, (3) draw in a variety of secondary predaceous species attracted to the original scavengers, and (4) at advanced stages of decomposition, serve as substrate for invertebrate grazers attracted to bacterial films on bones, or to the bones themselves as a source of calcium and other minerals.

## Independent Variables Influencing Postmortem Condition

A human body in the sea is subject to a variety of physical and biological forces that control its destiny. The density of seawater is much greater than that of freshwater and affects the timing of an object drifting passively down through the water column. Decomposition in the sea (see Table 1) may be slow or rapid, depending upon temperature, salinity, depth, currents, nature of the substrate, interactions between physical and chemical processes, and the number and type of scavenging organisms present. In general, cold temperatures of polar seas retard the processes of decomposition, especially microbial, and warm temperatures of tropical seas accelerate them. As in lotic, freshwater environments, dispersal of human remains in the sea is much more likely than in lentic or terrestrial sites. Tides, currents, wave action, and motile scavengers are the principal agents of distribution.

The multiple factors which can affect postmortem condition do not function alone but can interact in both predictable and unpredictable ways. For example, a body might start out with heavy clothing, but with deposition in a very high energy setting, the force of tidal or wave action could remove the clothing in the immediate postmortem interval.

In forensic cases, the questions most frequently necessary to answer are the identity of the victim, the time since death, and difference between perimortem and postmortem modification of the remains. Unfortunately, due to the multiplicity and interaction of independent variables, as well as the inability to reconstruct or measure these variables in specific forensic cases, the postmortem condition is usually not a very discriminating indicator of time since death. Just as in terrestrial settings, the ability to reconstruct the context of death and the postmortem sequence depends on painstaking attention to the full range of taphonomic variables which may have an impact.

Certainly, the variables which most influence our ability to identify the victim are those which affect disarticulation and transport. Unlike terrestrial scenes, both the discovery and recovery of remains from the ocean are often accidental. Although in some cases it may be

**Table 1    Independent Variables Influencing Postmortem Condition in the Marine Context**

| Variable | Influence on Skeletonization, Decomposition, and Disarticulation |
|---|---|
| Access to the water surface | More access: accelerate |
| Access to higher temperatures | |
| Access to scavengers | |
| Water and air temperature | Colder: decelerate |
| Season of death | |
| Geographic location | |
| Hydrology | |
| Body covering | Thicker, tougher, non-organic: |
| Access to scavengers | decelerate |
| Access to forces of dispersal | |
| Energy of water movement | Greater: increase |
| Inshore vs. offshore storms | |
| Biodiversity | Greater: increase |
| Access to scavengers | |
| Sea floor substrate | Muddier, softer: decrease |
| Ease of burial | |
| Sea floor geology | |
| Access to fishing operations | More bottom trawling: increase |
| Access to recovery | More recovery access: decrease |
| Time of death | Specific to scavenger species |
| Diurnal and nocturnal scavengers | |
| Seasonal scavenger cycles | |
| Surface area characteristics | |
| Surface area exposed | More surface area: increase |
| Breaks in surface continuity | Surface area breaks: increase |
| Thickness of compact bone | Compact bone thicker: decrease |
| Water chemistry | |
| Mineral solubility and saturation | Less saturation: increase |
| Oxygen availability | Specific to scavenger species |
| Time since death | Greater: increase |
| Season of death | |
| Probability of recovery | |

possible to send down divers, or even to use dogs on the water surface to locate remains in more shallow settings, more frequently it is not possible to visit the scene, or even to pinpoint its location with certainty. Thus, the forensic marine taphonomist must often reconstruct the depositional context indirectly.

## Marine Scavengers

Many marine organisms are scavengers on carrion, usually the remains of fish or marine mammals. Most of these species would respond similarly to human remains. In the sea, generally these scavengers are fishes, gastropod mollusks, crustaceans, and echinoderms. The feeding activities of a few species in other taxa may also aid in forensic interpretation of scavenging. Regardless of the specific agent, scavengers may affect a corpse in many ways. Biting, tearing, and chewing can alter clothing covering the body, quicken the course of disarticulation and dissemination of body parts, increase tissue surface area, encouraging a more rapid bacterial and microscavenger activity, and decrease time to skeletonization. The preference of some scavengers for particular body parts (e.g., crabs attacking eyes, facial flesh, and soft internal organs) can sometimes provide data on the sequence of events following the settlement of a body on the sea floor and thus aid in estimation of time since death. Frequently, however, human remains are found long after the primary scavenging sequences have occurred and the participants departed. It is then left to the invertebrate grazers and sessile forms to provide clues to the period of time remains have rested on the sea floor. Ojeda and Dearborn (1990, 1991) discuss the abundance and feeding ecology of some mobile predators in the Gulf of Maine and provide useful references.

## *Fishes as Scavengers*

Many marine fishes are scavengers or combine predatory-scavenging habits, although probably none are as adapted to skin and flesh eating as are the freshwater piranhas and certain African cichlids (Gerking 1994). Fish may significantly alter human remains at sea, especially once a body reaches the bottom.

It is likely that a body floating offshore at the surface or drifting slowly down through the water column might be investigated by such active and voracious feeders as the white shark, *Carcharodon carcharias*, shortfin mako. *Isurus oxyrinchus*, longfin mako (*Isurus paucus*), and blue shark, *Prionace glauca*. The latter species is known to be dangerous when injured persons are in the water (Robins and Ray 1986). A number of other sharks and rays may be important as first-order scavengers in coastal and estuarine waters; see Rathbun and Rathbun, this volume, for a case involving the tiger shark, *Galeocerdo cuvieri*. Another example, the bull shark, *Carcharhinus leucas* occurs worldwide in tropical coastal waters and is known to attack humans (Robins and Ray 1986). It is likely that this animal would respond to a body, especially if bleeding occurred.

Several groups of fish would respond to a human body recently arrived on the bottom. Species of dogfish, *Squalus*, and American eels, *Anguilla rostrata* occur in coastal waters from S. Greenland to northern South America and are notorious for their catholic diet of living and dead food, readily scavenging organic remains of any sort. Spiny dogfish *Squalus acanthias* have the frustrating habits of attacking other fish already caught in gill nets or seines and biting groundfish already caught on the hooks of longlines (Bigelow and Schroeder 1953), often dreadfully tangling the gear in the process.

Along the coastal waters of the western Atlantic reside a number of species of sculpins (Family Cottidae), several of which are known to be scavengers on organic debris in addition to feeding on live prey, primarily polychaetes, mollusks, and small crustaceans. Examples of these include the sea raven, *Hemitripterus americanus*, grubby, *Myoxocephalus aeneus*, longhorn sculpin, *Myoxocephalus otodecimspinous*, and shorthorn sculpin *Myoxocephalus scorpius*. Adult grubby feed primarily on sand shrimp (Lazzari et al. 1989) but readily pick at carrion when available. Longhorn and shorthorn sculpins feed on other fish and crustaceans (Gill 1905) and are particularly well known for their habit of gathering on the bottom under wharves, sardine factories, and lobster cars to feast on the flow of debris (Bigelow and Schroeder 1953).

Once the integrity of the human body surface is lost, these sorts of piscine scavengers would respond and consume soft tissue. No data are available on any possible feeding preferences of these various species to particular body parts or regions, and it is difficult, without direct experimental evidence, to predict the extent and nature of such scavenging behavior.

The response time of fishes to new carrion can be remarkably rapid. One of us (JHD) has experimented with the placement of bait bags on various external portions of research submersibles such that the bait is within view of the observer and can be photographed over time. At several locations on soft mud bottoms in the Gulf of Maine in depths below 90 m, tests with bags containing previously-frozen whole mackerel bodies, mostly 25 to 35 cm in total length, showed that Atlantic hagfish *Myxine glutinosa* arrived at the bait within less than 5 minutes. At one site, within 8 to 10 minutes, up to 12 individuals had arrived and invaded the bait bag, writhing within it, rapidly consuming the greasy mackerel, and producing great quantities of slime so characteristic of this hagfish. Fishermen often refer to them as "slime-eels." Hagfish have only vestigial eyes and are functionally sightless. They locate their food of dead or dying fishes and other carrion by extraordinary olfactory senses. They are especially destructive to commercial fisheries because they prey frequently on fish caught in nets or on lines and thus incapable of escape. According to Bigelow and Schroeder (1953:11) they generally bore first into the body cavity, eat out the intestines, then the muscle masses, leaving at the end "nothing but a bag of skin and bones, inside of which the hag itself is often hauled aboard…" In the Western Atlantic, hagfish reach a size of about 70 cm and range from the Arctic to North Carolina in 30 to 950 m depths (Robins and Ray 1986).

Fish scavengers are likely to be first-level scavengers, that is, agents which tear open the skin and, depending on the degree of ferocity, expose inner tissues to smaller and more numerous invertebrates.

## *Arthropod Scavengers*

The Phylum Arthropoda includes a huge assemblage of terrestrial and aquatic organisms. Insects and their allies dominate on land and in freshwater, whereas crustaceans dominate in marine habitats. The importance of insects to forensic science is well established (Haskell et al., this volume; Smith 1986). For practical, forensic purposes, the marine crustacean scavengers can be divided into two large ecological groups: (1) the powerful macroscavengers such as large shrimps, lobsters, and crabs, and large species of peracarids, particularly amphipods and isopods, and (2) the relatively small microscavengers, here defined as generally less than 2 cm in length, such as small amphipods (beach fleas, scuds), small isopods (sea lice and gribble), and small shrimps, all of which tend to occur in large numbers when attracted to carrion.

Large shrimp, lobsters, and crabs are much more powerful as individual scavengers or predators than are the smaller amphipods or isopods but would not occur in as large numbers on a human body. These macroscavengers are important in the decomposition process because it is their actions that open up a body recently settled on the bottom. The large chelate claws of lobsters and crabs can quickly tear open the skin and underlying muscle layers and expose the viscera and other organs to further attack. Along the New England coast, green crabs, *Carcinus maenas* and several species of *Cancer* are known to scavenge human remains and also use clothing on the corpse as a refuge (JHD, unpublished). The crab fauna along the Atlantic coast is diverse (Berrick 1986; Williams 1974, 1984) and depending on the location of a corpse, a number of other crab species could be expected.

Large species of peracarid crustaceans, e.g., certain gammarid and lysianassid amphipods and idoteid and serolid isopods may also act as macroscavengers, especially in the deep sea. They can occur at a food source in large numbers, often many hundreds per square meter of surface.

Photographs of bait cans lowered to the floor of the deep sea have been published by several authors (e.g., Gage and Tyler 1991 and references therein) and most show fishes and crustaceans, generally amphipods and isopods, swimming or crawling near the bait, thus demonstrating the attraction that exogenous energy sources have for deep sea scavengers. We believe a human body would receive the same response. Large food-falls may be rare events in the deep sea (Rowe and Staresinic 1979; Stockton and DeLaca 1982) although more recent authors suggest otherwise (Smith 1985; Smith et al. 1989). It is clear that large food-falls are a concentrated source of energy and despite being unpredictable in occurrence (Tyler 1988), elicit a rapid feeding response from scavengers, especially fish (Gage and Tyler 1991), amphipods and ophiuroids. The giant lysianassid *Eurythenes gryllus* which grows to 140 mm, and *Alicella gigantea* which reaches 188 mm, are quickly attracted in large numbers to carcasses and can rapidly consume them (see Hargrave 1985 and references therein). Some large lysianassids can be aggressive and have been known to drive off fish from around a carrion source (L. Watling and S. Sampson, personal communication).

**Figure 1** The giant Antarctic isopod, *Glyptonotus antarcticus*, an opportunistic scavenger.

Large isopods such as *Bathynomus* species, which live in deep temperate-tropical seas and can reach a length of 40 cm, and *Glyptonotus antarcticus* (Figure 1), which can reach 12 cm in length and occurs on the Antarctic Shelf, are also opportunistic scavengers. Lobsters and crabs are absent from the high Antarctic Shelf and their ecological roles as large predators and scavengers are taken by amphipods and isopods of various sizes. The normal diet of *G. antarcticus* includes ophiuroids, gastropods, other isopods, and to a lesser degree several other groups of benthic invertebrates (Dearborn 1967b). It is also, however, an opportunistic scavenger and, based on responses to traps baited with seal meat (Dearborn 1967a, 1967b), *Glyptonotus* would respond to human remains.

Smaller species of gammarid amphipods are especially important microscavengers and are found throughout the world from the intertidal zone to the deep sea. They can occur at a food source in large numbers, often many thousands per square meter of surface. Bousfield (1973) provides a taxonomic review and an extensive list of references on the gammarid amphipods of New England, and Barnard et al. (1980) review the amphipod fauna of California.

During benthic sampling at McMurdo Sound in the Ross Sea, Antarctica, 1958–1961, one of us (JHD) used wire fish traps baited with frozen blocks of seal meat about 20 cm square (Dearborn 1967a). These relatively large pieces of bait generally were consumed completely by scavenging amphipods (*Orchomenella* and *Orchomene* species) within 24 hours. These amphipods were taken literally by the bucketful (Dearborn 1967a) (Figure 2), and often fish that were also captured in the traps were partially eaten alive by the amphipods by the time the traps were checked, generally within 18 to 24 hours. The water temperature in McMurdo Sound during this work averaged –1.8°C and varied less than 1°C throughout the water column. Clearly scavengers in polar seas remain active at such low temperatures.

Idoteid isopods are also good examples of omnivorous microscavengers (Naylor 1955; Newell 1979). Although various seaweeds account for much of their diet, most species will utilize animal remains when available. Their mouthparts are adapted for a combination of scraping and biting, a feeding method well suited to scavenging on a variety of materials. Idoteids are especially common in intertidal and coastal waters.

## Molluscan Scavengers

With the exception of the bivalves (clams, mussels, oysters, and their allies) which are suspension feeders on microphagous particles, all other groups of living mollusks (e.g., chitons, snails, scaphopods, cephalopods) possess a unique anatomical feature, the radula, used in microphagous feeding, including herbivory, predation on live animals, or scavenging on dead material (Figure 3). Depending on the particular taxon, the radula usually consists of a ribbon of chitinous teeth which rides over a supportive base termed the odontophore. The number of rows of teeth, the number of teeth per row, and the position of the teeth within the row

**Figure 2** At McMurdo Sound, Antarctica, wire traps baited with frozen seal meat and set on the bottom attract both fish, e.g., *Trematomus bernacchii* shown here, and thousands of scavenging amphipods, particularly species of *Orchomene* and *Orchomenella*. If left in a trap for more than about 12 to 15 hours, fish of this size, about 20 cm in length, may be eaten alive and skeletonized by the amphipods.

**Figure 3** Scanning electron micrograph of the radula of the common waved or dog whelk, *Buccinum undatum*. Width of the radula shown here is 0.8 mm.

vary greatly depending on the group. Radular patterns are important characteristics in molluscan taxonomy and in interpreting feeding behavior (e.g., see general summary in Brusca and Brusca 1990). In general, those forms such as abalones which scrape algae from hard surfaces tend to have numerous rows with many teeth, including marginals, in each row; but carnivorous and scavenging forms often have both fewer rows and fewer teeth per row, generally lacking marginals.

From a forensic viewpoint, the most important molluscan carnivores and scavengers are probably the taxonomically advanced prosobranch gastropods (Neogastropoda) of which the common families Muricidae and Naticidae are examples. Members of these families generally

**Figure 4**    Two species of common scavenging gastropods in the Gulf of Maine. (A) and (B) are two views of *Buccinum undatum* with attached barnacles, total shell length 75.6 mm. (C) and (D) are two views of *Neptunea lyrata decemcostata*, the New England neptune, total shell length 71.1 mm.

feed on other mollusks by boring through the shell of the prey by mechanical action of the radula, augmented in some species by the secretion of acidic chemicals which further weaken the shell of the prey (Carriker 1943, 1959, 1961, 1981; Carriker et al. 1963). Many species of neogastropods are carrion eaters, and some species could be expected to feed on decaying human flesh or adipocere or to scrape microalgae or microbes from surfaces of bones. Particular species may even leave distinctive radular signatures, although this potential aspect has not been studied in the forensic context.

In the Arctic and North Atlantic, the waved or common northern whelk, *Buccinum undatum* (Family Buccinidae), is a common scavenger on dead fish and other organic debris and is considered a bait stealer by lobster fishermen. This is the edible whelk of New England, eastern Canada, Britain, and Europe. In England it is called the common whelk or buckie. It is this species and others such as Stimpson's colus, *Colus stimpsoni*, and New England neptune *Neptunea lyrata decemcostata* with similar feeding habits which are examples of larger gastropods most likely to be attracted to human remains on the sea floor (Figure 4). Other still larger whelks, up to 19 to 20 cm in shell height, e.g., species of *Busycon* (Family Melongenidae), generally feed on bivalves but are also attracted to lobster bait and presumably would also scavenge human remains.

In the intertidal and shallow subtidal zones in the northwest Atlantic several species of periwinkles (*Littorina*, Family Littorinidae) occur. The common periwinkle, *Littorina littorea* (seen in Figure 5B) is the edible species of North America and Europe. The Atlantic slipper-snail, *Crepidula fornicata* (Figure 6 a, b) is an example of another grazer which has been found associated with human remains (JHD, unpublished). These gastropods are generally herbivores, grazing on algal films. They can also scavenge corpses of fish, marine mammals, and humans, although whether they respond to algal and bacterial films which develop on the body or clothing, or to the decaying tissue itself remains an open question.

## *Echinoderm Scavengers*

The Phylum Echinodermata includes ar leastfive extant groups, the Crinoidea (sea lilies and feather stars), Asteroidea (sea stars), Ophiuroidea (brittle stars or serpent stars), Echinoidea (sand dollars, sea urchins), and Holothuroidea (sea cucumbers). Crinoids are primarily suspension feeders and most holothurians are either suspension feeders or deposit feeders. Neither group is important for forensic interpretation of scavenging activity, but local species of crinoids might use remains of clothing or portions of skeletal remains as a substrate for attachment and some species of holothurians could occur on clothing or body parts or in sediment accumulated in clothing. The other three groups all contain some scavenging species which would respond to human remains as a serendipitous energy source.

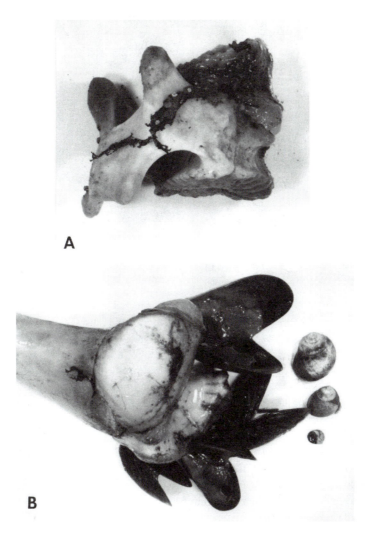

A

B

**Figure 5**    Remains of a whitetail deer, *Odocoileus virginianus*. (A) Vertebra with attached red algae with white tubes of the polychaete *Spirorbis* and encrusting bryozoan colonies. (B) Humerus with attached blue mussels, *Mytilus edulis*, and three specimens of the common periwinkle, *Littorina littorea*, which were originally grazing on the bone surface.

Many sea stars include carrion of various sorts in their diet (Jangoux 1982). Some of the common, larger species of New England sea stars in coastal waters, such as *Asterias rubens* (often referred to as *Asterias vulgaris*; see discussion in Clark and Downey 1992), *Asterias forbesi*, and two sunstars (*Solaster endeca* and *Crossaster papposus*) feed on a variety of living invertebrate prey but also are active scavengers, often found on and around the carcasses of fish or marine mammals. We expect they would also scavenge human remains, particularly after fishes and large crustaceans had begun the dismemberment process. Other nonscavenging species, especially smaller forms, might utilize for refuge clothing and skeletal remains after the disappearance of most soft tissue.

Much the same situation applies to brittle stars (Figure 7C). In his review of ophiuroid food and feeding mechanisms, Warner (1982) lists 6 out of 31 species (19%) worldwide which ingest carrion as a main food and 11 others (35%) for which carrion feeding has been recorded. Thus, for the 31 species listed, all of which had been studied in some detail, about 55% utilized carrion. Most of these are members of three families, the Ophiomyxidae, Ophiodermatidae, and Ophiolepidae. A variety of brittle stars thus is likely to be drawn to a human body on the sea floor.

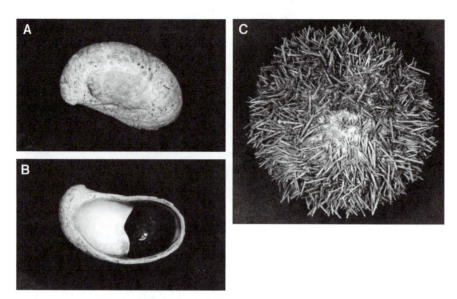

**Figure 6**    Two grazers. (A) The common Atlantic slippersnail, *Crepidula fornicata*, dorsal view, shell length 40.1 mm. (B) Same, ventral view of shell, soft tissue removed. (C) The common green sea urchin, *Strongylocentrotus droebachiensis*, aboral view, test diameter 72 mm.

Some larger species such as *Ophiura sarsi*, (Figure 7C) commonly found off the New England coast, normally feed on small organisms in the mud in which they live, but they also scavenge organic debris when the opportunity arises. Many species of ophiuroids would utilize for living space and shelter the clothing and microhabitat spaces formed by a decomposing corpse.

In their review of food and feeding mechanisms in Echinoidea, De Ridder and Lawrence (1982: 57) point out that "Of all echinoderm groups, regular echinoids seem to have the widest spectrum of food types…" and that "regular echinoids are opportunistic in their feeding." Thus herbivorous species may at times be carnivores or scavengers, and many species of echinoids might respond to a large food-fall such a human body, even though their normal behavioral food preference may be very different. De Ridder and Lawrence (1982) provide an extensive summary of foods of 205 species of regular echinoids from the world literature. Some of the most common species along the east and west coasts of the U.S. are those with especially catholic diets, including carrion at times, and they are thus of special interest in forensic investigations. Examples include the common green urchin, *Strongylocentrotus droebachiensis*, in the northwest Atlantic (Figure 6C), and *S. purpuratus* in the eastern Pacific.

Regular echinoids are equipped with a complex structure termed the Aristotle's lantern, which serves to grasp and chew food. It is made up of five teeth and 35 other calcareous pieces, together with muscles and connective tissue. There are four basic types of lanterns, with many variations, each associated with particular higher taxa. There are some modifications to particular foods and feeding behaviors but all lantern types are general enough in function to accommodate alternative foods when available. The scraping and biting of the tips of the teeth can leave distinctive marks on hard substrates, including human bones.

## Necrology in the Marine Context

### Decomposition of Submerged Remains

Although some research has been done on the process of decomposition of human remains which float in salt water (Boyle et al., this volume; Donoghue and Minnigerode 1977;

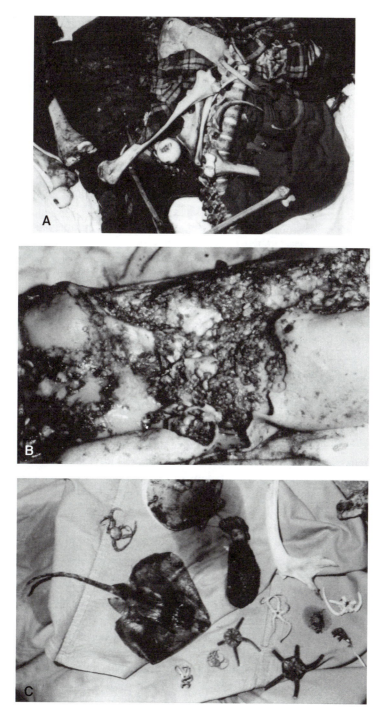

**Figure 7** Case #830040, postmortem interval 1 month. (A) Skeletonization of most soft tissue, preservation of cartilage, and partial articulation. (B) Skin of the foot and ankle. (C) Other associated marine organisms include: a sea scallop, *Placopecten magellanicus* (top center); sea cucumber, *Cucumaria frondosa* (right center); unidentified fish bone (upper right); a sea pen, *Pennatula aculeata* (lower right); a skate, probably the smooth skate, *Raja senta* (left center); and several species of brittle stars, *Ophiopholis aculeata* (upper left and center bottom) and *Ophiura sarsi* (two darker forms in lower center and right).

Ebbesmeyer and Haglund 1994; Giertsen and Morild 1989; Haglund 1993), we are aware of very few published studies which focus on submerged remains (Arnaud et al. 1978; Skinner et al. 1988; Sorg et al. 1995). As has been demonstrated in studies of water cases, many bodies will become submerged twice: once prior to bloating and once after the decomposition gases are released. Some bodies never float, and some may never sink prior to recovery.

Although it is possible to experiment with nonhuman remains (Payne and King 1972), taphonomic understanding of the processes of human decomposition in seawater can be greatly enhanced through careful documentation of human remains in forensic cases. Description of the condition of the remains should include data about the full range of taphonomic effects.

Table 2 presents a list of features important for taphonomic consideration, along with a proposed scoring system. Some of these variables were borrowed and adapted from research on taphonomic processes in modern marine environments, particularly other calcium-rich animal remains, such as bivalves (see Parsons and Brett 1991). The purpose of the scoring system is to promote comparison between cases, while keeping the framework simple enough to avoid inter-observer error, and descriptive rather than quantitative. The variables are not mutually exclusive. Their overlap is purposeful to accommodate a variety of possible observations. For example, both the presence of ligamentous tissue and joint articulation relate to the process of soft tissue loss; but since in some cases it may not be possible to evaluate the extent of articulation (perhaps only one bone has been found), observing the presence of ligamentous tissue affords an alternate access to that process.

## Biological Clocks and Postmortem Interval

Although there are no indicators of time since death comparable in precision to the use of insects in terrestrial cases, there are observations which can be useful in suggesting or ruling out an approximate postmortem interval. In particular, the time intervals needed for certain growth phases of marine plants or animals which attach themselves to the remains can be used to estimate a minimum time since death. The ecological context is, however, very important. Even within one species, variations in behavior may occur in slightly different habitats or different seasons. It is best to use research on populations and habitats similar to or the same as those within the taphonomic context.

We suggest that taphonomic research should focus on those sessile forms which literally attach themselves to the remains themselves or to body coverings. In these situations one can be sure that the organism was truly associated with the remains, despite sometimes haphazard recovery processes. Further, it is essential to work with local authorities to increase the care with which remains are received and transported. Attachments by some species may be lost by rough handling, or removed from the remains on purpose. The presence of a marine biologist is of critical importance for the initial examination. Not only should the location of the remains be identified, but each associated species should be identified; it will also be important to know where on the remains they were attached, how many of them were present (population size), their relative age(s), and their size(s).

## The Role of Sessile Invertebrates

After a human body has been in the sea for several months, the best exogenous biological indicators of time since death are sessile invertebrates which settle on bones or clothing or in some manner invade the remaining tissues. In some benthic communities, the amount of hard substrate available for larval settlement or growth of asexually reproducing forms is limited. Human bones cleansed by scavengers in the early stages of decomposition and dismemberment provide additional hard substrate and under appropriate conditions are readily

**Table 2  Taphonomic Variables Observable in Remains from Marine Settings**

| Feature | Comments | Variation |
|---|---|---|
| Location found | Location should include geographic as well as ecological factors | • Longitude/latitude<br>• Geophysical location<br>• Depth<br>• Access to scavengers |
| Season lost, if known | Seasonality should be based on known cycles of air and water temperature change for the location of recovery | |
| Remains recovered | The skull and distal extremities lose soft tissue and become disarticulated earlier than the bones of the torso and proximal extremities; the pelvis is the last area to become skeletonized | • Skull and/or distal extremities<br>• Torso and/or proximal extremities |
| Skin and muscle tissue | Since microenvironmental differences can apply within one set of remains, it is important to note the range of variation, including the maximum tissue loss | • No loss<br>• Loss with no bone exposure<br>• Some bone exposure<br>• Loss all elements |
| Articulation | This refers to joints which are held in anatomical position with soft tissue | • Present, all joints<br>• Present, some joints<br>• Absent |
| Ligamentous tissue | Ligamentous tissue may be present even though there is no longer articulation | • No loss<br>• Present, some articulation<br>• Present, no articulation<br>• Absent |
| Blood in marrow cavities | Can be found even when remains are skeletalized | • Present<br>• Absent |
| Cartilage | | • No loss<br>• Loss some elements<br>• Loss all elements |
| Decomposition odor | Often difficult to discriminate from odor of marine context | • Present<br>• Absent |
| Adipocere | The assumption is that the presence of saponification suggests the passage of some time beyond that usually necessary for soft tissue loss | • Present<br>• Absent |
| Abrasion | The wearing down of bone due to differential friction with sediments or body covering; found more often on remains collected from beaches or areas with strong currents or waves | • Absent<br>• Cortical thinning<br>• Cancellous bone exposure<br>• Marrow cavity exposure |
| Bioerosion (grazing, boring) | Grazing produces channels which resemble rodent gnawing or lytic lesions, usually concentrated at the metaphyses of major long bones; boring produces small perforations in the cortex — these frequently become enlarged by erosion or dissolution | • Absent<br>• Present |

**Table 2 (continued)   Taphonomic Variables Observable in Remains from Marine Settings**

| Feature | Comments | Variation |
|---|---|---|
| Dissolution | Changes in the chemical conditions (pH, pCO$_2$, temperature, saturation) can cause progressive dissolution of calcium carbonate; can be difficult to discriminate from abrasion, but tends to cause thinning of the cortex without marks of abrasion | • Absent<br>• Present, small amount<br>• Present, large amount |
| Encrustation | The growth on calcium substrates (bone) of certain sessile organisms such as barnacles; suggests the bone was not buried | • Absent<br>• Present, small amount<br>• Present, large amount |

colonized by sponges, hydroids, sea anemones, serpulid polychaetes, limpets and other gastropods (Figures 4 and 6), barnacles, encrusting bryozoans (Figure 5), ascidians, and other groups. Knowledge of the biology of these invertebrates whether solitary or colonial, can provide important insights into the length of time the body has been in the water, the degree to which it has been moved along the bottom by currents, and changes in the remains occurring during the recovery process. Specific knowledge of the reproductive cycles and rates of growth of sessile invertebrates will obviously provide the most useful evidence for a minimal estimate of time since death. Unfortunately, the timing and nature of the reproductive process and the specific rates of growth for the organisms involved may not be known or may be difficult to interpret because of the particular physical and biological conditions existing at the recovery site or problems related to the nature of the particular taxon.

Relating size of individuals to age is especially complicated for soft-bodied forms like sea anemones (Shick 1991). Within the same species there may be both isometric and allometric aspects of growth, further complicated by varying levels of growth efficiency and behavioral interactions in different habitats. Maximum body size of sea anemones of the same species can vary in high and low energy habitats and in fast current situations "may be constrained by mechanical limitations of the anemone's body plan" (Shick 1991: 217; Shick et al. 1979; Shick and Hoffmann 1980). The availability of food clearly affects the size of sea anemones (Lesser et al. 1994; Sebens 1981) and all other sessile groups, although the ecological literature on this and related topics varies greatly in detail and coverage for different taxa. Haderlie et al. (1980) review the sea anemones of California.

As with scavengers, the specific genera and species of sessile forms found associated with human remains will vary with geographic or bathymetric location. In some instances, these patterns of distribution may be of forensic importance. For example, members of the polychaete family Serpulidae are worms which produce calcium carbonate tubes which may be coiled or elongate. These are generally attached to algal fronds, shells, or other solid substrates, including human bones if available. Four species of *Spirorbis* occur along the East Coast, primarily from Long Island Sound to the Arctic (Gosner 1971, 1979). All produce small, limy tubes of rather tight coils. Two species are primarily intertidal and two are found only in deeper water. *Hydroides dianthus* occurs from the West Indies north to the Gulf of Maine but is more common south of Cape Cod. It produces elongate, snaky tubes. *Filograna implexa* is a common fouling species which occurs along the entire East Coast. It forms a colony of slightly curved, soda straw-like tubes. Each of these six species have more specific geographic and bathymetric ranges within which they are more likely to be found and substrate preferences which may also bear on the forensic problem.

The settlement of the larvae of sessile invertebrates on solid substrates, with subsequent metamorphosis to the adult form, followed by various patterns of growth have been studied in great detail for many taxa in many locations (e.g., see Giese et al. 1991; Newall 1979; Strathmann 1987; and Wilson et al. 1994 for extensive references). Marine scientists now know in detail the specifics of the life histories of many common and some not-so-common marine invertebrates, and certainly these data may be important to the forensic scientist as well. We emphasize, however, the interpretation of data from the marine literature on size–age relationships in particular species must be done with great care. Variations in the abundance and quality of food and in the temperature and level of energy in the specific habitat are just four parameters which affect rates of growth, yet can vary markedly between different sites even within a small geographic area. This does not negate these data as forensic clues. It does mean that a resulting estimate of immersion time must always be a minimal value often subject to large variance.

Two of the most important groups of sessile invertebrates from a forensic viewpoint are the barnacles (Arthropoda: Cirripedia) and bryozoans (Bryozoa, Ectoprocta, or Polyzoa).

## Barnacle Growth

In their development, barnacles go through a series of naupliar and cyprid stages before the cypris larva settles on a firm substrate and begins further transformation into an adult barnacle (Anderson 1994; Zullo 1979). The overall time for development to cyprid metamorphosis may be quite short, e.g., 7 to 13 days for *Balanus eburneus*, or much longer for other species (Costello et al. 1957). For forensic purposes the barnacles of most interest are members of the order Thoracia, which have external calcified plates as adults and generally remain attached to the same bit of substrate throughout their lifetime. In the intertidal zone barnacles usually live 3 to 5 years, depending on whether they are in the lower intertidal zone or higher on the shore (Zinn 1973). If the substrate to which a cypris larva attaches is a human bone, the size of the entire animal, e.g., the basal diameter of the barnacle, and the morphology of particular plates may provide evidence of the minimal time elapsed since soft tissue loss from the human remains. There is early precedent for using barnacles in this manner to aid in solving forensic cases, particularly the overall size of barnacles as an indication of the time of immersion of the corpse (Megnin 1894, cited in Smith 1986).

Anderson (1994) provides an extensive review of growth in barnacles. Many physical and biological factors influence the rates of growth in barnacles, and none of these factors is independent (Bertness et al. 1991). In general, within limits, growth rate increases with increased temperature, current flow, and, for intertidal species, daily immersion time. Growth rates can be lowered with increased population density, competition from other species, and during reproductive periods. A complicating factor for forensic interpretation of barnacle size as an indication of age is that considerable variation may exist within species depending on local conditions. Thus a barnacle with a basal diameter of 2 cm at one location may not be the same age as a 2 cm member of the same species at a different site.

Life spans of barnacles are equally variable. Species living high in the intertidal zone generally have long life spans (Foster 1987) while some species inhabiting the low intertidal may live only 2 years (Anderson 1994). In contrast *Calantica spinosa* (Order Pedunculata) may live up to 50 years.

Most of the common species of barnacles likely to be found on human bones are attached to the substrate by a broad section of their body, termed the basis. The basis is firmly cemented to the substrate and may be membranous as in most balanomorphs, or calcified into a flat, solid structure as in members of the common Family Balanidae. Even when the rest of the barnacle is missing, the diameter of the basis may still provide a useful forensic clue to the species involved and its minimum age.

A case from British Columbia provides a specific example of the potential use of sessile invertebrates in a forensic investigation. Mark Skinner (personal communication) brought these data to our attention and provided invertebrate specimens. The case involved a 26-year-old female who disappeared off a boat on November 8, 1980. The cranium and some long bones were found 5 miles away, in the intertidal zone, on July 28, 1982. The cranium was stained brown on the right side and exposure bleached elsewhere. Attached barnacles and

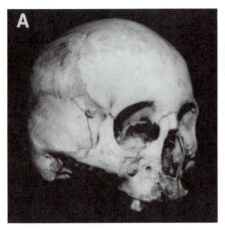
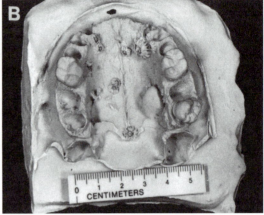

**Figure 8** Case from British Columbia. (A) Cranium with attached barnacles, probably *Balanum crenatus*. (B) Dental cast with barnacles. (Photograph courtesy of M. Skinner)

limpets were scattered around the cranium (Figure 8) and on the long bones, although several individuals became detached during photography.

All the barnacles were tentatively identified by one of us (JHD) as *Balanus crenatus*. The mean basal dimensions of six of these detached barnacles from the cranium were 9.1 × 7.7 mm, with a range of 10.8 × 9.6 to 6.4 × 5.1 mm. The dental cast (Figure 8B) included "fortuitously attached barnacles which stuck in the dental mould and transferred themselves to the cast" (Mark Skinner, personal communication). At least 13 individual specimens occurred on the dental cast, scattered over the palate, teeth and outer jaw. The largest of these was 10.2 × 9.4 mm in basal dimensions. *Balanus crenatus* is an abundant subtidal species in the northwest. Larvae may settle during most months of the year, and after settlement individuals can grow to a basal diameter of 20 mm in 1 year (Newman and Abbott 1980). Since the average size range of the sample was less than 20 mm, it is reasonable to assume that the time elapsed from exposure of the bone and discovery of the remains is under a year.

Two species of limpets were associated with the remains. They were tentatively identified by JHD as *Notoacmaea scutum*, the Pacific plate limpet, and *Collisella paradigitalis* ( = *C. strigatella*), sometimes termed the strigate limpet. Both species are relatively abundant in the intertidal zone of the Pacific Northwest. Shell lengths were 14.0 and 17.7 mm for two specimens of *N. scutum*, and 15.9 mm for an individual *C. paradigitalis* from the cranium. Shells of *N. scutum* can reach 63 mm in length (Abbott and Haderlie 1980), and so the specimens here may be considered juveniles or small adults. We could locate no specific data on growth rates of this species at this location; thus our interpretation must be based on limited data from *N. scutum* and other limpet species, suggesting only that the individuals found here appear to be small compared to maximum growth potential.

Based at least in part on the biology of these associated sessile invertebrates, the data in this case suggest that at some point in the intervening 20-month period the body apparently washed ashore and decomposed in the intertidal zone. Once the body was transported to shallow water and decomposition had reached an advanced state, the cleaned surfaces of the cranium and long bones became available as a substrate for settling barnacle and limpet larvae and perhaps juvenile limpets. We suggest that the sizes of both the basal diameters of the barnacles and the shells of the limpet are consistent with a postmortem period of 20 months, during the latter part of which the skeletonized remains were exposed in the intertidal zone.

In another case from British Columbia, barnacles were useful in establishing a minimum estimate of time since death. A lower jaw with attached barnacles was found about 2 years after recovery of the rest of the body (Skinner et al. 1988).

## Gastropod Growth Rates

Sutherland (1970) compared the dynamics of high and low intertidal populations of the limpet *Acmea scabra* on Bodega Head, CA. In the upper zone it took 11 years for individuals to reach the maximum observed size of 24 mm in shell length. Limpets in the lower zone reached 16 mm in shell length in 7 years, but did not grow as large as individuals in the higher intertidal. He suggested competition for food in the lower zone was a likely cause for the lower annual growth rate there (Sutherland 1970).

Abalones (*Haliotis* species) are important gastropod grazers along the west coast of the U.S. Young abalones average about 1 mm in size when they are 3 months old. Cox (1962: 148) noted that when "the first respiratory pore starts to form, their growth rate increases and by the time they are six months old they are approximately 6 mm long." *Haliotis discus* raised in the laboratory reached 18 mm in 1 year (Ino 1952). Earlier work on red abalone, *Haliotis rufescens*, by Curtner (1917) demonstrated that 1-year-olds were about 3 cm in diameter. He estimated growth at about 1.3 cm/year. Cox (1962) reviewed the growth data on California abalones and emphasized both the interspecific and intraspecific variations in patterns of growth in this group. Temperature and food availability were primary controlling factors.

Apparently the West Coast snails *Bursa* and *Kelletia* are about 7 to 8 years old when they reach 6.3 to 7.6 cm in length (MacGinitie and MacGinitie 1968).

In Britain, growth rates of the limpet *Patella vulgata* in different populations vary considerably (Lewis and Bowman 1975). Growth rates of *P. vulgata* are fastest during the first year, ranging from 5 to 15 mm/year (Bowman 1981), but decline to 3 to 10 mm/year by the 3rd year (Lewis and Bowman 1975). Growth rates remain relatively constant for several years until growth virtually ceases in oldest individuals.

## Bryozoans

Bryozoans or "moss animals" (Phylum Bryozoa, Ectoprocta, or Polyzoa, depending on the nomenclatorial system employed) are microscopic animals which form small to large, encrusting to foliaceous colonies generally on marine plant surfaces, rocks, or other firm substrates. As with barnacles and some other sessile groups, they are of forensic interest because the size of the colonies on human bones or clothing may provide supporting data on time since death. As with other examples cited however, rates of growth of the colonies of various species are not uniform and depend largely on local food supplies, quality of substrate, and physical microenvironmental parameters. Under favorable conditions colonies may cover several square centimeters or more. The microscopic individual animals are called zooids, generally about 0.5 mm in size. Each animal has an exoskeleton which may be calcified or not, and there may be a few thousands of individuals in a single colony. Some bryozoans produce rubbery or gelatinous colonies (e.g., *Alcyonidium* species), spongy, erect colonies (e.g., *Flustra* and *Flustrellidra* species), or low, encrusting colonies of tiny carbonate "houses" (e.g., *Membranipora* and *Electra* species), any of which may grow on human bones themselves or on algal fronds attached to the bones.

Bryozoans are a taxonomically difficult group (Gosner 1971, 1979; Soule et al. 1980), and a specialist may need to be consulted for specific, generic, or even familial determinations.

Especially useful references for two sessile groups of forensic interest not discussed here are Bakus and Abbott (1980) for sponges and Abbott and Newberry (1980) for urochordates.

We conclude that sessile invertebrates are potentially important forensic tools in estimating time since death. However, their biology is complex and high degrees of interspecific and intraspecific variation in the settling rates of larvae, rates of metamorphosis, and growth rates of juveniles and adults make forensic interpretation inexact. For many taxa, basic biological information is still not available. We hope this contribution will foster greater cooperation between the medical forensic community and marine biologists and that, over time, predictive databases will be established on rates of growth of sessile forms in various regions. More cooperative efforts and more careful recording of marine biological information in each case will aid that effort.

## Invertebrate Reproduction and Growth

There is a huge literature on the reproduction and growth of both pelagic and benthic marine invertebrates. Strathmann 1987, Giese et al. 1991, and Wilson et al., 1994 are just three of many examples of reviews that could be cited. Extensive references in these and other sources provide entry into the broad areas of marine invertebrate reproduction and growth. In an important contribution, Sebens (1986) reviews community ecology on rock surfaces in the Gulf of Maine and includes data on rates of colonization for a variety of encrusting inverte-brates, many of which might be useful forensic indicators. For any particular marine forensic case it is the close collaboration of a marine biologist or zoologist with the medical examiner, physical anthropologist, and other professionals who will determine what specific questions need to be addressed and what literature sources on invertebrates need to be researched.

# Forensic Taphonomy in the Gulf of Maine

## The Gulf of Maine

The range of marine environments within which a death assemblage may form are at least as varied as the range on land. Because observations and models developed for some marine settings may not be applicable to others, it is necessary to focus on particular locations and contexts in order to reap the most in terms of taphonomic potential (see, for example Ebbesmeyer and Haglund's 1994 research on the Puget Sound and Boyle et al.'s work on the Monterey Bay reported in this volume).

The Gulf of Maine, formed about 16,000 years ago, is a large (90,700 square kilometers) marine basin about 150 meters deep, with three-quarters of its perimeter created by the coastline from Cape Cod curving up along the coasts of Massachusetts, New Hampshire, and Maine, and around the Bay of Fundy along the coasts of New Brunswick and Nova Scotia (Apollonio 1979; Mountain and Jessen 1987). Beneath the water's surface, the eastern perim-eter of the basin is demarcated by the uplands of Georges Bank and Browns Bank, about 60 meters deep. Between them, the narrow Northeast Channel forms the only deep-water con-nection to the Atlantic Ocean, plunging down about 234 meters. The Gulf's main basin is itself composed of several smaller more smooth-bottomed basins separated by rougher, shal-lower areas. Thus, the topography generally restricts exchange with offshore waters and forms an ecologically distinct marine context. The bottom of the Gulf consists generally of bedrock overlain with glacial sediments, fine-grained mud, and sandy mud; the bottoms of the smaller basins tend to be sand covered and hard.

The Gulf of Maine receives fresh water from the drainage of rivers from the land which mixes with the salt water from the Atlantic. Its water column has three distinct layers: surface, intermediate, and deep. These exhibit different convection patterns which vary seasonally. The surface layer is replenished by cold, low salinity water which enters from the Scotian Shelf at the northeast edge of the Gulf, with maximum input during the winter. The salinity of the upper layer is greatest during late summer. The deep layer, approximately one third of the volume, receives warmer, high salinity slope water which enters via the Northeast Channel, with the maximum inflow during the summer. The intermediate layer is the remnant of winter-cooled surface waters which have sunk. During the winter the surface and intermediate layers merge into one homogeneous layer. The hydrography of the Gulf waters obviously influences water currents; it is also important ecologically. The slope water which forms the

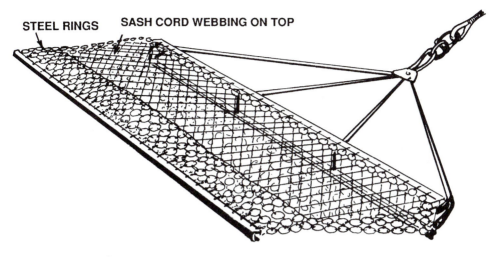

**STEEL RINGS**    **SASH CORD WEBBING ON TOP**

**Figure 9**  Typical scallop dredge used in the Gulf of Maine.

bottom layer brings with it a significant amount of the phytoplankton nutrients, perhaps as much as a third of all the nutrients needed for primary production in the Gulf. The water temperature of the Gulf of Maine is not homogeneous, and the annual mean has ranged from about 7 to 10°C during the last several decades.

The Gulf of Maine is fished by over 20,000 fishermen in the United States and Canada. However, a combination of increasing contamination and overfishing has tended to severely deplete the stocks of groundfish during the last decade. Campbell et al. (1991) report that the Gulf supports about 1600 commercial fishing vessels along with 4000 lobster boats. Of the nearly 1.2 billion pounds of fish taken in 1988, over 60% were fishes and invertebrates recovered from the sea floor, including the popular groundfish species of cod, haddock, and flounder, as well as scallops. Thus, the sea floor of the Gulf is heavily impacted by fishing activities.

## The Recovery of Human Remains from the Sea by Commercial Fishing Vessels

Human remains floating at sea may be sighted from aircraft or surface vessels or wash up on shore and subsequently be recovered, sometimes with minimal disturbance of the body. In contrast, remains which have become submerged and rest on the sea floor are generally recovered during commercial fishing activity. If trawls or dredges are involved, there is usually considerable dragging, tumbling, twisting, or other forms of severe disturbance to the remains before they reach the surface.

Figure 9 illustrates a chain-sweep dredge which is commonly used to harvest scallops from the ocean floor. The scallop draggers which operate these dredges are responsible for the accidental recovery of the majority of submerged human remains in the Gulf of Maine. Chain-sweep dredges vary in width from 0.6 to 4.5 m across; this chain-link bag is dragged along the ocean floor. Because the mouth of the dredge is only about 30 cm tall, it would be difficult for a whole body to be taken in; thus, scallop draggers are more apt to recover skeletalized remains. On the other hand, if defleshed remains are in the path of the dredge, the probability is high that some of the bones will be recovered. Because the rings of the dredge are about 8 cm in diameter, smaller bones will probably sift out.

The areas dragged by the larger gear tend to be hard and rather flat with sandy or muddy bottoms. Beam and otter trawls actually leave marks in the sediment, acting similar to a snow plow in reverse as they scoop up anything in their path. One pass might cover several miles, making it difficult to reconstruct exactly where remains were recovered along a narrow path.

This activity often results in the loss of body parts, the loss or shift in position of fish and invertebrates associated with the corpse, and sometimes the introduction of sediments into the clothing or body parts which does not represent the type of sediment where the original settlement of the body occurred. For these reasons, interpretations of the significance of associated fauna must be done with care and reasonable concern for alternative explanations.

## Gulf of Maine Skeletonized Forensic Case Series

The following discussion focuses on a series of 12 cases (Table 3) in which remains had been submerged and skeletonized, plus one which had been recovered in an intertidal area. Eight were recovered from within the 3 mile (4.8 km) limit, i.e., in-shore cases, and four from as far as 100 km from shore within the Gulf of Maine. Each of these cases was identified, and the time since death is known. Times since death range from 1 month to 32 years with most of the cases clustering between 8 and 18 months. Of the 12 found at sea, 11 were recovered by fishing trawl and one was recovered by divers.

Thirteen cases is not a sufficient number from which to make reliable generalizations, even about the Gulf of Maine. We present this series as a first step in establishing data ranges for a model of marine decomposition in this location. Just as in terrestrial cases, many variables can affect decomposition rates in the sea. In addition, just as on land, there are seasonal changes in the marine climate and idiosyncratic features of the geographic area or of the particular case — such as clothing worn and the presence of perimortem trauma — which can further complicate the decomposition process. For these reasons, we are presenting actual data on the condition of the remains. Because of the multitude of independent and interdependent variables which influence the process of decomposition, we believe it may be useful for other researchers to look at details from single cases as well as our summary of the range of variation across cases.

From a practical standpoint, few details about the taphonomic context could be reconstructed from our case files, emphasizing the need for more systematic data collection in the future. The Marine Patrol, usually involved in such cases, generally records only the type of vessel, the geographic location (e.g., near a certain island or the loran readings if available), and an approximate depth. As discussed earlier, some taphonomic information can be inferred from the fact that nearly all of the cases were recovered by bottom-trawling fishing vessels, most of them scallop draggers. This common factor is useful in interpreting the condition of the remains.

Fishing crews that discover human remains in their nets or dredging gear are obliged to report the discovery and bring the remains to shore immediately. There is a disincentive to report such discoveries, as it results in the loss of much valuable work time for the entire crew. Yet, compliance is the norm, probably because the individual whose remains are found may be known to the crew. Only occasionally do the discoveries turn out to be nonhuman. The Coast Guard is usually contacted first by the persons discovering the remains, but unless there are live people to be rescued, they turn the case over to the Marine Patrol — these State of Maine personnel are the marine equivalents of game wardens. The remains are then turned over to the Office of the Maine Chief Medical Examiner. Thus, the remains may be handled by several agents prior to our receiving them. Given the likely recovery by trawl and the usual chain of custody following discovery, the chance of disturbance of the remains is great.

## Place of Death and Taphonomic History

Examination of marine organisms can sometimes provide clues as to the place where death occurred, although bodies which float can confound such analyses. In one case (#880116, not included in Table 3 because it was not submerged or skeletonized), death had occurred 4 weeks previously. The body was recovered in the clam flats at the Damariscotta River's entrance into the Gulf of Maine. Bronchial washings were examined for evidence about whether death had occurred upriver or in the ocean. The presence of shell fragments and a spine from the common green sea urchin, *Strongylocentrotus droebachiensis*, strongly suggested that the death had occurred either in the estuary or in the ocean, but likely not upriver.

The circumstances of recovery, the condition of the remains, and the associated marine organisms may provide additional evidence about the taphonomic history. Bodies recovered by scallop draggers or groundfish nets are likely not to have become deeply buried, due to the nature of the bottom in areas where groundfishing is done. Water currents would be plentiful in such locations, and would probably have resulted in some movement of the body or parts from the place originally deposited. Scallop dragging is done in water from 30 to 200 m in depth, depending on the season. Estuarine or intertidal organisms associated with remains recovered by draggers would be inconsistent and suggest a more complex taphonomic history.

In some cases, however, complexity is introduced by variables unique to those remains and by an extended postmortem interval. Case #940421 was accidentally recovered by a goundfish trawler in off-shore waters. The death had occurred 32 years previously, but preservation of these skeletonized remains was enhanced by a Neoprene flight suit and antigravity apparel. Bones of the lower spine, pelvis, legs, and feet were present, although the bones of the upper body had been lost.

The condition of the remains, however, suggested that the upper body had experienced a different taphonomic history than the lower body. There was evidence of a dramatic gradient of erosion, with the lower body lacking erosional damage and the bones of the torso experiencing much erosion. Additionally, the presence of two sets of octopus eggs in the sleeves suggested a well-oxygenated environment with moving water, while the blackened condition of the legs and particularly the feet suggested an anoxic environment. The hypothetical picture which emerges is one in which only the lower body is buried while the upper body is subjected to moving water and sand. The organisms found were all consistent with the Gulf of Maine, a finding which was as confirmed when the details of the fatal accident were reconstructed, including its location off the coast of southern Maine. In fact, the body had not moved substantially from that location.

## Time Since Death

From a taphonomic perspective, keys to interpreting the length of the postmortem interval include the association of particular marine organisms with the remains and the condition of soft tissue and bone.

Table 4 summarizes hypothetical relationships between the process of decomposition and the association of organisms in marine settings generally. Birds are included in this table because of their likely involvement with floating bodies. There are two primary variables illustrated by this table. Exposure of the remains on the surface would increase the likelihood of soft tissue modification by birds, sharks, and certain microscavengers. Bone exposure, on the other hand, allows the association with motile grazers and sessile invertebrates.

Documentation of the association of marine organisms for Gulf of Maine cases has been difficult, due largely to their serendipitous recovery by nonprofessionals. Documentation of other variables related to the condition of the remains has been easier. Figure 10 illustrates the presence/absence of key variables according to time since death. Of particular interest are the facts that, in the Gulf of Maine context, (1) skeletonization can occur in under 3 weeks, even in deep offshore waters; (2) soft tissue and persistent articulation can be observed as long as 18 months after death, and decomposition odor as long as 3 years, at least in in-shore cases; and (3) soft tissue can remain intact within a heavy boot for nearly a year.

## *Phase 1: Loss of Soft Tissue*

Figure 5A and B shows a deer vertebra and humerus recovered in a tidal area. Although the time since death is not known, intervertebral disks are still present and there is an odor of

**Table 3 Taphonomic Variables Applied to Gulf of Maine Cases**

| Variable/Case# | 830040 | 840663 | 810312 | 910986 | 910990 | 911013 |
|---|---|---|---|---|---|---|
| Time since death (months) | 1.2 | 7.9 | 9.6 | 9.7 | 9.8 | 10.0 |
| Remains present | Most of skeleton | Cranium | Cranium Femur | Pelvis Sacrum L5 | Cranium | Femur |
| Econiche | Groundfish | Dragger (type ?) | Scallop | Scallop | Scallop | Scallop |
| In/offshore | Offshore | Offshore | Inshore | Inshore | Inshore | Inshore |
| Depth (m) | 137–182 | 137–182 | ? | ? | ? | ? |
| Season lost | Winter | Winter | Summer | Winter | Winter | Winter |
| Skin, muscle | Some bone exposure | Loss all elements (only cranium recovered) | Some bone exposure | Some bone exposure | Loss all elements (only cranium recovered) | Loss all elements |
| Articulation | Present, some joints | Absent (cranium) | Absent | Present, some joints | Absent | Absent |
| Ligaments | Present, some articulation | Absent (cranium) | Present, no articulation | Present, some articulation | Absent | Absent |
| Blood in marrow cavity | Present | ? | ? | ? | ? | ? |
| Cartilage | No loss | ? | Loss some elements | No loss | Loss all elements | No loss |
| Decomposition odor | Present | Present | Present | Present | Present | Present |
| Adipocere | Absent | Absent | Absent | Present | Absent | Absent |
| Abrasion of bone | Absent | Cancellous bone exposure | Cortical thinning | Absent | Cortical thinning | Cancellous bone exposure |
| Bioerosion | Absent | Present (probable) | Absent | Absent | Absent | Absent |
| Dissolution | Absent | Present (probable) | Absent | Absent | Absent | Absent |
| Encrustation | Absent | Absent | Absent | Absent | Absent | Absent |

| Variable/Case# | 840025 | 901043 | 840986 | 920974 | 850842 | 940421 |
|---|---|---|---|---|---|---|
| Time since death (months) | 11.3 | 16.8 | 18.0 | 36.6 | 140.0 | 384.0 |
| Remains present | Intact feet<br>Manubrium<br>Femur<br>Patellae<br>Tibiae<br>Fibuli<br>Few vertebrae<br>Few ribs | Mandible<br>Few vertebrae<br>Clavicle<br>Scapula<br>Innominates<br>Femora<br>Tibiae<br>Fibulae<br>Tali<br>Calcaneus<br>Few metatarsals | Innominate<br>Sacrum<br>L-5<br>Few ribs | Innominate<br>Femur<br>Tibia | Clavicle<br>Scapula<br>Vertebra<br>Few ribs<br>Innominate<br>Femora | Few vertebrae<br>Pelvis<br>Legs<br>Feet |
| Econiche | Scallop | Near-shore | Scallop | Scallop | Scallop | Scallop |
| In/offshore | Inshore | Inshore | Inshore | Inshore | Offshore | Offshore |
| Depth (m) | ? | 10 | 55–73 | 18–46 | 91–183 | 76–183 |
| Season lost | Winter | Summer | Summer | Fall | Winter | Summer |
| Skin, muscle | Some bone exposure | Loss, all elements | Some bone exposure | Loss, all elements | Loss, all elements | Loss, all elements |
| Articulation | Present, some joints | Absent | Present, some joints | Absent | Absent | Absent |
| Ligaments | Present, some articulation | Absent | Present, some articulation | Absent | Absent | Absent |
| Blood in marrow cavity | ? | Present (probable) | ? | ? | Absent | Absent |
| Cartilage | Loss, some elements | Loss, all elements | ? | Loss, some elements | Loss, all elements | Loss, all elements |
| Decomposition odor | Present | Present | Present | Present | Absent | Absent |
| Adipocere | ? | Present | Absent | Present | Absent | Absent |
| Abrasion of bone | ? | Absent | Cortical thinning | Cancellous bone exposure | Marrow cavity exposure | Cancellous bone exposure |
| Bioerosion | ? | Present | Absent | Present | Present | Present |
| Dissolution | Absent | Absent | Absent | Absent | Present, large amount | Present |
| Encrustation | Absent | Present | Absent | Absent | Absent | Absent |

**Table 4   Types of Organisms Which May Modify Human Remains in Marine Environments Under Different Conditions**

| Condition of Remains | Birds[a] | Macroscavengers (usually > 2 cm) | | Microscavengers (usually < 2 cm) Some gastropods, amphipods, isopods | Motile Grazers Some gastropods, sea urchins | Sessile Benthos Bacterial and fungal scums and mats, microalgae, some sponges, serpulid worms, barnacles, bryozoans, tunicates |
| --- | --- | --- | --- | --- | --- | --- |
| | | Fish at surface and in midwater | Benthic fish, lobsters, crabs, gastropods, amphipods, isopods, echinoderms | | | |
| **FOUND FLOATING** | | | | | | |
| *Never submerged* | | | | | | |
| Fresh | ++ | ++ | | + | | |
| Early decay | ++ | ++ | | ++ | | |
| Advanced decay with some bone exposure | + | + | | ++ | | ++ |
| *Previously submerged* | | | | | | |
| Early decay | + | ++ | ++ | ++ | + | |
| Advanced decay with some bone exposure | + | + | ++ | ++ | + | ++ |
| **FOUND SUBMERGED** | | | | | | |
| *Never floated* | | | | | | |
| Fresh | | | ++ | + | | |
| Early decay | | | ++ | ++ | + | |
| Advanced decay with some bone exposure | | | ++ | ++ | ++ | ++ |
| Skeleton disarticulated | | | ++ | ++ | ++ | ++ |
| *Previously floated* | | | | | | |
| Fresh | + | | ++ | + | | |
| Early decay | + | | ++ | ++ | ++ | |
| Advanced decay with some bone exposure | | | ++ | ++ | ++ | ++ |
| Skeleton disarticulated | | | + | + | + | ++ |

[a] Although birds are not discussed in this paper, they are an important modifier of floating human remains.

*Note:*   ++ modification likely; + modification possible.

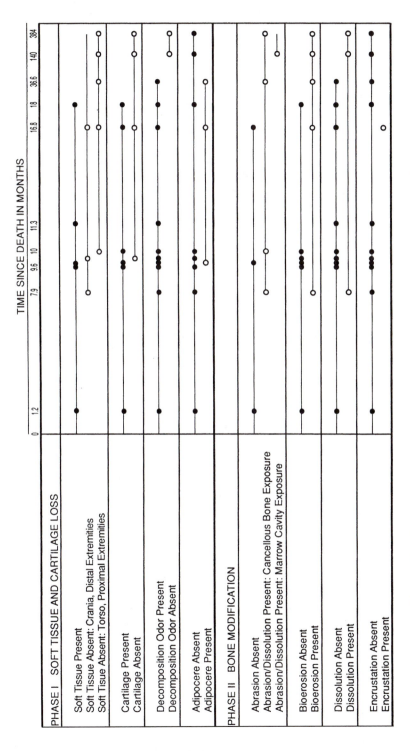

**Figure 10** Timing of marine decomposition variables among deaths in the Gulf of Maine.

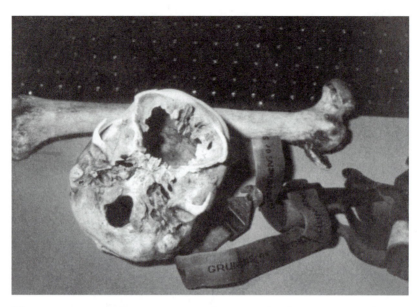

**Figure 11**   Case #810312, postmortem interval 9.6 months, has persistent soft tissue on the proximal femur.

decomposition. We show this case to illustrate that marine organisms are attracted to decomposing mammalian soft tissue. Due to careful recovery of these remains, we are able to demonstrate their association with attached and living scavengers and sessile forms. Three periwinkles (*Littorina littorea*), two adults and a juvenile, were attached to the humerus. Six blue mussels (*Mytilus edulis*) were also attached to the proximal end of the humerus by their byssal threads. Scars left by other byssal threads suggested that additional blue mussels had been on the bone at some time but had been lost. Most of the 12 vertebrae recovered had attached species of red algae, mostly *Chondrus crispus* and *Gigartina stellata*. Epifauna attached to several of the algal fronds included small bryozoan colonies and a few juvenile polychaete worms (*Spirorbis* sp.), which form coiled, carbonate tubes.

Although soft tissue can persist 11.3 months within a heavy boot, the bulk of the skeletonization can occur within the first month or less. Figure 7A to C illustrates an off-shore case (#830040) submerged 1 month. The clothing is intact and skeletonization is complete except for cartilage at the major joints (see Figure 7A) and skin on the foot and ankle (Figure 7B), which was encased in a heavy boot. The cartilage appears quite fresh, protected bones such as vertebrae remain articulated, and what appears to be fresh blood oozes from the long bone foramina. The cranium is multicolored with red, green, and blue hues. A number of teeth have been lost postmortem. The skin on the foot has a normal flesh color, but was covered by small gammarid amphipods which would have eventually consumed it. These remains were recovered by a net being used for ground fishing approximately 100 km offshore. Attached to the bones or within the clothing is a sample of the marine community associated with the bones (Figure 7C): a fish found in the underwear as well as crabs, brittle stars, and scallops.

Figure 11 shows all that was recovered of an individual who drowned 9.6 months previously (#810312). A scallop dragger in in-shore waters brought up the cranium, one femur, and a pair of foul weather gear suspenders. Although the postmortem interval for this individual is longer than that of the individual in Figure 13 (discussed below), there is no sign, at least in these bones, of similar cortical destruction, although the face is missing and there is damage to thin orbital areas. These remains exhibited a strong odor of decomposition as well as a small amount of persistent soft tissue on the proximal femur.

Four additional cases in this series had persistent, but minimal, soft tissue. Case #840025 had an 11.3-month postmortem interval and included a large number of bones from the torso and legs. Although the exposed bones were free of soft tissue, the feet were encased in heavy boots which kept the soft tissue intact. Case #840986, with a postmortem interval of 18 months, included bones of the pelvis, lower spine, and ribs. All of the bones had attached soft tissue, and the 5th lumbar vertebra was still articulated with the sacrum. These bones exhibited a blackish color, suggesting they may have been at least partially buried.

The difficulties in suggesting interpretive standards for partially skeletonized cases from marine environments are illustrated dramatically with a series of three cases recovered from in-shore waters by scallop draggers over a period of 1 week, and from the same general location. These three individuals were crew members of a single vessel. Their deaths occurred during a single event in the winter 10 months before recovery. Although deposition of all three bodies presumably occurred in the same place, and all three men were probably dressed in a similar fashion, the condition of the remains differed significantly. We suspect most variation is due to the fact that different body parts were recovered from each individual; thus, we cannot compare the condition of, e.g., three crania or three femora. The remains included no sessile organisms from which to derive additional information about time since death.

We were able to reliably discriminate each of the three individuals, despite the partial recovery. Case #910990 included just the cranium, characterized by a slight odor of decomposition, patches of greasy residue intermittent on the cranium, some nonmarginated abrasion to thin cortical areas and the occipital condyles, and postmortem loss of one molar. Case #910986 included the pelvis, sacrum, and the fifth lumbar vertebra. These remains had a small amount of soft tissue, cartilage on all joints, a small amount of adipocere, and body hair on the back, as well as being very odiferous, even after overnight soaking in a bleach solution. Case #911013 included only one femur which retained cartilage on the joint surfaces, but no soft tissue, and a very strong decomposition odor. Localized but nonmarginated abrasion, probably due to the dragger, was present.

Given the assumptions that time since death, season, location of death, and body covering were essentially identical, variation in the condition of the remains is more likely a function of the position of the bones within the body rather than idiosyncratic variation in the microenvironments. The cranium's relatively less soft tissue and clothing coverage probably contribute to its greater soft tissue loss and bone surface damage. Similarly, the greater soft tissue and clothing coverage for the pelvic area provided greater protection from maceration, disarticulation, and bone damage. The intermediate condition of the femur logically follows, due to its being part of an extremity, but more protected by soft tissue and harder-to-remove clothing than the cranium.

## Phase 2: Bone Modification

Loss of soft tissue exposes most bone surfaces to a variety of modification agents as early as 1 month after death. These may include: (1) gastropod rasping or boring (bioerosion); (2) encrustation by sessile invertebrates; (3) generalized abrasion and abrasion by moving water and sand; (4) localized abrasion due to friction with harder surfaces during the postmortem period or resulting from recovery by a dragger; and (5) eventual dissolution. Cortical destruction due to abrasion, particularly including damage to portions of thin, flat bones such as the maxilla and occiput, is observed in cases with an 8 month postmortem interval. It very likely may occur earlier, but this series has no cases between 1 and 8 months.

Figures 12A and B show off-shore case #840663 with the 7.9 month postmortem interval. Only this whitened cranium was recovered in a groundfishing net; a single tooth found in mud within the cranium enabled an identification. The maxilla, zygoma, and nasal areas are missing. The cranium is free of soft tissue, but retains some odor. Perforations of the orbits, occiput, and temporal can be seen in the basal view (Figure 12B), possibly due to tumbling

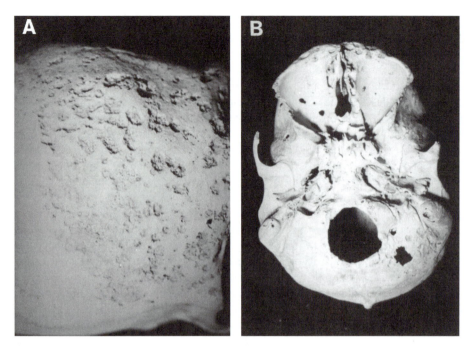

**Figure 12**    Case #830663, postmortem interval 7.9 months. (A) Superior view exhibits crater defects. (B) Basal view illustrates possible recovery damage.

and dragging within the net during recovery. Figure 12A, a close-up of the frontal bone, shows multiple, irregularly shaped craters, which have developed in the outer table exposing in diploe and occasionally penetrating the inner table. The cause of these defects is unknown, but they have been seen in numerous other cases and in long bone cortical surfaces as well as flat bones. Because of their irregular and sharp margins, the thinning of the cortical surface, as well as the occasional penetration through the bone itself, these defects are possibly due to abrasion and/or dissolution secondary to bioerosion by boring organisms. Figure 13A shows similar defects as in the proximal ulna of an unidentified case #910532; they are also seen in the proximal tibia and other bones of case #940421, after 32 years (see Figure 13B and discussion of this case below).

Figures 14A through D illustrate a case found by a diver in shallower in-shore waters, #901043. Because a diver can be more careful in recovery than a fishing trawler, much more of the skeleton was recovered. Although the postmortem interval was nearly 17 months, there is still an odor of decomposition, adipocere globules, and pinkish fluid in the marrow cavity. There is, however, no soft tissue present, although soft tissue was found in another in-shore case with an 18-month postmortem interval.

At first glance these remains appeared to have been modified by rodents. The distal tibia (Figure 14A) exhibits channels gouged from the metaphyseal area. The proximal femur (Figure 14B) and distal femur (Figure 14C) have a similar pattern. But these differ from rodent modifications in several ways. The damage is focused on the metaphysis or joint margin rather than the epiphyseal ends or bone ridges. It is roughly circumferential and has a channeled appearance. There are no identifiable tooth marks, nor are there scalloped cortical edges, and the flat bones do not exhibit any "window" formation. We believe these patterns may be due to bioerosion by sea snails, which rasp calcium substrates, as discussed earlier, in order to free up adherent organic material which they ingest. It appears that the rasping may have occurred while the bones were still articulated (perhaps by position only, rather than by soft tissue), thus limiting the snails' access to the epiphyseal surface.

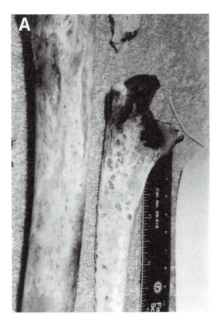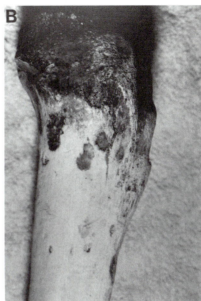

**Figure 13** Crater defects of cortical surface. (A) Proximal humerus shaft and proximal ulna of case #910532, unidentified. (B) Proximal tibia of case #940421, postmortem interval 32 years.

The time since death is consistent with observations of the sessile invertebrates which had settled on the bones. The barnacles (*Balanus crenatus*) (Figure 14D) ranged from 3.1 to 5.9 mm in diameter. The size suggests the bones were available for a seasonal release of barnacle larvae which settled on the bones and grew unimpeded for less than a year after that. The sizes of plant limpet *Notoacmea testudinalis*, 10.1 mm, and a juvenile common jingle (*Anomia simplex*), 6.3 mm, also found on these bones, suggested a similar time since death and availability of the skeletonized bone surface.

Generalized rounding of bones due to abrasion is not observed in one case at 36.6 months, or in cases with shorter postmortem intervals, although it is prominent at 144 and 384 months. Note, however, that this series from the Gulf of Maine is limited to only three cases with a time since death beyond 18 months. The presence of abrasion is related to both time since death and proximity to wave and current motion.

Dissolution of bone, characterized by changes in consistency, overall cortical thinning, and enhanced loss of bone in areas where there has been damage or exposure of spongy bone tissue, depends on local chemical environments, particularly the amount of saturation of calcium carbonate in the water. Abrasion and dissolution can occur simultaneously and are difficult to discriminate.

Figures 15A to C illustrate remains from case #840842, recovered by an off-shore scallop dragger. The bones were associated with an identifiable airplane seat from a P-3-Orion which crashed 12 years previously. The most salient feature of the bone, aside from the mottled dark brown and black coloration is the large amount of generalized, nonmarginated cortical destruction. The bone surface is soft and can be scraped with a fingernail, besides exhibiting a rather punky texture and irregular relief. The thin scapular body is nearly gone, the iliac blades are similarly eroded, the femora show remarkable destruction of the cortex which exposes the marrow cavity (Figure 15A), and the vertebrae have lost much of their morphological definition (Figure 15B). It is likely that this type of damage is produced by a variety of factors, including perimortem trauma, bioerosion, and subsequent abrasion and dissolution. The resulting erosional pattern is irregular and differs somewhat between the femora.

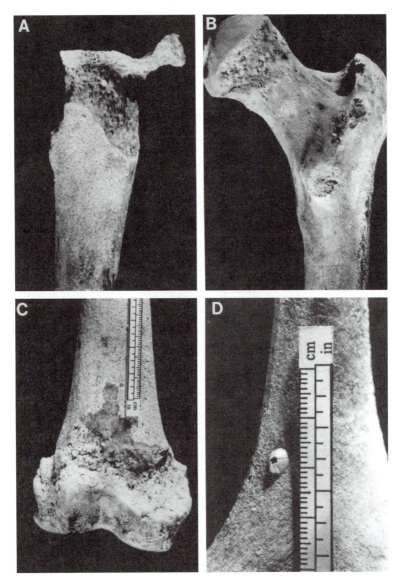

**Figure 14**   Possible damage due to snail rasping and barnacle encrustation in case #901043, postmortem interval 16.8 months. (A) Proximal tibia. (B) Proximal femur. (C) Distal femur, anterior aspect. (D) Distal femur, posterior aspect.

The end of the femoral fragments, possibly broken in the plane crash (see close-up in Figure 15C), are now heavily rounded, but cortical thinning is not uniform.

Figures 16A and B and Figure 13B illustrate case #940421, mentioned earlier, recovered 32 years after an aircraft carrier accident. Part of the lower spine and pelvis were present, as well as nearly all of the bones of both legs and feet; the patellae were missing. The only openings in the flight suit at the neck and wrists had apparently allowed the bones of the upper body to escape. Abrasion damage decreased from the lower spine (Figure 16A), and pelvis (Figure 16B) to the only lightly eroded leg bones (Figure 13B) and uneroded foot bones. Bones closer to suit openings had experienced greater abrasion and scattering agents such as moving water and sand, whereas the leg and foot bones were anchored and protected by the antigravity device and the intact suit itself.

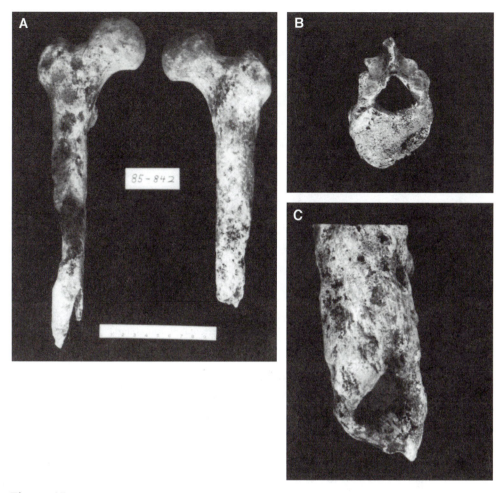

**Figure 15**   Case #850842, postmortem interval 12 years, showing cortical destruction. (A) Proximal femora. (B) Lumbar vertebra. (C) Close-up of midshaft femoral fragment.

No fish were found in or on the remains, nor were any species found which might have been responsible for saprophagous activity. Although we could find no diagnostic, macroscopic signatures of marine scavengers evident on the bone surface, the presence of irregular cortical destruction (Figure 13B) along with subsequent dissolution and abrasion suggest boring organisms had penetrated the cortex. This pattern is similar to that documented in bivalve shells by Parsons and Brett (1991). Although undiagnosed in their article, the same pattern of cortical destruction is illustrated by Arnaud et al. (1978) in bones submerged more than 1000 years.

The type and distribution of marine organisms recovered from inside the suit suggest it contained at least two microenvironments, as discussed earlier. The upper suit appears to have had more access to well-circulating and better oxygenated water than the lower part of the suit interior, which was probably nearly anoxic. The only motile invertebrates found were two specimens of the octopus *Octopus vulgaris*, one inside the waist area and one in the left sleeve. The octopods, which require well-oxygenated water, were using the inner suit as a stable habitat, as evidenced by the two egg masses found attached to the inner lining, one in each sleeve (Figure 17).

By contrast, no invertebrates were found below the pelvis attached to skeletal elements. A few bivalve shells (*Astarte* sp. and *Tridonta* sp.) were found in the gravel and mud within the external pockets. Numerous whole shells and fragments were found in the sediment within

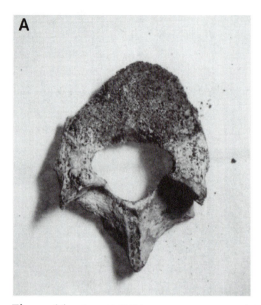
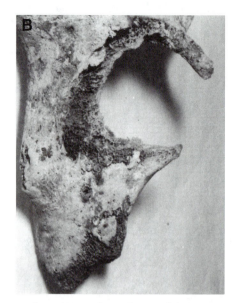

**Figure 16**   Case #940421, postmortem interval 32 years, showing a gradient of cortical destruction due to bioerosion, abrasion, and dissolution. (A) Lumbar vertebra. (B) Innominate.

**Figure 17**   Case #940421. Associated egg masses of *Octopus vulgaris*.

the suit legs and feet. Some of the bivalves may have been brought in by an octopus during feeding forays. Also found in the sediment were a number of ophiuroids, *Ophiura signata*. All species found are indigenous to the Gulf of Maine.

Analyses of other organisms found in this case suggest the remains had been on the sea floor for a minimum of 4 to 5 years in order to produce the colonies of the size found for several species of bryozoans and sponges. But, although this establishes a minimum postmortem interval, there is no evidence that would allow one to hypothesize several decades.

The condition of the remains, protected by the suit materials, is no worse than the condition found in the case submerged only 12 years, discussed above. The amount of corrosion on the metal valves also suggested a time since death of more than a few years. Thus, the condition of the remains may be more indicative of the type of body covering than the time since death.

As anticipated, based on this preliminary sample from the Gulf of Maine, the overall process of bone modification seems highly dependent on both micro- and macroenvironmental variables. Clothing and body covering, and probably burial, offer protection from both abrasion and animal modification. Small sample size and variation within the sample in terms of which elements were recovered place significant limits on comparability between cases.

## Conclusions

Forensic marine taphonomy is a newly developing field of inquiry, and as such is characterized by a number of significant research gaps. Although we have presented a general conceptual framework of interaction between marine environments and human remains, the details of these interactions need to be worked out for specific regions. Careful documentation of the condition of human remains as well as associated marine organisms is necessary in order to build sufficient case series from which models of postmortem change can be constructed. The use of sessile invertebrates to estimate postmortem intervals appears to be a promising new avenue of research, but one which will need considerable work. As in other areas of forensic research, interdisciplinary teamwork is an essential ingredient for adequate understanding of this complex topic.

## Acknowledgments

We would like to acknowledge with thanks the assistance of: Kelly Edwards, SEM Laboratory of the University of Maine, for SEM images and help in preparing the figures; Mark Skinner, Ph.D., Simon Fraser University, for contribution of information about two cases involving barnacles and gastropods; Judith Cooper, graphics artist, for illustrations; and Karen Turnmire and Marcella Joyce Sorg for technical assistance.

## References

Abbott, D.P., and E.C. Haderlie
   1980   Prosbranchia: marine snails. In *Intertidal Invertebrates of California*, edited by R.H. Morris, D.P. Abbott, and E.C. Haderlie, pp. 230–307. Stanford University Press, Stanford, CA.

Abbott, D.P., and A.T. Newberry
   1980   Urochordata: the tunicates. In *Intertidal Invertebrates of California*, edited by R.H. Morris, D.P. Abbott, and E.C. Haderlie, pp. 177–226. Stanford University Press, Stanford, CA.

Anderson, D.T.
   1994   *Barnacles. Structure, Function, Development and Evolution*. Chapman & Hall, London.

Apollonio, S.
   1979   *The Gulf of Maine*. Courier-Gazette, Inc., Rockland, ME.

Arnaud, G., S. Arnaud, A. Ascenzi, E. Bonucci, and G. Graziani
   1978   On the Problem of the Preservation of Human Bone in Sea-water. *Journal of Human Evolution* 7: 409–420.

Bakus, G.J., and D. P. Abbott

1980 Porifera: The Sponges. In *Intertidal Invertebrates of California*, edited by R.H. Morris, D.P. Abbott, and E.C. Haderlie, pp. 21–39. Stanford University Press, Stanford, CA.

Barnard, J. Laurens, D.E. Bowers, and E.C. Haderlie

1980 Amphipoda: The Amphipods and Allies. In *Intertidal Invertebrates of California*, edited by R.H. Morris, D.P. Abbott, and E.C. Haderlie, pp. 559–566. Stanford University Press, Stanford, CA.

Berrick, S.

1986 *Crabs of Cape Cod*. Massachusetts Natural History Series, Number 3. The Cape Cod Museum of Natural History, Brewster.

Bertness, M.D., S.D. Gaines, D. Bermudez, and E. Sanford

1991 Extreme Spatial Variation In The Growth and Reproductive Output of the Acorn Barnacle *Semibalanus balanoides*. *Marine Biology Progress Series* 75: 91–100.

Bigelow, H. B., and W.C. Schroeder

1953 Fishes of the Gulf of Maine, U.S. Fish and Wildlife Service. *Fishery Bulletin* 74: 577.

Bousfield, E.L.

1973 *Shallow-Water Gammaridean Amphipoda of New England*. Cornell University Press, Ithaca, NY.

Bowman, R.S.

1981 The Morphology of *Patella* spp. Juveniles in Britain, and Some Phylogenetic Inferences. *Journal of Marine Biological Association of the U.K.* 61: 647–666.

Brusca, R.C., and G.J. Brusca

1990 *Invertebrates*. Sinauer Associates, Sunderland, MA.

Campbell, L.A., K. Lignell, and M. Waterman

1991 Troubled Waters: Taking Stock of the Gulf of Maine. *Nor'easter* 3(2): 12–21.

Carriker, M.R.

1943 On the Structure and Function of the Proboscis in the Common Oyster Drill, *Urosalpinx cinerea*. *Journal of Morphology* 73: 441–498.

1959 Comparative Functional Morphology of the Drilling Mechanism in *Urosalpinx* and *Eupleura* (Muricid Gastropods). *Proceedings XVI International Congress of Zoology*, London, pp. 373–376.

1961 Comparative Functional Morphology of Boring Mechanisms in Gastropods. *American Zoologist* 1: 263–266.

1981 Shell Penetration and Feeding by Natacean and Muricancean Predatory Gastropods: A Synthesis. *Malacologia* 20(2): 403–422.

Carriker, M.R., D.B. Scott, and G.N. Martin

1963 Demineralization Mechanism of Boring Gastropods. *American Association for the Advancement of Science* 75: 55–89.

Clark, A.M., and M.E. Downey

1992 *Starfishes of the Atlantic*. Chapman & Hall, London.

Costello, D.P., M.E. Davidson, A. Eggers, M.H. Fox, and C. Henley

1957 *Methods for Obtaining and Handling Marine Eggs and Embryos*. Marine Biological Laboratory, Woods Hole, MA.

Cox, K.W.

1962 California Abalones, Family Haliotidae. California Department of Fish and Game, *Fish Bulletin* No. 118.

Curtner, W.W.
    1917   Observation of the Growth and Habits of the Red and Black Abalones. Stanford
    University, Masters thesis, Stanford, CA.

Davis, J.H.
    1992   Bodies in Water. Solving the Puzzle. *Journal of the Florida Medical Association* 79(9):
    630–632.

Dearborn, J.H.
    1967a Stanford University Invertebrate Studies in the Ross Sea 1958–1961: General Account
    and Station List. The Fauna of the Ross Sea, Part 5. *New Zealand Department of Science
    and Industry Research Bulletin* 176: 31–47.
    1967b Food and Reproduction of *Glyptonotus antarcticus* (Crustacea: Isopoda) at McMurdo
    Sound, Antarctica. *Transactions of the Royal Society of New Zealand* 15:163–168.

De Ridder, C., and J.M. Lawrence
    1982   Food and Feeding Mechanisms: Echinoidea. In *Echinoderm Nutrition*, edited by M.
    Jangoux and J.M. Lawrence, pp. 57–115. A.A. Balkema, Rotterdam.

Donoghue, E.R., and S.C. Minnigerode
    1977   Human Body Buoyancy: A Study of 98 Men. *Journal of Forensic Sciences*
    22(3):573–579.

Donovan, S.K. (ed.)
    1991   *The Processes of Fossilization*. Columbia University Press, New York.

Ebbesmeyer, C.C., and W.D. Haglund
    1994   Drift Trajectories of a Floating Human Body Simulated in a Hydraulic Model of
    Puget Sound. *Journal of Forensic Sciences* 39(1):231–240.

Foster, B.A.
    1987   Barnacle Ecology and Adaptation. In *Barnacle Biology*, edited by A.J. Southward, pp.
    113–133. A.A. Balkema, Rotterdam.

Gage, J.D., and P.A. Tyler
    1991   *Deep-Sea Biology: A Natural History of Organisms at the Deep-Sea Floor*. Cambridge
    University Press, New York.

Gerking, S.D.
    1994   *Feeding Ecology of Fish*. Academic Press, San Diego.

Giertsen, J.C., and I. Morild
    1989   Seafaring Bodies. *American Journal of Forensic Medicine and Pathology* 10(1):25–27.

Giese, A.C., J.S. Pearse, and V. B. Pearse (eds.)
    1991   *Reproduction of Marine Invertebrates*, Vol. 6, *Echinoderms and Lophophorates*. Box-
    wood Press, Pacific Grove, CA.

Gill, T.
    1905   The Sculpin and Its Habits. *Smithsonian Miscellaneous Collections* 47: 348–359.

Gosner K.L.
    1971   *Guide to Identification of Marine and Estuarine Invertebrates. Cape Hatteras to the
    Bay of Fundy*. Wiley-Interscience, New York.
    1979   *A Field Guide to the Atlantic Seashore. Invertebrates and Seaweeds of the Atlantic Coast
    From The Bay of Fundy to Cape Hatteras*. Houghton Mifflin, Boston.

Haderlie, E.C., C. Hand, and W.B. Gladfelter
    1980   Cnidaria (Coelenterata): The Sea Anemones and Allies. In *Intertidal Invertebrates of
    California*, edited by R.H. Morris, D.P. Abbott, and E.C. Haderlie, pp. 40–75. Stanford
    University Press, Stanford, CA.

Haglund, W.E.
  1993  Disappearance of Soft Tissue and the Disarticulation of Human Remains from Aqueous Environments. *Journal of Forensic Sciences* 38(4):806–815.

Hargrave, B.T.
  1985  Feeding Rates of Abyssal Scavenging Amphipods (*Eurythenes gryllus*) Determined *in Situ* by Time-Lapse Photography. *Deep-Sea Research* 32A: 443–450.

Ino, T.
  1952  Biological Studies on the Propagation of the Japanese Abalone (genus *Haliotis*). *Tokai Reg. Fish. Res. Lab.*, No. 5 (also Contrib. A, No. 3) pp. 102 [Japanese text, English summary].

Jangoux, M.
  1982  Food and Feeding Mechanisms: Asteroidea. In *Echinoderm Nutrition*, edited by M. Jangoux and J.M. Lawrence, pp. 117–159. A.A. Balkema, Rotterdam.

Lazzari, M.A., K.W. Able, and M.P. Fahay
  1989  Life History and Food Habits of the Grubby, *Myoxocephalus aeneus* (Cottidea), in a Cape Cod Estuary. *Copeia* 1989(1):7–12.

Lesser, M.P., J.D. Witman, and K.P. Sebens
  1994  Effects of Flow and Seston Availability on Scope for Growth of Benthic Suspension-Feeding Invertebrates from the Gulf of Maine. *Biological Bulletin* 187:319–335.

Lewis, J.R., and R.S. Bowman
  1975  Local Habitat-induced Variations in the Population Dynamics of *Patella vulgata*. *Journal of Experimental Marine Biology and Ecology* 17: 165–203.

MacGintie, G.E., and N. MacGintie
  1968  *Natural History of Marine Animals*. McGraw-Hill, New York.

Mountain, D.G., and P.F. Jessen
  1987  Bottom Waters of the Gulf of Maine, 1978–1983. *Journal of Marine Research* 45:319–345.

Naylor, E.
  1955  The Diet and Feeding-mechanism of *Idotea*. *Journal of Marine Biology Association, U.K.* 34: 347–355.

Newell, R.C.
  1979  *Biology of Intertidal Animals*. Marine Ecological Surveys Ltd, Kent.

Newman, W.A., and D. P. Abbott
  1980  Cirripedia: The Barnacles. In *Intertidal Invertebrates of California*, edited by R.H. Morris, D.P. Abbott, and E.C. Haderlie, pp. 504–535. Stanford University Press, Stanford, CA.

Ojeda, F.P., and J.H. Dearborn
  1990  Diversity, Abundance and Spatial Distribution of Fishes and Crustaceans in the Rocky Subtidal Zone of the Gulf of Maine. *Fishery Bulletin U.S.* 88(2): 403–410.
  1991  Feeding Ecology of Benthic Mobile Predators: Experimental Analyses of Their Influence in Rocky Subtidal Communities of the Gulf of Maine. *Journal of Experimental Marine Biology and Ecology* 149: 13–44.

Parsons, K.M., and C.E. Brett
  1991  Taphonomic Processes and Biases in Modern Marine Environments: An Actualistic Perspective on Fossil Assemblage Preservation. In *The Processes of Fossilization*, edited by S.K. Donovan, pp. 22–65. Columbia University Press, NY.

Payne, J.A., and E.W. King
1972 Insect Succession and Decomposition of Pig Carcasses in Water. *Journal of The Georgia Entomological Society* 7(3): 153–162.

Robins, C.R. and G.C. Ray
1986 *A Field Guide to Atlantic Coast Fishes of North America.* Houghton Mifflin, Boston, MA.

Rowe, G.T., and N. Staresinic
1979 Sources of Organic Matter to the Deep-Sea Benthos. *Ambio Special Report* 6: 19–24.

Schafer, W.
1972 *Ecology and Paleoecology of Marine Environments.* University of Chicago Press, Chicago.

Sebens, K.P.
1981 The Allometry of Feeding, Energetics, and Body Size in Three Sea Anemone Species. *Biological Bulletin* 161: 152–171.
1986 Community Ecology of Vertical Rock Walls in the Gulf of Maine, U.S.A.: Small-Scale Processes and Alternative Community States. In *The Ecology of Rocky Coasts,* edited by P.G. Moore and R. Seed, pp. 346–371. Columbia University Press, New York.

Shick, J.M.
1991 *A Functional Biology of Sea Anemones.* Chapman & Hall, New York.

Shick, J.M., W.I. Brown, E.G. Dolliver, and S.R. Kayar
1979 Oxygen Uptake In Sea Anemones: Effects of Expansion, Contraction, and Exposure to Air, and the Limitations of Diffusion. *Physiological Zoology* 52: 50–62.

Shick, J.M., and R.J. Hoffman
1980 Effects of The Trophic and Physical Environments on Asexual Reproduction and Body Size in the Sea Anemone *Metridium senile.* In *Development and Cellular Biology of Ceolenterates,* edited by P. Tardent and R. Tardent, pp. 211–216. Elsevier/North Holland Biomedical Press Amsterdam, Holland.

Skinner, M.F., J. Duffy, and D.B. Symes
1988 Repeat Identification of Skeletonized Human Remains: A Case Study. *Journal of the Canadian Society of Forensic Science* 21(3): 138–141.

Smith, C.R.
1985 Food for the Deep-Sea: Utilization, Dispersal and Flux of Nekton Falls at the Santa Catalina Basin Floor. *Deep-Sea Research* 32A: 417–442.

Smith, C.R., H. Kukert, R.A. Wheatcroft, P.A. Jumars, and J.W. Deming
1989 Vent Fauna on Whale Remains. *Nature* 341: 27–28.

Smith, K.G.V.
1986 *A Manual of Forensic Entomology.* British Museum (Natural History) and Cornell University Press, Ithaca, NY.

Sorg, M.H., J.H. Dearborn, K.G. Sweeney, H.F. Ryan, and W.C. Rodriguez
1995 Marine Taphonomy of a Case Submerged for 32 Years. *Proceedings of the American Academy of Forensic Sciences* 1:156–157.

Soule, J.D., D.F. Soule, and D.P. Abbott
1980 Bryozoa and Entoprocta: The Moss Animals. In *Intertidal Invertebrates of California,* edited by R.H. Morris, D.P. Abbott, and E.C. Haderlie, pp. 91–107. Stanford University Press, Stanford, CA.

Stockton, W.L., and T.E. DeLaca
1982 Food Falls In the Deep-Sea: Occurrence, Quality, and Significance. *Deep-Sea Research* 29A: 157–169.

Strathmann, M.F.
   1987 *Reproduction and Development of Marine Invertebrates of the Northern Pacific Coast.* University of Washington Press, Seattle, WA.

Sutherland, J.P.
   1970 Dynamics of High and Low Populations of the Limpet, *Acmaea scabra* (Gould). *Ecological Monographs* 40(2): 169–188.

Tyler, P.A.
   1988 Seasonality in the Deep-Sea. *Oceanography and Marine Biology, An Annual Review.* 26:227–258.

Warner, G.
   1982 Food Feeding Mechanisms: Ophiuroidea. In *Echinoderm Nutrition*, edited by M. Jangoux and J.M. Lawrence, pp. 161–181. A.A. Balkema, Rotterdam.

Williams, A.B.
   1974 *Marine Flora and Fauna of the Northeastern United States. Crustacea: Decapoda.* NOAA Technical Report NMFS CIRC-389.
   1984 *Shrimps, Lobsters, and Crabs of the Atlantic Coast of the Eastern United States, Maine to Florida.* Smithsonian Institution Press, Washington, D.C.

Wilson, W.H. Jr., S. A. Stricker, and G.L. Shinn (eds.)
   1994 *Reproduction and Development of Marine Invertebrates.* Johns Hopkins University Press, Baltimore.

Zinn, D.J.
   1973 *A Handbook For Beach Strollers.* University of Rhode Island, Marine Bulletin No. 12, Kingston, RI.

Zullo, V.A.
   1979 *Marine Flora and Fauna of the Northeastern United States. Arthropoda: Cirripedia.* NOAA Technical Report NMFS Circular 425.

# Human Aquatic Taphonomy in the Monterey Bay Area

# 38

SHELLEY BOYLE
ALISON GALLOWAY
RICHARD T. MASON

## Introduction

Taphonomy is defined as the transition of a body from the time of death through decomposition, destruction, transport or burial, to fossilization (Haglund 1991). The process by which bodily remains change depends on the region, local environment, and the circumstances in which they are deposited. The taphonomy of drowning victims, or victims whose death led to their deposition in water, differs from that of victims found on land, due to the radical differences in the environment.

The present study investigates the taphonomic processes undergone by victims of water-related deaths in the Monterey Bay area of the temperate central coast of California (36°59′N, 122°02′W). The northern portion of this bay is formed by the redwood-covered hills of Santa Cruz county. This area is renowned for its many water activities, including surfing, scuba diving, fishing, boating, and just "hanging out" at the beach. With unpredictable surf conditions, many people meet their deaths along the coastline when they are swept out by large waves. Rocky shores make getting back on land safely a difficult proposition. The waters are extremely cold, rapidly inducing hypothermia. In addition, strong rip tides can trap swimmers until they tire. Steep cliffs along the coast line invite sight-seers, but the soft, friable nature of the stone and strong erosion patterns cause frequent failures at the cliff's edge. As elsewhere, lakes, rivers, creeks, pools, bathtubs, and hot tubs also are involved in deaths from drownings and other causes.

This combination of features makes this region appropriate for evaluation of patterns of fatalities, transport, and change in human remains. Using coroner reports for the past 12 years, we review the causes and circumstances of death for all victims found in water, document a pattern of change, compare it to the "typical" sequence, and assess the environmental factors involved.

## Stages of Decomposition in Water

Bodies enter the water in many ways. Many people die as the result of accidental or suicidal drowning. Some die from natural causes or accidents while in or on the water, and their bodies are deposited and decompose there. Others may be deposited in water a long time after death. The cause and circumstances of the death and mode of entry play a role in the rate of decomposition. For example, perimortem damage to soft tissue provides a point of entry for scavengers, accelerating the decay process.

Since drowning is a common cause of death in water-related body recoveries, the likelihood of major perimortem injury is somewhat less than may occur with deaths on land.

Drowning is defined as "death due to submersion resulting in irreversible hypoxia of the brain" (Davis 1986). This causes damage to alveolar capillary endothelium, making it incapable of maintaining separation of water and protein from alveolar air spaces. Water may be present in the lungs and stomach, but this commonly occurs with submersion in water without drowning. There is a tendency for hemorrhages in the lungs, middle ears, and mastoid air cells due to the change in blood pressure, but, again, this is not specific to drowning. Water introduces microorganisms into the body, while hemorrhaging accelerates the process of autolysis within the tissues.

There are differences in the body due to immersion in ocean water or freshwater (Davis 1986). In the freshwater, water is absorbed into the circulation, resulting in an abrupt increase in blood volume. The body may take in up to 6 pints of water. Such massive intake causes tearing in the lungs and other tissues. In contrast, the high salinity of seawater causes fluids to be drawn from the blood into the lungs. This difference induces variation in the rates of autolysis and the spread of exogenous bacteria. Water temperature and other factors frequently alter these profiles.

Decomposition begins almost immediately (Haglund 1991, 1993; Payne and King 1972). The remains generally will sink, although clothing may trap air causing the body to remain afloat. Under submersion, the normal processes of decomposition (autolysis and bacterial breakdown) continue. One of the first changes is the appearance of "washerwoman's skin," seen as deep longitudinal grooves in the skin, which can be seen in as little as a half an hour in water 50 to 60°F.

The body will reappear when putrefaction has increased the buoyancy of the remains. Reappearance of the body is dependent on the temperature of the water. Putrefaction will occur slowly in salt water, because salinity retards bacterial growth. Once resurfaced, insect activity can begin, with eggs being laid in suitable exposed areas. Birds may also feed on the exposed body. As the decay progresses, most of the exposed flesh is lost and gone, while the submerged flesh remains intact, with the exception of skin slippage. Insects and other organisms can continue to feed on the remains below the water line. During this stage, the head, shoulders, abdomen, and legs frequently become separated. The remains continue to float until they lose their putrefaction-produced buoyancy through release of gas. Then, the body or segments will again sink.

The initial disappearance of the soft tissue usually occurs with the head, the hands, and the anterior lower legs (including the feet) (Haglund 1991, 1993). The appendages can be in contact with the sand, rocks, and other obstacles under water. Scraping occurs as the movement of the water pushes the remains back and forth over these surfaces. Other postmortem injuries can be caused by wildlife, propeller blades, fishing equipment, or other similar hazards.

The disarticulation of body segments, once the soft tissue has decayed, usually follows a sequence beginning with the hands and wrists followed by the feet, ankles, cranium, and mandible. The lower legs usually separate next, with the forearms following. The final separation is that of the upper arms and pectoral girdle, leaving the torso and pelvic girdle (Haglund 1991, 1993).

Once resubmerged, the process of decomposition may be hindered by the production of adipocere. This substance "consists of a mixture of fatty acids formed by the postmortem hydrolysis of body fats together with the mummified remains of muscles, fibrous and nervous tissues, and a little soap." (Mant 1957:18) It may take weeks, months, or years to materialize, but adipocere is typically a product of late decomposition. Its consistency is that of a gray-white, friable substance that does not have an offensive odor. The factors for adipocere formation consist of an excess of moisture, warmth, and the presence of skin and subcutaneous tissue. The process is absolutely dependent upon the presence of fat. Adipocere forms primarily in aqueous solutions, but may occur in terrestrially deposited remains if water obtained from the body is retained as humidity in the immediate environment of the remains.

Marine animal activity is difficult to distinguish (Mottonen and Nuutila 1970). In general, crustaceans cause the most commonly seen damage. These animals leave crater-like pits of varying size in the soft parts of the face, especially the area of the eye, nose, and cheek. Some smaller organisms enter the mouth and may pass into the lungs and stomach. Fish activity, when it occurs, may be more extensive, due to gnawing at the ears, lips, and soft areas of the face so that facial characteristics may be completely obliterated. Fish can reduce a body to a skeleton in a fortnight. Sharks are not known to typically "eat" a drowned victim. There have, however, been a few cases with tiger sharks, also known as "scavenger sharks," in which human remains were found in the shark digestive tracts (Rathbun and Rathbun 1984 and this volume).

## Materials and Methods

The Monterey Bay is a large semilunar bay approximately 20 miles across the mouth. Santa Cruz County forms the northern half of the bay and part of the coastline of the southern San Francisco peninsula. This coast is varied with wide beaches within the bay, rocky shores with sandy coves along much of the mouth of the bay, and steep cliffs interspersed by beaches along the ocean in the northern county.

The currents along this portion of the coast are generally in the southerly direction. This is in keeping with the flow of the California current which brings cold water from the Alaskan coast. This is particularly strong throughout the autumn but tends to move offshore in the other months. From late fall through midspring, there are occasional reversals of the nearshore currents. Wind direction is commonly toward the east, but seasonal changes are common, resulting in surface water being blown back out to sea. In such cases, colder waters well up from the deeper ocean to replace those at the shoreline.

The combination of coastal currents and the upwelling of deeper waters produces inhospitable water temperatures for the unprepared. These Pacific waters average 45 to 55°F year-round. The waters do warm seasonally, and there are also overlying cyclical changes. During the "El Nino" years the water temperatures will increase to about 60°F.

The coastline attracts a large amount of marine life. Sea lions and elephant seals maintain large rookeries at Año Nuevo State Park at the northern border of the county. These, along with seals, dolphins, and sea otters, feed on the rich marine life in the area, where the cold currents from underwater canyons produce upwellings of nutrient-rich waters. As the number of marine mammals has increased, so too has the number of predators. Great white sharks are a common predator off the rookeries and killer whales (orcas) have also been sighted in the bay. This coastline is also one of the best areas for sighting gray whale migrations.

Immediately offshore, along most of the coast, are dense kelp forests. These groves of vegetation are over 100 feet tall and serve as home for a host of small marine animals. They also play a crucial role in the wave and water movement patterns along the shore. Along the Santa Cruz County coastline there is a gently sloping plateau reaching depths of about 100 meters. In the southern portion of the bay, the offshore areas are characterized by deep channels and canyons which extend close to the shore. The Monterey and Carmel canyons are among the deepest accessible topographic features anywhere along the coast, reaching depths of 3.5 kilometers, and have a major impact on the types of marine life.

The combination of scenic attractions, wildlife, sporting opportunities, and proximity to major centers of residence has resulted in a relatively high frequency of water-related deaths. These fall under the jurisdiction of the local authorities at the place of discovery or recovery of the remains, but all such deaths in the county are referred to the Santa Cruz County Sheriff-Coroner's Office for investigation and autopsy. Officials from this office, in conjunction with the local representatives, work to establish the identification of the decedent as well as the cause and the manner of death. The movement of bodies in the coastal waters and decomposition sequences are, therefore, of interest for the estimation of the place and time of entry and exit.

**Table 1   Stages of Decay, Criteria for Classification, Duration of Time in the Water and Sample Size for Seawater and Freshwater Cases**

| Stage | Description | Freshwater | | Seawater | |
|---|---|---|---|---|---|
| | | Time | N | Time | N |
| Fresh | Absence of significant discoloration or bloating; rigor mortis and livor mortis may be present | 0–2 days | 38 | 0–3 days | 22 |
| Early decomposition | Significant discoloration and early to full bloating | 2 days–1 week | 11 | 2 days–1 week | 4 |
| Advanced decomposition | Beginning of adipocere development; sagging and bleaching of soft tissue; erosion of surface tissue | 1 week–1 month | 13 | ? | 2 |
| Skeletonization | Exposure of skeletal elements; often significant adipocere development | 1 month or longer | 2 | ? | 1 |

The Sheriff-Coroner's Office of Santa Cruz County granted permission for the authors to review the records of drowning victims and other water-related deaths for a 12-year period (1980 to 1992). The records contained full autopsy reports from the forensic pathologist (RTM), and full investigative reports from the Sheriff deputies. Many of these reports were available in the form of paper reports although the older ones were retained on microfilm.

Of the 105 water-related cases, 93 qualified for our purposes. Cases were excluded due to recovery of a living victim, followed by death during hospitalization or due to incompleteness of records. Our primary focus for the purposes of the present paper is upon those deaths that occurred in or on the saltwater areas. Sixty-four individuals were recovered from these situations. For each individual, we recorded the general characteristics of the victim: age, sex, ancestry, weight, and height. The date of recovery of the individual was documented. The date of disappearance, however, was sometimes estimated. As a result, the length of exposure could have been overestimated in some cases. Along with the cause of death, we recorded the places of disappearance and recovery. Information on the clothing at disappearance and recovery, if available, was noted to address the problem of wave action on the condition of the body. In some instances the duration of exposure was estimated based on the circumstances of the case.

The stages of decomposition were classified as fresh, early decomposition, advanced decomposition, skeletonization. Criteria for classification are presented in Table 1. These stages were parallel to those used previously in other studies of decomposition (Galloway et al. 1989; Rodriguez and Bass 1983). The circumstances of the recovery precluded assessment of the flotation properties of the remains which would have enabled the use of the stages of aqueous decomposition as outlined by Payne and King (1972) and Haglund (1991, 1993). In this study, the assessments were based primarily on the written descriptions of the remains, which were included in the autopsy reports. In some instances, there also were photographs of the individuals, which were consulted when available. In classifying the stages, a full description of the appearance and injuries of each individual was recorded.

## Results

The cases include 72 males and 21 females. The majority are adults, although 13 of the victims were subadult (less than 18 years) at the time of death. The manner of death was, in most cases, accidental (n = 75) or suicide (n = 12). Additional listed manner of death included accident or suicide (n = 4), homicide or accident (n = 1), and one unknown.

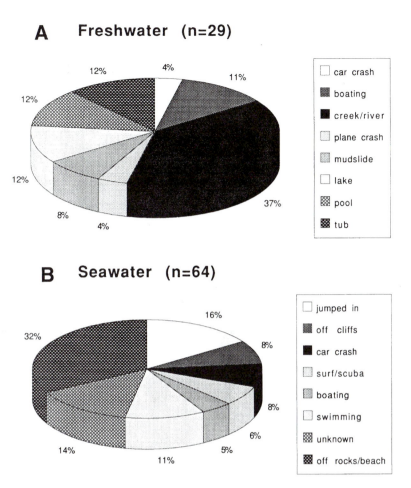

**A  Freshwater  (n=29)**

Legend:
- car crash
- boating
- creek/river
- plane crash
- mudslide
- lake
- pool
- tub

**B  Seawater  (n=64)**

Legend:
- jumped in
- off cliffs
- car crash
- surf/scuba
- boating
- swimming
- unknown
- off rocks/beach

**Figure 1**  Fatalities by the type of water and circumstances of the death. (A) Freshwater fatalities; (B) seawater fatalities.

The circumstances of death among the victims were quite varied. The majority of victims were involved in saltwater fatalities, with only 29 individuals dying in freshwater (Figure 1A and 1B). Of the latter group, most died in creeks and rivers. Another common location of drowning fatalities was bathtubs and hot tubs. The sea water deaths included those from water sports such as surfing (n = 3) and scuba diving (n = 1). However, the primary cause of entry into the water was from people being washed off the beaches or rocks by large waves (n = 21). Boating accidents were common, killing seven individuals, four of these in the coastal waters. Six individuals died as the result of car crashes, and one as the result of a plane crash. Additional fatalities (n = 5) are attributable to falling off cliffs or having the cliff collapse. For nine of the deaths, no known circumstances could be determined. The proportion of males dying in coastal waters was much greater than those in freshwater. Of the coastal victims, 86% were male, yet males constituted only 57% of the remaining deaths.

The time range for exposure was from a few minutes to fourteen months. Of the 93 cases examined, 64.5% (n = less than 60) were classified as fresh, 16.1% (n = 15) as early decomposition, 16.1% (n = 15) as advanced decomposition, and 3.2% (n = 3) were skeletonized. A sequence of decomposition could be estimated from the data recovered (Table 1). This is primarily applicable to remains from marine settings, as the freshwater victims were too varied to provide a discernible pattern beyond the initial period, and recovery of these victims was also more rapid.

In marine waters of this central California coastal region, fresh remains are seen in victims who are recovered from the water shortly after death and as late as 2 days of exposure to the water. After prolonged exposure, the victims are typically found with heavy wet lungs, pulmonary and cerebral congestion and edema, foam present in the respiratory system, and slight immersion changes in the palmar surfaces of the hands and feet. Depending on the amount of time in the water, appearances of minor predation from marine animals, abrasion from the movement of the body caused by the tides along the ocean floor, and sand and silt present in the esophagus, trachea and stomach are noted. The body is often in full rigor and exhibits dorsal lividity.

In the early decomposition stage, the body is found as rigor departs. The body tends to be bloated, with either marbling of the epidermis or a greenish-violet discoloration. Skin slippage is prominent in the scalp, torso, and limbs and most especially in the hands and feet. The marine animals and insects frequently will have almost completely eaten away the soft parts of the face, including the eyes, ears, and nose. The abrasions caused by the movement of the body across the sea floor are more extreme. The body will have begun readily noticable autolysis. This stage is evident in bodies up to 1 week after disappearance.

In this study, advanced decomposition is seen between 1 week and 1 month in seawater. In this stage there are no recognizable facial features as a result of marine animal activity and postmortem skin loss. There is a tendency towards bleaching of the exposed areas and discoloration of the present skin. Plants and animals are present in the respiratory tracts. There tend to be more postmortem fractures and the start of adipocere formation. Decomposition is slower when there is restrictive clothing present.

Skeletonization in portions of the body has been seen as early as 1 month. This is classified by exposure of skeletal material, but in some such cases adipocere formation was found in 90% of the body.

Of particular note is the rapid loss of clothing by individuals. Outer clothing such as jackets are most frequently missing at the time of recovery. Some of this loss may be due to the actions of the victims in attempting to rid themselves of weighty garments. However, even in victims whose death was instantaneous, the removal of clothing is common. Much of this is attributable to the strength of the wave action along this coastline. In at least one instance, the body was stripped of all clothing in a single day.

Among the victims, another point worthy of mention is the relatively short distances traveled by the bodies between the points of disappearance and recovery (Figure 2). Contrary to popular images, the vast majority of the bodies do not appear to drift far out to sea. With the exception of one body that entered the water north of Santa Cruz County, the victims' remains usually return within a mile or 2 of the entry point. In most cases, movement is toward the south, although occasional northward migration is also seen.

Despite the large number of sharks in the marine waters off the California coastline, no indication of shark predation on the remains is seen. Scavenging by smaller marine life is common, particularly about the face. Small pock-like depressions are probably the result of crabs and other crustaceans which fill the scavenger niche in the coastal kelp forests and rocky shores. Much of this postmortem damage appears to occur in the deeper, calmer waters, and most such scavengers are dislodged as the body is washed back into shore. Additional damage potentially may occur due to shoreline scavengers, although bodies are usually quickly recovered once they are washed ashore.

## Discussion

The causes and circumstances of death in water-related fatalities in the above survey show a contradiction with the more commonly held image of the dangers of this coast. In contrast

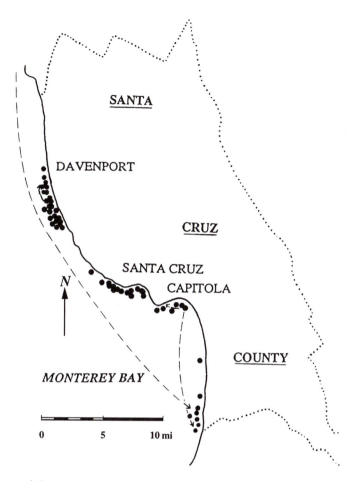

**Figure 2**  Map of the northern Monterey Bay area with dots indicating the entry and recovery points of the victims. When the entry and recovery points were separated, the direction of movement is indicated by an arrow.

to the media-attention attracting incidents in which surfers or divers are killed, the bulk of the deaths are due to people being washed from the shore by the action of waves. Despite signs warning of these dangers, the scenery, the opportunity to see marine mammals, and the fishing draws many to the water's edge. For the surfers, good waves are worth the wait but, for the unprepared visitor, they can be deadly.

A comparison of the sequence seen here and that outlined for water decomposition by Payne and King (1972) and Haglund (1991, 1993) shows some similarities and some differences. The decay process in the Monterey Bay area follows the same sequence, but the pace of decay varies, primarily due to differences in water temperatures. Seawater decay in the Monterey Bay area is considerably slower than reported in the study of feral pigs in South Carolina (Payne and King 1972), but roughly comparable to the results of Haglund (1991, 1993) in the Puget Sound region of Washington state for the more extreme durations of exposure. A notable contrast is the preservation of clothing with the material examined by Haglund, in that in this study, clothing was almost always lost soon after immersion into the water.

A major factor appears to be water temperature, the effects of which can be easily seen in comparison between the salt, fresh, and tub water deaths. The cold waters of the Pacific coast result in a slowing of decay from one stage to the next. The process of decay becomes more rapid as the water temperature increases. For instance, a drowning victim in a freshwater lake, where the water temperature averages 10 to 15°F higher than the coastal waters, resurfaced due to full bloating in only 2 days. Another victim showed massive edema, expansion of the lungs, and "washerwoman" skin after only 15 minutes or less in a covered hot tub. More advanced decay in a bathtub has been documented by Watanabe (1972).

In the Monterey Bay area, extent of the soft tissue damage due to predation and abrasion is relatively high. In general, however, the remains recovered in this county tend to be relatively intact, in contrast to the remains documented by Haglund (1991, 1993). It appears that the wave action is strong enough to bring the bodies ashore soon after they reach the bloated stage or adipocere is developed and before there is extensive dismemberment. Erosion tends to be confined to the most dependent areas which is of some benefit in the identification process.

Despite the images of shark-infested waters, the incidence of shark predation on humans is limited in this region. Shark attacks on surfers and divers have occurred and it has been suggested that the underwater profile of surfers is roughly similar to that of the seals and sea lions. Shark attacks on humans, however, often seem limited in duration. It is possible that the shark terminates the attack either because it dislikes the taste or because it is waiting for the victim to bleed to death. In either case, rescue efforts often intervene in the interim. For instance, during 1992 in the waters near Davenport, about 10 miles north of Santa Cruz, two surfers were attacked in separate incidents. These victims survived, pulled to safety by other surfers. Sharks are drawn to this area by the large number of sea lions, harbor seals, and elephant seals which now fish and breed in these waters. These are the primary prey of the large sharks, and as the mammal numbers increase the shark population is expected to follow suit. Unlike the case reported by Rathbun and Rathbun (1984), no reports of human remains recovered from sharks are known from this immediate region.

Since the point of entry into the water and the point of recovery tend to be in relatively close proximity to one another, there is often less difficulty in tracing the identity based on recorded entry points for persons presumed lost at sea. When no suspected identify is available, determination of entry needs to be assessed. Possible avenues for this investigation may include analysis of sand recovered from the internal organs. The varied geology of the coastline may allow identification of the beach sands. In addition, analysis of the microfauna may be helpful in isolating the particular area of the coast in which the individual's remains were immersed after death.

There are reports of individuals whose remains have not been recovered. There are, however, none of recent record in the Santa Cruz area. This suggests that the normal pattern of movement along this shore is severely restricted. The most likely explanation for this is the presence of the large kelp forests and the presence of rip tides which are frequent along the Pacific coast. These may "trap" the body as it is washed out to sea and hold it until decompositional gases form in sufficient quantities to allow the body to resurface. At this point, wave action carries the body back onto the coast. The absence of offshore canyons in this particular section of the coast also serves to prevent loss of bodies.

The local nature of the movement of bodies is seen in discussions with neighboring counties. To the north, bodies are often swept out of the San Francisco Bay and deposited along the coastline to the south (Cecil, personal communication). In the southern portion of Monterey Bay, some victims have been lost off or near the shoreline, and Monterey County authorities were not able to recover the remains (Hine, personal communication). It is possible that these have been pulled into deeper waters by currents generated through the Monterey and Carmel canyons.

A greater problem in establishing identification of the remains is the transient nature of the population in the coastal communities. This is compounded by the stripping of bodies by wave action and consequent loss of identifying clothing or items. It is not uncommon to recover a body with good preservation of soft tissue but to be unable to establish positive identification. Careful handling of the body during recovery becomes critical to ensure that fingerprints can be taken from the hand or from the "gloove" of sloughed skin which may still be adherent.

# Conclusion

Like the analysis of decomposition of human remains on land, it is important that studies of water decomposition be conducted regionally. Differences in water temperature, currents, wave action, fauna, and manner of entry into the water will all affect the overall decomposition rates. On irregular and highly variable coastlines, experimental models are limited and much can be gained from the retrospective approach taken here. This type of analysis can generate the questions and hypotheses which can be further tested and can allow for some general guidelines which are of more immediate application.

# References

Davis, J.H.
   1986 Bodies Found in Water: An Investigative Approach. *American Journal of Forensic Medicine and Pathology* 7(4):291–297.

Galloway, A., W.H. Birkby, A.M. Jones, T.E. Henry, and B.O. Parks
   1989 Decay Rates of Human Remains in an Arid Environment. *Journal of Forensic Sciences* 34:607–616

Haglund, W.D.
   1991 *Applications of Taphonomic Models to Forensic Investigations.* Ph.D. dissertation, Department of Anthropology, University of Washington, Seattle. University Microfilms, Ann Arbor, MI.
   1993 Disappearance of Soft Tissue and the Disarticulation of Human Remains from Aqueous Environments. *Journal of Forensic Sciences* 38:806–815.

Mant, A.K.
   1957 Adipocere — A Review. *Journal of Forensic Medicine* 4(1):18–35.

Mottonen, M., and M. Nuutila
   1970 Post Mortem Injury Caused by Domestic Animals, Crustaceans, and Fish. In *Forensic Medicine: A Study in Trauma and Environmental Hazards*, edited by C.G. Tedeschi, W.G. Eckert, and L.G. Tedischi, pp. 1096–1098. W.B. Saunders, Philadelphia.

Payne, J.A., and E.W. King
   1972 Insect Succession and Decomposition of Pig Carcasses in Water. *Journal of the Georgia Entomological Society* 7:153–162.

Rathbun, T.A., and B. Rathbun
   1984 Human Remains Recovered from a Shark's Stomach in South Carolina. *Journal of Forensic Sciences* 29:269–276.

Rodriguez, W.C., and W.M. Bass
   1983 Insect Activity and Its Relationship to Decay Rates of Human Cadavers in East Tennessee. *Journal of Forensic Sciences* 28(2):423–432.

Watanabe, T.
   1972 *Atlas of Legal Medicine.* J.B. Lippincott, Philadelphia.

# Burials at Sea

MARILYN R. LONDON
F. JOHN KROLIKOWSKI
JOSEPH H. DAVIS

# 39

## Introduction

There are more than two million deaths recorded each year in the United States (U.S. Bureau of the Census 1994). Of these, approximately 80% (Aiken 1994) are processed in the "traditional" manner, that is, embalmed, encasketed, and interred. The disposition of the remaining 20% is not well defined, but this number includes cremations and burials at sea. The term "burial at sea" is used to describe any purposeful disposition of human remains, including whole bodies or cremations (cremains), into a marine environment (Iserson 1994).

Burials at sea come to the attention of forensic science when they do not remain at sea. Several cases have been reported from various east and west coast jurisdictions, where remains have either been found along the coast (Florida) or were recovered by commercial fishing vessels (Rhode Island, Florida, Washington state). In certain cases, it may be relatively simple to determine that the remains are of no forensic interest; in others, a detailed analysis may be required. This chapter will discuss the taphonomic changes — or lack thereof — associated with remains after burial at sea.

## Scope of Problem

Most burials at sea — reportedly over 90% — are cremated remains. The exact number of these cases is unknown, because the final disposition indicated on a death certificate may read "cremation," but the location of the disposal of the cremains is not tracked (Comeaux 1989). While the popular conception of cremains is a container of ashes, it has been well documented that it is difficult to reduce bones totally to ash by burning alone (Birkby 1991; Suchey 1991). Individual bones and recognizable fragments may survive cremation and, if scattered at sea, may be snagged by fishing nets. One case reported from the Seattle area Environmental Protection Agency office was that of an entire urn of ashes recovered by a commercial fishing vessel. Two urns were recovered in Dade County, FL, as noted below.

The remaining 10% of burials at sea are whole body burials. The actual number of burials at sea per year in the United States is unknown. In accordance with the Environmental Protection Agency (EPA) regulations (see below), anyone who disposes of human remains at sea must notify the EPA by letter within 30 days. However, there is little or no enforcement of the law, although the National Funeral Directors Association reminds its members periodically of their responsibility in these circumstances. The Environmental Protection Agency offices for several regions on both the east and west coasts were contacted for estimates of reported burials, including cremains, at sea. These estimates ranged from one per year in the New England region to over 5000 — with a single report representing up to two dozen individuals — a year from the region which includes San Francisco. East coast EPA officials estimated fewer than 50 burials at sea per region per year, with a normal range of 10 to 15.

Various east coast EPA officials noted that they expected only 10% of burials at sea to be reported. The higher numbers reported on the west coast may be in response to a scandal in the 1980s, where various companies were accepting fees but were failing to scatter ashes at sea.

In Florida, the Medical Examiners Act requires medical examiners to approve all cremations, dissections, or burials at sea. In 1993 the 23 district medical examiners approved a total of 52,552 cremations, constituting 36% of the 147,634 total deaths from all causes. The number of cremations was actually greater, because approval was already granted if the medical examiner had prepared the initial death certificate. Cremation is considered final disposition. Where the cremains are distributed is not of concern to the medical examiners, nor to the Bureau of Vital Records. Accordingly, no state records exist to indicate disposal at sea of cremains. Whole body burials at sea are uncommon in Florida. Less than a dozen such requests could be estimated over a 39-year period in Dade County (District 11).

While burials at sea are usually dealt with by funeral homes, individuals may also take responsibility for the disposal of remains at sea. In these cases as well, the EPA regional office is to be notified by letter within 30 days. From the variability in the reported cases it is assumed that notification of the EPA is inconsistent.

Recent events suggest that other types of cases may be considered part of the same taphonomic category as "burials at sea." The extensive flooding in the American Midwest in 1993 and in Georgia in 1994 disturbed buried remains entombed in cemeteries, necessitating recovery and re-identification. Erosion may also expose and damage burial sites with historic value, such as old cemeteries along river banks (Rose 1985). In these circumstances, there may be evidence of embalming or other mortuary preparation, as well as water-related changes similar to those seen in burials at sea.

## Case Report from Rhode Island

In March of 1993, a commercial fishing vessel recovered human remains from 700 to 800 feet of water, 80 miles south of Block Island, due east of Long Island, NY. The fishing crew wrapped the remains in a large tarpaulin and notified officials upon their return to port the following day. The remains consisted of a skeletonized cranium with no mandible, and a torso. The cranium was attached to the vertebral column by several strands of soft tissue. Skin covered the torso, and the badly damaged proximal shafts of the humeri and femora protruded (Figure 1).

When the remains were viewed in the autopsy room, it was immediately noted (by FJK) that the torso had been incised in a typical "Y"-shaped autopsy incision, and neatly sewn closed. Over the left rib cage, a surgical incision was held together with staples; there was no indication of inflammation or of granulation tissue which would indicate healing (London and Krolikowski 1994).

When the Y-shaped incision was reopened, the torso was found to contain a stained, crumpled sheet and sawdust-like material; all of the internal organs had been removed. In addition, the anterior portions of the lower vertebrae had been sectioned.

The findings indicated that the individual had been autopsied. The fact that the skull had not been autopsied and the removal of the anterior vertebral bodies suggested that the postmortem procedure had taken place in a hospital rather than a forensic facility. The surgical incision around the rib cage suggested that the individual died after surgery.

The presence of the sheet and the sawdust-like packing material (hardening compound) is consistent with treatment of a body having undergone normal mortuary procedure where the organs have been removed (Strub and Frederick 1967; see also Berryman et al., this volume). The excellent condition of the skin implied that the remains had been embalmed. In support of this, there was no evidence of scavenger activity, although the soft tissue of the

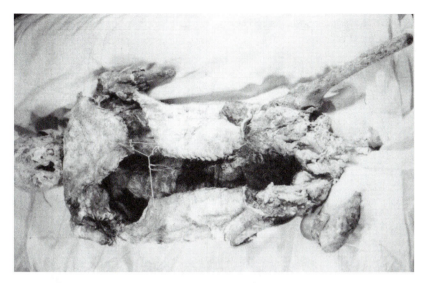

**Figure 1**    Head and torso of Rhode Island case, showing "Y" incision and stitching.

**Figure 2**    Femur of Rhode Island case, showing erosion of bone surface. No evidence of gnawing, crush, or fracture is present.

head and neck, as well as the external genitalia, were not present. There was very little odor detected in the remains, except for that associated with most cases from the marine environment.

There was severe damage to the cortical surface of the exposed bones of the skull and limbs, with extensive pitting and erosion into the cancellous bone. The shafts of the long bones present appeared to have been eroded away, rather than cut, broken, or gnawed (Figure 2). The marrow cavity was exposed. Damage — probably postmortem — to the left temporoparietal region of the skull resulted in the recovery of a portion of the left parietal bone from within the braincase.

A preliminary anthropological analysis of the remains (by MRL) indicated an adult male, probably caucasoid. The surgical incision was an indication of a major disease process, possibly involving the removal of the left lung. Vertebral sections were most likely removed for histological testing. It appeared that the individual had had major surgery, developed complications, and died. He was likely autopsied at a hospital, sent to a funeral home and embalmed, and then buried at sea.

At this point, the investigation was completed. The identification of the deceased would have served no purpose, and may have caused substantial emotional trauma to survivors.

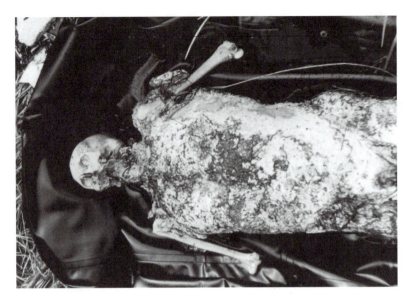

**Figure 3**    Florida case. Adipocere and skeletonization of skull and humeri.

## Case Reports from Florida

At least five sea burial remains, two urns of cremains, and three whole body burials, are known to one of us (JHD).

The urns were found by recreational divers in Biscayne Bay. One of these, a squat copper vase, had engraved on its lid (in German) the name of the person, the city and date of birth and death, and the date of cremation at the crematory in Munich. The other, a rectangular anodized aluminum box, had barnacles on its surface.

Two whole body sea burials were recovered in Dade County. One consisted only of the barnacle-encrusted skull, snagged by a deep sea fishing line off the coast. Prior to disposal, the calvarium had been removed during an autopsy. Identity of the decedent was not established. The other case was found on October 25, 1969 when a bottle hunter exploring mangroves along the western shore of Biscayne Bay reported a body. The following morning it was recovered from among the aerial roots of red mangroves in a few inches of water. When a detective and the medical examiner (JHD) carried it to shore, it was found to be an embalmed body, most evident by a remnant of pink axillary skin and an embalmer's trocar hole in the abdomen which carried the thread marks of the plastic button previously occluding the hole.

Adipocere was prominent. The forearms were missing, but the exposed humeri were intact (Figure 3). The skull was defleshed and the mandible lost, but the neck viscera remained. At autopsy, all internal tissues were well preserved, with excellent histological preservation of microscopic slide tissues (Figure 4). The cause of death of this elderly male was bronchopneumonia.

A search of the medical examiner's sea burial approval records led to the identity of the individual as an 85-year-old retired boat builder who had died of complications of cerebral atherosclerosis, according to the death certificate. Burial at sea had occurred on October 23, 1968, almost a year to the day prior to discovery. The body had floated up after disintegration of the wooden casket, had been carried by tidal currents from the edge of the Gulf Stream some 3 miles off the coast, drifted through the shallows into Biscayne Bay, and then drifted another few miles.

Most unusual in this case was artifactual shrinkage and dehydration of the embalmed brain and spinal cord. The brain was hard as stone and shrunken to a miniature orange-sized

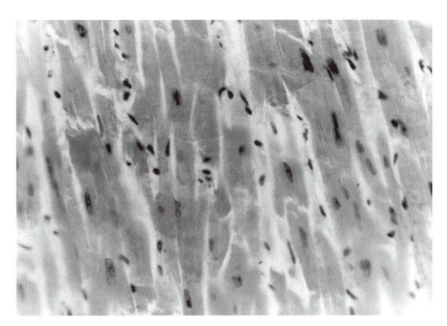

**Figure 4**   Florida case. Well-preserved myocardium. (H & E stain.)

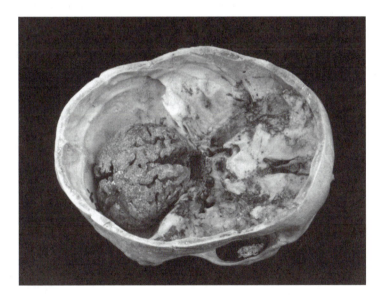

**Figure 5**   Florida case. Mummified shrunken brain inside skull.

replica of itself due to penetration of hypertonic sea water into the cranial vault (Figure 5). At the recovery scene, it was agreed to refrain from publicity, mainly to forestall legal solicitations. The body was quickly returned to the funeral home for repeat disposal.

The usual practice of burial at sea, as witnessed by one of us (JHD), is to place the body into a casket with holes drilled along both top and bottom. Cement bags are placed inside. The lid is strapped down, rather than depending upon the normal fasteners. The strapping is needed to prevent the lid from springing open, allowing escape of the cadaver. This occurred in one unfortunate local event, when the body floated away on the Gulf Stream, to the dismay of the funeral director and the amazement of passing fishermen.

The mystery of an autopsied body recovered from the ocean near Jacksonville was readily solved by Dr. Peter Lipkovik, District 4 medical examiner in Florida. He recognized the prior autopsy technique as his own, and the evidence of shotgun pellets in the neck. An X-ray of the recovered body matched his original autopsy X-ray in the pattern of residual pellets. The body had no head. This is explainable because the original injury had disrupted blood vessels in the neck, thus precluding adequate embalming, which usually deters marine faunal attacks.

## Laws and Regulations Pertaining to Burials at Sea

The Environmental Protection Agency is charged with protecting areas within a 3-mile limit of the coastline of the United States, including inland waters (lakes, rivers, wetlands, etc.). To prevent pollution of these areas, the agency controls "ocean dumping," which includes burials at sea (Federal Register 42[7], January 1977, Regulation 229.1). A general permit is granted by this regulation to anyone with a vessel or aircraft registered within the United States to transport human remains and bury them at sea. No permits, forms, or other paperwork are required in advance of such activity.

For whole body burials at sea, this regulation includes the stipulations that:

1. The burial must take place beyond 3 nautical miles from the coastline
2. Burial must be in water no less than 100 fathoms (600 feet) deep, except in certain parts of the southeastern coastline and the Gulf Coast, where it must be in water no less than 300 fathoms (1800 feet) deep
3. Materials which are readily decomposable in the marine environment may be placed with the remains (this precludes such items as plastic flowers; no stipulation is made regarding embalming fluid)
4. Measures should be taken to ensure that the remains sink to the bottom quickly and permanently; the EPA recommends a canvas body bag with a layer of heavy chain mesh surrounding it

Cremains may be disposed of beyond the 3-mile limit, without any water depth restrictions.

## Discussion

Information gathered from the Environmental Protection Agency, the National Funeral Directors Association, the Medical Examiners Office of the State of Rhode Island, and the Medical Examiner Department in Dade County, FL provides a list of factors involved for consideration when determining whether or not remains recovered from a marine environment are from a *bona fide* burial at sea. These include both physical and presumptive evidence.

Physical evidence which may be found in such a case includes:

1. The canvas body bag and chain mesh recommended by the Environmental Protection Agency;
2. Evidence of autopsy, such as a Y-shaped incision on the torso, the removal of the calvarium to expose the brain, and removal of internal organs;
3. Evidence of the application of mortuary techniques, such as trochar incisions, eye caps, and wiring of the jaws; this category also includes evidence of embalming, for which a test for the presence of formalin may be required;

4. An unexpected combination of postmortem changes in the remains, especially where mechanical damage is seen but scavenger activity is absent. For instance, all the proximal long bones in the Rhode Island case were eroded equally, down to only a few centimeters in length, but there was no indication of tooth marks or crushing fractures. This suggests that the limbs had all been exposed to mechanical erosion from tumbling or dragging on the ocean floor; and

5. The presence of an urn in which cremains are held.

Presumptive evidence includes:

1. Location of remains, e.g., outside the 3-mile limit and in a depth of water consistent with the regulations;
2. Absence of evidence of foul play and/or presence of evidence of major disease processes;
3. Lack of decomposition due to embalming of tissues; and
4. The presence of remains in an area where no drownings, accidents, or missing persons have been reported.

Once a case has been established as a *bona fide* burial at sea, there are issues associated with the analysis of the remains. Time since death may be difficult to determine if the body has been embalmed, although the extent of weathering may be taken into account. Evidence of outdated surgical procedures may also indicate a time frame of the burial. The location of the recovery of the remains may not reflect the original disposition of the remains, due to currents and faunal activity. However, if local records are available, as seen in the Florida cases, the time since death and even the identity of the individual may be determined.

Identification of the remains is unnecessary, unless it can be established that the burial violates Environmental Protection Agency standards or is associated with illegal activities such as homicide. Identification serves no purpose if the death has previously been recorded; recertification would only serve to create statistical errors. Furthermore, the survivors of the deceased may be subjected to further emotional trauma.

Responsibility for the final disposition of the recovered remains must rest with the medical examiner or other appropriate government agency which takes jurisdiction over the case.

# Conclusion

Burials at sea are thought to represent the final disposal of about 1% of the more than 2 million deaths in the United States each year. Up to 95% of these burials at sea are cremated remains; the other 5 to 10% represent approximately 1000 whole body burials at sea each year.

These remains, for the most part, will never come under the purview of forensic science. However, occasionally remains will be recovered from the marine environment by commercial fishing vessels, or may be carried in to the shoreline by strong currents. Remains which are illegally disposed of may require an analysis by a medical examiner and/or a forensic anthropologist.

Physical evidence, such as the presence of artifacts of autopsy or burial, must be reviewed to determine if the remains represent a *bona fide* burial at sea. Presumptive evidence, including the location of the remains and lack of scavenger activity, should also be documented. If the case is ruled a burial at sea, the investigation can be terminated and the remains disposed of properly at the discretion of the appropriate government agency.

Care should be taken to maintain the integrity of death statistics; these cases *should not be recertified*. In the future, a registry of burials at sea, such as the one maintained in Florida, should be considered. Tissue and/or DNA samples may be collected before burial at sea. Utilizing these tools, remains from burials at sea that return to land could be traced, and problems elucidated and rectified.

## Acknowledgments

The authors wish to acknowledge, with gratitude, the help provided by many employees of the Environmental Protection Agency; the staff of the National Funeral Directors Association; the staff of the Office of Medical Examiners, State of Rhode Island; the staff of the Medical Examiner Department, Dade County, FL; and the U.S. Coast Guard.

## References

Aiken, L.R.
  1994  *Dying, Death and Bereavement.* 3rd ed. Allyn and Bacon, Boston.

Birkby, W.H.
  1991  The Analysis of Cremains. Paper presented at the 43rd Annual Meeting of the American Academy of Forensic Sciences, Anaheim, CA.

Comeaux, M.L.
  1989  Burial: "Going Home." In *Encyclopedia of Death*, edited by R. Kastenbaum and B. Kastenbaum, pp. 36–37. Oryx Press, Phoenix.

Iserson, K.V.
  1994  *Death to Dust: What Happens to Dead Bodies.* Galen Press, Tucson.

London, M.R., and F.J. Krolikowski
  1994  The Return of the Native, or Protocol for Handling Recovered Burials at Sea. Paper presented at the 46th Annual Meeting of the American Academy of Forensic Sciences, San Antonio, TX.

Rose, J.C. (editor)
  1985  *Gone to A Better Land; A Biohistory of a Rural Black Cemetery in the Post Reconstruction South.* Arkansas Archaeological Survey, Fayetteville.

Strub, C.G., and L.G. Frederick
  1967  *The Principles and Practice of Embalming.* 4th ed. Frederick, Dallas.

Suchey, J.M.
  1991  Techniques in the Analysis of Cremains. Paper presented at the 43rd Annual Meeting of the American Academy of Forensic Sciences, Anaheim, CA.

U.S. Bureau of the Census
  1994  *Statistical Abstract of the United States: 1994.* 114th ed. U.S. Government Printing Office, Washington, D.C.

# INDEX

# Index